MW01148458

MEAN GENE KELTON'S

GIGS
FROM
HELL

# MEAN GENE KELTON

# GIGS
# FROM HELL

### IF THIS GUITAR COULD TALK...

## MEAN GENE KELTON

**FIRST EDITION**

Copyright ©2010 by Mean Gene Kelton

All rights reserved. No portion of this publication may be reproduced, stored in a retrieval system or transmitted, in any form or by any means, electronic, mechanical, photocopying, recording or otherwise, without the written prior permission of the author.

Every effort has been made to trace the copyright holders of the material and photos used in this volume. Should there be any omissions in this respect, we apologize and shall make the appropriate acknowledgements in any future printings if we are notified in advance.

I have tried to recreate events, locales and conversations from my memories of them. In order to maintain their anonymity in some instances I have changed the names of individuals and places, I may have changed some identifying characteristics and details such as physical properties, occupations and places of residence.

ISBN: 1453664785
EAN-13: 9781453664780

Printed in the United States of America

Editors: Denise Chatham and Joni Kelton
Front Cover: Michael Bohna, Kona Printing
Interior, Back Cover and Typography: Joni Kelton, Column Group Media
Mean Gene Kelton Illustration, opposite: ©Jim McDonnel 2008

Music, Lyrics and CD Citations from Mean Gene Kelton CDs, singles and videos are ©Gene Kelton Music, BMI except where noted.

Chuck Berry, "Back In The U.S.A." *Reelin' & Rockin'*, Chess, 1959.

First Edition

Contact Mean Gene Kelton at meangenekelton.com
Twitter: meangenerocks
Facebook: Mean Gene Kelton & The Die Hards

©2008 Jim McDonnel

# IF THIS GUITAR COULD TALK...

*If this guitar could talk, what do you think it might say*
*Would it tell you all my secrets – about my lowdown, sinful ways*
*Do you think you would be delighted with everything you heard*
*If you listen with your heart you can understand – each and every word*

*If this guitar could talk, it could tell you about elusive dreams*
*One night stands, all night jammin', hitchhikin' in the rain*
*Endless sacrifices, pawnshops and the blues*
*Every scratch has a story, this guitar tells the gospel truth.*

*If this guitar could talk – the tales that it could tell*
*About the cheap motels, small town jails, payin' our dues in hell*
*Late night, long distance telephone calls to someone waitin' lonely at home*
*And the night the phone rang off the wall, but the show must go on*

*If this guitar could talk – don't you think you might hear*
*How the road goes on forever, just follow the trail of tears*
*Its secrets might surprise you, it's time for show and tell*
*Cause this guitar is talkin', tellin' you about yourself*

## Special Thanks

Thanks to Deborah Smith McAllister for being a first-generation Die Hard and #1 Die Hard fan, and a great historian by providing many photos for the book from her vast collection.

Thanks to Helen Hughes [Mean Gene's mom] for scanning, typing and praying that God will forgive me for all the sins I confessed in this book.

Thanks to all our friends and fans who sent us pictures to include in the book.

Thanks to Elke Meyer for photo editing and scanning, and for providing most of the Southern Fried 4th Music Festival pictures, except where noted.

Thanks to Buddy Love for being our #1 Die Hard Road Manager, and for scanning hundreds of photos from the Die Hard archive for the book and website.

Special thanks to editor Denise Chatham for going above and beyond the call of friendship and working endless hours to make me sound intelligent, and for putting up with Joni.

To my wife "Even Meaner" Joni, thanks for everything: your dedication and passion, burning the midnight oil and working your little fingers to the bone. Thanks for kicking me in the ass when I needed it. Without you, this book would never have happened. Love, G.

# TABLE OF CONTENTS

## INTRODUCTION
What Is A Gig From Hell, You Ask? . . . . . . . . . . . . . . . . . . . . . . . . . . . . 1
Names Changed . . . . . . . . . . . . . . . . . . . . . . . . . . . . . . . . . . . . . . . . . 2
Texas Icehouses . . . . . . . . . . . . . . . . . . . . . . . . . . . . . . . . . . . . . . . . . 3

## BOOK ONE: GLORY DAYS 1961-1972
Mississippi Music Witch . . . . . . . . . . . . . . . . . . . . . . . . . . . . . . . . . . 9
Master of Ceremonies . . . . . . . . . . . . . . . . . . . . . . . . . . . . . . . . . . . 10
First Acting Gig . . . . . . . . . . . . . . . . . . . . . . . . . . . . . . . . . . . . . . . . 12
My First Guitar: April 1963 . . . . . . . . . . . . . . . . . . . . . . . . . . . . . . . 12
Sixth Grade Book Report . . . . . . . . . . . . . . . . . . . . . . . . . . . . . . . . . 12
First Band: The Continental Five . . . . . . . . . . . . . . . . . . . . . . . . . . . 14
Speech Class . . . . . . . . . . . . . . . . . . . . . . . . . . . . . . . . . . . . . . . . . . 15
Elvis and The New Kid . . . . . . . . . . . . . . . . . . . . . . . . . . . . . . . . . . 17
The Midnight Moonshiners . . . . . . . . . . . . . . . . . . . . . . . . . . . . . . . 19
The Moven Shadows . . . . . . . . . . . . . . . . . . . . . . . . . . . . . . . . . . . . 21

## BOOK TWO: WEEKEND WARRIOR YEARS 1973-1983
The Yellow Wagon Cafe . . . . . . . . . . . . . . . . . . . . . . . . . . . . . . . . . 25
The Brentwood Club . . . . . . . . . . . . . . . . . . . . . . . . . . . . . . . . . . . . 25
Drunk and Screwed . . . . . . . . . . . . . . . . . . . . . . . . . . . . . . . . . . . . 26
Quitting Jay's Club . . . . . . . . . . . . . . . . . . . . . . . . . . . . . . . . . . . . . 28
Escape From The 770 Club . . . . . . . . . . . . . . . . . . . . . . . . . . . . . . . 29
Not So Hot Shit . . . . . . . . . . . . . . . . . . . . . . . . . . . . . . . . . . . . . . . 31
Quitting the Band: 1974 . . . . . . . . . . . . . . . . . . . . . . . . . . . . . . . . . 32
Return Of The Weekend Warrior . . . . . . . . . . . . . . . . . . . . . . . . . . 34
Texas Country Bandits . . . . . . . . . . . . . . . . . . . . . . . . . . . . . . . . . . 34
    Back At Band Practice . . . . . . . . . . . . . . . . . . . . . . . . . . . . . . . . 37
Texas Fever . . . . . . . . . . . . . . . . . . . . . . . . . . . . . . . . . . . . . . . . . . 38
Cowboys In China . . . . . . . . . . . . . . . . . . . . . . . . . . . . . . . . . . . . . 39
Bayonet Blues . . . . . . . . . . . . . . . . . . . . . . . . . . . . . . . . . . . . . . . . 42
*Side Note: The Cimmaron Swingsters . . . . . . . . . . . . . . . . . . . . . 44

## BOOK THREE: ADVENTURES OF A ONE-MAN BAND 1983-1991
The Emporium Restaurant . . . . . . . . . . . . . . . . . . . . . . . . . . . . . . . 49
Shamrock Shrimp Singer . . . . . . . . . . . . . . . . . . . . . . . . . . . . . . . . 49
Roland The Wonder Drummer . . . . . . . . . . . . . . . . . . . . . . . . . . . . 50
City Club . . . . . . . . . . . . . . . . . . . . . . . . . . . . . . . . . . . . . . . . . . . . 51

Sunbright Bar . . . . . . . . . . . . . . . . . . . . . . . . . . . . . . . . . . . . . . . . . . . . . 51
The Beginning Of The Never Ending Hustle. . . . . . . . . . . . . . . . . . . . . . 51
Held Hostage By A Renegade Biker Gang . . . . . . . . . . . . . . . . . . . . . . . 51
    Renegade Biker Party . . . . . . . . . . . . . . . . . . . . . . . . . . . . . . . . . . 51
    Bear: The Cook. . . . . . . . . . . . . . . . . . . . . . . . . . . . . . . . . . . . . . . . 52
    On With The Show . . . . . . . . . . . . . . . . . . . . . . . . . . . . . . . . . . . . . 52
    Arriving Home: Almost Worse Than The Gig . . . . . . . . . . . . . . . . . . 55
Dorothy's Clock . . . . . . . . . . . . . . . . . . . . . . . . . . . . . . . . . . . . . . . . . . . 57
    Miss Ida . . . . . . . . . . . . . . . . . . . . . . . . . . . . . . . . . . . . . . . . . . . . . 57
    Time Is Not On Our Side . . . . . . . . . . . . . . . . . . . . . . . . . . . . . . . . 58
Alabama King Kong . . . . . . . . . . . . . . . . . . . . . . . . . . . . . . . . . . . . . . . 60
The Mine & Yours Club. . . . . . . . . . . . . . . . . . . . . . . . . . . . . . . . . . . . . 62
    Are You Gay? . . . . . . . . . . . . . . . . . . . . . . . . . . . . . . . . . . . . . . . . . 62
    The Mad Vet . . . . . . . . . . . . . . . . . . . . . . . . . . . . . . . . . . . . . . . . . . 62
Slasher . . . . . . . . . . . . . . . . . . . . . . . . . . . . . . . . . . . . . . . . . . . . . . . . . . 64
Stripped and Ripped. . . . . . . . . . . . . . . . . . . . . . . . . . . . . . . . . . . . . . . 66
Snow White Naked. . . . . . . . . . . . . . . . . . . . . . . . . . . . . . . . . . . . . . . . 67
    Snow White Part Two: Splinters. . . . . . . . . . . . . . . . . . . . . . . . . . . 70
The Bay-Deck Drive-In . . . . . . . . . . . . . . . . . . . . . . . . . . . . . . . . . . . . 72
Nashville . . . . . . . . . . . . . . . . . . . . . . . . . . . . . . . . . . . . . . . . . . . . . . . . 73
WSM Radio: Fired Before I was Hired . . . . . . . . . . . . . . . . . . . . . . . . 74
Looking For Gigs In Nashville . . . . . . . . . . . . . . . . . . . . . . . . . . . . . . . 76
The Madison Grill . . . . . . . . . . . . . . . . . . . . . . . . . . . . . . . . . . . . . . . . 77
Camel Country . . . . . . . . . . . . . . . . . . . . . . . . . . . . . . . . . . . . . . . . . . . 78
    Just Beat It! . . . . . . . . . . . . . . . . . . . . . . . . . . . . . . . . . . . . . . . . . . 79
    Gunfight At Camel Country . . . . . . . . . . . . . . . . . . . . . . . . . . . . . . 80
    Blood And Paint . . . . . . . . . . . . . . . . . . . . . . . . . . . . . . . . . . . . . . 80
Marcy's Pub . . . . . . . . . . . . . . . . . . . . . . . . . . . . . . . . . . . . . . . . . . . . . 81
    Ass Whuppin' In The Men's Room . . . . . . . . . . . . . . . . . . . . . . . . . 83
    She Ain't Bashful... She's From Nashville . . . . . . . . . . . . . . . . . . . 83
    Tip Jar Runner . . . . . . . . . . . . . . . . . . . . . . . . . . . . . . . . . . . . . . . 84
    Some Days Lucky, Some Days Not . . . . . . . . . . . . . . . . . . . . . . . . . 84
    Black Ice. . . . . . . . . . . . . . . . . . . . . . . . . . . . . . . . . . . . . . . . . . . . . 85
    You're Fired!. . . . . . . . . . . . . . . . . . . . . . . . . . . . . . . . . . . . . . . . . . 85
Back To Square One In Nashville . . . . . . . . . . . . . . . . . . . . . . . . . . . . 86
Back To Texas . . . . . . . . . . . . . . . . . . . . . . . . . . . . . . . . . . . . . . . . . . . 86
No Elvis Impersonator . . . . . . . . . . . . . . . . . . . . . . . . . . . . . . . . . . . . . 87
Whut Culler Is Mah Arm? . . . . . . . . . . . . . . . . . . . . . . . . . . . . . . . . . . 89
Mugged At The Silver Dollar. . . . . . . . . . . . . . . . . . . . . . . . . . . . . . . . 89
Pukin' Prom Queen . . . . . . . . . . . . . . . . . . . . . . . . . . . . . . . . . . . . . . . 90
    Prom Queen's Twenty-Year Reunion . . . . . . . . . . . . . . . . . . . . . . . 91
Rollin' & Tumblin'. . . . . . . . . . . . . . . . . . . . . . . . . . . . . . . . . . . . . . . . 93
Backyard Wedding. . . . . . . . . . . . . . . . . . . . . . . . . . . . . . . . . . . . . . . . 95
Naked Man Walking. . . . . . . . . . . . . . . . . . . . . . . . . . . . . . . . . . . . . . . 96
Tupelo TV Show . . . . . . . . . . . . . . . . . . . . . . . . . . . . . . . . . . . . . . . . . 98

## BOOK FOUR: THE GENE KELTON BAND 1988-1992

Fitzgerald's & The Reddi Room . . . . . . . . . . . . . . . . . . . . . . . . . . . . . 105
    The Reddi Room. . . . . . . . . . . . . . . . . . . . . . . . . . . . . . . . . . . . . . 106
Stepped in What? . . . . . . . . . . . . . . . . . . . . . . . . . . . . . . . . . . . . . . . . 106
Sold Out At Club Rave-On . . . . . . . . . . . . . . . . . . . . . . . . . . . . . . . . 108
Loggers. . . . . . . . . . . . . . . . . . . . . . . . . . . . . . . . . . . . . . . . . . . . . . . . 109

## BOOK FIVE: GENE KELTON & THE DIE HARDS

Blues Jams . . . . . . . . . . . . . . . . . . . . . . . . . . . . . . . . . . . . . . . . . 115
Die Hard Band Name . . . . . . . . . . . . . . . . . . . . . . . . . . . . . . . . . . 116
Our Fans Become Die Hards . . . . . . . . . . . . . . . . . . . . . . . . . . . . 117
The Great Louisiana Walkout . . . . . . . . . . . . . . . . . . . . . . . . . . . 118
Rebels Without A Chance . . . . . . . . . . . . . . . . . . . . . . . . . . . . . . 120
   No Paaakee Heeyah . . . . . . . . . . . . . . . . . . . . . . . . . . . . . . . . 120
   Hurry Up and Wait . . . . . . . . . . . . . . . . . . . . . . . . . . . . . . . . . 121
   Rockin' The Ball . . . . . . . . . . . . . . . . . . . . . . . . . . . . . . . . . . . 123
   Busboy Militia . . . . . . . . . . . . . . . . . . . . . . . . . . . . . . . . . . . . 123
Eastmart Blues Festival . . . . . . . . . . . . . . . . . . . . . . . . . . . . . . . 125
   The Crowd . . . . . . . . . . . . . . . . . . . . . . . . . . . . . . . . . . . . . . . 125
   Bubblin' Crude . . . . . . . . . . . . . . . . . . . . . . . . . . . . . . . . . . . 126
   The Sky Is Falling! . . . . . . . . . . . . . . . . . . . . . . . . . . . . . . . . . 127
Billy Blues . . . . . . . . . . . . . . . . . . . . . . . . . . . . . . . . . . . . . . . . . 129
   Billy Blues Arrives In Houston . . . . . . . . . . . . . . . . . . . . . . . . 129
   The Texas Blues Showcase . . . . . . . . . . . . . . . . . . . . . . . . . . . 130
   The Wizard: Billy Blues Sound Man . . . . . . . . . . . . . . . . . . . . 131
   The International Blues Band Rocks Billy Blues . . . . . . . . . . . 131
   Billy Blues Sells Out . . . . . . . . . . . . . . . . . . . . . . . . . . . . . . . 132
   What The Fuck is Texas Bluesrock? . . . . . . . . . . . . . . . . . . . . 133
   Last Gig At Billy Blues . . . . . . . . . . . . . . . . . . . . . . . . . . . . . . 134
Del's Lookout . . . . . . . . . . . . . . . . . . . . . . . . . . . . . . . . . . . . . . . 136
   Crash . . . . . . . . . . . . . . . . . . . . . . . . . . . . . . . . . . . . . . . . . . . 137
   Flying Tequila Glasses . . . . . . . . . . . . . . . . . . . . . . . . . . . . . . 137
   Skeeter Hell . . . . . . . . . . . . . . . . . . . . . . . . . . . . . . . . . . . . . . 138
   The Band House . . . . . . . . . . . . . . . . . . . . . . . . . . . . . . . . . . . 138
Michael's Ice House . . . . . . . . . . . . . . . . . . . . . . . . . . . . . . . . . . 139
   Pulling A Crowd . . . . . . . . . . . . . . . . . . . . . . . . . . . . . . . . . . . 140
   Jam Slutz . . . . . . . . . . . . . . . . . . . . . . . . . . . . . . . . . . . . . . . . 141
   Can A Chinese Man Play The Blues? . . . . . . . . . . . . . . . . . . . . 141
   Henry and The Mexicans . . . . . . . . . . . . . . . . . . . . . . . . . . . . 142
   Invasion Of The Stevie Ray Clones . . . . . . . . . . . . . . . . . . . . . 142
   The Count of Croatia . . . . . . . . . . . . . . . . . . . . . . . . . . . . . . . 143
   Our Biker Band Beginnings . . . . . . . . . . . . . . . . . . . . . . . . . . 144
   Crazy Women At Michael's Ice House . . . . . . . . . . . . . . . . . . . 145
   No More Blues Jams at Michael's . . . . . . . . . . . . . . . . . . . . . . 145
   Mr. Michael Sells Out To Fat Bob . . . . . . . . . . . . . . . . . . . . . 146
   A Call Back To Bob's . . . . . . . . . . . . . . . . . . . . . . . . . . . . . . . 147
   "The Texas City Dyke" . . . . . . . . . . . . . . . . . . . . . . . . . . . . . . 148
   Playin' Across The Street . . . . . . . . . . . . . . . . . . . . . . . . . . . . 148
Stump . . . . . . . . . . . . . . . . . . . . . . . . . . . . . . . . . . . . . . . . . . . . . 148
Fightin' Filly at Ken's Club . . . . . . . . . . . . . . . . . . . . . . . . . . . . 150
The Booze Brothers . . . . . . . . . . . . . . . . . . . . . . . . . . . . . . . . . . 151
Back To Back Bands . . . . . . . . . . . . . . . . . . . . . . . . . . . . . . . . . 152
Return To Billy Blues 1998 (A Second Chance) . . . . . . . . . . . . 154
   Third Time At Billy Blues . . . . . . . . . . . . . . . . . . . . . . . . . . . . 155
   The Lone Star Shootout . . . . . . . . . . . . . . . . . . . . . . . . . . . . . 156

## BOOK SIX: THE NOTORIOUS KELTONS

The Notorious Keltons . . . . . . . . . . . . . . . . . . . . . . . . . . . . . . . . 167
Evan's Camp: The First Gig For The Notorious Keltons . . . . . . . . 168
   Gas Station Cowboys . . . . . . . . . . . . . . . . . . . . . . . . . . . . . . . 171
Welders In The Bushes . . . . . . . . . . . . . . . . . . . . . . . . . . . . . . . . 172

Madness At Magnolia . . . . . . . . . . . . . . . . . . . . . . . . . . . . . . . . . . . 174
Deef & The Dumb Panty Man . . . . . . . . . . . . . . . . . . . . . . . . . . . . . . 177
Wadin' In Shit . . . . . . . . . . . . . . . . . . . . . . . . . . . . . . . . . . . . . . . . 178
Free Birds Fly . . . . . . . . . . . . . . . . . . . . . . . . . . . . . . . . . . . . . . . . . 179

## BOOK SEVEN: MEAN GENE ROCKS

The "Mean Gene" Name . . . . . . . . . . . . . . . . . . . . . . . . . . . . . . . . . . 185
Houston Livestock Show and Rodeo
  and The World Championship Barbeque Cookoff . . . . . . . . . . . . . . . 185
    Our First Cookoff . . . . . . . . . . . . . . . . . . . . . . . . . . . . . . . . . . 186
    One Year . . . . . . . . . . . . . . . . . . . . . . . . . . . . . . . . . . . . . . . . 187
    Championship Barbeque War Zone . . . . . . . . . . . . . . . . . . . . . 188
Tropical Storm Allison . . . . . . . . . . . . . . . . . . . . . . . . . . . . . . . . . . 189
September 11, 2001 . . . . . . . . . . . . . . . . . . . . . . . . . . . . . . . . . . . . 190
Diunna Does Dallas . . . . . . . . . . . . . . . . . . . . . . . . . . . . . . . . . . . . 191
A Bucket 'O Beer . . . . . . . . . . . . . . . . . . . . . . . . . . . . . . . . . . . . . . 194
Blow Up Doll And The Landlord . . . . . . . . . . . . . . . . . . . . . . . . . . . 197
King of the Urban Cowboys . . . . . . . . . . . . . . . . . . . . . . . . . . . . . . 199
T-Model Ford – Mississippi Blues Legend . . . . . . . . . . . . . . . . . . . . 205
Midland Mayhem . . . . . . . . . . . . . . . . . . . . . . . . . . . . . . . . . . . . . . 206
Wild Hogs . . . . . . . . . . . . . . . . . . . . . . . . . . . . . . . . . . . . . . . . . . . 207
Working For The King . . . . . . . . . . . . . . . . . . . . . . . . . . . . . . . . . . . 208
    No Elvis Songs At The House of The King . . . . . . . . . . . . . . . . . 209
    Jammin' At B.B. King's . . . . . . . . . . . . . . . . . . . . . . . . . . . . . . 210
    Back at Elvis Presley's . . . . . . . . . . . . . . . . . . . . . . . . . . . . . . 210
    The Building Has Left Elvis . . . . . . . . . . . . . . . . . . . . . . . . . . . 211
Tent Survival . . . . . . . . . . . . . . . . . . . . . . . . . . . . . . . . . . . . . . . . . 213
Kill Shorty . . . . . . . . . . . . . . . . . . . . . . . . . . . . . . . . . . . . . . . . . . . 215
Art Car Ball . . . . . . . . . . . . . . . . . . . . . . . . . . . . . . . . . . . . . . . . . . 218
80 dBs Of Hell . . . . . . . . . . . . . . . . . . . . . . . . . . . . . . . . . . . . . . . . 219
Kidnapped: "Stinkier Than Hell" Tour . . . . . . . . . . . . . . . . . . . . . . . 221
Continental Airlines Broke My Guitar . . . . . . . . . . . . . . . . . . . . . . . . 222
    In Mexico . . . . . . . . . . . . . . . . . . . . . . . . . . . . . . . . . . . . . . . 223
    Headline Goes Here . . . . . . . . . . . . . . . . . . . . . . . . . . . . . . . . 224
    Celine . . . . . . . . . . . . . . . . . . . . . . . . . . . . . . . . . . . . . . . . . . 224
    Returning to Houston . . . . . . . . . . . . . . . . . . . . . . . . . . . . . . . 225
    Second Trip To Continental Airlines Baggage Claim . . . . . . . . . . 225
    Continental Airlines Procedures . . . . . . . . . . . . . . . . . . . . . . . . 227
    A Die Hard Surprise . . . . . . . . . . . . . . . . . . . . . . . . . . . . . . . . 227
    Closure and Lettin' It Go . . . . . . . . . . . . . . . . . . . . . . . . . . . . 227

## BOOK EIGHT: GOOD HELP IS HARD TO FIND

Drugs And Alcohol, Etc. . . . . . . . . . . . . . . . . . . . . . . . . . . . . . . . . . 234
Fired! . . . . . . . . . . . . . . . . . . . . . . . . . . . . . . . . . . . . . . . . . . . . . . . 235
Fishnet Surprise . . . . . . . . . . . . . . . . . . . . . . . . . . . . . . . . . . . . . . . 235
Speedy . . . . . . . . . . . . . . . . . . . . . . . . . . . . . . . . . . . . . . . . . . . . . . 235
Grits In The Pits . . . . . . . . . . . . . . . . . . . . . . . . . . . . . . . . . . . . . . . 236
Sneezy . . . . . . . . . . . . . . . . . . . . . . . . . . . . . . . . . . . . . . . . . . . . . . 236
Homeless . . . . . . . . . . . . . . . . . . . . . . . . . . . . . . . . . . . . . . . . . . . . 236
Toker . . . . . . . . . . . . . . . . . . . . . . . . . . . . . . . . . . . . . . . . . . . . . . . 236
Milkshake Nelson . . . . . . . . . . . . . . . . . . . . . . . . . . . . . . . . . . . . . . 236
Fistfight at The Cactus Moon . . . . . . . . . . . . . . . . . . . . . . . . . . . . . 237
The Smokin' Team . . . . . . . . . . . . . . . . . . . . . . . . . . . . . . . . . . . . . 238
Bud Wiser Knife Fight . . . . . . . . . . . . . . . . . . . . . . . . . . . . . . . . . . . 239
Tubby . . . . . . . . . . . . . . . . . . . . . . . . . . . . . . . . . . . . . . . . . . . . . . . 240

Redneck Mothers . . . . . . . . . . . . . . . . . . . . . . . . . . . . . . . . . . . . . . . . 241
Enemas Anyone? . . . . . . . . . . . . . . . . . . . . . . . . . . . . . . . . . . . . . . . . . 241
Mail Box . . . . . . . . . . . . . . . . . . . . . . . . . . . . . . . . . . . . . . . . . . . . . . . . 241
Offended Flamingo . . . . . . . . . . . . . . . . . . . . . . . . . . . . . . . . . . . . . . . 241
Locking Horns at The Hop. . . . . . . . . . . . . . . . . . . . . . . . . . . . . . . . . 242
Drummer Takes Tips . . . . . . . . . . . . . . . . . . . . . . . . . . . . . . . . . . . . . 242
Amps For Drugs. . . . . . . . . . . . . . . . . . . . . . . . . . . . . . . . . . . . . . . . . . 243
Happy New Year . . . . . . . . . . . . . . . . . . . . . . . . . . . . . . . . . . . . . . . . . 243
The Return Of Tubby . . . . . . . . . . . . . . . . . . . . . . . . . . . . . . . . . . . . . 243
Ten Bucks A Smoke . . . . . . . . . . . . . . . . . . . . . . . . . . . . . . . . . . . . . . 243
300 Pound Canary . . . . . . . . . . . . . . . . . . . . . . . . . . . . . . . . . . . . . . . 244
Burn That Bridge . . . . . . . . . . . . . . . . . . . . . . . . . . . . . . . . . . . . . . . . 244
Quickie. . . . . . . . . . . . . . . . . . . . . . . . . . . . . . . . . . . . . . . . . . . . . . . . . . 244
Doc Bass. . . . . . . . . . . . . . . . . . . . . . . . . . . . . . . . . . . . . . . . . . . . . . . . 246
Mad Sax . . . . . . . . . . . . . . . . . . . . . . . . . . . . . . . . . . . . . . . . . . . . . . . . 247
Beer For Sax. . . . . . . . . . . . . . . . . . . . . . . . . . . . . . . . . . . . . . . . . . . . . 247
Walking Off the Stage . . . . . . . . . . . . . . . . . . . . . . . . . . . . . . . . . . . . 248
Two Bulls In The Same Stall . . . . . . . . . . . . . . . . . . . . . . . . . . . . . . . 248
    Bash . . . . . . . . . . . . . . . . . . . . . . . . . . . . . . . . . . . . . . . . . . . . . . . . 248
    Bass With A Case . . . . . . . . . . . . . . . . . . . . . . . . . . . . . . . . . . . . . 249
    Lead Bass . . . . . . . . . . . . . . . . . . . . . . . . . . . . . . . . . . . . . . . . . . . 249
Dippin' and Chewin' . . . . . . . . . . . . . . . . . . . . . . . . . . . . . . . . . . . . . 249
No Styrofoam Products . . . . . . . . . . . . . . . . . . . . . . . . . . . . . . . . . . . 250
Real Die Hards Only . . . . . . . . . . . . . . . . . . . . . . . . . . . . . . . . . . . . . 250
Mutiny . . . . . . . . . . . . . . . . . . . . . . . . . . . . . . . . . . . . . . . . . . . . . . . . . 250
Stepper's Teeff . . . . . . . . . . . . . . . . . . . . . . . . . . . . . . . . . . . . . . . . . . 251
Melt Down . . . . . . . . . . . . . . . . . . . . . . . . . . . . . . . . . . . . . . . . . . . . . . 251
Worst Band . . . . . . . . . . . . . . . . . . . . . . . . . . . . . . . . . . . . . . . . . . . . . 251
Who Dressed J.R.? . . . . . . . . . . . . . . . . . . . . . . . . . . . . . . . . . . . . . . 252
All Dressed Up. . . . . . . . . . . . . . . . . . . . . . . . . . . . . . . . . . . . . . . . . . 252
Flip-Flop . . . . . . . . . . . . . . . . . . . . . . . . . . . . . . . . . . . . . . . . . . . . . . . 252
Lester the Mo' Lester . . . . . . . . . . . . . . . . . . . . . . . . . . . . . . . . . . . . 253
The Reverend B . . . . . . . . . . . . . . . . . . . . . . . . . . . . . . . . . . . . . . . . . 253
Mid-Wife . . . . . . . . . . . . . . . . . . . . . . . . . . . . . . . . . . . . . . . . . . . . . . . 254
Middle-Aged Crazies . . . . . . . . . . . . . . . . . . . . . . . . . . . . . . . . . . . . . 254
Disappearing Musicians. . . . . . . . . . . . . . . . . . . . . . . . . . . . . . . . . . . 255
    Ghost. . . . . . . . . . . . . . . . . . . . . . . . . . . . . . . . . . . . . . . . . . . . . . . . 255
    Slippery When Drunk . . . . . . . . . . . . . . . . . . . . . . . . . . . . . . . . . 256
    Shaggy . . . . . . . . . . . . . . . . . . . . . . . . . . . . . . . . . . . . . . . . . . . . . . 256
    The Mercenary . . . . . . . . . . . . . . . . . . . . . . . . . . . . . . . . . . . . . . . 257
Pu-King Donuts and The FNG! . . . . . . . . . . . . . . . . . . . . . . . . . . . . 258
    Music Related . . . . . . . . . . . . . . . . . . . . . . . . . . . . . . . . . . . . . . . . 260

## BOOK NINE: Insignificant Others

Band Wives and Girlfriends . . . . . . . . . . . . . . . . . . . . . . . . . . . . . . . 263
He Said, She Said. . . . . . . . . . . . . . . . . . . . . . . . . . . . . . . . . . . . . . . . 263
Punkin' . . . . . . . . . . . . . . . . . . . . . . . . . . . . . . . . . . . . . . . . . . . . . . . . 264
Sha-Moo. . . . . . . . . . . . . . . . . . . . . . . . . . . . . . . . . . . . . . . . . . . . . . . . 264
Crack Wife . . . . . . . . . . . . . . . . . . . . . . . . . . . . . . . . . . . . . . . . . . . . . . 264
Cum To Me . . . . . . . . . . . . . . . . . . . . . . . . . . . . . . . . . . . . . . . . . . . . . 265
Swang Yer Partner . . . . . . . . . . . . . . . . . . . . . . . . . . . . . . . . . . . . . . . 265
Swap Meat . . . . . . . . . . . . . . . . . . . . . . . . . . . . . . . . . . . . . . . . . . . . . 265
The Unwritten Rule . . . . . . . . . . . . . . . . . . . . . . . . . . . . . . . . . . . . . . 265
The Pipe . . . . . . . . . . . . . . . . . . . . . . . . . . . . . . . . . . . . . . . . . . . . . . . . 266

Bar Tab . . . . . . . . . . . . . . . . . . . . . . . . . . . . . . . . . . . . . . . . . . . . . . . 266
Sloth . . . . . . . . . . . . . . . . . . . . . . . . . . . . . . . . . . . . . . . . . . . . . . . . . . 266
Psycho Sisters . . . . . . . . . . . . . . . . . . . . . . . . . . . . . . . . . . . . . . . . . . . 267
Let Buster Sang! . . . . . . . . . . . . . . . . . . . . . . . . . . . . . . . . . . . . . . . . . 267
Social Calender . . . . . . . . . . . . . . . . . . . . . . . . . . . . . . . . . . . . . . . . . . 268
Insignificant Others Today . . . . . . . . . . . . . . . . . . . . . . . . . . . . . . . . . 268

## BOOK TEN: DOOR DEALS FROM HELL
What Is A Door Deal? . . . . . . . . . . . . . . . . . . . . . . . . . . . . . . . . . . . . . 271
Die Hard's First Door Deals . . . . . . . . . . . . . . . . . . . . . . . . . . . . . . . . 271
VFW Takes All . . . . . . . . . . . . . . . . . . . . . . . . . . . . . . . . . . . . . . . . . . . 271
Whites Park – Anahuac, Texas . . . . . . . . . . . . . . . . . . . . . . . . . . . . . . 272
Texa-Vegas . . . . . . . . . . . . . . . . . . . . . . . . . . . . . . . . . . . . . . . . . . . . . 273
Cookie Bitch . . . . . . . . . . . . . . . . . . . . . . . . . . . . . . . . . . . . . . . . . . . . 274
Radio Airplay Makes A Band Worth More Money . . . . . . . . . . . . . . . . 275
Working Clubs For The Door . . . . . . . . . . . . . . . . . . . . . . . . . . . . . . . 275
    Door Person Stealing Money . . . . . . . . . . . . . . . . . . . . . . . . . . . . 275
    Mustang Sally's . . . . . . . . . . . . . . . . . . . . . . . . . . . . . . . . . . . . . . 276
    Show Me Your ID! . . . . . . . . . . . . . . . . . . . . . . . . . . . . . . . . . . . . 277
    None O' Yer Biz! . . . . . . . . . . . . . . . . . . . . . . . . . . . . . . . . . . . . . 278
    Where Eagles Dare . . . . . . . . . . . . . . . . . . . . . . . . . . . . . . . . . . . 278
    Just For The Record: Regarding Lodges . . . . . . . . . . . . . . . . . . . 279
    The Door Deal Agreement . . . . . . . . . . . . . . . . . . . . . . . . . . . . . . 279

## BOOK ELEVEN: SICKER 'N HELL
The Creepin' Crud . . . . . . . . . . . . . . . . . . . . . . . . . . . . . . . . . . . . . . . 285
Heat Stroke . . . . . . . . . . . . . . . . . . . . . . . . . . . . . . . . . . . . . . . . . . . . . 286
Operation Bass Player Removal . . . . . . . . . . . . . . . . . . . . . . . . . . . . . 286
Food Poisoning . . . . . . . . . . . . . . . . . . . . . . . . . . . . . . . . . . . . . . . . . . 287
Falling Off Stage . . . . . . . . . . . . . . . . . . . . . . . . . . . . . . . . . . . . . . . . . 287
Toxic Fog . . . . . . . . . . . . . . . . . . . . . . . . . . . . . . . . . . . . . . . . . . . . . . 288
Band Members Sick . . . . . . . . . . . . . . . . . . . . . . . . . . . . . . . . . . . . . . 289
    Dog Bites Drummer . . . . . . . . . . . . . . . . . . . . . . . . . . . . . . . . . . 289
    Always Sick Keyboard Player . . . . . . . . . . . . . . . . . . . . . . . . . . . 289
    Back Surgery . . . . . . . . . . . . . . . . . . . . . . . . . . . . . . . . . . . . . . . 290
    Crash Test Winner . . . . . . . . . . . . . . . . . . . . . . . . . . . . . . . . . . . 291
No More Sicker 'N Hell . . . . . . . . . . . . . . . . . . . . . . . . . . . . . . . . . . . . 291

## BOOK TWELVE: BENEFITS AND FUNDRAISERS
Fundraisers . . . . . . . . . . . . . . . . . . . . . . . . . . . . . . . . . . . . . . . . . . . . 295
    Flight Of The Wheelchair King . . . . . . . . . . . . . . . . . . . . . . . . . . 295
    Honda Drop . . . . . . . . . . . . . . . . . . . . . . . . . . . . . . . . . . . . . . . . 296
    Fire In The Hole! . . . . . . . . . . . . . . . . . . . . . . . . . . . . . . . . . . . . 297
    Hotter'n Hell At The Hawg Stop . . . . . . . . . . . . . . . . . . . . . . . . . 298
Benefits . . . . . . . . . . . . . . . . . . . . . . . . . . . . . . . . . . . . . . . . . . . . . . . 299
    Mr. Liver Transplant . . . . . . . . . . . . . . . . . . . . . . . . . . . . . . . . . 300

## BOOK THIRTEEN: RUNNIN' FROM THE LAW
Locked Up In Liberty . . . . . . . . . . . . . . . . . . . . . . . . . . . . . . . . . . . . . 305
Christmas Eve 1985 . . . . . . . . . . . . . . . . . . . . . . . . . . . . . . . . . . . . . . 306
Mayberry – Maybe Not . . . . . . . . . . . . . . . . . . . . . . . . . . . . . . . . . . . 306
Cop Rock . . . . . . . . . . . . . . . . . . . . . . . . . . . . . . . . . . . . . . . . . . . . . . 307
Mother's Day 1999 . . . . . . . . . . . . . . . . . . . . . . . . . . . . . . . . . . . . . . . 308
Cops Request Stevie Ray Vaughan . . . . . . . . . . . . . . . . . . . . . . . . . . . 309
The Natchez Trace . . . . . . . . . . . . . . . . . . . . . . . . . . . . . . . . . . . . . . . 310

## BOOK FOURTEEN: DIRTY TRICKS

The Joy Of Sax. . . . . . . . . . . . . . . . . . . . . . . . . . . . . . . . . . . 315
Guitar Hero. . . . . . . . . . . . . . . . . . . . . . . . . . . . . . . . . . . . . . 316
Getting The Jump On Johnny Dee . . . . . . . . . . . . . . . . . . . . . . . 317
Vanessa & The Wild Cactus Band . . . . . . . . . . . . . . . . . . . . . . . 318
Shit Pills. . . . . . . . . . . . . . . . . . . . . . . . . . . . . . . . . . . . . . . 321
Marking Their Territory . . . . . . . . . . . . . . . . . . . . . . . . . . . . . 322
Wet Money . . . . . . . . . . . . . . . . . . . . . . . . . . . . . . . . . . . . . 322

## BOOK FIFTEEN: SKIN TO THE WIND

Painted On Smile . . . . . . . . . . . . . . . . . . . . . . . . . . . . . . . . . 325
Mama's Boy . . . . . . . . . . . . . . . . . . . . . . . . . . . . . . . . . . . . . 325
What Big Titties You Have, Grandma! . . . . . . . . . . . . . . . . . . . . 326
Spread 'em, Granny! . . . . . . . . . . . . . . . . . . . . . . . . . . . . . . . 326
Tangled Tits . . . . . . . . . . . . . . . . . . . . . . . . . . . . . . . . . . . . . 327
Nudist Resorts . . . . . . . . . . . . . . . . . . . . . . . . . . . . . . . . . . . 328
    Fire Dancers . . . . . . . . . . . . . . . . . . . . . . . . . . . . . . . . . . 328
    A Taller Table . . . . . . . . . . . . . . . . . . . . . . . . . . . . . . . . . 328
    Does The Band Play Naked? . . . . . . . . . . . . . . . . . . . . . . . 328
Swingers . . . . . . . . . . . . . . . . . . . . . . . . . . . . . . . . . . . . . . . 329
    Swang Yer Pardner . . . . . . . . . . . . . . . . . . . . . . . . . . . . . . 329
    Strap-on Cucumber . . . . . . . . . . . . . . . . . . . . . . . . . . . . . 330
    Raining Rat Shit . . . . . . . . . . . . . . . . . . . . . . . . . . . . . . . . 331
    Swingers House Party . . . . . . . . . . . . . . . . . . . . . . . . . . . . 332
Vampire Swingers . . . . . . . . . . . . . . . . . . . . . . . . . . . . . . . . . 333
    Vampire Swingers Eat At Joe's. . . . . . . . . . . . . . . . . . . . . . . 333
    Vampires Howl At The Cactus Moon . . . . . . . . . . . . . . . . . . 334

## BOOK SIXTEEN: MISCELLANEOUS

Devils Rob Angels . . . . . . . . . . . . . . . . . . . . . . . . . . . . . . . . . 337
Purse Snatcher . . . . . . . . . . . . . . . . . . . . . . . . . . . . . . . . . . . 338
Kick Pedal Goes Swimming . . . . . . . . . . . . . . . . . . . . . . . . . . 339
Don't Touch My Wife . . . . . . . . . . . . . . . . . . . . . . . . . . . . . . 339
Drummer's Truck Stolen . . . . . . . . . . . . . . . . . . . . . . . . . . . . 339
Stranded . . . . . . . . . . . . . . . . . . . . . . . . . . . . . . . . . . . . . . . 339
    Jumpa Cayba No Reesch . . . . . . . . . . . . . . . . . . . . . . . . . . 340
    No Brakes! . . . . . . . . . . . . . . . . . . . . . . . . . . . . . . . . . . . 341
Coffee In My Peavey . . . . . . . . . . . . . . . . . . . . . . . . . . . . . . . 341
Ethnic Slurs . . . . . . . . . . . . . . . . . . . . . . . . . . . . . . . . . . . . 341
Biker Wants Tip Money Back . . . . . . . . . . . . . . . . . . . . . . . . . 343
Konk. . . . . . . . . . . . . . . . . . . . . . . . . . . . . . . . . . . . . . . . . . 343
Breeeeathe, Mutherfuckerrrrrrr! . . . . . . . . . . . . . . . . . . . . . . . 344
I'll Kick Yer Ass. . . . . . . . . . . . . . . . . . . . . . . . . . . . . . . . . . . 345
Butcherin' The Hag . . . . . . . . . . . . . . . . . . . . . . . . . . . . . . . . 345
A Cross Canadian Redneck . . . . . . . . . . . . . . . . . . . . . . . . . . 346
The "C" Word. . . . . . . . . . . . . . . . . . . . . . . . . . . . . . . . . . . . 346
Bus Trips From Hell. . . . . . . . . . . . . . . . . . . . . . . . . . . . . . . . 347
    Blind Drunk at Blind Lemon . . . . . . . . . . . . . . . . . . . . . . . 347
    Another Drunk Drives The Bus . . . . . . . . . . . . . . . . . . . . . . 347

## BOOK SEVENTEEN: GROUPIES FROM HELL

Groupies or Fans: What's The Difference? . . . . . . . . . . . . . . . . . 351
Just Do It!. . . . . . . . . . . . . . . . . . . . . . . . . . . . . . . . . . . . . . . 352
Sneakin' Out. . . . . . . . . . . . . . . . . . . . . . . . . . . . . . . . . . . . . 352
Bonus Plan . . . . . . . . . . . . . . . . . . . . . . . . . . . . . . . . . . . . . 353

Maggie May . . . . . . . . . . . . . . . . . . . . . . . . . . . . . . . . . . . . . 353
Jailbait!!! . . . . . . . . . . . . . . . . . . . . . . . . . . . . . . . . . . . . . . . 354
Scrapbook . . . . . . . . . . . . . . . . . . . . . . . . . . . . . . . . . . . . . . 354
Danita . . . . . . . . . . . . . . . . . . . . . . . . . . . . . . . . . . . . . . . . . 355
Working Groupie . . . . . . . . . . . . . . . . . . . . . . . . . . . . . . . . . 356
Eighty And Crazy . . . . . . . . . . . . . . . . . . . . . . . . . . . . . . . . . 356
70 Year Old Stalker . . . . . . . . . . . . . . . . . . . . . . . . . . . . . . . 357
Kicked Out . . . . . . . . . . . . . . . . . . . . . . . . . . . . . . . . . . . . . 357
    Naked In The Dashboard Lights . . . . . . . . . . . . . . . . . . . 357
The Shrine . . . . . . . . . . . . . . . . . . . . . . . . . . . . . . . . . . . . . 358
Down and Dirty . . . . . . . . . . . . . . . . . . . . . . . . . . . . . . . . . 359
Backfired Booty Bluff . . . . . . . . . . . . . . . . . . . . . . . . . . . . . 359
Thanksgiving Dinner . . . . . . . . . . . . . . . . . . . . . . . . . . . . . 360
The Pirate's Daughter . . . . . . . . . . . . . . . . . . . . . . . . . . . . . 363
Nadine The Whiskey Queen . . . . . . . . . . . . . . . . . . . . . . . 364
    Who The Fuck Are Ya'll? . . . . . . . . . . . . . . . . . . . . . . . . . 366
Zena . . . . . . . . . . . . . . . . . . . . . . . . . . . . . . . . . . . . . . . . . . 367
    A Naked Zena Donut . . . . . . . . . . . . . . . . . . . . . . . . . . . 368
LolliPop . . . . . . . . . . . . . . . . . . . . . . . . . . . . . . . . . . . . . . . 369
The Sorceress . . . . . . . . . . . . . . . . . . . . . . . . . . . . . . . . . . . 371
Wanda The Witch . . . . . . . . . . . . . . . . . . . . . . . . . . . . . . . 371
Swingin' From The Rafters . . . . . . . . . . . . . . . . . . . . . . . . . 373
Curb Service . . . . . . . . . . . . . . . . . . . . . . . . . . . . . . . . . . . 373
That's Him! That's Him! . . . . . . . . . . . . . . . . . . . . . . . . . . . 374
Cow Tang Sisters . . . . . . . . . . . . . . . . . . . . . . . . . . . . . . . . 374
Freida Freakenstein . . . . . . . . . . . . . . . . . . . . . . . . . . . . . . 376
    Outlaw Dave Plays The Backwoods Rant . . . . . . . . . . . . . 378
Psycho Sybil . . . . . . . . . . . . . . . . . . . . . . . . . . . . . . . . . . . . 378
    Escape From Sybil . . . . . . . . . . . . . . . . . . . . . . . . . . . . . 378
    Sybil Calling . . . . . . . . . . . . . . . . . . . . . . . . . . . . . . . . . 379
    I Quit . . . . . . . . . . . . . . . . . . . . . . . . . . . . . . . . . . . . . . 379
Can Men Be Groupies? . . . . . . . . . . . . . . . . . . . . . . . . . . . 380
    Mad Max . . . . . . . . . . . . . . . . . . . . . . . . . . . . . . . . . . . 380
Tor-let Paper . . . . . . . . . . . . . . . . . . . . . . . . . . . . . . . . . . . 383
Starman Rides Again . . . . . . . . . . . . . . . . . . . . . . . . . . . . . 383
My Wives: Groupies? . . . . . . . . . . . . . . . . . . . . . . . . . . . . . 385

## BOOK EIGHTEEN: MUSICIANS COMMANDEER FUNERAL, R.I.P. TONY LEE

Musicians Commandeer Funeral and Send Preacher Packing . . . . . . . . . . 393
    At The Gravesite . . . . . . . . . . . . . . . . . . . . . . . . . . . . . . . 394
    Monica Goes Head-To-Head With The Reverend . . . . . . . . . . . . . . . 395
    Monica Marie Owed A Public Apology . . . . . . . . . . . . . . . . . . . . 396
In Closing . . . . . . . . . . . . . . . . . . . . . . . . . . . . . . . . . . . . . . 397

# Introduction

I never really gave much thought to writing a book. Especially a book about my gigs from hell – because all musicians have gigs from hell. I just talk about mine more than most.

As I would tell my stories, many people suggested I write a book about all the misadventures in my life as a professional musician.

Reluctantly I started making notes and giving each story a title. I never realized how many wild, crazy, hilarious, dangerous and sometimes life threatening experiences I had been involved in until I had written over two hundred titles… and *Gigs From Hell* was born.

## WHAT IS A GIG FROM HELL, YOU ASK?

Do you remember that scene in *Blues Brothers* where the band is on a stage behind a chickenwire fence while drunk rednecks threw beer bottles at them? That scene may be funny to you, but to musicians who have actually experienced that sort of disrespect that shit ain't funny!

That, my friends, is a *gig from hell*.

Do you remember the movie *Roadhouse?* It featured The Jeff Healey Band, performing behind a chickenwire fence while the joint was destroyed by barroom brawls. Those scenes are exciting on the silver screen, but in real life can be terrifying and sometimes tragic. For a band, they are *gigs from hell*.

Unlike Hollywood depictions of bands and band life, my *Gigs From Hell* are *all true*.

If you have a problem with graphic descriptions of nudity, sexual activity, tales of violence, drunkenness, drug use, extreme profanity, political incorrectness and the use of words that start with N, C, P, F and many others, then throw this book down now: run, bury your head in the sand and pretend the world is perfect. This book is not a whitewashed, candy-coated collection of happy little music fairy tales where shit don't stink and people live happily ever after.

*Gigs From Hell* is a documentary of real life events written in the same attitude and voice in which I experienced them – hard, rough, sometimes dangerous and often unfair.

I have written in such a way that you will feel your eyes burn from clouds of second-hand smoke.

You'll smell the cheap perfume and beer breath of an aging barfly hanging all over you trying to be your date for the night.

You'll feel the rush of a standing ovation on nights when you can do no wrong, and the cold fear of gettin' your ass stomped when an angry redneck crowd turns into a lynch mob.

You'll feel the tequila set your brain ablaze, you'll taste the blood on your lips, and feel the tears in your eyes.

You'll know the anxiety and anguish of dreams dashed. You'll experience the ecstasy of being live, onstage, alone and in the spotlight.

You'll fight beside me against the devil himself in a barroom brawl and run with me for our lives from possible death and destruction.

You'll go *with* me – *next* to me – center stage. Under the glare of the bright lights, you'll face the crowd and bare your soul to the critics, hecklers, groupies and worshippers.

Chasing your dream like a hobo chasing a freight train, you'll feel victorious from conquering the neon world with nothing but a song and a guitar and then the loneliness of a cheap motel after a show.

Riding with me on the road, you'll take your turn driving all night when your eyelids feel like lead and dawn is a million miles away.

You'll call me a *liar*.

Everything is *true*.

Welcome to the trenches, the front lines of my life.

Welcome to Mean Gene Kelton's *Gigs From Hell*!

## NAMES CHANGED

Because people grow up, move out, move on, get religion, get married, get remarried, have kids, raise grandkids, move on to different careers, die, and so on, I have either purposely omitted or changed the names of many people, places and venues in this book in order to protect them, their memories, their reputations and their families from the repercussions of all the stupid shit they did.

Me? I confess… *I did it all!*

## TEXAS ICEHOUSES

Since many *Gigs from Hell* took place in Texas icehouses, I figured I'd explain what an icehouse is right here in the beginning so I wouldn't have to explain it every time. Traveling and touring around the country we discovered people outside of Texas – especially in northern states – had no clue when we talk about performing in Texas icehouses. They always asked, "What the hell is an icehouse, and how do you play a gig there?"

For those folks outside of Texas, this chapter is dedicated to you.

In Texas today, the term *icehouse* refers to what most people would call a beer joint. Not a nightclub. *Nightclubs* serve liquor by the drink. Icehouses serve only beer, wine, setups and soft drinks. Its counterpart would be what people up north call a *pub* or *tavern*. In other parts of the South they are called *beer joints, juke-joints, roadhouses* and *honky-tonks*.

During the early part of the last century, an icehouse was where giant blocks of ice were kept. Ice men with horse-drawn wagons would make the rounds through the neighborhoods, delivering blocks of ice to residents who then stored the ice in their *iceboxes.* (The term *icebox* was coined long before the word refrigerator.)

Working men on their way to work every morning began the habit of leaving bottles of beer at their local icehouse so they could enjoy a cold one as soon as they got off work. As the years passed, men congregating at icehouses after work to drink cold beer became a tradition. Icehouse owners soon realized they could make a lot of money by keeping cold beer readily available at all times. Thus – the *Texas Icehouse* was born!

Today the majority of Texas icehouses are big metal buildings with large, sliding, overhead garage doors that make the place look more like a muffler shop than a drinking establishment. With tin roofs, icehouses are hotter than nine kinds of hell in the summer because most do not have air conditioning. The garage doors are kept open to allow the air to flow through. Most icehouses keep a few industrial shop fans on hand to blow hurricane force winds across the room.

It's a great time when the music is loud, the beer is ice cold and tattooed waitresses are flashing their tits – so much fun no one notices the roar of the shop fans, the suffocating heat, or the fact that their clothes are soaked with sweat.

The open doors also allow street noise, mosquitoes, flies, birds, wasps, bees, wind, rain, dirt, sand, pollution and fumes to blow through. Oh yeah, then there are the occasional stray dogs that wander in looking for a handout.

During southern winters most icehouses are heated with warehouse-type ceiling-mounted heaters or newer floor-stand propane heaters. Those tall, giant, mushroom-shaped heaters really stink up a place. Some icehouses still burn firewood in iron wood stoves.

Unlike nightclubs, icehouses can open as early as 7am, but must close at midnight six nights a week, except Saturdays, when they can close at 1am. It's not uncommon in shift-worker towns for an icehouse to have a packed house of beer-guzzling graveyard shift workers at 8am.

Most Texas icehouses have bare concrete floors – easier to sweep with a leaf blower or wash off with a water hose. Rarely do tables and chairs match. Parking lots are either gravel or ground-up oyster shells, always dotted with potholes. When it rains those parking lots become mud bogs full of water. Any icehouse with a paved driveway is considered a high class joint. I once saw a sign: *"Pickups in the front. Bikes on the side. Horses in the back."*

Texas icehouses are very earthy places that cater to a clientele of multi-cultural, blue-collar beer drinkers and hell raisers: construction workers, refinery workers, veterans, cowboys, roughnecks, rednecks, truck drivers, bikers, aging hippies and literally people of all sizes, shapes, creeds and colors. Anywhere you find real men still in their work clothes (which signifies they have a job and a paycheck), you'll find real women ready to help them spend it. Tough women. Women who can out-cuss a sailor, bang your brains out or beat your brains out. If they're wearing a Harley t-shirt, chances are they ride their own bike.

Bikers love Texas icehouses. They can have a few beers, hang with friends, shoot a game of pool and still see their bikes only a few feet away through the giant open doors. Many icehouses have an outdoor seating area with picnic tables and a protected bike parking area.

Anywhere you find a rowdy drinking crowd you'll find a smoking barbeque pit cooking up some Texas-style, flamed-broiled brisket, burgers, sausage or chili. Sunday afternoon crawfish boils are popular, in season of course.

I've seen people sit at the same bar stool for years as if they personally owned it. Lord knows they paid for it, one beer at a time! I've seen people meet, court, dance, get laid, get married, have babies, fight, get hit, beat up, stabbed or shot, shoot back, get naked, get caught and busted, go to jail, get paroled, get religion, backslide, move away, move back, get divorced, lose their wife, lose their husband, get drunk, get high, fall down, get dragged, get sick, get sober, get run over, catch fire, run, hide, crawl, cuss, cry, pray, bleed, shit, puke, laugh hysterically, throw fits of rage, have heart attacks and I've seen them die.

I've seen it all happen in the glow of an icehouse neon light while the band played on.

I have played fancy uptown gigs where I was treated like disposable white trash and never made anything in my tip jar. At a good ol' Texas icehouse we musicians are treated like family. As far back as the early '70s I could make a couple hundred bucks a night in my tip jar alone from the generosity of "real folks" who know what it's like to earn their daily bread by the sweat of their brow and appreciate a journeyman's labors.

There is a line in my song "Too White To Play The Blues" that says, *"when the oil fields ran dry, this guitar fed my family."* That line describes a time around 1979 when I was laid off from my oil field job in the middle of the winter and unemployed for months. I had a wife and two little sons to feed. Finally out of sheer desperation I took my guitar down to a little icehouse in Liberty, Texas, and played for tips. The next day my wife bought groceries and we kept the lights on for another month.

I have seen benefits and fundraisers held in Texas icehouses where hard working folks poured out their hearts and wallets to raise money for some unfortunate family when snooty, high-fallootin' religious or charity organizations refused to help.

Depending on where you are in the Lone Star state, you'll hear some of the world's greatest musicians and aspiring bands playing everything from classic country and Texas Swing to Cajun, Zydeco, Mexican, German Oompah, '50s and '60s Oldie-Goldies, Southern Rock and Texas Blues. You'll meet the most unique characters in the universe, drink the coldest beer on the planet and have the most fun you'll ever have in your life.

If you're not careful you may come away with the worst ass-whupping you ever had – all in one afternoon – all in a Texas icehouse.

Many of the stories documented in *Gigs From Hell* took place in Texas icehouses. I've seen the good, bad and the ugly. The wild side of life. I've tasted cold beer and my own blood, breathed first-hand dust and second-hand smoke and felt the sting of honest sweat in my eyes. I've wiped the spit of a sputtering drunk from my face and nursed a knot on my head from a flying salt shaker. I've performed with – and learned from – the best and worst musicians in the world. Regardless of their level of ability, they always played with a big smile and had a limitless passion for the music.

Through it all I've had a blast! I love my job!

Would I do it again? *Hell yeah!!!!!!*

# BOOK ONE

# Glory Days

## 1961-1972

## MISSISSIPPI MUSIC WITCH

My first introduction to the entertainment business was a traumatic experience that affected me even into the early years of my professional career.

I was seven years old in January of 1961 when we moved to Moorhead, Mississippi. That January, as I became the new kid in Mrs. Dinwiddie's second grade class, rehearsals for the annual "Spring Show" in May were already underway. The show featured first through sixth grades in skits, singing, dancing and performing a series of synchronized marches in the gym.

Since I started school in the middle of the year long after rehearsals for the spring show had begun, I figured I would not be involved in the production. Being a very shy kid, the thought of sitting it out did not bother me at all.

One very cold morning a week or so after starting school the classroom door flew open. The school's music teacher materialized as if by some supernatural means. A very tall, thin woman, she had pasty-white, corpse-like skin. She was probably in her late forties, but to my young eyes all grown-ups may as well have been a hundred.

She wore a long, dark dress buttoned tight around her neck and long sleeves that fit tight around her wrists. Her dress hung nearly to the floor, but I could see her black lace-up boots (like the ones my grandmother wore with her stockings rolled down). Her hair was dark and pulled straight back. She didn't smile. She reminded me of the wicked witch in *The Wizard of Oz.*

She marched to the front of the class. Interrupting Mrs. Dinwiddie, she waved her long, skinny finger like a magic wand. In a crackling sneer she asked, "Which one is the *new boy*?"

The class fell silent as everyone turned and looked at me! I wished I could turn invisible and run out of the room as the old witch's squinty eyes burned a hole in me. She curled her index finger in a "come here" gesture and in a high-pitched voice like fingernails on a chalk board, she cackled, *"Eugene Kelton! Come with me!"*

A streak of fear ripped through my stomach. I was terrified. What had I done to deserve whatever punishment lay in store for me? I was instructed to be quiet. I was herded across the small elementary school campus, feeling like Hansel and Gretel being led to the oven (my only point of reference at that time). We entered an old, large metal building that was ice cold.

I was ushered into a small, freezing room where twenty-five other kids from different classes and grades huddled together in heavy coats, ear muffs and gloves. They stood in an area that had several seating levels, much like a choir loft in a church. It was so cold in the room I could see my own breath.

The old Witch sat down in front of an antiquated, upright piano and started banging away at the splintered keys, yellowed by years of abuse and neglect. The notes boomed like thunder in the small room. Even at that young age my untrained ears were offended – no – *violated* – by her sour notes. I remember thinking how horrible she played. Looking back, the old piano was probably a hundred years old and severely out of tune. The Witch and the piano were certainly just as cold as the children.

She played a melody line. Children who had already been picked to sing in the spring event stood and sang the phrase: "I've got a great big pair of boots." After demonstrating the melody line and their vocal abilities, the old Witch leaned forward, glared at me through her gold-rimmed spectacles, raised her eyebrows and with her eyes wide open she snapped, "Now you do it, Eugene!"

Again, streaks of terror shot through me like lightning! I had never sang in front of anyone in my life. I was speechless. She played the melody as if expecting me to sing along. I stood silent, frozen with fear.

She turned her evil eyes toward me and screeched, "*Sing!*"

Frightened by her explosive outburst, I jumped backwards. The other kids snickered at my reaction. "*Silence!*" she screamed at the other children without ever taking her icy stare off of me. I felt as though she was about to turn me into a frog and devour me. It's a damn wonder I didn't pee down both legs right there in front of everybody. I could feel my lower lip start to tremble. Again she played the melody and squinted in my direction daring me to sing. I barely squeaked out the line, "I-got-a-great-big-pair-of-boots."

In one startling, sweeping motion the old Witch leaped to her feet, jerked open the door, pointed her long, skinny index finger toward the opening and screeched, "You can't sing! Go back to class! You're wasting my time!"

I bolted out of the room embarrassed and humiliated. I could hear the kids roar with laughter behind me as I raced back to the main room. Just before the door slammed I heard her scream, "SHUDDUUUP!" I ran for my life back to the safety of my nice warm classroom.

The rest of the day I brooded and vowed I'd never sing in public for the rest of my life.*

## MASTER OF CEREMONIES

Since I apparently could not sing and had enrolled at the school too late to be included in the marching routines, the teachers were in a dilemma as to how to include me in the Spring Show. They decided to appoint me "Master Of Ceremonies" to introduce one of the events. After the singing portion of the program was over, my job was to march to the center of the gym and introduce the grand finale like an announcer in a three-ring circus.

It was easy enough in rehearsal. I had practiced my one line in the empty gymnasium.

On the day of the show I stood underneath the bleachers with the teachers watching the event come to life before my eyes. I was mesmerized at how different and magnificent the show seemed with everybody dressed up and the gym full of people. I listened to the enthusiastic applause and cheering of what sounded like a thousand people in the stands above my head.

When it was time for me to do my stuff I marched like a perfectly trained toy soldier to the center of the gym, placed my right toe behind my left heel as instructed, and made an abrupt about face. The sudden sight of a thousand people staring at me slammed the air out of my lungs like getting hit in the chest with a shovel. I gasped! I was speechless! I wanted to run like hell, but my mother was in the audience and I wanted to do a good job for her.

Somehow, I managed to suck in enough breath to shout in a shaky, terrified little voice: "*Ladieeees and gentlemen, the first and second grade will now perform some marching drills!*"

At the precise moment of my last word, the powerful "Stars And Stripes Forever" exploded from the outdated public address system and reverberated through the gym at an earsplitting volume. The roar of a thousand people cheering and jumping to their feet in a thunderous, standing ovation almost knocked me off my feet. A hundred school kids marched proudly in perfect formation around the gym waving the Mississippi state flag and the American flag to the sound of the music and applause. My young soul was swept up in a tidal wave of excitement as if being carried through the skies on the wings of a thousand screaming eagles! It was an exhilarating, overwhelming feeling to be a part of something that seemed so massive and so important.

I hurriedly marched off the gym floor and back under the bleachers where all the teachers hugged me and patted me on the shoulder making me feel like my performance was the key to the success of the entire event. It was my first time to experience the rush of adrenaline from being in front of an excited audience. My little heart was beating like a sewing machine.

I was elated and felt ten feet tall.

I guess there is a certain level of star status associated with being the center of attention. Later that afternoon two of the prettiest girls in the second grade, Scottie Harpole and Virginia Ann Hughes, and their little girlfriends, showed up at my house on their bicycles to tell me they were impressed with my performance. As the weeks passed, my mother kept a gallon of cherry Kool-Aid made at all times because my house became *the* place where all the girls (my first groupies) hung out.

At that time I didn't know why I was getting a massive rush from the attention I was getting from the girls. It was a different kind of rush than being in front of an audience, but I somehow sensed the two experiences were closely related.

While other boys my age were trying out for baseball and joining Boy Scouts, I was under the tree in my backyard or behind the school playing kissing games with the girls.

However, my sudden celebrity status with the young ladies came with a price – all the boys in school labeled me a "sissy" because I preferred hanging out with the girls instead of playing baseball with the boys.

On numerous occasions I had to prove my manhood in fights with other boys. Win or lose, the girls still hung around to cheer me on to victory or to feel sorry for me when I got my ass kicked. I wore my bruises like a badge of honor. I still have a chipped front tooth to remind me of those days.

Later that summer when we moved away from Moorhead, Mississippi, I took with me many lessons learned:

1. I loved the entertainment business and the roar of the crowd.
2. Chicks love the guy who gets the glory.
3. I'd rather kiss girls than play baseball.
4. Chicks still dig you even when you get your ass whipped.

*When I turned 18 (a mere ten years after the humiliating vocal audition described above) I reluctantly started singing in my first band out of necessity when it became painfully obvious that our lead singer sucked worse than I ever did. For many years into my adult life my experience at the old Witch's audition haunted me so much that every time I would see someone laughing in the back of the room I just knew they were laughing at me like those kids in that ice-cold room. For years I would get pissed off and confront people demanding to know what they were laughing at. Naturally, they thought I was crazy.*

*It took a long time to out grow that feeling of inferiority.*

*Whether I can sing or not is a matter of opinion, but I finally got over my fear of singing in public and never let it stop me from pursuing my dreams.*

## FIRST ACTING GIG

When I was nine years old we moved from Greenville, Mississippi, to a garage apartment in the Heights section of Houston, Texas. That year I started fourth grade at Cleveland Elementary on Jackson Hill Street. I was given the lead role in the fourth grade play about the origins of Thanksgiving. Remembering the humiliation I experienced when I was forced to sing in the second grade, I had fully decided that if I was required to sing I would run away from home! Once I realized that I did not have to sing, I recalled the elation I felt as the announcer for my second grade musical and the female attention I received from it. I anxiously looked forward to dressing up like a pilgrim, standing in front of an audience and reciting my well-rehearsed lines with the "purdiest" girl in the class and then reaping the glory!

Unfortunately for me we moved to Splendora, Texas, only a month before my acting debut.

I felt robbed of the glory I thought would surely be mine as the star of the Thanksgiving Play. I made my mother promise to take me back to see the play. On the day of the play Mom kept her promise. I found myself sulking in my seat in the back of the auditorium, green with envy as I watched another boy wear my costume, say my lines, steal my thunder, get my girl and reap my glory. I was really pissed that I didn't get to be in that play! I remember thinking, "I coulda done better than him!" I missed out on impressing my leading lady who was "nine-and-a-half-going-on-ten." She was a real knockout by my standards.

## MY FIRST GUITAR: APRIL 1963

The following year my mother married Bruno Acker (an illegal German immigrant – more about him later) and we moved again to be near his job in Bellaire, Texas.

It was in Bellaire that Mom gave me my first guitar for my tenth birthday. It was a beautiful sunburst Sears & Roebuck F-Hole Silvertone acoustic guitar, complete with a *Mel Bay Guitar* book. Over the next few months I wore that book out and broke hundreds of Black Diamond strings in my effort to master my new found passion.

My new stepdad had a friend named David Schindler. David had a red-hot rock 'n roll band called "The Nomads." When David and his girlfriend Bonnie came over, David would show me chords and licks. I was a fast learner. By the end of the summer of 1963, I would sit on a picnic table in the park next to the Bellaire swimming pool playing the theme from *Peter Gunn*, *The Twilight Zone*, "Honky Tonk" and bits and pieces of this and that.

I soon discovered my guitar was a chick magnet. After the first few licks I would be surrounded by young girls from the swimming pool (some as old as fourteen and wearing *two piece bathing suits!*) who thought this little burr-headed, ten-year-old guitar player was cute and cool! Wow! Life was great.

I became addicted to the girls' attentions and worked harder and harder to learn more songs to impress them. I didn't understand what that "flush-all-over-feeling" was when the girls came around. I only knew something was giving me a great rush and it only seemed to happen when I played the guitar.

I can't say that getting a guitar was a life changing experience – because at ten years old, I had no life to change. However, the guitar did show me a road I could take, and I loved the scenery along the way.

## SIXTH GRADE BOOK REPORT

The following year we moved again, this time to southwest Houston. I spent sixth grade at Almeda Elementary. During oral book report week, showbiz came calling for a third time.

All week long students sat in the non-air-conditioned room nervously sweating at the thought of speaking in front of the class. I suffered along with the other students who stammered, stuttered and even cried, and who were consumed with the terror of public speaking in front of an unforgiving classroom full of mocking and giggling sixth graders.

The night before it was my fate to give my oral book report, I grabbed my library book, skimming through it for the first time just enough to get the jest of the story.

My palms were dripping wet as I dreaded my turn as much as everybody else. I was willing to take an "F" if I could just forget the whole thing. When my name was called, I slowly trudged forward to receive my dose of public humiliation. I reached the front of the class, turned and stared back at a room full of faces glued on me anxiously waiting for me to make a fool of myself. I was scared to death. Taking a deep breath, I mustered up my best announcer voice learned from my second grade musical in Moorhead, Mississippi.

"Ladieeees and gentlemen, I'm gonna tell you about the best book I ever read! It's about…"

As I heard the sound of my own voice begin to speak with power and authority, something inside me clicked *on*. The more I talked, the easier it got. Suddenly, through no will or plan of my own, I became very animated. Instead of standing still as other kids had done, I walked excitedly back and forth across the front of the room. I flailed my arms around. I dramatically dropped down to one knee. I changed my voice and stance, acting out different characters in the story. I was not nor have I ever been a class clown, but the class rolled with laughter over and over at my performance. I was winning them over and instinctively leaned into the characters, accents and gestures that seemed to garner more laughter.

Out of the corner of my eye I saw two sixth grade teachers from down the hall standing at the door. They wanted to see why tidal waves of laughter were disrupting their classes. They watched my entire delivery with great interest.

I ended my performance to a rousing round of cheers, applause and an A+. I should have realized it then – *my destiny was calling.*

The next day Mrs. Simon told me the other sixth grade teachers wanted me to give my oral book report in the same fashion to their classes. She scheduled my performances to follow immediately after lunch for the next two days. Looking back, this was my first experience with a successful *opening night*, then two more *shows* negotiated by my *agent* (the teacher) who *booked* me for two *one-night stands on the road* (the classes down the hall).

In the days before integration, my class was made up of kids just like me: average middle class white kids from blue-collar working class families. We all wore jeans, tennis shoes or cowboy boots, and rode the school bus. They related to the humor in my story. Class #2 was also kids from working class families, but considered to be "slow learners" that needed special attention. When I did my show – I mean my oral book report – class #2 rolled with laughter. I didn't know if the kids understood what I was talking about or just laughed at my animated delivery. Regardless, I was happy with their response to my performance. Mrs. Simon was beaming with pride.

In those two performances I discovered I could think on my feet, speak in public and make people laugh. It never occurred to me I might have a future in show business.

The next day after lunch I was escorted by my entourage (now I had an *escort* and an *entourage*): Mrs. Simon, the other sixth grade teacher and the school's principal. We went to the #3 sixth grade class, which was made up of uppity kids from very wealthy and well-to-do families. They wore fashionable clothes and were dropped off and picked up by their parents in long, shiny new cars.

Whenever we were at recess the kids in class #3 never associated with the rest of the sixth graders. It was obvious they looked down their snobby little noses at what they believed was Almeda Road white trash. We saw them as a bunch of sissies.

Confident with my two-for-two winning track record, I sincerely believed I would win over those uppity snots and have them rolling in the aisles in no time. The teacher of class #3 introduced me, giving rave reviews about my show in the class next door.

I stepped to the front of the class and began my routine. In places where the other classes laughed, class #3 never made a single sound. *Not even a peep!* Even in the funniest places they sat in stone-cold silence. It was the first time I ever felt the pangs of dying on stage in front of an audience. I fought back the overwhelming desire to jump out the second-story window. But from somewhere, natural instincts kicked in and I somehow knew that no matter what *the show must go on*.

It was my first gig from hell and I felt horrible. I finished my routine to dead silence. No applause, no laughter. Nothing. I was embarrassed and humiliated. Mrs. Simon patted me on the head and offered a kind, forced smile. I left the room to the sound of a lackluster applause initiated by the host teacher in a futile effort to be polite.

I was too young to understand that the uppity kids, who had already heard the laughter of the "lower" classes blowing down the hall, weren't about to lower themselves and laugh at the same story that white trash kids and "retards" thought was funny. I was crushed. I was a flop! My tour of the fifth grade classes was canceled. My career as a stand-up comedian was nipped in the bud in only three shows.

Little did I know that bad experiences were part of what entertainers call "payin' yer dues." Hurt and discouraged by my last performance I wasn't mature enough to realize I had a two-out-of-three winning streak going. I wasn't strong enough to shake it off and keep going. As a result I refused to ever try to be funny in public again. I even quit doing impersonations of Gomer Pyle and Gabby Hayes at backyard barbeques. However, I would soon learn showbiz was not through with me yet.

That Sears & Roebuck Silvertone was sitting at home, and it was calling my name.

## First Band: The Continental Five

I was fourteen in 1967. Doug, a flamboyant and highly excitable young drummer I went to school with wanted to start a rock band and was holding open auditions at his "private studio." I showed up to my first audition on my bicycle with my Sears & Roebuck acoustic guitar slung across my back. In my mind I looked as cool as Elvis with his guitar and motorcycle in *Roustabout*.

I could hear amplifiers and drums from the driveway. I coolly dropped my kickstand, adjusted my collar and ran a comb through my Brylcreem-drenched hair.

I entered Doug's so-called studio which obviously served a double purpose as his bedroom. There were a dozen other boys my age already there, dressed in psychedelic t-shirts with Beatle bangs combed down over their pimply foreheads.

I sat down on the bed feeling very out of place. I observed total chaos, frustration and flaring tempers.

Doug showed off his drumming talents by pounding away on a set of Western Auto kiddie drums as loud, hard and fast as he could hit. He was oblivious to the other musicians struggling to find common ground on their electric guitars for the first time in their lives. Nobody seemed to know a whole song all the way through. Untried and untrained male voices going through the voice change from boys to men screeched and squawked in unknown keys and butchering songs by popular rock bands of the day.

Doug disappeared. A few moments he later bound back into the room wearing a homemade Colonial-style Revolutionary War jacket and a black cowboy hat he had customized into a three cornered "minute man" hat. He stole the look from Paul Revere & The Raiders.

"The band is gonna be called The Continental Five," he announced. His enthusiastic speech about the world's greatest rock band yet to be seen came to an abrupt halt when someone asked if he could score a matchbox. (You old hippies that survived the sixties will certainly remember what a matchbox was. Later generations will just have to look it up.)

Doug had apparently been sniffing too much model airplane glue, believing his own hallucinations regarding the rock star band he created in his mind. I didn't like the arguments, the chaos or the sissy-looking Paul Revere costume. I also didn't like Doug's self centered, egotistical, self-appointed dictator approach telling us how things had to be his way because it was "his band" and he owned his own "studio."

As more heated arguments ensued about the songs, song lists and costumes, I slipped unnoticed out of the room full of red-faced, peach-fuzzed, cursing fourteen- and fifteen-year-olds. I threw my guitar over my shoulder, saddled my trusty Schwinn and rode home disenchanted, gunning my imaginary motorcycle throttle as my one little Elvis curl danced on my forehead.

My first band experience lasted less than twenty minutes and I didn't even get to play.

## SPEECH CLASS

I was sixteen in the summer of 1969 when my family moved from the big city of Houston to the small town of Liberty, Texas. It was only fifty miles away, but it was a culture shock – like going back in time to Mayberry in the '50s.

When school started in the fall, the first thing I noticed was the small town kids were a lot more laid back than what I was used to in Houston. Most of the kids had grown up together since first grade. There were no gang fights. Nobody skipped school. Nobody smoked dope or dropped acid in the restrooms. Nobody talked back to the teachers.

Being the new kid, fresh from the violence of the Houston school system, I exuded a cocky, defensive attitude. I didn't make friends very quickly at first.

My only friend at that time was my guitar and I couldn't wait to get home every afternoon and wear grooves in the fretboard, dreaming about the day I would play music for a living.

Knowing I wanted a career in the music business, I knew I would have to learn how to act and speak properly in front of an audience. I signed up for Mrs. Southgate's Speech 101.

Public speaking came easy for me. After all I had done pretty well a few years back with my sixth grade book report. I jumped at every chance to get in front of the class and do an impromptu two-minute speech on whatever subject Mrs. Southgate pulled out of her hat. I was having a blast honing my newly discovered talents.

One day Mrs. Southgate announced we would be required to bring an object to class and give a five-minute demonstration speech about it. She compared a demonstration speech to a salesman explaining the virtues of a new product. We would be timed and graded on originality, showmanship and our ability to get our point across in the given time limit.

The following week I watched as a surfer brought in a surfboard, explaining about its length, shape, contour and the purpose of different types of fins. He took off his shoes and demonstrated how to catch a wave and hang ten.

A young cowboy and member of the FFA brought in a saddle, threw it over a chair and explained the purpose of the different parts like the saddle horn and stirrups. He demonstrated how to saddle and ride a horse.

As the days passed I was amazed at how everyone seemed to have some special talent or ability to do something very unique. I racked my brain trying to figure out what I could do. Maybe I could demonstrate how I sacked groceries at Snappy's Grocery where I worked after school. Or maybe I could demonstrate how to tie a hangman's noose with thirteen rings, shuffle a deck of cards, rack a set of pool balls or throw a knife and stick it in the wall. I finally came to the conclusion that I couldn't do a damn thing except forge my stepfather's name to perfection, and play my guitar. *That's it!* I'll bring my guitar and play for five minutes! But wait! By doing so my secret would be out and I would open myself up to the same teasing the "Elvis" kid Bert Owen endured on a daily basis.

Like me, Bert Owen was an aspiring musician. In Bert's case he was consumed by the music of Elvis so much that he patterned himself after The King. Kids at Liberty High teased Bert unmercifully and called him "Elvis." When I saw him being made fun of because of his interest in music, I decided to remain silent about my personal musical interests and my ability to play guitar. I knew if anybody ever teased me like they teased him I would be kicked out of school for knocking somebody on their ass. Now I was faced with the decision of whether or not to bring my guitar to speech class and take a chance on being mocked like Bert. I decided I'd just have to take my chances. Playing the guitar was all I knew how to do.

On the day of my demonstration speech I didn't want to carry my guitar around with me all day and take a chance on getting in a fight if somebody popped off. I skipped all my earlier classes and showed up just in time for speech class. As I entered the school building the bell rang and the hallway filled with students rushing to their next class. I swaggered through the crowded hallway in my black leather jacket and aviator shades with my guitar over my shoulder trying to look cool. Kids stepped aside to let me pass as if I was carrying a loaded shotgun. I could hear their murmuring as they stopped and stared.

Once in the classroom, I propped the guitar behind the teacher's desk before the rest of the class arrived. When it came my turn to speak, I picked up the guitar, sat down on the front of Mrs. Southgate's desk and laid the guitar across my leg. The room fell silent. My palms were sweating, my hands were shaking and I didn't know what to say.

Somehow, I just started talking. "This is a Silvertone F-Hole acoustic guitar," I said.

I explained different parts of the guitar: the body, the neck, what frets were and their purpose. I explained that guitar strings come in different gauges and each one makes a different sound. You could've heard a pin drop as I slowly plucked each string separately, then placed my fingers on the strings at different positions along the neck to make an even greater variety of sounds.

I told how the guitar was a very versatile instrument and capable of playing many different styles of music. I demonstrated by playing a simplified version of an old Spanish instrumental tune I'd seen Roy Clark play on TV called "Malaguena." When I finished the tune I was blown away when the class exploded in an enthusiastic cheer and round of applause. Until then, none of the other students had received that kind of response. I'm sure they cheered more out of surprise that I could play – not because of my expertise (or lack of) with such an intricate piece of music.

In an era when psychedelic rock reigned supreme, I took a chance and played a medley of country instrumentals: "Wildwood Flower," "Under The Double Eagle" and signature licks from Johnny Cash's "Folsom Prison Blues." Again I was surprised when the class cheered. I then played instrumental versions of several old blues riffs, "Johnny B. Goode," "Honky Tonk" and "Heartbreak Hotel." No, I didn't sing.

I figured my five minutes of fame was about up so I tried to make an exit. I was taken by surprise when the class yelled, *"More! More!"* Even Mrs. Southgate insisted I continue! Five minutes turned into thirty and I exited to a standing ovation. *I knew I had found my calling.*

Even though I'd gone over my time limit Mrs. Southgate wrote me a note. "Thank you for bringing your guitar and entertaining the class. A+."*

By sixth period word spread around the school like wildfire about my guitar playing.

*I carried Mrs. Southgate's note in my billfold for many years, then kept it in a book for another twenty-plus years. Every time my career in music was at a low point I'd get it out and re-read it, reminding myself who I really was and why God put me on this planet, to make a joyful noise – a noise that helps people forget their troubles even for just a little while.*

## ELVIS AND THE NEW KID

After my guitar demonstration in speech class word spread fast through Liberty High School that I could play. I was very suspicious of anyone who asked me about music – I had promised myself no one was going to make fun of me as they did that Bert Owen kid.

Bert was a skinny kid about fifteen years old. It was obvious by his appearance that he did not fit into any of the cliques that revolved within the Liberty High School teenage social groups. The country kids wore cowboy boots and jeans while the city kids always looked like they were on their way to church. Bert was always dressed like a rock musician about to go on stage: multi-colored shirts with white cuffs and collars like the The Monkees wore, tight fitting, striped jeans like Sonny Bono and pointy-toed, high-heeled zip-up Beatle boots. He always wore sunshades and his hair was combed back like they did in the '50s. Even after moving from Houston where *everybody* looked weird, Bert definitely stood out in the crowd of FFA cowboys and small-town preppies.

Liberty High School kids may have been easygoing compared to their Houston counterparts, but when it came to Bert some were unmercifully cruel in their razzing. On numerous occasions I watched as kids relentlessly teased and made fun of Bert. Before school, after school, during lunch and between classes kids would yell, "C'mon Elvis, sing us a song!" It was always those uppity rich kids that made fun of Bert. I never saw any of the country kids bother him.

Whether or not Bert realized they were making fun of him I don't know. Bert was always a good sport. He would jump on a chair or a park bench and break into his impromptu Elvis routine, singing the King's hits complete with imaginary microphone and hip gyrations.

I'm sure Bert thought the laughter and hoots were sincere, but I knew better. It infuriated me to see a bunch of spoiled brats making fun of someone who had guts enough to do his own thing. Maybe it made me angry because I was influenced by Elvis as much as Bert, but not a fanatic about it. I saw Bert as a kindred spirit and those kids could have just as easily been making fun of me.

After seeing the harassment Bert went through, I had kept quiet about my musical interests, ability and desire to play until my speech class debut. When I stepped off the school bus the morning after my guitar demonstration, Bert was waiting for me.

News had reached Bert that the new kid played guitar. He met me at the bus stop to tell me he was looking for guitar player. I gave him a glance and walked away. I did not want to be around when kids started making fun of him. He followed, got in front of me, stuck out his hand and introduced himself.

Bert told me he wanted me to perform with him in the upcoming Liberty High School Talent Show. I found him to be a very likeable kid and I noticed right away that he was very passionate about his music. I said, "Okay. Let's give it a shot."

I showed up at Bert's house a couple of days later for a practice session. He ushered me into his bedroom which would serve as our practice room. As I entered the room I was blown away. Every square inch of wall, ceiling and door was covered with album covers and full color posters of Elvis.

While I tuned up my guitar, Bert plowed right into playing bits and pieces of different songs. With each song he'd excitedly ask, "Do you know this one? Do you know this one?"

I was amazed at his musical versatility and ability to play songs by Elvis, Chuck Berry and '50s rockers, as well as the Beatles, Bob Dylan, Johnny Cash, Merle Haggard, and Hank Williams. At that time most teenagers were into rock. Bert was the first kid I had met in my age group that played country.

Growing up in the southern music meccas of Mississippi, Tennessee and Texas had given me a lot of exposure to many different kinds of music: '50s rock, country, hillbilly, and blues. I never missed a single episode of *The Johnny Cash Show* or *The Glen Campbell Goodtime Hour*. Rarely did our household miss the *Ed Sullivan Show*. My stepdad kept the family radio set on country stations while I kept my little transistor set on rock stations. As a result I only knew one other musician that could relate to Bert's wide repertoire – *me!*

I asked Bert about the rest of the band. He said there was no band, just him and me. We ran through a lot of songs that afternoon. We settled on two songs to play at the talent show auditions to be held in the auditorium the very next day after school. We would play "Mama Tried" by Merle Haggard and "Whole Lotta Shakin'" by Jerry Lee Lewis.

The next afternoon at the auditions we set up Bert's amplifier and both plugged into it. Bert was the only singer and would use the house mic. It was one of those old style "potato masher" mics screwed onto the stand like the ones popular in the '50s.

The room was full of students waiting their turn to audition and their families, as well as curious onlookers who came to see what "Elvis" and "The New Kid" were going to do. We played "Mama Tried" and it went *great!* Bert's voice rang through the old high school auditorium speakers as clear as a bell. We sounded like a Saturday Night at the Grand Ole Opry. People actually applauded!

I kicked off "Whole Lotta Shakin' Going On" with a Chuck Berry/Johnny B. Goode style guitar intro. In his excitement to do his best Elvis interpretation of the song, Bert grabbed the mic stand and dropped on his left knee with his right leg stretched out across the floor. He cradled the mic in his left hand inches below his well-planned Elvis sneer. His right hand flew straight up in the air with his fingers twitching back and forth. It was just like I'd seen Elvis do in some old black and white newsreel. There, in all his glory, in front of half the school stretched out across the stage in his Elvis position – *Bert forgot the words!* He yelled into the mic, "HEEEEEEY BABY…" *The wrong words!*

Bert had gone completely blank! He looked up at me from his outstretched position. I saw the fear in his eyes. His face turned white with terror. I kept playing, waiting for him to remember the words. I yelled, "Bert, it's *'come on over baby'*!" He finally started singing "Come on over baby, whole lotta shakin' going on…" Bert then jumped up and started dancing and shaking all over the stage like he had been struck by a lightning bolt. I was dumbfounded! I couldn't look at the audience for watching Bert wondering what the hell he was going to do next. He didn't warn me about his Elvis dance routine and it was just as much a surprise to me as it was to the audience. They were screaming, shouting and rolling in the aisles laughing their asses off. I could feel the heat running up the back of my neck. I wanted to throw the guitar down and *run*.

Somehow we made it through the first half of the song. While I played my lead guitar solo Bert was convulsing all over the stage. The audience was screaming hysterically. The second verse came around and, once again, Bert stretched out across the stage in that classic Elvis position and yelled into the mic, "HEEEEEEY BABY!" Once again it was the *wrong words*! Once again, Bert went blank! Once again, he turned white as a ghost! Once again, I yelled "it's *'come on over baby'*!" Bert took my cue, finished the second verse and we ended the song. By the end of the song, people were literally falling out of their seats!

My face felt like a third-degree burn. I could not look at the audience. On my last note I yanked my guitar cord right out of the amp and bolted out the side door of the auditorium as fast as I could run with my guitar still strapped over my shoulder.

Bert called me later that evening. We didn't pass the audition. How did I already know that? I just knew we would be the laughing stock of the whole school and my biggest fear of being made fun of would come true. I went to school the next day prepared to fight.

Apparently we were not as bad as I thought. Even though we flubbed our audition I was surprised by the positive reviews and I got a lot of compliments on my guitar playing. Fellow students gained a new respect for Bert. He may have forgotten the words, but he put on a hell of a show.

In the weeks that followed, people talked about our audition more than the actual talent show. Bert's teasing from the other students stopped. I was offered a job as lead guitar in a couple of bands at school that I did not even know existed.

After graduation Bert moved to Houston. He became a respected full-time entertainer at the World Famous Gilley's Club in Pasadena, Texas. He has performed all over the country, rubbed elbows with the stars, cut records, produced his own CDs, been on TV and radio and even performed as an Elvis Impersonator. Imagine that.

Even to this day, Bert will say he went blank at the audition because, according to him, when he leaned over, a girl on the front row was wearing a mini-skirt and no panties. That's as good an excuse as any I've ever heard.

Bert Owen and I have remained great friends through the years and have done many shows together. We often joke about our flubbed audition. Each time we do a show together, just before the first song, I always turn to Bert and say, "remember it's *come on over baby*!"

## THE MIDNIGHT MOONSHINERS

After the flubbed talent show audition, over the next year I met and jammed with a number of musicians at Liberty High School.

One of the musicians was Billy Touchet (too-shay) who was a fantastic country singer. On weekends he and I would tell our parents we were working late at our grocery store jobs. Instead of working late we'd sneak off to the Wagon Wheel Club where Billy would sing a few songs with the band. We were both only seventeen, but learned you can talk your way into about anything if you show up carrying a guitar. I wasn't good enough to play with a professional band yet, but I'd watch in amazement as Billy's songs would pack the dance floor with boot-scootin' two-steppers.

One evening Billy stopped by my house and told me he was on his way to audition for a band in rural east Liberty County in a community called the Fregia Settlement (pronounced Free-jay).

Thirty minutes later we arrived at a small building in the middle of nowhere. Cars and pickups were parked up and down both sides of the road. As we stepped out of the car we could hear a live band blasting old time rock 'n roll through the open doors and windows.

We made our way between several men standing outside the front door drinking beer. Stepping inside, the room was dimly lit with Christmas tree lights and was full of people of all ages dancing to the music. I was surprised to see such a big party on a weeknight. It was my first introduction to the Cajun culture. As time passed, I learned that whenever music is playing, Cajuns will throw an instant party!

As Billy and I entered the building the band quit playing and the room fell silent. Being strangers in their midst, the Cajuns eyed us suspiciously. I recognized a couple of guys in the band from school. With shouts of greetings, Billy was immediately invited to the stage to sing. I sat down in the back of the building on a wooden bench that was nailed to the wall.

After a few songs Billy motioned me to the bandstand. He had told them I played lead guitar. He introduced me to the band: Junior Crouthers on drums and Charlie Adams and Donny Roberts on rhythm guitar. I played three songs with them and they offered me my very first job as a lead guitar player in a real band, called The Midnight Moonshiners.

I was ecstatic. Later that night I told my parents the great news, but they were not very excited. I didn't realize my mother's tepid response came from the fact her second husband, Bob Allbritton from Moorhead, Mississippi, had been a professional lead guitarist who had once played for Conway Twitty. She still had a bad taste in her mouth from her brush with the music business. She knew far better than me the trials and tribulations that lay in my path.

My stepdad (Mom's third husband Bruno Acker) was quick to resound from his big recliner in front of the TV. "What the goddamn hell is wrong with you? You better stick your nose in yer goddamn school books, boy, you got shit for brains!"

I knew I was on my way to stardom so I paid no attention to them.

Billy quit the band almost immediately. Since none of us sang, The Midnight Moonshiners were forced to become an all-instrumental band. We played our first gig in the spring of 1971 at a beer joint called Curley & Opals on Houston's notorious McCarty Drive. We thought we had hit the big time when we arrived to see our band name written in magic marker on white butcher paper stapled to the front door. We played our twenty songs over and over, making a grand total of $13 at the door. That was three dollars each and a buck to Donnie's brother David Fregia, who was our manager.

With Billy gone we needed a lead singer. No one volunteered. Remembering my traumatic singing experience from the second grade I reluctantly said, "I ain't no damn singer, but I'll give it a shot."

In that same small building that always filled up with people every time we practiced, I was scared to death at the next band practice. I didn't want to sing, but somebody had to. I had no idea how to sing. I might as well have been trying to fly an airplane blindfolded.

We kicked off the first song. My untried voice was all over the map. I had no idea what key I sang in so I was constantly changing. I felt stupid and embarrassed. In my mind I could hear all those kids back in my second grade class rolling with laughter. When I sang Elvis' "One Night With You," a beautiful, dark-haired sixteen-year-old Cajun girl in the back of the room started squealing. I knew I had it right!

Before the night was over, I was The Midnight Moonshiners new lead singer. I was also going steady with the Cajun girl.

## THE MOVEN SHADOWS

Within a few weeks The Midnight Moonshiners broke up.

The drummer Junior and I stuck together and decided to form another band. Having difficulty finding new members in such rural surroundings, my mom insisted we let my kid brother Ray play.

I argued. "But Mom, Ray is only fifteen! He can't play guitar good enough and his Magnus Chord organ is a toy!"

Nonetheless, we agreed to let Ray play if Mom would buy him a bass guitar. My brother became our reluctant bass guitar player.

James Nugent became our rhythm guitarist and eventually his girlfriend, Barbara Johnson (a rodeo queen from Hardin, Texas), became our lead singer. Together we became the Moven Shadows. Too young to play in bars, we spent the rest of our high school days performing anywhere we could: house dances, barn dances, on front porches, in back yards, at community centers, on the back of hay trucks and at benefits.

After my graduation in 1972, to my great disappointment the band broke up. I guess it was a part of growing up, but I wanted a career in music.

Ray moved off with some hippie girl and grew his hair down to his ass.

Junior got married and got a day job operating a bulldozer.

James married the Rodeo Queen and they both gave up music.

Me? I was suddenly a dreamer without a band, without a plan and without a direction. But I still had a dream. And I still had the Cajun girl.

*Barbara Johnson and James Nugent, 1972*

*The Moven Shadows Circa 1972, L to R: Gene Kelton, Guitar; Junior Crouthers, Drums; Ray Kelton, Bass. Not pictured: James Nugent, Guitar*

*Me, age 7 in Moorhead, Mississippi where
I had my first Gig From Hell.*

*At 14 with my Sears Silvertone. After my
twenty-minute career with the Continental Five.
May 1967*

*The Moven Shadows circa 1971, L to R: James Nugent, Guitar; Junior Crouthers, Drums;
Ray Kelton, Bass; Gene Kelton, Guitar*

BOOK TWO

# Weekend Warrior Years

## 1973-1983

One week after graduation my stepdad gave me two choices: move out or be thrown out by the following weekend. I moved out that same day. Twenty bucks a week got me a hole in the wall room with a bathroom down the hall at Liberty's Ott Hotel.

I spent my first year out of school working as a laborer for Brown & Root Construction at Mobay Chemical in Baytown, Texas, making $2.40 an hour. After taxes I brought home eighty bucks for forty hours of busting my ass digging ditches in the blazing August sun or pushing wheelbarrows through the mud with icicles hanging off my hard hat in the winter. My life was not what I thought it would be after spending thirteen years in school to earn a diploma (I failed one year) and learning every one of Chuck Berry's licks on my guitar. Didn't those Brown & Root assholes know I was a *star*?

Any time I talked about having dreams of playing music for a living those redneck Brown & Rooters would rake me over the coals. They all sounded like my stepdad.

"Dreams are for kids," they said.

## THE YELLOW WAGON CAFE

I worked my first winter out of high school at Mobay. I hated my day job. Every day I suffered in anxious desperation and depression wondering what the hell I was going to do about my music career.

In the spring of 1973 I got a solo-acoustic gig at The Yellow Wagon Cafe, a small truck stop cafe on Almeda Road twenty miles south of Houston. I played every Friday and Saturday night from 6pm to midnight sitting on a bar stool. I got free beer, a hamburger basket and a salary of ten bucks a night. I usually made another forty bucks in tips from truckers who either requested an old country classic or offered to pay for my next haircut. Except for the long hours it was a good gig, a good time and a great learning experience.

I actually thought all those sexy gals who hung around the truck stop were there because of my singing! How stupid I was in those days.

## THE BRENTWOOD CLUB

After a few weeks at The Yellow Wagon Cafe, I graduated to a three-night-a-week gig at a little mixed-drink bar called The Brentwood Club in southwest Houston. I played every Thursday, Friday and Saturday from 9pm to 1:30am. I was paid an unbelievable salary of $25 a night! The salary plus tips put me earning over a hundred bucks a week playing a guitar.

When I weighed the $80 a week I made busting my ass for Brown & Root against the money I was making playing guitar three nights a week in a nice air-conditioned nightclub filled with hot, young, lonely housewives, I told Brown & Root to kiss my ass. I quit my day job. I spent the next couple of months reveling in my youth, and that less than a year out of high school I was making a living playing music. I was having a blast!

One night a long-haired guy about my age sat at the bar at The Brentwood Club. His intense interest in my performance alerted me that he was probably a musician. My suspicions proved to be correct. On break I invited guitarist/singer Mike Sicola to sit in.

He was very talented and sang great. After about four songs, he headed out the door without saying a word. When I returned to the stage I saw the reason for his hasty exit. He had broken three strings off my new Yamaha twelve-string guitar.

About three weeks later Mike snuck back in the club.

The moment I saw him I immediately took a break and demanded payment for a new set of strings. We argued but I couldn't help but like the guy. This time he brought his own guitar and we did a set together. It went great.

The following week Mike brought in his keyboard and I invited a drummer (whose name I don't remember) and my brother Ray to sit in on bass. Together we rocked the Brentwood Club for the next several weeks. Since I was the only one on salary, I let the guys split the tip money. Sometimes they made as much as me.

Every night the manager repeatedly told us to turn it down. We wondered why. What right did she have to tell us what to do? After all, we were the reason the place was packed! The place would've been empty without us! Why should we let a beer-slinger tell us what to do? *Didn't she know we were going to be superstars?*

Finally Mike had enough. "Bitch! We're musicians, you're just a fuckin' barmaid, you mind your fuckin' bar and we'll take care of the music!"

That night I got fired from The Brentwood Club. Yep. It truly was a learning experience.

Though unemployed I had hope. Ray, Mike and I had formed a new band called the "Firecreek Boogie Blues Band." We practiced every minute we could and played a lot of free gigs just to be playing.

We played a gig for a wild, private party in the clubhouse of the Citadel Apartments. Over a hundred people were shitfaced and girls were "pulling chains" in the sauna. Everyone was openly smoking marijuana, a definite no-no in public back then. I had never smoked grass while playing music. That night I learned the hard way that I could not – and should not – *ever* smoke dope and try to play music. I became sluggish, tone deaf, and couldn't even *tune* my guitar. While hitting one string I tightened another and broke several strings before I realized what I was doing. I was unable to finish the night. After that night I rarely ever toked more than a drag or two at a gig if anything at all.

With our band in practice mode with no paying gigs my unemployment situation soon became critical. I cringed at the thought of crawling back to my old job with Brown & Root. I started working in a sweltering insulation manufacturing warehouse. Every night I came home itching after being impaled with millions of minuscule fiberglass particles.

## DRUNK AND SCREWED

I was twenty years old in the summer of 1973, and ready to conquer the world as lead guitar player with the newly formed Firecreek Boogie Blues Band. The band name was later shortened to Firecreek for marquee purposes. Our band played for free three nights a week at a jumping little nightclub on Telephone Road near Pearland, Texas, called Jay's Club.

The owner Jay was the stereotypical, middle-aged, greasy-haired sleazeball club owner who made us a lot of promises about future employment – and money-making potential – as his full-time house band. Being country boys from the small town of Liberty, we blindly trusted everybody. We believed ol' Jay when he said, "If you boys will work a couple of weeks for free, when ya'll get the crowd built up, I'll start payin' you a salary."

Believing we would soon be making big money, we made and hung posters in area businesses, passed out flyers and got on the phone to everybody we knew inviting them to shows. On our breaks during the show we made it a point to go around to each table meeting people and making them feel welcome. We busted our asses promoting that gig and our promotion campaign worked! Within a couple of weeks we were playing to a packed house every Thursday, Friday and Saturday night!

I was very proud of Firecreek. We were a damn good band. There were far better bands out there, but our enthusiasm was contagious and that alone kept the crowd coming back.

During that era most young white-boy bands played rock music. Country music was played by middle-aged, beer-gutted, country-western bands in VFWs and cowboy honky-tonks. Firecreek was probably the first band (and the first band in our age group) to promote themselves as a Country-Rock band, meaning we could go from playing songs by Three Dog Night and Jimi Hendrix to Merle Haggard and Johnny Cash. Songs like "Sleepwalk" or "House Of The Rising Sun" would always pack the dance floor and a good old '50s rocker would always fire up the audience.

While most bands drew a following their own age, we noticed we were drawing a wide variety of people – hippies, cowboys, recent Vietnam vets, bikers and so on. This made for a potentially volatile mix when alcohol was added. We were serenading a time bomb.

One night at Jay's Club I was singing a very popular new song called "Why Don't We Get Drunk And Screw" by young singer/songwriter Jimmy Buffett. Radio stations would not play the song, but it was blasting from every jukebox in the country every fifteen minutes. It became our most requested song. Every time we sang it the entire audience would join in on the chorus.

As I finished the song an older gentleman approached the bandstand. Thinking that he wanted to shake my hand and make a request I extended my hand. He jumped back and yelled, "I ain't shakin' yer goddammed hand you hippie piece a shit! You gotta be the most vulgarest human I ever seen! You offended me and my wife with that damn screwin' song! We don't wanna hear that shit!"

I was caught completely off guard. Up to that point we had great reviews and accolades from our audiences. Now a drunk old redneck was cussing me out in front of my audience!

He kept yelling. "You apologize to my wife you asshole! Apologize to my wife you asshole! I may be an old man but I'll whup goddamn hippie ass!"

My first impulse was to jump off the stage and smack the guy. Instead I yelled back. "Look, Pop, this ain't no church! It's a beer joint! Take your old lady and get out! If you wanna kick my ass, when we take a break I'll meet you in the parking lot!"

I could not believe I actually challenged the old guy as if I were back in high school. I thought he was going to take a swing at me as the band went into the next song. He stood in front of one of our speakers as if he were about to dowse it with his drink. Ray unfastened his guitar strap ready to spear the guy with his bass.

I kept my eyes on the old dude as we played out the set. I sized him up for the impending fight. Then reality hit me. He was at least 65, I was 20. If he got the drop on me, I'd look like a candy-ass getting my ass kicked by an old man. Then again, if I whipped his ass every redneck in the place would stomp the shit out of this "young hippie" for beating up a poor, old grandpa. I was in a lose-lose situation. There was no way for me to get out of this predicament with any dignity and not get my ass kicked, one way or the other.

I grabbed the mic. "Hey people! This old man wants to whip my ass for singing 'Why Don't We Get Drunk And Screw'!" The crowd roared with laughter and started booing him.

"He says I offended him and his wife and that I'm the most vulgarest human he ever met!"

The crowd rolled with laughter.

"Ya'll like that song?"

With a rousing, pep-rally like cheer the crowd yelled, "YEAH!"

"Then you're all vulgar humans and he's gonna whip all your asses!"

Worked into a frenzy the crowd started yelling at the old guy. The guy stood at the front of the stage glaring at me like a mad bull. I saw his mouth moving but the crowd drowned him out. The band joined me in ridiculing the old man.

Mike yelled, "Take your stupid old lady and your redneck ass and get the hell outta here!"

The crowd was loving it! They joined in calling the old guy every filthy name in the world.

The club manager was a big, football player-looking guy. He jumped over the bar, grabbed the old man by the shirt collar and seat of his pants and tossed him into the parking lot. The crowd was on their feet cheering. Suddenly a high pitched, shrill scream penetrated the roar of the cheering crowd. "You son-of-a-bitch, that's my husband!"

The manager grabbed the old lady by the arm, dragging her toward the door. She was screaming at the top of her lungs as if he was killing her. Shoving her out the door was like trying to shove a cat into a pail of water. It was hilarious watching her grab the door and claw at him with her free hand. She fought back trying to kick the manager in the balls, all the while screaming, "My purse, my purse!"

Somebody threw her purse across the room and it landed by the door. The manager pushed her out the door then kicked her purse out behind her.

The excited audience broke into a rousing cheer and gave the manager a standing ovation. With a big grin on his face he bowed to the crowd like a Broadway actor after a hit performance. We kicked off into the chorus of "Why Don't We Get Drunk and Screw." The rowdy audience sang along with us louder than ever.

Except for the owner shooting himself in the foot with his own gun, nothing that exciting happened again until a month later.

## QUITTING JAY'S CLUB

We were promised a big salary once we built up a clientele for the club. Two months into the gig we were packing the house and still working for tips. Every time we'd talk to Jay about a salary he refused to pay us saying we didn't have a regular following yet.

We knew it was bullshit. Every weekend fire marshalls arrived and threatened to shut the place down because too many people were inside. Jay would station himself at the door and turn people away. Our enthusiasm turned to contempt.

One Friday night we played to a packed house. We waited until the middle of the second set and with the dance floor packed, we abruptly stopped in the middle of a song. People on the dance floor thought the power went off. I stepped to the mic. "We quit! The owner won't pay us so we quit! We refuse to keep playing for free!"

The room filled with loud protests from the audience, booing the owner and insisting he pay us to keep playing.

As we shoved our amps out the door, well-meaning fans desperately tried to get us to stay by offering to pass the kitty. We thanked them, but we were tired of passing the kitty while the owner raked in the bucks and refused to pay us. It was no longer just about the money. We vowed not to sell any more whiskey for Jay unless he paid us.

It was only 11pm. As the packed house cleared out Jay still refused to pay us. He went out of business two months later.

Performing at Jay's Club was not a total loss. The experience served its purpose. Working three nights a week for most of the summer had forged Firecreek into a super-tight show band with great three-part harmonies and a song list a mile long. By trial and error we learned the art of spontaneous, creative jamming that spawned arrangements I still use to this day.

The experience also taught us lasting and valuable lessons about dealing with nightclub owners: never play for free, never bid low and expect to ever get a raise and club owners are not in the music business – they are in the *alcohol selling business.*

We learned how to promote our own shows and how to be *entertainers,* not just play instruments. We learned how to win over an audience and the power of rock 'n roll.

## Escape From The 770 Club

In October 1973 my new bride and I moved from our little apartment in Pasadena, Texas, into a trailer house we bought and set up in the middle of her daddy's cow pasture in Liberty. My music career was put on hold while I became domesticated, housebroken and root-bound. After about a year without playing music I was like a drug addict who needed a fix.

The rest of the band still lived on the northwest side of Houston about seventy miles away, doing little gigs here and there. In an effort to get the band together they would camp out at my house in Liberty on weekends. We would immerse ourselves in grueling practices from Friday night until Sunday afternoon, preparing to unleash the all new Firecreek on the world.

All musicians know you can practice until you are blue in the face but you never really get tight until you play in front of a live audience. After months of tedious practicing with no live performances we were edgy, short-tempered and getting on each other's nerves. We needed the release only playing live would bring.

One Sunday afternoon after a weekend of hard practicing we were restless and itching to play in front of people. I remembered the old 770 Club in Raywood, Texas. It was only a few miles away and one of the few places open on Sunday that had a bandstand. We jumped in the car and headed to the 770 in hopes we could jam for a couple of hours, blow off some steam and test drive our new song list.

The 770 was a dilapidated, wood-frame beer joint located on a deserted stretch of Highway 770 between Raywood and Daisetta. There were always a few pickup trucks parked out front, and sometimes even a couple of horses tied next to the building. The 770 had a reputation for being a "blood-bucket," meaning fights were common. There were always bloody fistfights. Drunk or sober, oilfield roughnecks, rednecks and cowboys love to fight! If there was nobody to fight they'd just put their fist through the wall for the hell of it.

I figured since it was a Sunday afternoon we'd be able to do a short jam session without any trouble. There were several pickup trucks parked around the building when we arrived.

As we four long-haired musicians strolled into the building, a hush fell over the room – just like a saloon scene in a Clint Eastwood movie. I never thought about what we must have looked like to the indigenous rednecks until we walked through the door.

In the days before cowboys wore long hair and earrings it was still considered open season on long-haired, hippie-looking males whenever a redneck felt like starting a fight for sport. In those days there was no discrimination between being black and being a long-haired white guy. Both were fair game to a redneck out to start trouble.

As we walked past the pool table toward the bar I heard one of them say, "Gaaaaddamn! Whut-tha fuck we got here? A buncha got-damn hippies!"

Another one hollered. "Da-a-a-ammn, she's a purdy one!"

We ignored their catterwalling and insults and walked straight to the bar where I spoke to the bartender. I recognized her from previous gigs. Her name was Tiny. That was ironic because she weighed about 400 pounds. She always wore all black, matching her mile high, teased-up jet black hair. She said we could set up and play since we offered to play for free.

Suddenly a slobbering, spit-spurting, snaggled-toothed drunk redneck grabbed my left forearm, pressing it down on the bar and stabbing his index finger into it.

"You look like one a-them thar gaw'damn hippiefied dope fiends! I bet 'chu been a-poppin' that thar gaw'damn merry-jee-wanna!"

Knowing it was pointless to tell the toothless creep you don't "pop" marijuana, I jerked loose from his grip. "Naw, man, we're a band, we're just here to play some music."

A commotion to my right got my attention. Our lead singer Mike Sicola, drummer T.J. Austin and my brother Ray were being hassled at the bar. In an effort to provoke us to fight, the rednecks flipped Mike's long hair and called us fags, queers, hippies, niggers and so on.

Mike and T.J.'s solemn expressions indicated they were well aware of the seriousness of our predicament. Ray, on the other hand, seemed somewhat lackadaisical and disconnected from the reality of the situation and was actually cracking jokes with our aggressors.

A streak of terror ripped through me like lightning. I remembered my brother Ray had stitches in his stomach from an emergency operation for a ruptured appendix just a week before. He was on antibiotics and pain killers. One punch to the stomach and Ray's guts would spill all over the floor. He could die!

I looked around for Tiny hoping she would call off the rednecks, but she had disappeared to the other side of the room pretending not to notice shit was about to hit the fan.

I turned to the mob and yelled, "Whoa! Whoa! Hold on! We don't want no trouble! We're just a band here to play ya'll some music!"

"We don't wanna hear nun-na-yer goddamn hippie shit!"

I knew right then the rednecks were out for blood and there was no way to avoid a fight. In fear for my brother's life I grabbed him by the arm and pushed him along the wall behind the pool table toward the door. "Let's go, let's go!" Mike and T.J. followed behind us.

The lynch mob of drunk rednecks armed themselves with beer bottles and pool sticks, pinning us against the wall. I wasn't worried about Mike and T.J. I knew they could fight.

At 25, Mike was a husky Italian who grew up on Houston's tough north side. In his teens he had spent a couple years in Gatesville prison for teenage boys. He got out only when the judge gave him two choices: be transferred to an adult prison for two more years or spend two years in the Army. Mike chose the Army. The scars on his face and knuckles and the self-applied tattoos on his hands were proof he could handle himself.

I was not concerned about T.J. either. He was a tall, lean kid about 18 with a short fuse and a bad-ass James Dean attitude. He was a street fighter with some jail time under his belt as well. He could play machine gun drum rolls with lightning fast precision. I knew he could beat the shit of any slobbering drunk in the place. As tough as we thought we were, being outnumbered was a concern. Ray's handicap put Mike, T.J. and me against eight or nine rednecks. Winning or losing a bar fight was nothing compared to the fact that a single punch to Ray's stomach could kill him.

The four of us inched our way toward the front door with our backs against the wall. The mob took turns taking practice swings at us with pool sticks, coming within inches of our faces before pulling back, shrieking with maniacal laughter and showing their rotten teeth every time we threw our arms up to block the blows.

I stood between Ray and our attackers. I positioned my left hand in front of me protecting myself from an attack and my right hand behind me holding Ray's belt buckle, dragging him toward the door. Ray's pain medication was in full effect – he seemed oblivious to the danger. He kept cracking jokes as if we were in a *Saturday Night Live* skit. I remember him pointing his finger in the air, quoting that famous line from *Cool Hand Luke*: "What we have here is a failure to communicate!" Funny now, but not then.

We finally made it to the parking lot. Our car was parked twenty feet from the front door, but it seemed like a hundred miles. Huddled together back to back, we inched toward the car at a snail's pace. The mob followed us outside calling us names and still taking practice swings with their pool sticks.

Somehow we made it to the car without incident. While bantering with our antagonists I slowly opened the backdoor and shoved Ray into the back seat. The rest of us slid into the car real slow, expecting an attack at any moment. We slammed the doors. I fired up the engine, threw the car in reverse and spun out of the driveway, throwing mud and rocks all over the rednecks. As we sped away Mike leaned out the window raising his middle finger in the air and yelling, "Fuck you, you buncha redneck cocksuckers!"

The rednecks, laughing like hyenas, returned Mike's parting gesture and threw rocks at us as we burned onto the blacktop. On the ride home we were overwhelmed by the adrenaline rush of a very intense and close call. Mike and T.J. were exploding with the stereotypical macho male rhetoric. T.J. yelled, "Man, we shoulda took those pool sticks away from them son-of-a-bitches and stuck 'em up their asses!"

"They're lucky they didn't fuck with Firecreek!" yelled Mike. "We'd a beat their fuckin' redneck asses to a pulp!"

"Yeah!" exclaimed T.J. "We oughtta go back in there and whip their asses!"

Mike shouted, "Man, don't cha know they'd shit in their cowboy boots if we busted back in the door and kicked their ass!" (Laughs all around.)

Me? I drove home in silence. My hands were shaking as I considered that Ray's guts could have been splattered all over the floor back at the 770.

Ray's pain medication had caused him to be completely disconnected with what just happened. He reached into his pocket, retrieved half a joint and fired it up. In his best redneck impersonation, he said, "Hey! Any a-you hippiefied dope fiends wanna pop some merry-jee-wanna?" We all cracked up laughing.

## Not So Hot Shit

In the early seventies, most hotels had lounges and hired bands. The big, ritzy hotels featured Las Vegas quality show bands. Hotels like Ramada and Holiday Inn hired smaller combo groups like our four-piece band. Due to the hotels' wide range of customers, "Holiday Inn bands" (as I referred to them) were required to play a variety of middle of the road, watered-down, candy-coated music. No hard rock or dirt road country by any singer with a name like Hank, Johnny or Merle. Because of the large number of hotels hiring bands and the work available, Firecreek became a Holiday Inn lounge act. Our song list included "Tie A Yellow Ribbon," by Tony Orlando, "I Believe In Music" by Mac Davis, "Behind Closed Doors" by Charlie Rich and other yawnable songs. We hated our song list but we worked steady.

One day I got a call from a club in Kemah called The Bamboo Hut. The owner said he had a house band called "Bert, Art & Beaver" who had been there a long time and he was ready to make a change. We agreed to come in for an audition.

The other band's gear was set up onstage when we arrived, so we set up on the dance floor. At 7pm we kicked off our forty-minute audition. Having been playing Holiday Inn lounge act songs, we did our usual lounge-lizard routine to the small, unappreciative audience.

After the audition the owner came over. "Look, you boys are pretty good, but that bullshit ya'll just played ain't gonna cut it here. Ya'll got anything with a harder groove to it? More of an edge? If ya'll wanna give it another try, the house band don't play for another hour."

We went back up and played "Johnny B. Goode," "Smoke On The Water," "Long Train Runnin'," "Ramblin' Man" and some blues. By that time a few more people had come in and the response was very enthusiastic.

After we quit and loaded our equipment, the owner told us he would use us provided we build a better song list. We were elated to have landed a gig outside of the Holiday Inn circuit. Feeling cocky and thinking we were hot shit we decided to stick around and see the band whose job we just took.

We didn't know it but throughout our entire audition the house band was sitting in the back of the room checking us out. At 9pm Bert, Art & Beaver surprised us when they rose from a table in the corner, climbed on stage and exploded into a high energy version of Willie Nelson's "Bloody Mary Morning." My God, they were *great*! They sounded like a ten-piece band! The lead guitar player sounded like three lead guitar players and a steel player all playing at the same time! We were blown away.

Their following turned toward us with looks that said, "They just kicked your ass!"

In an effort to make a joke of our public humiliation I literally crawled under the table. It was a funny stunt, but I really wanted to be invisible and run out the door!

I told the owner that his house band was a hundred times better than us and he'd be crazy to get rid of them. Out of respect for their musicianship I refused to take their gig.

"It don't matter how good a band is," the owner said. "Any band will get burned out if they stay too long at one place. It's not your problem. I'll bring 'em back when I get ready. They need a break. Do you want the gig or not?" I reluctantly accepted the gig, knowing we had big shoes to fill.

I don't know whatever happened to Art and Beaver, but as the years passed Bert Wills became a Gulf Coast legend. He and his band The Cryin' Shames became one of the hottest bluesrock bands in Texas. Throughout the '80s and '90s, any blues band working the Texas Gulf Coast owed a great deal of gratitude to Bert Wills. It didn't matter where you played, Bert done been there and got that cherry!

Bert Wills & The Cryin' Shames was Texas' original Biker Band and were playing the blues long before The Blues Brothers made their first movie and before anyone ever heard of Stevie Ray Vaughan.

I am proud to say that through the years Bert and I became great friends and have done a lot of shows together. He hardly remembers The Bamboo Hut incident, but then again it wasn't he who got his ass kicked that night.

When I grow up, I wanna be just like Bert Wills.

## QUITTING THE BAND: 1974

By fall of 1974 I was twenty-one years old. My first wife and I had been married for about a year and we lived in Liberty. I was working a full-time construction job. We bought a new truck, a mobile home and had a half-acre of land. Meanwhile, I was still handling the promotion and management duties as band leader for Firecreek.

My brother Ray and lead singer Mike Sicola shared an apartment in Houston. They were always unemployed, broke, out of gas, driving piece-of-shit cars and getting evicted. Somehow they never failed to have money for the necessities of life: alcohol, cigarettes and marijuana. They slept all day and stayed up all night writing songs on their acoustic guitars – songs that did not make a damn bit of sense to me nor fit into Firecreek's format. I vetoed every effort to incorporate their fog-brained songs into our show.

It did us no good to rehearse as Firecreek. No matter how much we practiced, not a single song was played at a gig the way it was rehearsed. I grew angry and frustrated that my musical dreams were being dashed by two guys who were great musicians but chose to stay fucked up all the time.

In December of 1974 my wife announced that she was "late." That announcement caused me to give serious consideration to the pursuit of my musical dreams, especially since I couldn't get any cooperation from the band.

A week or so after my wife's big announcement, Firecreek played a gig at The Bamboo Hut. On the first break, Ray and Mike had their usual parking lot smoking session and ridiculed me for not joining them. I had already learned the hard way I could not smoke dope and play music.

Just before going back on stage for the second set, Ray and Mike, with their bloodshot eyes and Cheech & Chong impersonations informed me they were taking over the band. From that point on *they* would be running the band and were going to play *their* songs, *their* way and *people were going to love it*!

"You just step aside and watch!" said Mike. "People will sit up and take notice at the all-new Firecreek!"

Without argument, I moved my mic stand to the back of the stage. "Please, by all means, do it your way! I can't wait to see people sit up and take notice."

Neither the drummer T.J. Austin nor I had a clue what Ray and Mike were going to do.

They attempted to play their fog-brained dope songs. After several false starts, they stopped in the middle of each song to argue about keys, arrangements and so on – right there in front of the audience. I sarcastically said, "Hey, Mike! You were right, man! People are sittin' up and takin' notice!"

After the most embarrassing twenty minutes of hell I've ever spent on stage, Mike asked me to take over so we could finish the show with some dignity.

At the end of the night I packed up. I told them my wife was pregnant and I had more important things to think about than to waste my time with their dope-smoking bullshit.

As I walked out Mike said, "Man, you're gonna be sorry cause in six months you'll be watchin' us on *The Midnight Special*!"

I wished them luck and drove away. I arrived home around 3am, sat down on the couch and told my wife what happened at the gig, and that I quit the band. I wept as if I had lost a loved one in death. I felt it was the end of a dream I had nurtured since I was ten years old. I was hurt and angry because my time, hard work, sacrifice and everything I had worked for was up in smoke! Literally. I knew Ray and Mike were great musicians when they wanted to be, but staying stoned had robbed them of their talents, skill, good sense and ambition. It robbed us all of a damn good band.

The following week I sold my band equipment, got a haircut and began preparing for our new arrival. I did not pursue music again as a full-time performer for nearly twelve years.

Ray and Mike never did get on *The Midnight Special*.

Drummer T.J. Austin disappeared off the face of the earth. We figured the rowdy young outlaw had either gone to prison or had been murdered by some of the unsavory characters he ran with. To my amazement as I was writing this book, an email popped up on my screen from the prodigal drummer himself. It had been thirty-three years.

There is a lesson here. I'll let you figure it out.

## Return Of The Weekend Warrior

After getting disgusted and quitting Firecreek in December 1974, I spent the next several years concentrating on taking care of my family.

By 1978 my first wife and I had been married five years. We had two little boys, a new home in the country and two cars in the driveway. I was making a damn good living selling life insurance for American National.

Even with the good life there was something deep down inside gnawing at me so strong I couldn't sleep at night. No matter how hard I tried to ignore it, it would not leave me alone. It haunted my dreams. It was music and my destiny was calling.

After nearly five years of no public performances, I gave in to my inner calling. I bought a new electric guitar and amp and started practicing.

## Texas Country Bandits

By the summer of 1978 the newly formed Firecreek was a weekend warrior, outlaw country band. We played the hits of the day by Waylon, Willie, Charlie Daniels, Johnny Paycheck and others in little honky-tonks around southeast Texas.

During the week my brother Ray and I, along with our life-long friend and drummer, Charlie "CT" Taylor, struggled at our miserable dead-end day jobs while pursuing a music career on Friday and Saturday nights.

While performing at a drag boat racing event at Mizell's Lake in Liberty, the event promoter John Terry, a boisterous hotshot in his mid-thirties, took an immediate liking to us. He claimed he was a personal friend of music producers and famous celebrities involved in the drag boat industry. He offered to introduce us to the "right people" if we would be willing to play a few private parties for his celebrity friends and drag boat sponsors.

Desperate to do whatever it took to hit the big time, we accepted.

John offered us the use of a large warehouse behind the western clothing store he owned in Houston. He suggested leaving our band equipment set up all the time. He said it would cut down on practice setup time and serve as a place where he could bring potential talent buyers to hear us.

Even though we didn't need the practice space, we accepted his offer. From our point of view it gave us a good excuse to hang out with John and get in good with him and all his high-powered friends.

I had always been our unofficial band manager, but as the weeks passed John's interest in the band slowly evolved into management and promotion. We allowed him to take over, leaving us to concentrate on the music.

As practice sessions got underway John's true colors began to surface. On his own turf he became a very aggressive control freak who obviously suffered from a bad case of short man's syndrome. Practicing at his warehouse put us at his mercy. He could do and say anything he damn well pleased and we became the brunt of his raging temper tantrums and scathing insults.

According to John we were just a group of ignorant country boys from Liberty County who didn't know shit about the real world and he alone held the keys to our success. We tolerated his humiliation and dictatorship believing he would lead us to the promised land. Whenever we disagreed with him, he threatened to send us back to Liberty with no hope of ever making it without his help.

At every practice John would bring important-looking "financial backers" claiming they were promoters of major events. They'd sit at one end of the room ignoring our audition, filling the room up with smoke, sipping expensive whiskey and laughing at God knows what.

In an effort to display his power over us John would show off in front of his visitors. He would stop us in mid-song, waving his arms and yelling "Whoa! Whoa! Whoa! What the fuck was *that*? That sounds like shit! Play it again, this time, goddammit, get it right! I didn't spend all this goddamn money so ya'll could fuck up!"

It was really embarrassing in front of strangers who supposedly held the keys to our future.

Not only was the room full of John's friends but also John's wife "Chrissy" and her entourage. Chrissy was a drop-dead gorgeous strawberry blond and former model. She liked our band and loved parading her high class socialite hottie girlfriends around in front of us and John's friends. If I didn't know better, I'd say Chrissy's friends were *auditioning* also. Then again, what the hell did I know? I was just a dumb country boy from Liberty County.

Our practice sessions soon turned into John's private Playboy party with high-powered money guys and red-hot bombshells – all drinking, smoking and dancing to our music two and three times a week.

We felt like trained sideshow monkeys performing at John's whim. I began to understand what blues singer Robert Johnson must have felt like after he supposedly sold his soul to the devil at The Crossroads. Our lust for fame and fortune had caused us to be tempted by the devil's promises – and the devil's name was John.

John insisted on changing the name of the band from Firecreek to a name that identified the band as being from Texas, that played country music and that projected an outlaw image.

From that came the name Texas Country Bandits. We didn't want to change our name but John was the money man. John also demanded that we wear clothes from his western clothing store. "If you're gonna be Texas outlaws you need to look like Texas outlaws," he said.

There was nothing wrong with what we were wearing, but John wanted to use the band to advertise his store. It was his money so he became our clothing sponsor. His fashion-conscious wife became our "image consultant." Along with the clothes, John insisted we wear western hats. Ray's hat was very cool. With his shoulder length dark hair, he looked like a character in a Tom Selleck/Sam Elliott western. Charlie's hat was a very cool black top hat. With his beard and rugged Clint Eastwood looks, Charlie looked like a sinister, old west snake oil salesman.

I was given a hat that was too damn big for my height and stature. The brim was as big as an umbrella and the crown was too tall and rounded on top. Even Hoss Cartwright would've looked silly wearing that damn hat. John adamantly insisted I wear it, along with a pair of suspenders to add to the look. Instead of a Texas Outlaw I felt like a cartoon character. I hated the look. I told John I would not be the comic sidekick for the band. Ray and Charlie suggested I just go along with it. After all, *again*, John was the money man footin' the bill for the duds.

I believed that John was trying to be the dominant male in our little organization, and purposely trying to make me look like a stupid idiot.

Further exercising his power over us, John brought in a beautiful, blond model and told us she was our female singer whether we liked it or not. We protested. We were an all-male band and it would mean endless rehearsals to learn a whole new female-oriented song list. According to John we needed her to do all the female hits of the day and it would be easier for him to book a band with more to offer than "just a bunch of hard dicks."

We relented when John again tempted us with untold riches if we would just "shut the fuck up" and do things his way. He also said the girl singer was his "private stock" and told us to keep our hands off her and our mouths shut. He always made it a point to brandish his automatic pistol whenever he was discussing her.

She certainly was a beautiful woman and looked great in the designer jeans John bought her. No doubt she would have looked great on stage, *but she could not sing a single note.* After a few very painful practice sessions, I called her and fired her. She cried like a baby. In between sobs she asked how I could fire her when, according to her, John had put the band together *just for her* so she could pursue her lifelong dream of being a country-western singer.

I explained it was not John's band. He was only our manager with no say-so whatsoever about who we hired or fired. "Fuck you!" she yelled as she slammed the phone down.

Within minutes John called me raising hell and threatening to whip my ass for firing his singer and messing up his piece of ass. He said he'd kill me if the girl went to his wife. I told him that she might look good, but even he knew she couldn't sing. He agreed she was a terrible singer. John told me from that point on he'd make all the hiring and firing decisions.

John still insisted we needed a girl singer as well as a fiddle player and a keyboard player to round out our Texas Country outlaw sound. I found a keyboard player from Houston's west side. He was a nice, easy going guy in his mid-twenties, very intellectual and a great musician.

As fate would have it we found "Lizzy Gold," a girl singer who was also a red-hot fiddle player. She was truly an undiscovered star!

Regardless of her amazing talents John constantly complained that Lizzy did not fit his vision of what he thought a showbiz vixen should look like. Lizzy wore faded jeans, denim work shirts, and lace-up work boots. She had waist-length straight brown hair that she parted in the middle and let the wind do the rest. She never wore makeup.

What Lizzy didn't have in the glitz and glamour department she made up for when she played and sang. Her focus was on sound, not shine. When she rosined up her bow and unleashed her amazing talent, she captured the heart and soul of everyone listening. Her version of "The Orange Blossom Special" brought people screaming to their feet!

In an effort to give Lizzy a more show-biz look, John bought her an entire wardrobe of the latest western fashions: skin tight designer jeans, sparkly blouses, fancy new boots and a fashionable western hat. He insisted she let her long, brown hair fly during her performance, saying it was an exciting look. Actually he was trying to cover her face since she refused to wear makeup.

Lizzy seemed to appreciate the new clothes, but was not at all interested in John's vision of glitz and glamour. She was the real thing – a true musician and a great entertainer. Even though the band members were about the same age, Lizzy was the only pro. Having already toured with many great bands she was much more experienced than the rest of us. She forgave our amateur efforts and always remained professional, polite and patient as our group of ignorant country boys struggled to keep up with her. She taught us how to be a professional concert showband instead of just a honky-tonk bar band.

After several weeks of grueling practice sessions, John booked the first gig for The Texas Country Bandits at the world famous Sam Houston Coliseum in Houston. We were ecstatic! We were willing to forgive John's ass-holiness because he had come through for us.

In 1978 the Sam Houston Coliseum was Houston's biggest and hottest concert arena. It had hosted Elvis in 1956 and the Beatles in 1965, as well as hundreds of other major concerts and events. We felt as though we were on the brink of stardom.

"Who are we opening for?" we asked. "Willie and Waylon? Johnny Cash?"

"Neither!" came John's reply. "Ya'll are the opening act for a boxing match!"

Though disappointed in the nature of the event, we were still glad to be playing where Elvis and the Beatles had played. It would look good on our resume and we would be paid $500 for one forty-minute set. Wow! That was $100 a man. The average pay in those days was $30 to $50 a man for a four-hour show. We thought we had finally hit the big time.

We set up on a makeshift stage fifty feet from the boxing ring. The building had a capacity of 10,000 people but, except for the ringmaster's announcement mic, there was no house PA or sound system to accommodate a live band. We had to set up and use the same gear we used when playing in little beer joints, with no monitors. Our efforts to tune up by ear were drowned out by boos of the raucous, multi-ethnic crowd there to see a fight, not a country-western band in fancy cowboy clothes and big hats.

We turned up as loud as we could and kicked off with "The South's Gonna Do It Again" by The Charlie Daniels Band. Lizzy's fiddle was screaming. As the crescendo of the first accents exploded and echoed throughout the old building, a thousand people rushed toward the stage. They danced wildly as if possessed by demons. They knocked each other down and fell in piles of thrashing bodies on the floor. The seething mass screamed so loud we could barely hear ourselves play.

Though we were a country-western group, we played with the intensity of a rock band. Lizzy's hat was pulled down tight over her eyes covering her face. Her long hair was whipping like a willow tree in a hurricane. I don't know how she kept her hair from getting tangled in her bow.

During our performance several of Chrissy's bikini clad girlfriends appeared on stage and threw out stacks of John's cheap, caribbean-style straw hats into the crowd. I was amazed at the level of violence as the crowd reacted like sharks in a feeding frenzy, fighting over the free hats and ripping them to shreds.

We were all reeling from the adrenaline rush as we finished our one and only set. As the boxing matches started, I remember thinking it wasn't the first time I'd played the soundtrack for a fistfight. That night I met world famous Houston boxing champion Termite Watkins.

We've been friends ever since.

**Back At Band Practice**

Basking in the glory of our first successful show, our next band practice a few days later at John's warehouse started with a flood of enthusiasm until John entered the practice room. He immediately ripped us to shreds, ridiculing our performance and finding fault with everything we had done or not done.

"The response was phenomenal!" we argued.

"You were playing to a bunch of fuckin' niggers and wetbacks!" John yelled. "And mostly kids! What the fuck do they know about country music? Not a goddamn thing. They weren't there to see you, they were there to see a fight! All I heard was shit!"

We knew we had played good, but John was not going to admit it. After his demoralizing rant I sat down to tune up and we proceeded with our band practice. John stopped us with his usual overly-dramatic hand waving and yelling.

"Get up!" he yelled, glaring at me. "Get the fuck up on your goddam feet! You will perform at every practice just like you were at a show!"

"Hey, man!" I snapped back. "I don't need to stand up to figure out a chord pattern!"

His face turned beet red. I had defied his orders in front of everyone. "I said get on your goddamn feet! *Now!*" He screamed.

The room fell silent. The band was waiting to see if I would give in. John's face turned from red to purple and veins bulged out of his neck. Realizing we were on the verge of fistfight I remembered the pistol he kept on his desk. I did not want to provoke the guy. I knew we'd end up whippin' his ass and he'd probably go for the gun. Reluctantly I stood up to keep the shit down. Everyone was noticeably upset and the tension could be cut with a knife. It was short practice.

The next day I went to see John. I knew it would be only us in the store and no witnesses for him to show off in front of. Few words were spoken, but all were well placed. He was a different man when it was just him and me. I packed up my equipment, tossed that stupid-looking cowboy hat at him and walked out.

I hated to leave Ray and Charlie, but it was their choice to stay. After a few more weeks of John's tyrannical bullshit and endless auditioning of new lead guitarists, they too walked out. Except for some old posters and a couple Texas Country Bandit t-shirts mounted under glass at Charlie's house, that was the end of The Texas Country Bandits forever.

Through the years Ray, Charlie and I have jammed together many times. We never heard from John or the keyboard player again. We lost track of Lizzy until, while writing this book, I looked her up on the internet. She had gotten married, given up her stage name and moved to another country where she has a successful career writing, performing and recording religious music for children.

Lesson learned. After the experience with John I never again allowed myself, my music, my band or my career to be under someone else's rule.

Since then I have ripped up numerous management contracts and walked away from many small-time record deals, sometimes wondering if I made a mistake. Maybe. I always went with my gut feeling. Like Elvis and Frank Sinatra once sang, "I did it my way."

## TEXAS FEVER

In 1979, along with Junior Carouthers on drums, Donny Roberts on bass, Mutt Fingleman on rhythm guitar and lead vocals, and John Beasley on lead guitar and fiddle, I co-founded and played lead guitar for Texas Fever, a weekend warrior country-western band in Liberty.

We were a good band considering our limited musical ability at that time. However, we had a fantastic following. Whenever we played the local lodges or the legendary Wagon Wheel Dance Hall located in the Trinity River Bottom between Liberty and Dayton, we'd pack them to capacity. We also did a lot of shows for trail rides, rodeos, country fairs, grand openings and private parties in the backyards of some of Liberty County's oil and agriculture tycoons. We did a lot of street dances set up on the back of flatbed trucks and 40-foot semi truck trailers.

For some reason it seemed every gig we played was a gig from hell. Probably because of our youth and inexperience in life itself. Take a group of cocky, young bulls, fill 'em full of ego and alcohol and then put 'em in the same stall. Add to that a gaggle of cackling, blabber-mouth band wives, girlfriends and jealous groupies who kept shit stirred up between each other as well as the musicians and see what happens. It's a damn wonder we survived.

John Beasley was an excellent fiddle player but he and I butted heads time and time again when it came to the lead guitar spot. On several occasions he and I headed out the door to settle our differences the cowboy way. Thankfully we always came to our senses and never locked horns. We are still friends to this day.

Mutt Fingleman was a great singer whose amazing, super-star voice should have been cranking hits out of Nashville instead of being lost on the ears of in the East Texas hecklers. I was a restless, guitar-slinging show-off (let's say "showman") who would drop to my knees in the middle of the dance floor and play "Johnny B. Goode" behind my head. The band (and my wife) hated for me to take the spotlight like that and tried to censor my performance. The crowd loved it so the crowd won.

Mutt and I lusted for fame and fortune and we were not content to be hometown heroes. We knew it was time to move on when the rest of the band insisted we dress in matching orange t-shirts and red baseball caps. Mutt and I argued that we were a band, not a baseball team. Our protests fell on deaf ears. We quit to start our own band. No orange t-shirts and I could play "Johnny B. Goode" any way I wanted. We used my old band name, Firecreek.

## Cowboys In China

In the summer of 1980 Firecreek consisted of Russell Shelby on drums, Charlie Adams on bass and Mutt Fingleman on rhythm guitar and lead singer. We were booked at a private party in China, Texas, a mere spot in the road, a blink of an eye, on Highway 90 between Liberty and Beaumont. We were hired by a very prosperous feed store owner from Liberty. I don't remember his name so I will refer to him as "Mr. Feedstore."

We were excited about performing at this particular party because many of Liberty County's "rich and famous" were supposed to be there. Rich business owners, wealthy rice farmers, cattle barons, oil field millionaires and so on. We were told many of those rich folks were personal friends with Willie Nelson and had connections to other major country music stars. Mr. Feedstore was willing to introduce us if we agreed to perform at a discounted rate. We were also promised more and better paying private parties in our future if we played for a discounted rate *this first time.*

Being young, dumb and desperate for fame and fortune, we believed everything Mr. Feedstore said. We booked the party for basic expenses and practiced our ass off in an effort to make a good impression.

The directions to the party led us down several blacktop backroads. We came upon a cardboard sign nailed to a fencepost with the word "PARTY" and an arrow pointing down the dirt road. We crossed a cattle guard onto a narrow, dusty dirt road with cows grazing in the pastures. At the end of the road, nestled in a grove of giant oak trees draped in spanish moss, sat a stately southern-style mansion straight out of *Gone With The Wind.*

We parked alongside Cadillacs, Lincolns, new pickup trucks and a few saddled horses tied to a white rail fence that kept wandering cattle out of the yard. As we climbed out of our cars we were slapped in the face by the blended aroma of barbeque and cowshit.

Mutt went to find Mr. Feedstore and get the setup details. He came back a few minutes later and said we had to leave the cars outside the fence and carry equipment across the huge, manicured yard to the large front porch – our stage.

As we hauled in our gear we noticed dozens of picnic tables strategically placed around the yard, neatly covered with red and white checked tablecloths. Washtubs and ice chests were filled with ice and beer. Smoke billowed from a giant barbeque pit, drifting over the buffet table covered with piles of ribs, briskets and sausage links. Bowls of potato salad, cole slaw, beans and banana pudding sat covered with foil.

Our wives sat down at one of the picnic tables. Mr. Feedstore was not pleased.

"The tables are for invited guests only," inferring our wives had not been invited to his event. He reluctantly allowed us have a table over by the front gate, farthest from the rest. In other words, "the help (and their wives) ain't allowed to sit with the guests."

At 8pm the Texas sun was setting as we kicked off the first song. Multi-colored Chinese lamps strung between the trees made the place look more like a used car lot than the intended effect of being J.R. Ewing's back yard at Southfork. Regardless, the party had begun.

The crowd of tobacco spitting farmers and ranchers passed around bottles of whiskey. Their wives, with their beehive hairdos, sat at the tables looking uncomfortably stuffed into designer jeans too tight to be healthy.

Summer evenings on the Texas Gulf Coast are always miserably hot. It was so humid you could cut the air with a knife. Cold beer and whiskey on the rocks were the only remedy for the sweltering heat. Soon the inebriated crowd was dancing the night away on the front lawn. We performed top country hits, throwing in an occasional '50s rock 'n roll song for added excitement. The crowds hoots and hollers told us they liked us. We knew more lucrative parties and an introduction to Willie Nelson was in our future.

Everyone was having a great time except, of course, for our disgruntled wives. Understandably they felt disrespected when their table was purposely quarantined far from everyone else. The high society women at the party would not associate with them at all. It is common in the music business. Until a band/artist reaches star status, most band wives and girlfriends are often treated like lepers. Our girls sat smoldering in their exile. They were ignored by everyone – except the mosquitoes!

It is a known fact that mosquitoes on the Texas Gulf Coast are big enough to stand flatfooted and screw a chicken. As the darkness snuffed out the last defiant ray of sunlight, swarms of ravenous chicken fuckers invaded the party like Kamikazes in a feeding frenzy. Thanks to their massive intake of beer and whiskey the drunken guests did not seem to notice the vicious attack of giant mosquitoes or the suffocating heat, but the band and our wives did.

Our poor ladies sat there dressed in sparkly blouses, with Farrah Fawcett hairstyles and sprayed-on Calvin Klein jeans looking as sexy as Sue Ellen on Dallas, all the while sweating profusely and being eaten alive by millions of horrendous mini-vampires! From the stage we could see the fires of hell blazing in their eyes as they solemnly stewed in their discontent. They were furious.

Through gritted teeth and clenched fists our wives fervently expressed their extreme unhappiness to us at every break. They were in a highly exaggerated state of being pissed off and blamed us for their every discomfort. Then they did what all band wives do – made us (the musicians) feel guilty for having a good time performing for an appreciative audience. They bombarded us with complaints about the heat and humidity ruining their hair and makeup. They ragged on us about the treatment they received from the "snobby bitches" who shunned them. And, of course, the mosquitoes were eating them alive. How *dare* we have fun playing music while they were in such *misery*?

In self defense we reminded our wives that it was *they* who had begged to tag along because *they* wanted to mix and mingle with Liberty County's so-called elite. There was nothing we could do about their predicament but offer them insect spray. They adamantly refused saying it would cover up their perfume.

Not only did our wives treat us like shit because we were having fun, but as we mingled with our employer and his guests, we too were suddenly treated like field hands who didn't know our place. Our employer had kissed our ass to get us to play his party at a discounted rate and as long as we were on the stage we were superstars. The moment we took a break, we were treated like white trash. We felt as if we had been lied to and screwed. Quitting time couldn't come soon enough.

Our clothes were soaked with sweat and our bodies covered with insect bites. We were angry from the disrespect and exhausted from complaints from our wives. We were miserable and our enthusiasm for this event was *gone*.

As the evening wore on older folks went home early. From the stage we watched the party go from a down home country-western dance to a raucous, free-for-all redneck frat party, complete with arm wrestling, chug-a-lug contests and ear splitting rebel yells. The aroma of marijuana drifted from the backyard and blended with the smells of barbeque and cowshit. We played our last set to thirty very drunk drugstore cowboys in their mid-twenties. They were full of whiskey and recklessness.

At exactly midnight on the dot we announced our last song. That was the cue for our wives to go to the cars, start the engines, roll up the windows and turn on the air conditioning. On our last note we immediately set about pulling plugs and rolling up cords with great haste. Being out in the middle of nowhere, the sudden silence caused a rumble of discontent to rise up from the small but rowdy crowd.

"Aw c'mon, play one more!" they yelled. "Play one more! Last year's band played until four in the morning!"

Any other time we would have gladly played a few more songs and even suggested they pass the hat for another set, but this was not one of those times. We were hot, tired, bitten up by mosquitoes, lied to, disrespected and ripped off by our employer. We refused to play one more. There would be no encores.

Some of the macho assholes in the crowd felt they could motivate us by making threats. We were suddenly surrounded by a dozen or more angry young cowboys itching for a fight. They blocked our way out, calling us names and shouting, "If you sum-bitches don't keep playin' we gonna whup ya'll's ass!"

We ignored their insults and continued to break down the equipment. We carried our gear across the yard to the cars in pairs through the gauntlet of angry cowboys. The loudmouths shadowed our every step cussing us all the way. Out-numbered we never spoke a word or made an aggressive gesture. We just loaded our gear as fast as we could while keeping one eye on our shitfaced antagonizers.

Our wives, realizing the situation, climbed out of the cars and stood anxious for a cat-fight. Though their intentions were commendable, I told them to get back in the cars, aim them down the road and leave the doors open and motors running. I convinced them to stay in the cars. We didn't want one of them to get hurt or lost in the confusion when it was time to make our getaway.

While we loaded cars Mutt was busy distracting the pack of loud, angry drunks surrounding him like they were about to string him up. He convinced them we would play one more set if they just backed off. Judging from the extremely loud profanity coming from his direction, I knew we had to hurry before the lethal mixture of alcohol and hot tempers exploded setting all hell loose on us.

I knew Mutt couldn't walk away from the frenzied pack without getting sucker punched. I ran into the mob, grabbed him by the arm and pulled him free from the group while yelling as loud as I could, "C'mon man, let's play another set!"

Free from the huddle we bolted toward the cars with the angry lynch mob in hot pursuit. We bailed through the open doors like the Duke Boys, stomped the gas pedal and threw gravel all over the pursuing posse. Our four cars fishtailed back and forth between the ditches all the way to the blacktop. It was a close call and a narrow escape.

Fortunately Mr. Feedstore paid Mutt before we started playing. We never got a call back for another party, and never got an introduction to Willie Nelson.

## BAYONET BLUES

By December 1981 Firecreek had completely dissolved. I had not played a gig in over a year. I couldn't seem to stay with any band without getting fired, pissed off or quitting. I drove a delivery van for a hotshot service during the day until the company went bankrupt. I was unemployed and, on top of that, separated from my first wife.

I felt like I needed to get the hell out of Houston and go where no one knew me and no one could find me. I needed space to clear my head so I threw a dart at the map. On December 12, 1981, my new girlfriend and I rolled into the small town of Stillwater, Oklahoma, with nothing but a guitar and a suitcase full of clothes.

Our first night we got a room – and I got a job – at the Holiday Inn. Over the next few weeks I ripped out old carpet, laid new carpet, unclogged toilets, moved furniture, grouted bathrooms, painted walls, did yard work and then some.

One night we went to a local club hosting a jam session. Before the night was over I was the new lead guitar player for The Cimmaron Swingsters, a Bob Wills-style western swing band.*

With two kids and a soon to be ex-wife back in Texas and a new live-in girlfriend in Oklahoma, the measely salary I was earning at the Holiday Inn and the few bucks I was making with the band on weekends was not enough to survive on. I contacted a local employment agency for help finding a better paying job.

I filled out the necessary paperwork and soon found myself sitting across the desk from a very unique and interesting employment counselor I will call "G.I. Joe." Why? G.I. Joe didn't dress in the usual suit and tie like other employment counselors. He dressed head to toe in camouflage, complete with US Army issue Vietnam jungle boots. This was long before camo clothing became fashionable street dress for civilians.

I noticed Joe's hands and face were badly scarred from serious burns and he was obviously wearing a wig. He noticed my curious stare and proudly told me he wore camouflage to remind people of lives lost in Vietnam. He wore the wig because while serving in Vietnam he suffered traumatic burns over his entire body when the jeep he was driving was blown off the road. He held up his hands, showing me the fingers on his right hand were fused together. With all that said we got to the job interview.

During the interview I noticed several guitar picks laying on his desk. Our conversation turned to a mutual interest, music. He seemed fascinated with tales of my playing music in Texas. I felt I had made a friend who could also help me find work.

Joe called me later in the week and invited me to stop by his house to see his music room and guitar collection. He also said we couldn't let the employment agency know we were hanging out after hours on a social basis. It would be considered a conflict of interest and he might be accused of showing favoritism if he got caught finding jobs for his musician friends. I remember thinking it was an advantage to have a fellow guitar player looking out for me.

A few days later I stopped by Joe's house. He brought out a couple of guitars and we jammed awhile in the living room. His bitchy wife raised hell the whole time about the noise. His rude, obnoxious kids ran through the house, fighting and screaming at each other like maniacs. Joe seemed oblivious to the ruckus and insisted on singing songs he had written.

As he played I struggled to add some lead guitar licks to his melodies. All his songs were morbid, gross descriptions about death, destruction and dismemberment in Vietnam. When I had heard enough of his blood-splattered lyrics, I stood up to leave. He told me he was also a painter and insisted I see some of his paintings before I left. We went to the back of the house where he had gutted a couple bedrooms building a makeshift recording studio. The walls were lined with aquariums full of snakes and big spiders. Freaked me out!

Joe brought out his paintings. I was thinking he painted pictures of flower arrangements or sunsets in an effort to think about something besides being burned up in Vietnam or his lunatic family. The first painting he showed me was a watercolor of an M-16 machine gun. The next was a Sherman tank. Other paintings depicted airplanes dropping bombs or spraying Napalm on burning villagers. There was one of a Chinook helicopter gunship blasting rockets into grass huts and scenes of truckloads of men being blown to bits with bloody body parts scattered across the canvas. He painted scenes of men being impaled on bamboo poles, run through with bayonets, beheaded with axes and so on. The quality of the paintings equaled the doodlings of a ten-year-old child. How the hell was I supposed to react to that?

Suddenly it hit me. I was in a total stranger's house, surrounded by snakes and spiders, looking at paintings of dead bodies painted by a guy who wore camouflage combat gear seven days a week and wrote songs about blood and guts dripping off the end of a knife! I fought the urge to run before I got stuffed in a pot, cooked and served on a platter to his vicious, demon offspring.

As the weeks passed Joe called me with a job here and there. To keep on his good side I would occasionally stop by his house to see his latest gory painting or hear his newest death song. They all sounded the same.

One Friday evening Joe called. His wife and kids were out of town and he invited my girlfriend and I over for drinks and to strum on the guitars. I had been telling her about this weird guy, so we decided to stop over for a few minutes so she could see for herself.

Joe was already shitfaced when we arrived. He poured us each a glass of wine and gave my girlfriend the grand tour: snakes, spiders, recording studio, bloody paintings and all. Occasionally, she looked at me and winked as if to say, "You're right, this guy is crazy!"

Back in the living room Joe brought out a guitar and a bottle of Jack Daniels. He drank straight from the bottle. He was getting nasty mouthed and obnoxious so I tried to keep him busy singing his war songs.

Sensing my girlfriend was getting uneasy I mentioned it was time for us to go. Joe got up, left the room and returned with a genuine Army bayonet that looked to be at least a foot long. In a flash he raised the bayonet into the air and brought it down with such force that it went completely through the center of the coffee table! Sitting beside me on the couch my girlfriend almost jumped clean through me, squeezing my hand so hard she almost broke my fingers. We were scared shitless. We both thought we were going to die and be buried under Joe's house or worse.

"Ya'll ain't going no fuckin' place!" he yelled. "We still got a whole bottle of whiskey and some more wine to drink!"

Joe turned the stereo up as loud as it would go. When he grabbed my girlfriend's empty wine glass and headed into the kitchen we saw our chance. She and I bolted out the front door. When we looked back Joe was standing in the doorway, a full wine glass in his hand, yelling at us as we backed out of his driveway and burned rubber down the street.

I never saw or heard from G.I. Joe again.

## *Side Note: The Cimmaron Swingsters

I performed with The Cimmaron Swingsters for four months. As of this writing, to my knowledge drummer Mark Freeman and bass player Tim Smalley still reside in Oklahoma.

The sax player was Larry McWhorter, the son of Frankie McWhorter, fiddle player for the legendary Bob Wills and the Texas Playboys. Larry was a real cowboy who had worked cattle ranches around Oklahoma. He taught himself to play the sax while "ridin' herd" on the long, lonely days on the wide open Oklahoma Plains. He was fantastic!

Larry went on to write and record albums of superb cowboy poetry. Among the many awards and honors he earned was *1998 Cowboy Poet of The Year* awarded by the Academy of Western Artists and *Cowboy Poetry Album of The Year 1999*. Unfortunately, Larry McWhorter lost his battle with cancer in March 2003.

The keyboard player was a beautiful young lady named Kelly Glenn. She was far too gifted and refined to play with us roadhouse honky-tonkers. She eventually went to work as keyboard player for country superstar LeAnn Rhimes.

*From top, l to r: The two top pictures are the original Firecreek Boogie Blues Band. Me, T.J. Austin on drums, Mike Sicola on guitar, and Ray Kelton on bass.*

*Bottom left: Bert Owen sitting in, T.J. Austin on bass.*

*Hardin Community Center, Hardin, Texas Winter of 1973*

Texas Fever, 1978

Texas Fever, 1978, l to r: Me, Junior Crouthers, Donny Roberts, Mutt Fingleman. Front, l to r: Manager. Tom Snell, John Beasley. Mutt and I refused to wear orange t-shirts and red caps onstage.

Charlie Taylor

Mutt and me.

Texas Country Bandits, 1978, l to r: Ray Kelton, the girl singer I fired, Charlie Taylor and me.

The last ride of Firecreek, New Years Eve 1979. Me, Mutt, Charlie and Ray.

Me, Ben Sterling on drums and Ray Kelton on bass at Boondocks, Humble, 1978.

# BOOK THREE

# Adventures Of A One-Man Band

## 1983-1991

In December 1982, one week after marrying my second wife, I was fired from my day job as an advertising salesman at KBUK radio in Baytown, Texas.

At first my new wife accused me of quitting my job on purpose so I could lay around the house playing my guitar while she earned our living. She changed her tune when she realized the station had been sold and everyone had been fired by the new owners. One month later she too was fired from her job.

There we were. January 1983, newlyweds and both unemployed. With a recession plaguing the nation, especially in oil industry-based Texas, my frantic search for employment turned up nothing. By April our unemployment checks were running out. Child support was behind and adding up fast. There were no jobs to be had and the bills were piling up. We were getting desperate.

A guitar player friend, Bert Owen, was getting steady work as a single act in nightclubs all over southeast Texas. I went to see him a couple times. I figured if he could it, I could do it. Average pay for a single act was about fifty bucks a night in those days. Not a lot of money but enough to get by on until I found a full-time day job.

I had a Fender Telecaster. With the last of my unemployment money I bought a small four-channel Peavey PA system: the PA, two Peavey 112 speaker boxes, a mic and a mic stand. I started looking for work.

## The Emporium Restaurant

In April 1983 I landed my first one-man gig playing background music during lunch hour Monday through Friday at The Emporium Restaurant in Baytown. It was the first time I had played solo since the Brentwood Club nearly ten years before. I was nervous as hell!

I only knew beer drinking, house rockin' honky-tonk songs. I had to do some quick woodsheddin' and learn to play easy-listening songs. Yuk!

I was paid $35 a day plus free drinks and a meal. The owner liked me and booked me Friday and Saturday nights for an additional $50 a night. Wow! A whopping $275 a week for playing a guitar. That was as much as my base salary at KBUK. And food! And drinks! And tips! I was off and running.

## Shamrock Shrimp Singer

When the Emporium gig played out I landed a gig as the happy hour singer at one of the ritziest places in Texas – the world famous Shamrock Hilton in Houston.

I was excited to be playing a place that hosted kings, queens, movie stars, famous politicians, notorious gangsters, industry giants and legends of the sports world. I was greeted at the front door by a big, black valet/doorman wearing gold gloves, a long olive green coat, a hat and a smile that looked like a row of piano keys on a baby grand. His big smile faded and his attitude became very matter of fact when I told him I was the happy hour singer. He pointed toward the side of the building and snapped, "You can't cay'ry yo' stuff through here. Whuss wrong wit chu? Git 'round back and go through da kitchen!"

I made my way around back, rang the delivery buzzer and stepped into a world of chaos. Cooks, chefs, janitors, waiters, waitresses, busboys, housekeepers, maintenance people and garbage collectors scurried around like worker bees running to and fro.

Everybody was yelling in various languages. I finally found my contact, the Food and Beverage Director, who gave me a stern lecture about what songs to sing, how to act, what to say, what not to say, and a bunch of other bullshit. He instructed me to set up on the dance floor in the small lounge. I was disappointed I didn't get to play in the large showroom.

I managed to drag my gear through the confusion and set up. Just before start time at 5pm the room filled with men and women of all ages and races dressed in expensive business suits and evening attire. The high society ladies were dripping in diamonds. Millionaires, I presumed. I set out my tip jar thinking I'd do well amongst all these high dollar rich folks.

As I started to play two Mexican busboys dressed in fancy green Shamrock Hilton green uniforms rolled out a huge fifty gallon tub filled to the rim with boiled shrimp. They parked it on the dance floor just two feet in front of me. *Two feet!* I could have reached out and grabbed a handful of shrimp as I was playing. I was annoyed to be singing to a tub of shrimp.

As soon as the bus boys stepped away the room full of high class rich folks in their fancy clothes and diamonds made a mad dash for the tub like hogs to a trough! With their little plates in hand they pushed, shoved, bumped and cut in front of each other in the worst display of rudeness I'd ever witnessed. It looked like a scene from a sitcom.

People crowded around the shrimp tub forcing their way into the small space between me and the tub. The back of their heads literally bumped into my mic as I was singing! I sang six inches from the rolls on the back of a fat man's neck – it was disgusting and embarrassing.

The moment the patrons finished gorging themselves on free shrimp, the room cleared out. I played the second hour of my two-hour gig to the same two Mexican busboys as they cleaned up the room. It looked like the remains of a feeding frenzy at a fish cannery.

Good thing I was on salary. I left there with zero in my tip jar.

I learned two things that night. Rich folks don't tip and food and beverage people need to stay in the kitchen and out of the music business. I never went back to the Shamrock Hilton, but I'm glad I got to play there at least once. It was torn down four years later.

## ROLAND THE WONDER DRUMMER

Shortly after the Great Shamrock Hilton Shrimp Event, a booking agent told me if I bought a drum machine he could book me for a hundred bucks a night.

I did some research and bought a Roland Electronic Drum Machine. It was about the size of a cigar box and with dozens of buttons indicating various pre-set rhythms and beats it looked like an adding machine. I could set the tempo and an LED readout gave me beats per minute (how fast I was playing). Once the desired drumbeat and tempo were set, I stepped on a footswitch. The computer-generated drum sounds came thumping through my PA system. With my harmonica and guitar I almost sounded like a full band.

Just for the record, I never used background tapes or soundtracks. "Roland The Wonder Drummer" just gave me a beat. That's all. I wanted people to hear *me*, not the latest technology.

If an agent could book me I could book myself. I hit every joint with a neon beer sign within a twenty mile radius, booking myself for a hundred bucks a night. Playing music came easy for me and a hundred bucks a night was like getting paid to breathe.

I was a hustler. Within a couple of months Roland and I were working seven nights a week and it was taking its toll on me. I had to take time off just to let my voice rest.

## City Club

One Sunday afternoon at a small club in Baytown called The City Club, owner Bobby Reynolds told me he didn't hire musicians, but I was welcome to set up and play for a half hour for tips. I walked out four hours later with $300. I played the City Club every Saturday night for two years.

I learned that if I could get an audition I could usually get a gig.

## Sunbright Bar

After The City Club I landed a gig every Friday night at a little beer bar in Pelly called The Sunbright Bar. It was the oldest bar in the region. It was called The Sunbright because since the early '40s it opened every morning at 7am. There were usually two or three slam-bang, knock-down, drag-out fights every time I played there. I saw people get beat up, stomped, hit with chairs, dragged out by their feet, dragged out by their hair, get barred, run off or get hauled off to jail. A Vietnam vet, who had been a POW, would eat roaches that ran across the bar then chase 'em with a gulp of beer just to freak people out.

What a great place for an aspiring entertainer to hone his craft.

## The Beginning Of The Never Ending Hustle

With Roland The Wonder Drummer my ability to get out and hustle and my ability to entertain an audience once I got the gig, I was soon making more money and having more fun than I ever had in my life.

For nearly a decade I averaged 200+ shows a year, playing every kind of event imaginable: nightclubs, icehouses, storefronts, tents, on the back of trucks, on boats, at campsites, in malls, backyards, living rooms, barns, new and used car lots – you name it, I played 'em all – from the shittiest to the ritziest.

Each gig brought with it the potential to be another *Gig From Hell*.

## Held Hostage By A Renegade Biker Gang

When I turned thirty in April of 1983 I was the happiest man on the planet. I had a new wife who seemed at that time tolerant of me playing music for a living. I was pleased I had achieved my life-long dream of being able to play music for a living even though I was just a one-man band with a drum machine.

Being a one-man band has its pros and cons. You never have to worry about band members missing a gig, showing up late or getting drunk. On the down side, a one-man band has no one else to back him up.

### Renegade Biker Party

By early summer of 1983 I was starting to get the hang of being a one-man band, and I was playing a lot of private parties. One particular party was a backyard party in a rural section of northeast Harris County near Crosby, Texas. Arriving around 1pm on a beautiful Saturday afternoon, I set up for my 2pm to 6pm gig. The party was at a very nice brick home on a blacktop road located in the middle of a three-acre yard. The nearest neighbor was a quarter mile away.

I pulled into the driveway and was met by my employer's wife. She told me to set up underneath the carport. Before she walked away she reached in her pocket and pulled out a hundred dollar bill, shoved it in my hand and said, "Oh yeah, here's your money."

With a wink and a big grin she said, "I better go ahead and pay you now, cause I don't know what condition I'll be in by the time this party is over."

We both had a little chuckle and she went on her way. I did not see her again for the rest of the day. At the time I did not realize she had taught me a valuable lesson that would stay with me for the rest of my career.*

I backed my car down the driveway and parked next to the carport. The area was cluttered with tool boxes, a welding machine, engine parts, stacks of tires and work benches. A small area had been cleared out in the center for me.

## Bear: The Cook

I set up, did my little sound check and decided I would walk around, get myself a beer and meet a few folks.

The first guy I met was the cook. He stood barefoot, rotating a full-sized hog over a large fire pit. He was a big, husky guy wearing a pair of overalls with only one strap fastened over his shoulder and no shirt. He proudly exposed his bare arms, shoulders and chest which were as thick with body hair as a bristle welcome mat. His face was covered with a werewolf beard that grew almost over his cheeks. I could barely see his eyes obscured by unkempt curly hair that dangled over his forehead like a cluster of grapes. He looked like a giant Chia Pet. He stood next to the fire pouring beer over the hog from the same bottle he was drinking.

I walked over, introduced myself and tried to make small talk about the massive hog he was roasting. He did not even acknowledge my existence. He ripped off a big chunk of the steaming meat and shoved it in his mouth. The beer marinade, combined with hog grease and barbeque sauce, painted his mustache and beard with an orange liquid that oozed between his fat fingers, covered his chin, ran down his arm and dripped from his greasy elbow.

With his jaws gorged with his kill, he yelled loud enough for everyone to hear, "Fuckin' meat's ready!"

He wiped his mouth with his forearm and looked at me with contempt. With his mouth still full of hog meat he growled, "They call me Bear!" I did not need to ask why.

## On With The Show

I retreated to the carport, put on my guitar and started playing promptly at 2pm. The next four hours were completely uneventful. I watched as the yard filled up with about a hundred motorcycles.

The bikers who attended this party were not at all like the RUBS (Rich Urban Bikers) we see today. These bikers were stereotypical motorcycle gang outlaws as depicted in Hollywood movies like *The Born Losers*. None of them were wearing identifying colors that would tie them to any certain motorcycle organization or club. They seemed to be a bunch of rowdy independent riders coming together to enjoy a beautiful day, barbeque and beer. Live music and motorcycles have always gone hand in hand and having ridden a bike myself and done many performances for bikers, I thought nothing more of this party than any other biker event I had played.

From my view underneath the carport there wasn't a single person listening to me. The bikers were scattered around the yard in small groups involved in various activities. Some were standing under the trees passing something around. Others were ripping meat off the hog. Some played games on their bikes or had wrestling matches. A few were on blankets on the ground with their girlfriends. Overall everyone seemed to be having a good time.

I must have sounded like a transistor radio. I was drowned out by the roar of Harleys as the bikers rode around the yard revving their engines and playing biker games. Not a single person paid any attention to the little one-man band. Not until my quitting time at 6pm.

I played my last song and said my traditional "thank you and goodnight" to no one in particular. I took off my guitar and put it in the case. Out of professional courtesy I walked down the driveway where my employer and some of his buddies were sitting in lawn chairs. I extended my hand. "Thanks for inviting me to play your party. I had a great time. I'll see you guys down the road."

When my employer had approached me a few weeks before and asked me to play his party he was a real nice guy. Now, as he sat there in the midst of all his biker buddies, his demeanor completely changed. When he did not return my handshake I knew there was a problem. He sat there in his lawn chair staring at me with his eyes half shut, one hand on a longneck beer, with no expression on his face.

Finally, in an ice-cold voice reminiscent of Clint Eastwood in *Dirty Harry* he said, "Ya know, we really like yer music. In fact, we like yer music so much we think ya oughtta play s'more. *Ain't that right boys?*"

They all laughed, nodded their heads and said, "Yeah, play s'more, man."

My employer's tone of voice and gunslinger stare, along with the sadistic grins of his buddies, told me everything I needed to know. *They were not going to let me leave.*

A cold streak of fear ran through my gut as I realized what was happening. I tried not to show fear as I pretended not to notice I was being threatened. I forced a laugh and replied, "Sure man! Anything for the fans. I'm glad ya'll like the music. Hell, I'm always glad to play a little longer when people are diggin' it! As soon as I take a leak and get a beer I'll…"

He stopped me in mid-sentence and said, "Play! *Now!*"

I tried not to look at him or his buddies straight in their eyes. I knew I had no choice but to pick up my guitar and play another set or get my ass kicked. As I turned and walked back toward the carport they all busted out laughing. Silent rage, humiliation and total helplessness washed through me, all at the same time. I felt like the old prospector in a '50s western where the outlaws would shoot at his feet while laughing and yelling "*Dance! Dance!*"

Underneath the carport I piddled around. I tuned my guitar, straightened tangled cords and got something to drink. Trying to prove I would not be bossed around, wasting time was the only thing I had to fight back with. After fifteen minutes I noticed the group on the driveway watching me. I picked up my guitar, set my drum machine for a shuffle beat and started doing some old Jimmy Reed songs.

I played a very lackluster set for about an hour and a half, hoping if I played really bad and bored them to death they would get tired of listening and tell me to leave. Believing the bikers had gotten their harassment of me out of their system, around 8pm I again announced "Thank you and goodnight."

"Hey! C'mere!"

This time my employer and his buddies stood in a circle around me. I felt like a dwarf surrounded by six mean Klingon Warriors from Star Trek. He put his finger in my chest.

"Keep fuckin' playing!"

"Man, I can't keep playing! I have been singing since two o'clock. I was supposed to quit at six. It's past eight now. I'm just a one-man band, and my voice is worn out."

"Hey dude, we paid ya to play a fuckin' party. *This party ain't fuckin' over yet.* Ya know what I'm sayin'? If yer tired, we got shit here that'll keep ya goin' fer days. If yer hungry, eat some of that fuckin' pig. If ya wanna drink, we got plenty a whiskey 'n beer! If ya want some pussy, just pick you out wunna them bitches over there and go fuck her behind the shed! But yer ass ain't leaving 'til I say so! *Y'understand that, muthafucker?*"

A cold chill ripped through me. I was truly being held captive against my will. My mouth was so dry I could hardly swallow much less reply. I just shook my head yes. My heart pumped adrenaline through my body at a hundred miles an hour. I was on fire with fear, rage and humiliation. Although I was terrified, somehow I managed to keep my cool and not piss down both legs. I was well aware of the reputation these guys had on the street for violence. I told my employer I needed to call my wife and let her know that I'd be late.

He said, "*No!*"

"Look, if I don't call her, she might think I was in an accident and send the cops out looking for me."

I knew he didn't want any cops at his party. He motioned for his buddies and me to follow him into the house into what looked like a den. I noticed dozens of hunting rifles, handguns and a large collection of knives and swords mounted on the walls. He picked up the phone, asked for the number, dialed it and then stood next to me holding the phone to my ear.

My wife answered. With bikers all around me, I said, "Hi honey! Everybody here is enjoying my show and have asked me to keep playin'. I'm gonna hang around awhile."

She bluntly replied, "You were supposed to be home an hour ago!"

In an effort to alert her something was wrong, I tried to give her clues that I was in a serious predicament by changing the subject to something unrelated to our conversation. I answered her by saying, "Raining? No, it's not raining here. Is it raining hard there?"

She said, "What? Raining? Are you drunk? You need to come home *now*!"

"You be sure and tell your mama I said hi."

Instead of realizing my conversation was a little weird, all she said was, "You're drunk!"

Then she started screaming into the phone. "I'm not gonna live like this! If you wanna stay out all night, get drunk and fuck around, you can pack your shit and get the hell out!"

As she yelled at me I looked at my captors standing around me. I was so scared it was all I could do to keep from shouting, "You stupid bitch, can't you tell I need help? I'm being held captive, call the cops!"

I couldn't say anything that might cause my captors to attack me on the spot. My wife slammed down the phone and sealed whatever fate might lie in store for me. **

Consider this. Any other time most women would read between the lines of a man's words like a detective looking for clues to his possible indiscretions or true thoughts concerning a particular subject… *but not this time!*

Escorted by my guards I was ushered like the prisoner I was out the back door to my designated holding area underneath the carport. One of my biker guards looked at me and sneered, "Play some David Allan Coe!"

Not wanting another confrontation with the "Guardian Assholes," I picked up my guitar and played a ninety-minute set of mostly slow blues and old country. As I played I watched my captors sitting in their lawn chairs getting drunker and more stoned by the minute.

By this time most people still coherent enough to drive were starting to leave. Those that stayed were passing out under the trees or falling asleep around the campfires.

It was after 9pm. I decided to take a break.

My captors, now content I was not going anywhere, were not paying any attention to me. I knew it was not my music they cared about. It was the fact they held power over another human being that gave them a thrill. In their extreme state of inebriation they were distracted by a couple of biker chicks who were teasing them with tit shots and dancing to David Allan Coe blasting on the stereo system.

Thankfully my car was right next to the carport. Although I could have easily inserted the key, fired up the engine and burned rubber out of the driveway making a quick, clean getaway, I couldn't just drive off and leave my guitar and $3,000 worth of band equipment. I sat down in the front seat, contemplated my situation and planned my escape.

One good thing about being a one-man band is you don't need much equipment to get the job done. When packed properly, all of my gear would fit neatly in the trunk of my 1980 Oldsmobile Cutlass. However, I knew if I raised the trunk my captors would be on me in a flash. I considered how to load my gear without calling any attention to myself.

There was so much accumulated junk under the carport the absence of my equipment might not be noticed. The only thing that made my presence obvious was my Fender Telecaster propped up against the workbench. With its light-colored, natural wood grain finish and chrome hardware it stood out among the clutter, shining beneath the big neon shop light like a diamond in a portacan full of shit. I knew as long as my captors could see that guitar they would think I was coming back to play again.

Working very slowly and methodically so as not to be noticed, I unplugged the cords. I pulled them together in a big tangled mess and tossed them on the front passenger side floorboard. Next was the compact 4-channel Peavey PA head. I slowly put it on the back floorboard. I had a rag and pretended I was cleaning the two small speaker boxes. I slid them into the backseat on the burgundy velour upholstery. The drum machine, being no bigger than a cigar box, slid easily behind the driver's seat along with my mic stand and my guitar case.

One more piece to go. My Telecaster.

As I sat in the front seat pretending to fumble with the radio, my mind flashed to all the firearms I saw in the house. In fear for my life I retrieved my Smith & Wesson .38 pistol from underneath the seat, placing it on the seat beside me. I put my money in my sock.

I walked over to my guitar. I picked it up pretending to tune it. I sat down in the front seat of the car, sliding the guitar over to the passenger side. I immediately put the key in the ignition, fired up the engine, slammed my door, put the car in drive and burned rubber out the driveway onto the blacktop and headed for home!

In mortal fear I would be chased down by the renegade bikers, I kicked that Oldsmobile in the ass and let her rip. I kept checking my rearview mirror, slowing down only after I was sure no one was after me. My senses slowly returned. I was covered in sweat and my heart was beating like a freight train. My hands were shaking and I could hardly catch my breath. Keeping an eye on my rearview mirror, I saw nothing. Thank God.

My brain must have gone on automatic pilot. To this day, I don't remember driving the twenty-five miles home.

### Arriving Home: Almost Worse Than The Gig

Pulling into my driveway around 11pm I snapped out of my daze.

As my headlights lit up the front of the house I saw something on my front porch that looked like bodies. It was piles of clothes. *My* clothes! My wife had taken all my clothes out of the house and thrown them out on the porch.

I tried to go in the house but the deadbolt was locked from the inside. My new bride was screaming at me through the door. "Go away! All your shit is on the front porch! Get it, and get the fuck out! I wish I had never married you!"

Believing I'd been at a party having the greatest time of my life, getting drunk and screwing other women, she had thrown all my worldly belongings outside and locked me out.

I told her to open the door or I'd break it down. Naturally she threatened to call the law if I did. Finally she let me in and I tried to convince her that her suspicions were wrong. She didn't believe my story about being held captive by a renegade biker gang. She would've believed an alien abduction over the story I told her.

I reminded her of my strange comments during our phone conversation that she failed to pick up on. She just shrugged her shoulders. "You sounded drunk."

I took her to the car and showed her how the gear was in a state of disarray which was certainly not my usual way of loading gear. It was obvious I loaded the car in great haste. I would never put speaker boxes on her precious burgundy velour seats. I pulled my boot off and retrieved the money from my sock. I showed her the loaded pistol in the seat. To this day I don't think she believed me or realized the seriousness of the situation I'd escaped from.

Our conversation took a new direction. Instead of being glad I was home safe and sound, she threw a fit about me playing music for a living.

"You got just what you deserved!" she yelled. She insisted I get out of the music business.

"Why? It's the only thing making us a living right now!"

The conversation escalated. One screaming tirade led to another.

Finally I'd had enough. I had been held captive all evening in fear for my life only to get home and find my clothes on the porch. My wife was yelling at me to get the fuck out. She was threatening to call the law. She would only let me stay *if I quit playing music!*

In a blind fury I grabbed my poor innocent Telecaster. I smashed it against a tree in the front yard and threw the pieces at her feet.

"There! Now I'm outta the music business! Are ya happy now, bitch?"

She was squalling like a scared cat and trembling with fear over my violent outburst. She had never seen me act that way. I didn't like it either. Sometimes a woman can drive a man over the edge, especially after the day I'd had. Through her sobbing she yelled, "Why'd you do that? How are we gonna make money?"

"You shoulda thought about that before you wanted me out of the music business. Guess you'll have to get yourself a job!"

After things calmed down she told me go pick up my clothes off the porch. That wasn't gonna happen. I told her, "Hell no! You threw 'em down, you pick 'em up!"

Three days later she finally put my clothes back in their proper place.

Since my job as a musician was our only income I was losing money every day as a result of busting my guitar. My wife magically produced another of her secret credit cards and bought me a new Fender Telecaster.

I have played music for a living ever since and I ain't looked back. The marriage lasted twelve years. The music is forever.

*\* To this day, whenever I play a private party I always get a contract with a 50% deposit at least thirty days in advance. I pick up 100% of the balance prior to the performance upon arrival at the location before I ever unload the first piece of equipment. I often provide my own security.*

*** Phone/code – Since we now live in the age of cell phone technology, incidents like this rarely happen. It's too easy to document situations with video phones or call for help. It's a good idea to have a code word to alert friends or family when you are in a situation where you can't talk freely. Always let someone know exactly where you are going to be.*

# DOROTHY'S CLOCK

One night in the winter of 1983, a very confident, rough talking woman named Dorothy approached me as I performed as a one-man band at The Sunbright Bar in Baytown. She offered me a gig at her little beer bar called Dorothy's Place in Liberty County.

Dorothy's Place was located on a dangerous, narrow stretch of FM 1409, a two-lane blacktop road that winds its way some twenty miles through a thick jungle of moss-covered trees and Trinity River backwater swamps between Old River and Dayton. Through the years, many lives have been lost on that stretch of road due to drunk driving, hitting deer or other animals or overconfident teenagers whose lack of driving experience was no match for wet pavement and a dead man's curve.

I pulled into the parking lot of Dorothy's Place for the first time and saw a small one-room wooden building sitting on blocks beneath the overhang of giant moss-covered trees. The muddy parking lot was dotted with huge potholes. Junk cars with weeds growing around them sat decomposing next to a dilapidated storage building with a caved-in roof. Firewood was piled up between the buildings. The entire area was covered with trash scattered by stray dogs or other starving varmints scavenging for food.

The interior of Dorthy's Place was reminiscent of western saloons in movies. Rough talking customers stood elbow-to-elbow at the bar. There was only enough seating for about thirty people at the mismatched tables and chairs. An ancient pot-bellied woodstove in the corner kept the place filled with smoke. The floor was a gritty, dusty mess with tracked-in mud ground to a fine powder on its hardwood planks.

Dorothy's clientele consisted of rugged folks who lived in the backwoods of the undeveloped Old River Road region: oil field workers, construction workers, outlaw bikers, hell-raising rednecks, loggers, truckers, Mexican migrant workers and a few eccentric backwater recluses. Anywhere you find rough and rowdy men, you'll find rough and rowdy women. When a fight broke out the women were right there with the men, fists flying. They could go from dirty dancing to dirty fighting in the blink of an eye.

It took me a while to figure out why I became sick every time I played at Dorothy's. I finally figured out taking long, deep draws on my harmonica would give me a shotgun of wood smoke, second-hand cigarette smoke and finely ground dust particles stirred up every time dancers would kick up a dust cloud. I quit playing my harmonicas unless I absolutely had to and took my breaks outside to get some fresh air.

## Miss Ida

Of all the rough and rowdy women I met at Dorothy's Place, one of the most memorable was a lady known by all as Miss Ida. Miss Ida and Dorothy were good friends and she was at Dorothy's every time I played there. She was a small woman, around 5' 2" and close to eighty years old when I met her in 1983.

Always very well dressed, she wore thick makeup and kept her hair dyed jet black. She was very loud and outspoken and could out-cuss a sailor. She was well-respected and revered by all. People stepped aside for Miss Ida the minute she came through the door cause Miss Ida didn't take any shit from *anybody*. If there was a particular seat she wanted she'd tell the fellow sitting there, "Get the hell up and let an old lady sit down! Ain't you got no goddamned manners?"

The answer always came back, "Yes, Miss Ida!!" It was a badge of honor to be cussed out or scolded by Miss Ida.

In the heyday of the oil boom along the Texas Gulf Coast it was rumored Miss Ida operated a number of profitable whorehouses. "If it weren't for Miss Ida's whorehouses," said one admirer, "they wuddn'ta got no oil outta the ground 'round here!"

Miss Ida was no stranger to dealing with roughnecks and cowboys. Her advanced years didn't slow her down when it came to telling someone to kiss her ass. Whenever one of the rowdy young men got out of hand she would call them down saying, "Sit down and shut up you little son-of-bitch! I knew your short-dick daddy and your grandpa too. They wuddin' shit and you ain't either!"

Miss Ida quelled a number of fights by shaming the young bucks out the door, tails between their legs like whipped pups. It was always hilarious to watch her do her stuff, pointing her walking cane at the ruffians.

I was one of Miss Ida's biggest fans. Often I'd sit with her on my breaks, enthralled by her tales about wild times in the early days of the wildcatters, roughnecks, crooked politicians and promiscuous preachers she did business with. I felt honored that Miss Ida was one of my biggest fans. She had her list of favorite songs I would sing. On many occasions, she would stand and yell at the audience. "Shut the hell up! That boy is trying to sing!"

One particular night at Dorothy's Place a fight broke out. The whole place turned upside down. Tables and chairs were knocked over, beer bottles hit the floor. Women were screaming, and people were falling all over each other.

One of the men accidentally bumped into Miss Ida's chair. She leaped to a fighting stance with the speed of an old mama lion. Her eyes were solid black with fury as she raised her walking cane over her head and yelled at the man, "Come on you son of a bitch! I'll whup yer goddamn ass with this here walking stick!"

The man turned white with fear.

In Texas, if a man hits a woman, especially in a beer joint, every man in the house will stomp a mudhole in his ass! The man immediately started backing up, profusely apologizing, "I'm sorry, Miss Ida... I'm sorry, Miss Ida..."

Someone yelled, "The law is on the way!"

"I don't need no goddamned law," yelled Miss Ida, "I'm a-fixin' to put this here stick across this son-of-a-bitch's ass!"

Everybody cracked up laughing and the fight was over before the law arrived.

## Time Is Not On Our Side

I arrived at Dorothy's Place one Sunday to set up. By 7pm an all-day barbeque had turned into a rowdy party. The crowd was drunk and bouncing off the walls. I kicked off the music at 8pm playing the loudest and fastest old-time rock 'n roll songs my little drum machine and I could crank out.

Somebody must have doctored the barbeque sauce because everyone in the place was jacked up and acting full-moon crazy! Voices seemed louder than usual, laughter seemed more hysterical and people danced every dance with the reckless abandon of a tribal celebration.

I played hard all night. I started my last set at 11pm and planned to stop at closing time at midnight. Since I did not wear a watch I checked the big clock mounted on the wall to my immediate left every few minutes. I played four or five songs, at least a twenty-minute set. I glanced up at the clock and it was only 11:10pm. Bewildered, I thought I must have cut those songs short. I played another half dozen songs, at least twenty-five to thirty minutes of music.

The clock read 11:20pm.

I was exhausted. I remember thinking the night sure was dragging on. I played another set of at least thirty minutes and glanced back at the clock. It read 11:30pm.

Before I had time to even consider why I was experiencing a time warp, the front door flew open. A full battalion of armed Liberty County Constables burst into the room screaming and yelling like a swat team on TV.

"Everybody against the wall, *now*!" they yelled. "Put that beer down! Raise your hands! Put your hands behind your head!"

One officer approached me and yelled, "You! Stop the music! *NOW!*"

In all the excitement I didn't realize my drum machine was still whipping out a beat.

"I said put the guitar down now and turn and face the wall!" he yelled again.

"Hey man, I'm just the guitar pla…."

"Shut up! Turn and face the wall!"

With the music off the room was silent except for Dorothy yelling, "What the hell is this all about?"

One of the officers yelled, "You are all guilty of being in here after hours and consuming alcohol after hours. You're all going to jail! I wanna see everyone's ID!"

Objective moans and cursing came from the patrons lined up around the perimeter of the room. They stood facing the wall, arms raised, their fingers interlocked behind their heads.

Dorothy continued to argue with the officers, pointing at the wall clock and yelling, "It's only 11:30!"

The lead officer yelled back, "The time is 1am ma'am, and you and everyone in here are all going to jail!"

Beer bars in Texas only have a midnight license except on Saturday when they can stay open until 1am.

One of the young rookie constables was a girl named Sandy Vogel who was a distant cousin to my first wife. In school we had often rode the same bus. She was in the seventh grade when I was a senior. Now here she was, all grown up and standing in front of me in full battle gear and wearing a gun.

Trying to appear very professional she came over to talk to me. I told her I was hired to play a gig and I had nothing to do with closing time. "If everyone is going to jail," I asked, "could I at least load up my gear and lock it in the trunk of my car?"

She spoke to her superior officer who checked my ID and interrogated me about what part I played in keeping people after hours.

"Man," I told him, "I'm just the guitar player. As long as they're puttin' money in my tip jar, I keep playing."

Sandy stood up for me to her superior officer and gave me a good reference. The officer handed me my driver's license and told me I could load my gear but told me, "Don't try to leave. Everybody here can tell their story to the judge."

As I was loading my gear in my car Dorothy was still in a heated argument with the officers about the time on the clock. Other officers were checking IDs and interrogating people. A couple of suspicious male patrons were in handcuffs and some of the women were bawling their eyes out, on the verge of hysteria.

When I loaded the last piece of gear and slammed the trunk, an officer standing on the porch told me to get in my car, drive away and don't look back. I started back up the steps to enter the building to thank Sandy. The officer stepped in front of me, put his finger in my face and barked, "I said, get the hell outta here, NOW!" I jumped in my car and hauled ass.

I never went back to Dorothy's Place. I found out later a couple of pranksters confessed to the officers that they kept turning the clock back as a joke. They were threatened with fines, but nothing ever happened. Dorothy was not fined and no one went to jail.

I never saw Sandy again after that. Sandy, if you ever read this, many thanks for sticking up for me. I hope some day I can return the favor.

## ALABAMA KING KONG

In the summer of 1984 the Silver Spur on North Main Street in Baytown was just another hell hole icehouse where denim-clad, blue-collar workers went for a couple beers after work. On the weekends bands set up on the makeshift stage in the back of the building. The performance area was a giant screened-in porch with a concrete floor. None of the tables and chairs matched.

As with most icehouses there was no a/c. During the summertime it was hotter than hell. During the day the sun would beat down on the corrugated tin roof making it feel as though you were sitting in an oven. For whatever reason, people would sit there drinking beer enduring the discomfort and dripping with sweat like they had just stepped out of a shower.

The Silver Spur had a violent reputation. Every time I played there I would get a gnawing, sick feeling in my gut. The fifty bucks they paid me to play four hours on Sunday afternoons was my motivation to endure the heat, the mosquitoes and the aggressive nature of drunken rednecks. I always kept a loaded .38 pistol in my guitar case and a tire tool behind my amp in the event a situation occurred that required the service of such items.

Bikers, aging hippies, rednecks and blue-collar workers were usually no trouble at all. They just wanted to be left alone. Young cowboys were the first ones ready to "whup somebody's ass" – and any reason was a good reason.

Since most blue-collar workers stayed at home with their families on weekends, my Sunday afternoon performances were usually attended by bored cowboys looking for something to do and shift workers who, because of their crazy schedules, often had no clue what day it was.

Part of my Sunday afternoon audience at the Silver Spur was a pipeline crew from Alabama that had been working seven days a week in the Baytown area for months. They would take Sunday afternoons off to do laundry, go grocery shopping and then stop by the Silver Spur for a few beers. They were just a bunch of good ol' down home southern boys a long way from home, who wanted to hear "Sweet Home Alabama" over and over. Every time I sang it, they would jump up and dance around with their beer bottles in the air and cut loose with their earsplitting rebel yells.

One afternoon the pipeline crew was already there drinking when I arrived. They were celebrating having finished their job in Texas and were going back to Sweet Home Alabama the very next day. There were eight or nine of them sitting together at a table getting loud and rowdy. They all had a pocket full of money and were taking turns buying rounds, tipping the waitress and throwing money in my tip jar demanding to hear "Sweet Home Alabama" one more time. Everybody was having a great time.

At the beginning of my last set the biggest one of those Alabama boys stood up. He was about forty, well over six feet tall and probably weighed 275 pounds of solid muscle. He looked like King Kong as he raised both arms in the air pretending to stretch and yawn.

Suddenly his right arm came down in a blur, his giant fist busting the nose of the guy sitting to his left, sending him rolling end over end, blood spewing everywhere. He brought his right hand around, backhanding the guy seated to his right, flipping him backwards out of his chair. Blood splattered from that guy's mouth and nose as well. Before the rest of the crew had time to respond, "Alabama King Kong" grabbed the side of the table turning it over on the men seated on the other side, pinning them to the floor.

The sounds of tables crashing, metal chairs hitting the cement floor, beer bottles breaking and desperate screams of terrified men getting their asses whipped – combined with screams of other patrons running toward the door – made the scene look and sound like the world was coming to an end. In fear for their lives, grown men screamed, "No! No! No!"

The Alabama King Kong beat the hell out of every one of those guys with the speed of Superman and the fury of a shark attack. He threw full grown men left and right like rag dolls. He grabbed one victim by the throat, lifted him off the ground, pounded his face and tossed him across the room, and then grabbed the next guy. Blood was everywhere.

Broken beer bottles, broken furniture and battered bodies were strewn all over the room. A couple of guys who landed on their backs crawfished backwards across the floor, screaming and kicking at Alabama King Kong as he grabbed their flailing legs, coming down on them with a smashing sledgehammer body blow.

In less than ten seconds it was over. The room was completely cleared except for Alabama King Kong – and *me*. It happened so fast that instead of running, I stood motionless on the stage, dumbstruck by what I had just witnessed.

Alabama King Kong slowly turned looking straight at me. Had it not been for his crew yelling "fuck you" out the windows of their company trucks as they burned rubber on the street, it was completely silent in the bar.

When Alabama King Kong started walking toward me, I felt my nuts draw up. My stomach was in a knot. I remembered my gun and tire tool but they were completely useless in my guitar case. I'd never reach them in time. As Alabama King Kong walked closer I unhooked my guitar strap. I was ready to start swinging my Fender Telecaster like Davy Crockett swung "Old Betsy" at the Alamo. Halfway across the floor, King Kong stopped.

He looked me dead in the eyes. In his slow southern drawl, as tender and calm as a preacher saying a prayer at a funeral, he said, "Gene, I shore am sorry I had to mess up your sangin', but every one a-them sorry sum-bitches needed they ass whupped, and they got jes whut they deserved. Man, ah'm real sorry."

He extended his huge hand. He took my trembling hand covering it with both of his big, giant gorilla paws. With a sincere heartfelt look, he said, "Yor a real good sanger and I shore hope you may-kit big some day. I shore have enjoyed yer music, but I reckon I better git 'fore the law gits here. You take care now, ya hear?"

I was completely speechless. Alabama King Kong moseyed out the door as if he had all day. Suddenly I felt as though my lungs were about to burst. I must've been holding my breath through the entire event and didn't even know it. I let out a great sigh of relief as I watched him walk calmly to his truck, climb in and slowly drive away.

My knees were so weak I sat down on the front of the stage. I played my last set to nobody except the waitress as she mopped up blood and broken glass.

## The Mine & Yours Club

In 1985 the Mine & Yours Club was a huge, country-western mixed-drink dance hall in an old shopping center in Baytown. It would hold a thousand people and usually did seven nights a week. I performed there as a one-man band every Monday from 7pm to 11pm. I have no idea why they asked me to play there. There was no way a single act could fill that room with enough sound to be interesting. I must have sounded like a transistor radio.

### Are You Gay?

Except for a few middle-aged divorcees in a singles club that met at the Mine & Yours on Monday nights, nobody paid much attention to me. Every time I took a break the DJ would crank up the house PA so damn loud it could peel paint off the walls. The dance floor would pack out with dancers doing the Texas Two-Step and the Four Corners.

The overweight divorcees would always ask me to dance when I was on break, but I always respectfully declined. Being that I was a married man, I ignored them and spent my breaks hanging out with some of the fellows I knew.

One evening a lady from the singles club came over to my table. She sat down next to me, took my hand, looked me straight in the eye and asked, "Are you gay?"

"WHAT??!! GAY? Hell no! What the hell makes you ask a question like that?"

"I didn't mean to offend you," she said, "but all the women in our club come to see you every week, and you never talk to any of us, or ask us to dance. You are always hanging out with the guys. We were just wondering if you were gay."

"Hell no, I'm not gay!" I snapped. "I'm happily married, and I plan to stay that way."

I pointed at my wedding ring. "Look, I appreciate your interest, I'm honored and flattered! But how would you like it if your husband was hanging out in a beer joint, dancing with all the women in a singles club?"

"How do you think I ended up single?" she replied sarcastically and politely excused herself and walked away.

"My point exactly." From then on I made sure to be a little more cordial to the ladies.

My sexual persuasion was never questioned again.

### The Mad Vet

Since I performed every Monday at the Mine & Yours, Memorial Day 1985 was just another day at the office for me. The place was packed when I kicked off at 7pm. The club had promoted a Memorial Day celebration featuring live entertainment and drink specials. To me all that meant was I would play my usual Monday night single act gig and alcohol was at happy hour prices all night.

There was a large group of young soldiers in the club that night dressed in their camouflage uniforms. Another large group of people were wearing camouflage as a show of their support for the U.S. military. As the night wore on the party got louder and wilder. The lower booze prices had everyone drunk as hell early on.

I stood on the stage singing my songs with my trusty little drum machine. As usual not many people in the huge room were paying much attention to me. From out of the crowd a big, burly middle-aged fellow walked up to the stage and stood in front of me. He was about six-foot-four, dressed in camos. In a voice as rough as a WWF wrestler he demanded, "Gimme the gawddamn mic, I got sumpum needs sayin'!"

Before I had a chance to reply the guy jerked the mic from the stand.

"Move!" he barked at me as he barged on the bandstand. He was a human wall with an attitude. I did not argue with him. This guy was twice – no *three times* – my size and with his scraggly beard and tattered camos he looked like Fidel Castro with eyes like Charles Manson. I knew he meant business.

He stood for a moment staring at the audience caught up in their revelry. Sweat ran down the side of his face, his chest heaved like he had been running and his knuckles were white as he clutched the mic. I could see his jaw muscles quivering as he clenched his teeth.

Suddenly he screamed into the mic as loud as he could, "Fuck everybody in here! I'll whup ever gawddamn one of you sons-a-bitches!" The room immediately went dead silent.

"I'll whup all you sorry muthafuckers!" he yelled. "Ya'll are all a buncha pussies! My buddies died in Vietnam so ya'll could come in here and drink 'n dance, 'n pretend nuttin' ever fuckin' happened! They're dead! *Dead*! Ya hear me ya sorry muthafuckers? I seen 'em get their arms and legs blowed off so ya'll could come in here 'n chase pussy! Fuck you! While you're out there dancin', there's vets th'ain't got no fuckin' legs! Fuck all you bastards for not rememberin'! They're the reason you fuckers can come here and fuck off!"

While the Veteran was making his rant, the owner came to me on the side of the stage and demanded that I take the mic away from him.

"Do I look that stupid to you?" I replied. "You want the mic, *you* get it."

"If you want to keep your job, you better take that mic away from him, *now*!" he yelled.

"I ain't your damn bouncer. Get it yourself."

"Then turn it off!" he yelled.

"You're standing next to the plug. Just yank the plug outta the wall, but let me get off this stage first cause he's gonna whip your ass!"

While the owner and I were arguing about taking the mic away from the Mad Vet, the Vet had walked out to the middle of the vacant dance floor as far as the microphone cord would allow. He was still yelling and threatening the audience. That's when my old friend "Mad Max" walked up face to face with the Vet.

Mad Max was a big, husky guy about forty years old and six feet tall. He was a notorious scrapper with a red-hot temper and a short fuse that would go off like a bottle of nitro. He was no stranger to bar fights and would gladly fight the devil himself for sport. One night at another club Mad Max fought with a guy over a pool game. The crowd had to pull Mad Max off of the guy. Mad Max had him in a headlock trying to force a billiard ball into his mouth.

Now here at the Mine & Yours Club, Mad Max stood directly in front of the maniacal Vet who was on the verge of going ballistic.

The Vet leaned into Mad Max's face and screamed. "Who the fuck are you, asshole? I'll beat yer gawddam ass!"

I figured Mad Max was going to deck the guy and the shit would be on. Instead, in the stone cold silence, everybody in the room could hear Mad Max softly say, "Let me stand by you, brother. I'm a vet just like you. Let me stand by you. I'm on your side."

Mad Max moved to the Vet's left side. He stood shoulder to shoulder with the Vet, facing the audience. Mad Max slipped his right arm around the Vet's shoulder. "You're right, brother. Let me tell 'em. I was there, man, just like you, I was there. Brother, I'll stand with you. We'll both tell 'em."

Mad Max cautiously took the mic and gently removed it from the Vet's grip.

The audience, expecting a fight, could not take their eyes off of Mad Max and the Vet. Mad Max, now holding the mic, started talking very softly to the audience.

"Ladies and gentlemen, who'll stand with this man? Who'll come stand with us? Come stand beside us. Let us know you remember our fallen brothers and sisters who gave their lives so we could be here today enjoying our freedom. Come here and stand with us. Show this man how much you love him and appreciate the sacrifices he and our fallen soldiers made."

Not even Billy Graham himself could have given a better alter call than Mad Max did that night in that smoke-filled honky-tonk. Everyone came forward gathering around the Vet, who was now sobbing and weeping like a lost child. Everybody was crying and hugging.

From the midst of the cluster of bodies I saw Mad Max's arm rise into the air, holding my microphone. I made my way into the crowd and retrieved it. With his other arm still around the Vet, Mad Max looked over his shoulder and whispered, "Play something."

I got back on stage and started playing Amazing Grace on my harmonica. Max looked over his shoulder shaking his head no, motioning for me to pick up the tempo. I dispelled the tension in the room by breaking into "Old Time Rock 'n Roll" by Bob Seger. People dispersed back to their seats or started dancing. Thanks to Mad Max the rest of the night was somewhat uneventful and nobody got hurt.

Mad Max was truly the hero of the evening.

## SLASHER

By the winter of 1984 I had grown bored working as a one-man band and tired of being limited by what I could do with a guitar and a drum machine. Even though I could make more money as a single act, I couldn't stretch out and play lead guitar solos or play music the way I was feeling it. I desperately wanted to start playing with a real band again. I was always on the lookout for a good bass player and drummer.

One night a guy came into The Sunbright Bar in Old Baytown and introduced himself as a bass player looking for a job. He said he had some band equipment set up in his apartment, and we could meet there for a jam session.

The following Sunday afternoon a freezing rain had started falling. My second wife dropped me off at the guy's apartment with the understanding she would pick me up in the same spot in two hours. I kissed her bye and she drove off toward the mall. With my Telecaster in hand I bound up the steps to the bass player's apartment.

Just as I reached the door and raised my hand to knock I heard someone yelling on the other side of the door. I listened for a moment and reluctantly knocked. No answer. I knocked harder. No answer. I pounded on the door with the palm of my fist. The door flew open. The bass player stood there with a phone in his ear, his face red as a beet from an obviously heated phone conversation. Before he realized it was me, he yelled, "What the fuck do you want?! Oh, sorry man, it's you. Come on in."

He motioned me toward the back bedroom as he continued yelling into the phone. Judging from the words he was using and the fact there was not a single stick of furniture in the house, I concluded the person on the other end of the phone was his wife. She had apparently moved out the night before and taken everything he owned while he was gone.

I found my way to the back bedroom and sat down cross-legged on the carpet next to the only piece of furniture in the room, his bass amp.

I heard him scream, "You fuckin' bitch! You fuckin' bitch! I'll kill you! I'll kill you!"

He slammed down the phone. A split second later he burst into the practice room waving a hunting knife over his head. He ran past me to the back wall of the room, viciously attacking the wall and stabbing it over and over. Chunks of sheetrock flew around the room.

"That fuckin' bitch! That sorry fuckin' bitch! I'm gonna kill that sorry fuckin' bitch!"

Realizing I had walked into a war zone, I got up to leave and suggested maybe I should come back at another time.

"Naw, man, naw! We're gonna jam!" he insisted. "Fuck her! Her bullshit ain't gonna stop us from jammin'!"

He grabbed his bass guitar and sat down cross-legged facing me. We both plugged into his bass amp and started jamming on a three-chord blues progression.

The phone rang and he ran to the kitchen to answer it.

I could hear him yelling at his wife. It was a repeat of the previous explosive conversation. Moments later he charged back in the bedroom in a blind rage. Again he made several furious stabs in the wall with his hunting knife sending more pieces of sheetrock flying and screaming "I'll kill her! I'll kill that fuckin' bitch!"

I was scared shitless.

In his fury the guy could have easily turned on me and cut me to pieces as I sat completely defenseless on the floor holding my guitar. I was freaking out. What if my wife came back early from her shopping trip and came knocking on the door looking for me? What if in his rage he tried to hurt her? I knew I had to get out, but how? I was on the second floor and there was no back door. I felt trapped and was on the verge of panic. I was looking for an escape and I still had to pack up my guitar.

Again, the phone rang.

When he headed for the kitchen, I jumped up, pulled the knife out of the wall, and quickly sat down with the knife hidden under my thigh just in time as he came back ranting and raving. In an effort to distract him from the fact I had his knife, I yelled, "C'mon man, let's jam." I fell into a fast, loud, blues rock shuffle.

Agitated and uninterested he fumbled with his guitar, trying to figure out the chord progression.

The phone rang again. He leaped to his feet and bolted toward the kitchen. This was my chance to escape, but there was only one way out: through the kitchen and right past him. I jumped up, tossed the knife behind the amp, shoved my guitar in the case, slammed it shut and latched the lid in one quick move. I shot past the guy as he stood with his back to me at the kitchen counter yelling into the phone.

I jerked opened the front door and bolted down the stairs into the courtyard. As I made my way down the sidewalk, he stood in the open doorway screaming, "Where the fuck you going? Muthafucker, you ain't leavin'! Muthafucker, you ain't leaving!"

I was in the guy's apartment less than twenty minutes and still had an hour and a half to wait in the freezing cold before my wife was scheduled to pick me up. I could have waited in the nice warm leasing office, but I didn't dare take a chance my wife might come back early and go to that maniac's apartment. Since there were no cell phones in those days, I was forced to stand in the freezing cold and drizzle waiting for my wife.

To top it all off, she was twenty minutes late. "I know how you love to play so I was just giving you a little extra time to do your thing."

Chilled to the bone and my teeth chattering I told my wife what happened. Instead of being happy I was safe and appreciative of my concern for her all she said was, "Well, maybe now you'll forget all this music business crap and get a real job."

She always said that.

## STRIPPED AND RIPPED

In the summer of 1985 I was performing a Sunday afternoon gig as a one-man band with my drum machine at an icehouse on Bayway Drive in Baytown called Jay Walkers.

As I was setting up my equipment, three girls in the early twenties, Big Brenda and the two cuties she ran with, Becky and Jeannie, sat at the front table. For several months they had followed me as I performed at different beer joints in the area. They were always alot of fun, clapping and singing along from the moment I kicked off the first song.

As the day wore on and the beer loosened them up, I tried to coerce them into showing some skin as I played "Don't It Make You Want To (Take off Your Clothes)." They insisted I go first. I laughed off their remarks and continued playing.

I have a habit of closing my eyes whenever I play the harmonica on a rack around my neck. While in the middle of a harmonica solo I didn't see Big Brenda when she snuck around behind me. She wrapped her sweaty, wrestler-like arms around me and pinned both of my arms down to my sides. She gave me a big squeeze and started lifting me off the floor. I'm sure my eyes flew wide open with a look of shock and surprise. Everybody in the place burst out laughing.

I'm 5' 6" and weighed 155 at the time. Big Brenda was at least 6' and must have weighed about 250 pounds.

With her hands firmly locked in a death grip across my chest, Big Brenda lifted me off the floor as if to make a present of me to her two smaller girlfriends. My feet dangled in the air like a small child. The more I struggled to get loose, the tighter Big Brenda's boa constrictor arms squeezed. I couldn't breathe! She obviously didn't know her own strength. The crowd roared with laughter.

With me held tight in a helpless position, Becky clawed at my shirt. Seams ripped and buttons popped like popcorn. Up to then it was all fun and games. I quickly realized it was a serious when Jeannie unbuckled my belt, unzipped my pants and started yanking my jeans down. Feeling my pants start to slide off, I jerked violently like a fish caught in a net. My yells for help were lost in the laughter of the crowd.

I managed to get my left thumb through a belt loop and held on for dear life while my right hand clutched my guitar.

I knew the girls were just having fun. Even so, they were scratching me all to hell as they mercilessly pulled at my clothes off. No one was coming to my aid. I had to get loose or be stripped right there in the front of the crowd.

The amiable crowd of afternoon beer drinkers had turned into a screaming mob of raving maniacs, standing on tables and chairs and cheering the girls on. My mic stand was knocked over. The mic was screamed with feedback and added to the noise of the frenzied crowd.

My music stand was knocked over and pages of song lyrics were caught in the jet stream of shop fans. Paper blew around the room like debris in a hurricane. It must've been a hell of a sight. Through it all my drum machine was still pounding out a beat. My guitar was still strapped over my shoulder and responded with muffled sounds of the struggle. It was total chaos – and the crowd loved it!

My biggest fear was not the embarrassment of being undressed in front of an audience by three wild women. If anything, that would have been a great publicity stunt and great for my reputation. But the possibility of my guitar falling to the concrete floor and busting into a million pieces was my main concern. I yelled to my old friend and fellow musician Mad Max to come help me. I hoped he would snatch my guitar and then pull the girls off of me.

Mad Max safely rescued my guitar from the seething mangle of sweaty arms and legs and the train wreck that was about to happen.

With the guitar out of the way I began thrashing wildly. Suddenly I heard my guitar being played. Instead of putting the guitar down and coming back to help me, Mad Max started playing it. Again I yelled to him for help. He stood there with a big ol' shit-eatin' grin and said, "Tough luck, buddy! You're on your own!"

Realizing no one was going to help me, I kept jerking and twisting until I finally broke free and bolted out the big open garage doors.

People followed me screaming with hysterical laughter as I ran across the parking lot. I stopped at the edge of the highway and fastened my pants. When I looked back, everybody was outside the building laughing their asses off! They raised their beers to me, toasting my great escape.

I began to examine myself for damage. My shirt was ripped to shreds. My arms, chest and neck were covered with claw marks and long, red welts. I looked like I had been in a fight with a barbed wire fence and lost.

I finally heard my guitar and drum machine stop playing. The laughter died down and the crowd went back inside. Country songs resumed on the jukebox. After a long break I went back in and finished my gig. The gang of lusting felines sat grinning and said, "Just wait 'til next time."

*Next time* was not my immediate concern. My immediate concern was how the hell was I going to explain to my wife my torn clothes and scratches all over my body? She already had a severe dislike for me playing music for a living. This experience was only going to give her more anti-music business ammunition. She interrogated me like a POW every night when I got home, especially if some female had given me a hug and there was a faint whiff of perfume on me.

I knew I was going to catch hell this time when I got home covered with scratches and torn clothes. I never had a reason to lie to my wife before, but as I drove home I considered a dozen possible tales. None of them were any good.

When I walked in the door my wife immediately asked, "What the hell happened to you?"

I replied in a very cool, matter-of-fact tone, "I was attacked by three crazy girls who tried to rape me right there on stage."

"No you were not!" she snapped. "What really happened?"

Whew, I thought. I told her the truth and she didn't believe it. I teased her with my "three-girl" story for a little while longer. When she grew tired of it I nonchalantly told her Mad Max got in a fight and I helped him out. Since she knew Mad Max and his reputation as a hot-headed barroom brawler she never asked me about it again.

## SNOW WHITE NAKED

In the fall of 1985 I performed as a single act for a Sunday afternoon show at a very nice, upscale bar in Clear Lake. I'll call it "Hank's Place."

The yuppie clientele at Hank's Place was not interested in my southern rock/outlaw country song list and continually requested songs by Jimmy Buffett, Kenny Rogers and Lionel Richie. I didn't know any of their requests, but tried to accommodate their taste by playing my most easy-listening set of music.

I was bored to death. People ignored me as they played video games, shot pool or just sat and chatted quietly. After two hours of playing background music a young woman about twenty five years old walked up to the bandstand to make a request. She was tall, had beautiful snow-white blond hair and was drop-dead gorgeous.

She was wearing slacks and a tight fitting, pullover sleeveless sweater that made her breasts look humongous. Her slurred speech cued me that she was beyond shitfaced. She made her request and awaited my response. Mesmerized by her appearance I didn't comprehend a single word she said. I just said, "Huh? I mean, what'd you say?"

She just smiled. I had been busted for staring at her tits.

Considering her inebriated condition I thought I might be able to have some fun with her (musically speaking of course). Before she walked away I said, "Hey, Snow White, have you ever wanted to be in show business?"

She looked at me and very bluntly stated, "I *am* in show business! I'm a *model*!"

"That's great, but can you *dance*?"

"Well of course I can dance, but I don't *have* to. They just take pictures of me," she replied in a very uppity fashion.

"Well then, honey, I tell you what. You just stand right there on the side of the stage and when the music starts you just do whatever comes natural."

I kicked off into a song I wrote with a very swampy, funky groove to it. She immediately fell in with the beat as if she had stepped on a live wire. The moment she started moving, the guys in the audience started howling like wolves in heat. The more they yelled the more she would gyrate and tease them.

It was obvious she was not a dancer. She had no natural rhythm and the alcohol made her awkward and clumsy as hell. But damn, she was good to look at.

After a couple of minutes of instrumental music I started singing the words. Real low at first, barely a whisper only she could hear, like a subliminal suggestion, I sang, "Don't it make you want to... don't it make you want to... take off your clothes, take off your clothes..."

That song had a 95% success rate at getting women under the influence of whatever they were under to take off their clothes in public. It was my secret weapon and it worked like a charm. I repeated the line over and over, getting louder and louder so the audience could hear.

As I continued repeating this hypnotic suggestion, the guys in the audience started yelling, "Take it off, take it off!"

Snow White's friends started sending tequila shots to her. I was on my second Hurricane. As the music, the tequila and prodding from the excited crowd took possession of her she started to flash her bra covered breasts at the audience.

I leaned over and said, "Hey babe, they can see a bra in a Sears catalog."

She asked, "Well, how am I gonna get my bra off without taking my shirt off?"

"Like this," I said. With my drum machine never missing a beat, I slid my right hand up underneath the back of her shirt and unsnapped her bra strap with one hand (a trick all young men learned back the era of drive-in movies).

Feeling her bra go loose, she jerked her head around and stared at me in total surprise. Before she could say a word I pulled her shoulder strap down past her left elbow. She automatically pulled her arm out. She then slipped her other shoulder strap down off of her other arm. With the bra loose I pulled it out from the side of her sweater. Feeling the bra being dragged across her breasts she clutched both hands to her cleavage, looked at me and said with a gasp, "My, aren't we the little expert?"

I laughed and handed her the bra, which she swung round and round over her head a few times and flung it into the applauding audience.

With her bra off she flashed the audience the real thing. And they were *real*! Hugh Hefner would've paid a million bucks to photograph those babies. The crowd was going wild!

Over the next few minutes Snow White became more and more daring. She started bending over, dropping her pants and mooning the audience. Needless to say, the crowd had forgotten about playing pool and other activities. All eyes were on Snow White.

About that time another young woman, also in her mid-twenties, ran up to the stage. "That bitch can't dance! I'm a professional dancer! Let me up there!"

Hippie Girl was a very cute, small framed girl about 5' 2" with long, straight, brown hair parted in the middle, hanging to her waist. She reminded me of hippie girls of the '60s. In a split second she peeled off everything except her tiny panties. She was obviously a professional dancer. With her long hair flying round and round, she was bumping, grinding and driving the crowd wild! With Snow White on one side of me and Hippie Girl on the other, I realized at that moment how much I loved my job!

With Hippie Girl stripped down to her panties, Snow White was not about to be outdone. She eyed the newcomer with contempt. Snow White took her shirt off and threw it into the crowd, followed by her designer shoes. She turned her back to the crowd, slid her pants down to her ankles, exposing a perfect heart-shaped ass covered by a sheer pair of bikini panties. She turned around and kicked her pants into the crowd. The audience was going berserk!

With both girls wearing only panties, patrons were throwing money at me and yelling "Keep playing, keep playing!" I would need a rake to pick up all that money.

As the two girls tried to out-dance each other, a third girl stripped down to a pair of lace panties, jumped on the stage next to Hippie Girl and started dancing. A cheer went up from the audience and more money came raining down on the stage.

Apparently, Hippie Girl and Lace Panties knew each other. They probably danced at the same titty bar. In an effort to steal the show from the inexperienced Snow White, the two titty dancers started humping each other's legs and rubbing their nipples together. Wow, what a show! And the money continued raining down...

A fourth woman decided to join the festivities. She was much older, probably in her late fifties. She was twice as large as the other girls, about 250 pounds. "Big Mama" jumped to the far end of the stage, taking off her shirt and bra. Saucer-sized brown nipples covered half of her huge breasts that sagged across an huge, fat stomach like two cantaloupes in a tow sack. Her big, wide ass was covered with a pair of grandma panties that could have been used for a boy scout tent.

She was completely uninhibited, not at all intimidated by the writhing lovelies half her age. She was having the time of her life. It was obvious by her mocking dance moves she was making fun of the other girls. Whatever the other girls did, she would mimic. Her size, age, physical appearance and mockery of the other girls made the show hilarious. People were rolling on the floor with laughter.

Aggravated that they were being made fun of and that Big Mama was stealing the show, the three younger women peeled off their panties, threw them into the audience and danced around the stage completely naked.

Across the room I saw the bar manager pull the shades over the windows and lock the front door. People were screaming and going crazy. Snow White grabbed my mic and yelled, "Hey all you guys, now that you've seen us naked, we want to see ya'll naked!"

That's all it took for the men and women in the audience to start ripping off their clothes. Within seconds, clothes were strewn all over the room. The fancy nightclub looked like a laundromat hit by a tornado. Fueled by raw lust, people were getting out of control. Men were dancing around the room in their underwear. Women danced topless, wearing only their panties. The energy in the room was about to turn the place into a frenzied sexual feast, rivaling the tales of the legendary Roman orgies.

The bar manager ran to the stage and yelled in my face. "Stop playing now, goddamit! I said stop playing *now*!"

The crowd booed him away from the stage. By this time I had been playing the same song for almost an hour. More money was being thrown at me to insure that I kept playing.

The bar manager ran to the back of the building and flipped off the electrical breakers to the bandstand. The music went silent and the party came to an abrupt halt. The bar manager returned, yelling, "We're closed! Everybody get the fuck out!" He shoved my pay in my hand, and said, "You'll never work here again! Pack your shit and get the fuck out!"

The naked women on the stage scattered. Tables and chairs turned upside down as patrons frantically looked for their clothes. I raked up the money, cramming it into my guitar case.

A skinny, nerdy kid about twenty-two, wearing nothing but his underwear and a pair of thick, blacked-rimmed glasses, walked up to the bandstand. In a voice as nasally as Steve Erkle he said, "I never been to a place like this before. I've never done this kinda thing before. Does this happen all the time? I'm gonna to tell all my friends!"

I looked at him and yelled, "Get your fuckin' pants on boy and get the fuck outta here 'fore the cops show up!" In a flash he was gone.

By the time I got loaded up the place was empty. The bar manager was still cussing me from behind the bar for instigating and inciting a riot and causing him to close early.

The next day I got a call from the bar owner, Hank himself. He was a rough-talking old cowboy-type who looked like the Marlboro Man. I picked up the phone, said hello and Hank yelled, "What the goddamm hell happened at my club yesterday, boy?"

"I don't know, sir," I replied innocently. "What do you mean?"

"What happened? Don't play dumb with me boy! They tell me you got my goddamn fat-ass ex-wife and three other women butt-ass naked on my stage! Hell boy, I heard you had ever-goddamned-body in the whole goddamn place naked!

"I just play music," I said. "If people wanna get naked, that's them. I'm not responsible for what your customers do. Your manager could've stopped 'em anytime but he didn't."

"Yeah, well you instigated the whole goddamn thing! I coulda got shut down!"

After ol' Hank blew off some steam, he offered me a another gig at his other bar. It was a slightly bigger place and he wanted me to bring a full band.

He said, "Now boy, I like you, and I like your music. You're pretty damn good. But this time, don't try to get everybody naked. Just get 'em drunk! I can't make any money if they're naked. I only make money if they're drunk! You understand? The last thing I need is for my fat-ass ex-wife to show up and get naked and run all my goddamn customers off!"

We made our deal for me to bring a band to his other place, which became another *Gig From Hell: Splinters*

## Snow White Part Two: Splinters

After Hank cooled off over the events at Hank's Place, he asked me if I could bring a band to play for a crawfish boil at the other bar that he owned called Hank's Too.

With a bass player named Leroy and a drummer named Barney, we threw a band together and played at Hank's Too on a beautiful Sunday afternoon for about 150 people. Over all the day was pretty much uneventful. Being a throw-together band we weren't exactly setting the world on fire, but we weren't bad and we had a lot of fun.

As the afternoon progressed a couple of pretty young ladies started flirting with Leroy and me. One girl was a cute little brunette who had her eyes on Leroy. The other girl, giving me the come hither look, was equally as cute with thick, curly, blond hair. The two of them took it upon themselves to make sure we had whatever we needed: drinks, snacks, etc. Every time the blond would bring us a drink, I noticed she walked with a slight limp. I figured she probably sprained her ankle and didn't give it another thought.

At the end of the night as we were loading up the equipment, the girls cornered Leroy and me asking us about our plans for the rest of the evening. While Leroy talked to the brunette, I told "Blondie" I appreciated her interest, but I was happily married (as if she couldn't see the ring on my finger) and planned to stay that way. I suggested she get acquainted with our drummer, Barney, who was single. As I drove away the four of them were talking in the parking lot.

The next day I got a call from Leroy who was laughing as I picked up the phone. "Hey, man!" he yelled. "When you hear from Barney, ask him if he got all the splinters out! Haaaa ha haaaaa!!" Without further explanation he hung up.

A few hours later I got a call from Barney. The first thing I asked him was, "Hey, man, did you get all the splinters out?"

"Fuck you!" he yelled and slammed down the phone. I called him back but he would not answer. I called Leroy back and told him what happened with Barney. Leroy roared with laughter!

"So what's up?" I asked.

According to Leroy, he and Barney and the two girls ended up at Blondie's small one-bedroom apartment where one thing led to another. Leroy and the brunette were going at it on the couch in the living room, while Barney and Blondie were in the bedroom. Right in the middle of Leroy's throes of ecstasy, the brunette let out a blood curdling scream. Leroy opened his eyes and there was Barney, completely naked, standing right next to him. "Get the fuck outta here!" yelled Leroy. "Can't you see I'm busy here?"

"But what do I do with *this*?" pleaded Barney. Barney was holding a *wooden leg!* It belonged to Blondie. That explained her limp.

"I don't know!" yelled Leroy. "Put it down and go fuck her!"

"But I can't!" whined Barney. "I just *can't*. We gotta go!"

"Go fuck *yourself*!" yelled Leroy. "Now get outta here! We don't want you watchin' us!"

Leroy went on to tell me that Barney retreated to Blondie's bedroom and did not come out again until the guys were ready to leave.

Barney was so shocked when Blondie took off her wooden leg he could not "rise to the occasion." Blondie was embarrassed that her handicap was a hang-up for Barney causing him to become impotent. Barney was also very embarrassed he could not get it up, which was why he yelled at me on the phone when I asked him about the splinters.

Later that day I received another call from good ol' club owner Hank.

When I said hello he yelled "Boy! What the god-damned hell am I gonna do about yer sorry ass?"

Playing dumb I asked what he was talking about. "Two weeks ago, you played my first club and you got four women, including my ex-wife and half the club naked! Yesterday, you played my other club and ended up screwing my daughter! And she's *crippled*!"

"Whoa! Wait a minute! I didn't screw anybody! I'm married!" Still playing dumb I said, "I don't even know your daughter!"

"Yeah you do! She was the little blond girl that walks with a limp. She's got an artificial leg. Remember now? If it wuddin' you screwin' her, it was one o' yer goddamn band boys!"

I denied any knowledge of his daughter. "I don't know what happened after I left," I lied.

"Son! You wreak havoc every fuckin' where you go! You ain't never playin' for me again!"

With that Hank hung up on me. From that point on Barney's nickname was "Splinters."

We picked at Barney unmercifully about how he discriminated against that poor little handicapped girl by not giving her the same good screwing he would have given any other girl. Because of his hang-ups and lack of performance, he left Blondie embarrassed and disappointed. She apparently ran and told her daddy that a band member had taken advantage of her. If Barney had just given the girl a good screwing to start with we might still be in good standing with old Hank. Barney hated us for ribbing him about that. After all, handicapped girls need love too.

Leroy eventually gave up the music business and became an oil-industry technician. Barney moved to California, became a car salesman and disappeared off the face of the earth.

I never heard another word from ol' Hank.

## THE BAY-DECK DRIVE-IN

In the summer of 1985 the Bay-Deck Drive-In was a small wood framed building that sat on the corner of Bayway Drive and Decker in Baytown. It was a tiny place no bigger than a two-car garage. It had double garage doors that stayed open from 7am to midnight. The bar seated about ten people and had room for only two pool tables. If there were more than ten customers, the rest sat outside behind the building on picnic tables, concrete blocks and logs. It was the kind of place where refinery workers would rush in after work on pay day, get their check cashed, grab a beer and a Slim Jim and rush out.

In an effort to hold some of the check cashers I was asked to bring my one-man band show every Thursday, a busy check cashing day, and play from 6pm to 10pm.

The place was so small there was not enough room for me to play inside. After kicking a big stack of cardboard beer boxes out of the way, I set up outside next to the back door. As I started to play, refinery workers cashing their checks hung around to see what was going on. Within a couple of weeks the place looked like a giant tailgate party. It was always packed.

Alot of women were starting to work refinery jobs and construction in those days so after-work parties often got wild. There's nothing like a long-haired girl in tight jeans and a hard hat pouring beer over her sweaty t-shirt while doing the hoochie-coo on top of a picnic table. You can imagine the reaction of the crowd. It was a blast.

Through the summer and into November, people showed up in pickup trucks, motorcycles and even on horseback. It all came to a halt as cold weather moved in since the building was too small to accommodate me and my guitar.

I played in the little Bay-Deck building only once more, many years later after it became Mac's Boot & Shoe Repair. When I stopped to pick up a pair of boots, the owner, Mac Choate, refused to take my money. Instead he called his family to come to the shop, and I played my guitar and sang for one hour to pay for my boots.

# NASHVILLE

One night in the early spring of 1986, my second wife and I were propped up in bed in our apartment in Baytown, watching a country music awards program on TV.

Though I never fit the hard-core country-western mold, the country music of the mid-eighties included some house-rocking artists I could relate to: Exile, Sawyer Brown Band, and Hank Williams, Jr. The blue-eyed soul of country bluesrockers T. Graham Brown and Ronnie Milsap were burning up the charts.

I knew I could play the hell outta that blues-rocking country, so I turned to my wife and blurted, "Let's move to Nashville!"

I'll spare the details regarding our numerous heated discussions about picking up and moving. On June 1, 1986, we rolled into Music City USA in a 1984 Dodge Ram van with the bare necessities of life and the tools of my trade, my band equipment.

We spent the first nights in Nashville camped out in an RV park sleeping in the van. We spent our days studying the classifieds looking for a small house. I insisted we rent a house instead of an apartment so I could practice without disturbing the neighbors.

We finally found a very nice unfurnished two-bedroom cottage on a quiet dead-end street in Madison, a suburb of north Nashville. It was perfect. We moved in with nothing but our clothes, a foam mattress, a box fan and a 19" portable color TV.

The little house did not have any air conditioning. We thought being that far north of the humid Texas Gulf Coast we wouldn't need air conditioning. Wrong.

The summer of 1986 turned out to be one of the hottest summers on record for Middle Tennessee. I suggested we buy a small, one-room air conditioner to at least keep the bedroom cool. My wife insisted we move to an apartment with central air. I didn't blame her for constantly complaining about the heat and sleeping on a foam mattress on the floor. It was uncomfortable compared to what we were used to. I reminded her that all the great superstars started out like this so I knew we were on the right track.

She did not share my optimism.

Next to the little house was a wooded area where a small stream made gentle tinkling, gurgling sounds as it flowed over the smooth, round river rocks and on down the hill. The scene was as pretty as a picture in a puzzle.

One afternoon three weeks after we moved in, a gentle summer rain passed through. We welcomed the drop in temperature. I dozed off in my underwear in front of our little box fan. Within minutes my wife woke me. The room was dark. I looked outside. The sky had turned pitch black with big, dark clouds rolling treetop high. The wind was blowing so hard trees were being jerked back and forth, as if caught in a giant washing machine.

*KA BA BOOOM!* Thunder rocked the tiny house like an earthquake. Lightning flashed like strobe lights at a rock concert. The gentle summer rain had turned into a torrential downpour. I was watching weather bulletins on TV when my wife yelled from the living room, "The water is coming up and you'd better move the van!"

"Move the van? We're on the side of a hill, it's not going to flood on the side of a hill!"

She kept yelling at me until I got aggravated enough to take a look.

"Goddaaamn!"

The picturesque little babbling brook had turned into a raging river over a hundred yards wide and was rushing down the hill like the Colorado River. Garbage cans, lawn furniture, toys, beer coolers and all sorts of items washed past our front door with tidal force.

My van was parked with the rear end toward the oncoming current as the water came down the hill. The water was already up to the bumper. I jumped into my pants, grabbed my keys and charged into two-foot deep water making my way to the van. I started the van, put it in reverse and stomped the gas pedal – but the van would not budge. The water was pushing against the back doors with such force the van couldn't move. All my band equipment was in the van. I yelled, "Come on baby, come on, you can do it!"

Water was rushing up the tailpipe and in through the seals around the doors. The wheels were spinning as the gravel driveway washed away from underneath. As I kept one foot on the gas to keep the water blown out of the tailpipe, I saw blue smoke bubbling from under the water. I yelled to my wife to call a tow truck. A few minutes later she yelled back saying all the tow trucks in Nashville were busy. Then she screamed, "Water is coming in the house!"

The water was rising fast. I could feel the rear of the van lift off the gravel and float like a pontoon boat! I knew if the van got caught in the current it would be sucked down the hill and underneath the bridge on the next street.

While I was dealing with the van, my wife was busy stacking our belongings on the kitchen counters. "There's four inches of water in the house!" she yelled from the door.

Just then I heard the "beep, beep, beep" of a tow truck backing down the street. The driver had stopped at the water's edge near the top of the hill. I climbed out of the van and waded the swift current to where he was parked. The driver just stood there with his hands in his pockets.

He spit out a big, black squirt of tobacco juice, shook his head and said, "Sorry mister, I can't get mah truck down yonder in nat deepa wadder." He also refused to wade the water and take a winch line to hook to the bumper.

Desperate I yelled, "Just gimme the goddamn winch line! I'll swim out there and hook it up myself!"

"Fer fifty dollars in cash, and no ree-ceet cawse I ain't s'posed to let 'chee do thayat."

I gave the guy fifty bucks, took hold of the winch line and waded into the current. In order to hook the line around the bumper, I had to kneel down in waist-deep rushing water which left only my head sticking out of the filthy, swirling sewage. The current could have easily pulled me under the van, but I managed to hold on with one hand as dirty diapers, dead rats, and sticks covered with ants floated past me. I was also watching for snakes.

With the van hooked up I jumped behind the wheel and motioned to the wrecker driver to reel me in. By now the rear of the van was completely floating, nose down from the weight of the motor. The wrecker driver pulled me up the hill, unhooked the van and drove off with my fifty bucks without saying a word. I checked the oil. It was milky white. The next day we put the van in the shop. It came back a week later as good as new.

My wife and I felt very discouraged by the flood. She saw it as an omen and we almost moved back to Texas right then. We had been in Nashville less than a month and I was not going to let one little thunderstorm run me off. However, I conceded we should move before another storm caught us in that little house. The following week we found an apartment nearby, on the *third floor*. Let it rain.

## WSM Radio: Fired Before I was Hired

After getting settled in Nashville I set about finding work. I started looking for gigs at all the famous entertainment venues that I had read about or had seen on TV: The Nashville

Palace at Opryland, the Opryland Hotel, Kitty Wells Restaurant, Ernest Tubb's Record Shop, numerous hotels and bars and, of course, the world famous Tootsie's Orchid Lounge.

Tootsie's Orchid Lounge is a small bar located on Nashville's South Broadway Street. It sits back-to-back across the alley from the stage door of the old Ryman Auditorium, the location of the original Grand Ole Opry.

In the early days of the Grand Ole Opry, country music stars would hang out, drink and have impromptu jam sessions at Tootsie's while waiting to go on stage at the Opry. Performing at Tootsie's, whether you were paid or not, was a rite of passage for any aspiring musician who planned to make a career in Nashville.

A few blocks away a row of nightclubs lined Printer's Alley, another famous place where musicians played hoping to be discovered. World famous sax player Boots Randolph had a showroom in Printer's Alley and performed there four to five nights a week. I walked in and hit the manager up for a job as Mr. Randolph's opening act. No luck. The same guy had been Mr. Randolph's opening act for years and had no plans of leaving. Eventually I did get a call to audition for the gig. The opening act was booked to go on the road with Barbara Mandrell, but unfortunately their gig fell through. I just marked it up to another in a long line of music business disappointments. I learned that most steady gigs in Nashville had been held by the same acts (or house bands) for *years*! The chances of getting a gig was slim to none.

Money was running short so I decided to find a day job. With my radio experience and proven track record in advertising sales, I went straight to the King of Country Music Broadcasting, WSM Radio.

WSM has featured the Grand Ole Opry since its beginning. WSM was also a part of everything from The Nashville Network (TNN): Hee Haw, Opryland Amusement Park, The Opryland Hotel and who knows what else. I knew if I had a job at WSM I would have an opportunity to meet every famous country-western singer in the world and pitch them my original songs. Wow, what a great plan! So I thought.

To prove I could sell advertising I walked into WSM carrying a briefcase full of signed advertising contracts from my days with KBUK Radio in Baytown. Within fifteen minutes of looking over my contracts and sales credentials, I had a job. The sales manager took me on a tour of the station, introduced me to the staff and showed me my desk, the restroom and the kitchen. After the tour he poured me a cup of coffee.

Back in his office we sat down to fill out some paperwork. He placed a big, black binder on his desk which I figured was the company's hiring policies, employee health plan info and maybe their advertising rate sheets.

I remember thinking, "I made it! I made it! I've only been in Nashville a few weeks, and I already have a job at the greatest country radio station in the *whole damn world*! Wait 'til the folks back home hear about this."

I could hardly contain my excitement and professional composure. I wanted to jump up and down like a kid on Christmas morning.

Flipping pages in his binder, the sales manager snapped me out of my momentary daydream and back to reality. "Well, Gene, what brings you to Nashville?"

"I'm a professional musician and songwriter," I proudly announced, thinking that would impress the guy. "I write country music."

His expression and friendly demeanor toward me changed in an instant. He slammed his binder shut, stood up, thrust out his hand and said, "Thanks for stopping by. We wish you well with your music career. Good luck."

I'm sure I looked like a little kid after a big bully steals his candy when I said, "What's going on? I thought I had a job."

"We don't hire musicians or songwriters who plan to use this station as a means to further their music career." he announced. "Good day!"

I walked out of the WSM World Headquarters like a man going to the gallows. I was so high a few minutes before, then the rug was jerked out from under me, by *me*! Why did I tell this guy I was a *musician*? Then again, I didn't know I had to keep it a secret. After all, I was in Music City, USA.

I learned the hard way that if you are going to work a day job in Nashville, don't tell anyone you are a musician.

I spent the next month in Nashville loading and unloading trucks.

## LOOKING FOR GIGS IN NASHVILLE

While working days on various Nashville loading docks, I'd hurry home after work, clean up, and go back out on the streets looking for places I could get a gig as a single act.

Being new in town I didn't know the protocol of getting a gig. I plowed into places with my Texas bulldozer attitude, the way I was used to doing in Texas.

I hit all the tourist places in Printer's Alley, Opryland Hotel, the Blue Bird Cafe, the Hall of Fame Hotel, Tootsie's Orchid Lounge and other places along South Broadway. To the club owners and managers I was just another in a long line of starstruck kids with dreams of hitting the big time.

The club owners were right. I had no luck until I started hustling gigs at small pubs and taverns on the outskirts of Nashville that catered to locals. Those places were not on any tourist map and were alot more like the beer joints and icehouses back in Texas.

Club owners and managers gave me the usual brushoff by asking for a demo tape. Demo tapes of a one-man band sound thin so I always insisted on doing a live audition. I was already a seasoned entertainer and did not come across like the average, shy and timid Randy Travis wannabees from the mid-west singing about their Grandpa's dead dog or Granny's family Bible.

I knew if I could show off a little bit and bullshit with whatever audience that might be there, chances were I'd get the gig. Conceited? No. Confident? *Yes!*

I made a hundred dollars a night back in Texas. In Nashville they laughed at me when I asked for that. Whole bands in Nashville, made up of A-team players, didn't get more than a hundred bucks to divide between four or five band members.

In Nashville a good single act in 1986 averaged about twenty bucks a night, plus tips.

Nightclubs, as a rule, have one thing in common. They all want to sell drinks. That's all. They don't care if the band is made up of one or ten little green men from Mars as long as the cash register is full of money at the end of the night. I knew I could sell drinks. I would tell club owners my goal was to sell more drinks than their five-piece bands. A drink costs about the same in Nashville as in Texas, therefore I didn't see why I couldn't make as much as I made in Texas. Most club owners had never heard a musician make a pitch like mine and that usually sparked their interest enough to let me audition.

I started getting gigs paying $40 a night on weeknights and $75 a night on Friday and Saturday nights.

Not a hundred bucks a night, but a damn good start.

## THE MADISON GRILL

Late one Sunday afternoon in July of 1986, I walked into a little beer joint in Madison, Tennessee, called the Madison Grill. It was the equivalent of a Texas icehouse except there were no big garage doors.

Not more than a dozen people were there drinking and soaking up the air conditioning. The songs that poured out of the old jukebox – which still played 45rpm records in 1986 – were pure honky-tonk gold: Patsy Cline, Johnny Cash, George Jones, Loretta Lynn, Ray Price, Hank Williams, Sr. and other classic country hits from previous decades.

I made a mental note that the clientele was well over fifty. The men who still had hair were wearing Brylcreem and the women had their hair teased high and wore too much makeup for a hot, summer afternoon.

The owner, in her mid-fifties, was skinny as a rail. Her skin looked as rough as leather. The look in her eyes and the tone of her voice told me she'd seen my kind before and was not impressed by another transient guitar player seeking fame and fortune at her expense. She spoke "at" me in her deep southern hillbilly drawl, with a cigarette hanging out of one side of her mouth as she went about her duties behind the counter.

"We don't hire no git-tar pickers 'round here, but if ya wunna play fer tips, you kin play anytime yount'to. But if ya sound like shit, y'ain't playin' a'tall cause we don't listen to no bullshit, even fer free. We had some boys in here awhile back whut sounded like shit and we run their sorry asses off!"

I was amused by her comments. I knew I didn't sound like shit, but then again, one person's shit is another person's, well, whatever. She hollered over the jukebox to her small crowd, "Hey! Ya'll wanna hear this boy from Texas sang some songs?"

The crowd cheered. I was getting desperate for cash so I rigged up and did my usual audition hoping to make a few bucks in the tip jar. I kicked off my first song, "Hey Bartender," and started blowing my harmonica like my life depended on it. People started screaming and yelling. They jumped up and started dancing around the room like maniacs. Within minutes my tip jar started filling up.

I finished the song to a rousing ovation. I guess I didn't sound like shit. The more I played the more money the small crowd put in my tip jar. The owner got on the phone and called everybody she knew. Within an hour the placed was packed. I played for *eight hours.*

I had $150 in my tip jar by the time I quit at midnight. I could hardly talk. The owner asked me to come back the following Sunday from noon to 6pm, for tips only. I agreed.

My head was in the clouds as I drove home that night with my pocket full of Nashville money. I took my success at this small venue as an omen I'd been accepted in Nashville and things would only get better from here. To celebrate my small victory I stopped and bought a gallon of Chocolate Goo Goo Cluster ice cream my wife and I'd seen advertised on TV. Apparently it was only sold in the mid-south because we never heard of it in Texas.

I got home feeling like a victorious conqueror. I dumped all the money on the floor next to our foam mattress and handed my wife the gallon of ice cream. She screamed with delight! Money and chocolate, what more could a girl want, right?

The following Sunday I returned to the Madison Grill and started playing at noon. Again the place packed out. People danced, screamed and went crazy. It was as if they'd never seen a musician play. I saw "clogging" for the first time. People in their sixties would actually jump up on the tables, start clogging and let loose hillbilly Rebel yells as loud as they could. I could not believe the level of excitement.

I was supposed to quit at 6pm. Every time I announced it was quitting time, they would pass around the tip jar for another set. Again I played until midnight. Twelve hours. I took home over $300 dollars in tips. No matter how much money I made I couldn't continue to do a twelve-hour shift as a one-man band. My voice was ravaged. I told the owner the best I could do was 4pm to 10pm. She understood and even offered to pay me a salary to go along with my tips, $25 a day and a free hamburger.

The most interesting gig I ever played in Nashville was at the Madison Grill. A local factory wanted to throw a party for the graveyard shift and I was asked to play from 7am until noon on a weekday. The party was scheduled so the graveyard shift would have time to sober up before returning to work that night. Once again, what a party! It was the first time I had to get up at 5am in years and the first time I ever had to play a gig at 7am in the morning.

I played at the Madison Grill every Sunday until I left Nashville.

## CAMEL COUNTRY

While performing in Nashville I landed a Thursday night gig at a dirty, seedy, smelly, country-western bar called Camel Country, an unusual name for a bar. The bartender told me the original owner's last name was Camel so the bar name remained through the years. It was a big place with high ceilings and dark as a dungeon even in the daytime. It had no air conditioning. It was like playing in an oven.

Camel Country was located in an area known as East Nashville. In 1986 East Nashville was a low-rent district, populated mostly by white, low-income hillbillies from the south who moved to the big city seeking work. I always referred to East Nashville as a "Hillbilly Ghetto." But, if you're thinking Beverly Hillbillies, don't.

There were no pretty little Ellie Mays with their doe-eyed, innocent looks. No lovable good old boys like Jethro. No wise, old Uncle Jed-types spouting homespun wisdom. Nope! These were hell raisin', fist fightin', family feudin', gun totin', knife wieldin', moonshine guzzlin', snake handlin', revenuer killin' hillbillies.

I was surprised at how many people came into the club barefoot. One old man who appeared to be the "Grandpappy" in charge of a clan of about twenty of his "kin" always showed up wearing nothing but a pair of worn-out overalls – no shirt, no shoes – just overalls. No one in his group made a move without first talking to Pappy.

The ages of the women varied and they were either extremely obese or skinny to the point of looking anorexic. The older women wore long dresses, no makeup and had extremely long hair either piled high on their heads (like Pentecostal women) or pulled straight back and tied in a bun. Everybody – men and women alike – had a "chaw" of chewing tobacco or a dip of snuff. Few people had a full set of teeth and the teeth they had were yellow, brown, black and rotten. That didn't stop them from grinning big tobacco-stained grins (with a stream of brown spittle running down their chin) when something struck them funny.

The young men who *had* jobs always came in wearing whatever clothes they'd worked in that day. Some would be covered in drywall dust, dried mud or grease and oil. They wore their sweat-stained, dirty clothes like a badge of honor that meant they had a job and a pocket full of money.

Generally the men were a lean, brawny, proud lot. Heavy drinkers and tough as nails. Any one of them could go bear hunting with a switch if they desired. From beneath their hats their dark, hollow eyes watched everyone in the room with cautious suspicion, especially the young guitar player from Texas.

Having been born in Booneville, Mississippi, and raised by hillbilly grandparents before moving to Texas, I knew a little about how to get along with the hillbilly clientele. On my breaks I made my rounds introducing myself like the new preacher in town. It was too dangerous to talk to hillbilly girls who giggled whenever I approached their table so I spoke only to the menfolk. Even then I talked first with the one who seemed to be the alpha male or leader of his particular clan. The men never said much and kept a keen eye on me the whole time – usually with one hand in their pocket.

After a few weeks the hillbillies started warming up to me. I asked where they were from and what kind of work they did. As I got to know them I would tell them a little about my Mississippi upbringing – how I picked cotton as a kid and how my Grandpa Kelton had run-ins with the law for making moonshine. Those were things they could relate to and their attitudes toward me loosened up a bit.

Every time I played songs with an uptempo bluegrass beat the hillbillies would go into a uninhibited dancing frenzy. The dance floor would become a wild, packed-out hillbilly mosh pit, folks arm-and-arm, a-swingin' their partners round and round and clogging in their bare feet. They'd clap, stomp and scream "Y-e-e-e-h-a-a-a-w!" It was a hoot. Or, should I say, a *hootenanny*?

One night I was told I was a "purdy good gee-tar picker," but they wanted to hear some songs *they* liked instead of the usual stuff I played. They requested "Rocky Top," "Foggy Mountain Breakdown," "Wildwood Flower" and insisted I learn "Knoxville Girl."

I learned all the songs except "Knoxville Girl." It was a sad old mountain folk song, handed down from the 1800s about a young man who murdered his girlfriend by beating her to death with a stick and then threw her body in a river. I just couldn't make myself sing that song.

Occasionally someone in the audience would get up and sing it a Cappella. Each time a haunting, eerie silence fell over the room. People would sit motionless, paralyzed, as if it was the first time they had ever heard the song. It seemed understood that nobody had better make a sound until the song was over or they might get their ass whupped.

**Just Beat It!**

On another night, one of the hillbilly boys offered to help me load my equipment after the gig if I would give him and his little sister a ride home. They were both in their mid-twenties and lived about a mile away. I had seen them in Camel Country many times. They were always friendly so I agreed.

All night long Hillbilly Boy had been dancing with a "city woman" who appeared to be twice his age. They were bumpin' and grindin' all over each other, practically doing the nasty on the dance floor all night.

I played the last song and started to load up. Hillbilly Boy said he was going to walk the woman to her car and would be right back to help me. I loaded all the gear by myself and was ready to go. Hillbilly Boy had still not returned. Little Sister and I climbed in the van and waited, and waited, and waited.

Finally I backed up the van so we could see down the alley where Hillbilly Boy and the woman were last seen. Suddenly, Little Sister screamed, *"What the hell is he doing?"*

I looked down the alley and saw Hillbilly Boy standing beneath a street light with his pants down around his ankles. With one hand he pressed the woman against the building, while he masturbated with the other. The woman stood paralyzed, her purse drawn up under her chin and a look of horror on her face. Evidently she had changed her mind about Hillbilly Boy.

Little Sister leaned out the window and screamed, "You stupid mutherfucker, ever-body kin see yer stupid ass!"

I hit the gas and left Hillbilly Boy standing in the alley with his dick in his hand. I drove Little Sister home as fast as I could.

It was 2am when I pulled up in front of her house. She invited me in for a beer and to meet the family. Visions of *Deliverance* and a shotgun wedding flashed through my head. "No thanks!" I said. She leaned over and tried to kiss me goodnight, but I turned my head just in time for her to collide with my cheek. She got the message and slid out of the van. I drove away as fast as I could.

I don't recall ever seeing them again.

### Gunfight At Camel Country

*All* hillbillies carry guns. At least in Nashville in 1986 they all carried guns. They were *born* carrying guns. *Grew up* carrying guns. Survived in the wilderness by carrying guns. When they moved to the big city it was only natural for them to continue to carry guns. They carried guns for two reasons – to kill something to eat or to kill whatever was about to kill them – whether it be a snake, a bear, a mountain lion or another hillbilly with a gun.

The hillbillies of East Nashville not only brought their guns, culture and beliefs to the big city, they brought their attitudes, their Hatfield and McCoy-type family feuds and their own style of hillbilly justice.

In Hillbilly Ghetto, man's worst enemy was another man, especially when alcohol was involved. Almost every night there were knock-down, drag-out fistfights at Camel Country. Everybody fought. Women, men, young or old. Didn't matter.

One night the fight went out the front door. In a few minutes I could hear gunfire. Concerned about my van I peeked out the front door. One group of hillbillies was shooting at another. They were hiding behind trees, cars, telephone poles and laying in the gutters. It sounded like a war zone. It *was* a war zone!

Within seconds a dozen cop cars slid sideways into the intersection with tires screeching and sirens blaring. The cops jumped out of their cars with shotguns drawn. All became silent. The hillbillies disappeared into the darkness like ghosts and the cops drove away empty handed.

My van was parked right outside the front door. I ran out to check for bullet holes and fortunately there were none. Other cars parked around me weren't so lucky.

### Blood And Paint

Another night at Camel Country, a customer was so drunk he kept passing out at his table. Every time the bartender would wake him up, he would lift his head just long enough to cuss the bartender, then his head would fall back down on the table with a loud *thunk*! Finally the bartender picked the guy up by the collar and the back of the pants, guided him to the front door and gave him a shove, sending him into the night.

From the stage I couldn't see outside the front door, but I could tell from the grimace on the bartender's face something serious had happened. With my van parked by the door I became concerned. I took a break and ran to check on my van.

The drunk had collapsed face down on the sidewalk next to my van, apparently breaking his nose and knocking out his front teeth. Blood was splattered on the concrete like somebody had gutted a hog.

With blood spewing from his injuries, the drunk struggled to his feet by climbing up against my van. My white van looked like a painted Indian pony with bloody handprints and blood smeared all over the side. I drove home in fear of getting stopped and being accused of a hit-and-run. The next day I made a beeline for the car wash with a pocket full of quarters to scrub off the dried blood. I never saw that drunk fellow again.

I don't remember my last night at Camel Country. I only remember being glad I never had to go back. I quit Camel Country when I was offered a full-time gig at Marcy's Pub.

## MARCY'S PUB

One Monday, after loading semi-trailers all day at a shower curtain factory, I drove out past the Nashville Airport to a place called Marcy's Pub. The owner, Larry, told me on the phone he already had a girl singer working Wednesday through Saturday and was not looking for any more musicians. He accepted my offer for a free audition.

I walked in like any other customer, ordered a beer and checked the place out before asking for Larry. Marcy's Pub was small. Seventy-five people would pack the place. It had the atmosphere of a nice little cocktail lounge, but it was only a beer bar.

I introduced myself to the gorgeous dark-haired beauty working behind the bar. She turned out to be Larry's wife "Marcy."

Marcy asked, "What kind of music do you play?"

Here I'm standing in a country-western bar in Nashville, Tennessee, wearing cowboy boots and jeans and this lady asks me a question like *that*? As straight-faced as possible I sarcastically replied, "Reggae-disco-acid-rock-polkas!"

Without missing a beat Marcy clapped her hands together, jumped up and down and squealed, "Oh-oh-oh-oooh, we *love* that kind of music here!"

I should have walked out the door right then.

My thirty-minute audition turned into a two-hour set. Customers kept tipping me so I would keep playing. Larry was very blunt in reiterating that he did not need my services.

"I got a dyke bitch that sings here four nights a week," he said. "She brings in a lot of her dyke friends. Men come in just to watch them bitches put on a floor show. You can't top that! But, my customers like you. You can play every Monday and Tuesday from 8pm to midnight. I'll pay you forty bucks a night." I accepted his offer.

Combined with my other gigs I was working seven nights a week averaging $700 a week. I had only been in Nashville a couple of months. My body was exhausted and my throat stayed sore from singing every night, but at least we were not starving as friends predicted prior to my leaving Texas.

Now that I was working seven nights a week, I was too tired to canvass Music Row during the day to pitch my songs to publishing companies. The A&R guys at the record companies would not take or return my calls. All the "stars" and music business people I met when I worked at KBUK radio station in Baytown – the ones who said "call me when you get to Nashville" – would not take or return my calls. It was very disheartening.

The only person who gave me his time, advice, returned my calls and treated me with respect was one of the greatest country music songwriters of all time, the pride of Crosby, Texas, Rodney Crowell. Thanks, Rodney.

Since nobody on Music Row would return my calls, I resigned myself to play seven nights a week until the powers that be in Nashville discovered me – or I dropped from exhaustion.

One Saturday night I was performing in a little beer joint on the north side of town. I had started to build a following around Nashville and a dozen regulars from Marcy's Pub started following me from place to place. Also in the audience was Larry, the owner of Marcy's Pub. It was obvious Larry was pissed about something. He walked up to the bandstand and said,

"You see those fuckin' people? Those are *my* fuckin' customers from *my* fuckin' bar! If my people want to see you they can see you at *my club*. I'm firing that fuckin' dyke bitch and I want you to play my place every Wednesday through Saturday, exclusively. *My* people can buy *my* beer at *my* bar if they want to see *you*!"

Larry guaranteed me a hundred bucks a night four nights a week. By Nashville standards that was a helluva deal. Most single acts were barely making twenty bucks a night or working for tips. Our deal was he would pass the tip jar several times a night. At the end of the night if the tip jar totalled less than a hundred dollars, he would make up the difference. If it was over a hundred dollars, it was all mine and he didn't owe me anything out of his pocket. It was an open-ended, handshake deal. We agreed I wouldn't play any other place in Nashville, and I had a full-time job at Marcy's Pub as long as I could keep a crowd coming in. Since Marcy's was closed on Sundays we agreed my Sunday gig at the Madison Grill would continue.

By August 1st I had been in Nashville for only two months. I was working five nights a week, knocking down five to seven hundred dollars a week. Once again I saw this as a good omen. I knew fame and fortune were just around the corner.

Working at Marcy's Pub I got to know Larry real well. For some strange reason Larry and I hit it off as if we had known each other all our lives. He didn't beat around the bush with me. Most of the time I appreciated his frankness. Other times I knew he just wanted to hear himself rant. His crudeness was down right comical like Archie Bunker. Sometimes, his bluntness was very painful to whoever it was aimed at.

He was a rough talkin', arrogant, self-appointed king of his own little one-room empire. At Marcy's Pub he was god and let everybody know it. He disrespected struggling musicians who came in looking for a gig. Larry would even make fun of musicians who worked for famous artists who just stopped in for a beer. He'd make fun of their employers, whether it was a rising young star or a Grand Ole Opry legend. I don't know how he stayed in business because he never had anything good to say about anybody.

Larry's arrogant nature sometimes got him in trouble. Mexican immigrants were just starting to infiltrate Nashville in those years. One night after an argument with some Mexicans, Larry made a group of them leave. Before leaving a couple of them went in the men's restroom, ripped the toilet out of the floor and threw it out the men's room window.

Marcy's was built on the side of a hill. The front door was at street level but the back of the building was three stories above the rear parking lot. When water flooded the club, the commode was discovered in a million pieces in the rear parking lot.

When he wasn't being a jerk Larry and I made a great team. Every time he popped off some long line of arrogant bullshit pretending to be my worst heckler, I came back with a stinging one-liner. Together we kept the crowd stirred up. They loved it!

Larry had a talent for the spoken word. He'd lay down a line of bullshit as slick as a snake oil salesman in a traveling minstrel show. He also had a talent for getting women to do things they ordinarily wouldn't do. If Larry could get a girl into the kitchen, he'd produce a bottle of tequila or white lightning and the party was on. Larry would say, "I bet Gene five bucks that you had pretty little pink nipples, and Gene says he bets you have big, brown ones."

Some girls would take the bait and show their tits right away. Others would just point to the winner, but we told them that hearsay was inadmissible. Either way, Larry had a special talent for getting the most straight-laced woman to show her tits before the night was over.

Larry had a handle on *Girls Gone Wild* long before it became a video fad. I learned a lot from good ol' Larry!

## Ass Whuppin' In The Men's Room

One night as I was a taking a break at Marcy's Pub, a pretty young woman in a very low-cut dress walked up to the jukebox which sat right next to the bandstand. As she leaned over the jukebox, she looked up and smiled ever so sweetly. She knew from the stage I had a great view of her voluptuous twin peaks. She blinked her big, innocent bedroom eyes and cooed, "we really like your music."

"Thanks," I replied. "Hope ya'll are having a good time."

I sat my guitar down and walked straight to the restroom.

As I was standing in front of the only urinal, two guys came in and stood between the door and me. I thought nothing of it at first. "Take a number guys, I'm going as fast as I can."

Their solemn expressions alerted me that something was wrong. I recognized them as being with the young woman I had spoken to at the jukebox.

Finally one of them said, "Whad'ya say to the lady, asshole?"

"What lady?"

"Don't play stupid, mutherfucker, we're gonna kick yer fuckin' ass! You don't talk to our women!"

"Hey, easy pal," I said. "I work here. It's my job to speak to everybody that comes in. That's what they pay me for – it's called public relations."

"Fuck you!"

They were on a mission to whip my ass and I knew nothing was going to stop them. They stood between me and the door. With my pants unzipped and my hands busy, I pondered: What to do? What to do? *How would James Bond get out of this?*

"At least show a man enough respect to let him get through taking a piss!"

The guys leaned back against the wall watching me, their arms folded.

"C'mon guys, I can't piss with ya'll watching me. Can't a fellow have a little privacy?"

"Just piss, mutherfucker!" one yelled.

I was already finished but I had to think fast or get my ass whipped. I stalled for time. I zipped up my pants, jumped back from the urinal and yelled, "Gawddamn it! Ya'll made me so nervous I pissed all over my hands!"

I threw both hands up in front of me and lunged toward my assailants as if I was going to rub urine in their faces. They quickly jumped out of the way and I was able to sidestep and escape out the door and back into the club. I told Larry what happened. We each picked our target and made our way across the room to their table. Now it was two against two. Larry gave the boys two choices. They chose to leave. They cussed us all the way out the door, but they never made a move toward us.

Larry told me their freaky girlfriends came in all the time trying to start a fight. He said violence turned them on sexually, that's why Twin Peaks was flirting with me at the jukebox. She was trying to stir up shit. That was the first time I'd ever heard of stupid crap like that.

## She Ain't Bashful… She's From Nashville

While most Nashville entertainers were working for nothing at half-empty tourist traps cloning themselves after Randy Travis and George Strait, I was packing the house at Marcy's Pub. I was having a blast playing songs by Creedence Clearwater Revival, Elvis, Chuck Berry, Johnny Rivers and, of course, the blues.

Naturally, being in Nashville I played a lot of country. There must have been a law you couldn't play in Nashville if you didn't play "Rocky Top," so I had to finally learn it.

One of the many original songs I played was "Don't It Make You Want To (Take Off Your Clothes)." Nashville girls had never heard such a sexually suggestive song. Every night when I played it they went nuts. They would dance around flashing their tits, teasing the audience and pretending to strip. They became more and more daring with each passing night.

One night three girls were competing with one another on the dance floor, each one going a little further than the last. All three ended up dancing completely naked. Larry locked the front door and would not let anyone in unless he knew them personally.

The strip show became a nightly tradition. Around midnight Larry would lock the door and give me the signal to play "Don't It Make You Want To."

One of the many sayin's I learned about Nashville women I found to be true was, "she ain't bashful, she's from Nashville." Every night more and more women from the audience would strip down and dance completely naked.

As word about our strip shows got out customers would make sure to be inside before midnight. I was supposed to quit at 1am, but with a hell-raising party going on, my tip jar would fill up and the extra bribery often kept me playing until closing time at 3am. Some nights I played six hours.

Larry finally told me that we had to stop the strip shows. It was just a matter of time before we all got busted.

In a way I was glad to see the change. Those six-hour gigs were kicking my ass.

**Tip Jar Runner**

The tip jar gimmick turned out to be very profitable for Larry. I had built a good following at Marcy's Pub. Every night my tip jar would fill up with over a hundred dollars and rarely did my performance cost him anything. One night a customer said, "Hey man, let me pass the tip jar around for you."

He took the tip jar and walked through the crowd a couple of times. When it filled up, he dashed out the door with the tip jar full of money under his arm like he was running for a touchdown. I jerked the guitar off my shoulder and bolted out the door after the guy. I caught him at the end of the long parking lot. I demanded the tip jar. He was a greasy little guy. Shaking like a leaf he kept repeating, "I'm sorry man, I'm sorry man!"

The crowd poured out of the bar and ran in our direction. I knew they wanted to see a fight.

"That crowd is gonna wanna see me whip your ass! Gimme the gawddamn tip jar and I'll let you go!" He shoved the tip jar in my hand and bolted just as the crowd arrived.

"Did you whip his ass?" someone yelled.

"Naw, he was too fast for me," I said. "But I got my money back." The crowd cheered.

**Some Days Lucky, Some Days Not**

The longer I worked for Larry the more I learned to deal with his sudden mood swings. He enjoyed raking me over the coals and telling me everything he thought I was doing wrong. He took pleasure in telling me I was getting too old to make the big time. I was thirty three.

Larry seemed to have the attitude that owning a bar in Nashville made him an expert in the music business. He often bragged about high-powered people he knew at record labels. He assured me that when he thought I was ready he would introduce me to his record producer friends. I knew it was just a ploy to keep me selling beer for him.

As the winter months arrived business slowed down. When Larry was in one of his good moods he would shove a hundred dollar bill in my hand and say, "Put your guitar in the box and let's go downtown!" He would grab a bottle of tequila and we'd hit the streets. Party time!

Larry would take me to the famous clubs in Nashville where he would pretend to be my manager. In no time his gift for talking shit would land me a guest spot on stage with musicians that played for Hank Williams Jr., Reba McIntire, Alabama and many others.

One night at a very famous hot spot called The Stockyards, Larry told the band he was my manager and I had just signed a recording contract with RCA Records. Within minutes I was on the bandstand jamming away with some of the greatest musicians in the world. It was a blast! I felt like I was home.

Larry sat watching from a table three rows back from the stage, knocking back tequila shots and being obnoxious. He made fools of both of us by yelling slurred requests to the band as loud as he could.

After my second song, when the applause subsided, the whole room heard the splattering sounds of Larry puking his guts out on the Stockyard's concrete floor.

To drown out his gutteral heaving and belching sounds I kicked into "Johnny B. Goode." By the time the song ended, Larry was slumped over and wiping the slime off of his chin with his forearm.

One of the musicians turned to me and asked, "Isn't that guy with you?"

"Nope."

I jumped off the stage and headed toward the door. As I passed Larry I hit him on the shoulder and yelled, "Let's go. I'll meet you in the parking lot."

## Black Ice

On the way to a gig at Marcy's Pub in the winter of 1986, I saw a car in the ditch along Briley Parkway. Then another, and another.

Briley Parkway is a winding, hilly road in suburban Nashville. As I applied my brakes in a curve on top of a high ridge, the van began to slide sideways without slowing down.

"Oh shit!" I shouted. I then understood why so many cars were off the road. Being from the Texas Gulf Coast I was not used to ice on the roads. I had no clue.

Eventually I regained control. I slowed to a crawl and fell in line behind cars trying to make it up an ice-covered hill. The hill was too steep. Not a single car could make it.

Teenage boys with four-wheel drive pickups were towing people to the top of the hill who were willing to pay them five bucks a tow. Then they'd return to hook up to the next person.

When it came my turn I asked the kid, "What happens when I get stuck at the bottom of the next hill?"

"Just sit thar till I get thar, it'll be a 'nuther five bucks ta gitcha to the top o' the next hill."

There were thousands of cars stranded and hundreds of ice covered hills. Those kids were making a fortune. After four hours on the ice, I finally made it back home.

I missed my gig at Marcy's Pub that night.

## You're Fired!

I had some great times at Marcy's Pub. For the entire time I worked there, four nights a week for seven months, most nights the house was packed and it was always a rowdy party.

Late one night in February 1987 I had just ended my last song when a young bass player came up and wanted to jam. I had been hoping to find a bass player and start a band so I put my guitar back on and we jammed on a some old rock 'n roll and blues. *The kid was great!*

His bass lines, with my guitar and drum machine, made us sound like a full band. Everybody was dancing and having a great time.

Marcy yelled from behind the bar, "Play 'Pretty Woman'!" She loved that Roy Orbison song and I had to sing it for her at least twice a night. The bass player didn't know "Pretty Woman" so I announced we couldn't do it right then. We continued to jam on other songs.

The moment we quit Larry called me to his corner table. Judging from the response of the crowd, I thought he was going to tell me to hire the bass player. He looked at me with the cold stare of an executioner. "Pack yer fuckin' shit and git the fuck outta my place!"

Thinking this was another one of his pranks, I started laughing.

It was February, yet he was sweating profusely. He glared at me from across the table, his eyes like black marbles. "Pack yer fuckin' shit!" he yelled as he slammed his fist on the table.

"What the hell is this all about?" I asked, "I thought we were friends! Are you really firing me?"

"You goddamn right I'm firing you! You insulted my wife in front of her friends. She told you to play 'Pretty Woman' and you said *no*! You don't say *no* to *my* wife, motherfucker!"

I couldn't believe what I was hearing. In an effort to keep my job I replied, "Larry, I was playing after hours on my own time, for the sole purpose of auditioning the bass player. He didn't know 'Pretty Woman' so we couldn't play it. You gonna fire me for something I did on my own time?"

"This is my club and I do what the fuck I want. Now get the fuck outta here!"

I was stunned. Never before had I been fired from a club where I was packing the house.

Before I loaded up Larry got real nasty. He accused me of stealing money out of the tip jar which, according to our deal, would cause him to have to pay me out of his pocket.

"Bullshit!" I said. "Keep the fucking tip jar and everything in it!"

As I drove away I thought, "First, they [club owners] treat you like you walk on water and you can do no wrong, then they screw you over and treat you like shit!"

I vowed to never trust another nightclub owner again for as long as I lived.

## Back To Square One In Nashville

I was back to square one, like the first day we arrived in Nashville.

Over the next couple of weeks I hit every beer joint, hotel and tourist trap trying to get a gig. February is not the best time to look for a job as a guitar player in snow-covered Nashville. Times got tough. I even went on a job interview for selling encyclopedias.

As fate would have it, my wife had a family emergency so we packed up and returned to Texas to help her mother with her ailing eighty-four-year-old father.

I didn't want to leave Nashville. I wanted to stick it out even if it meant going back to work on the loading dock until springtime. After having been starved, broke, froze, stranded, snowed in, flooded, fired, and constantly arguing with my wife about the loyal following of attractive young groupies I had developed, I agreed to return to Texas without further protest.

Late one freezing February night we snuck out of town still owing back rent, and headed for Texas. Just as we passed the Nashville City Limits sign, "Pretty Woman" came over the radio. My wife turned to me and in her usual sarcastic tone said, "There's your omen for ya!"

## Back To Texas

A couple of weeks after we arrived at my wife's parents home in Center, Texas, her dad passed away. Her parents had been married for fifty years. We didn't want to suddenly leave her mother all alone so we settled in for an indefinite stay. I went about trying to book gigs in East Texas.

## NO ELVIS IMPERSONATOR

I quickly learned that East Texas was not conducive to the career of a full-time musician and I needed to work at least five nights a week.

Being fresh from Nashville impressed East Texas club owners and booking Friday and Saturday night gigs at the Lake Country Inn in Center was no problem. However, in that rural region of Texas where chicken farming and logging were the main industries and people went to bed at the crack of dark, booking weeknight gigs proved to be much more difficult.

I scoured the countryside from Center to Marshall, Longview to Lufkin and Nacogdoches, then all the way to Shreveport, Louisiana, hitting every little bar and beer joint along the way. Wherever I saw a flashing neon beer sign I stopped, made my sales pitch and offered to do a free audition. I had learned if I could get an audition I had a 99% chance of getting the gig.

One afternoon I stopped in Lufkin at a club called Dudes. The club was inside a hotel next door to a 24-hour truck stop, where the Lufkin Loop meets Highway 59 North.

The bar manager was a big, burly guy from New York City. With his heavy Brooklyn accent he sounded just like the mafia wise guys portrayed in the movies. He also had an obnoxious, holier-than-thou Yankee attitude and showed a great deal of disrespect for his southern customers. As I started to give my sales pitch about being a musician from Nashville he butted in. "Okay! Okay! Yous hired! Yous kin play next Tursday night, seven to eleven."

"Just like that?" I asked. "No audition?"

"Yeah! Juss like dat! Look, I ain't got no time ta hear ya schpiel or watch no audition. Yous said yous from Nashville, right? So I figgas ya muss be pretty good, else ya wuddn be askin' me for a job. Nashville is whaya all dem cowboy singers is from, right? Dat's all we got round heah, deese cowboy country bumpkin' fucks. If yous kin sing that hillbilly bullshit, yous hired. If yous ain't wert a fuck, I fire ya on da spot. Capiche?"

I knew I could handle most anything so I agreed.

As I walked away he yelled, "Hey! One udder ting, ya do any Elvis songs?"

"Sure do."

I arrived at 5pm the following Thursday to set up. When I walked in with my guitar in hand, a cheer went up from the crowd like the Beatles had just walked in the door. To my surprise Dudes Club was packed. Dumbfounded by the unexpected greeting, I returned to my van to bring in more equipment. I happened to look up at the marquee that stood twenty feet in the air next to Highway 59. What I saw took my breath away and pissed me off all at the same time. There, in big, black letters seen by thousands of vehicles, was a statement that stopped me dead in my tracks. It said, "Tonight Only! Gene Kelton, Elvis Impersonator."

What??!! *ELVIS IMPERSONATOR???!!!*

I slammed my van door and went straight to the office of that damn Yankee bar manager.

"What the hell is that bullshit on the marquee? I ain't no goddamn Elvis Impersonator!"

"Hey, yo!" he said, holding his hands out to calm me down. "Take it easy. Didn't ya say yous could sing Elvis songs?"

"Yeah! Everybody sings Elvis songs, but I ain't no goddamned Elvis *Impersonator*! That crowd out there is expecting a big, Las Vegas-style production! I'm just a one-man band!"

With his patronizing reply, he was cool as cucumber. "Hey, wassa big fuckin' deal? Juss sing 'em some fuckin' Elvis songs! Deese country fucks dunno da fuckin' diff'rence. Forgettaboutit! Just go out dere and sing! Fuck it!"

"I want the sign taken down, *now*!"

"Hey, tough shit, buddy!" he replied, "da fuckin' maint'nance guy is gone for da day, an my fat ass ain't climbing dat fuckin' sign."

"Where's a ladder? I'll climb up there myself!"

"Da ladder is locked in da maint'nance building and I ain't got time to fuck wid it. Like I said, tough shit! Da sign stays! Now, shuddup 'n play or get da-fuck outta here, cuz I don't givashit!"

I stormed back outside ready to drive away. I looked at the marquee. It was mounted on two steel I-beams twenty feet high with a catwalk on each side. I had been an iron worker back in the late '70s and knew how to scale an I-beam. I just hated to in a pair of snakeskin boots and my good clothes. In my pissed-off state of mind I scaled the I-beam like a spider. I ripped the letters "ELVIS IMPERSONATOR" off the sign, threw them to the ground and then slid down the beam just like in my construction worker days.

I barged into the Yankee's office and whizzed the plastic letters across his desk. The letters caught air and flew like a handful of frisbees bouncing off the walls. He seemed amused at my irritation. "Lotta good dat'll do ya," he smirked as he tossed me a copy of the *Lufkin Daily News*. I choked as I read the half-page ad. "Appearing Thursday Night at Dudes Club – Live From Nashville, Tennessee – Gene Kelton – ELVIS IMPERSONATOR!"

"Dat paper goes to a dozen counties round here," he said with a big sarcastic grin. "I don't tink yous gonna be able to go all ovah da fuckin' country and tear dem all up."

I was on the verge of a meltdown. The club was packed. The crowd was expecting to see a full-fledged Las Vegas-style Elvis show, complete with a full orchestra, background singers and rhinestone jumpsuits. There I was, just a one-man band in faded jeans with a drum machine.

I had two choices. Walk away or play and risk the fury of a disappointed East Texas crowd.

Not one to run from a challenge, I decided to do my one-man band show and hope for the best. Besides I really needed the measely hundred bucks. I finished setting up and started tuning my guitar. The heckling began. "Hey, guitar man! Where the hell's yer band?"

A lady yelled, "Let's see ya shake that ass, ya little hunka, hunka burnin' luv!"

Finally, I was ready. I stood there, all alone, facing a packed house of at least 200 rowdy, beer-guzzling East Texans fired up and ready to see an authentic Elvis Impersonator.

The room fell silent as a tomb. The near-frenzied crowd realized the advertised Elvis Impersonator Show was not going to happen. There was no big orchestra, not even a band. No background singers and no light show. No thundering "2001 Space Odyssey" intro. No rhinestone suit or silk scarves. Nobody on stage except lil ol' me, in my sweaty western shirt, blue jeans and boots, holding my trusty old Fender Telecaster.

My hands were shaking. I took the mic and said, "Good evening folks, my name is Gene Kelton. There has been a major misunderstanding here tonight. I am *not* an Elvis Impersonator. Never have been, never will be. As you can see, there's nobody here but me and this guitar. If anyone has a problem with that, or with the false advertising, please see the management."

You could have heard a pin drop. After a moment of silence some cowboy yelled, "Aw, hell, we're already drunk, just do whut 'cha do, 'n git on with it!" The crowd cheered.

With that I cranked up my little 4-channel Peavey PA as loud as possible, stomped the drum machine pedal and blasted off into a fast version of "The South's Gonna Do It Again" by the Charlie Daniels Band. My two little 12" speakers were doing all they could to impress the crowd. With my harmonica mounted on a rack around my neck, I closed my eyes and started blowing like a freight train. The crowd started screaming. I opened my eyes. I was surprised that the dance floor was packed. For the rest of the night they danced every song.

On break I met alot of nice folks who were very complimentary about my music. The gig turned out great, and the Yankee was pleased.

I played there every Thursday night for several months.

## WHUT CULLER IS MAH ARM?

One Saturday night at The Lantern Restaurant in Etoile, Texas, I was playing a lot of blues and old time rock 'n roll. The small group of East Texans in attendance seemed to be having a good time.

Suddenly from the back of the room, one of the whiskey-drinking rednecks stormed to the stage, rolled up his sleeve and shoved his fat forearm in front of my face.

He looked at me real mean and angrily asked, "Whut culler is mah gawddamn arm?"

I knew what he meant by his question so I posed my answer as if I was guessing. "Uh, lemme see, white?"

"Yeah," he growled. "I don't wanna hear no more a-that gawddamn nigger music. You better play sumpin' I kin dance to. I didn't come here to listen that shit 'chu been playin'!"

"You like Willie Nelson?" I asked.

"Hell yeah!" he roared, with a big snaggled tooth grin, "Now we tawkin'!"

As he walked away I announced, "This next song is an old, obscure Willie Nelson song. I found it on the B-side of an old album my mama had." I was lying.

Instead of playing a Willie Nelson song, I played another old blues shuffle called "Baby What You Want Me To Do" (aka "You Got Me Running, You Got Me Hiding") by Mississippi blues legend Jimmy Reed.

The short stumpy redneck and his equally short stumpy wife, believing that I was playing a Willie Nelson song, came two-stepping past the bandstand grinning like possums eatin' saw briars. He gave me the thumbs up and yelled, "Yeaaaaah Buddy! That's better! Naw you jus keep on playin' that kinna music and we'll git along jus fine"! If he had only known.

## MUGGED AT THE SILVER DOLLAR

In the summer of 1987 I landed a weekly Sunday night gig at The Silver Dollar in Lufkin.

One particular night was slower than usual. The bartender yelled at me from behind the bar to quit early and come get my money. I took my guitar off, put it in the case and started rolling up cords. Again the bartender yelled. "You wanna get paid or not? I'm closing out the register! C'mon, let's get the hell outta here!"

I went to the bar. He counted out my money on top of the bar – in plain sight of two very drunk, thirty-something-year-old rednecks who looked and smelled homeless. They were arguing with the bartender protesting his decision to close early. The bartender ordered them to get the hell out. I ignored their comments about how much money "gee-tar pickers" make and returned to the stage to load out.

My van was parked next to the stage door behind the building. As I started to move my gear to the van, the anxious bartender came over. "Hurry up! Just set the shit outside the door so I can lock up, *then* you can put it in your van!"

Just as I set the last piece of equipment outside, the bartender slammed the big, metal back door with a *bang.* I heard the clicking of the lock as he bolted the door from the inside.

There I was. Alone and locked out of the building, in the dark with a ton of equipment to load. I spotted the two drunk rednecks walking around the end of the building. My inner voice was screaming like the robot from *Lost In Space* "Warning, Warning! Danger, Danger!"

I didn't have time to load my gear before the drunks were in my face. As they approached one of them yelled, "Hey, man, we gonna help you load yer shit. Then we wanna tawk to ya!"

"No thanks! I do this every night. I don't need no help."

I knew there was no way to avoid an impending confrontation. I reached inside the van and grabbed my hunting knife from the floorboard next to the driver's seat. It was a large, chrome-plated buck knife with a six-inch serrated blade, a built-in bottle opener and a compass in the handle. I pulled my knife from the holster and slid it into my belt under the front of my shirt. As I turned around the two rednecks were in my face breathing their stinking beer breath on me.

I knew they saw me get paid at the bar and were going to try to rob me. I watched their every move looking for signs of a weapon. I was ready to go for the knife. Believe me, I knew how to use it.

In my early twenties I lived in rural Liberty County and had raised hogs. Every winter, we would butcher the hogs and make sausage. I learned to ram a knife blade through the tough skin of a hog's throat and slice its heart in half with split-second timing. Unless those two shitfaced drunks had a gun, they wouldn't stand a chance against my experience with a knife.

Only inches apart, face to face and eye to eye, their stench filled the air. I realized I might be forced to kill them to save my own life. Deep down I didn't want to hurt them. I only wanted to get away. Before I had time to think, I jumped into the open side door of the van.

"Hey! Whar the hell you goin'? We wanna tawk to ya!"

"Sure," I said. "Just as soon as I get loaded up. Ya'll hand me the gear and I'll set it in place. It's gotta go a certain way or it won't fit. When I get loaded, I'll come back out and we'll talk."

As soon as the last piece was in the van I told them to slam the side doors.

"But you said you wuz gonna come back out here 'n tawk!"

"I am! But those old doors only shut from the outside, so give 'em a good hard kick." I was lying about the doors.

They slammed the doors with me inside. I hit the locks, moved to the driver's seat, started the van and drove away. They were running along side beating their fists on the van, yelling, cussing and shooting me the finger. I smiled and waved. I thought, "Go ahead and cuss me, you sorry bastards, you could be lying there dead."

They didn't realize I had probably just saved their lives.

On the way home I said a silent prayer thanking God for once again sending His Guardian Angel to protect this guitar-playing sinner and seeing to it nobody got hurt.

Since that night my contract states that all money transactions take place in private. By paying me at the bar in plain sight that bartender's stupidity almost got two men killed – maybe three.

## PUKIN' PROM QUEEN

During the winter of 1988 a group of people in their late thirties came to see my show at Rangers on Spencer Highway on the west side of La Porte, Texas. They were auditioning me for their twenty-year high school reunion. They were well-dressed and looked completely out of place in the sleazy little honky-tonk.

One of the women was extremely gorgeous. She looked like Marilyn Monroe with perfect bleached blond hair teased high like Dolly Parton. She was extremely overdressed in her low-cut lacy blouse, miniskirt and high heels. At Rangers, muddy boots and faded coveralls were considered after-five attire.

I was introduced to the group and learned the blond was the chairperson of the Reunion Committee. I also learned she had been the Head Cheerleader, Valedictorian, Prom Queen, and FFA Queen. In fact, she was *"Miss It."* Now, she was a full-time housewife who seldom left the confines of her quiet, rural community near Beaumont, Texas, where she was still considered a local celebrity.

Trying to impress them, I played an extended set of oldies, taking them back to their high school glory days. They danced the night away, guzzling longnecks as if recreating spring break.

The beer was having a major effect on the Prom Queen. She was obviously out of practice in both drinking and dancing. She was doing moves I had not seen since the last episodes of *Shindig* and *Hullabaloo*, like The Twist, The Watusi, The Jerk and The Swim, complete with holding her nose like she was going underwater. While the Prom Queen commanded full attention on the dance floor, my biggest fans at Rangers – the beer-guzzlin' fat girls – stewed in silent rage, glaring at the bouncy vixen who stole my attention.

As I finished each song, the room got quiet except for the crack of billiard balls and the ringy-ding-ding of the pinball machines. Suddenly running toward me at full gallop across the dance floor was the Prom Queen. At first I thought she had an urgent song request. Then I thought to myself, "Surely, she's not gonna do one of those cheerleader cartwheel things?"

No. She was headed for the large trash can that sat in plain view of the audience on the right corner of the stage. With a wild-eyed look of terror she slammed on the brakes and slid toward the trash can. Just before she hit it, the room filled with the sound of a-r-r-w-a-a-a-k!

The Prom Queen spewed vomit though the air like a fire hose. It blasted the side of the trash can with the splattering sound only projectile vomit can make. She grabbed the edges of the trash can like a giant steering wheel, and buried her head as far as she could go. Bent over, her miniskirt slid up over her backside displaying her assets to the world. She raised her head from the rim of the trash can and peered at me through half-closed eyes, as melted mascara and dark blue eye shadow ran down her face.

The Prom Queen gasped for breath, wiping the slime from her lower lip and chin.

My better judgment was screaming, "Don't look!" It was like watching a train wreck and I couldn't turn away.

The fat girls cheered as the "Queen of Every Damn Thing" was dethroned by the public humiliation of standing spread-legged puking her guts up in front of her adoring audience.

Amid hoots and laughter, her embarrassed group of friends dragged her toward the front door like Medics dragging a wounded soldier off the battlefield. The jealous fat girls screamed with vengeful laughter. They gave the Prom Queen a standing ovation and yelled, "Serves you right you snobby-ass bitch! You ain't so fine now, you uppity slut!"

Within a few minutes things went back to normal. I took a break while the fat girls line danced to "Stars On The Water" on the jukebox.

The legend of the Pukin' Prom Queen was the talk of Spencer Highway for months.

And yes, I got the gig to play the Pukin' Prom Queen's reunion the following summer.

**Prom Queen's Twenty-Year Reunion**

The next summer the reunion was held in a small community building in a rural rice farming town near Beaumont. Most everyone was in their late thirties and early forties and had known each other since first grade.

The Prom Queen offered me a slight smile and embarrassed hello. Understandably she kept a low profile in my presence and stayed out of my sight. After all, I had seen her in her most glorious moment. Her friends pulled me to the side and asked me not to mention her "performance" at Rangers Club.

There was plenty of food, drinks, hugs and handshakes. The atmosphere was festive. Speeches were made, prizes and awards were given to those who had driven the farthest or who had the most kids. Heartfelt toasts were made to those who had passed on.

There was no stage. I set up at the end of the room at the edge of what would become the dance floor. As I played golden oldies, I watched the beer and whiskey resurrect the lost spirit of the Class of 1968.

Most people were reluctant to dance to the fast songs, except one guy. A tall, skinny cowboy, "Slim." He never missed a song. From what I learned about Slim, he had been a nerd and a nuisance in high school. In years since he had obviously learned to dance in order to become more socially acceptable. He danced as if he had taken advantage of free country-western dance lessons nightclubs offered during Monday night Happy Hour.

The reunioners (*I made that word up*) "ooohed" and "aaahed" and responded with cheers and applause every time Slim wowed them with his fancy spins, whirls and dips.

The drunker Slim got the more daring he became. Instead of asking a woman to dance, he would simply grab her by the hand and drag her protesting and giggling onto the dance floor. No doubt, Slim was a good dancer. This was his night of glory he must have dreamed about for twenty years.

An hour into Slim's daredevil dance routine it was obvious he was exacting sweet revenge on the former popular kids who once considered him a nerd. He had danced the breath out of every woman who had held some social rank in high school and who would not give him the time of day back then. Tonight was his night to shine. He could do no wrong.

After dancing with the once popular, now overweight cheerleaders, the Honor Roll girls that now worked at Wal-Mart and the fat girl who refused to dress for P.E. but now looked like a porn star – it was time to go for the grand finale. It was time to shed the last of his schoolboy inhibitions and ask the girl of his teenage fantasies – the girl who made him stutter – the girl who never spoke to him after sixth grade – to dance.

It was time to go in for the kill. *A dance with the Prom Queen.*

The crowd cheered as Slim dragged the Prom Queen to the dance floor. She shrieked when he spun her around like a top and gave her a whirl every bit as good as John Travolta in *Urban Cowboy.* The crowd encircled the dance floor, clapping in time with the music as Slim and the Prom Queen put on a show. The Prom Queen loved the spotlight any way she could get it. It was Slim's finest hour.

As they passed in front of me Slim gave the Prom Queen a fast spin, changing sides and reaching to catch her hand as she came out of her spin. He missed. The perpetual motion sent her spinning across the room and slamming into the buffet table. Her screams started a chain reaction with fifty other women, and a group shriek ensued.

The screams blended with the sounds of the buffet table, loaded with bowls of food, crashing to the floor.

Slim was a blur as he went past me inches from my face.

He tripped over my floor monitor and went airborne, taking out my mic, mic stand and music stand. The mic hit the floor with an explosive boom amplifying the crashing sounds of the equipment and sending feedback squealing into the room. With women screaming, my drum machine still beating out a "bump-ba-da bump" and food bowls hitting the floor, the scene sounded like a train wreck.

Slim slid flat on his back across the linoleum floor. The men roared with laughter. Embarrassed and humiliated the dance king jumped to his feet ready to vent his rage on the first person he saw.

The first person he saw was *me*.

Slim bowed up in the stereotypical cowboy fight stance. With an angry scowl on his face and gasping for air, he balled up his fists. "I'll whup your fuckin' ass, motherfucker!"

Completely surprised by his threat, I jerked my guitar from around my neck and got ready for his charge.

Before Slim had a chance to take a step in my direction, several men jumped him, taking him to the floor. Slim was kicking and fighting like a wild animal, screaming that I had tripped him. One of the men yelled, "You drunk bastard, you fell on your ass on your own! That's whatcha get for showin' off!"

I followed as the men dragged Slim outside where he scuffled with them, screaming that I had tripped him and he was going to whip my ass. They told him to shut up and leave.

Still reeling from the embarrassment of being demoted from Dance King to dumb-klutz, Slim jumped in his truck. He revved the engine, slammed it in gear and stomped the gas. The truck fishtailed across the manicured community center lawn, digging ruts and throwing sod, careening toward the deep ditch on the side of the road. The truck jumped Duke-boy style across the ditch, only making it half way, landing with the front wheels in the air and the tailgate stuck in the mud at the bottom of the ditch. Slim kept the pedal to the metal. His engine screamed to the point of explosion. The spinning tires sent blue smoke billowing into the clear night sky.

The men ran to the truck yelling at Slim to cut the motor. They managed to get the door open and pull Slim out and turned the truck off. Slim refused assistance cussing everybody. He lit a cigarette and stormed off on foot into the darkness down the long, dark blacktop road.

I went back inside. The ladies were cleaning up the mess. The Prom Queen was nowhere in sight. Several men were laughing, retelling and already embellishing the tale of what just happened as they put away folding tables and chairs.

I loaded up my gear, said my goodbyes and drove away.

A couple miles down the road I caught up with Slim. He was staggering along at a pretty good clip. As I approached him I blew my horn. In my headlights I saw his hand go up in a one-finger salute.

I couldn't help but laugh and think – *someday I oughta write a book about all this crap.*

## Rollin' & Tumblin'

Around 1989 a friend of mine who was a very successful entertainer always seemed to have his name in the paper for the most unlikely of reasons. If he bought a new car, there'd be a story and photo of him shaking hands with the sales manager at the dealership. If he took his kids to the zoo, there'd be a story and photo of him and his kids, petting a llama. When I asked him how he always got his name in the paper, he told me he had hired a public relations firm to publicize anything he does at every opportunity.

He gave me the number of his PR agent. I gave the guy a call.

The PR agent, "Mr. Jones," turned out to be very well-known and respected, working for numerous celebrities, corporations and professional sports organizations. He offered to take me on as a client for $1000 a month. There was no way I could afford that, so I thanked him, hung up and forgot about it.

A few days later Mr. Jones called me with an offer. He promised to put my name in the paper next to some high class celebrities if in turn I would perform at a private birthday party at his house for his daughter who was turning forty years old.

As I arrived at Mr. Jones' multi-million dollar estate in River Oaks, Houston, my blue-collar Baytown ass felt very much out of place. Former Presidents, movie stars, Arabian princes and middle-eastern oil tycoons have homes in River Oaks.

As a one-man band, I didn't need a lot of space. Mr. Jones pulled a couch away from the wall and I set up in a three-foot wide area behind the couch.

Over the next hour, Houston's elite filtered in. The men had perfect haircuts and perfectly tailored suits. The women looked fashion-magazine perfect, dripping in diamonds and pearls.

People mingled and chatted, sipping wine from crystal glasses. The women gave each other little mid-air kisses, pretending to "absolutely love" their dress or jewelry. Nobody paid any attention to the musician behind the couch trying to sing softly in a tone to fit the occasion.

On my first break I made my way to the buffet and tried to make small talk with a couple of people. The society folks looked at me as if they were surprised that a lowly, hired peasant like me would have the gall to step out of my social class and try to converse with them. Without even a reply they turned up their noses, turned their backs to me and moved away like I had the plague. Finally, a middle-aged guy in khakis, a sport jacket and no tie – looking as out of place as me – came over and pulled me aside.

"Look, I don't know how you ended up here, but don't try to be friends with these snobby bastards. They all think their shit don't stink and they ain't gonna talk to ya. I like your music, man, but then again I lived in a hippie commune in the sixties where I smoked dope, dropped acid and shit in a hole in the ground. These people don't have a clue about real life. Personally, I hate all this stupid shit. But I married into it, so I've got be here. Just do your thing and don't pay any attention to all the snotty fucks."

I felt I'd found a kindred spirit among the glitz and glamour and I went back to work.

During my second set everyone gathered at the foot of the grand spiral staircase, raising their glasses as the birthday girl appeared on the landing above. Looking like Jackie Kennedy-Onassis, she waved to the crowd below as they cheered, clapped and broke into a verse of "Happy Birthday."

With one hand on the rail and the other waving as if she were Queen of the Rose Bowl Parade, "Jackie" slowly started down the staircase, savoring every moment of the attention, posing for the cameras as I played something fitting for her grand entrance. At the third step Jackie tripped, let out a blood-curdling scream and tumbled head over heels. As she fell, she sounded like a wheelbarrow full of bowling balls rolling down a staircase. She screamed all the way down. Still holding their wine glasses in one hand, the crowd rushed to her aid.

Automatically, my honky-tonk musician experience kicked in. In a honky-tonk, whenever there is a fight or some other emergency, bands turn up the volume and keep playing as a distraction until the emergency is over.

As Jackie lay screaming in pain on the floor, totally embarrassed – her hair a mess, makeup smeared and her dress up around her waist – I kicked off into a rousing version of something fast. I don't remember what it was but it was *fast*!

The former non-speaking, no-shit-stinkin' uppity snobs suddenly turned into an angry mob rushing toward me like a tidal wave. Thank God I was behind the couch or they would have knocked me down.

"You stupid son-of-a-bitch, stop playing! Can't you see we have an *emergency*!"

"Have you no compassion?" yelled one lady, angrily shaking a pointy finger in my face.

"How utterly *rude*!" another lady snapped. "That poor girl is hurt and you continue to play. How rude! *What kind of person are you?*"

Other people continued to ridicule me. The old hippie, sitting on the other side of the room, just smiled and raised his glass to me as if he understood my reasoning and predicament.

There was no way I could explain that where I come from, when shit happens musicians are expected to create a distraction. I loaded up and left.

Mr. Jones kept his promise. The next week my name appeared in the society section of the Houston Chronicle. I got six words for my efforts. *"Music was provided by Gene Kelton."*

I never heard from Mr. Jones again. There was no mention of his daughter's fall down the stairs.

## Backyard Wedding

In the summer of 1990 I performed for a backyard wedding in a upscale neighborhood in west Houston. The large brick home was decorated to perfection.

White lace curtains hung arch-like over the doorways, scented candles burned in every room and flower arrangements were strategically placed throughout the house. Silver trays were piled high with fruit, vegetables and various kinds of cheeses, crackers, chips and dips on linen-covered tables. Soft drinks, whiskey, imported beers and wine sat next to a large punch bowl filled with Kool-Aid. The small backyard was surrounded by a six-foot wooden fence, decorated appropriately for the occasion. Rented white chairs sat in exact rows on carpeting spread out over the well-manicured lawn.

Next to the garage, tables were stacked with plates, silverware, linen napkins and a three-level wedding cake complete with a bride and groom figurine on top.

The white lattice archway where the bride and groom were to say their vows stood in the middle of the yard covered with red and white roses and surrounded by plants. The backyard looked like a movie star wedding you'd see in the pages of *The Enquirer*.

Dressed in their finest clothes, everyone mingled around sipping drinks and sneaking munchies from the kitchen until the big event. The preacher finally arrived and was led to the archway in the backyard. He stood, Bible open, looking very solemn and reverent.

The bridesmaids in their matching dresses, along with the groom and his groomsmen, took their proper place. Family and guests were seated.

The bride's brother gave me the official "nod," signaling me to begin with a couple of sappy love songs chosen for the momentous occasion. As I softly strummed my guitar, crooning the first few notes of some obscure wedding ballad, the bride entered the backyard arm in arm with her father.

The beaming bride, who looked like Lulu from Hee Haw, was maneuvered through the cyclone fence gate like a large ship squeezing through a canal opening. Several women held various parts of her flowing white wedding gown trying to keep it from getting snagged on the metal fence. Her father firmly held her hand and led her across the uneven, carpeted ground toward the archway.

The groom, along with his groomsmen, still reeling from the bachelor party the night before, stood in a line at the archway trying to focus on the approach of the lovely bride. They placed their hands over their bloodshot eyes in an effort to protect them from the afternoon sunlight. They looked like they were either all saluting or about to break into a chorus of "Y-M-C-A" by the Village People.

Cameras flashed and video rolled, documenting the event for all time.

Ah, the million things that must be considered when meticulously planning such a wonderful occasion. Engraved invitations, the reception dinner, deciding on a bridal gown and matching bridesmaid dresses, flowers, rented furniture, the perfect wedding cake, table linens, the guest list and a wedding singer (me) performing the perfect love songs.

Then suddenly – *an unexpected surprise!*

In all their planning, the wedding planners forgot to inform the Rottweiler that lived on the other side of the fence there would be a wedding and to please keep his damn loud mouth shut. Just as I started to sing and father and daughter stepped onto the carpet leading to the archway, the dog on the other side of the fence started to bark. Long, loud and incessant. "Arf! Aaararararrf! Arrarararf! Arf! Arf! Arf! Arf! Ararararaarf!"

The Rottweiler's barking sounded like cannon blasts. He alerted every dog in the neighborhood that there was a party going on. Within seconds the entire neighborhood sounded as if a cat got loose at a dog kennel.

It was definitely an *America's Funniest Home Videos* moment as everyone looked at each other, bewildered and embarrassed.

Although I was laughing on the inside, I couldn't help but feel sorry for the happy couple, especially since everyone worked so hard to make the wedding a success.

I kept singing and video cameras kept rolling.

The preacher began to speak, "Dearly Beloved…"

"Arf! Ararararf!"

He could barely be heard over the Rottweiler's cannon blasts.

"We are gathered here today…"

"Arf! Arf! Arf!"

Everyone was snickering, trying to hold back their inappropriate laughter.

"To join this man and this woman…"

"Arf! Arf! Ararararaarf!"

Finally, the preacher closed his Bible. Through clenched teeth, he muttered, "You may now kiss the bride…"

"Ararararararf! Ararararaarf!

The video looked good but sounded like a wedding set to the music of a pack of dogs barking and howling over my guitar. Disappointing then, hilarious now.

The bride and groom should have taken a hint from the dog's warning. The marriage went to the dogs about seventy dog-years later.

## Naked Man Walking

In the fall of 1985 I was working as a one-man band with my drum machine at a little nightclub on Preston Road in Pasadena called The Rambling Bushes.

The club got its unusual name because it sat next door to another club called The Rambling Rose. When people got kicked out of The Rambling Rose, they simply "rambled" across the parking lot through the bushes to The Rambling Bushes (thus the name) and stayed until they got kicked out of there as well.

Most of the customers were regulars and had known each other for years. There was alot of camaraderie and people were like family. Performing at The Rambling Bushes was always unpredictable and *just plain fun*!

Almost every time I played the song "Don't It Make You Want To (Take Off Your Clothes)," some female in the audience would get the message and start bumping, grinding and taking off her clothes. The crowd would offer applause as each button came undone. Soon the dancer might be dancing around the room wearing nothing but a smile.

It was *wild*!

On many occasions women would compete for the crowd's attention and the place would go into hysteria. That one song sometimes lasted an hour, with various women taking turns trying to outdo each other. The men were usually just appreciative spectators encouraging the willing women with catcalls, whistles, applause – and sometimes a dollar or two stuck in their panties. Some would instigate the women by being the first ones to pull their shirts open and flash some skin, hoping the women would return the gesture.

One night a tall, young biker in his mid-thirties named Quiz was one of the instigators.

In an effort to get the women to follow his lead, he began prompting them by raising up his Harley t-shirt. Quiz was a good looking guy with shoulder length dark brown hair, a mustache and a sly grin. His biker image made him seem a little dangerous and the ladies were going wild, focusing their attention on his tanned, toned body and gyrating hips as he did his best male stripper impersonation.

Quiz unbuckled his belt, the women screamed. He took off his belt, the women screamed. He straddled the belt and started sliding it back and forth between his legs, the women screamed. He kicked off his boots, the women screamed. He started pretending to slip off his jeans, the women screamed!

When it became obvious he was not wearing any underwear, some of the women started flashing their tits and screaming like they were being tortured. Some started yelling, "Come on baby! Show mama whatcha got!" and "Yeah baby, go for it!"

As Quiz became more caught up in his own performance, I continued playing "Don't It Make You Want To." I thought the women would jump in and take over the performance any minute saving Quiz from any further involvement.

I couldn't believe how frenzied the women were getting over Quiz's impromptu performance. There was such a sexual energy in the room, I thought the place was going to explode into a million pieces. Everybody was yelling so loud I could hardly hear my own music. Every woman in the room was as hot as a firecracker, ready to jump the bones of anyone who would stand still long enough.

Quiz removed his shirt, tossed it in the air and fastened his belt around his waist. He hung a bar towel over the front of his belt and another over the back, making two flaps like an Indian loincloth. He slid out of his jeans, leaving them in a pile on the floor.

The women were screaming to the point of losing their minds and their voices. Some were on the verge of passing out. Quiz was completely naked, except for the two flaps that hung from his belt. He stepped onto a chair, then on top of a table. The frenzied room was exploding! I didn't know people could scream so loud!

Even though the air conditioning was on, women were ringing wet with sweat. Some were crying and clawing at their own faces. They screamed louder and louder as Quiz started walking across the table tops. They made a game of trying to look under his loincloth.

Out of nowhere, a big, beer-gutted fifty-something-year-old redneck charged the crowd. The redneck plowed through the women like a rogue elephant gone berserk in a circus parade, knocking them down left and right. He slammed into the table Quiz was standing on, flipping it over and throwing Quiz into the air. Quiz's makeshift loincloth flew off exposing his naked ass and family jewels as he rolled across the floor. The women's screams of delight turned into shrieks of terror as the good time suddenly turned violent.

A dozen angry women tore into the redneck with their razor sharp fingernails. What little hair he had was ripped from his scalp. He was pounded in the face by the tough, fist fightin' honky-tonk honeys who knew how to pack a wallop. Flailing his arms as if being attacked by killer bees, the redneck fought back. The men in the club took over and beat the redneck to a bloody pulp. The last time I saw the redneck, he was leaving a smeared trail of blood across the floor as he was dragged out of the building by his feet. The concrete floor ripped scalp from the back of his head while women kicked him in the ribs as he was dragged past them.

I was still playing the same song, watching the excitement unfold.

Quiz, somewhat disoriented and embarrassed, found his clothes amid the chaos. He went out the back door, straddled his Harley and disappeared. I didn't see him for several weeks.

To this day, every time I run into to someone who used to come see my show at The Rambling Bushes, they say, "Hey, remember that time Quiz walked naked on the tables and a big fight broke out?"

Quiz and I are still great friends and reminisce about the old days with a few laughs every time we see each other.

## TUPELO TV SHOW

In the summer of 1990 I took my second wife and my two sons to visit relatives in my hometown and birthplace of Booneville, Mississippi. Since Booneville is only a half-hour north of the Tupelo, some of my relatives suggested that while I was there I should try to do a performance on a show that aired at 6am every weekday on Tupelo's WTVA.

*The Mornin' Show* was hosted by the husband and wife team of Buddy and Kay Bain. Buddy and Kay were singers and entertainers who'd performed with numerous major celebrities during their career, as well as appeared on *Hee Haw* and *The Grand Ol' Opry*.

*The Mornin' Show* featured community information pertinent to northeast Mississippi. Births, deaths, marriages, who was in the hospital and what they were suffering from, who had just been released from the hospital, local church functions, birthdays, family reunions, school menus, charity events and other local *news* was covered.

Every morning after announcements and interviews with local movers and shakers, Buddy and Kay, along with their fantastic four-piece house band, performed gospel songs. Special celebrity guests often dropped in to do a few songs.

After a few phone calls I connected with Buddy Bain himself. He turned me over to his lead guitar player who served as music director. Mr. Lead Man instructed me to send a cassette tape with two songs along with lyric sheets and chord charts two months prior to my scheduled date so the band could learn my songs well in advance of the show. He went on to say the show went live at 6am and I should be at the stage door at 5:30am with my amp and guitar. He informed me he would play all lead parts and my guitar would only be a prop.

I wondered at the time if they would have said that to Chet Atkins or Roy Clark.

Two months later we were in Mississippi, staying at my Aunt Frankie and Uncle Harold's house in Rienzi. We were awakened at 3:30am on the morning of my performance to the down-home smells of hot coffee, fresh baked biscuits, eggs, bacon and country ham. We filled up on a great home-cooked breakfast and, at 4:30am, headed for Tupelo.

It was still dark when we arrived at the studio entrance behind the building at 5:30am. The stage door was locked. We knocked but nobody came. We waited and waited. At about five minutes before show time, three cars whipped into the parking lot. It was the drummer, bass player and Mr. Lead Man. They all looked as though they had just woke up.

After a few quick introductions we were escorted into the small studio and told to be quiet. The weather girl was on the air doing the weather, live. During a commercial during the weather segment I set up my amp and guitar. I was told to play very quietly because the band would carry all the music heard over the air.

Mr. Lead Man asked me what songs I planned to sing.

"The two on the cassette I sent you two months ago," I replied.

He slapped his forehead with the palm of his hand. "Oh crap, I forgot all about that!" He suggested I sing a couple copy songs the band already knew. I refused, stating I had complied with his instructions to the letter and had come a long way to sing my own original songs.

"Are they hard songs?" he asked.

"Only if you don't know 'em," I replied.

"In that case, you just play where I can see your hands, and I'll cue the rest of the band."

With seconds to spare before air time, I hurriedly set up my guitar and amp while the band took their positions. I was seated off-camera with my family as the intro music began. From out of nowhere, Buddy and Kay appeared behind their desk. It was my first time to see them.

Back in Texas, I'd worked for several radio stations and been associated with various DJs and TV personalities. They all had big, booming, authoritative broadcast voices that commanded attention as they delivered their messages with a sense of urgency and articulate perfection. There were no pretend broadcast voices here in Tupelo. As *The Mornin' Show* intro music subsided, Buddy and Kay began to speak slowly and calmly in their slow, natural southern drawls as if they were ordering pancakes at Shoney's.

Both appeared to be in their sixties. Buddy Bain was just a good ol' boy who could've easily passed for a southern TV preacher. Kay Bain was gorgeous. She looked like a movie star and I couldn't take my eyes off of her. She was the epitome of southern class and charm. I was captured by her soft, sultry, southern drawl as her words oozed like honey into thousands of living rooms across Mississippi and Alabama. No wonder their little local show was so popular. I imagined every farmer in Mississippi was probably spilling his coffee at the very moment when Kay smiled into the camera and cooed, "Mornin', ya'll."

During the first commercial I was instructed to take my place with the band. For some reason I was expecting a studio audience. At that hour there was no one in the studio except Buddy and Kay, three sleepy-eyed musicians, one camera operator, a weather girl and somewhere behind a tinted-glass wall, an engineer. And of course my wife, two sons and me. Standing at the mic facing the camera, all I could see was the one big camera.

As the show got underway I realized I had to sing to that *one* camera as if it was an audience of thousands. After all thousands were watching, I just couldn't see them. There would be no warm up, no sound check, no practice set. No first set to get the mood right like in a nightclub performance, and no monitors.

Coming back from the commercial, Buddy and Kay segued into my introduction. Knowing the band had not listened to my demo tape, I couldn't believe I was about to perform on live television with a band who had never even heard the two songs we were about to play.

I kicked off my first song knowing my entire family in northeast Mississippi was watching. My only regret was my Dad was not alive to see me and reap the glory of his prodigal son performing on the most popular television show in Mississippi.

Somehow we got through the first song with the band successfully faking their way through. Buddy and Kay sat smiling as we ended the song. I expected them to cut to a commercial. Instead, right there on live TV, Buddy said, "Why don't 'cha do another one?"

I was caught totally off guard.

I kicked off my second song. Again the band struggled along behind me, trying to follow the chord progression they were supposed to have learned. They did great. Only a true professional could tell they didn't know the song.

In the middle of the second song the piano player showed up. Out of sight of the camera he crawled on the floor past my feet on his belly and slithered onto his piano stool. I couldn't help but be distracted. I tried to maintain my focus. After all, *thousands were watching.*

Out of the corner of my eye I could see the piano player signaling Mr. Lead Man to give him the key the song was in. Suddenly the obvious sound of a phantom piano that previously had not existed interjected itself in the middle of my song.

I couldn't believe this was live television, but then again that's what happens.

*The Mornin' Show* always ended with Kay and Buddy and their guests standing together and singing an old-time gospel song while the credits rolled. Buddy invited my wife and sons to join us. My boys, who were twelve and fourteen, jumped from their seats and bolted towards the stage door. I couldn't help but laugh. The door was locked. The boys returned to their seats and refused to join us even with Buddy's prodding.

We left the station with autographed pictures of Buddy and Kay and a souvenir VHS tape of my performance. I wish I would have pursued another appearance on *The Mornin' Show,* but I never did. Buddy passed away in 1997. At the time of this writing, Kay continues the legacy with *Kay Bain's Saturday Mornin' Show.* And she is still absolutely gorgeous!

To see my 1990 performance on *The Mornin' Show,* go to youtube.com/meangenekelton.

My 1984 Dodge Ram van, only 17,000 miles.
After the flood, I drove it another quarter-million
miles. By the time I sold it, the heater quit
working, the a/c caught fire, and the roof was
caved in from the band standing on it. It smoked
like a mosquito fogger but still ran on seven
cylinders when I sold it $600 in 1996.
Man, I loved that old van.

From middle, clockwise l to r: All photos at Marcy's Pub, Nashville, 1986. Me;
Danita playing tambourine; Me showing off. Miss Marcy herself with me. Marcy's Pub owner Larry.
His t-shirt says it all – he should be a poster boy for club owners.
Photos courtesy of Danita Dorris, Nashville.

*Ray and me, Sunbright Bar, Baytown (Pelly) 1983.*

*Me at the Sunbright Bar, Baytown (Pelly).
Photo courtesy of Janelle Phillips and
Jean McCartney Thompson.*

*Little Jimmy Chandler, Ramblin' Bushes, 1988.
He played the washtub bass til his fingers bled.
He grew up to star in shows in Branson and
Dollywood. Now lives in Nashville.*

*The Silver Spur Club, Baytown. The first time
I saw my name on a sign – I thought I made
the big time. Summer 1983.*

*February 1986. Interviewed by John Davenport
for a feature on Houston Channel 13's
"J.D.'s Journal." RIP.*

# BOOK FOUR

# The Gene Kelton Band 1988-1992

By 1988 I had been a one-man band for five years. I had grown tired and bored with it. In fact, I was sick of it. Sick of the stigma that went with it. Sick of being a hotel lounge act and feeling like a side show act at little country-western bars. Sick of being limited in my ability as a musician and the type of songs I could play.

Being a single act was a means of survival back in 1983, but after five years I was aching to crank up the volume, bend some strings and tear up some butt-bumpin', house-rockin' Texas Blues with a full band. I tried for the umpteenth time to put a band together.

I hired drummer Gerald Handwright and bass player Terry Dry.

There weren't many blues joints in Houston in those days where a local, white-boy blues band could work and make a decent salary. In an effort to make a living and work the band into a tight group, I booked every country-western shithole in southeast Texas as much as possible. The pay was only about fifty bucks a night per man, but it was steady. We'd play a couple country songs, then slip in a couple blues songs. Stevie Ray Vaughan was just starting to make some noise on country jukeboxes in those days and that helped our efforts.

After months of interspersing blues songs at our country-western gigs, I felt the band was ready to emerge as Houston's answer to The Fabulous Thunderbirds. With demo tapes in hand, I relentlessly pursued gigs at every blues joint in Houston.

## FITZGERALD'S & THE REDDI ROOM

One of the most highly coveted places for a blues band to get a gig in Houston in the '80s was a huge, old two-story beer hall called Fitzgerald's. Famous blues rockers from all over the country either got their start or still played there on a regular rotating basis. Any local blues band that could get a gig at Fitzgerald's earned the instant respect of the local blues community.

After months of pursuing a gig at Fitzgerald's, I finally booked a weeknight as The Gene Kelton Band. We naively believed we'd be on the big concert stage upstairs and playing to a packed house of frenzied blues lovers. Instead, we were directed to set up on the tiny stage downstairs where unknown, untried bands played during the week.

Salary: *Zero.*

Fitzgerald's gave us 100 preprinted "tickets" that were really only discount door fee coupons to give away to our fans. The coupon was worth $1 off the cover charge. The coupons looked official with our band name printed on them. We were going to be paid a whopping one dollar per person for every ticket returned to the door for our performance. We made seven dollars.

Fortunately, it was not money I was after.

I wanted the notoriety and instant credibility I thought a gig at Fitzgerald's would give us. With a Fitzgerald's gig on our resume, other blues clubs would be clamoring to book us. Not so. With Fitzgerald's reputation of hiring unknown "coupon bands," it only meant we were desperate – and willing to play for free.

**The Reddi Room**

In the '80s, former B.B. King bandleader and Texas Blues legend Milton Hopkins packed the house at The Reddi Room in Houston, a red-hot jumping little blues club two doors down from Fitzgerald's on White Oak Street. It was the most famous *pure* blues club in Houston at that time.

After our gig at Fitzgerald's, I approached The Reddi Room. The man who ran the place, a big, tough, white man named Bill, reminded me of John Wayne. He interrogated me about my ability to play *nothing but blues*. I kept referring to our recent gig at Fitzgerald's. I never told him we had only pulled seven people. He booked us for Sunday afternoons for a hundred bucks total to be split by the band.

The Reddi Room was tiny, tiny, tiny. The stage was no bigger than two sheets of plywood. When we set our main speakers on two cocktail tables on each side of the stage to give us more room, Bill roared from the bar, "Put all your toys on the stage, boys! All your toys go on the stage, not on my tables!"

There was absolutely no room on the stage. We stacked gear all the way to the ceiling.

We played every blues song we knew. At our first performance not more than twenty people wandered in all afternoon. I was crushed when Bill told me we sounded like a country-western band trying to play the blues.

Within three weeks we were fired.

## STEPPED IN WHAT?

In the late summer of 1988, I received an offer to do a show at a ritzy, high class jazz club's mid-week happy hour in the Town & Country Mall in west Houston.

It was still daylight when drummer Chris Bernhard and bass player Bubba B. Badd and I arrived. The parking lot was already packed with Cadillacs and Lincolns. The first thing we noticed as we stepped inside was everyone looked a hundred years old. They appeared to be Houston's old money. Everyone was dressed as if they were attending a Broadway premier. The men wore suits and ties, the ladies wore evening gowns and fur coats, and it was summertime! We felt seriously out of place in faded jeans and cowboy boots.

The club was a beautiful with lush carpet, crystal chandeliers and soft lighting. The music of Frank Sinatra, Dean Martin and Tony Bennett crooned from hidden speakers mounted in the ceiling. The waitresses were scantily dressed young hotties who shamelessly flirted with the rich old men. The place was like stepping into an old Humphrey Bogart movie.

The stage was great. It was huge and designed to accommodate a full orchestra. We set up around a full size, solid black Baby Grand piano which was a permanent fixture. We were not allowed to touch it. It was used by the jazz band that played on the weekends. Being only a three-piece band we still had plenty of room.

We were not familiar with playing at a jazz club so our first set consisted of soft versions of blues songs by Jimmy Reed, B.B. King, T-Bone Walker, Sam Cooke and others.

During our first break I was paraded around by the owner and introduced to his regular customers who raved on about the band. Judging from the crowd's lackluster response while we were onstage, I didn't think anyone even knew we were playing – except one damn little dog somewhere in the back of the room that barked during all our songs.

I was introduced to a very large, okay – *fat* – and boisterous seventy-something-year-old lady painted up like Tammy Faye Baker. Her physical appearance and bawdy sexual innuendos also reminded me of Mae West. She was dripping with diamonds and wearing a white boa. She had snow white hair piled high with long curls that fell on her equally snow white bare shoulders.

I couldn't help but notice her low-cut evening gown that barely covered her giant breasts and exposed more cleavage than the Grand Canyon. I'm sure she noticed me noticing.

In her lap sat the damn little dog that obviously hated our music. Fifi was a yipping, yapping, snapping, barking, discontented, squirming, perfectly-groomed white French Poodle with a diamond collar. Being a regular, "Mae" was allowed to let Fifi have the run of the club.

As the owner, Mae and I talked, she placed the spoiled, tiny terror on the floor. "Sit down, Baby, and be good." Fifi shot off like a rocket to snap up food dropped under the buffet table.

We started our second set with more energy, playing three-chord boogie shuffles and blues. As we were playing, a dapper-looking gentleman sat down at the Baby Grand. He looked to be in his mid-sixties with perfectly coiffed silver hair and wearing a black tuxedo.

He started jamming along with us and it sounded great. At the end of the song he told us he was the piano player with the jazz band that played on weekends.

"Hope you guys don't mind me sitting in. This is a blast! I haven't played in a major key in years!" (Musicians will understand.)

During the next song, I caught a glimpse of Fifi as she darted under the piano. I saw her spinning around in circles and sniffing the floor right next to the piano player's feet that were busy keeping time to the music. Before I could react and shoo her from the stage, Fifi arched her back and humped up in the canine shitting position. I stepped forward to warn the piano player. I stopped. "Naw, this is gonna be *toooo damn funny.*"

I signaled Bubba and we both watched as the little monster squirted a quick blast of doggie diarrhea onto the carpet and then hauled her furry ass back to Mae. The rich food from the buffet must of given her the shits. The piano player, patting his foot in time to the music, was stomping, smearing and grinding fresh dog shit into the lush carpet.

Laughing like maniacs we never missed a beat as we waited. The piano player didn't know what we were laughing at. He just grinned from ear to ear, happy to be jamming with us. He was the first to get the full force of the pungent fumes rising up from the floor. Suddenly his happy-go-lucky expression turned very solemn. His face contorted, his eyes squinted. We knew the smell had hit him.

We were laughing so hard we couldn't sing. The piano player's posture became very staunch and erect. Realizing that we were laughing at *him*, he glared at us as though we were to blame for the aroma that was wafting across the stage which made the situation even funnier. Chris couldn't see what was happening and yelled, "What? *What?*"

Finally the piano man looked down. His expensive shoes were covered with dog shit. The expression on his face was priceless! Even over the volume of the music we could hear him yell, "*Awwwwwwww, shit!* I'm gonna kill that damn dog!"

He wiped his feet on the carpet and stormed toward the restroom tracking dog shit across the club's shiny hardwood dance floor.

We laughed so hard tears rolled down our faces. The disgusting, nauseating smell of fresh dog shit filled the entire room like a toxic gas. People were gagging and making faces. Angry customers cornered the bar owner, poking him in the chest and screaming in his face about Mae's dog shitting on the floor and pestering customers.

The fiery confrontation continued between the owner and the waitresses who refused to clean up the dog shit and threatened to walk out. The owner was furious. He grabbed Mae by the arm and dragged her to the piano like she was under arrest. He then forced her down on her hands and knees, threw her some cocktail napkins and yelled, "Clean up that shit, then get that damn dog outta my club!"

Embarrassed and humiliated, Mae crawled around underneath the piano. She was wailing and crying as if she was being beaten to death. She did her best to clean up the dog shit with the tiny cocktail napkins that kept disintegrating.

I turned to Bubba and said, "These high-class sons-a-bitches ain't no different than anybody else. We come all the way from Baytown to play this high-class joint just to see a dog shit in the floor, a bar fight and people cussing each other!"

No matter if you're in an icehouse, a juke-joint or a high-class jazz club, all people get down to the same level where alcohol is involved.

Whiskey and dog shit. *The great equalizers.*

## SOLD OUT AT CLUB RAVE-ON

In the early '90s Club Rave-On in Baytown was one of the top live entertainment venues in southeast Texas. The perception was if you played there you must be a star, or on your way to becoming one. It was one of those places we musicians tried to get on our resume. We believed it would lead to other high-profile gigs.

Club Rave-On brought in hot regional acts like Ezra Charles, Miss Molly & The Whips or Bert Wills & The Cryin' Shames. They also brought in unknown blues bands from Austin. In the first few years following the death of Stevie Ray Vaughan, any unknown white-boy blues band from Austin meant a guaranteed full house for Houston area clubs.

I'd been trying to get a gig at Club Rave-On for a long time and was constantly turned down because I was known as a local, hometown boy. Club Rave-On wasn't interested.

In June of 1992, Club Rave-On's management decided to give me a chance on a Saturday night. They charged $5 a person at the door.

My friends, James Haarmeyer and Gloria Bashrum from Baytown showed up early to get good seats. Expecting several more people to join them, they pulled a couple of tables together for their group. Immediately the waitress working that section rudely reprimanded them for moving *her* tables and chairs. She grabbed the tables, dragging them back where they came from.

"We have other people coming!" argued James and Gloria.

"Well, they're not here yet!" the waitress barked. "Nobody moves my tables and chairs until they are bought and paid for!"

James got up, calmly went to the bar and bought every seat in the rude waitress's section.

The crowd started coming in. With the seats in that section all reserved by James, no one was allowed to sit where the rude waitress worked. Customers stood along the back wall with nowhere to sit.

We played our first set to an empty front of the club. The people in the back loudly protested that they were not able to sit at the empty tables. With no customers in her section except James and Gloria, the rude waitress shot past the stage, purse under one arm and other in the air giving everybody the finger, as she flew out the front door.

After the rude waitress left, James released his reservations and the crowd filled the front of the club.

We played the rest of the night to a packed house.

# LOGGERS

In the summer of 1992, the Ranch House Cafe on Highway 321 north of Dayton was a typical Texas roadhouse. It was a sagging wood-frame building with a gravel parking lot full of potholes.

By day the Ranch House cooked up genuine, home-style burgers and fries. Gallon jars of pickled pigs feet and pickled eggs sat on the bar. It was the type of place where locals would sit all day, smoking and drinking and solving the world's problems. Ancient country music blared out of an equally-ancient jukebox. When the sun went down, the Ranch House became a hell raisin' honky-tonk, serving up ice-cold longnecks, set-ups and free ass whuppin's.

The Ranch House's flashing neon sign was like a beacon to late night truckers who pulled in for a burger to go or to fill their thermos bottles with the burnt swill the club passed off as coffee. Once inside they would often get caught up in the revelry and stay. At closing time, it was common to see loaded semi trucks parked on both sides of the road, emergency lights flashing and engines idling while drivers were sleeping off too many longnecks or being visited by truck stop angels.

One night while performing at the Ranch House, a very drunk middle-aged woman staggered to the bandstand to request a song. Just before she reached the stage, she tripped and fell forward. She instinctively grabbed my mic stand to keep from falling. With her forward momentum and full weight falling against it, the microphone slammed into my face busting my bottom lip. Excruciating pain shot through my face. I felt myself become consumed with blind rage.

I grabbed the mic stand with one hand and pushed it and the woman upright, who was still holding on for dear life. With my other hand I felt my lower lip for blood and broken teeth. Blood ran down my chin. The pain was so intense my eyes watered. My bandmates asked if I was alright.

"Hell, no! That stupid bitch just knocked the shit of me, and I'm bleedin' like a stuck pig!"

I stepped away from the mic and wiped blood from my lip. The woman was so drunk she was oblivious to what had happened. She kept standing there yelling, "Play a Patsy Cline song fer mah huzzbun."

I was furious. With my hand over still over my lip trying to stop the bleeding, I yelled, "Get the hell away from me! Can't you see you busted my lip? *Get the hell outta here!*"

She was not listening. "I wunt 'chu to play a song fer mah huzzbun. He said tell ya'll to play 'Crazy'."

In my rage I grabbed the mic. "I don't sing Patsy Cline songs! Somebody get this crazy, drunk bitch away from my stage, *now*! She just busted my goddamn lip with the mic stand!"

The drunk woman turned and slowly wobbled back to her table and sat down with several men. With lighted beer signs on the wall behind them all I could see was their silhouettes, but I could tell alot of intense conversation was taking place at their table.

While I waited for the swelling in my lip to go down, we played a couple of instrumentals. Two or three songs later the woman's equally shitfaced "Huzzbun" meandered up to the bandstand and glared at me. At the end of the song he shouted, "Mah wife told you to play a gawddamned Patsy Cline song and by-gawd you're a-gonna fuckin' play it!"

I looked the man squarely in the eye sizing him up. He was tall, skinny and prematurely old with deep ruts carved in his face from years of hard living. His thinning, greasy, gray hair was slicked back and needed an oil change. He didn't seem to be the kind of fellow that would ordinarily go looking for a fight, but then again, I had just insulted his wife in front of his friends. He had to do the *man thing* and challenge me to defend her honor.

The Huzzbun's hands were shaking and his lower jaw quivered as he made his ultimatum.

Three big bubba log truck drivers at the drunk couple's table stood up ready for a fight. They had obviously put him up to confronting me and must have assured him they would be his backup. They were bowed up in a big bubba "I'll whup yer ass" stance and ready to charge me like a herd of boar hogs.

I knew that Huzzbun would be no problem, but I wasn't ready to ruin my new Fender Telecaster playing baseball with a bunch of fat-ass log truck drivers.

I looked to my right to see if my band was ready and willing to stand with me against the big bubbas and Huzzbun.

The bass player, my brother Ray, had backed up to the stage door that led outside. The drummer Dennis Forbes was hunkered down on his hands and knees behind the drums peering out from between the cymbals. I stood completely exposed on the front of the stage with nothing between me and the loggers, except a ghostly haze of cigarette smoke.

I realized I was on my own.

This was no time to wimp out. I yelled into the mic, "Do I look like fuckin' Patsy Cline to you? I told your old lady I didn't know the gawddamn song. Now I'm tellin' *you*! I wouldn't play the son-of-a-bitch now even if I knew it. Now get outta my face!"

Trembling from head to toe, Huzzbun swallowed hard and stuttered, "Y-y-you gonna play tha-tha-that sa-song."

He walked backwards all the way back to his table, yelling at me the entire time. The closer he got to his table the louder and more confident he became. By the time he reached the safety of his logger buddies his stuttering stopped and he bravely yelled, "You better play that gawddamn song, you mutherfucker!"

I kicked off into the fast, rocking riff of "The House Is Rockin'" by Stevie Ray Vaughan. I suddenly realized I was playing the song alone. I turned to my two petrified bandmates.

I yelled, *"Play, goddammit!"*

Ray and Dennis finally started playing. We went from one loud, rocking song into another until the loggers and the Drunk Woman and Huzzbun left. The rest of the night was uneventful.

The next day I washed the mud from The Ranch House Cafe parking lot off of my van and never went back.

*From top, l to r: Ray Kelton, Sid Kelton (14) and me, 1992. Sids first professional gig, photo courtesy Deborah McAllister; Gerald Handwright, Terry Dry and me at Fitzgeralds, 1988; Reddi Room sign, 1988; Receipt showing we made $7 at Fitzgeralds, 1988.*

**• NO REFUNDS •**

FITZGERALD'S

Houston Music Alliance Presents
THE GENE KELTON BAND
Wednesday        October 26, 1988        8 PM
Adult Gen. Adm. $4.25/With this ticket $2.25
18 - 20 yrs.old $4.25 w/Ticket AND VALID I.D.

2706 WHITE OAK at STUDEMONT in HOUSTON HEIGHTS  Call 862-7580

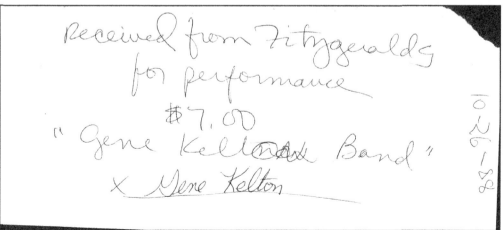

Received from Fitzgeralds
for performance
$7.00
" Gene Kelton Band "
x Gene Kelton

10 26 88

*Show poster for Fitzgeralds, 1988. I hand-drew the posters back then, doing all my own artwork. This was the first time I ever used "Mean" Gene as my stage name.*

# BOOK FIVE

# Gene Kelton

# &

# The Die Hards

## Blues Jams

By the spring of 1991 I was making more money a night as a single act than most full bands. Still I was restless and bored and chomping at the bit to start a blues band. I was willing to sacrifice a night or two if I had a chance to play what I was feeling in my soul.

I had been doing a one-man show at the City Lites Club on Texas Avenue in Baytown on Saturday nights for a couple years. I approached the owner Bobby Reynolds about the possibility of starting a Wednesday Night Blues Jam with a full band. He was extremely reluctant to have a full band in his small club and even less enthusiastic about the blues.

Based on my successful track record as a one-man band at City Lites since 1983, he said, "Gene, you know this is a country-western place. All the songs on my jukebox are country. You've always done a good job for me, so I'll give you three weeks to draw a crowd. If you can't pull a crowd by then, you're out! Deal?"

We shook hands as Bobby said his famous line, "A deal's a deal!"

From the first night I played at The City Lights with a full band, the club was packed and stayed packed for fifty-five consecutive Wednesday nights. We finally had to quit.

The fire and police departments threatened to shut Bobby down for having too many people in the place.

After those fifty-five weeks, without missing a single Wednesday night, I moved the blues jam to Club Rave-On and played to a full house every week. However, the owner kept calling, complaining about low sales totals and threatening to fire the band. I told him I couldn't understand why he wasn't making money because we drew plenty of people.

Over the next couple of weeks I figured out why the band was being blamed for low sales.

With the band set up next to the kitchen door, I witnessed first hand how waitresses spent their time hiding in the kitchen, smoking, sneaking drinks, doing their makeup and bitching about their job. They should have been serving their customers and selling drinks.

The next time the owner complained to me about low sales totals I fired right back at him about his goof-off waitresses, their piss-poor service and their disrespect to the customers. I told him if he'd do something about his lazy waitstaff, he'd see an increase in sales. But who the hell was I? Just a stupid ass musician. What the hell did I know about customer service?

As usual the band got the blame for low sales and got fired. Club Rave-On went out of business a year later.

Again, without missing a single Wednesday night, I moved my blues jam to Frankies Club, owned by my old friend Frankie DeSabatino. The club had plenty of parking, service was great and there were no problems with law enforcement. We packed the house every Wednesday night for the next year.

In December of 1993, after hosting a non-stop blues jam in Baytown every Wednesday night for two and a half years, then at Frankies for over a year, I turned the jam over to my old friend Professor Blues with his band The Doctors Of Love featuring Thurman "P-Funk" Robinson on bass and Larry Kintz on drums.

I moved on to create and host *The Texas Blues Showcase* at the new Billy Blues Club in Houston.

In an effort to create work through the '90s, I hosted blues jams three to five nights a week and still played regular showcase gigs on Friday and Saturday nights.

Club owners tried to get me to work for less money on weeknights. In their thinking it was a weeknight instead of a weekend and as host I was on stage only about half the time. I refused to work for less. A packed house on a Wednesday night should pay the same as a packed house on a Saturday night. Many times the Wednesday night shows had better attendance than Friday or Saturday nights.

As the jam host I had to be on location from start to finish. I had to coordinate the jam, deal with bullshit egos, attitudes and immature amateurs and take a chance some drunk wannabe would tear up my gear. If a club refused to pay my price I found a club who would.

I never missed any work and being asked back year after year speaks for itself.

## DIE HARD BAND NAME

I am often asked how the band became known as "The Die Hards." Some people think we took the name from the Bruce Willis *Die Hard* movies, while others think we named ourselves after the battery. Neither of these are correct. However, the spirit of the name is the same. In the Bruce Willis movies, McClane never gave up his relentlessly pursuit of a positive outcome in the face of great odds. The Diehard battery has a reputation for dependability and starting every time regardless of the circumstances. Similarities? You bet!

It was our fans who gave us the name "Die Hards," back in the summer of 1992.

Every Sunday afternoon from March through October, The Gene Kelton Band hosted a blues jam on the top deck of the Flamingo Cafe. It was a floating, double-decker party barge moored on Clear Lake next to the Hilton Hotel on Nasa Road One in Clear Lake, Texas.

It took over two hours to unload and set up. Every week we hauled our gear the length of the 100-foot pier, down to the lower deck of the barge, then up a winding staircase to the top deck. We double-teamed the big stuff like a crew of Mayflower movers to carry the gear up the stairs. We each had to make several trips to get our gear from the parking lot to the top deck. I was thirty-nine years old at the time and in the best shape of my life. I welcomed the strenuous set up as a workout. I laughed at some of the fat boys in the band who dreaded the gig and faced a near-death cardiac event every week.

Our biggest challenge was not the physically demanding set up, but the heat. There was no shade. Every week we performed in the open facing directly into the blazing Texas sun.

While loading in and setting up we had to work around the Clear Lake yuppie snobs that frequented the Flamingo. They sat staring at us from underneath their shaded canopies and sipping their candy-colored drinks and imported beer while we fried like eggs on a hot tin roof. The yuppies had no respect for a bunch of sweaty, blue-collar musicians struggling with tons of gear. They kept getting in our way and acted offended when we asked them to move.

In Houston, summer temperatures can hit 100 degrees by noon and heat indexes are deadly. The management refused to give us any kind of protection from the sun for the entire season. We took it personal. The gig became a weekly challenge to prove to ourselves how tough we thought we were.

By the first of July our will to survive and conquer this *Gig From Hell* began earning the respect of our growing yuppie following. Many began to join us by sitting at tables in the sun and sharing our pain. Many traded in their sissified fruity drinks for the official drinks of the

Die Hards, double shots of Crown for the bass player, 151 for the drummer, Jose Cuervo straight up and lots and lots of ice-cold Bass Ale for me.

As news of our blues jam spread we were soon packing the upper deck with jammers. I was told that some weekend warrior bands refused to perform a regular gig at the Flamingo because of the pier, the stairs and the heat, but they looked forward to jamming with us on Sunday afternoons. Our jam became a sort of weird rite of passage for both seasoned musicians and weekend warriors as the rowdy weekly party grew.

As our audience grew I heard people say, "Man, you guys are a bunch of *die hards* to keep coming up here and playing in this heat every week." The name "Die Hards" stuck and we became known as "Gene Kelton & The Die Hards."

The band began to take pride in the fact we wouldn't back down from the Flamingo gig because of the load-in or the heat. Soon we were accepting gigs regardless of circumstances, especially gigs that other weekend warrior bands wouldn't play. It solidified our reputation as Die Hards. Taking inspiration from the Bruce Willis movies, our motto became "never give up, never surrender, never quit." That's the way it's been ever since.

Just like the battery we pride ourselves in being dependable and able to get the job done, no matter what.

Like I say to the ladies, "If you ever need a jump, call The Die Hards!"

## OUR FANS BECOME DIE HARDS

As time went by we noticed many of the same people showing up at every gig, regardless of distance or how scarey the joint was. They would recognize each other from previous gigs and began referring to themselves as Die Hards.

Soon our shows became a traveling party. Just like the Grateful Dead had "Deadheads," we had "Die Hards."

The Die Hard fans soon developed their own Die Hard Code, complete with a list of requirements of what it took to be a part of their elite group. Some of the requirements:

*1. Die Hards always bring a bottle of Jose Cuervo to the gig and always offer the band a shot.*
*2. Die Hard women never wear panties to a Die Hard show.*
*3. Die Hards look out for each other.*
*4. Die Hards encourage dancing and always ask other people to dance.*
*5. Die Hards always invite other people to become a Die Hard.*
*6. Die Hards always pass the tip jar for the band several times a night.*
*7. Die Hards attend 75% of all gigs, no matter where they are.*

There were many more of these rules, some hilarious and some sexually suggestive.

Since 1992, I have seen all kinds of Die Hards come and go. Some were desperate, lonely groupies, while others became lifelong friends. Some have passed on, others got married or got religion, had kids, moved away or grew out of their infatuation with the band and faded into a lazy boy recliner somewhere. As one moves on, new ones take their place. Through it all, the Die Hard train keeps rolling down the track. People get on and ride for awhile, then they get off and others get on.

As the '90s gave way to the twenty-first century, the internet introduced Gene Kelton & The Die Hards to millions of people worldwide who now wear our t-shirts and play our CDs for their friends and family.

Me, I'll be here throwing the coal, blowing the whistle and burning up the tracks for as long as I can.

## THE GREAT LOUISIANA WALKOUT

On Friday, July 31, 1992, the band and I were excited to embark on our first weekend-long road trip. I crammed an old couch in my 1984 Dodge Ram van, rented a covered U-Haul trailer for our gear and the four of us – me, "Tubby" the bass player, "Dooley" the drummer and "Lips" the sax player – hit the road. Our mini-tour would take us from Baytown to Lake Charles, Louisiana, and on to New Orleans. Our first stop was a show at the Louisiana Opry House. For the first time in our careers we felt like real road warriors.

Just before dark we pulled up to the Louisiana Opry House. It was a huge, red brick, turn-of-the-century cotton warehouse converted into a giant nightclub, covered with vines, and stood four stories tall. In the fading light of a Louisiana sunset, it was one of the most intimidating and scariest looking places I'd ever seen.

The interior had been gutted, leaving nothing but a cavernous room and a ceiling open all the way to the roof. The manager told me Delbert McClinton had performed the previous week pulling in a thousand people and still didn't fill it up. Wow! If Delbert couldn't fill the room, what the hell did he think an unknown band from Houston was going to do?

The room had two bars that stretched the length of the sides of the club. Each bar could comfortably seat at least a hundred people.

The stage was five feet high, with as much floor space as a double-wide mobile home. We joked that the stage alone had more space than most nightclubs we'd played.

The Louisiana Opry House was the first club I ever played that gave us a private dressing room, washtubs filled with iced-down beer, bottles of whiskey and tequila and food trays. Feeling like superstars we attacked the feast like ravenous vultures.

We could not believe our eyes. By 8pm the club filled up with hundreds of people who paid the $5 cover charge to see an unknown band from Texas. We kicked off at exactly 9pm to what looked like a thousand people.

Having never played shows on the road, I didn't know to discuss or negotiate sound requirements with the talent buyer. We performed using our own little nightclub PA system. I'm sure we sounded like background music in that gigantic reverberating building, but we turned up and played as loud and as hard as we could. The crowd danced every dance.

I remember thinking, "Wow! These Louisiana folks sure know how to party!" Strangely enough they all kept yelling, "Stevie Ray! Stevie Ray!"

Stevie Ray Vaughan had been dead only two years. His memory and influence were still fresh in the hearts and minds of blues lovers who worshipped his high-energy, guitar-driven bluesrock sound. In those days bands from Texas had to contend with audiences constantly yelling "Stevie Ray" so at first we thought nothing of it. Like most bands we loved and respected Stevie Ray and had learned a few of his songs.

That night we played every SRV song we knew as hard as we could. We noticed when we finished a Stevie Ray song, the crowd would again yell, "Stevie Ray! Stevie Ray!" They didn't want to hear anything else. Just Stevie Ray.

After a ninety-minute set of hard-driving southern bluesrock that included every SRV song we knew at least twice we took a break. While the rest of the band headed for the dressing room and the free food and booze, I headed for the bar hoping to meet some new people and win some new fans. I always felt musicians should meet, greet and campaign like a politician if they want to build a following.

This is the one time in my career I should have gone to the dressing room.

While I ordered a drink, a man came up to me and excitedly asked, "What was it like playing with Stevie Ray Vaughan?"

"I never played with Stevie Ray," I replied.

"*Never?*" he asked in a surprised tone.

"No, never."

"But you *knew* him, right?"

"No, I never even met him."

The guy shook his head in disbelief and walked away.

A minute later an attractive well-dressed lady approached me and asked the same questions about Stevie Ray Vaughan. She also walked away disappointed with my answers about my lack of association with Stevie Ray Vaughan.

"This is too weird," I thought. "Why are people asking me about Stevie Ray Vaughan?"

I decided to move to the other side of the room to get away from the Stevie Ray freaks.

At the other bar I was approached by two very excited young men in their early twenties. By their dress and questions about my guitar and amp, I assumed they were musicians. They hit me with the same question, "What was it like playing for Stevie Ray Vaughan?"

I told them I never played for Stevie Ray. I'd never met him. The young men mumbled to each other and walked away looking as if someone had let the air out of their tires.

I headed to the dressing room. I told the band something weird was going on and suggested we get back on stage immediately.

We hit the stage like gangbusters for our second set. As we played we watched a mass exodus of the formerly lively crowd who had turned into a disgruntled, angry mob and demanded their money back. We had no clue why they were  leaving. By the end of the second set we were playing to *ten people*.

In a room that would hold a thousand people, there were only two people left in the club by our last set. They dragged their table to the middle of the dance floor and sat directly in front of the stage.

While the band loaded the gear, I went to the office to get paid. I apologized to the owner about running off his crowd, especially a crowd that demanded their money back.

"I guess they didn't like us." I sat with my head down, staring at the floor. "It was weird! All they wanted to hear was Stevie Ray Vaughan songs. They kept asking me what it was like playing for Stevie Ray. Hell, I never played for him, never even met him. What gave them an idea like that?"

"I guess that's my fault," admitted the manager. He handed me a recent copy of the Lake Charles newspaper.

There in big, bold, black letters was the reason people kept harassing me about Stevie Ray:

*NOW APPEARING!*
*GENE KELTON*
*FORMERLY WITH STEVIE RAY VAUGHAN!*

"What the hell is this shit?" I yelled in disbelief. "I never played with Stevie Ray!"

"Aw, hell!" said the manager. "Don't worry about it. Nobody 'round here ever heard of you, so I had to do something to get people to come in. I figured all you Texas boys played in each other's bands at some time a'nother. I guess my idea backfired. It don't matter, I'm still gonna pay you."

No wonder people kept asking me about playing with Stevie Ray. No wonder a thousand people walked out on us. The owner had lied to the public in his advertising campaign. When I told the crowd the truth, they walked out feeling betrayed and ripped off. After seeing the results of his false advertising I didn't feel so bad about taking his money.

We loaded up, drove off into the night and headed for New Orleans.

## REBELS WITHOUT A CHANCE

Leaving our Friday night gig in Lake Charles around 3am, we drove straight to New Orleans. We had been hired by The Children of the Confederacy to play their annual Confederate Ball on Saturday night, August 1, at the DoubleTree Hotel in downtown New Orleans. We arrived at the hotel at the crack of dawn Saturday morning.

Our plan was to get to the DoubleTree early, check into our rooms the group provided, sleep all day and play the gig that night. After the gig we planned to load up our equipment, go party on Bourbon Street for a couple hours, go back to the hotel for some sleep and hit the road to Houston around 10am Sunday morning. A perfect plan, so we thought.

Things started going wrong the minute we pulled up at the hotel.

Being inexperienced road musicians it never occurred to us people had to check out of our rooms before we could check in. The hotel desk clerk told us to come back around 11am. Imagine our frustration. We had already been up for twenty-four hours. Now we had to kill four hours in downtown New Orleans before we could get a shower and some sleep.

We spent the next few hours driving around a strange city looking for a place to park. Not a single parking lot in New Orleans would allow us to park while towing a trailer. Everywhere we tried to park we were threatened with police action and forced to leave. We explained to the parking lot attendants we needed a parking space only until 11am when we could move to the hotel loading dock.

### No Paaakee Heeyah

As we pulled in to a parking lot near downtown with plenty of empty spaces, a short, wiry oriental man who could barely speak English immediately started yelling at us.

"Noh paaakeee heeyah, gho whey! Gho whey!"

I offered to rent two spaces, one for the van and one for the trailer. He just kept yelling, "Noh heeyah! Gho whey! Gho whey!"

Frustrated, Lips leaned out the window, shot the guy the finger and yelled, *"Fuck you, you fuckin' gook!"*

The oriental guy turned purple. Furious, he ran toward the van shaking his fist and screaming at the top of his lungs, *"No fuckee meee, fuckeee yuuuu, fuckeee yuuuu!"*

As we pulled out of the parking lot, Lips was still leaning out the window yelling, "C'mon you fuckin' gook! C'mon!"

Tubby grabbed Lips by the belt and pulled him back inside before he fell out the window.

After hours of being verbally abused and run off by parking lot attendants, we finally found a parking space about four blocks from the hotel in an abandoned warehouse district. We didn't realize it was where tour buses parked to load and unload tourists. Within minutes of us parking, tour buses started arriving.

One giant, black bus driver waddled out of his bus and over to the van. In an effort to intimidate us he yelled, "Move it! Move it *now*! These spaces are for tour buses!"

"This is a public street. Anybody can park here. I ain't movin'!"

The yelling went back and forth, but I refused to move. The bus driver threatened to call the cops and have me towed. I still refused to move on the grounds it was a public street and anyone could park there. Bus drivers congregated across the street, pointing their fingers, shaking their fists and threatening us, but we still refused to move.

We didn't know we'd spend the next eight hours parked right there. Every hour or so I walked the half mile to the hotel and asked about our rooms. Tired of seeing me at the front desk, I was finally told our rooms would not be ready until after 4pm. We were wore out, overheated and miserable.

Walking back and forth, I became aware of the homeless vagrants and panhandlers roaming the streets begging for handouts and pestering the hell out of the tourists. Thugs and prostitutes lurked in alleys between the buildings like vultures waiting on easy victims.

As the day wore on, the blazing August sun beat down. The van was an oven. The heat rising from the concrete was unbearable. We were exhausted. We needed showers, clean clothes, food and rest, but there was no hope in sight until after 4pm.

With fatigue taking its toll on us, Tubby, who was a big fellow of about 260 pounds, took off his shirt, climbed in the back of the van and fell asleep. Since we couldn't let a gasoline engine idle all day to keep the air working, we took turns checking on Tubby to see if he was still alive. Sleeping in a hot van on a 100-plus degree day, he could have suffered a heat stroke. Tubby seemed to be perfectly content basking in his own juices like a Christmas ham.

We took turns guarding the van while the others explored Bourbon Street, Jackson Square and other area shops to find some shade and get some food and cold drinks.

It was around 5pm when the hotel desk clerk told me our rooms were finally ready. Since it was so late on Saturday and no more deliveries were expected, we would be allowed to park the van and trailer at the loading dock until Sunday morning. I walked back to the van to get the guys and move the van and trailer to the loading dock.

All the streets around the DoubleTree were one-way and packed bumper-to-bumper with tourists. When I finally got the van and trailer into position to back up to the loading dock, the four-lane street was gridlocked. Dooley and Lips got out of the van to block traffic. Tubby stayed in the passenger seat. As I whipped the trailer crossways in the street it sounded like every horn in Louisiana was blasting at us.

Being inexperienced at backing a trailer, I zig-zagged left, zig-zagged right, jackknifed left and jackknifed right. The car horns were deafening.

Tubby was leaning out the passenger window and shooting the finger at the traffic screaming, *"Fuck you… fuck you!"* In the excitement of the moment he yelled, *"Waaa-hooooooo! Man, ain't this a great adventure?"*

After several efforts, I finally backed the trailer into the loading dock. Whew!

## Hurry Up and Wait

After we got parked it took another hour to find our employer for instructions about where to set up. We were told to use the freight elevator to move our gear to the banquet room on the sixteenth floor. No problem. We began to unload and looked for the freight elevator.

As fate would have it, there were several conventions taking place at the DoubleTree in New Orleans that weekend and the place was packed with convention-goers and tourists. There were hundreds of kids running loose in the hotel like wild heathens. Total chaos.

We tried to carry small gear like guitars and suitcases up the regular elevators but were told by hotel staff that we had to use the freight elevators.

Because of all the convention guests and activity in the hotel, the waiting line to get on the freight elevator was fifteen minutes every time. We had to stand in line behind hotel workers with stacks of food trays, bins of laundry and carts of clean linens, soap and toilet paper. Maintenance men with tool boxes on their way to remedy some emergency waited as well.

Some of our equipment was so heavy it took two guys to carry it, one piece at a time. We all carried as much as we could on each trip to the elevator. The hotel officials adamantly refused to allow us to use even one luggage cart. We were told the carts were for guests only, and we were not considered *guests* even though we were staying at the hotel that night.

One person had to stay behind guarding the van. Freaks and weirdos kept hanging around the loading dock and were constantly ran off by the security guards.

It took us two hours to move the band gear from the loading dock to the banquet room on the sixteenth floor. We still had to set up and do a sound check. We were still wearing the same stinking, sweaty clothes we had on when we left Houston the day before.

While we got set up the banquet room was being prepared for the party. We were told to hurry because guests were arriving and a formal dinner would be served shortly. The band was supposed to be out of the way. There was no time for a sound check.

I asked about getting something to eat for the band. I was told we were not allowed to eat with the guests and that we had to eat at the restaurant downstairs.

Dooley and Tubby got finished setting up first. I gave them their room key, told them to go shower and a get couple hours sleep, and that we'd kick off at 9pm. I told them I'd call at 8:30pm. Lips and I hurriedly finished setting up and did a quick sound check before being shooed out of the banquet room.

We had requested two double rooms. When Lips and I opened the door to our room, we were pissed off to find only one bed. I called room service and they brought up a small roll-a-way. After a quick shower I called the front desk for an 8:15pm wake-up call. I passed out on the little bed.

I had been up thirty-six hours straight with no sleep and no shower. No sooner had I closed my eyes than the phone jarred me from a death-like slumber. At least I slept an hour. Still exhausted, I woke Lips. I told him I was going to the lobby for some coffee and would see him in the banquet room.

When I got to the lobby I was surprised to see Dooley. He was drinking coffee and looked really tired. I asked him if he had gotten any sleep. "No!" he snapped. He told me when he headed for the room, Tubby went to the bar. When he opened the door to the room, there was only one bed and he went to sleep. A few minutes later he was awakened by what he called a "funk that would gag a maggot off of a gut wagon."

Dooley said he was in such a deep sleep he didn't hear Tubby enter the room. Tubby then stripped down to his underwear and laid down on the bed next to Dooley.

"I smelled something so bad it woke me up!" said Dooley. He said when he opened his eyes he was face-to-face with Tubby's stinking, hairy armpit.

"I gagged!" exclaimed Dooley. "Almost puked in the bed!"

Dooley said he jumped up, grabbed a pillow and tried to sleep on the floor. "But the whole room reeked of funk!" He then went in the bathroom, closed the door and tried to sleep in the bathtub. When that didn't work, he gave up on sleeping and went to the lobby for coffee.

I told Dooley he should of called me. Housekeeping could of brought a roll-a-way to their room. I told him we'd get one after the show.

I told Dooley to go wake up Tubby and meet us at the banquet room.

## Rockin' The Ball

About 8:45pm the four of us entered the banquet room ready to rock The Children of the Confederacy Ball. As we walked in someone was giving a speech and presenting awards. We were ushered back into the hall and told to wait outside until we were called.

The room was decorated to the hilt with Confederate Flags and decorations. Some of the young men were dressed in Civil War uniforms while others wore period costumes. The young ladies were dressed in beautiful Antebellum plantation gowns and displaying lots of eye-popping cleavage.

We kicked off our first song around 9:30pm to about 150 people. With the exception of only a few older people, almost everyone in the room was between fourteen and nineteen years old. A few were in their early twenties.

I was thirty-nine years old. I felt too damn old to be playing for a bunch of kids. One thing for sure, those kids were full of energy and enthusiasm and danced every song with reckless abandon. Their enthusiasm made us forget we had been up for two days and had just spent all day on the street with a heat index of over 115 degrees.

As we played a set of '50s and '60s rock 'n roll and Southern Rock, the kids reacted as if they were hearing this kind of music for the first time. As young as they were, it was probably their first exposure to live music. Everyone was having a blast. I envisioned Jerry Lee Lewis, Elvis and Chuck Berry having this same sort of experience back in the '50s.

We had been asked to learn two songs for the party, "Shout" by Otis Day & The Knights, and "Dixie." By request, we played each one at least a dozen times that night.

Every time we played "Shout" the kids would scream, wave their arms in the air, then throw themselves backwards onto the floor kicking their feet and rolling around.

Each time we played "Dixie" they would march around the room singing along as loud as they could. It was like a scene out of *Music Man*. I thought the South really *was* going to rise again that night. Wow! What a party.

The hotel staff serving the party was extremely rude and disrespectful. I guess the fact the waitstaff was black and having to serve a Confederate organization, complete with Confederate uniforms and flags, along with having to hear "Dixie" every third or fourth song, really pissed them off!

## Busboy Militia

The banquet room was reserved for the Children of the Confederacy until 1am.

At exactly 1am on the dot, in the middle of yet another rousing version of "Dixie," about forty pissed-off black waiters, busboys and security guards burst into the room like stormtroopers! They crossed the room, lined up at the opposite end and started herding the crowd toward the exit. As they forced the partygoers out of the room, the Busboy Militia jerked tablecloths off the tables as they went. Everything on the tables was dumped into trash bins, including fresh drinks, plates of food, wine glasses, silverware, dishes and articles of clothing, as well as the decorations bearing the Rebel flag.

The Children of the Confederacy ran screaming out the door as their party was ambushed. In less than a minute it was over. The room cleared out so fast that we were left standing on stage holding our guitars with our mouths open like a bunch of scarecrows.

All the white people were gone. The room fell silent. The only people left in the room were forty angry black men – and four bewildered white guys that had played "Dixie" all night.

The chief of security, a fat, sweaty guy who was so black he glistened purple in the stage lights, walked up to the band and scowled, "Ya'll gots fit-teen minutes to git ya'll's shit outta heah! If ya'll ain't outta heah in fit-teen minutes, I pressin' chaages fo' truss-passin' cause ya'lls in heah adda hours!"

I knew the chief was just trying to scare us. I told him there was no way we could load out in fifteen minutes. It would take at least an hour.

"Not good 'nuff," he said. "Thirty minutes or we's press'n chaages!"

What he was really saying was he and his busboy militia wanted a fight. They kept popping off racial slurs about "honkys," the Civil War, and how "deese honky muthafuckas (the band) gon' git dey ass whupped up in heah fo dis night's tru!"

The chief got on his radio reporting our every move to somebody somewhere, while several busboys were commanded to keep an eye on us. The uniformed busboys weren't kids. They were grown young men who looked and acted more like "gangstas" than busboys. They hung too close for comfort, giving us dirty looks and talking trash loud enough that we could hear their threats. They would "sign" to each other in gangbanger sign language.

At that late hour we commandeered a couple of luggage carriers and started carrying out equipment as fast as we could. I sent Lips and Tubby to the van with the first load. I told them to stay with the van while I brought down another load. I told Dooley to stay in the banquet room with the last of the gear until we got loaded.

Once at the loading dock, the security guard there told me to move the van or he was going to have it towed. I protested, "Hey man, the hotel manager told me we could leave the van right here overnight since there are no deliveries on Sunday. We have rooms here tonight and we'll be outta here by ten o'clock in the morning."

"Day manager ain't here! I say wazzup on my shiff. Ya'll needs to park dat muthafucka at ta curb else I calls my cousin. He gossa tow truck. He do aww da towin' fo dis hotel!"

There was no way we would park a van pulling a U-Haul loaded with thousands of dollars' worth of band equipment on the street in downtown New Orleans on a Saturday night. I'd already seen thugs operating in broad daylight and I knew it'd be stripped clean before morning. With no more than one hour of sleep in the past two days we only had one option. Forfeit our rooms and head to Houston, *ASAP*!

I still had at least three more trips to the van. On my next trip to the loading dock Lips and Tubby were furious! They had been in a verbal confrontation with the two busboys assigned to stand guard over them at the loading dock. Lips and Tubby informed me that just before we left the hotel they were going to beat the hell out of the busboys and throw them behind the dumpster.

"Hell no!" I said. "Don't do that!"

The loading dock security guard was already watching every move we made from the window of the guard house, looking for any excuse to call his crew down on us. I reminded the guys we were in a strange town and there was absolutely no way to make a quick getaway pulling a bright orange U-Haul. I didn't even know how to get to the freeway.

It seemed like everyone in New Orleans was related. The last place I wanted to be that night was in jail in New Orleans for beating the hell out of one of the policeman's cousins. The Busboy Militia already wanted to whip our ass for playing "Dixie" all night. I told the guys not to fuck up or we'd be alligator shit by daylight.

Thank God the guys agreed with me. We finished loading up, climbed in the van and headed to Houston. We had been up for two days straight. We got home around 9am.

That afternoon, we kicked off on time at 5pm at The Flamingo Cafe.

With the exception of a phone call a few days later from our employer complaining that Dooley had ordered porno movies and charged them to his room, I never again heard from the Children of the Confederacy.

# EASTMART BLUES FESTIVAL

In 1993 Eastmart was a giant indoor flea market on the southeast side of Houston. Hundreds of small shops and booths lined the endless maze of aisles, selling every type of merchandise known to man. In an effort to draw bigger crowds, my band was asked to perform every Saturday from 1pm to 6pm.

Each week we had to wade through and move tons of nasty, filthy garbage dumped behind the building during the week just to get to the big sliding doors to unload. The loading dock, located just inside the shipping and receiving area in the back of the building, made a perfect ready-made stage. Our concert area was the size of a showroom at a car dealership. Plus, being inside meant it was an air-conditioned gig, and would never be rained out.

The purpose of performing in the back of the building was to force people to walk from the front door through the maze of booths to get to where the music was coming from. The owner built a plywood wall eight feet high around the perimeter of the concert area to shield the vendors from a direct hit of loud music. Since the ceilings were at least fifteen feet tall customers could still hear the music, but would have to walk through the maze to find us behind the "Great Wall of Eastmart." In theory, as people passed the booths on their way to the stage they would be tempted to buy more merchandise.

The manager instructed the maintenance crew to set up picnic tables, a snack bar and a popcorn machine and to hang streamers in the concert area to create a festive atmosphere. The weekly event was christened "The Eastmart Blues Festival" and we invited blues musicians from around the city to come out and jam. I distributed flyers and copies of *Texas Blues Magazine,* featuring a full-page ad promoting our show to the surrounding neighborhoods. I posted 100 circus-style colored posters in store windows and on telephone poles in the area.

After all that promotion we kicked off our first show to a crowd of *one*. The Eastmart manager. As we played, a few curious shoppers found us behind the Great Wall. They came as far as the entrance to the concert area, watched a couple of minutes and then left.

Most of the Eastmart clientele were low-income Blacks and Hispanics who had no interest in us white boys playing the blues in the back of the building. After a couple of weeks a few musicians started showing up to jam with us. Each one was allowed to sign our "Eastmart Wall of Fame" behind the stage.

After a few weeks of playing to nobody, the manager and I agreed to move the show outside on the sidewalk next to the entrance of the building where we could attract people from other stores in the shopping center. She instructed her crew to build a portable stage that could be easily assembled and moved with furniture dollies before and after each show. Each section was three feet tall, ten feet deep and four feet wide. When put together, we had a great stage that was 10x20. In the middle of April we moved the show outside.

## The Crowd

Our first Saturday afternoon outside went great. Hundreds of people gathered in front of the stage to enjoy the outdoor festival atmosphere. The band cranked up and we rocked out. We had hit on a winning combination.

As the weeks went by, our Saturday afternoon Eastmart Blues Festival grew bigger and bigger with people bringing their entire families. They brought their own lawn chairs and ice chests and gathered around the bandstand. Many would sit in the back of their pickups making a tailgate party out of the event. It was a great way for people to enjoy live entertainment with their families without having to sit in a smoky bar or venture out in the middle of the night.

Musicians from all over Houston showed up every week to jam with us and entertain the enthusiastic crowd. As word of the jam got out, musicians from Dallas, Beaumont, Galveston and Austin would show up to jam at this most unique live entertainment venue.

All sorts of people attended the free event and we musicians were as entertained by the audience as they were by us. We saw the good, the bad and the ugly of society pass before us. We saw purse snatchers grab ladies' bags and run like hell. We saw hit and run accidents in the parking lot. We saw shoplifters being chased out of the market by angry shop owners.

Drug dealers, pimps and "hos" made their presence known. One older black man always hawked the services of his teenage daughter to us like a K-Mart Blue Light special: *"Blowjob, only five dollars!"* he would announce, *"Blowjob! Five dollars!"*

We were offered every kind of drug you could imagine. We declined.

Occasionally a skanky female crackhead with no respect for children in the audience would leap onto the stage and start taking off her clothes. We'd promptly kick her off to the boos of the males and cheers of the mothers with children. It wasn't pretty, but it was *funny*.

One day a woman was mercilessly beating her child near the side of the stage. My bass player was a big guy known only as "Reverend B" who looked like Jerry Garcia of the Grateful Dead. He put down his bass in the middle of a song, jumped off the stage, grabbed the woman and dragged her away from the child, all the while screaming at her, "How'd you like for me to beat your ass like that, bitch!" The crowd applauded. Reverend B had three daughters of his own, and told me later he didn't tolerate people beatin' up on kids.

There was a guy who showed up every week. He was a Cuban boxing match announcer. He claimed to have barely escaped Cuba after being sentenced to death under Castro's regime. He loved being onstage and in the spotlight. Every week he would insist on introducing the band. Out of curiosity, we let him. He would take the mic and yell like a master of ceremonies at the Barnum & Bailey Circus. "Laaadeeees ant Jent-ta-muns! Aye intro-dooz to jew, Geeeeeeeenah Kill-o-tooone!" For years after that every time I ran across drummer Dennis Forbes he would yell across the room or a parking lot "Geeeeeeenah Kill-o-toooone!"

We never had any trouble with any musicians or bands except one that was so bad, even the Eastmart manager gave me the cut-throat signal. I told the band to stop, but they continued to play. I had no choice but to pull the power cords out of the wall. The lead singer yelled, "Hey! We lost power!"

I held up the unplugged power cords and motioned his band off the stage. As bad as I hated to do it, sometimes I was forced to be an asshole.

## Bubblin' Crude

One sweltering July afternoon the Texas sun was beating down so hot the asphalt in the Eastmart parking lot started to bubble. The crowd in front of the stage seemed oblivious to the heat. We kept them preoccupied with a fast-paced, high-energy show.

Suddenly, shrieks of horror came from the audience. Men and women screamed. Parents snatched up their kids and ran in all directions. The crowd parted like the Red Sea.

From the bandstand we were dumbfounded. Was somebody getting mugged? Was there a mad dog loose? What? What? *What?*

Within seconds our questions were answered. The thick July air suddenly filled with the nauseating stench of raw sewage. From the bandstand we saw murky water, shredded toilet paper and raw sewage bubbling up from a four-inch clean-out drain twenty feet in front of center stage. We never noticed the four-inch hole before because it was always covered with trash. That day it made itself known to all by belching its hidden treasures like Old Faithful.

Our drummer Dennis Forbes was laughing so hard he turned red. I was so embarrassed in front of our musician friends waiting to jam that I wanted to jump off the stage and run. So I did. I ran inside to find the Eastmart manager.

She instructed her maintenance crew to pour two gallons of industrial-strength Pine-O-Pine into the drain to kill the gagging stench and to wash the parking lot off with a water hose. If you've ever cleaned with Pine-O-Pine, you know that when it mixes with water it turns white like milk. When the maintenance crew hosed down the parking lot, the mess turned into a milky-white, stinking slop that ran down underneath the cars. The stench of shit and Pine-O-Pine filled the air. Dennis yelled, "Smells like somebody shit in a Christmas Tree!"

We had a good laugh, but it wasn't funny to people coming out of the stores unaware of what just happened. When they realized they were stepping in shit, they hurled obscenities at the maintenance crew washing down the parking lot. We watched with great amusement until the manager told us to get back on stage and continue playing.

In a short time we drew a fresh crowd to the front of the stage. Within minutes Old Faithful started blowing shit out of the ground again. Once again, the audience ran screaming like they were in a Japanese Godzilla flick. Once again, the manager told us to keep playing. I refused. She insisted we tear down all our gear, move inside, set back up and keep playing. Again, I refused.

The day was already half over. It would take more than an hour to move inside, leaving only thirty minutes until quitting time. The manager argued with me and threatened to deduct two hours from our pay. I told her it was not our fault that Eastmart's plumbing ruined the show and the day had literally gone to shit. She paid me in full and the band went home.

Riding home, Dennis turned to me and said, "Man, what a shitty day."

We laughed all the way to Baytown.

## The Sky Is Falling!

When I arrived at Eastmart at noon on Saturday, August 7, the first thing I noticed was the stage was set up three feet off center from where it usually was. I started to say something about it to the maintenance crew, but a little voice inside me told me to forget about it and not be so damn picky. I figured what the hell, it's already set up. The music is going to sound the same whether it's three feet off center or not.

The stage sat under an overhang with an open skylight four feet wide and thirty feet long. Because the stage was off center, during midday the scorching Texas sun beamed through the skylight frying our drummer. The band on the front of the stage was in the shade.

To get the drummer some shade, I asked the Eastmart manager to cover the opening. She sent her maintenance crew to cover the skylight with a blue plastic tarp. The roof of the Eastmart building was flat and covered with pea gravel and nothing on the roof to tie the tarp to. The crew carried large, round, concrete flagpole stands, 16" in diameter, 8" thick and 80 pounds each up to the roof to hold the corners of the tarp down over the skylight.

At around 5:45pm, Professor Blues was on stage leading the band. Ron Long was on bass, and Dwayne Warnock was sitting in on drums. Tha Lady D was center stage singing her heart out. I had just stepped on stage to lower a mic stand for sax player Ricky Ford when suddenly *KA-BOOOM*! The whole stage shook like an earthquake!

A crashing, metallic sound of jolted reverb screamed out of the speakers with an earsplitting pitch. A low-end roar sounding like a freight train plowed through the stage.

In a split second it was over. Everything went silent. The musicians and the audience stood absolutely still, all staring at each other wondering what the hell had just happened.

"Was that an earthquake?" somebody yelled. It happened so fast we were all in shock.

I looked around to see if anyone was hurt. I saw amplifiers and mic stands turned over and knocked down. Harmonicas, guitar tuners, drink cans and personal items were scattered all over the stage as if we'd been hit by a bomb. Since the stage was just a few feet from the parking lot, I looked to see if a car had hit the stage. There weren't any cars close by.

We started looking at the damage. Ron Long's Peavey bass amp was lying face down and the stand it had been sitting on was crushed flat. My Peavey Bandit 112 was knocked off its stand onto its side. The top of my Bandit was smashed and a big chunk of the wood cabinet was knocked out in the shape of a shark bite. Speaker cabinet material was splintered and scattered about the stage like mulch. Several speaker cords were severed and the bass guitar case was smashed flat.

My new Fender Telecaster, which had been innocently leaning against the back wall, had the neck ripped from the body. Large gaping holes were gouged out of the back of the neck.

Thank God no one was hurt. *What the hell happened?* It wasn't an earthquake, and we didn't get hit by a car. *What did all this damage?*

Looking through the debris, we discovered two of the 80-pound concrete flagpole stands had fallen through the skylight from roof, twenty feet above. But how? We figured high gusts of wind that day must of caught the tarp and jerked it like a giant sail. The pea gravel on the roof acted like ball-bearings allowing the concrete blocks to be dragged closer and closer to the edge of the roof with each gust of wind, until they fell through the skylight.

As I stood looking at where the concrete blocks had landed on the stage, I realized the severity of the situation. I said a quick prayer, *thank you, God, that nobody was hurt and for giving me enough sense to listen to my inner voice.*

When I arrived that day I noticed the stage was set up off center. Had I insisted the maintenance crew reset the stage and center it between the columns as it usually was, the concrete block that fell on the bass amp would've made a direct hit on drummer Dwayne Warnock, surely killing him instantly.

If the stage was where it should of been, the concrete block that fell on top of the my amp would have instead made a direct hit on our 12-channel Peavey PA mixing board. That would've been a $1500 loss.

Peavey amps proved once again that Peavey products are truly the workhorse of the music industry. After taking a direct hit from the 80-pound concrete blocks after a twenty-foot fall, the amps continued to work without a problem.

The owners of Eastmart paid for a new bass guitar case and the repair to my Fender Telecaster. I took the Telecaster to Airline Vintage Guitar where Guitar Doctor Huey Wilkinson – who also does custom guitars for ZZ Top – did a superb job of reattaching the neck and filling in the gouges.

Six years later I recorded my first CD, *Most Requested,* with that same Telecaster.

If there is a moral to this story it would be, "If something in your life seems a little off center, leave it alone and don't worry about it. There's probably a good reason, and the situation will remedy itself in its own time."

We played Eastmart Blues Festival every Saturday, April through September. Our only obstacle was the deadly heat wave during July and August that got the best of some of our musicians. Other than that, it was always a blast.

Never dull, never the same, and a different adventure every week.

## BILLY BLUES

Shortly after the death of Texas bluesrocker Stevie Ray Vaughan in 1990, hundreds of Stevie Ray clones and white boy blues bands flooded the Texas music scene, cashing in on the surge of public interest in the blues. Especially Texas Blues.

For me the Texas Blues Explosion of the early nineties enabled me to make a damn good living doing what I loved and what I had always wanted to do – play nothing but the blues! Hosting blues jams enabled me to play nothing but the blues five and six nights a week. I was doing exactly what I loved. I was in heaven.

Blues jams sprang up like mushrooms in a cow pasture after an East Texas downpour. On any given night, there was a blues jam just about anywhere there was a neon beer sign. Even country-western bars had "Blues Night."

While us white boys played Stevie Ray covers in strip centers, the only places you could hear real, pure, live blues played by Houston's black blues legends was in little juke-joints, hidden in the back streets of the lower income sections of town. Blues lovers, in need of a "true blues" fix, often put their lives, wallets and cars in danger when parking on dark streets and trying to scurry down the block into a blues club before being approached by the "welcoming committee."

To put it very bluntly, white folks going to black neighborhoods to hear real blues were at the risk of getting mugged (or worse) by drug addicts and crack whores. Once inside the club, there was safety among fellow blues lovers. Getting back to their car after midnight always proved to be an adventure.

### Billy Blues Arrives In Houston

In February of 1993 Billy Blues opened in Houston, taking the blues out of Houston's seedy neighborhoods and bringing it into the spotlight on the hot Richmond Strip.

Billy Blues was a combination restaurant and nightclub where customers could sit on matching upholstered chairs in air-conditioned comfort, order a plate of barbeque ribs or a gourmet Blues Burger and wash it down with an exotic mixed drink or an imported ale while listening to hot rockin' blues bands, seven nights a week.

Fashionably dressed yuppies valet parked their yuppie-mobiles in the large, paved, lighted parking lot without concern. Once inside the yuppies discovered *real blues* for the first time, performed by Houston blues legends that not only performed around Houston, but had been performing around the world for the past twenty, thirty and forty years.

To the yuppies it was a whole new experience. For Houston's blues acts it was the exposure and recognition they had sought and deserved all their lives. Blues music was suddenly *cool and hip*. Billy Blues became to the blues what Hard Rock Cafe is to rock.

A one-of-a-kind giant saxophone, the "Smoke Sax," stood in front of Billy Blues. The Smoke Sax could be seen from several blocks away. It graced the cover of numerous magazines and was featured in news stories around the world. It was a fantastic piece of art, made from Volkswagen car parts, surfboards and beer kegs. The bell of the Smoke Sax was an upside-down '60s-era VW Beetle. The Smoke Sax became the iconic symbol for Billy Blues and the Houston blues scene.

Opening night was phenomenal, like a Hollywood premier. Limousines lined up delivering celebrities decked out for the gala event.

Miss Molly & The Whips opened for The Fabulous Thunderbirds who performed to a standing-room-only crowd. The joint was packed and rockin'!

The following week I approached the general manager, Steve Miller, about hosting a weekly blues jam. I thought I was the Jam King in Houston in those years, but Houston blues legends Clarence Green (RIP) and "Guitar" Slim (RIP) rightfully earned the coveted Monday night jam slot. I felt I had lost an opportunity to host the best blues jam in the most famous blues club in Texas since Antone's in Austin.

I was honored when Clarence and Guitar Slim asked me to be their very first guest on their very first Monday Night Blues Jam. I still lusted for a steady, weekly gig at Billy Blues. I had to come up with a new idea.

Steve Miller told me Billy Blues was looking for new bands to fill their weeknights and bands to use as openers for national touring acts. Since Billy Blues was new in town, the managers didn't know which local bands met their standards and they didn't trust demo tapes.

Being the publisher of *Texas Blues Magazine,* I was asked to recommend some of the better local bands from around Southeast Texas.

**The Texas Blues Showcase**

I came up with an idea for a weekly show that was basically a glorified audition with two local bands, each performing one thirty-minute set of their best songs for Billy Blues' audience and booking agents.

Since the bands would be playing for free, I insisted that Billy Blues furnish all sound equipment and a sound man, and give the bands a free dinner. I also insisted that a Billy Blues booking agent attend every show to consider bands for possible bookings. I would serve as producer and MC, and my band would open and close each show. The event would be called "The Texas Blues Showcase."

Billy Blues loved the idea and bought it.

For the next year and a half Billy Blues was *the* place to be every Wednesday night. The place would pack out to a standing-room-only crowd of enthusiastic blues lovers. We could do no wrong. The Texas Blues Showcase was kicking everybody's ass in town. All the bands I booked were great and most landed coveted rotating gigs.

The media was all over us. Houston's ABC Channel 13 sent its reporters and featured us on the ten o'clock news. Local newspapers and music trade magazines covered our showcase. Radio personalities from KPFT, KTSU, KLOL and other stations were always in attendance. Celebrities dropped by to sit in with us. Not only were we fanning the flames of the Texas Blues explosion, we were helping ignite the fire – and loving every minute of it.

With A.J. Fee on bass and Russell Shelby on drums, we felt ten foot tall and bullet proof. When I announced that since some people had to leave early we were going to play our last set first, people thought I was trying to be funny. What the audience didn't know was before each show, we'd sneak a bottle of tequila into the dressing room and pass it around until it was empty. It was like throwing gasoline on a roaring fire. We'd hit the stage fired up from an explosive mix of supercharged adrenaline, over-inflated egos and straight tequila. Damn, we were cocky bastards! We had more fun than the law allowed.

Every night when I announced that Jose Cuervo was the official drink of the Die Hards, tray after tray of Cuervo shots were delivered to the bandstand by hottie little waitresses who then became the target of our sexual innuendos, all in the name of the fun and entertainment. The crowd loved it. The audience would order tequila shots and do them with us. Time and time again Billy Blues sold out of tequila before the night was over. I really miss the excitement of those days, but I don't miss the hangovers. Thank God I quit drinking before I ended up on a liver transplant list.

## The Wizard: Billy Blues Sound Man

Billy Blues had an in-house sound man who had an evil, sadistic mean streak a mile wide. "Wizard," like the character in *The Wizard of Oz*, reveled in the fact – and often bragged – that from his control board he held the power to make or break a band. He was a frail, skinny guy who looked like an mad scientist with in his thick, wire-rimmed glasses and waist-length gray hair that flew out behind him as he zipped back and forth from the stage to the sound control booth.

When Wizard had a grudge against a band he would tamper with their sound, making even the best band sound like a muddy wall of garbled noise. He would dance around behind the soundboard, shrieking with maniacal laughter when showing off his dark powers and yelling "Those son of a bitches will never play here again!"

When Wizard was in a good mood he was one of the best soundmen in the business. Unfortunately, his good moods were few and far between. When he was pissed, which was most of the time, he would mess with our sound, then hide and ignore any requests for assistance. Several times we had to stop the music and go find him. He was usually outside smoking his brains out (if you know what I mean). No wonder our sound sucked so much of the time.

Whenever a musician so much as touched a mic, a mic stand, or even slightly moved a stage monitor, Wizard would fly into a rage. He'd make a spectacle of himself in front of the audience by screaming at the top of his lungs, "Keep your fuckin' hands off my shit!"

Wizard would clench his teeth and fire razor-sharp insults at bands, warning them about the consequences of touching the house gear. The only thing that kept someone from beating the hell out of him was he was so frail it would have been like beating up an ugly little girl.

## The International Blues Band Rocks Billy Blues

One of my proudest moments at Billy Blues was the spontaneous formation of "The International Blues Band."

One night during the summer of 1993, we were playing our last set. The house was packed not only with fans and blues lovers, but with dozens of musicians who came out every Wednesday night to see and be seen hanging out at the hottest blues venue in town.

After noticing the variety of musicians in the room, I told my bass player and drummer to take a break. They shrugged their shoulders and left the stage. They never knew what I was going to do next.

I started calling musicians to the bandstand. They were of different nationalities, races, backgrounds and from different parts of the world. All under the same roof, they were brought together by their love for the Blues. Once they were all on stage I introduced them individually to the audience.

On lead guitar was Houston's own Chinese Blues Man Rick Lee, a third-generation Texan.

Also on lead guitar was David Brown from Dallas, a Native American from the Sioux-Creek Indian Nation.

I introduced Pierre Stoot, an African American accordion player in a local Zydeco band who I jokingly said was from "The Nation of Louisiana."

On drums was Osama Raad from Lebanon.

On bass guitar from Jerusalem, Israel was Nuri Nuri, a radio DJ known as "The Big Bad Boss Man of The Blues" on Houston's KPFT 90.1 FM.

On harmonica, I represented the white folks.

Once we were ready, I stepped to the mic and announced, "Ladies and gentlemen, I give you the *International Blues Band*!"

The band kicked off and the crowd went wild. To this day it still sends chills down my spine and brings a tear to my eye. That night The Blues erased all barriers of race, religion, color, creed, nationality, culture and personal attitude, bringing everyone in the building together in one common groove. It was love, man, in the purest sense.

When the house lights came on we were still jamming and the crowd was yelling for more. People were coming to the bandstand shaking hands with the International Blues Band like they got saved at a tent revival!

The Blues had conquered again.

Ten years later in 2003 at the beginning of the war in Iraq, I would recall the International Blues Band experience and write a song called "If Everybody Loved The Blues, There Wouldn't Be No War."

**Billy Blues Sells Out**

Every Wednesday night for a year and a half the Texas Blues Showcase packed the house.

In the fall of 1994 Billy Blues was sold without warning. The new owner was from the Middle East.

We were flabbergasted and hurt to think the original owner had sold out! He was known for his love of the Blues and we were told he was going to build Billy Blues locations all over the country and around the world. We understood that business is business, but the blues community could not help but feel betrayed.

Overnight our good friends and staunch supporters of the blues, manager Steve Miller and all his great staff, disappeared like Jimmy Hoffa. New management took over.

It seemed the new owner didn't have a clue or didn't give a damn about the people who patronized Billy Blues for live music. There were many changes at Billy Blues. We were told by the new regime to "turn down, or else!"

Most bands who played Billy Blues, including us, were powerhouse bluesrockers that played with a lot of energy and volume. All bands, from the local weeknight bands to the famous weekend headliners and Houston's legendary blues royalty, were disrespectfully scolded by the new management. They were told to "play quietly" as if they were little children at a church social. Bands started canceling their shows left and right.

If there is one thing we musicians will not tolerate, it's unqualified, non-music industry management telling us how we should play. *We* are the experts on what we do. That's why we're hired in the first place. Food and beverage people should stick to carving tomatoes into flowers and making cute decorations with dead shrimp.

One night when the new manager told me to turn my amp down the third time, I yelled back, "Goddammit! The amp is set on *one*! There is no setting lower than *one*! It won't go any lower than *one* without being *off*! Trying to make this equipment operate properly on *one* is like trying to fly a jet plane at 50 miles an hour! It won't work!"

"We don't care what you have to do," he replied very coldly, "but like it or not, you *will* turn down!"

I constantly argued with the new management. When volume is turned down, bands lose their energy. When bands lose their energy, the audience gets bored. When an audience gets bored, they leave.

We had worked very hard building a great show and a great following. Being forced to play at a lower volume cost us attendance at every show. People came to Billy Blues to rock, not to be put to sleep. As attendance dwindled, naturally the new management blamed the bands. Typical stupid club owner ignorance.

Management threatened to fire Wizard if the bands got too loud. With his job on the line, Wizard turned into a vicious "volume nazi" and would scream at the bands more than before. He'd even turn off the PA if a band's stage volume exceeded the newly-imposed sound limits.

Over the next few months, Wizard and I had several serious confrontations when my audience would yell, "Turn it up!" One night we got into it again over the volume. Wizard screamed, "You want volume, I'll give you volume!" He then pushed all the volume and graphic mixing controls to maximum levels and bolted out the back door in a dead run. The room exploded with shrill, high-end feedback and a loud roar that sounded like a F-5 tornado screaming through the building. Needless to say, Wizard and I exchanged more heated words.

To save his job Wizard would march his skinny ass to the new management like a stool pigeon every time he and I had a confrontation. He made sure management understood it was Gene Kelton who was fully to blame for any defiant acts and volume indiscretions.

The *Texas Blues Showcase* was not fun anymore.

An uneasy vibe engulfed the showroom like an evil spirit the moment you walked in the room. I kept the faith our track record of attendance would prove to be our salvation.

**What The Fuck is Texas Bluesrock?**

In January 1995, I was called to a meeting at the corporate headquarters of Billy Blues with the new Vice President of the corporation. I had met the big shot VP once when he showed up one night to check out my show. He was a middle-aged, fat white guy whose aloof, sarcastic tone expressed his dislike for me.

I was under the impression Mr. Big Shot wanted to talk to me about the future of the *Texas Blues Showcase* and live entertainment in general. As I arrived at the chrome and glass tower on the west side of Houston, I felt very confident. With my briefcase full of newspaper clippings I was prepared to proclaim the virtues of my show.

The receptionist announced my arrival. I was promptly shown to Mr. Big Shot's office. Mr. Big Shot and I exchanged friendly small talk while the receptionist brought us coffee. The moment she left the room, Mr. Big Shot closed his office door, turned to me and roared, *"What the fuck is Texas Bluesrock?"*

His sudden loud blast of profanity caught me off guard. I almost threw my cup of coffee in the air. Realizing this was not going to be a business meeting but rather an ass-chewing, I felt ambushed.

My years of experience dealing with irate hecklers in juke-joints automatically threw my defense system into fight mode. I was not about to let some fat ass corporate asshole intimidate me.

I jumped to my feet and yelled back, "What kind of stupid fuckin' question is that?"

I figured if he could use profanity, I could too.

"Stevie Ray Vaughan, Albert Collins, The Fabulous Thunderbirds, ZZ Top and Johnny Winter! That's Texas Bluesrock!" I yelled.

Seeing I was not intimidated by his surprise attack, he sat down and glared at me.

"I don't give a fuck what it is!" he said, grinding his teeth. "There will be no more Texas Bluesrock at Billy Blues! Billy Blues will no longer be run like a goddamned beer joint. It is no longer a blues club that happens to serve food. It is now a restaurant that just happens to have bands until we can get rid of 'em. Bands are no longer the focus at Billy Blues. We're a fuckin' *restaurant*!"

He continued his rant. "In Atlanta, we had little black blues bands who sat in the corner and played quietly because they knew their fuckin' place. They didn't bother anybody. Unfortunately Billy Blues has a reputation of having bands. We'll have to deal with it for a while. For right now all bands will just be window dressing. They'll shut the fuck up and play quietly so people can talk while they're having a meal."

"Window dressing? Little black blues bands that know their *place*? Man, what kind of talk is that?" I asked. "People don't come to Billy Blues for the food! Hell, man, you can eat anywhere. People come to Billy Blues cause they love the music!"

Mr. Big Shot turned red. "This meeting is over!" he announced, "and, by the way, you're fired! *Tomorrow night is your last night!*"

"You called me out here to give me a ration of shit, knowing you were going to fire me?"

"Yep!" He laughed. "Sue me!"

Walking toward the door I held up a copy of *Texas Blues Magazine*. "Naw, but I'll be sure to let people know how your little black blues bands need to know their *place*," I calmly said.

I left him screaming threats at me as I exited the office and headed toward the elevator.

## Last Gig At Billy Blues

The next day I called my band and told them what had happened. I told them not to show up at Billy Blues that night. We were going to walk our last gig. It was never my style to walk a gig, but it was the only way I could fight back.

The following night I showed up at Billy Blues at the usual time. I told Wizard it was our last night. He exploded with hysterical laughter and started jumping around. "Yeah, I know, I know! I heard all about it. You got your fuckin' ass fired! Haaaaaaaaaaaaa!"

I was furious with Wizard's ridiculous mockery, but stayed calm. "Since tonight is our last night, I don't want you running sound for us. We'll be setting up our own equipment, including our PA. So move all your house-band shit outta the way. My guys will be here any minute to start setting up."

"Great! That means I'll have the night off!" Wizard leaped from his seat behind the control board and ran like a madman to the stage, unplugging mics and dragging the house drums and other equipment into a pile at the side of the stage.

At exactly 8pm, the time our band was supposed to start, I was sitting at the bar sipping a beer, observing a packed house that seemed bewildered there was no band about to play. I thought about how this great gig had gone to hell, about the disrespect I received from Mr. Big Shot, Wizard and the new owners and about everything I had done to promote Billy Blues. I had packed the house every week. It had all come down to this.

By 8:20pm the stage was absolutely bare. The crowd was getting restless. Most of them were Wednesday night regulars, and knew we always started on time – *no matter what.* The crowd had paid to get in. They demanded their money's worth and they wanted it *now*.

Bartenders, waitresses and customers kept asking, "When's the band gonna start?"

The fans and employees became outraged when I told them the new owners had fired us. When the news spread around the room, the crowd turn into an angry mob, ready to overthrow the current regime on our behalf. My work was done. That was my cue to leave, but I had one last thing on my agenda.

For my last act of defiance, I walked over to Wizard who was sitting behind the soundboard for the sole purpose of slapping the shit out of him. I was actually pissed off enough to instigate violence. In my opinion, Wizard was past due for an ass whipping and I was about to bring his account up to date.

I stepped in front of the soundboard and began a verbal barrage of insults. My plan was to piss him off enough to make him attack me first, then bitch slap him. Because he was so frail and wormy, I didn't want to hurt him, just embarrass him.

To my surprise Wizard embarrassed himself by throwing himself against the back door with his hands in the air and squealing like a girl, "Please don't hit me, please don't hit me!"

I heard a man's voice from my left side. "What the hell's going on here?"

I turned to see a slick-headed bald guy about forty years old in a gray suit and tie. "Why don't you mind your own fuckin' business there, Slick?!"

"This *is* my business. I'm the new regional manager of Billy Blues and I'm in charge of yadda yadda blah blah blah…!"

I was not impressed or intimidated with Slick's suit, corporate title or bullshit mumbo-jumbo. I took a big slug of my beer, looked him straight in the eye and said, "I got two words for ya there, Slick, *fuck you!*"

He gasped. Clutching his hands to his chest like a sissy he stammered, "I-I-I can't believe you said that to me! I-I-I'm the new regional manager, and I-I-I want you outta here, now!"

I fired back at Slick. "After I kick *his* fuckin' ass, *you're next* if you get in my way!"

Just for the record, I don't try to pass myself off as a tough guy, but I knew I could whip both of those candy-asses. I was reveling in the moment.

With that, Wizard bolted out the back door screaming at the traffic on Richmond Avenue, "Help, help! We need help!"

Slick yelled for the bartender to call the busboys to throw me out. In seconds I was surrounded by six or seven Mexican busboys.

Slick yelled, "Throw him out! Throw him out *now*!"

What Slick didn't know was that after having played Billy Blues for a year and a half, I knew all those guys and they knew me. They were all good guys just trying to make a living, and didn't want to fight me. I knew they could lose their jobs if they didn't obey Slick's orders. I told the ones who could speak English to call off the others and I would leave peacefully without causing them any trouble with the new owner. The busboys retreated.

Slick kept screaming, "Throw him out! Throw him out, *now*!" He ran toward me and tried to jerk my beer from me. I drew back and offered to shove the bottle down his throat if he touched me.

I moved slowly toward the stage door nonchalantly sipping my beer and grinning. I waved to the crowd who sat silently and stared in disbelief as I was being thrown out of the place whose reputation I had helped to build.

All the while, Slick walked along behind me screaming, "Get the hell outta here! Get the hell outta here *now*!!"

I reached the stage door, turned and bowed a farewell to the crowd that supported my band and Billy Blues for a year and a half. I exited the building with Slick still hot on my heels.

My van was conveniently parked in the musician's loading zone right behind the stage for my premeditated quick getaway. A crowd converged on the deck watching Slick as he followed me down the steps to my van yapping at me like an aggravating ankle-biter.

I climbed into the van and fired up the engine. Slick stepped next to my door, pointed toward the driveway, leaned in my window and screamed in my face, "Off the premises! Off the premises!"

I threw my door open and jumped out, yelling, "I'm gonna whup yer ass, boy!"

Slick bolted back up the steps and into the building screaming, "Call the cops! Call the cops!"

I saluted the crowd that had flooded out onto the deck and climbed back into my van. I slowly pulled into the traffic on Richmond Avenue.

"The end of an era," I said to myself as I drove away.

In the months that followed, exaggerated rumors flooded the Houston music community, proclaiming that Gene Kelton had started a fight at Billy Blues, beat up the soundman and the manager and had been barred from Billy Blues *forever*.

It was rumored that police action would be taken if I ever set foot on the property again. Wow! I felt like a real Texas Outlaw.

It would be three years before I stepped foot back in Billy Blues.

## DEL'S LOOKOUT

During the mid '90s we performed several times each summer at a bar in Surfside Beach, Texas, called Del's Lookout. Performing there was always an unpredictable adventure.

We didn't know what to expect the first time we arrived at Del's Lookout. Not more than 100 yards from the crashing waves of the Gulf of Mexico, it was a large nightclub built on crooked stilts right on the beach at was two and half stories high. The area underneath the building was packed with tons of discarded rotting building materials, rusting sheets of tin, rolls of rusty wire, stacks of old tires, car motors, rusted 55-gallon barrels, trash cans, crab nets and mountains of debris that washed up during high tide. Dozens of stray cats, frantic sand crabs and rats darted in and out of the debris.

We were slapped in the face by the putrid smell of dead fish and cat piss the second we got out of our vehicles. The humid, salty wind pelted us with a fine powdery mist of sand. We were immediately attacked by giant saltwater mosquitoes.

Being so close to the ocean, at high tide the water washed up under the building. We had to park a short distance away down the sand-packed street and hand-carry our equipment through pools of ankle deep water.

After carrying equipment down the road, we had to maneuver our gear up very steep stairs it the back which were practically straight up, almost like a ladder. Every other step was missing and others creaked and threatened to break under our weight. Some did.

The building was not air conditioned. We thought the evening gulf breezes would blow through the building and keep us cool in the 100-plus degree Texas summer. Wrong. The air inside the building was still and stifling and the heat and humidity was excruciatingly miserable. Any breeze coming in the wide-open front windows that faced the beach never reached the bandstand at the rear of the very long building. With the heat and humidity melting us, we looked like a bunch of wet, drunk rats weaving in the wind atop the three-foot high stage.

Two giant industrial shop fans were mounted at an angle over the stage, blowing hot air with a blinding, hurricane force so powerful it would knock us off balance. Hats and hairstyles were out of the question. The shop fan wind noise and the roar of the fan motors were magnified through our mics making the band sound like we were performing in a typhoon. Lowering the air blast would lower the roar, but would increase the heat on stage. We cranked up the amps as loud as we could and kicked it in the ass.

The clientele at Del's was always a mixture of yuppie vacationers in their designer beach attire and sun-parched, local, barefoot beach bums who lived in dilapidated beach houses and abandoned cars along the beach. It was a great cross-section of cultures, yet everyone at Del's coexisted peacefully sharing their love of the beach, cold beer and live music.

I did not require the band to adhere to our usual band dress code at Del's. It was always too damn hot to try to dress nice. We performed in shorts, tank tops, bathing suits and sometimes even barefoot. Everyone in the club, including the band, was always covered with a glistening sheen of sweat and a thin, gritty layer of wind-blown sand. The fine-grit sand had to be meticulously cleaned out of our equipment after every Del's experience.

## Crash

One night at Del's, my son Sid was playing drums. Rick Lee was sitting in with the band. Sid became extremely angry when he realized we had borrowed one of his cymbal mics to mic Rick Lee's amplifier. Right in the middle of Rick's first song, we suddenly heard *"Cccrrraassssssshhh!"* It sounded like an airplane had crashed though the ceiling.

In a fit of anger for having his drum sound tampered with Sid had heaved his huge crash cymbal from the back of the stage into the air. It landed in the middle of the dance floor with a loud, brassy explosion, so loud every woman in the audience screamed. It was hilarious! The band kept playing.

A drunk customer stumbled to the middle of the dance floor, dropped to his knees and wrestled with the cymbal, trying to get his fingers under it. His inebriated state caused this simple task to become a hilarious event reminding me of a skit from the Red Skelton Show. The drunk finally picked it up, staggered to the rear of the stage and handed it to Sid. "Hey Buddy, ya dropped yer thing-a-ma-jig!"

Sid took the cymbal and immediately flung it back into the air and onto the dance floor with another crashing explosion. The audience roared with laughter and cheers of approval.

Realizing the audience was digging Sid's performance, we started throwing everything that wasn't tied down off the bandstand onto the dance floor. The crowd was screaming. The owner, Del, sitting at the front table, was laughing his ass off.

Bass player A.J. Fee laid his bass guitar on the floor of the stage and played it with his fist and bare feet like a piano.

Rick Lee, obviously aggravated that we interrupted his performance, moved as far away from the rest of us as he could get on the small stage. The minute the song and the antics ended, he was gone.

## Flying Tequila Glasses

The unbearable heat at Del's always gave us a good excuse to drink excessively. In those days we drank excessively anyway. Del always kept us well supplied with tequila. He said he enjoyed our antics after we "got greased up." One night, caught up in the excitement of the moment, I downed a shot of tequila and flung the glass across the room. It smashed against the wall with a loud, shattering "ka-splash!"

I've always found it strange that the piercing sound of shattering glass can be heard over the thunder of a loud, rockin' band at full concert volume. When the glass slammed against the wall, everyone in the bar turned to see if there was a fight. Del came running, bowed up and ready for battle.

Del was a big biker guy, about forty years old, 6' 6" and 250 pounds of lean, mean muscle. He had long, bushy, brown hair that hung past his shoulders and a thick, dark brown beard. He looked like a WWF superstar.

I had a sudden "oh shit" moment, expecting him to jump my ass for throwing a shot glass.

Instead, Del cracked up laughing and bought us another round just to see us throw the shot glasses. Soon everyone in the place was throwing shot glasses. It was a hoot!

After a few months, Del said it was getting too expensive to keep restocking shot glasses. He started serving us our favorite beverage in plastic jello-shot cups.

Throwing plastic cups just didn't have the same effect.

## Skeeter Hell

One hot night after a gig at Del's, Sid decided to drive back to Houston by way of the narrow, blacktop beach road that ran along the Gulf from Surfside to Galveston. After too much partying Die Hard style, I chose to stay at the band house and drive back the next day. I took a shower and passed out.

An hour later I was awakened by someone pounding on the front door. "Gene, Gene, get up! It's an emergency!"

It was Del. He had received a phone call that Sid's truck had broke down somewhere on the long stretch of deserted highway between Del's Lookout and Galveston.

With my head still reeling from tequila, I got dressed and headed up the beach road toward Galveston. Since Del didn't know the exact location all I could do was drive until I saw Sid's truck on the side of the road.

After about fifteen miles, my headlights spotted two figures stumbling along the side of the road towards me. It was Sid and A.J. They were wind blown, dehydrated and ate up by thousands of ravenous saltwater mosquitoes.

According to Sid, two ladies driving by pulled over and asked if he and A.J. needed some help. Naturally the ladies would not pick up two strange, stinking, shirtless men on a highway in the middle of the night. Instead, they offered to call Del's from a payphone in Surfside to get help. Walking, Sid and A.J. would've never gotten back to Del's before daylight and there wouldn't of been much left of them after the humidity and mosquitoes took their toll.

The next day we tied a rope to Sid's truck and towed it back to Houston.

## The Band House

The band house served as the overnight residence for touring bands. Whenever the band was on a break it was convenient to retreat to the band house for a quick shower to cool off, or just to sit in the air conditioning for a few minutes. The band house was where the real party took place. We always had plenty of smoke, beer and tequila and plenty of girls who knew we had plenty of smoke, beer and tequila! It seemed like a great situation.

The band house was a deteriorating, three-bedroom, one-bath beach house on stilts directly behind Del's. It was connected to the club by a narrow, rickety, wooden catwalk fifteen feet high. Years of bombardment by hurricanes, high tides and shifting sands made the place very unlevel and unsafe. In other words, it was a crooked house that rocked when the wind blew.

More often than not when we arrived the place had not been cleaned since the last band the week before. Sheets were always covered in sand and who knows what else. Trash cans were full of last week's beer cans, pizza boxes and chicken bones. The place was crawling with roaches and flies, flies, *flies*.

And junk, junk, *junk!* Every inch of the band house was piled high with crap that should have been thrown out years ago: old TVs, stereos, ceiling fans, space heaters, car batteries, mooring rope, weedeaters, broken furniture, piles of old clothes, busted speakers, and buckets filled with all kinds of tools, nuts, bolts, car parts and motorcycle parts.

Some of Del's employees lived at the band house during the week, but when bands came in on weekends, Del made the employees leave. Some slept in abandoned cars around the club. Del would always apologize for the mess in the band house and send someone to clean while we set up.

The first night we stayed in the band house it came a torrential downpour. Rain poured in at a dozen places including our beds. We set out buckets and pots and pans to catch as many leaks as we could. Joni and I found a big old greasy nasty crab pot in the junk and positioned it at the end of the bed to keep the bed from being soaked. We were kept awake all night from the tink-tink-tink sound of water dripping into the pots and pans and from having to get up to empty the pots before they overflowed.

I'm not complaining. With all its faults, we appreciated Del's Lookout and its rickety band house. It's what we call *payin' our dues*. Del was always a great friend and a great employer, and he loved the blues.

Del's Lookout was another adventure in the never ending saga of our musical lives.

## Michael's Ice House

In the spring of 1994 A.J. Fee, Russell Shelby and I played a gig at Michael's Ice House in Texas City, Texas. Like most icehouses, it was a big metal building with a concrete floor, high ceilings and giant garage doors on all sides.

The owner of Michael's was a hard-nosed, crusty old Greek around seventy years old. Mr. Michael was a shrewd businessman who hated musicians. To him we were a necessary evil.

Because his Sunday afternoons were real slow, I convinced Mr. Michael to hire us to host a Sunday afternoon blues jam. At that time I was the publisher of *Texas Blues Magazine* and used it to help promote the jam. Thanks to our shameless promotion efforts, our first Sunday Blues Jam was packed. An endless line of musicians showed up to take their turn on stage.

We kicked off at 3pm. For the next four hours it was a non-stop, house rockin' blues party.

It was an extremely hot, humid day. After running nearly an hour overtime in order to let every musician have a chance to play, we were exhausted and ready to shut it down. As we were about to play our last song, five cocky young men in their early thirties walked in and rudely demanded that their band be allowed to play. I told them we'd already played an hour overtime and they could play *one song only*. They agreed.

The five arrogant assholes proved to be a very good band, but the moment they ended their *one* song they immediately kicked off into a second. Not cool!

Attitudes in Texas saloons have not changed much since the days of the wild west. Disrespect still begets the same consequences. The defiant looks from the five players told me all I needed to know, they didn't intend to stop playing until they were damn good and ready. I couldn't allow them to walk in and take over my show or it would happen all the time. Basically they were calling me out. Shit was about to hit the fan.

There were five of them and three of us. Actually, it was five of them, against *two* of us. A.J. was preoccupied at the bar and didn't see what was happening on stage.

I sized up the five players. I calculated which two would run like scared jackrabbits when the fight started. I knew I'd have to tangle with the husky lead singer since I was about to yank the mic from his hand. I knew my drummer Russell, a former nightclub bouncer, could beat the hell out of the remaining two players with one hand while eating a hamburger with the other.

As the band finished their second song, their drummer clicked his sticks together to count off a third song. I bounded onto the stage and yelled at the drummer, "STOP!" I jerked the microphone from the lead singer's hand.

In an effort to remain professional and avoid tipping the audience off to the impending barroom brawl, I shouted, *"Ladies and gentlemen, how 'bout a big hand for this great band!"*

As the crowd applauded, the lead singer bowed up. "Mutherfucker! Nobody takes my fuckin' mic! I'll whip yer fuckin' ass right here!"

I pretended not to hear him. "Thanks for comin' ya'll, see you right here next week!"

The lead singer was yelling at me like a drill sargent. I stepped in his face, poked him in the chest and yelled back, "The deal was *one* song. You fuckin' blew it. *Get the hell off my stage!"*

"Fuck you! You're just pissed cause the crowd was diggin' us! We'll whip yer fuckin ass!"

"Yeah!" yelled the rest of his band as they joined his threats.

The old plywood stage floor shook when Russell jumped on the stage. "Ya'll can whup *his* ass, after ya'll whup *mine!"*

The two players I had predicted would run did exactly that. Russell's imposing 6-foot, 250-pound frame, along with his steamroller attitude, forced the remaining three players to reconsider their threats.

"We got no fight with you, man," the lead singer said to Russell. "He's the one tha…" he said pointing at me.

Russell shut him down mid-sentence. "You sum-bitches was playin' my fuckin' drums! *You want some shit? Step up to the plate!"*

The three remaining musicians made a hasty exit, cussing us as they burned rubber out of the parking lot. We never saw them again.

**Pulling A Crowd**

Our Sunday afternoon jam sessions at Michael's Ice House became an instant success from both a musical standpoint as well as the attendance. Mr. Michael was happy with his cash register receipts every week. As news of our Sunday afternoon jam spread, people from all over southeast Texas packed in every week for the free show and to cheer for musicians of every who rocked the house.

In order to keep the show interesting and people coming back, we experimented with new ideas. Russell, A.J. and I became notorious for our unexpected and unpredictable antics. With our wireless guitars, we'd walk out to the parking lot and into the street. We'd climb on top of tables, chairs and on top of the bar. We always encouraged the customers (especially the women) to climb on the bar with us.

On one of those bar-climbing stunts, Russell's snare drum fell off of the bar and slammed to the concrete floor. Pieces flew in every direction. In his effort to catch the drum, he lost his balance, fell off the bar and landed on top of the drum. His expression told us he was in severe pain. His stomach was gashed wide open and he was bleeding like a stuck pig. Like a true Die Hard, Russell grabbed what was left of the drum, put it in a headlock under his left arm and beat the hell out of it with one stick until we finished the song.

One night, with our wireless guitars and a snare drum, we took the show outside. The crowd followed. Russell, A.J. and I climbed on top of my van. The combined weight of the band caused the roof to cave in and from then on the roof made a nice birdbath.

One hot, steamy afternoon the crowd was in a listless mood. There seemed to be nothing the band could do to get them excited. We climbed on the bar and I performed guitarist Danny Gatton's famous beer bottle slide trick.* Beer was foaming and spewing all over my Telecaster! The crowd went wild! They thought I was going to get electrocuted. Fortunately I was playing wireless.

*I highly recommend the video of Danny Gatton's beer bottle slide trick on "Honky Tonkin' Country Girl" at dannygatton.com. That guitar trick became part of our show from then on.

### Jam Slutz

There were never any *extremely* bad musicians at our weekly Sunday Blues Jam. Some were obviously much better players than others. Some just smelled worse than others. Regardless, we always tried to make room for everyone who showed up to play. There were regular "jam slutz" who showed up almost every week and soon became recognized as local celebrities. They were known by their nicknames: Red Fred, Still Bill, Starvin' Marvin, Hollywood, Professor Blues, Sweet Mama Cotton, and many more – including a bass player who called himself Blind Lemon Pledge. Three of the hottest guitar players who consistently blew everybody away were Matt Johnson, Louis Cressy and Craig Schneider.

There was an amazing sixty-something-year-old black singer, named Bo Young. Bo always wore denim overalls and his hair was often twisted into dozens of little "Liza Jane" pig tails. Though he was a sight, he had true superstar talent. His electrifying soul voice equalled Otis Redding, Wilson Pickett or James Brown. The moment he started singing, people were on their feet going absolutely crazy. It was always a pleasure to play for him.

Why he never hit the big time I'll never know, but he was *big* at Michael's Ice House.

### Can A Chinese Man Play The Blues?

One Sunday afternoon Rick Lee showed up at Michael's Ice House. Rick had his own band, Rick Lee & The Night Owls. A third-generation Texan of Chinese ancestry, Rick was making a name for himself in southeast Texas with a song he had written called "Can A Chinese Man Play The Blues?"

As Rick tuned up, one of the rednecks in the audience yelled, "Hey thar Buddy! Play that thar song a-yors 'bout kin a Chinaman play tha blues!"

Rick grabbed the mic and unleashed an angry tirade on the unsuspecting crowd, lecturing them about the political incorrectness of the word *"chinaman."*

"The proper term is Asian-American or Chinese!"

The guy making the request did not intentionally mean to offend Rick by using the word *chinaman.* Most people were not aware "chinaman" had become politically incorrect. After all we'd been indoctrinated by re-runs of Bruce Lee movies and David Carradine's *Kung Fu* TV series for decades. Who knew?

Rick was offended at being called a "chinaman." The crowd of rednecks, bikers and blue-collar workers were equally offended by Rick's glaring chastisement of their ignorance regarding politically correct terminology. I saw the mood of the happy, drinking crowd change to one of anger and resentment. Several rednecks bowed up ready to fight.

I yelled to Rick, "Shut the fuck up, man! They're gonna kick your ass!"

Rick continued his rant. The redneck that made the original request stormed toward the stage, obviously embarrassed at Rick's belittling of him. His buddies grabbed him and pulled him back. I drowned out Rick's fiery sermon by ripping into Chuck Berry's "Johnny B. Goode." The dance floor filled up and Rick's ass was saved. After several well-accepted songs, Rick finished his set with a rousing version of "Can A Chinese Man Play The Blues."

### Henry and The Mexicans

One Sunday afternoon three ancient-looking, rough-cut Mexican men, probably in their late sixties, asked if they could sit in. I thought they were joking. They looked like they had just gotten off work because they were still wearing their paint-splattered uniforms.

One toothless old guy, speaking for the trio, introduced himself as Henry Garza. The men's age and appearance made me reluctant to let them play. I told them to stick around and I'd try to work them in. I humbly confess, I purposely kept putting them off, hoping they would get tired of waiting and leave. They stayed and stayed, all the way till the end of the jam.

Finally I called them to the bandstand. I cringed as I placed my Telecaster in Henry's calloused, paint-speckled hands. Henry beamed a broad, toothless smile from ear to ear as he examined the guitar as if it was made of solid gold. Without any warning or introduction, the trio exploded into "Evil Ways" by Santana. As I was walking away from the stage, I stopped dead in my tracks. Turning around I stared in disbelief at what I was hearing. The crowd, watching the three unassuming paint-splattered old Mexicans, leaped to their feet in a rousing cheer. *The three old guys were fantastic!* Santana would've been proud.

Although it was near quitting time, we were mesmerized by the trio's amazing sound and encouraged them to keep playing until they got tired. The crowd offered one standing ovation after another. From then on every time Henry and his guys came in, paint splattered or not, they were treated like celebrities by the audience and revered like royalty by the musicians.

That night I learned a serious lesson about judging, or *not* judging, a book by its paint-splattered cover.

### Invasion Of The Stevie Ray Clones

During my five-year stint at Michael's Ice House, I grew more as a musician and lead guitarist than at any other place before or since. I was constantly challenged by young guns who showed up every week trying to cut my head off. I often felt like an old gunfighter being called out at high noon by the new fast draw in town.

In the early '90s the Texas music scene was flooded with hundreds of young, arrogant, Stevie Ray clones wearing the look-a-like SRV hat and playing the official SRV Strat. Most were pretty damn good players as long as they played only Stevie Ray songs. For whatever reason, every week I was called out by young guns half my age, wanting to challenge me to a *Crossroads* style head-cutting duel.

My Fender Telecaster, loaded with razor-sharp, glass-shredding Lace Sensor pickups, sounded like Albert Collins on steroids. I played through a 100-watt Peavey TransTube, patched into a 300-watt Peavey Combo with a 15" speaker. My friend and fellow musician Benny Brasket once said, "Man, I've seen Marshall *stacks*, but that's the first time I've ever seen a Peavey *Pile!*"

The SRV clones ripped Stevie Ray licks from their shiny new Strats. I'd crank up my Peavey Pile and fired back at the little bastards. I was there to jam, they were there to kill. A few were formidable opponents.

What the young guns didn't realize was that we older players knew exactly what they were going to do before they did it. Whenever they tried to play all SRV, we'd take them into uncharted territory that didn't exist note-for-note on their tab sheets. They were lost.

Most of the young players had not yet learned how to improvise to play from the heart and shoot from the hip. The band and I would rip their little heads off and send 'em packing. I admired the ones who kept coming back week after week. They eventually developed the necessary skills. Many have stayed in music, becoming successful players.

Facing the young guns in a head-cuttin' guitar duel every week kept me on my toes, sharpened my skills, increased my speed and made me a better player. It was a fantastic adrenaline rush.

## The Count of Croatia

Speaking of being called out for a serious head-cuttin' duel…

Slaven was an over-confident player in his late-twenties. From Croatia, an Eastern European country, his strong accent sounded like a cross between Arnold Schwarzenegger and Bela Lagosi. For some reason he absolutely refused to jam with anyone else but *me*.

Being a very talented young guitarist, he applied blistering, lightning-fast, speed-metal shredding ability to his new-found love, Texas Blues. He would arrive with an entourage of groupies. Dressed in a long black trench coat, he'd march straight to the stage, stand directly in front of me, point his finger in my face and yell, "Ey vant du blay wit *chew*!"

Slaven was dead serious about cuttin' my head off. Each song became a death match. It's a good thing we weren't dueling with swords or I would have been cut to ribbons. Slaven wielded his white-hot ax like a *Star Wars* light sabre. Compared to his warp-speed expertise, I felt I was playing a two-by-four with cooking mitts. The situation reminded me of *Rocky IV* when Rocky fought the Russian. I felt I was playing for the honor of the good ol' USA!

My only salvation was that Slaven always played so many notes, so fast, and with so much distortion, that he was his own worst enemy. Playing like that didn't allow the music to breathe. Slaven's performance often sounded like one long, grinding, distorted chain saw.

After performing one of his trademark a-million-distorted-notes-in-ten-seconds solos, Slaven looked at me with the sly smirk of an arrogant MiG pilot who had me in his crosshairs, as if to say, "Now, leez zee jou do dhat!"

Instead of making a fool of myself by trying to play like him, I motioned for the band to bring the volume down. I hit one single note, letting the sustain ring out. I allowed the feedback to carry that one single note all the way through to the chord progression. The crowd exploded into hysterical laughter!

Humiliated by my one-note solo, Slaven was furious. He jerked his guitar cord from the amplifier and stormed off stage. I felt victorious, as though I had beaten the Evil Empire with *one note*!

I knew Slaven was an excellent player, but his talent was being buried under a myriad of distortion pedals and effects boxes. A few weeks later I suggested he unplug his effects, plug straight into my Peavey and play without leaning on all those effects. Reluctantly, he tried. He discarded his heavy metal enhancements right then and there and became one of the best blues rock players I have ever heard.

The last time I received an email from Slaven, he was spreading the gospel of Texas Blues back in Croatia. Keep on Bluzin', Slaven! You rock! You can check out his music and his band MojoHand at mojomusic.net.

## Our Biker Band Beginnings

During the '90s the band tried hard to be strictly a blues band, but every time our southern-rock roots mixed with adrenaline and alcohol, the combination created a high energy, volatile mixture. To our disappointment, we were shunned by most blues lovers, especially hardcore blues purists. Bikers on the other hand, loved us.

As the weeks and months passed, we noticed more and more bikes coming to Michael's Ice House on Sundays to hear our Southern bluesrock sound. Bikers seemed to gravitate toward the bad-boy blues we were dishing out. That was the beginning of our biker following. Over the next decade, we became well-known as a "biker band."

In 1994, most bikers that frequented Michael's were not like the RUBs (Rich Urban Bikers) that became prominent in later years. These bikers were *real* bikers. Some were just good ol' boys who worked in the refineries, but most were associated with outlaw motorcycle clubs. Regardless they were all tough mo-fos and didn't take shit from anybody. I was glad they liked our band and our music.

Most of the bikers we saw on a regular basis became good friends of the band. *Most.*

It's always been my policy to meet, greet and introduce myself to customers wherever we played. Since the bikers were diggin' the band, I felt I should show some respect for their interest and make the rounds, introducing myself and personally saying thanks for coming.

One particular time as I was making my rounds, I approached a table of bikers, leaned over and extended my hand. "How ya doin', fellas? I just wanted to say thanks for hangin' out and supporting the band."

They all sat up erect and stared at me in stone cold silence. No one offered to shake my hand. No one moved. The awkward moment of stillness seemed like an eternity. Finally one of them said in a very flat tone, "Jes cause we like yer music, don't mean we like *you.*"

I got the message. I slowly backed away from the table. My bass player, who was a biker himself and knew some of the guys at the table, told me later I was lucky I didn't get my ass kicked for intruding on their conversation without an invitation. He enlightened me on proper biker etiquette.

Never interrupt bikers when they're talking. When approaching a group of bikers, if they stop and stare at you without speaking that usually means you're not welcome to be part of their private conversation. Keep your distance, keep walking and deny you heard anything.

When walking past a biker or group of bikers you don't know, it's best not to make eye contact. Nod respectfully and keep moving.

If you accidentally bump into a biker, show your hands and back away immediately. Apologize, accept the blame for being a clumsy idiot and move on quickly. Never be so stupid as to bump into the same biker twice.

Never ask a biker about his bike. If you must say something, just say, "Nice bike." If he wants you to know any more than that, he'll tell you.

Never *ever* touch, move or sit on a biker's bike. Touching a bike is usually followed by a near-death experience.

Never act overly interested in a biker's bike unless it has a "For Sale" sign on it. It's the same as staring at his old lady. Sometimes worse.

Never ask a biker questions about his private life, his job, his old lady, his real name, how he got his road name, and so on. In other words, mind your own damn business.

No matter how wild and crazy biker women get or how interested they seem to be in *you*, never purposely talk to them or act overly interested in them, no matter what.

When a biker chick starts flirting and flashing her tits at the audience or the band, just smile and nod approvingly, that's all. But, don't ignore her while she's showing off. She and her old man might take your lack of interest as an insult to her charms and her effort to show off what "good stuff" her old man is privy to. Like I said, just smile and nod, then buy her old man a beer.

A lot of biker girls would come to the bandstand to request songs. They would dance by themselves while their men were discussing business. Sometimes a girl would flash her tits just to mess with us and to make her ol' man jealous. We'd just nod gratefully and grin, but to save our butts from appearing too interested we'd kick off into the next song as soon as possible and keep on rockin'.

## Crazy Women At Michael's Ice House

There were alot of women who came to Michael's during our Sunday jams. Most were there with dates or friends to enjoy the music, but the ones that stand out in my memory were the crazy ones. By the time the sun went down, the music and alcohol would have some of them really charged up.

Whenever we played "My Baby Don't Wear No Panties," "Let Me Pump Your Gas" or "Don't It Make You Want To (Take Off Your Clothes)," the crazy women would start flashing their tits and throwing panties on the stage. One girl got on stage, pulled everything off except her t-shirt and raised it over her head. Use your imagination. The place went wild. She got off the stage when the bass player stuck the headstock of his guitar in the crack of her ass.

Another girl always wore a short skirt, cowboy boots and no panties. She would sit at a front seat facing the band and "take our picture"!

Some girls danced together, humping each other's thighs. An endless supply of girls would dance on the tables, showing everything they had to the approving cheers of the audience. Never a dull moment.

As the news of our wild Sunday afternoon shows spread, Michael's would pack out with people coming to hear some hard-driving blues and see the girls put on a show. We knew the wilder our shows were, the more the place would pack out, guaranteeing our job.

We learned by trial and error how to keep a crowd motivated, stirred up, and coming back for more. I earned my PhD in Hellraisin'!

## No More Blues Jams at Michael's

Mr. Michael fired me a couple of times during the first year. Thinking he had a good Sunday afternoon crowd built up, he'd hire cheaper weekend warrior bands that undercut my salary. Each time, Mr. Michael lost his audience and within a few weeks he would ask me to come back. Each time he hired me back, he gave me a small raise.

From then on, every time I mentioned quitting, Mr. Michael would kick in another twenty bucks a week to entice me to stay. We had become the highest paid unknown three-piece band in Texas at that time.

By the spring of 1998, four years into our jam at Michael's, a demo of "My Baby Don't Wear No Panties" fell into the hands of local DJ Joe Montes from KPFT 90.1 FM. His show, "Joe's Roadhouse," played the hell out of the "Panties" song along with "Texas City Dyke." The airplay sent hundreds of new customers into Michael's looking for the band that played the "Panties" song. Instead of hearing the band they heard on the radio, they new customers were bombarded by several hours of unqualified jammers before my band finished the night with "Texas City Dyke" and "My Baby Don't Wear No Panties."

I was growing tired of running jam sessions, tired of playing nursemaid to a bunch of amateurs and tired of putting up with the egotistical bullshit that comes with running a jam. It wasn't fun anymore. I wanted to be a real band. I told Mr. Michael he could fire me if he wanted, but I wasn't going to back up another beginner or cut heads with one more hot-headed SRV wannabe clone.

Mr. Michael got real quiet for a moment. I thought he was about to fire me. "Boy! That's the best news I've heard. You've had some sorry son of a bitches up there sometimes! Tell you what, I don't give a shit what you do as long as you keep the people coming in!"

From that point on our jam was by invitation only. We pissed off a lot of the wannabe jammers when they were not invited to play and they complained to Mr. Michael. He'd say, "If Kelton don't want you to play, you must not be worth a fuck!"

We culled a lot of players, improved the quality of our show and never lost our audience.

## Mr. Michael Sells Out To Fat Bob

Around October or November of 1998, after four and a half years of Sunday afternoon shows, Mr. Michael called me into his office. He broke the news that he was retiring. He had sold Michael's Ice House to a guy named Bob who would be taking over the following week. Mr. Michael thanked me for never giving him any trouble, always putting on a good show and keeping the crowds coming in.

Before Mr. Michael left he gave me a fifty dollar a week raise and backdated his booking calendar to make it look like I had been making that amount for the past year.

"When the new owner sees this," he said, "it'll look like I've been paying you that much all year long. Don't tell him any different. You've always pulled me a damn good crowd and you deserve more money."

I hated to see Mr. Michael go. Through the years he and I had developed a mutual respect. I liked him because he let me do as I damned well pleased with the music. He never gave me any trouble because, as he put it, we consistently packed his house and put money in his pocket. I thanked him, we shook hands and I never saw him again.

The following week the new sign on the building read "Bob's Ice House."

I went in and met Bob. At 5' 2" and 300 pounds, Bob was a short, fat, obnoxious white guy in his mid-thirties with a flat-top haircut like Sargent Carter on *The Gomer Pyle Show*.

At the end of our first night under Bob's regime, he handed me my pay and scowled, "This is bullshit!" I can get a six-piece band, hell for that matter, I can get a ten-piece band for this much money!"

"Mr. Michael didn't pay me for how many players are in my band, he paid me for how many people are in the audience. He kept me around five years because I put money in his pocket. As a businessman, you oughtta appreciate that. Try hiring ZZ Top, they're a three-piece band. See what they'll cost you!"

The following week Bob shoved a cash register receipt in my face. "This is all the beer you sold and it ain't worth shit! If you can't sell any more 'n that, yer ass if fuckin' *fired*!"

"I ain't no beer salesman!" I snapped back. "I'm a musician. You're the beer salesman. My job is to pull the crowd. Your job is to sell 'em beer! I'm still pulling the same crowd I pulled when Mr. Michael was here and he never complained. If you ain't making any money, you better watch those skanky bitches you hired. They're stealing you blind!"

Bob had fired all of Mr. Michael's best waitresses. They had been loyal and trustworthy to Mr. Michael and their customers for years. Some were hardworking, single moms with two and three part-time jobs, just trying to make ends meet. The regular customers were pissed because Bob fired their favorite waitresses, especially one very sweet, old lady who all the customers loved. She was about seventy years old and everybody called her "Mom."

Bob said the place needed new, hot, young babes to attract a bigger crowd of men from the local refineries. Bob's new female staff was a motley crew of burned out, ex-titty dancers, crack whores and aging prostitutes. In my opinion, the skanks were more interested in selling their ass and drugs than selling beer for Bob. It was obvious they were stealing from Bob and naturally my band was getting the blame for the low cash register receipts.

When getting paid at the end of the night, it was always my policy to count the money with Bob in his office. One evening Bob shoved a wad of money across the bar into my hand and hastily turned and walked away. I hollered for him to come back so we could count the money together. He walked back and I counted the money out on the bar. It was $50 short. He insisted I had either stuffed the fifty in my pocket when his back was turned or dropped it on the floor. He made a big show of pretending to look for the phantom fifty behind the counter and under the beer cooler. We both knew it would never be found.

For the duration of the Sunday gig at Bob's I would never accept any money from Bob unless he counted it out on top of his desk in the privacy of his office. That is a policy I still live by today with *all* talent buyers, especially club owners.

After talking to the other bands who worked for Bob, we learned he was shoving sales receipts in everybody's face and playing the "lost money game" with every band. We all agreed to ignore his bullshit when he presented the cash register receipts. The other bands began demanding to be paid in the office like I did.

Bob was furious with the new payment trend I started. He took every opportunity to blast me with offensive, personal insults in front of the audience during our show. He soon learned that it was difficult to out-step a stepper.

In a bold act of arrogance, Bob parked his candy-apple red, fully-dressed Honda touring bike on the dance floor in front my spot on the stage. People looking at the band had to look over the Honda to see us. Since the band was drawing a large biker crowd who mostly rode Harleys, the crowd, as well as the band, saw this as an act of complete disrespect. Bob quickly lost favor with the bikers.

One afternoon in January of 1999 two hours before I was to leave for Texas City, I received a call from Bob. He screamed into the phone, "You're fuckin' fired! You can't draw a crowd, and nobody likes your music!" Bob hung up before I could reply.

It's a mystery to me why a man with thousands of dollars invested in a club would rip off, insult and fire a band that was making him money, fire his best waitresses that customers loved, hire a bunch of thieves to handle his money and disrespect his clientele.

That was the end of our five-year stint at Michael's and Bob's Icehouse.

### A Call Back To Bob's

Two years after being fired by Bob, he called me and acted like my long, lost friend. He asked me to come back and play for a biker wedding reception at Bob's Ice House on an upcoming Wednesday night. "There's gonna be six hundred, seven hundred bikes here!" exclaimed Bob. "They insist that you play! How much you gonna charge me?"

Knowing he would never pay what I was worth, I calmly said, "A thousand dollars."

"A thousand dollars? I ain't payin' no gawdamm band a thousand dollars. Wednesday nights are my slowest nights!"

"Didn't you just tell me you were expecting *seven hundred bikes*?" I asked.

"Yeah, but, but…"

"Six or seven hundred bikes on any night is *not* a slow night. The price is a thousand dollars, half up front and the other half on arrival."

Remembering our conversation two years before I asked, "Why the hell are you calling me, anyway? Don't you remember telling me *nobody likes my music and I can't draw a crowd?*"

It gave me great satisfaction to slam the phone down in Bob's ear. That was the end of my relationship with Bob's Ice House.

### "The Texas City Dyke"

Nine months after I was fired from Bob's Ice House, I recorded *Most Requested* that featured a song I had been singing for over ten years, "The Texas City Dyke."

I felt the song needed more to make it complete. At the last minute, I scribbled out two more verses about a guy named Fat Bob who got his ass whipped and his wife stolen by a diesel dyke at an icehouse in Texas City.

Any similarities to persons living or dead was purely coincidental. Draw you're own conclusions.

### Playin' Across The Street

As years passed, Bob's Ice House was plagued with constant changes in management and new lessors. Each one would solicit my band's services. I'd tell them all the same thing. "I'll play across the street for free before I'll ever work a paying gig where money made from my performance eventually finds it way into Fat Bob's pocket!"

## STUMP

In 1996, the band and I started a Thursday night blues jam at a large country-western nightclub in Galveston County called Marguerite's. We had no idea the gig would last nearly three years. It was a blast while it lasted. Every week the crowds kept getting bigger and bigger. Many times we would still be playing when the house lights came on, with the crowd yelling for more.

Over time we got to know the regulars. We learned who to hang with, who liked which songs, who didn't give a damn about the band, who showed up only for the dart tournament and who to watch out for.

There was one guy named "Stump" who we were warned about. He was a short, stocky dude in his early thirties who stood about 5' 6" and weighed about 225 pounds. He had shoulders as wide as a 1960 Pontiac. His arms were as big around as my waist. Rumor had it he had a short fuse and loved to fight. We were told to step lightly around him until he got to know us. Even some of the most notorious big guys stayed clear of Stump. They'd say "He's like fightin' a wild hog."

One evening my girlfriend Joni sat alone at a table near the stage. The table next to her was crowded with a rowdy group of good ol' boys having a few beers after work. One of them was Stump. As the alcohol mixed with testosterone, Stump and his friends began to push and shove each other the way most young guys do in a rite-of-passage ritual. Every other song they'd raise their beers in the air in a rousing, rebel battle cry and yell *Skynyrrrrd!*"

While on break I was sitting with Joni when suddenly Stump, in his revelry, backed into our table. Our drinks sloshed out of our glasses, but we grabbed them before they turned over. No harm done. I moved our table over a couple of feet.

Again, Stump backed into our table, tipping it slightly and sloshing our drinks. I knew it was an accident and the young guys were just having fun. I had no plans of making a big deal about it and, once again, moved our table a few more inches away.

Joni took offense to the second incident and placed her foot against the chair directly across from her and gave it a mule kick as hard as she could. The chair rammed into Stump's back, causing him to spill his drink.

"Owwww!" he yiped and grabbed his lower back as if he'd been shot. He spun around ready to fight and there *I* was, standing next to our table. I'm sure I looked petrified. Naturally, Stump assumed it was me that had struck the blow, not the petite young lady now sitting quietly.

Stump glared at me like a demon from hell. His upper lip curled like a mad dog and he bowed up, ready to charge. I realized he thought I was the one who had just kicked the shit out of him. My "O-o-o-o-oh shit!" alarm sounded in my head. I knew an ass whuppin' was about to occur and the ass getting whupped was going to be mine.

There was no way to get out of this situation with any dignity. I could have said, "She did it!" Even though it would have been the truth, I would have looked like a chickenshit if I put the blame on Joni.

Stump pointed his index finger at me and yelled "I'm gonna kick your fuckin' ass!"

Expecting him to charge, I took one step back on my right foot and assumed a sideways stance in order to protect any vital organs from a direct hit. I kept both of my hands loose at my sides and didn't make a fist so as not to appear to be making any aggressive moves.

He continued to yell, "Muthafucka! I'll whup your fuckin ass!" I stood completely silent and didn't respond to his verbal threats. We stared at each other eye to eye like two gunfighters in a spaghetti western. Neither of us blinked. The room fell silent.

Stump seemed to relax when I didn't vocally respond to his verbal assaults or make an aggressive move toward him. He turned slowly and eased away. I stood motionless, watching for his unexpected charge. He turned toward me and yelled one last time, "Mutherfucker, I'll whup your goddamned ass!" I kept a cautious eye on him as he slowly moved away.

When I felt he was no longer a threat, I grabbed Joni by the arm and dragged her out of her chair. "C'mon!" I snapped, "Your ass is gonna sit at one of those empty tables in the back! You almost got me killed!"

Joni jerked loose from me and charged toward Stump yelling, "If you can't kick his fuckin' ass, I will!"

I grabbed her and dragged her to the back of the room and forcefully sat her down at a secluded table. I held her there until she cooled off.

"Why didn't you tell him I was the one that hit him?" she asked.

"Because! I'd look like the world's biggest chickenshit and never live it down if I blamed it on my *girlfriend*!" I snapped. "And your little ass ain't whuppin' nobody! Now sit down and shut up before you get my ass kicked!"

As the months went by Stump and I slowly formed an uneasy truce. One night about a year later, we were drinking tequila shots together. He said, "Hey, man, remember that night I almost kicked your ass? Well, I'm glad I didn't cause I like you better as a friend."

We had a good laugh. I never told him it was Joni who kicked the shit out of him. As long as he thought I had balls enough to stand up to him, I had earned his respect.

Now he knows.

## Fightin' Filly at Ken's Club

In the fall of 1994 the band was performing in a small mixed-drink lounge on the west side of Houston called Ken's Club.

The little corner stage was far too small, even for our three-piece band. The club itself was too small for our high-energy bluesrock power trio sound, but it didn't seem to matter. Everybody in the place belonged to the "Geritol For Lunch" bunch. We should have been playing Frank Sinatra and Dean Martin instead of ZZTop and Stevie Ray Vaughan. There seemed to be no way to motivate the audience. They just sat staring at us, a drink in one hand and cigarette in the other.

Sitting at the bar one night was a lady about thirty, with long, brown hair that hung down past the butt cheeks of her sprayed-on jeans. Her seventy-plus-year-old male escort was pumping tequila shots into her one after the other. She was beyond shitfaced. She danced wildly across the dance floor all by herself. Her long hair whirled behind her like the mane of a wild, spirited filly. In her drunken state, she fell on her ass several times.

Caught up in the music, The Filly tried several times to get onto the bandstand and grab my microphone. Each time she stepped on stage, I would get between her and the mic and shove the head of my guitar into her stomach like a bayonet, forcing her back onto the dance floor. After several tries, she sidestepped me and went to A.J.'s mic. We were in the middle of a song when A.J. yelled, "Get the fuck away from me, you stupid bitch!"

I didn't want to grab her or shove her off the stage with the same force I would use on a man. I had to be gentle, but firm. Trying to get her attention, I pinched a strand of her long hair between my fingers and gave it a slight tug, hoping she would move away from the mic.

Instead of giving in to my slight tug, The Filly let out a blood-curdling scream. She went into a frenzied spin, swinging her arms wildly like a street fighter. A.J. and I stepped back as she spun around and around, kicking over mics and mic stands. She was tangled in the cords. She tripped over the stage monitor. She was going *down*.

The Filly's freaked-out reaction caught us by surprise. In the commotion, I didn't realize I still had a grip on her hair. As she fell my instinct was to hold on to her hair to keep her from hitting the floor and busting her head wide open. She turned on me, swinging her arms like a windmill, knocking monitors and mic stands onto the dance floor, all the while screaming like a banshee.

The half-asleep Geritol crowd missed the beginning of the episode, but her sudden screams woke everybody up. They looked up just in time to see what must have appeared to be a violent scene of me dragging her off the stage by the hair of the head.

Realizing what it must look like to the audience, I instantly turned loose of The Filly's hair just as she jerked away from me. She hit the dance floor and rolled. It appeared to the crowd that I had thrown her down. She was still screaming at the top of her lungs as if she was being murdered. Even though the band knew it was just one of those things, we stood ready for some macho asshole to challenge us for what might have been perceived as us "whuppin' up" on a woman.

Nobody made a move toward us.

Crawling around on her hands and knees on the dance floor, The Filly was screaming, "Fuck you, you son of a bitches, you pulled my goddamn hair, you mutherfuckers! Fuck you, *you fucking assholes!*"

I got on the mic and yelled to her old boyfriend. "Hey Pop, come get your stupid bitch and keep her off the bandstand!"

Old Pop was sitting at the bar just as shitfaced as The Filly was. He was completely oblivious to what had happened. He barely raised his head enough to look our way and waved us off as if to say, "Aw, to hell with her."

We kicked off another song and spent the next set trying to keep The Filly off the stage. It became a game to her to get back onstage and a comedy act to the audience. My cousin Chazz Evans happened to be in the audience that night and inherited the job of keeping The Filly off the stage.

Finally, the manager threw the Filly and Old Pop out of the place. Good riddance.

## The Booze Brothers

In December of 1996 we were booked to play a Christmas Toy Drive at Lloyd's Bar in Humble, Texas. Since Lloyd's is a small neighborhood bar – where everybody knows your name – it was too small for my six-piece band which included A.J. Fee on bass, a drummer, a three-piece horn section and me.

The owners of Lloyd's, David and Terrie Plummer, decided to turn the event into a street dance. They blocked off the street. For a stage, they set up a thirty-foot-long heavy duty equipment trailer, the kind that transports tractors and bulldozers. Giant tubs filled with iced-down beer were placed on the sidewalk. Folding tables and chairs were set up in the street. The scene looked like a small festival.

As darkness fell, a couple of hundred people gathered and the party was on. We kicked off the music and people started dancing in the street. My friends Charlie Taylor and Biff Cole were scheduled to perform with us as "Jake & Elwood – The Blues Brothers." On our second set, we introduced our Blues Brothers tributaires, kicking off with the trademark Blues Brothers song "Gimme Some Lovin."

With longneck in hand, Jake (I mean Charlie) bolted toward the front of the stage in a dead run from across the street. He planned to leap onto the front of the stage in a single bound. At a full sprint, his foot slipped on loose gravel just as he pushed off. His body slammed into the front of the stage (the trailer) with a thud loud enough to be heard over the music. He hung there, one arm and one leg draped over the stage. The rest of his body was plastered against the trailer wheels like a bug on a windshield.

Charlie slid to the ground with an expression I'd only seen on Wile E. Coyote after a failed attempt to catch the Roadrunner. He had the breath knocked out of him and his black suit was covered with dust, dirt and beer from his now broken beer bottle. Except for a little embarrassment, he was okay. We all got a big laugh.

In the meantime Elwood (I mean Biff), who had imbibed far more than his legal limit of liquid courage, somehow managed to navigate his way up the ramp on the rear of the trailer. As he traversed his way across the stage through the obstacle course of amps, mic stands and scattered chords, he tripped and fell into the whole damn horn section.

In the chaos Biff knocked the sax player off the back of the three-foot high stage. The other two horn players tried to keep their balance, hold onto their horns and catch the sax player at the same time, but to no avail. Just as Biff followed the sax player over the edge, the drummer grabbed him by the arm and saved him from falling on top of the sax player who was already laying on the ground.

Though unhurt, except for his bruised ego, the sax player was furious. He jumped up screaming he was going to sue everybody involved – Biff, Lloyd's Bar, the trailer owner and me. As it turned out, a small rod was slightly bent but the horn was still functional.

We got through the show just fine. Biff paid the sax player $400 to shut him up. That was the end of that. Through it all, the show went great, the band sounded great, everybody had a great time.

The stage survived unharmed.

## BACK TO BACK BANDS

During the Christmas season of 1997, A.J., Sid and I performed a Saturday night show in the very elegant and world-famous Galvez Hotel in Galveston, Texas.

The nightclub was very posh. I don't remember how we got the gig, but it was certainly a long way up from the beer joints we were accustomed to playing. The club manager said he wanted to bring in some serious drinkers and figured we were the band for the job.

As we were setting up we noticed the wall behind the stage was not really a wall at all. It was merely a folding glass partition. When the partition was open, it made the club twice as big. With the partition closed and stretched across the middle of the stage, it created two separate stages and two separate rooms: a banquet room on one side and a nightclub on the other. We set up on the nightclub side.

On this night the partition was closed. To our surprise, another band was setting up on the other half of the stage on the other side of the glass directly behind us. We could see them and they could see us. When the two drummers set up their kits, it was obvious they'd be playing less than a foot apart, back to back, with only a thin wall of glass separating them.

Dressed in faded denim and black leather, we were hired to rock the club with our own brand of Southern Rock. The other band was wearing tuxedos. They were hired to play easy listening Christmas music for the Alvin State Bank Christmas party.

We recognized a couple of musicians in the Tuxedo Band and walked around the partition to say hello. We all agreed this was not going to be an easy gig for either band, but would all try to keep a professional attitude and get through the night as best we could.

The Tuxedos, featuring my old friend Bill Parrish on guitar, were scheduled to play 8pm to midnight. We were to play from 9pm to 1am. That meant the Tuxedos had a one-hour head start on us and we would play an hour longer at the end of the night.

At exactly 8pm, pleasant jazz-flavored renditions of "Jingle Bells," "Deck The Halls" and "Frosty The Snowman" wafted gently through the thin glass partition and into the nightclub side as if the partition between the two didn't exist.

Occasionally the Tuxedos would look over their shoulders into the nightclub. They could see us sitting at the bar, downing tequila shots and anxiously awaiting our time to play. With big smiles we toasted their efforts by raising our shot glasses. They would immediately face forward without acknowledging our greeting. They seemed embarrassed to be seen dressed in their monkey suits and playing Christmas music. It was their inevitable fate to be blown off the stage by us and we all knew it.

From our perch on the bar stools, we observed the bank employees and their spouses eating their nice Christmas dinners at their nice little tables, decorated with nice scented candles and nice Christmas arrangements. Each time the Tuxedos finished a song, their audience politely offered an obligatory, lackluster golf clap.

At exactly 8:45pm, the Tuxedo Band took their first break just as the bank employees were being served coffee and dessert. Until now, all was well in Christmasland.

At 9pm, both bands took the stage. Sid mounted his drums. He was no more than eight inches, back to back, from the other drummer with nothing between them but the partition.

The Tuxedos peered at us through the glass with a deer-in-the-headlights look. Both bands knew if the Tuxedo's little Christmas melodies could be heard with the partition closed, then the Die Hards were about roll over them like a steamroller.

Our nightclub crowd sat grinning like fans in an ancient Roman arena, waiting to see us destroy the Tuxedos. We felt bad for them. It wasn't our desire to disrespect fellow musicians, but there was no way around doing what we were hired to do. The situation was the result of poor planning. The club manager didn't give a shit. "Kill 'em!" he said.

Our sympathy for the Tuxedoes was short-lived. I reminded Sid and A.J. the manager told me the Tuxedoes were making three times more than we were to sing limp Christmas songs. "Let's rock!"

When the Tuxedos kicked off their second set of Christmas dinner music, we gave them a thirty-second head start and exploded into "Tush" by ZZ Top. I looked over my shoulder to see the Tuxedos glaring back at us with hate in their eyes. We were blowing through the glass wall like a tidal wave. There was no way they could hear their own instruments.

The bank group had no idea another band was about to play until we blew them out of their seats. They leaped to their feet and peered at us through the glass as if we had set off a bomb.

The situation only got worse. Every time we ended a song, we could hear the faint sounds of Christmas music drifting ever so sweetly through the partition. We retaliated with another barrage of supercharged Southern rock.

As the night wore on, the alcohol began to work its magic on the young ladies at the Christmas banquet. Some gave in to the call of the wild and our music, and found the passageway between the rooms. They were soon shaking their asses on *our* dance floor.

Not to be left behind, the rest of the banquet party followed. Soon they were gettin' down and dirty, doing the hoochie-coo on our side of the glass. I looked over my shoulder and saw the Tuxedos, now playing to an empty room and giving us some serious go-to-hell looks.

In the meantime, the little bank teller girls pulled off their shoes, let their hair down and were rockin' to our band. Suddenly our dance floor cleared as if an invisible alien force had teleported all the bank employees out of the nightclub. They scurried back to their seats in the banquet room like school children caught misbehaving while the teacher was gone. They spent the rest of the night staring blankly at the Tuxedos, looking very bored and unhappy. I was told later the bank president ordered all employees to return to their seats and listen to the band that he paid for, or else don't come to work on Monday.

At exactly midnight, the very punctual Tuxedos quit. By 12:01am the bank employees filled our dance floor once again. The alcohol, mixed with the pent-up frustration of being forced to listen to the Tuxedos all night, sent them uninhibitedly dirty dancing across our dance floor. What a party.

The Tuxedos were still giving us serious go-to-hell looks as they packed their gear. We hoped they realized no disrespect was intended and we were just doing our job. We'd extended an invitation for them to join us on stage for a rockin' jam session as soon as they finished their Christmas gig. They repaid our invitation by giving us the finger as they left.

We rocked our last set out to a packed house. The lady claiming to be in charge of the entertainment committee with the bank approached the bandstand. Wiping sweat from her brow, she enthusiastically promised to call me the following week to set up some company parties. Alas, as all things go, when the alcohol wears off, so does the enthusiasm. Taking the initiative, I made several calls to Alvin State Bank, but none were ever returned. So be it.

To this day, every time I see former members of the Tuxedos they are still pissed.

# RETURN TO BILLY BLUES 1998 (A SECOND CHANCE)

After being barred from Billy Blues in January of 1995, it was three years before I set foot back in the place. I had heard there had been a constant turnover in management and staff and that any good busboy or waitress could move up to general manager within six weeks. I took a chance no one currently employed knew me, my reputation or the circumstances of my being barred in 1995. I was right. None of the old employees were still there but that same wormy soundman Wizard. Slick and Mr. Hot Shit were no longer with the company.

The new manager "Marko" was dedicated to bringing back the blues. I saw my chance. I explained to Marko about my previous success with the *Texas Blues Showcase*, conveniently omitting the details of my final exit. We agreed to bring the *Showcase* back. I was in!

I went to Wizard, shook hands and made peace. We both agreed not to talk about the incident three years before to the new management. He promised not to mention my fight with Slick and I promised not to mention any of the things he was allegedly smoking behind the building. Done deal.

Within a few weeks, the *Texas Blues Showcase* was back. This time I added a new twist, *television*! In my absence from Billy Blues I had become a certified television producer with Houston's public access TV station. Today it's called Houston Media Source.

Every Wednesday night the new *Texas Blues Showcase* featured my band as the opening act. Two guest bands performed a thirty-minute set each and then my band closed the show. The entire show was taped and edited into thirty-minute segments and aired the following week. It was a great exposure for the bands and for Billy Blues.

Billy Blues had lost its original blues-loving client base and the new audience didn't seem to be excited about the blues. Try as I might, I could not rekindle the same excitement of years past. In an effort to ignite our performance, the band and I returned to our ritual tequila shots in the dressing room before every show. With each *Showcase* taped, we could review our performance. We learned to play to the cameras, not to the half-dead audience who froze every time the cameras were turned on.

Guest bands on the show often got lost in the blah-ness of the dead audience instead of doing their best performance for the cameras. Most of the taped performances were uninspired. Many bands wondered why their performances never made it to television. Sometimes the lighting was horrible. Sometimes the old cameras we leased from the station were faulty. Sometimes the sound was terrible. Sometimes everything just plain *sucked*. Every taping was a learning experience.

There were some exciting highlights. Every time we played "My Baby Don't Wear No Panties," I would invite girls from the audience to dance on stage. The wilder they danced, the more excited the audience became. It was good for business. Sex sells.

Eventually we started drawing bigger crowds and they got used to the cameras. The crowds also looked forward to the girls on stage. The manager ruined the party when he banned anyone onstage that was not in the band. "Insurance purposes!" he said.

One night fans bought tequila shots for the band, a dozen at a time, tray after tray. I was wound up and roaring like a freight train. At the end of the night I raised my glass to the audience, thanking them for helping bring back the *Texas Blues Showcase*. The audience raised their glasses and we all sucked down the demon liquor together in one big cluster-gulp.

After doing the shot, I gave into an overwhelming urge to fling my shot glass against the stage door, a habit I picked up earlier that year at Del's Lookout in Surfside Beach. The sound of shattering glass fulfilled an inner primeval need to destroy something! *It was beautiful!*

The violent act charged up the audience as if someone stuck them with an electric wire. They cheered! Suddenly dozens of glasses exploded against the back wall as the audience followed my lead. Again, they cheered and applauded. Wow, what a party!

For the next hour, the audience went into riot mode. They were screaming, yelling and dancing at a fever pitch, giving into to the revelry of the moment. The band was rockin'! People were buying shots just to throw the glasses. Tequila was selling faster than the bartender could pour it. It was great. Then, a waitress delivered a note from the manager. In big, bold letters, it said, *"QUIT NOW!"*

The house lights came on an hour early. Against audience protests, the party was shut down. I went to the office. The manager paid me. He said throwing shot glasses against the wall was the most unprofessional thing he'd ever seen and then yelled, "You're fired!"

"Unprofessional! Fired?!" I yelled. "Bullshit! I was just trying to get the crowd excited. You're turning this place into an old folks home. Man, you sold out of tequila tonight. So it cost you a few cheap shot glasses. Big deal! All those people had a blast. They'll be telling everybody. This place will be packed next week!"

"Next week they'll see a professional band, not a bunch of white trash throwing shot glasses!"

"Are you nuts?" I yelled. "Man, you might know food and beverage, but you don't know shit about show business! What we did tonight was *showbiz*! No different than Ozzy bitin' the head off a bat or Hendrix setting his guitar on fire!"

"Hendrix wasn't throwing *my* shot glasses! If he did, he'd be fired too! *Now get the fuck out!*"

It was October 1998 and my second stint at Billy Blues had lasted four months. For a second time my hellraisin' ways had gotten me banned from performing at Billy Blues.

## Third Time At Billy Blues

Knowing the management was subject to change every six weeks at Billy Blues, I waited until Marko was gone and until a couple of managers had come and gone before I made an effort to get back in to perform at Billy Blues.

About a year later, the new manager was a cutesy young lady about thirty years old who had worked her way up from waitress to manager in the usual six weeks. She was oblivious to my history and hired me without question for a series of Wednesday night shows.

On my first night back, as I was counting off the first song, the manager came running to the stage. She stood in front of me, her hands clenched under her chin and blurted, "I just found out I was not supposed to hire you! It says so on our computer. It says, '*Gene Kelton is a troublemaker. He starts fights, incites riots and throws shot glasses. DO NOT HIRE!*' "

I cracked up laughing. "I didn't know I was such a notorious outlaw!"

"Oh please, pleeeeease, pleeeease, pleeeease," she pleaded in her little girl voice. "I'm begging you, pleeeeease don't throw any glasses tonight or do anything to get me fired. I didn't know I wasn't supposed to hire you."

I laughed and told her everything would be okay. I was tired of trying to help promote a big, exciting show. I told her I just wanted to play the blues. The night slipped by uneventfully. It was so uneventful that I was booked for several more uneventful gigs. Each successive gig was also uneventful.

The new owner had obviously lost all interest in making Billy Blues the exciting venue it once was. The place was dying a slow, agonizing death. After a few more uneventful shows, I saw no point in trying to ride a dead horse.

I moved on and never pursued a gig at Billy Blues again.

**The Lone Star Shootout**

The last time I stepped foot into Billy Blues was Sunday, June 4, 2000. The Houston Blues Society (HBS), under the leadership of president Steve Sucher, sponsored a major event called *The Lone Star Shootout*.

The Lone Star Shootout featured the guitar-slinging talents of three Texas Blues Legends: Lonnie Brooks, Long John Hunter and Phillip Walker. They were flown in from Chicago and California to play the show. Their backup bands were a hand-picked group of A-team Texas session players from Austin.

Joni and I were members of HBS and volunteered to help with the event. Joni's job was to make sure the performing artists had water, towels, ashtrays and such. My job was simple. I was to pick up three amplifiers donated by Rockin' Robin music store in Houston and deliver them to the stage for the three headliners to use. After the show I was to return the amps to Rockin' Robin. In between my delivery and pickup duties, I had planned to sit at the bar, drink tequila and enjoy the six-hour, $20 per person event for free.

Joni and I arrived at Billy Blues two hours before show time. We were surprised to see the parking lot already packed with cars. As we entered the restaurant area of the building, it was packed with Middle Eastern people wearing formal, traditional attire. The women wore Berkas (long gowns with head coverings and veils). The men were all well-dressed in modern suits and ties. Middle Eastern music whined through the Billy Blues house PA system. We were dumb struck. "What the hell is this shit?" we both asked at the same time. "This is supposed to be a *blues* club!"

The owner sabotaged the HBS event by commandeering the restaurant half of Billy Blues for a Middle Eastern wedding reception on the same frickin' day as the Lone Star Shootout.

On the other side in the showroom musicians were milling around on the stage, also wondering what the hell was going on with the all the middle-eastern activities in the restaurant and "that irritating noise" blaring through the intercom.

I told myself it was not my problem and I wasn't going to worry about it. I delivered the three amps to the stage. Ta-daaa! My work was done. I made my way to the bar, ordered a beer and a shot of tequila. I was ready to enjoy the all-day blues extravaganza.

At one point, I headed for the restroom. The usual route from the showroom was through the double doors, then through the dining area to the restrooms near the main entrance. I walked from the showroom through the double doors to the restaurant area. As I entered the dining room, I was immediately stopped and ushered back into the showroom by two Middle Eastern guards who rudely informed me I was intruding on a private affair. To get to the restroom, I was told I would have to exit the stage door, walk around the outside of the building, through the parking lot and re-enter through the front door.

For the rest of the event, everyone attending the Lone Star Shootout would be forced to walk outside, around the building and come back in the front door to get to the restroom. Inside the main entrance, they were met by a row of solemn faced Middle Eastern men standing guard between the restrooms and the entrance to the restaurant. The men were dressed in black suits, each sporting a thick, black mustache and one, long, woolly black eyebrow that lay across their foreheads like a big, black caterpillar.

After using the restroom, blues patrons were immediately ushered back out the front door by the stern-faced Middle Eastern Gestapo.

Blues lovers were furious that our precious Billy Blues had been taken over and occupied by a foreign country. There was nothing any of us could do about it.

Buddy Love, who eventually became our Die Hard Road Manager, was stationed outside the stage door as our Blues Guard. He collected door fees and checked IDs. The stage door, which usually served as the musicians' load-in door, was now the main entrance to the Lone Star Shootout. Good thing it wasn't pouring down rain that day.

Blues lovers are usually very easy-going, but tempers flared that day. I was very proud the blues people showed respect to the Middle Eastern wedding reception, even though the Middle Easterners openly expressed a great deal of rudeness and disrespect for the HBS event.

From my viewpoint at the bar, I was entertained by the frantic HBS President Steve Sucher. He was engaged in screaming matches with numerous people regarding the wedding reception. Bewildered and angry blues lovers blamed Steve for scheduling an HBS event on the same day as the reception. Truth was, the owner purposely sabotaged the HBS event. Steve could have easily got in his car and drove away, but he hung in there like a trooper even though he was catching hell from every side.

Steve spotted me sitting quietly at the bar, sipping my beer and amused by the chaos playing out around me. He forced his way through the crowd in my direction. Gasping for breath and sweating profusely, he stopped in front of me. He was so pissed off I thought he was about to pop a blood vessel. He had just been in a heated verbal confrontation with the owner who gave him and HBS two choices: cancel or shut up and deal with it.

"So what do you wanna do, Steve?"

Gritting his teeth, Steve took a deep breath. He glared toward the wedding reception in the dining room and blurted, "Let's blow 'em outta the goddamn building!"

It took a couple minutes to become clear why Steve was telling *me*, the humble amplifier delivery guy, what was going on. No one had thought to arrange for a stage manager and stage crew. Apparently Wizard had been fired. The new soundman was freaking out over the magnitude of the event and was about to walk off the job.

Through Steve's insistence, I reluctantly agreed to be the stage manager. This meant that I was a crew of *one*. I went from sipping a cold beer and minding my own business to being in charge of the confusion and chaos onstage.

I was suddenly responsible for everything that had to be moved in, moved out, moved on, moved off and moved around the stage. Everything had to be properly placed, propped up, and leaned back, with chords moved, taped down and plugged in, mics and mic stands put in proper positions, any faulty equipment identified and removed and all gear had to be sound-checked. For the next hour I was a sweaty grunt, crawling around on my hands and knees on stage. Whew! Now that the soundman had me there to do the stage duties, he decided to stay. All he had to do was sit behind the soundboard and turn knobs.

There were six different bands and at least a dozen special guests. All arrived with bad attitudes and inflated egos. My experience with hosting live radio shows, TV productions, jam sessions and the *Texas Blues Showcase* kicked in. I went on automatic pilot.

Every musician in the show bitched, griped, moaned, complained and yelled at me about *everything*. I had expected true professionalism from the Austin A-team musicians, but I was disappointed to see most were egotistical, arrogant assholes consumed with their own self-worth. Believing I was just a common laborer hired to move their equipment, they talked down to me like I was an ignorant field hand. Several musicians took great pride to inform me they had once played with Stevie Ray Vaughan, expecting me to be impressed enough to kiss their ass and do their bidding. "When I played with Stevie, we did it like this, blah, blah, blah…" Finally I had enough of their holier-than-thou bullshit.

Since they all looked too old, too worn out and too fucked up to fight, I barged into their group conversation on the deck next to the stage door and yelled, "Hey!"

They all turned, looking annoyed by my intrusion. I started handing out my business cards. "I'm a musician just like ya'll and I'm not taking any more of ya'll's shit! I don't care who the fuck you are, who you played with or where you're from. You're here now and I'm not your fuckin' flunky! I'm with the Houston Blues Society, and we're the ones *paying* you. Now, unless ya'll wanna move your own shit, how 'bout showing a little more respect to all us folks trying to help you do a good show here today?"

Things got real quiet for a moment, then they went right back to jabbering amongst themselves as if I'd never said a word. Although they pretended not to hear me, nobody crossed me the rest of the day. I still had to contend with the cantankerous attitudes and egos of the stars of the show. Lonnie Brooks and Long John Hunter were on my ass like chickens on a junebug. They bitched about every detail. They mercilessly expressed their extreme discontent about the amplifiers provided for them.

"That ain't what we ordered!" one of them barked.

"I ain't playing on that shit!" yelled the other.

Already aggravated from dealing with the Austin musicians I snapped. "Gentlemen! You have two choices, play or don't play. I can't squat down and shit you a new amp! These amps are all we have. Take 'em or leave 'em."

Mr. Phillip Walker just smiled from the side of the stage at my predicament. He never said a single unkind word.

The show started right on time. It was fantastic. All the bands were great and the event ran like clockwork. No one could tell the stars had any attitude or any issues with the amps. Everyone played great and the amps sounded fine. The audience cheered every song. Judging from the smiles on the performers faces, everybody was happy.

After the show, Mr. Phillip Walker, a true blues legend, presented himself as a true gentleman as well. He handed me his card and shook my hand. He thanked me for a great time and for my assistance on stage. In fact, he told me to look him up if I ever got out to California. I was honored.

Two of the Austin musicians approached me with a handshake and few kind words which changed my negative attitude toward them. They were Antone's Records session guitarist extraordinaire Derek O'Brien and Texas Tornadoes/Delbert McClinton drummer Ernie Durawa. Both men are top-notch Texas musicians and both are super nice guys. They thanked me for my help and suggested I visit them in Austin.

A few months later, in the fall of 2000, Billy Blues closed forever.

At the time of writing this story, the "Smoke Sax" still stands tall on Richmond Avenue as a monument to the Blues and to the short-lived glory of what could have been.

Long live the blues!

*Eastmart Blues Festival indoor stage. Houston, 1993. Stage, l to r: singer unknown; Thurman "P-Funk" Robinson, bass; Barbara Pope, singer; drummer, unknown; me. The stage was the old loading dock and the walls became the "Eastmart Wall of Fame" that all musicians signed when they performed.*

*Eastmart Blues Festival, outdoor stage. 1993. Left: Chris Gould, aka Professor Blues, RIP. Above, l to r: Ray Kelton, bass; drummer unknown; Vanessa, singer; me.*

*Bottom three photos, l to r: One of the 80-lb. concrete flagpole stand that fell on the stage; Me making fun of myself – my picture was on the poster yet I had to wade through garbage every week to get to the stage door. Two photos by Thurman "P-Funk" Robinson.*
*All other Eastmart Photos Courtesy Deborah McAllister*

*From top, l to r: Me, A.J. Fee and Russell Shelby standing
on top of my van at Michael's Ice House, 1995.
Me and the official drink of the Die Hards, Jose Cuervo
A.J. Fee showing his Die Hard ink.
Partyin' on top of the bar at Michael's Ice House
with Linda the waitress. Russell's drum fell off the bar
after this picture was taken.
Me and A.J. jamming on the bar at Michael's. I'm doing my
show-off "Danny Gatton beer-bottle-slide" trick.
It was always a party at Michael's Ice House.
Pictures courtesy Deborah McAllister.*

*From top, l to r clockwise: Me, Stevie Wilson on drums and Chinese Bluesman Rick Lee playing the One Tongue Blues; Me with Slaven from Croatia; Me and Dave Miller, writer for North of the Border Magazine; The Blues Brothers Tributaires – Biff Cole and Charlie Taylor; One of the greatest soul-blues singers of all time in his trademark overalls, Bo Young. Drummer behind Bo is Dwayne Warnock.*

*Slaven and Bo Young photos courtesy Deborah McAllister.*

*The International Blues Band, Billy Blues, January 1994.*
*Nuri Nuri (Jerusalem), bass; Gene Kelton (representing the white folks); Pierre Stoot (Louisiana),*
*accordian; Osama Raad (Lebanon), drums; Rick Lee (third-generation Chinese-American), guitar;*
*David Brown (Native American Souix/Creek Indian), guitar.*

*From top to bottom, l to r: Houston Blues Society President Steve Sucher at my CD Release Party for*
*Most Requested at Cactus Music, Houston, 2000; Die Hard drummer Dennis Forbes;*
*The Die Hard crowd at Billy Blues. Billy Blues debut of Tha' Lady D with the Professor Blues Band.*
*Opposite page: The Billy Blues sign and the infamous Smoke Sax.*
*Photos courtesy of Deborah McAllister*

# BOOK SIX

# The Notorious Keitons

## THE NOTORIOUS KELTONS

In January of 1995 my band was riding high as a top regional band when suddenly, without warning, both my bass player and drummer quit at the same time. Overnight I was without a band. My search for new players was futile. All the good players in my genre who could play full time were already working.

During that same time, my ex-wife had been calling me for months saying our two teenage sons, who had lived with her all their lives, were both out of school and refused to get jobs or help around the house. She said they slept all day and stayed up all night running with their hoodlum friends and practicing with their rock band. Her desperate request was, "Pleeeesse! Take 'em! Take 'em! Take 'em!"

My sons' band, Chaotic Order, was a hot little rock band with a large following of teenage groupies in Liberty County. They packed the local skating rink every time they played there, but like most young rock bands they were wrought with, well, *chaos*.

Jamie was nineteen years old. He was a hot lead guitarist and an excellent bass player. Sid was seventeen years old and a damn good drummer. He'd been subbing for me on drums since he was fourteen. Both boys had been sitting in with my band when they came for weekend visits, so they knew most of my material. I knew they were good musicians.

Since I needed a band and their mom wanted them out of her house, I made the boys an offer. They could move to Houston, live with me and play bass and drums in my band. I offered to pay them $50 a night per gig, plus free room and board with kitchen privileges. But, there were rules. They would have to help out around the house, clean up after themselves and wash their own clothes.

You'd think two unemployed young musicians would jump at the chance to step into a ready-made job with a top band, but not them. They hem-hawed around for two weeks before reluctantly accepting my offer. My sons moved in with me on the northwest side of Houston around the first week of February. I bought Jamie a new bass guitar and a used amp. I bought Sid a set of used drums. We started practicing right away. From the get go, it was *hell*.

With the exception of weekend visitations and summer vacations, we hadn't lived together as father and sons since Jamie and Sid were seven and five years old. At nineteen and seventeen the boys were young men, with attitudes and ideas of their own. After so many years of being just a weekend dad, I was hoping to reconnect with my sons. I naively thought we'd live happily ever after like a '50s sitcom.

The boys turned out to be notorious young rebels with short tempers and hair triggers. Living with those two young guns was like living with a couple of pissed-off red wasps. The slightest thing set them off like nitroglycerin. I'd never seen that side of them. I had my work cut out for me in more ways than one.

Both boys were in the habit of sleeping until 2pm every day. While living with their mother they'd watch TV, smoke cigarettes and drink coffee until dark, and then play music until daylight.

The boys had gotten used to their mother doing all the household chores. They refused to do anything I asked. To their utter disdain I changed all that.

I rolled them out of bed by 9am with the stereo blasting. I shoved coffee in their faces and had them practicing by 11am for eight hours a day seven days a week. They hated me for it. We fought like pit bulls, verbally of course, but at times I wondered if the young bucks were going to gang up and whup ol' Dad's ass.

Not only did I have to be their employer and band leader, I was still Dad. In a situation like that, its hard to draw the line between family and business. Living under the same roof for the first time in many years and practicing together every day, caused family business and band business to become intertwined. Every family discussion ended in a heated argument about the band. Every band discussion ended in a heated argument about a family matter.

Pissed off attitudes were brought to the practice sessions. If I raised hell about them leaving dirty dishes in the sink, they raised hell because I rolled them out of bed earlier than they were used to. Disagreements about song arrangements mixed with arguments about housekeeping. I expected them to clean up after themselves. I didn't allow smoking in the house. Whenever I found ashtrays running over and dirty dishes or fast food wrappers laying around, I'd put the trash in their beds. When they pulled back the covers of their unmade beds and found their sheets covered with cigarette butts, dirty dishes and trash, the fight was on.

I told them if I had to pick up after them, then they were gonna pick up after me, especially if they wanted to sleep in a clean bed. They finally got the message. Tuff love. I believe in it.

Though the official band name was still Gene Kelton & The Die Hards, people quickly realized we were definitely *not* the Partridge Family. We were called "Flesh & Blood" for awhile, but we soon changed the name to "The Notorious Keltons."

After two months of grueling seven-day-a-week practice sessions, I felt The Notorious Keltons were ready to take the new band out for a test drive. A friend got us our first gig at a small beer joint/bait shop on the east side of Lake Houston called Evan's Camp. I'd never heard of it and didn't know what to expect.

Evan's Camp would turn out to be the first of many *Gigs From Hell* we would have as The Notorious Keltons.

## EVAN'S CAMP: THE FIRST GIG FOR THE NOTORIOUS KELTONS

It was getting dark and a light drizzle fell as we turned off the pavement and descended into the thick, dark East Texas jungle somewhere north of Huffman, Texas. We drove down a maze of winding, muddy back roads trying to decipher directions given to me by a very drunk customer who had answered the phone earlier that day at Evan's Camp.

Lost in the pitch-black undergrowth of the swampy backroads, the area looked like a third-world country. Most of the housing in the area in 1995 was either dilapidated camper trailers or make-shift shanties that appeared to be made from scrap lumber, sheets of tin and old road signs. Many roofs were covered with tarps.

Finally, we found Evan's Camp.

In the dim, misty glow of naked light bulbs dangling from the moss covered trees, the dreary-looking building appeared to be several smaller buildings that had been shoved together.

I parked the van in the mud next to a few mud-splattered ATVs. We could see from the vans headlights that the gravel driveway continued past the building down to a natural boat ramp to a swampy inlet a couple hundred feet away. We could see people with flashlights trying to pull their small fishing boats out of the water before the heavy rain began.

After carefully considering the situation, I reluctantly bailed out of the van and went in. The place smelled like cigarette smoke and dead fish. The concrete floor was covered with mud. The place had apparently started off as a bait camp many years before where fishermen could stock up on supplies before embarking on a day on the lake. Somehow it evolved into a beer joint that happened to sell fishing supplies.

Evan's Camp consisted of three rooms built in a row like a trailer house. The front room was a full-fledged beer bar with tables and chairs and a jukebox playing vintage honky-tonk country music. The back room housed a pool table and served as a storeroom for cases of beer which were stacked along the walls.

We were instructed to set up in the middle room which was the bait room. Anyone going between the bar and the pool room had to walk through the bait room. It was 10x10 with a large double sink, a couple of refrigerators, brooms stashed in the corner and a big, open gurgling water tank filled with live minnows.

The room reeked of dead fish.

I set up next to the side entrance and had to deal with people coming in and out all night, tracking mud on my guitar cords. Sid's drums were set up next to the pool room door. People going back and forth between the pool room and the bar had to walk right between Sid and me. Jamie was set up in the far corner opposite me and next to the stinking minnow tank.

Sid and I had limited visibility through the doorway to the front room where customers sat. Jamie had no visibility of anything except the room we were in.

As we neared start time, the place filled to capacity with people who lived in those little make-shift shanties we'd passed. Denim overalls, yellow rain jackets, camouflage clothing, orange hunter's vests and mud-covered rubber boots were accepted dress for the evening.

Somehow we managed to start The Notorious Kelton's first musical adventure on time. For the next three hours we rocked the joint playing southern rock and blues.

My sons were excellent musicians and took to my style of music naturally. They did a great job considering this was our first paying gig together. I had crammed a lot of music in their heads in a short time.

As the night wore on we made a lot of mistakes, which was to be expected for a first-time gig. I attributed our mistakes to the distractions of an inconvenient setup, the stinking fish smell, unpleasant working conditions and an unappreciative audience. The whole situation was affecting our attention span and draining us of energy.

Evan's Camp was a good trial run before I booked high-profile shows. If we made a mistake no one would notice or give a shit. I knew this gig would bond us and make us stronger. Anything we did after this would be easy.

Every time we ended a song the crowd would sit stone-faced and silent with no response at all. Nothing! Blank faces stared back at me through the doorway. About the third set, the crowd began to get real drunk and real mean. The heckling began.

"Play some kunt-tree! Play some kunt-tree! Don't 'chall know inney kunt-tree?"

We ignored them and kept on rockin'.

A big redneck in overalls yelled, "We ain't a buncha fuckin' niggers! Play some old Hank!"

We ignored him and kept on rockin'.

The bartender stuck her head around the door and yelled, "Play some country, goddammit! These people don't wanna hear that fuckin' shit!"

We ignored her and kept on rockin'.

In between songs, the crowd started beating on the tables with their fists, ashtrays, beer bottles and whatever else they could find to make noise with. They chanted at the top of their lungs, "No more nigger music! No more nigger music! No more nigger music!"

Sid looked up at me from his drum stool with a very puzzled look. "Dad, what are they talking about? We're not playin' rap!" (in reference to the "nigger music" accusations.)

The moment he said that, inside my head the noise in the room went totally silent like a movie dream sequence. I stared at my son in disbelief. His simple yet profound statement made me realize I had never explained to my sons that the blues songs we were playing were of black origins.

My boys had grown up listening to me and my white musician friends play songs by B.B. King, Jimmy Reed, Muddy Waters and others. We were the boys' only point of reference when it came to those songs. In their minds, how could we be playing "nigger" music? I realized I needed to have a long talk with my boys about the history of the blues if we ever got out of this place alive.

"Get the fuck outta here, you buncha fuckin' freaks!"

I snapped out of my brief daydream.

A screaming cuss fight broke out in the front room between people who liked our music and the rednecks who were calling us names. From the bait room we heard the sound of chairs hitting the floor as people jumped up ready to fight while others were trying to get out of the way of flying beer bottles. People were shaking their fists at us and giving us the finger.

Jerry Springer would have been proud.

The boys were as white as ghosts and their eyes were as big as saucers. In a flash I remembered how they used to pour over rock magazines, dreaming of being rock stars and being worshipped by legions of voluptuous groupies. I remembered their skating rink gigs with their high school rock band surrounded by screaming little teeny-boppers.

Here they were, with *me*, playing their first gig as professional musicians in the muddy armpit of hell, being cussed at, screamed at and threatened by a pissed-off lynch mob of drunk backwoods rednecks who wanted to kick our ass. The boys never knew bands were treated like this.

I yelled at them, "Welcome to the real world of rock 'n roll boys! This is what's called payin' yer dues! Now crank it up and let's kick some ass!"

For the next hour we rocked loud and hard, not allowing any dead space between songs and not giving the rednecks a chance to yell at us.

At quitting time, I ordered the boys to load up as fast as possible before shit hit the fan. I headed for the bar, expecting to have a serious problem collecting our paltry $200.

I was surprised when the barmaid shoved the full amount of money at me. As I counted out the money she glared at me and said, "Ya'll ain't never playin' here no more. I know all the places round here whut hires bands and ah'm gon' ta see to it that ya'll don't play no-whurs round here."

With my money in my hand I replied "Thanks, lady, you be sure and do that. You'll be doing me a favor."

The boys, anxious to get out of that shithole, were already loaded and standing at the van when I returned with the money. We jumped in the van and hauled ass before the rednecks came outside looking for us. When we finally reached the highway, I breathed a sigh of relief. I was thankful we got through that experience without any of us getting hurt.

Regardless of the circumstances, we had played our first official gig together as a band. We rocked 'em pretty good and certainly left an impression. I was very proud of my sons. Technically, they did everything right but they still lacked the confidence and grit that only comes with on-the-job experience.

Even though Jamie and Sid were above-average musicians, they were still young and not at the level of musical maturity I was accustomed to. It would take years of seasoning to bring them up to my level. I had two choices. I could either send them out into the world to sink or swim like I did. Or, I'd have to slow down, wait for them and work with them, teaching them so they could catch up with me. It would take at least two more years of grueling practice sessions and hard, steady gigging to accelerate their musical growth to earn the respect of our peers and be serious contenders in the music business, not just a father-son novelty act. It meant dragging them into every beer joint, hell-hole icehouse and honky-tonk imaginable, four to five nights a week, for them to mature musically and become polished professionals.

I knew the time would come when the call of the wild would take them away from me and they would go out into the world chasing their own rock 'n roll dreams. I decided that being with my sons at that moment in our lives was far more important to me than anything else in the world.

I had already lost out on too much of Jamie and Sid's young lives being divorced from their mother and a being part-time, weekend Dad. I didn't want to miss this last once-in-a-lifetime chance to experience their youth with them, to perform with them and guide them into manhood and their chosen career – the music business. I knew they had the talent, all we had to do was mold it. These thoughts were spinning in my head as we pulled into an all-night gas station in Huffman, Texas.

Little did I know the night still held another memorable event for The Notorious Keltons.

## Gas Station Cowboys

After escaping from Evan's Camp, my sons and I headed for the nearest beacon of civilization, which happened to be a Chevron station at the corner of Highway 2100 and FM 1960 in Huffman. Around 1:30am, we pulled in and parked around the side. I went in the station to get some cold drinks, snacks and change to pay the boys. Jamie and Sid hung out by the van to smoke a cigarette.

When I rounded the corner of the building on the way back to the van, the sight I saw sent a wild streak of fury up my spine. It was the first time I could recall feeling my natural, protective "papa bear" instincts kick in full force.

Three young cowboys, complete with ten-gallon hats, license plate size belt buckles and John Wayne attitudes, were about to jump Jamie and Sid.

Two cowboys squared off around Jamie, next to the van. Sid was pinned against the building by the third guy who was twice his size and giving him a serious cussing out about something.

I thought the cowboys followed us from Evan's Camp, but I didn't remember seeing them there. I then figured they were some redneck boys looking for a good fight on a Saturday night who thought my two long-haired sons standing in the parking lot were fair game.

It was all I could do to keep from throwing a body slam on a couple of those guys. Then again, I couldn't rescue my grown sons all the time. I needed to leave them some room to get out of the situation on their own with some dignity.

Very nonchalantly I walked past the group and said, "Howdy boys, looks like ya'll are out for a little fun this evening."

The cowboy pressing Sid against the wall replied, "This ain't nunna yer fuckin' business! This is 'tween me and this piece a shit! I'm gone whup his fuckin' ass!"

"If anybody's gonna do any ass whuppin' round here tonight, it's gonna be *me*," I replied.

I opened the driver's side door of the van, reached behind the seat and pulled out the aluminum baseball bat I carry for just such festive occasions. The young cowboys must have thought I was going for a gun. The moment I turned around with the baseball bat in my hand, they jumped into their pickup truck. The screaming tires left a cloud of blue smoke in the air as the truck fishtailed across the intersection. They shot us the finger as their taillights disappeared into the darkness.

My boys and I stood there laughing and returned their parting gesture. "They ain't so damn tough when you show 'em a baseball bat," I said. "Now, one of ya'll wanna tell me what that was all about?"

The boys reluctantly confessed to knowing the cowboys from Liberty and there had been some bad blood between them. When the cowboys spotted Jamie and Sid standing in the parking lot, they were out to settle an old score.

I never did find out exactly what the old score was, but I heard rumors about a girl.

## WELDERS IN THE BUSHES

It was a miserably hot summer afternoon in July 1995 when Jamie, Sid and I arrived at the Rambling Bushes Club in Pasadena to do an early afternoon setup and sound check.

It's always been my routine to set up equipment at a venue during the day when there are fewer people to contend with and it's easier to get a good parking space to unload. That way we can return to the gig that evening looking like professional entertainers instead of a crew of sweaty furniture movers.

A blast of ice-cold air hit me as I opened the door and stepped inside the Rambling Bushes. I told the day manager behind the bar we were there to set up the band for that night's performance. She just nodded.

The only customers at that time in the afternoon were four large, rough looking construction workers in their early fifties sitting at the end of the bar. Noticing their starched khaki uniforms and skull caps, I figured they were welders. It was not uncommon to see construction workers of every craft hanging out in a bar in the middle of the day in Pasadena, where refinery crews worked rotating shifts 24/7.

With longnecks in hand, they turned around to see what I was doing. I propped open the front door and we started bringing in band equipment. Within seconds one of the welders yelled, "Shut the goddamn door! You're letting all the cold air out!"

Another one piped in, "We didn't come here to sweat our fuckin' ass off! Shut the goddamn door!"

"We'll be through in a minute, fellas," I yelled back.

They yelled at the bartender, "What the hell is this shit? We come in for a cold beer and gotta put up with a buncha fuckin' hippies lettin' the a/c out! This is bullshit!"

The beer, combined with their redneck attitudes, had them all worked up. They continued their verbal assault on us calling us hippies and queers. "Hey, why don't ya'll go somewhere and suck each others dicks, you long-haired pieces of shit!"

"C'mere 'n suck my dick, you little bitch!" one yelled.

The welders all burst out laughing.

My angry glances only fueled their laughter.

Jamie and Sid had grown up believing everything they had seen on MTV where musicians were treated as gods. Working for me they were getting a taste of the real world of the struggling, starving musician and what the music business was really like.

The boys looked at me to see what I was going to do about the barrage of vulgar insults.

"Boys, welcome to the music business! This is exactly the way it was back when I first started playing. Elvis, Willie Nelson and all the famous musicians went through this same shit on their way to the top. Look at it this way. When you're gettin' cussed out, you know you're on the same path. Just hang in there and keep your cool. We'll drown 'em out with a sound check and get the hell outta here."

Within a few minutes we were ready for the sound check and I asked the bartender to turn off the jukebox. We quickly ran through several songs. In between songs, the redneck welders continued to entertain themselves by trying to out-do one another with non-stop verbal assaults directed toward us.

With the sound check over, I put my guitar in its case and told the boys to stay on the stage. I walked to the bar and stood face to face with the biggest welder in the bunch. He was as big as Hulk Hogan and could have easily killed me with one crashing blow.

Realizing I was probably going to get my ass kicked in front of my sons, I looked Hulk square in the eye and said, "Hey, mister, we ain't queers and we ain't hippies. Those two young men over there are my sons. I don't appreciate ya'll calling us queers. We're just trying to make a livin'!"

I was prepared to be knocked on my ass. To my surprise, the room fell silent. The other men watched to see if ol' Hulk was going to knock the shit out of me.

Hulk glared at me. I was terrified, but stood completely still. Then, he slightly bowed his head, squinted his eyes, rubbed his chin, and in a very humble tone he whispered, "Them's yer sons?"

"Yeah. They're nineteen and seventeen, and they work for me. We're working men just like you guys. Only difference is we play music for a living. You called us queers and hippies? Hell, man, even Willie Nelson's got hair down to his ass and he ain't a queer or a hippie. You like Willie, right?"

You could have heard a pin drop.

Hulk stared straight at me. His chest began to heave as he took a few slow, deep breaths. His big nostrils flared like a angry bull. His jaws flexed and he pressed his lips together tight. I'm sure his friends expected him to slap me silly.

I gritted my teeth, waiting for him to charge at me. Instead, his eyes welled with tears. He slowly reached out to me with his giant, leathery hand which was as big as a baseball glove. He clasped his sausage-sized fingers around my hand. In a low, slow, apologetic voice he murmured, "Sir, I am so very, very sorry. I didn't know them was yer sons up there."

He turned to his buddies and snarled, "Ya'll shut the fuck up 'bout this man! Them's his sons up there playing with 'em!"

"What? His sons? No shit!"

Hulk threw his big, tree trunk-sized arms around me in a bear hug. "Man, I'm so sorry, please forgive me. I been drankin' and I let my big mouth get away from me. I'd never insult a man's children on purpose."

The other men also started apologizing.

"We'd like to meet yer sons."

I called Jamie and Sid to the bar. In an instant they were beside me like two young soldiers ready to defend their ol' man, not knowing if we were about to be in a gang fight with a bunch of rednecks or if they were going to have to carry me out.

The boys looked surprised when the men started their shaking hands, hugging them and apologizing for the nasty things they'd said. Hulk looked at both boys, put his huge hands on their shoulders and delved out a big dose of his own fatherly wisdom.

"Boys, we didn't know ya'll was father and sons when we went to tawkin' shit. We're sorry. Yo' daddy come up here and jumped our ass on ya'll's behalf. Takes a big man to stand up for his family and we respect him for that."

Big tears streamed down his face as he continued. "You boys got it made playing music in this nice cool building here with yer daddy. My boy is thirty years old and he's out there right now swinging a sledgehammer in that hot sun. It kills me to see him have to do that cause there ain't a goddamn thing I can do to help him. If ya'll stick with yer daddy here, he'll never steer you wrong. It's a wonderful thing ya'll can play music together. Me and my boy? Shit. We can't hardly talk without fightin'."

One of the other men stepped forward and apologized while he cleaned his glasses and wiped away his tears. He also shook our hands and hugged us. After composing himself he said, "I buried my oldest boy last year. He was almost thirty. He got on them goddamn drugs when he was a teenager and I was never able to get him off. We tried everything. I can't play music, but I think if I'd a spent more time with him (he began to cry) when he was younger, if I'd a-took him fishin' or somethin' – (he was sobbing) – maybe he'd still be here today."

He threw his arms around me. "Stay by your boys, and you boys, ya'll stay by your Dad!"

It was a strange feeling, hugging and sobbing with total strangers in a honky-tonk when just a few minutes before they were cussing at us.

Hulk looked at me. "One dad to another, would you let me buy your boys a beer, and would ya'll mind doing a couple more songs for us 'fore ya'll leave?"

We returned to the stage. For the next hour the men sent more beer to the stage than we could drink. We performed a one-hour concert for the formerly hardened redneck welders who now watched our performance with a whole new appreciation. They clapped and cheered enthusiastically at every song. It was a very spiritual experience.

We left feeling as though something very profound had happened. I personally felt as though I had been baptized. The four hardened rednecks were crying like babies because I was performing with my sons.

I realized right then and there Jamie, Sid and I had something very special that touched people in a unique way. I didn't know what *it* was, but whatever *it* was, *it* was a good thing.

Now, if we could only keep it *together*.

## Madness At Magnolia

The Magnolia Bar and Grill in Houston has always featured live bands outside on their deck when the weather permits. In Houston, that's about nine months out of the year.

Located at the corner of the very busy intersection of Richmond Avenue and Fountainview, bands performed on a triangle-shaped stage with their backs to the street, putting Richmond Avenue about thirty feet to their left and Fountainview thirty feet to their right. The large deck could accommodate about a hundred people.

The Magnolia was big on print advertising. Bands not only got alot of exposure in local music magazines, but with thousands of vehicles passing during the week the bands got great exposure on their big marquee. The pay was always a little better than average so performing at The Magnolia was always a high-profile, well-paying gig coveted by Houston bands.

In the fall of 1995, The Notorious Keltons were elated to land an unheard of open-ended gig every Friday night at The Magnolia. No band had landed a house gig there before.

We always arrived at the beginning of afternoon rush hour to set up for the 6pm gig. The traffic noise was unreal as Friday afternoon traffic rolled by only a few feet from the stage. Motorcycles revved their engines and blasted off like rockets from the intersections. Big, sluggish city buses would roar deep, painful moans while struggling to gain momentum. Westbound buses would blow smoke all over us. Lowriders, sitting at the intersection with high-wattage sound systems, jarred the fillings out of our teeth with their boom-ba ba-boom! ba-ba-boom! Every other car was laying on their horn for some reason.

People passing by thought it was funny to roll their windows down and yell "Fuuuuuucckk yooouuuuuuu!" at the band and the customers sitting at outdoor tables.

On our first night, friends, fans and customers filled the seats. My sons and I had a reputation for rockin' out at some very rowdy east Harris County juke-joints and weren't about to be drowned out by motorcycles, buses, car horns and disrespectful drive-by hecklers. We cranked up the volume with the intention of giving our fans what they came for, a kick-ass, high-energy show.

As soon as we kicked off, a waitress came running to the stage yelling, "Turn it down! Turn it down!" She disappeared before we finished the song. We turned down, but soon she was back again, and again, and again.

The rest of the night was a nightmare. We tried to play at a volume deemed acceptable by the management. I was extremely embarrassed every time a waitress was sent to reprimand *me*, a professional musician, in front of my fans. For the next few weeks we played at lounge-act level and drowned out by traffic noise. Joni even created and distributed t-shirts to our fans that said "Turn It Up!" on the front and "No Dinner Blues!" with a red circle with a line through it and on the back.

Finally one night I'd had enough of the street noise, the smart-mouthed waitresses, the management's constant harassment and our fans yelling "turn it up!" I turned my amp around facing the street, turned it up to ten and told Jamie and Sid to kick it in the ass.

We rocked out as my amp cut the heads off people in the intersection waiting for the light to change. They rolled their windows up as fast as they could. Crotch rockets tried to compete by revving their engines, but the light would change and they'd disappear like a shot. Our fans loved our defiant performance and patrons of the pizza joint across the street were dancing in the parking lot.

With my wireless guitar transmitter, I jumped over the rail of the deck, walked onto the median on Richmond and challenged the honking cars. Fans on the deck cheered me on.

Returning to the stage I saw the general manager standing inside the restaurant glaring at me from behind the plate glass window. He motioned me to come to his office. The audience thought it was funny when I told them I had to go to the principal's office to take my licks for playing too loud.

The general manager was mad as hell. He scolded me like a small child.

"What the hell did I tell you about playing too loud? We have a sound ordinance, *blah, blah, blah...*"

I was pissed to the tenth power. I had already heard his lecture about the sound ordinance. The street noise was louder than the band. There were kids walking by with boom boxes on their shoulders that were louder than the band. Car horns and radios were louder than the band! The general manager knew what kind of band we were when he hired us and I didn't need a food and beverage guy telling me how to play and entertain my fans.

My argument did not matter to him.

"Play the way I tell you or get out!" he commanded.

I needed the money from the guaranteed weekly gig so we decided to try to muddle through until I found another one. We turned down the volume until we were barely audible over the street noise. My fans were pissed. They drove from all parts of the city and paid big bucks for high dollar food just to be bombarded by street noise and to barely hear us. They wanted to rock!

The following week as we were setting up, a skinny blond marched to the bandstand. Without even a proper introduction she announced, "I'm the new manager and I've already heard all about you. If you get too loud, you're fired!"

With that, she made an abrupt about-face and marched off. I told Jamie to turn his bass rig down to where only he could hear it. Sid has a foot that kicks like a mule so I told him not to use the kick drum or the cymbal and to play only rim shots.

We were all pissed. You may wonder why musicians get pissed when they can't play as loud as they want. Is it just an ego trip? Power trip? No. It depends on the occasion and style of music being played. Some bands are geared to play at a low volume for background purposes and that's fine, but don't hire a freight train when all you need is a hearse. Our equipment is designed to perform properly at higher energy levels.

Another week went by. The new little blond manager turned out to be a tyrant on her own power trip. Every time a car went by with the boom box thumping, she would come running out to the deck thinking it was the band.

Finally I had enough of her charging across the deck and embarrassing me by sticking her boney little finger in my face in front of my audience. The next time she approached the stage and started her schpiel, I shouted, "We quit!"

Surprised by my announcement she yelled, "You can't quit, look at all these people! We'll lose our clientele!"

"First, you threaten to fire us. Then tell us we can't quit! Lady, I was playing music before you were shittin' yella and I'll be goddamned if some kid is gonna tell me how to play!"

I turned to the band. "Roll up, boys. Let's get the hell outta here!"

I ripped my guitar from my shoulder. The manager took my sudden and unexpected gesture as an act of aggression and ran like hell. Moments later the armed guard who watched the parking lot approached me with a very serious look on his face.

The guard was a big, fat, white guy in his mid-thirties, obviously suffering the ill effects of too many donuts. During our stint at the Magnolia, he usually hung out in the shade at the edge of the deck sipping a Diet Coke. He always joked around with the band as we were setting up. Since the arrival of the new manager, I noticed he never hung out in the shade anymore. Instead he was constantly pounding a beat in the parking lot. His jovial smile and friendly demeanor was gone. The hot afternoon sun had him sweating his ass off.

The guard started interrogating me in a very official, police-like manner. "Did you use profanity on the young lady? Did you threaten her in any way?"

"Look, dude, I didn't say shit to her except I quit. And, just like you, I'm tired of her shit. She don't let you hang out in the shade anymore, does she?"

"No," he replied.

"She's making you walk a beat in the hot sun in the parking lot, right?"

"Yeah," came his humble reply.

I could see the manager gleefully watching us from the corner of the building, expecting her "hired boy" to do her bidding and slap me in handcuffs.

"My friend," I said, "you don't like that bitch any more than I do. You can hang around here and keep taking her shit if you want to, but we're outta here. You can go back and tell her that you chewed my ass out and threatened to have me arrested or whatever you want to say, I don't care. If you'll just back off, I'll get my gear loaded and we'll be out of your life forever in about fifteen minutes."

He knew I was right. He also knew if he wanted to keep his job he'd have to report something to the manager. For a few moments we stood silently staring at each other. Finally he winked and stepped back out of our way. He said, "You guys get outta here as quick as you can." I knew that meant he would run defense for us until we left.

"Thanks, man," I said.

As we rolled out of the parking lot, the guard and the bitch were on the front sidewalk. I could tell she was ripping him a new ass for letting us go without a fight.

I never set foot back in the Magnolia Bar & Grill again. It closed in the spring of 2010.

## DEEF & THE DUMB PANTY MAN

In 1999, my band was invited as guest performers for a benefit show at a popular Houston blues club called Shakespeare's. Jamie couldn't attend, but, with many bands on the bill that day, Sid and I showed up ready to jam with whoever was available to play bass.

For several hours we watched musicians and bands come and go. We were especially amused by a seventy-something-year-old black bass player who performed with several bands. He sat on a bar stool with one foot firmly planted on the stage and the other on a rung of the stool. He propped his bass guitar on the seat between his legs with the neck sticking straight up in the air like an upright bass.

When the old guy played, he became so excited that he swayed back and forth, so far to the left and right that the headstock of the guitar made a five-foot swath through the air in time with the music. He was so animated with his black shades and big, uninhibited smile that we thought he was drunk. We expected him to go flying off the barstool with every beat.

When Sid and I were called to the bandstand, we told the stage manager we didn't have a bass player and would like to borrow one from another band. The old black man was still sitting on his barstool. The stage manager shrugged and said, "Use *him*," and walked away.

Sid and I just looked at each other as if to say "Uh-oh!"

I tuned up, and turned to the old bass player to tell him what we were going to play and what key it was in. He never seemed to acknowledge my presence. He sat staring down at the floor through his dark glasses. He replied to my instructions with a slight nod and an unconcerned, "Uh-huh, uh-huh."

The old man sprang to life when we played a couple of blues standards. So far, so good. The crowd started yelling "My Baby Don't Wear No Panties!" I turned to explain the song to the old bass player and he surprised me. "Oh yeah! I knows dat song! I heared it on da radio."

When he realized I was the guy on the radio, he got real excited. He started yellin', "You's da panty man! You's da panty man! I heared ya on da radio, I can't bleeb I'm playin' wit da *panty man*!"

I cringed at the thought of being stuck with the name "Panty Man" and continued my explanation of the song. "When you see me do this with my guitar (I demonstrated a chopping motion with the headstock of my guitar) that means to *break*."

At that moment the old bass player turned to me for the first time. In a voice loud enough for the whole room to hear he barked, "Boy! Can't 'chu sees I'm a *bliiiind man*?"

The crowd burst into laughter. I must have looked stupid and embarrassed by his announcement. I stepped back and stared at him in awe. That explained his dark glasses and his animated Ray Charles/Stevie Wonder movements on stage that made Sid and I think he was drunk.

I turned to Sid and before I realized what I said, I blurted, "This motherfucker's *bliiind*!"

"I may be blind, but I ain't *deeeef*!" the old bass player snapped back.

I apologized for calling him a "motherfucker" and told him it wasn't personal, I was just surprised that he had fooled me.

"You surprised dat a blind man kin play good as a seein' man?" he asked. "Dey tell's me lotsa folks play wit dey eyes shut, so whuts-sa diffence? You jes play da song and I be's rite in der wit-cha!"

"Okay! Okay!" I said, "I ain't deef either. I'll make you a deal. You don't call me the *Panty Man* and I won't call you *motherfucker*." We both laughed.

Sid clicked his sticks together. The three of us brought the house down with a gut-bucket version of "My Baby Don't Wear No Panties."

## Wadin' In Shit

During the late '90s Jamie, Sid and I performed at least twice a month at a small beer joint in the bayside community of San Leon, Texas, called Ol' Henry's.

In the summertime we performed outdoors on a large patio, which meant dealing with stifling humidity, ravenous mosquitoes and dust. The patio was next to the parking lot made of pulverized oyster shells. Every time a vehicle pulled in or out, clouds of white dust would choke us half to death. The dust would settle on us, our gear, our vehicles and the people sitting at picnic tables, lawn chairs and on the tailgates of pickup trucks.

Most people who attended our shows at Ol' Henry's were a hardy, rowdy lot of shrimpers, fishermen, bikers and pirate-types who lived in the makeshift beach houses in the area. They never seemed to notice the dust, heat and mosquitoes. For those rough folks it was a way of life. Their remedy? More alcohol. *Haaarrrrrr!*

In bad weather we set up indoors. Ol' Henry's didn't have a stage so each time we played we'd be in a different corner of the building.

Once during a summer rainstorm, we were set up just inside the front door which was left wide open. The placed filled up with people, mosquitoes, flies and dogs. That's right, dogs. Stray dogs wandered in to get out of the rain and made themselves at home sleeping underneath the tables. I was amazed at how dogs could sleep while a band played. There's nothing like singing a love song while smelling the stench of a wet dog.

There was a big screen TV on the wall and as we played, someone found a porno channel. The crowd was mesmerized by the action on the TV. The sound was off, but every time we ended a song the room would be stone-cold silent. Everyone was staring at the TV. Finally, someone changed the channel.

Another time on a cold, rainy, winter afternoon, we were told to set up in the back room because the folks in the front room were watching a ball game on the big screen.

We pulled around behind the building to unload. As we rounded the corner, there was a covered flatbed lowboy trailer with an industrial size barbeque pit permanently mounted on it. There were two cooks standing on the trailer tending to the meat. The trailer sat between us and the back door where we had to load in. There was absolutely no moving the trailer.

The back door was blocked by several 55-gallon drums, overflowing with beer bottles, trash, raw chicken parts, rib bones and used paper plates covered with leftover potato salad and meat scraps soaked with barbeque sauce. The stench was sickening.

We had to move trash cans, old tires, car batteries and discarded beer cases in order to clear a path to the back door. Once inside, the back room looked like an old storage room. There was barely enough space for the band.

We began the task of unloading and carrying our gear in the drizzling rain through muddy slop two inches deep, around the barbeque trailer and across the soggy backyard. We had to maneuver our equipment dolly between overflowing trash cans to our so-called showroom.

While dragging a dolly load of equipment, the soggy ground caused the dolly to tilt to one side, and *splat!* One of my monitors tumbled off, falling face down into the disgusting muck. Nasty, brown goo covered the monitor and splattered all over my clothes. I was pissed.

One of the cooks standing on the barbeque trailer cracked up laughing. "Ya better git that cleaned up quick, boy! The sewer is backed up and that box just fell in a puddle a shit! Ha! Ha! Ha! You boys are *really* gonna sound like shit! Ha, ha, ha!"

I was furious. I had no idea we were wading in shit. I was disgusted. The thought hit me about all the shit musicians literally go through to play a gig. They call it payin' yer dues. If I hadn't needed the measely hundred bucks so bad and we hadn't already half-way set up, I would have driven away.

We suffered four hours of pure hell. The gas heater was turned up on high and the air was so hot and stuffy we could hardly breathe. The air on the concrete floor was freezing. We were wet from the rain and our feet were freezing. Our boots were soaked with raw sewage. We were breathing overheated gas fumes from the space heater.

There was no seating in the back room, so we played all night long to nobody. The few customers that came in on that miserable afternoon were in the front watching the game and eating free barbeque. They had no idea it had been cooked over a lake of shit.

I counted down the minutes until we could play our last song and get the hell outta there. I vowed I would never, never, *never* return to Ol' Henry's, nor would I ever again play a gig where I had to fight my way through garbage and literally wade through shit.

And I haven't.

The next day I sprayed the monitor with a water hose, not caring if it ever worked again. I let it dry out for a week. When I plugged it up again, it played great for another five years.

It was a Peavey!

## Free Birds Fly

Through the years, many people have asked me what it was like having my sons in the band and performing with them and if I only hired them because they were my sons.

Parents working with their children is not a new concept. Since the beginning of time parents and children have worked side by side, especially in rural farming communities. Many parents go into business with their adult children or raise their children in the family business to pass it on to them when the time comes.

For some reason, being in show business with your children seems extra special.

Family bands featuring parents and children have always been part of music. The Carter Family, The Kendalls, The Judds, Pops Staples and The Staple Singers, and so on.

I watched Jamie and Sid develop an interest in music from the moment they struggled with their first notes until they were rocking at teenage hangouts with their high school band.

When the time and circumstances were right I offered them a job. I did not hire them because they were my sons. I had a job to do and it had to be done *right*, regardless of who was on stage. I hired my sons because they had the talent, ability and desire to do the job. They were willing and ready when I needed someone to fill empty positions. For me, the fact they were my sons was a bonus. I can't speak for them, but for me, it was an experience of a lifetime I will always cherish.

My years of experience and discipline, combined with their youthful energy, unbridled enthusiasm and talent for putting rock 'n roll arrangements to my blues songs made for a volatile and undeniable combination. We became a force to be reckoned with.

Jamie and Sid were a powerhouse rhythm section and performing with them was like sitting on the front bumper of a runaway train doing 200 mph! It was a rush.

For five years we were The Notorious Keltons. We played together, drank tequila together, raised hell together, fought off those who would fight any one of us and fought each other.

We were an inspiration to many and to each other. We sometimes got cross when weird groupies with twisted minds tried to play us one against another. We often argued about song arrangements. The lines between band leader, employer and Dad criss-crossed and got tangled when tempers flared.

I purposely dragged Jamie and Sid through every sleazy, cut-throat shithole beer joint and dive in an effort to season them for the inevitable journey I knew lay ahead of them. I also took them in the recording studio, put them on television and got them their first movie parts in *The Passage*.

In the fall of 1999, Jamie and Sid and I recorded our first CD together, *Most Requested*. It features them playing on twelve songs. Thanks to their participation and unique arrangements, six of those songs hit #1 on various independent bluesrock charts worldwide.

The January 2001 issue of *Bass Player Magazine* did a write up on Jamie's unique bass pattern on "The Avon Man" on *Most Requested*.

By 2001, Jamie and Sid were tough, experienced, seasoned and restless. It was time for my young freebirds to fly and do their own thing.

It's a treat whenever we get a chance to perform together. The boys have moved on and are busy with their own lives, families and careers. They have a successful music career doing their own original music. I will always cherish those times when my sons and I played together, including our *Gigs From Hell*. I hope they feel the same. I only hope I was a good band leader and a good Dad as well.

I wish them great, great success. Someday, they'll be picking out my old folks home, and I want a damn good one.

*The Notorious Keltons*

*From top, l to r: Sid (1yr)
and Jamie Kelton (4 yrs)
Musicians in the makin', 1979;
Sid on drums, Jamie on bass,
Me (Dad)
Left: Sid
Middle: Jamie (4 years old)*

*Bottom photos: Jamie and Sid
sitting in at Thunder On The Trinity,
Liberty, Texas, 2006.*

*The back cover of the original release of Most Requested, 1999.*
*Jamie and Sid played on twelve of the fifteen songs on the CD.*
*CD Photos by: Joe Faulkerson*

# BOOK SEVEN

# Mean Gene Rocks

## The "Mean Gene" Name

Many people have asked me through the years why I'm called "Mean Gene." After people have met me, they tell me they expected to meet someone 6' 8" and 500 pounds. Some guess I might be a former heavyweight fighter or a professional wrestler. One guy thought I must be an ex-con.

Nope, I'm just lil' ol' me.

The music business has always been filled with performers known by nicknames derived from where they come from, their size, their color, the instrument they play, their style, etc. "Blind Lemon" Jefferson, "Smokey" Robinson, "Fats" Domino, "Texas" Johnny Brown, Joe "Guitar" Hughes, "Muddy" Waters, "Blues Boy" (B.B.) King, Lightnin' Hopkins, Pete "Love You Madly" Mayes, Jimmy "T-99" Nelson, Teddy "Cry Cry" Reynolds and the list goes on.

During the early nineties I noticed more and more people at my shows saying, "Man, you sure play a *mean guitar*." As a musician, that was the greatest compliment I could ever hope to hear. It gave justification to the thousands of hours of practice and the sacrifices it took to be a good player. Knowing there are literally thousands of guitar players half my age that could play circles around me, I would politely say thank you and write it off to the excitement of a show and the alcohol content of the complimenter. *(Complimenter? Is that a word?)*

One night at Billy Blues in the early nineties I was invited to the dressing room by Texas Blues legend Joe "Guitar" Hughes to meet his lifelong friend and fellow Texas Blues legend, Johnny Clyde Copeland. As Mr. Hughes introduced me to Mr. Copeland he said, "I calls 'im Mean Gene, cause he play a mean git-tar."

Mr. Copeland extended his right hand, and with his trademark ear-to-ear smile, simply said, "Well, Mean Gene, pleased ta meet 'cha."

The name stuck.

From that point on, I officially became known as "Mean Gene," a name bestowed upon me by two great Texas Blues Legends I was proud to have known.

## Houston Livestock Show and Rodeo, and The World Championship Barbeque Cookoff

Every year in February, millions of people from all over the world attend the three-week long Houston Livestock Show & Rodeo held in Houston's sprawling Reliant Park. Along with it comes the thousands of vendors hawking everything from belt buckles to cotton candy. A giant carnival is erected in the parking lot that features dozens of thrilling, chilling rides, booths to win prizes like stuffed animals and fun houses full of mirrors.

Next to the carnival is the World's Championship Barbeque Cookoff that lasts about a week. The Cookoff features several hundred cooking teams. When the teams set up in their booths and tents, the parking lot looks like a wild west mining town. Each team tries to win coveted bragging rights as #1. Along with trophies for the best Texas chili or barbeque, showmanship awards are also given.

Many teams build elaborate sets rivaling the most elaborate western movie sets ever created by Hollywood. A booth space may be as small as a 10x10 spot of asphalt barely big enough for a barbeque pit. It may be as spacious as a big top revival tent complete with a temporary floor and able to accommodate several hundred people. Various themes and outrageous costumes add points to the team's efforts.

A few years ago cooking teams started hiring their own bands to perform in their booths to add even more points toward a showmanship award.

Most of the shows we've done at the Cookoff have been inside mid-sized tents that hold about 300 people comfortably and 500 who cram in when it rains. Sometimes we've been lucky enough to play in a tent that has a floor, other times we've had to stand on the asphalt. Only a couple of times have we had a stage. Tents are not heated, meaning we are subject to the chill of the February weather. Most cookoffs are a wet, soggy, ice-cold hell. In Houston, the humidity will cause the damp cold to seep right through you and it's almost impossible to put on enough clothes to stay warm.

No vehicles are allowed on the premises after the gates open to the public around 11am. We were instructed to bring our equipment in early and get the van back out by 10am or the van would have to sit stationary until 4am the next morning. Every year for the next six years, we arrived by 7:30am on Friday to set up for our two-night performance.

Live music stops at 11pm in order to clear the general public off the grounds by midnight. Herding 100,000 people out the gates in an hour is impossible.

Bands are not allowed to bring vehicles in to pick up equipment until after 4am on Sunday. Before leaving Reliant Park we would tear down the equipment and have it ready for load out before making the one-mile hike back to our vehicle. Since I live about thirty minutes from the site, after the gig we usually went home, caught a few hours sleep and went back the following morning around 7:30am to pick up our gear.

**Our First Cookoff**

We performed at our first Cookoff in February of 2000. My first CD, *Most Requested*, had been out for about a month and was getting lots of publicity and airplay all over Houston. I was excited and really looking forward to being associated with the Cookoff, especially the wild parties I'd heard so much about.

What an education we received!

When we arrived to set up at our first Cookoff, guards stopped us at the entrance refusing to let us in because we didn't have a vendor permit. They instructed us to drive to a satellite parking lot about four miles away to obtain a permit from the "permit guy." The permit guy looked at my business card, took my word that I was with a band and made a mark on my windshield in crayon. Evidently that was my official pass into the Cookoff grounds. In all the years I've played this event, I've never seen the permit guy except for that one time. Since then, I just tell the guards at the Cookoff entrance there was no one at the satellite lot and the guards let me in anyway, no questions asked.

Once inside the Cookoff grounds, it was total chaos and confusion. People were frantic, running around like chickens with their heads cut off trying to remedy last minute emergencies in order to get their booths ready before the gates opened.

There was a constant parade of garbage trucks either emptying trash barrels and dumpsters, or delivering even more trash barrels and dumpsters. Porta-can trucks unloaded new porta-cans, and shit-sucking vacuum trucks cleaned used porta-cans. The stench was horrendous.

Pickup trucks towing lowboy trailers delivering building materials attempted to back between the previously mentioned parade of trucks. More pickup trucks delivered ice, firewood, booze, food and breakfast to the crews who stayed all night guarding their booths.

Hundreds of officials were speeding around on golf carts with their plastic-covered cowboy hats, clipboards and official Houston Livestock Show badges trying to look important. I was amazed that the women riding in the golf carts at that early hour in the morning, regardless of age, looked like a million bucks.

Amid the chaos, hundreds of bands were driving around lost, trying to find their booth to set up, do a sound check and get the hell out before the gates closed at 11am.

Cooking booths are numbered and laid out in "streets" side-by-side and back-to-back, like houses in a subdivision. No electricity is provided, so each team must provide their own generators. That means as many as 500 teams have at least 500 gas or diesel generators, ranging from small to industrial size. All 500-plus generators run at the same time throughout the entire event. When the exhaust fumes mix with barbeque smoke and the stench of porta-shitters being cleaned, there is a reeking stench and non-stop, horrendous noise.

Are we having fun yet?

The constant roar of the generators, the rumbling of delivery trucks revving their engines, the "beep, beep, beep" of trucks backing up, horns blowing, traffic directors blowing whistles, people yelling instructions at each other, carpenter saws buzzing and hammers hammering added to the chaos. Just wait until dark when the carnival is roaring full tilt and some 500 bands crank up.

Every booth played country music as loud as possible to drown out the sound of the booth next door doing the same thing. Somewhere a 100,000-watt sound system blasted Eddie Arnold's "Cattle Call" while hundreds of bands did their sound checks.

In the congested "streets" hundreds of people were walking around with cell phones and walkie-talkies, with a finger in one ear, and simultaneously yelling, "What? What?!"

And it was only 8am.

We eventually found our booth, got unloaded, set up, did a sound check and got back out of the gate before the 10am cutoff. After going home to get some rest, we returned that afternoon fighting Houston traffic and trying to get parked in the vendor parking lot by 5pm. Even with our parking pass, we were still parked a mile from the stage. We learned to walk the distance in tennis shoes and put on our boots when we got to the stage.

At exactly 7pm, hundreds of gasoline generators roared to life, providing juice for hundreds of bands who all started cranking out live music at the very same time. Canvas tent material does not contain the sound of generators parked outside tents or the sound of other bands performing only a few feet away. Every time we ended a song, the muffled roar of hundreds of generators and the sound of the band next door invaded our space like a derailed freight train coming through the tent walls. I'm sure we were doing the same thing to them. It was frustrating and annoying to the bands and confusing to the listeners. It caused bands to sound off beat, out of time and out of tune. Basically, everybody sucked. All night, bands fought for sound dominance and by quitting time, every bands' PA systems were maxed out and blowing speakers.

**One Year…**

One year a sudden storm blew through the site while we were setting up our gear. The tent was not yet secured and gusts of wind lifted it up several times about ten feet off the ground. The tent was flapping in the breeze like laundry on a clothesline. The two-inch metal tent poles slammed back into the asphalt like spears, tearing out chunks of the parking lot. We all ran to the center of the tent to keep from being skewered by the poles. A crew of teenage Mexican boys hired as a maintenance crew grabbed onto the poles to hold them down. The wind was so strong it picked the boys up and slung them around like puppets. I just knew one of them was going to be shish-ka-bobbed before it was over.

Another year we didn't have a stage and set up on the asphalt just a few feet away and on the same level as the crowd. People were drunk, whip dancing and falling all over the band. We attempted to barricade the band from the rowdy crowd by tying a rope across the front of the band. Our Road Manager, Buddy Love, with his grizzly bear frame, stood guard in front of the band, literally bumping and maneuvering people out of the way to keep them from knocking over mic stands and monitors.

One year we played standing on the asphalt during a blinding rain storm. Streams of rain, mixed with overflowing porta-cans, ran under our tent. Drunk people danced and splashed about in the puddles of the ice-cold filth. Thanks to the whiskey the audience didn't notice that they were dancing in sewage. Our gear sat in a half-inch of water. I lost three hundred dollars worth of guitar effects pedals. After that experience I refused to play for any team that didn't provide a stage.

One year after a show it was raining so hard that we confiscated clear plastic 55-gallon trash can liners. We cut out holes to see through and wore them like raincoats in an attempt to keep dry on our twenty-minute walk back to our vehicles. Marching into the blinding rain, we must of looked like a bunch of giant condoms.

## Championship Barbeque War Zone

Returning to the site on Sunday morning to pick up equipment is just as hectic as the previous Friday. Total chaos, only *in reverse*. Sunday mornings there are no guards blocking traffic at the gate and vehicles buzz in and out like the Indy 500.

Once again, trash trucks, shit trucks, street sweepers, pickups with trailers, pickups with campers, flatbed trucks, wreckers, RVs, sound company trucks, golf carts and hundreds of band vans are vying for position in the narrow streets to retrieve, move, push, pull, load and haul *something*. People are yelling and cussing each other, horns are blasting, whistles are blowing and gears are grinding. "Beep, beep, beep" is everywhere.

The tent city looks like a war zone in various stages of demolition. Some crews stay up all night tearing down, others arrive early in the morning. All crews have been on location for the past week and everyone is tired, miserable, exhausted, cold, wore out, sore, aggravated, pissed off, short tempered, either still drunk or hungover and ready to fight with anyone for any reason. But, they'll still offer you a cup of coffee with a shot of Jack Daniels just to get the day kicked off right, Texas style!

We eventually worm our way into position at our booth, get loaded and worm our way back out again and onto the freeway. It takes several weeks for the smell of hickory smoke, barbeque and generator fumes to wear off our equipment.

The World's Championship Barbeque Cookoff is a major pain in the ass with all its chaos and difficulties, but it's still one of the greatest parties I've ever played. The gig is always fantastic, the party is always wild and the people are always crazy. Our employers treat us like movie stars. The food is great, the booze is free and the women are hot!

Every year, I swear I'll never, never, never do it again, but by October or November, the phone rings. Once again, I'm ready for another great adventure! *Yeeee-haaaawwww!*

## TROPICAL STORM ALLISON

On June 8th and 9th in 2001, one of the worst tropical storms in history hit southeast Texas. Tropical Storm Allison, a slow-moving mini-hurricane stationed herself over Houston, dumping rain of Biblical proportions. I'll spare you the historical facts and meteorological records, you can research it on the internet, and see some amazing photos of the devastation.

Joni and I had been watching the news and Weather Channel all day Friday. Houston was flooded and more rain was coming. We repeatedly called The Rhythm Room on Washington Avenue inquiring about the show status for that night. Each time the club manager would say, "We're on high ground! We ain't gonna flood, and we ain't canceling! We got tables reserved! Come on in!"

Around 6pm we left Baytown. In a blinding rainstorm, Joni and I headed for The Rhythm Room, north of downtown Houston some 30 miles away. Driving east on I-10, we drove right into the worst of the storm. By the time we reached the Houston city limits, I-10 was covered in a foot of water. Bumper-to-bumper traffic was backed up for miles in both directions. The side roads were flooded and there was no way to get off the freeway to turn around without driving into four feet of water. Stalled and abandoned vehicles lined the roadside. Semi trucks plowed through the deep water like tugboats on the exit ramps.

Our van was loaded with thousands of dollars worth of band equipment, boxes of our newly released CDs and all of our merchandise, and we were stuck in the traffic. The rain was pouring down and the water was rising. We became very concerned about the van, our gear and our lives. We didn't want to be another statistic on the ten o'clock news.

When we crawled across the overpass on I-10, we looked down at the ten-lane 610 East Loop below. The water on the 610 underpass was almost level to the highway on I-10 and hundreds of cars and semi trucks were submerged. That was an incredible sight!

We were constantly on the cell phone, explaining our situation to The Rhythm Room manager. He kept insisting we get to the club any way possible. With rising water threatening to stall us on the freeway with no escape, we had two choices: sit there and drown or take our chances on the side streets. After two hours of crawling along I-10 and traveling less than one mile, we took an off ramp that exited at an incline to an intersection on top of an overpass where we could make a U-turn and head back to Baytown. With I-10 west blocked in flooded downtown Houston, the traffic going back was minimal.

We made our last call to the club manager who was furious that we were not coming. With predictable club manager rhetoric, he shouted, "You'll never work here again!" and slammed down the phone.

That night The Rhythm Room sat empty. How do I know? Even though our drummer Kevin Reed and bass player Mike "Lowboy" Leubner were stranded, our keyboard player Norm Uhl had somehow managed to make it to the gig from his home on the far north side of Houston before the downpour. He arrived two hours early, set up his keyboard and waited. He said no one was there except him and the angry manager who had foolishly insisted we play. Not only did Norm have to deal with the wrath of the pissed-off manager as he loaded his gear in the pouring rain, but he narrowly escaped the fast-rising flood waters.

Joni and I made it back to Baytown.

We turned on the news and saw most of Houston was flooded, the worst in its history. All of downtown and Houston's world-famous Medical Center had as much as eight to ten feet of water, completely crippling the city and the hospitals. Only a few blocks from the Rhythm Room, I-10 looked like the Mississippi River. Hundreds of cars and semi trucks with trailers were completely submerged under ten to fifteen feet of water. Had I complied with the manager's demands, we would've certainly lost the van and thousands of dollars worth of equipment and maybe even our lives.

The only thing we lost was the income from gigs booked at several venues that were completely destroyed, and that never went back in business.

## SEPTEMBER 11, 2001

September 11, 2001, started out to be just another ordinary, late-summer day in our quiet neighborhood in the small, working-class town of Baytown. I got up early to put the trash on the street before the garbage truck came, fed my dogs, poured myself a cup of coffee and turned on the morning news. I was shocked by the horrible images that burst from the TV.

My heart sank as I realized so many innocent people had just been murdered and life as we knew it here in the good ol' USA had changed forever in the blink of an eye.

Like every citizen on planet Earth with a TV, Joni and I sat dazed by the unbelievable scenes. By afternoon we forced ourselves away from the TV to make a necessary trip to the grocery store to stock up. We expected to see stores jammed with people ripping provisions from the shelves like they do when a hurricane threatens the our Gulf Coast area. To our surprise, the stores were deserted. We assumed most people were home watching the news.

While shopping we bumped into some old friends. Fears of whatever lay ahead were evident by their solemn expressions and hollow stares, mirroring our own. Asking "how ya doing" seemed like a stupid question when thousands of fellow Americans lay dead in the aftermath of the attacks and thousands more searched for them while all America grieved.

By day's end on September 11th, booking agents, club owners and promoters from all over the country called, canceling all shows and events all the way through Christmas. All gigs near downtown Houston were canceled for fear airplanes would crash into the skyscrapers. We were suddenly 99% unemployed. Only a handful of local icehouses on the outskirts of the county stayed open, but even they canceled all bands until further notice.

After several weeks of zero cash flow, we finally played our first show at a giant icehouse on the west side of Houston. We were surprised when a couple hundred bikers filled the place just before our show time.

As I stood on the front of the stage with my guitar over my shoulder, prepared to play my first song since 9/11, I felt extremely guilty for not being more than merely a guitar player in a honky-tonk. I wished I could somehow make a difference in the world besides being known for singing the "Panties" song. I felt sick at my stomach knowing that, at that very moment, thousands of emergency workers and volunteers from all over the world were still digging out bodies at Ground Zero.

What was going to happen when we kicked off? How the hell was I going to instigate a party atmosphere and act as if nothing ever happened? Were people going to boo us off the stage for filling the night air with up-beat rhythms of southern-fried rock 'n roll instead of playing sad laments in tribute to our lost Americans? I wouldn't blame them if they did. For the first time in my career, I did not know what to do.

As the somber crowd sat quietly sipping their beer, I took the mic and thanked them for coming. I went on to say that never before in my career had the first song we were about to play meant so much to me as it did right then.

We kicked off with Chuck Berry's "Back In The USA." The crowd exploded in a rousing cheer when I sang the line *"...anything you want... is right here in the USA!"*

From the first thunderous strains of that rock 'n roll anthem, the band was off and running. For the next four hours, beer and sweat poured as people danced wildly to every song as if it was the first time they'd ever heard rock 'n roll and it was the last dance of their lives.

I didn't understand the crowd's overwhelmingly positive reaction to the music, nor did I understand why, at the end of the night, people swarmed the bandstand and inundated us with hugs and handshakes. It was like an alter call at a tent revival.

Finally, one lady with tears in her eyes, grabbed my hand and said, "Thank you for your music. Thank you for taking our minds off all the bad news and helping us think about something else, if even for just a little while. Tomorrow will be another day. But, right now, I feel recharged and energized! I feel alive!"

Her comment was such a simple yet profound statement, it turned my soul inside out. In a flash my second stepfather's insults echoed in my head as I remembered how he screamed I had "shit for brains" regarding my youthful desire to play music. I recalled my first wife's accusations of being possessed by the devil and his demons and "playin' the devil's music."

At that very moment, I realized it was God who gave me my talents and instilled in me a desire to play music and entertain people for the very reason the lady suggested – to help them forget their troubles, recharge their lives and help them feel alive. Seeing the response of that audience, weary from recent events and seeing the effect my music had on them, made me feel very proud to be merely a guitar player in a honky-tonk.

To all entertainers who stand before an audience: whether you are a comedian, singer, musician, actor, writer, whatever – we as entertainers are blessed with God-given talents, and entrusted with the great responsibility of taking people away from their everyday troubles, even for one night, one show, one side-splitting joke or one footstompin' song. There is a reason there are sayings like "music soothes the savage beast" and "laughter is the best medicine."

Entertainers, get out in the limelight and make 'em dance in the aisles, sing along with the band, laugh 'til they pee, cry heartfelt tears of joy and jump to their feet with standing ovations. You keep the money and give the glory to God.

*"Everyday I give my thanks to God, He lets me do what I love and I LOVE MY JOB!"*

## DIUNNA DOES DALLAS

Houston Blues Diva Diunna Greenleaf is a larger-than-life, black blues singer who demands, commands and expects attention, respect and red carpet treatment everywhere she goes and from everyone she meets. Pity those who blow her off. She has a notorious reputation for charging into every situation head-on like a rhino through a Land Rover. Absolutely nothing stops her when she has made up her mind to sing at an event or get herself invited on B.B. King's tour bus.

When it comes to singing the blues, Diunna is definitely one of the most dynamic entertainers I've had the honor of sharing the stage with. I've witnessed first hand how her soul-wrenching renditions of blues standards bring blues purists to worship at her feet. I've seen new blues converts give her rousing ovations when she sings a Capella with her powerful voice. Being on stage with Diunna is a religious experience, which is why I accepted the offer when Diunna called and asked if Mean Gene Kelton & The Die Hards could serve as her back up band for a New Year's Eve show, December 31, 2001, in Dallas.

My band consisted of A.J. Fee on bass guitar and Russell Shelby on drums. Russell had relatives in Dallas and said he would drive up a few days early to visit with family. A.J. and

I planned to make the four-hour drive from Baytown to Dallas on the morning of the event and drive back the next day.

A couple of days before the show, Diunna called. "I forgot to tell you, you gon' hafta furnish the PA and furnish me transportation to Dallas, cause I ain't drivin'. That was included in that price I quoted you."

I knew it was pointless to argue with Diunna so I just agreed.

At that time I had just purchased a brand new, long wheelbase one-ton Dodge Ram van. Being a cargo van, it only had two seats up front and it sat high off the ground. With Russell driving his own car, transportation for A.J. and me was no problem. But now, since Diunna had commandeered a ride with us, I had to figure out where to put her and how to get her *in* and *out* of the cargo door. There were no steps or running boards.

A.J. loaned me a bench seat from his van, and we secured it to the floor of the van with bungee cords. With no seat belts it was very unsafe, but at least Diunna had a place to sit.

We arrived at Diunna's house in northwest Houston around 9am. She took one, long look at the high step at the sliding side door of the van, cocked her head toward me and with a raised eyebrow said, "You gots to be kiddin!"

After much huffin' and puffin' and her yelling, "Help me now! Help me now!" we finally got Diunna into the van, but only after being forced to lay hands on the Queen's behind and shoving her in the door. Once she was in, we were off to Dallas.

Getting Diunna in and out of the van each time we stopped, which seemed like every twenty minutes, was an experience in itself. Each time stopped she would shove her purse at one of us and force us to carry it. She then insisted we hold her hands and lead her (as she balanced herself on her high heels) to the restroom, where we were instructed to "stand guard," and then we escorted her back to her waiting chariot. It was truly a show.

As we neared Dallas snow began to fall. By the time we arrived at the gig in mid-afternoon to set up and do a sound check streets were covered with ice and snow. It was a struggle to keep Diunna upright in her high heels as she tip-toed through the snow and into the club. If she went down, we would *all* go down.

Russell met us for the set up and sound check. Afterwards, we were ready to go to our rooms, get cleaned up, grab a bite to eat and maybe take a nap before our 9pm start time. Diunna had other plans. She had brought a jambox cassette player and told us we were going to spend our afternoon listening to her songs so we'd know what to do later that night.

Around 5pm, the four of us arrived at a very ritzy hotel near the gig where our employer had reserved our rooms. Russell seemed amused when A.J. and I, now well trained, automatically assumed our stations as the Queen's attendants and assisted her into the hotel. Once inside, Diunna went to the front desk to see about our reservations. Russell, A.J. and I waited in the lobby with her luggage and the giant jambox.

At first we thought nothing of what we must have looked like. We realized everyone in the lobby was staring at us. Occasionally the desk clerk would strain his neck to peer around Diunna's large frame to take a look at us. Diunna was shaking her head and was pissed off when she came back to where were waiting.

"What's going on?" I asked.

"He wanted to know what a big, black woman like me was doing checking into a hotel with three white boys!" she snapped.

We rolled with laughter! Then she added, "He seen that jambox and wanted to know if I was gonna dance for *ya'll*, or if ya'll was gonna dance for *me!*"

We laughed as we followed Diunna to the elevator. With jokes flying back and forth I asked, "Well, what did you tell him?"

"I told him I was a famous blues singer and ya'll wuz mah bodyguards!" I laughed until tears rolled down my face.

As we exited the elevator, Diunna announced, "There's one other thing, ain't but one room, and we all gonna have to stay in it!" A.J and I stopped laughing. That meant he and I had to share the room with Diunna. Russell was now the only one laughing because he would be staying with relatives.

We entered the room. It was actually a small, one-bedroom studio with a kitchen. The tiny, cramped bedroom contained only one bed and we were pissed. Diunna immediately laid claim to the foldout couch in the small living room and commanded us to stay off of it. Again, Russell rolled with laughter as he cracked jokes about A.J. and I sleeping together in that one damn bed. I volunteered to sleep on the floor.

After spending the afternoon listening to Diunna's tapes, we were well prepared when we kicked off the New Year's Eve show at 9pm sharp. The show went great. Diunna brought the house down time after time as she waded through the aisles, wailing the blues. She motioned for the band to stop playing. She put down her mic and peeled the paint off the walls as she strolled through the building, arms spread out singing a Capella. At times we couldn't see her, but we could hear her powerful voice roaring from the back where patrons burst into numerous rounds of applause. Diunna kicked ass. The crowd didn't know what hit 'em.

We played until 1am. After loading up, Russell went back to his relatives' house. We arrived back at our hotel room around 3am. A.J. and I had been up since 6am the day before. We were exhausted and could have slept on a pile of rocks. Before either of us could make a beeline to the bed Diunna locked herself in the bedroom claiming she needed it for a dressing room after her bath. Again, she told us to stay off of her fold-out couch and she would be out in a few minutes. A.J. and I looked like a couple of red-eyed zombies as we tried to stay awake, sitting in the straight back chairs at the dining table and watching TV.

An hour passed.

We could still hear Diunna splashing water in the bathroom. A.J. crawled under the table and passed out on the carpet. I fell asleep in the chair. We were awakened around 5am when Diunna finally came out of the bathroom, and yelled, "Hey! Ya'll need to git outta here, cause I need to go to bed!"

Aggravated and too tired to fuss, A.J. and I, still fully dressed in our stinky stage clothes, crawled on top of the bed, stuck a pillow between us and passed out.

Two hours later my eyes popped wide open. Daylight burst through the window like a spotlight. I jumped off the bed, hit A.J. with a pillow and yelled, "Wake up! Let's go to Houston!"

I went into the living room. Diunna lay blissfully sleeping on the foldout couch. "Get up!" I yelled. "We overslept! It's check out time. They're gonna throw us out! We gotta roll!"

Of course I lied to Diunna about the checkout time, but I was tired of being bossed around. I was not about to sit around and watch her sleep 'til noon, then still have to drive four hours back to Houston. Diunna struggled to sit up on the couch, all the while protesting my insistent demands to rise and shine!

"We'll pick you up at the front entrance in fifteen minutes," I yelled as I slammed the hotel room door behind me.

"But who gon' carry my lugg…?"

*Bamm*! The room door slammed, cutting her off in mid-sentence. A.J. and I headed for the elevators and a continental breakfast and coffee in the lobby.

Twenty minutes later, Diunna struggled into the van under her own power and began ripping me a new ass for waking her up too early and lying about checkout time. As soon as her butt hit the seat I hit the gas and we headed south.

She continued her rant about being rousted from her beauty rest as we rolled past little towns and crossings. She bluntly commanded, "Pull ova at da nex' Denny's or IHop. I wunt sum bacon 'n eggs!"

Stopping for breakfast was the last thing on my mind. I was in a hurry to get home before the second wave of exhaustion hit. I had been up for two days with only two hours sleep.

A.J. pointed out a large Denny's sign that loomed in the distance. I looked over my shoulder. Diunna had fallen fast asleep. I mashed the accelerator and passed Denny's at 80mph. A.J. grinned, knowing Diunna was gonna kick my ass when she woke up and realized I passed a Denny's.

Diunna woke up a few minutes later and asked if we had passed a restaurant. "Nope," I replied. She fell back to sleep.

For the next three and a half hours I passed every restaurant at warp speed. When Diunna finally woke up and looked out the window, we were only fifteen minutes from her house.

"What the hell is this?" she yelled. "We's in Houston! I told you to stop and git me sum bacon and eggs!"

A.J. sat scrunched down in his seat, snickering at my predicament and obviously wondering how I was going to get us out of this one.

"Diunna," I replied, "I know you wanted some bacon and eggs, but when I looked back there and saw how you was sleeping so peacefully and knowing how tired you were after last night's show, I just didn't have the heart to wake you up."

"Sounds like bullshit to me!" she snapped. "You just didn't wanna pull ova 'n git me some bacon 'n eggs!"

Busted! A.J. and I cracked up laughing.

"Me 'n A.J. is dog tired and we ain't stoppin'! You're almost home and when you get home you can make all the bacon 'n eggs you want!"

Fifteen minutes later we tossed Diunna's luggage on her living room floor and drove away. That was New Year's Day 2002.

I can't speak for A.J., but I have never performed with Diunna since. No hard feelings, our careers just went different directions. I performed at a benefit in Diunna's honor at the Big Easy in Houston on February 20, 2007. Diunna was in the audience when blues historian and videographer, Kenne Turner, captured me telling the story about our hotel check in experience. There is a link to the video on my website.

In the years since that New Year's Eve experience, Diunna Greenleaf's career has exploded. She has a great band that features my guitar playing friend from Baytown, Jonn Richardson, winner of numerous blues guitar awards. Jonn's guitar wizardry, together with Diunna's magnificent voice have delighted blues fans around the world.

Hey Jonn, where ever you go, be sure to stop and git Diunna some bacon 'n eggs!

## A BUCKET 'O BEER

In July of 2002 the band was invited to perform at a bike rally hosted by the Southern Indiana Chapter of the American Legion Riders (ALR).

We found southern Indiana to be absolutely beautiful with rolling green hills dotted with picturesque little farms. Traffic? Occasionally we'd have to slow down to get around a tractor or a horse-drawn Amish carriage. There was never a single piece of trash on the meticulously manicured rural highways.

We arrived at our concert location mid-afternoon under a clear, blue sky. The ALR welcomed us with open arms and treated us like royalty. We were escorted to an outdoor stage to set up for the evening's performance.

The stage was a covered, flatbed trailer set up at one end of a large, grassy hilltop overlooking a lake surrounded by tall trees. I expected Indiana to be cooler than Texas. Instead, the heat and humidity was as hot as a Texas heat wave. I thought the temperatures would cool off at sundown.

As we were setting up our gear, we realized there was no PA system and no stage lights. The opening band that had agreed to provide the gear had unexpectedly pulled out of the event at the last minute, leaving us with no PA and no lights. The ALR had assumed we would bring our own PA system and lights as backup. However, most touring bands travel as light as possible, carrying only instruments and personal amps. Concert events always provide PA so naturally we assumed the promoter would provide all the PA and lights.

With only a couple of hours before show time, the ALR promoters went into a frenzied search scouring the countryside trying to find a PA system. After numerous frantic calls to every music store and musician in southern rural Indiana (which there are few and far between) no gear was found. The DJ hired to play music during the day agreed to let us use his sound system. Thanks to the DJ our PA dilemma was remedied but his small system was not designed for a live band. We still didn't have any lights or monitors.

What are monitors? Monitors are the wedge-shaped speakers placed on the stage, allowing us to *monitor* our own performance so we can stay on key and hear exactly the same thing the audience is hearing. Without monitors we can't hear our own singing and tend to overcompensate by singing louder and harder, which can result in singing off-key or, even worse, rupturing a vocal cord.

At show time, the sun was just starting to set so we were still had some light. After performing the first couple of songs with no monitors, we criss-crossed a couple of the mains (the front speakers facing the audience) setting them at an angle so the bass player and I could hear our own voices. The idea backfired resulting in massive, squealing feedback.

What is feedback? Feedback is the loud, shrill, high-pitched squeal heard when a microphone is too close to the front of a speaker. The sound emitting from the speaker gets recycled back through the mic, then back out the speakers, then back through the mic and so on. As the endless cycle of sound circulates faster and faster, it creates a high-pitched squeal called feedback. We were plagued with feedback and forced to re-direct the main speakers back to the forward position.

Our bass player "Hollywood" Steve Rangel and I could barely hear our own vocals. Our drummer Curtis Craig, positioned on the rear of the stage, couldn't hear anything except the lead guitar and bass. To him every song sounded like an instrumental. To help him hear our vocals, someone brought out a small home stereo system and patched it into the PA from an output on the mixer. Two small, cigar box-sized home stereo speakers were mounted on each side of Curtis's head just a few inches from his ears. Our vocals were so distorted through those little speakers that we sounded like we were singing over a CB radio with a lot of static. After a few minutes the home stereo, speakers and all, fried like Kentucky Fried Chicken!

As the sun set, with no lights, the stage and concert area became pitch black. We couldn't see the audience and they couldn't see us. Every time we ended a song, the sound of a rousing wave of applause would wash over the stage from an unseen crowd somewhere out in the darkness. As the night wore on, the sound of applause grew louder and louder. We knew the crowd was growing, but in the moonless, pitch black darkness we could not see them. "Now I know how Ray Charles feels!" I remarked.

Someone brought a string of red Christmas lights and hung them across the front of the stage. They emitted a dim crimson glow just enough so that the audience knew where the stage was, but the band still could not see the audience.

The freakish heat wave smothered us like a blanket. We were soaked with sweat and were suffocating in the humidity. My friend and ALR member Keith Jones, aka "Dawg," called it "air you can wear."

At one point Dawg and Steve Hemmer, aka "Baron," approached the stage asking if we needed anything to drink. I yelled back, "Yeah! Just bring us a bucket of beer!"

With raised eyebrows and a puzzled expression, Dawg and Baron looked at us as if we were nuts. They shrugged their shoulders and took off toward the community building. In a few minutes they returned carrying a five-gallon plastic bucket filled to the rim and sloshing over with beer. We cracked up laughing. Something was lost in the Texas-Indiana translation of what a *bucket of beer* was.

In Texas, a bucket of beer means six to eight longnecks sticking out of a bucket full of ice. In Indiana, a bucket of beer literally means *a bucket filled with beer*. After explaining the difference between a bucket of beer in Texas as opposed to a bucket of beer in Indiana, we all got a good laugh.

Curtis, Hollywood and I dipped plastic cups into the bucket, hoping it had not been used for mopping the floors in the community building and took a big gulp. Holding the beer in our bulging cheeks like mouthwash, we stared at each other. Not wanting to appear rude and ungreatful to our hosts by spitting out the nasty stuff, we managed to swallow the beer without making a face.

"What kind of beer is that?" I asked, trying to sound appreciative.

"Busch Light Draft!" they replied. We politely thanked them for the beer and set the bucket on the back of the stage, never to be touched again. We joked with the ALR about their unlikely choice of beer for a bike rally. Sipping Busch Light Draft didn't seem to fit their rowdy biker image.

Almost in unison, Dawg and Baron said, "Well, maybe you'd like one of *these*?"

They were grinning from ear to ear, dancing around in front of the stage and teasing us with cans of Lone Star, *The National Beer Of Texas*.

Tramp, an ALR member from Texas, saved the night. He arrived with a couple cases of The National Beer of Texas iced down in his saddlebags. Thanks to Tramp we all had a Texas good time on an Indiana hilltop.

After chugging a couple of Lone Stars, Dawg and Baron introduced us to a potent, homemade brew called "Apple Pie." It was the northern equivalent to White Lightnin'. It tasted just like mom's homemade apple pie, but it kicked like a mule.

Throughout the entire event every few minutes someone would yell, "What do we like about Hemmer?" Several hundred people always yelled back, *"Not a goddamn thing!"*

I never did find out what that was all about, but Mr. Hemmer was the raucous ALR member who took a lot of razzing from his friends all in fun.

Near the end of our show, several ALR members, including Dawg and Baron, climbed on stage to sing backup for us. Reeling from the effects of the heat wave, the long days and nights without sleep preparing for the rally, and too much Apple Pie mixed with Busch Light Draft, they were hilariously funny. They jokingly referred to themselves as the "World's Ugliest Chorus Line." Their jokes, songs and antics had the crowd rolling with laughter.

Our show in Southern Indiana was a blast. Our friends Dawg, Baron, Tramp and all the American Legion Riders of Southern Indiana were some of the greatest people and the most fun-loving hosts we have ever known.

So what do we like about Hemmer????

## BLOW UP DOLL AND THE LANDLORD

A song on my first CD *Most Requested* is called "My Blow Up Lover."

The original idea for that song belongs to a songwriter friend named Bob Albright. Bob came to one of my shows back in 1988 and said, "I have an idea for a funny song about a blow up doll." We had a few laughs about his idea. Then he reached in his shirt pocket, retrieved a small spiral note pad, tore a few pages out and handed them to me. The few lines scribbled on the pages described the benefits of owning an inflatable, life-sized, anatomically-correct female blow up doll. He asked me to take a look at his lyrics and add whatever ideas I had to turn them into a song.

Bob showed up every other week asking, "How ya doin' on that song?"

After six months of messing around with various lyrics, ideas and chord progressions, I woke up one morning and got out my guitar. Seven hours and three pots of coffee later, "My Blow Up Lover" was finished. "My Blow Up Lover" became very popular in the dives and honky-tonks I played in so I included it on *Most Requested*.

In April 2001, my friends threw a big birthday party for me at one of my Sunday afternoon shows. I was on stage when someone came up behind me and wrapped the arms of a life-size blow up doll around me in honor of the "Blow Up Lover" song. It was hilariously funny. Everybody took turns getting their picture made with her. She was passed around the room. Everybody copped a feel, fondled her breasts and bent her into various positions. It was a fun party. By the time the party was over, the doll had been signed by everyone in attendance wishing me happy birthday.

As usual for me in those days, I drank too much tequila. Joni drove me to her house where I spent the night. Joni had a beautiful house in a very nice section of the Heights in Houston.

Her landlord was a famous Texas judge who lived two houses down from her. The old Judge was about eighty years old, sharp as a tack and still presided over court cases on a part-time basis. He had a razor-sharp wit and was always razzing me when he saw me at Joni's house during the day while she was at work.

The Judge would often comment about how he "never saw me hit a lick at a snake" and that I "wasn't worth shootin' for lettin' that little girl take care of me" while I "laid around the house and did nothing." I explained to him many times I was a professional musician and worked at night. His comment, "Musician! That's even worse!"

I know he meant it all in fun.

Joni had to work the next day after the party. When we got home from the gig that night, I took the blow up doll out of the car and tossed it on the couch in the living room.

The next morning Joni was already gone when a loud banging at the front door roused me from my tequila-induced coma.

In my hangover haze, I leaped out of bed. I hastily grabbed Joni's housecoat – too small and pastel pink – threw it around me and headed for the front door.

My head was spinning from the sudden jump out of bed. A wave of nausea hit me as I wavered down the hall toward the living room with one eye half-open and one hand pressed against the wall.

I had all the usual symptoms of a hangover: dizziness, dry mouth, shaking hands and blurred vision. The pressure in my throat and under my jaws warned me of an impending volcanic explosion that required an immediate visit to the Porcelain god. But first, I had to force myself to hold back long enough to take vengeance on whoever was pounding on the front door, forcing me from my blissful, comatose state into the living hell of physical awareness and retina-searing daylight.

The thunderous pounding on the front door was splitting my head like an axe. I jerked open the door, and yelled "What that f-u-u-u...?!!!"

The force of yelling and the sound of my own voice caused my head to explode. My eyes retreated to the back of my head as I squinted in the blinding daylight that burst through the open door. I raised my hand over my brow and realized I just yelled at two serious-looking men, the Judge, and another man wearing denim work clothes.

Trying to sound apologetic for my outburst I said, "Oh hey, Judge, mornin' sir. Sorry 'bout that. I was asleep. What's up?"

"Obviously you ain't!" came the Judge's dry reply. "The day's half over and I see you're still layin' round the house while that little girl o' yers is out working her fingers to the bone to support you, you lazy dog. How do you live with yourself?"

My explanation about my occupation and working at night fell on deaf ears.

The Judge introduced the contractor he had brought over to take measurements for some sort of repair to the house.

I invited them in and we stood in the living room talking about the necessary repairs. Suddenly both men went silent. It wasn't like the Judge to *ever* be silent about *anything*. Something over my shoulder had them hypnotized. I automatically turned to see what had captured their attention.

Horror shot through me.

I saw that damned blow up doll sitting there on the couch in all her glory, legs spread wide, exposing her obvious femaleness through a pair of crotchless panties someone had put on her. Her eyes were wide open in an expression of "surprise" and her puffy, candy-apple colored lips were permanently affixed in the shape of an "O."

I turned and said, "I know what ya'll must be thinking, but..."

The Judge overruled my defense. "Yep, I had you pegged right all along, you pervert! And don't tell me you got her for the HOV lane!"

There I stood half naked, Joni's pink housecoat wrapped around me exhaling fermented tequila fumes, looking like death, with dark circles under my eyes, my hair in disarray – and a blow-up doll on the couch. It took some serious talking to convince the Judge that I was innocent of his suspicions when the circumstantial evidence proved otherwise.

Good thing I wasn't on trial.

The Judge threw his hands in the air, shook his head and repeated, "Like I said, boy, how the hell do you live with yourself?"

## KING OF THE URBAN COWBOYS

I was twenty one years old in the in the fall of 1974 when I saw a local honky-tonk piano player named Mickey Gilley banging the hell out of an old piano on a Saturday morning TV show. The show aired every week on one of Houston's independent stations. I never missed it. I liked Gilley's upbeat, '50s rock 'n roll style which reminded me of Jerry Lee Lewis. I wanted the job as Mickey Gilley's lead guitar player.

One morning after watching the show, I loaded my guitar and amp in the back of my Ford Courier pickup and drove sixty miles from Liberty to Pasadena, to Mickey Gilley's nightclub aptly named Gilley's Club.

When I walked through the wide-open double doors sometime around noon, I paused to watch the house band rehearse. From out of nowhere, a denim clad security goon stepped in front of me. He was as big as a house, with a short, scruffy beard and a ten-gallon hat. "Club ain't open!" he growled. "Come back later!"

"I want to see Mickey Gilley about a job playin' guitar with the band," I said.

"Gilley don't hire musicians," he said gruffly. "Ya need ta see the owner, Sherwood Cryer."

The news someone other than Mickey Gilley owned Gilley's Club was a surprise to me. After getting directions to Sherwood Cryer's office at another location, I was off and running.

A few minutes later, I pulled into the shell parking lot of a two-story, dilapidated garage apartment on Red Bluff Road. Damaged pool tables, jukeboxes and barroom furniture were stacked up underneath the carport. A stocky, gray-haired man, about fifty-something and wearing blue coveralls was walking up the stairs carrying something in his hand. I stepped out of my truck.

"Howdy! I'm looking for Sherwood Cryer!"

The man gave me a quick glance, darted up the stairs and disappeared around the corner on the top deck. I quickly climbed the rickety, wooden stairs and found the door the man had just entered. It had a small, one-way mirrored glass window at eye level, protected by a separate, outer door made with steel bars. I knocked.

"What the hell ya wunt?" yelled an angry male voice from the other side of the door.

"I'm a guitar player," I yelled. "I'm lookin' for Sher…"

"We don't need no goddamn gi-tar players!" the voice interrupted.

"But I just wanna see Mr. Cryer about…"

Before I finished my sentence, the one-way window jerked open. A big, black automatic pistol jutted out between the steel bars and stopped right between my eyes. A man's voice from behind the pistol yelled, "I said we don't need no goddamn gi-tar players! Now get the fuck outta here!"

I barely caught a glimpse of a blue coverall shirtsleeve as I spun toward the stairs. Seconds later my truck tires threw gravel and shell dust as I fishtailed onto Red Bluff. I never again pursued a gig at Gilley's Club or any other establishment Sherwood Cryer owned.

Within a few years Mickey Gilley became a country music superstar and Gilley's Club landed in the Guinness Book of World's Records as the World's Largest Honky Tonk. Sherwood Cryer became one of the world's greatest music promoters. Sherwood single-handedly changed the course of country music when he insisted *Urban Cowboy* be filmed at Gilley's Club instead of on a Hollywood set.

*Urban Cowboy*, starring John Travolta and Debra Wringer, ignited a world-wide interest in country music and created a nationwide fad that ruled country pop culture through the '80s.

I learned Sherwood Cryer was not only the owner of Gilley's Club, he was also Mickey Gilley's manager. Sherwood also supposedly owned almost every establishment in Pasadena that sold alcohol, including convenience stores, liquor stores and icehouses. He was literally the king of his own Urban Cowboy empire.

As the fame of Gilley's Club spread around the world, local rumors began to surface regarding Sherwood's questionable business methods that were being compared to mafia tactics. Many Southeast Texas musicians talked about the risks of working for Sherwood.

According to them, a musician could sell his soul to Sherwood in exchange for a good paying, full-time house gig at one of Sherwood's many live music venues. I was told by many musicians that getting out of line, quitting or getting fired often came with a serious ass-whuppin' by Sherwood's redneck goon squad. There was no such thing as leaving Sherwood's employ under any circumstances without serious consequences.

News stories and interviews with Gilley's Club personnel confirmed to me that the man in the blue coveralls, who had put a pistol between my eyes years before, was none other than the notorious Sherwood Cryer himself. I couldn't believe I had tried to work for him.

According to news reports, Mickey Gilley and Sherwood Cryer parted company in the mid-eighties. The world's largest honky-tonk mysteriously burned down in 1989. It was end of an era, but just another day at the office for Sherwood.

Nearly three decades passed from the day I looked down the barrel of Sherwood's pistol until the day when my home phone rang and brought me full circle back into the world of Sherwood Cryer.

A crusty, smoke-cured male voice with a strong East Texas accent asked, "Hey, is you that sum-bitch whut sangs 'at goddamn song 'bout tha girl with no panties?"

"Yes, I am," I replied.

"Is you that same sum-bitch whut sangs 'at goddamn song 'bout that goddamned dyke?"

"Yes, I am."

"This is Sherwood Cryer. You know who I am?"

"Yes, sir. I sure do."

"Well lemme tell ya one goddamned thang. I hate them goddamn songs. Mah customers play 'em on all mah goddamn jukeboxes, in all mah goddamn beer joints, all the goddamn time! I gotta listen to 'em all goddamn day. Now, way I figger it, if mah customers wunna hear you sang, then by-god you oughtta be sangin' at mah place, G's Icehouse. You be here ten o'clock in-na mornin'. I wunna see whut the hell you look like, and we'll juss see 'bout 'chu sangin' here."

G's Icehouse was a long, white metal building nestled between petrochemical refineries along Highway 225 in Deer Park, Texas. Everybody knew Sherwood owned the place. I had driven past it for years, but the memory of Sherwood's pistol between my eyes reminded me to never stop there.

Curiosity got the best of me. At 10am the next morning I turned into the shell parking lot between two decomposing delivery vans that sat drowning in high weeds marking the entrance. They were used as permanent billboards advertising upcoming shows at G's Icehouse.

Trash blew across the parking lot like tumbleweeds as I dodged the potholes and came to a stop. I noticed the entire property was littered with broke down and wrecked vehicles, rusting lawn mowers, 55-gallon drums and discarded building materials that sat rotting in high weeds all around the building. An awning ran the entire length of the front of the building. Underneath the awning was a fenced-in area cluttered with discarded jukeboxes, damaged pool tables, broken barroom tables, busted chairs, old couches, paint cans, ladders, more 55-gallon drums and stacks of lumber.

In the middle of all that junk, in all its faded glory, sat the world famous *El Toro*, the mechanical bull that had been tamed so well by Debra Wringer in *Urban Cowboy*. Judging from the dusty, stained pads scattered on the floor to catch falling riders, I presumed El Toro still worked.

I made my way between the picnic tables where several Mexican laborers were already drinking at that hour. Dressed up in my stage clothes, they eyed me suspiciously. Once inside the bartender led me to a smokey back room. Sitting at a cocktail table, wearing his trademark blue coveralls, was the man some called the devil himself, Sherwood Cryer.

The years had reduced him to a small, frail old man near eighty. He wore gold-rimmed spectacles. His hair was snow white and his arms were as thin as toothpicks. He was immersed in stamping huge stacks of one dollar bills, one at a time, with a rubber stamp. In permanent, blood red ink, Sherwood stamped each one dollar bill with a message that read "G's Icehouse – Deer Park, Texas."

Sherwood motioned me to sit down in the chair directly across from him. In the chair next to him lay a pump shotgun, aimed directly at me. Glancing over the top of his glasses, he commented, "Ain't never seen a musician on time before." He then added, "Ain't never seen one up at ten o'clock in the morning, 'less he's gittin' bailed outta jail."

He pulled out a pen and spiral notebook and for the next two hours Sherwood interrogated me in great detail about my life, career and personal interests as if he were taking notes for a trial. He may have looked like a frail, old man, but his questions were sly and tricky. His mind was lightning fast and razor sharp. He took notes as I calmly answered his questions with the coolness of someone taking a lie detector test.

I knew Sherwood was looking for my weaknesses as he needled me about my personal life. He asked if I screwed bar whores that usually followed bands. He asked if I had any sexual perversions. Did I have any ex-wives, ex-girlfriends or illegitimate kids I owed money to? Did I have any enemies, bill collectors or bounty hunters looking for me? Did I own my house, car and music equipment? Did I smoke, drink, do drugs or have a police record? Was I wanted by the law in any state? Did I, or my wife, have any diseases? How many kids did we have? How many relatives or other musicians lived at my house?

Ordinarily, I would have told someone asking those questions to kiss my ass. Oddly enough, I found Sherwood to be entertaining, fascinating and intriguing. His questions, comments and commentaries regarding musicians and the music business were laced with hard truth and dry wit. To my surprise, I actually *liked* him.

After the two-hour interrogation, Sherwood reviewed his notes. "Boy, I don't know whether ta b'lieve you or not. Y'ain't never been ta prison. Ya don't smoke, drink or do drugs. Ya show up on time. Ya say ya don't chase pussy, 'cause yer happily married. Sounds like bullshit to me! I never met a musician yet, married or not, whut didn't chase pussy 'less he wuz a goddamn queer. All I gotta say, boy, is what the fuck's wrong with ya? Ever-body's got vices! What's yers?"

"Just music, sir," I replied, laughing.

Sherwood then suggested I come off the road, cancel all my previously booked shows and play for him exclusively. "Boy, thar ain't no goddamn reason ya oughtta hav-ta play anywhur's else when I kin give ya a full-time gig right here. Way I see it, if the world wants ta see Mean Gene, let 'em sum-bitches come here!"

I told him I couldn't do that because I was already contractually obligated for several road shows throughout the summer and had local gigs booked whenever I was home. Sherwood insisted I book every open Saturday night at G's Icehouse whenever I was home. But by the end of the summer, he wanted my band to perform four nights a week at G's Icehouse, exclusively. When I was twenty, I would have gladly quit my day job, canceled every gig and jumped in blindfolded for a chance to work for Sherwood Cryer. A seasoned road warrior sees through different eyes.

I agreed to book all available Saturday nights at G's Icehouse through the summer, and promised to consider his house band offer starting in September. As I stood to leave, I again noticed the shotgun pointed at me. "You ever have to use that thing?"

Sherwood looked over his glasses. He flatly stated, "Ain't never shot nobody whut didn't need shootin', never whupped nobody ass whut didn't need whuppin'."

I knew Sherwood meant every word.

Sherwood proudly took me on the grand tour of G's Icehouse to show me the stage and load-in area. The first thing I noticed was that there was no air conditioning. It was only April, yet the place was already as hot as a Chinese laundry. The second thing I noticed was the building had two sections, a bar area and a dancehall.

The bar was at the front entrance. Wooden picnic tables lined one wall with a narrow aisle between the tables and the bar. The wall behind the bar was a shrine to the glory that was once Gilley's Club. Memorabilia decorated the bar walls and cheap souvenirs were for sale.

The dancehall area was as big as an airplane hanger. The concrete floor was covered with rows of folding tables and metal chairs. Dust-covered trophy saddles, tires, expensive chrome rims, lawn mowers, outboard motors and even a small bass fishing boat hung from the ceiling fastened to steel I-beams with heavy chains. Apparently those items had belonged to people who still owed money to Sherwood.

Along the front of the building were several large garage doors, open to allow the southern breeze to blow in. Unfortunately the breeze also blew in dust from the shell parking lot.

At the far end of the building sat a huge stage approximately twenty-feet deep, twenty-feet wide and five-feet high. I climbed the steps to examine it for sturdiness and electrical outlets. The stage floor was covered with a threadbare red carpet with thousands of rips, cigarette burns and strips of duct tape.

Standing on the high stage, I felt the heat radiating from the metal roof which was already baking in the morning sun. The air onstage was stifling. On the wall behind the stage, directly behind where the drummer would sit, was a large sign with over a hundred high-powered, red light bulbs arranged to read: G'S  I C E H O U S E.

As I started to leave, Sherwood and I shook hands on our deal. He said, "By the way, I sell beer 'til two o'clock. You start at nine, play 'ta two, on the dot. Don't go over fi'teen minutes on break. Ya pay full price fer y'own drinks."

I cringed at the thought of a five-hour gig in that hotbox, but a deal's a deal. We started our Saturday night shows at G's Icehouse on May 25, 2002. The Texas summer had set in and showed no mercy. The building was like a giant oven. The heat index onstage was deadly.

The bulbs on the lighted sign behind the drummer flashed like a side-show at a parking lot carnival, greatly distracting us and the audience from our performance. The heat emitted from the hundred odd light bulbs added to the already sweltering heat on stage. The lights roasted our drummer, Curtis Craig, like a chicken under a hot light at KFC. When I asked Sherwood if he would turn the sign off, he just chuckled and walked away.

We had a full house when we kicked off our first set on our first night. Our fans showed up more out of curiosity about G's Icehouse than to see us. The unbearable heat caused everyone to be covered in a sheen of sweat that ran down their foreheads, glistened on exposed cleavage and soaked through clothes. When the dust blew in from the parking lot, it stuck like glue to their sweaty bodies, caked on their exposed skin and caused a gritty feeling all over. The open doors also allowed for big, hungry ship channel mosquitoes to come in and feast. Everyone was miserable. By the second set we were playing to about twenty people.

By our third week I regretted my agreement to play so many shows at G's Icehouse. Heat, dust, mosquitoes and inflated beer prices caused attendance to drop to under twenty people a night. People would come in, have one beer and leave. Sherwood called me in his office.

"Boy, whur's all yer people? I thought you's sum big shot."

As usual, a club owner always blames the band for lack of attendance. I told him my following didn't like the miserable heat, mosquitoes and being covered with shell dust.

"Aw, hell, boy, they ain't nuttin' but a buncha goddamn rednecks 'n meskins. They just wunna git drunk and chase pussy."

"Sir, all due respect." (I couldn't believe I was arguing with the notorious Sherwood Cryer.) "You built your empire forty years ago when Pasadena was a wild-west boom town and people came from around the world to build the refineries. Yeah, they were mostly rednecks and Mexicans in those days, but nowadays, most of my following are RUBS."

"Wha-ta goddamn hell is *rubs*?" he asked.

"R-U-B stands for Rich Urban Bikers. Doctors, lawyers, CEOs, engineers and people who carry gold cards and ride expensive motorcycles, mostly on weekends. They'll go to biker bars where I do afternoon shows. They like to be home by dark, and don't much like to sit in a sweaty bar 'til 2am."

"Tell ya whut," he said, "you jus' play yer gittar, 'n I'll worry 'bout dem fuckin' bikers."

The next day Sherwood called. "I got sumpin' fer yer fuckin' bikers. I booked David Allan Coe, 'n you gon' be his openin' act."

It was obvious Sherwood was still thinking old-school bikers, not RUBS.

"You also gon' be tha closin' act," he said. "That crazy sum-bitch might take a notion to walk off tha goddamn stage after jus' thirty minutes. I wunt 'chu ta be ready ta jump up 'n start playin' the minute he quits, so you kin hold the crowd 'til closin' time."

With that, he hung up. Sherwood's call meant my band would have to be there early to set up and play an opening set from 8pm to 9:30pm. Coe would play from 10pm to whenever he decided to quit. My band would start playing immediately after Coe left the stage and play until 2am, all for opening act pay.

On the day of Coe's show we arrived early only to find out we weren't allowed to perform on the stage or be allowed to play through Coe's giant concert PA. Coe's roadies and sound crew had completely taken over. Sherwood told me to set up my own gear on the concrete floor in front of the stage. Extra tables and chairs were brought in, covering every square inch of the room. We barely had enough room to set up on the floor in front of the main stage. The audience was sitting close enough for me to set my drink on their table.

As Joni began to set up our band merchandise table next to the back door, a couple of Sherwood's female managers forced her out of the building. The aging witches, left over from the Gilley's Club days, told Joni the club was for paying customers only, not for someone selling merchandise other than Sherwood's.

Joni had to set up the merchandise table outside underneath the awning in the dark, alone and lost among the accumulated junk. As vehicles circled the parking lot, Joni and our merchandise were covered with shell dust.

When the doors opened at 7pm, the crowed poured in. Sherwood bragged that he had pre-sold over a thousand tickets at $20 each. There was not enough room in the building for that many people. The place was packed beyond capacity, standing room only, elbow to elbow, fat-gut to fat-gut. The sweltering humidity, combined with the body heat of a thousand sweaty, smelly people crammed together made it nearly impossible to breathe. People standing in line outside the building were furious they had spent twenty bucks and could not get in. They were actually the *lucky* ones.

We kicked off at 8pm to a packed house of hellraisin' David Allan Coe fans and Die Hards. The crowd screamed so loud we could hardly hear ourselves through our monitors. Except for the heat and the fact Sherwood charged us (the opening act) four dollars a bottle for every half-pint of generic bottled drinking water, it was a musician's dream. Curtis Craig, Steve Rangel and I could do no wrong. We quit at 9:30pm.

At 10pm, without any introduction, the legendary David Allen Coe walked on stage and the room fell silent. Coe picked up his guitar and, without a single word to his fans, broke into a medley of vintage country songs by Merle Haggard, Hank Williams and others. Coe ignored requests from fans who shouted out titles of his hits. About an hour later, without warning, Coe sat his guitar down in the middle of a song, walked off stage, out the door and climbed in his big red tour bus and drove away. His band abruptly stopped playing and began rolling up chords and moving speaker boxes.

Realizing Coe was not coming back, the crowd, feeling ripped off and betrayed by their idol, went into an frenzied uproar. Coe's band became the brunt of the crowds' angry rantings. The band hurriedly tried to get loaded and get out.

Per Sherwood's instructions, we grabbed our instruments and kicked off "My Baby Don't Wear No Panties." Within seconds, the crowd was gyrating to the beat and yelling back, "how do you know, how do you know?"

It was a long, hot night and we were glad to see it end.

The following week Sherwood called me in for another interview. He told me he wanted to make a star out of me like he'd done for Mickey Gilley and Johnny Lee. He said "Boy, I'll git 'cha on ever radio station in Houston. Every one 'o them sum-bitches owes me favors. Half of 'em wuddin' even be in business if it weren't fer me!"

I reminded Sherwood I was not a *boy*. I was fifty, not twenty. Times had changed since the days he paid off local DJs to play Gilley's records. I explained that local radio stations were not interested in a fifty-year-old singer that never had a radio hit. They were interested in younger artists. Most radio stations in Texas that played my genre of music were already playing my songs.

Sherwood had not promoted an artist in many years and had no knowledge of computers or the internet. He refused to listen when I tried to explain that the internet had distributed my music around the world. He only knew one way to do things, *his* way, the way he had done it all his life. He was obviously tired of working around my schedule and told me point blank to cancel all my other shows right then and there and play for him exclusively.

I cringed when he informed me my next CD would feature a photo of him and me on the cover standing in front of the G's Icehouse sign that stood in the weeds next to the highway. He pulled out his calendar and pointed to a date. "You gon' start ever weekend right here!"

I knew he was a control freak and was trying to take over my life. I needed a way out before I got in too deep.

Over the next couple of months, we played another show with David Allan Coe and an Urban Cowboy Reunion with Johnny Lee, Johnny Williams and a number of other former Gilley's Club entertainers. At the end of every show it always took Sherwood over an hour to pay me because he took his own sweet time counting out my pay in one dollar bills, each one personally hand-stamped in blood red ink with his famous advertisement.

As soon as I played my last show at G's Icehouse, I called Sherwood. I explained I had worked too long and too hard in my career to settle down at his icehouse. He was furious, and told me I was making the wrong decision by not accepting his offer.

Maybe it was a mistake. I'll never know, but I had to go with my gut feeling. As much as I had grown to like the feisty old coot, I knew he still had a notorious controlling streak and wanted to dictate my every move. I never went back to G's Icehouse, and to my regret, never spoke to Sherwood again.

I wish I would have patched things up with Sherwood. I would have loved to have written a book about his colorful life and learned some of his promotion secrets. His passing in 2009 sealed that possibility forever.

I still have a one-dollar bill stamped in blood red ink. G's Icehouse – Deer Park, Texas.

## T-Model Ford – Mississippi Blues Legend

In 2002 we played a show at the Walnut Street Blues Bar in Greenville, Mississippi. T-Model Ford, a true Mississippi Delta Blues Legend, came in and was making the rounds shaking hands and saying hello to people he knew. According to him, he had just returned to his hometown of Greenville from a successful European tour and he was wound up on adrenaline and enthusiasm. He demanded in no uncertain terms to sit in with the band.

I usually don't take lightly to musicians or their friends making demands of me where I earn my living, blues legend or not. I've always felt that a certain etiquette should exist between professional musicians. I've met many who seem to think that a little notoriety gives them an excuse to discard plain ol' good manners. In T-Model's case I made an exception, considering his excitement about his successful tour. He was on cloud nine. I would be too. Also, I considered the fact that old blues guys like T-Model are the very ones who paved the way for white boys like me. I stepped aside and invited him to my bandstand.

"Ya'll go s'down," he commanded. "I don't needs no band."

He plugged into my amp and played half a song. He twisted every knob on the amp. With every twist he yelled, "I can't gits mah *tone*! I wants mah *tone*! Dis ain't mah *tone*!"

At his insistence, we lugged T-Model's raggedy old amp up on stage (a Peavey I think) that looked as if it had been salvaged from the bottom of the Mississippi River. He plugged in and started banging away on his guitar. He got *his tone*!

My eyes welled with tears as I sat mesmerized by T-Model's raw-gut wailings and gritty guitar riffs. Having grown up in the Mississippi Delta, the sound took me back to my musical roots, where I first heard the blues when I was six years old, to back-country dirt floor juke-joints like Elmer Green's Place near Charleston, with its parking lot paved with bottle caps. Places my grandpa took me as a kid, where he would satisfy me with an RC Cola and a moon pie while he sipped white lightnin' with the black plantation hands he supervised at the Mabus Cotton Plantation where we lived. He and I would sit and watch real blues bands play long before blacks and whites were allowed to mingle in public in Mississippi.

I snapped out of my daydream down memory lane when Joni elbowed me. She was appalled at the reaction of the crowd to T-Model's playing. I looked around the room. None of the local white folks in the club were paying any attention to T-Model. To them, he was just another old black man with a guitar they had seen round these parts for years.

To us, T-Model Ford, and others like him, will always be a national treasure.

## MIDLAND MAYHEM

It was another wild Saturday night at The Bar (yes, that's the name of it, "The Bar") in Midland, Texas, sometime in 2003.

The Bar was packed with a rowdy crowd of middle-aged, hell-raisin' West Texans that always came to see us when we played there. They danced to every old rock 'n roll song we threw at them. Most were involved one way or the other in the oil "bid-ness." There were always a few local radio DJs checking out our music, as well as local musicians curious about the touring band invading their turf.

Then there were people originally from the Houston/Galveston area who, for whatever reason, ended up on the barren plains of West Texas. They sought us out to talk about how they missed the simple things in life like green grass and tall pine trees swaying in the breeze. They hungered for the latest news about the Gulf Coast and riddled us with questions as if we were intergalactic travelers bringing news from the Mother Planet.

One night around 11:30pm a fleet of limousines pulled up to the curb of The Bar, carrying fifty college kids who squeezed into the already-packed place. They were dressed to kill. The young men wore tuxedos and the women wore long, white evening gowns with lots of cleavage and high heels. They had just come from a wedding reception and were plenty drunk, fired up and ready to rock.

There was no place for them to sit. They stood crammed together on the small dance floor, all the way to the edge of the stage. As we played, they screamed, yelled, spilled booze on each other and danced as much as the cramped conditions would allow. A few girls climbed on the stage and started humping each other's legs, bumping, grinding and flashing their tits. They started humping my leg and our bass player's leg as we played. Two of the girls raised their long dresses like can-can dancers to reveal garter belts and thong panties. It was wild and crazy!

The sexual energy washed over the room like a tidal wave. Some of the young men could no longer contain themselves. They jumped on stage to dance with the writhing young women. Women dancing on my stage is okay, but out of control frat boys, *absolutely not*!

The guys were shitfaced. They slammed into me and the bass player, knocking us off balance. They stomped on my guitar pedals and knocked our mic stands over. One guy grabbed my mic and screamed into it as loud as he could before I could tear it from his hands and shove him off the stage. The bass player and I nodded to each other and started pushing the guys off the stage.

I bayoneted one guy in the kidneys with the headstock of my Telecaster. He jumped down to the dance floor, turned and started toward me. I stepped forward as if I was about to run him through with the neck of my guitar. He stopped and yelled something at me, but the sound of our music drowned him out. Through it all, we never missed a beat.

Alerted by the drunk screaming on the mic, the general manager saw our predicament, made his way to the stage and started throwing people off like ragdolls. An hour later, the kids suddenly made a beeline for the limos and the place cleared out. Wow! What a party.

## WILD HOGS

After a gig at The Bar, we left Midland at the crack of dawn one Sunday summer morning for the ten-hour drive back to Houston.

At that hour we were the only vehicle cruising across the desert on the two-lane blacktop that connects with I-10. As the sun came up we couldn't help but notice the large number of rattlesnakes on the road. Since nights in the Texas desert are very cool, even in summer, the snakes lay on the warm pavement after sundown to absorb the heat from the road. Some of the snakes were alive. Many had been run over and were being feasted on by vultures.

Every time we approached a flock of vultures feeding on the dead snakes, the vultures would wait until the very last second before spreading their wings, giving a couple of flaps and, in slow motion, barely clearing the top of the van as we zoomed inches beneath them.

"I hope we don't hit one of those damn things!"

No sooner had I said that then *baaaam*! A bird hit the center of the windshield. Blood, guts, shit and feathers flew everywhere. The sudden impact scared the hell out of us.

It's a miracle the windshield didn't break, splattering nasty, stinking guts and broken glass all over us.

We composed ourselves and started talking about other wild creatures we'd seen dead along the road, deer, rabbits, coyotes, etc. The very second I said "I hope we don't hit a wild hog," a pair of Javelinas walked onto the road, 200 feet ahead. We were traveling 80mph, and loaded down with band equipment.

I knew the van was too heavy and going too fast to stop in time. Hitting a large hog can flip a vehicle. I couldn't slam on the brakes and swerve for fear of rolling the van. These thoughts raced through my mind in a split second. In an effort to slow down, I pumped the brakes. My biggest fear was throwing the band equipment forward and crushing us.

The first hog (or Javelina) abruptly stopped on the yellow line. The second hog hesitated, then began to mosey into my lane.

The van had slowed to about 40mph, but with the weight and momentum I still couldn't stop in time. I tried to go between the two hogs. Suddenly, the second hog darted in front of the van and I nailed it dead center of the front bumper. It sounded like we ran over a giant bowling ball.

In the hard stop, all the equipment, probably weighing at least a ton, came sliding forward, and it slid forward *fast*.

Between the equipment and the front seats were two cheap-ass recliners we had for the band to sit in, with room between them and the front seats to let out the footrests. Joni was in the seat directly behind me as I drove. Seeing we were about to have a collision, she pulled herself up in a fetal position in the recliner and hung on. Good thing. When the equipment slid forward, it pushed the recliner right into the back of my seat. If Joni hadn't pulled herself up in the recliner, her legs surely would've been crushed.

We finally came to a stop a hundred feet past where we hit the hog. I envisioned the bottom of the van ripped out, oil and fuel leaking everywhere and being stranded in the desert surrounded by a million heat-seeking rattlesnakes.

I opened the door and climbed out to inspect the damage. I got down on one knee and looked under the van, expecting to see the drive shaft hanging, muffler dragging, oil pan ripped out and transmission fluid leaking. Nothing. Believe it or not, everything was okay.

Joni leaned out the window and yelled, "Get in, get in! The other one's coming back!"

The first hog had run into the brush, but was coming back looking for its mate. It spotted me in the road on my hands and knees looking under the van. Javalinas are extremely fast, extremely vicious and are notorious for attacking humans. I jumped in the van in the nick of time. We snapped a couple of photos and continued on our way.

We agreed to not mention any other situations that might conjure up a negative physical manifestation. It seemed every time we mentioned something like hitting a bird or a hog, it would happen, *immediately*! We started talking about finding a suitcase full of money on the side of the road. We must have passed it, we didn't see one. But, our adventure wasn't over.

As we headed east on I-10 toward San Antonio, we found ourselves behind a tanker truck. His fuel tank had burst and was spraying diesel all over our van. Fortunately, diesel fuel doesn't ignite like gasoline, but there is still danger of fire. It was a tense situation, but we managed to signal the driver and he pulled off the road. Problem solved.

We came to the conclusion that the Good Lord was trying to warn us about some impending danger, trying to slow us down by throwing obstacles in our way, even if it meant He had to sacrifice a bird, a wild hog and spray us with a flammable liquid. Why else would these situations have happened, yet we suffered no damage? Who knows what might have happened had we arrived somewhere too soon? We heeded His warnings and slowed down.

When we arrived in San Antonio, we decided to take a couple hours off from our race to Houston. We took a leisurely stroll along the famous Riverwalk, visited the Alamo and enjoyed some excellent Mexican food. Sometimes ya just gotta stop and smell the margaritas, eat some fajitas and drink some ice-cold Mexican beer.

Thank ya Je-e-e-z-z-u-s-s-sah! Amen.

## Working For The King

In 2002 the band and I performed a series of seven-night-a-week shows at the Sheraton Casino in Tunica, Mississippi. Tunica is about twenty miles south of Memphis.

We used our time off to scout the region for other potential gigs. Our quest led us to the world-famous Beale Street in Memphis. Beale Street was a happnin' vibrant place where wall-to-wall restaurants, nightclubs and gift shops pumped Memphis music into the street through open doors and outdoor loudspeakers, day and night. Street musicians played blues in alleys, parks and along the sidewalks. Live music blared out of every club, day and night. At night we were overwhelmed by the energy, the excitement of the crowded street and the sound of red-hot guitars spewing blistering blues riffs from nightclub stages out into the crowds like fireworks.

Then of course, there was the aroma of world-famous hickory-smoked Memphis barbeque wafting through the air, tempting the inner desires of even the most staunch vegetarian's secret, carnivorous lust.

On one of our scouting missions to Memphis, we stopped for dinner at Elvis Presley's Memphis (EPM). We were surprised that EPM was a very upscale venue with a sterile and calculated atmosphere compared to the more earthy blues joints down the street. It felt more like a sophisticated museum instead of a Beale Street hotspot named after the original bad boy of rock 'n roll.

Dark hardwood floors were polished as slick as a mirror. Walls were decorated with gold-framed photos of young Elvis and glass display cases housed many of his costumes and guitars. Linen napkins and polished silverware were placed with perfection on tables covered with starched tablecloths. White and yellow half-moon shaped leather booths made the dance floor area look like a scaled-down Vegas showroom. The giant crystal chandelier that hung over the main dining room added a touch of palatial elegance. Easy listening Elvis ballads crooned from hidden speakers. Behind the stage, a retractable screen intermittently dropped to show scenes of Elvis in concert.

After our meal we gave the waitress a big tip and a business card, along with a copy of *Most Requested* asking her to pass it on to the manager. To be perfectly honest, I never expected *that* venue, with its clinical atmosphere, to be interested in hiring a rough-edged biker band that sang songs like the "Panties" song and "The Texas City Dyke."

A few days later I was surprised to receive an email from the EPM manager, Judith Parra, offering us a gig.

By February 2003, as the snow fell on Beale Street, we were playing our first gig at Elvis Presley's Memphis.

**No Elvis Songs At The House of The King**

Before our first show Judith gave me explicit instructions, "Whatever you do, don't play *any* Elvis songs."

I did not question her or her instructions.

I knew it was probably because so many copy bands had tried to impersonate Elvis and fell short. I told Judith we already played several songs Elvis was known for, but performed them in our own original style. She agreed to let us play them with the understanding we would delete them from our song list if she requested.

We were accustomed to playing biker bars across the South where rowdy, Harley-ridin' rebels danced, yelled and raised hell. We found it difficult to play to the EPM audiences who just sat there, staring at us like zombies, while we threw our best rockin' songs at them. Like us, they too seemed intimidated by the perfect, ultra-polished museum atmosphere.

After throwing our high-energy, biker-band versions of "Polk Salad Annie," "Hound Dog," "Blue Suede Shoes," and "Jailhouse Rock" at them, the audience were soon yelling, dancing and singing along. Our versions of "Elvis songs" were a hit!

Without my knowledge, Judith had contacted someone at Graceland about our Elvis set and a representative from Graceland sat incognito in the audience during a show. He liked what he saw. Because of the audience's response and participation, Judith informed me that Graceland insisted from that point on 90% of our show would be *our* versions of Elvis songs. The remaining 10% could be other '50s rock 'n roll, or our originals. The "Panties" song could only be played as a last song, if there were no children in the audience. We already knew "Texas City Dyke" was never to be played.

Judith immediately booked us for half of EPM's open dates for the rest of the year. The other half were divided between four other bands.

Judith and her entire staff of bartenders, waitresses, cooks and even cleaning people rolled out the red carpet for us. The club furnished a house PA, stage lights, a full-time sound man and all the gear we needed. We preferred to use our own amps and drums. Whenever we arrived, Judith would send her busboys to help us unload. All our food and drinks were free and every night we were treated to the most expensive dinner on the menu. Joni and my personal favorite was the Pecan Encrusted Catfish.

Since EPM was a tourist venue, there were never any complaints about slow nights. On Tuesday or Wednesday nights during the winter we'd often play only one set and the place would close by 10pm.

It felt great to be top dog in the House of The King, on the most famous music street in the world, in the most famous city in the history of music. We tended to strut our stuff a little bit as we walked up and down Beale Street and decked out in our show clothes just before going on stage.

## Jammin' At B.B. King's

Whenever we got off early from EPM, we'd hit the clubs along Beale Street and listen to other bands. B.B. King's Blues Club sat caddy-corner across the street from EPM.

One night we asked if we could sit in and do a couple of songs while the house band, made up of all black players, was on break. An older black gentleman in charge of the stage interrogated us about our ability to play the blues. On the way to the stage he stopped three times, turned and asked, "Ya'll's sho' ya'll kin play da blues?"

Standing on stage at B.B. King's in Memphis was another dream come true for us. We were only allowed to play *one* song. We pulled out our secret weapon, guaranteed to rock the house and get everyone's attention on the first line, "My baby don't wear no panties!"

By the second verse the dance floor was packed with hip-grinding, thigh-humpin' tourists, screaming at the top of their lungs and yelling the trademark call back, *"How do you know? How do you know?"*

Members of the house band stood at the side of the stage staring in disbelief at the response three white boys from Texas were getting from *their* audience. The instant we played our last note, they rushed the stage like a SWAT team and yanked the instruments from our hands. The crowd mobbed us as we left the stage, asking for business cards and autographs. The house band jumped in and played *their* secret weapon, "Brick House." I should have asked them if *they* could play any blues.

A few weeks later we stopped at B.B. King's again, hoping for a chance to play during their Sunday afternoon jam session hosted by a different band. There were no other jammers that day, but we were being ignored by the host band until the bartender insisted they let us play after we tipped him a few bucks.

Once again we were interrogated by an elderly black blues man about our ability to play the blues. "We don't git many white boys up in hee-ah what kin play da blues," he said. "We don't wunt none-a dat hard rock shit! Dis hee-ah be's a bluuues place!"

We assured him there would be no problem. Once again we were told we could play only *one* song. With a new audience to play for since our last visit, again we played the "Panties" song. Again, the crowd went wild.

The old black blues guy rushed onto the bandstand, grabbed his ancient-looking electric guitar and started jamming along with us. His horn players and keyboard player quickly joined us. Our one song turned into a thirty-minute, house rockin' jam session. Again, we were mobbed by the audience as we left the stage. I gave the manager our card and we left feeling confident that we would soon be performing at B.B. King's.

## Back at Elvis Presley's

Each night as I stood on the fancy Vegas-style stage at EPM, I felt all the sacrifice and hell I had endured in my life to become a respected, professional entertainer had finally been justified.

I stood gazing into the audience who applauded our every song. I thought, "Ain't it funny, here in Memphis we're treated like superstars for playing the very same music, the very same way we always played it for so many years in beer joints in Texas."

Our drummer Curtis Craig and I appreciated the steady work, the high-class atmosphere and red carpet treatment. Our bass player A.J. Fee constantly complained we were getting soft and becoming a lounge act and losing our Texas biker band edge. However, he never bitched about the superstar treatment, the free room and board, the free drinks and the free steak dinner he enjoyed every night.

Since EPM hired mostly Memphis area bands, the club did not furnish hotel rooms. To help cover the cost of motel rooms for the band, Judith was able to boost our pay.

With fifty percent of our time spent in Memphis, it was cheaper to rent an apartment on a monthly basis than pay for motel rooms by the night. We rented a very nice, two-bedroom apartment on the tenth floor of a mid-rise building near downtown in Central Gardens. The apartment was all bills paid and included a secure parking garage, 24-hour closed-circuit security, a swimming pool, a workout room, a game room, a laundry room and an in-house convenience store.

Joni and I furnished the place with Salvation Army furniture. She and I took the small bedroom and gave A.J. and Curtis the big bedroom with two beds.

The view was fantastic. Every morning we sat on the balcony, overlooking Memphis. Most of the residents in the building were in the music business and several were musicians who worked for Isaac Hayes and Bobby "Blue" Bland.

As the months passed, rumors spread that EPM was set to expand across the US, then on to Europe and Japan like the House of Blues and The Hard Rock Cafe. We felt confident we would soon be gigging around the world, representing Memphis and the legacy of the King of Rock 'n Roll. Joni and I started looking for a house in Memphis.

During the two weeks a month we were off from EPM, we toured the South, performing at motorcycle rallies and biker bars across Arkansas, Louisiana, Mississippi, Tennessee, Kentucky and Texas, using either Houston or Memphis as our home base.

**The Building Has Left Elvis**

Late one Monday afternoon in August of 2003, the band left Houston and headed for our apartment in Memphis for a two-week run at EPM.

The next morning while the band slept, I was up early and out the door to run some errands and pick up a few groceries before getting ready for the show. As I stepped into the elevator and pushed the ground floor button, an elderly lady on her way down to the lobby said, "Isn't it a shame about Elvis Presley's Club closing?"

"DO-O-O-O WHAT?!" I snapped.

Frightened by my sudden outburst, the poor lady backed into the corner of the elevator. "I'm sorry, sir! I'm so sorry! I didn't mean to bother you!"

Realizing I'd just scared the shit out of her, I lowered my voice, apologized and told her I was employed at Elvis Presley's and had not heard the news.

"It was on the front page this morning," she said as the elevator door opened.

I bound out the door and snatched a copy of the morning paper from the lobby. I stared in disbelief at the big, bold letters. *ELVIS PRESLEY'S: CLOSED.*

I felt my guts ripping out in panic.

To me, the headline really said, *"Mean Gene Kelton's Music Career Down The Shitter!"*

To me, the news meant our livelihood, our apartment in Memphis and braggin' rights to the coolest gig we ever had were *gone*. Gone! Gone! *Gone!* Our association with Elvis Presley Enterprises was *gone*! Any dreams of touring the world with the expansion of EPM was *gone*!

It also meant that with no other gigs booked in the Memphis area, we'd have no choice but to go back to Texas with our tails between our legs and try to salvage the rest of the year playing any shithole gig we could scrape up just to cover our losses.

I was in shock as I read the paper. With the band upstairs sound asleep, they were oblivious to the fact we were unemployed and our paycheck for the next four months was gone.

Within minutes, I pulled up outside EPM. There was a flurry of activity as an army of workers loaded moving vans with furniture, bar equipment and Elvis paraphernalia. Beer trucks were picking up unsold beer. Employees stood on the sidewalk, clutching their personal belongings, weeping and hugging each other and as if someone had died.

I found Judith sitting at her desk in her office. It was obvious she had been crying. We embraced like old friends comforting each other at a time of great sorrow. Holding her in my arms, I felt tears welling up and realized it was not the gig, the prestige or the money. I was mourning the loss of sharing a common dream with people like Judith who had welcomed us into their lives and had become our family.

At that moment I realized how much I would miss the magic of Memphis, the music and Judith – with her zest for life and undying support of our band.

Judith told me neither she nor anyone else had any idea that EPM was closing. Apparently Graceland officials had marched in like stormtroopers at midnight the night before, ordered all the employees to gather their personal belongings and get off the premises immediately under the watchful eye of armed guards and Graceland management.

Out of the kindness of her heart and risk of possible wrath from ruthless lawyers that guard the Graceland Estate and Elvis Presley Enterprises, Judith paid me in full for the upcoming week that we were losing.

I returned to the apartment, broke the news to the band and paid them in full for the canceled week. I told them the rest of the thirty-five weeks booked at EPM were gone. I gave them the option of quitting the band with no hard feelings, no questions asked.

Except for the loss of income, both A.J. and Curtis insisted they were true Die Hards to the core and would stay no matter what. A.J. seemed relieved our cushy gig was over, saying "It's time we got back to Texas and back to being real Die Hards!" He insisted we pack up and leave for Texas immediately.

We weren't due back in Texas for two weeks. I told the guys to consider the next week a paid vacation in Memphis. They could go to blues clubs, casinos or hang out at the pool. I would get on the phone and get the band booked.

I spent the next week on the phone hustling gigs around Memphis. I tried to use the TV publicity EPM was getting and the status of being one of the top bands there to try and get other Memphis gigs. In fact, every time a TV reporter was shown during a news clip standing in front of EPM the cameras showed my name, still on the marquee.

Memphis booking agents and talent buyers treated us like infected rats leaving a sinking ship. Not a single club, venue or booking agency in Memphis would see me in person, accept a promo pack or return my calls.

I called Graceland and asked for referrals to management companies or booking agents in Memphis. After all, Graceland was the reason we were unemployed and I felt they still owed us for thirty-five canceled dates. That was the least they could do. All I got was a brush-off.

Even though the band had received a fantastic response at B.B. King's, when I called the manager he bluntly stated, "Tourists don't come to Memphis to hear a Texas band!"

The phone went dead.

After ten days of hopelessly scouring the Memphis area for gigs, we sold or gave away everything in the apartment. We packed up and headed back to Texas. We rode along in silence feeling like we had just come from our own funeral. Just outside of Little Rock my cell phone rang. It was a TV news man in Memphis who insisted we turn around and get back as soon as possible to be interviewed for the evening news broadcast.

Over the previous week I'd seen how Memphis reporters made distraught EPM employees look like angry, disgruntled fools. "No thanks," came my emotionless reply.

I hung up and kept the van aimed for Texas.

## Tent Survival

It was a blazing hot summer day in 2002 when we turned off the freeway into an east Houston neighborhood, searching for the location of our early afternoon show. We were scheduled to perform for a builder's open house event in a newly-developed subdivision.

We re-examined our directions when we found ourselves driving through one of the worst poverty stricken, crime-infested ghettos in the city, where the narrow streets were lined with overflowing trash cans and abandoned cars. Homeless vagrants leered at us from the porches of dilapidated crack houses that sat so close to each other there was barely enough room for someone to walk between them. Old people sat on buckets and wooden boxes in bare dirt yards underneath shade trees, fanning themselves with pieces of cardboard. They eyed us suspiciously as our caravan slowly drove past like lost explorers drifting down an ancient river past their village. Little children, who seemed oblivious to the heat, stopped playing games, ran along beside our vehicles and waved at us as if we were a parade. We waved back.

The massive skyscrapers of Houston's majestic skyline looked down on us from a distance. We couldn't believe such wealth existed so close to so much poverty.

At the end of a long line of crumbling rowhouses, a giant concrete wall with two massive columns and a large, impressive iron gate appeared. An armed guard stepped from a small guard shack next to the gate. He stepped to my driver's side window where I handed him my business card. He opened the gate and motioned us to drive through. I could hear him saying something on his walkie-talkie as we drove past.

Entering the iron gate was like stepping through a Stargate to another planet.

We suddenly found ourselves materialized in an all new, beautiful, resort-style luxury community with wide, spacious streets, million dollar condos and perfectly manicured landscaping. Apparently, the builder had bought up many acres of the near-downtown ghetto, bulldozed the shanty-town and built million-dollar homes. Progress.

As we turned onto the street, we saw an army of Mexican laborers sweeping and picking up tiny bits of trash and cigarette butts. There were dozens of construction vehicles parked along the street, indicating a variety of craftsmen busy making last-minute adjustments. Sanitation trucks, with their constant "beep, beep, beep," were removing the unsightly portacans used by construction crews.

We made our way between the vehicles and laborers to the end of the street where a large canopy had been set up for the afternoon's festivities. I parked my van, jumped out and headed toward the canopy to meet our contact for instructions on where to set up the band.

Smoke billowed from barbeque pits under the canopy as chefs in white aprons and chef hats prepared genuine Texas barbeque with all the trimmings. Caterers had laid out dozens of trays of finger foods covered with plastic wrap. Workers packed cases of sodas and beer in ice while others set up tables and chairs for at least two hundred guests.

After asking who was in charge, one of the salesmen went to get the boss. A few seconds later, a pudgy-looking guy with greasy hair, wearing an out-of-date leisure suit, stepped out of the sales office. He demanded to know who I was and what I wanted.

"I'm the band," I said, "and if you guys want us to set up under this tent, you're gonna have to make some room."

"You outta your fuckin' mind? This tent is for our customers, the band don't set foot under here! You got that?" He pointed to cul-de-sac. "Set your shit up out there!"

"I don't know what we need a fuckin' band for, anyway!" He mumbled as he walked away.

Suggesting that I was "out of my fuckin' mind" was not the professional greeting I had expected from someone representing a multi-million dollar real estate developer. Without even a handshake or introduction, ol' Pudgy set off my Incredible Hulk auto-response. I felt my myself start to bust loose at the seams.

Looking in the direction he pointed, I saw a small stage set up about fifty yards away at the end of the cul-de-sac, out in the open, with no protection from the blaring sun.

When I motioned for the band to drive around the canopy to the stage, Pudgy started screaming, "Stop those vans! Stop those vans! All vehicles need to be outta here, *now*!"

I told him they were my vans, and asked how the hell did he expected us to unload a ton of band equipment if we couldn't get to the stage?

"When you get unloaded, get those vans outta here!" he yelled. "Park 'em over on the next street! All parking on this street is for our guests!"

I told Pudgy we'd move the vans as soon as we could and went to check out the stage. The stage was a makeshift 20x20 plywood platform, two feet tall and covered with black indoor-outdoor carpet. It had no cover, therefore, there was no shade to protect us from the blazing sun. With no cover and black carpet, the stage was nothing more than a giant frying pan. Just a year before, I had suffered from a severe heat stroke and didn't want a repeat of that experience.

Our drummer Curtis Craig was as mad as we'd ever seen him. He had recently bought a brand new set of custom-made drums. We all knew they would warp if he performed in direct sunlight and 100-plus degree heat.

I returned to the tent and told Pudgy we needed a case of iced-down bottled water for the band and that he needed to send his workmen to put a tarp over the stage to give us some shade. Pudgy went ballistic.

"Hell no!" he screamed. "All the fuckin' water is for our invited guests! Hired help don't touch the fuckin' water. All my crews are busy getting million-dollar houses ready to sell, and we got more important things to do than worry 'bout a fuckin' band!"

All the cooks, caterers and laborers stopped in their tracks. The fires of hell raced through my veins as I endured Pudgy's humiliating remarks. I noticed the dirty looks he was getting from his crew and the caterers. He had probably been an asshole to them as well.

I reached in the nearest cooler and grabbed a bottle of water.

"Put that back!" yelled Pudgy. "Food and water is for the guests, not the help!"

Defiantly I stared Pudgy in the eye, twisted off the cap and took a big gulp, purposely letting the water run down my chin. Wiping my mouth I yelled, "Get me a fuckin' tarp! Right now, or we leave!"

I snatched up a few more bottles of water and headed toward the stage. As I walked away, Pudgy continued yelling. He was not going to furnish us with a tarp, or water.

At the stage, the band had already unloaded most of the gear on the ground next to the van.

"Load up!" I yelled. "We're leavin! Fuck these son-of-a-bitches!"

For a moment, the band just looked at each other without saying a word. We all knew leaving meant no payday.

"Fuck 'em!" I yelled. "You guys wanna die out here in this heat for a little chump change? They refuse to put a cover over the stage and refuse to give us water! I'm not gonna be treated like shit and take it up the ass just cause we're musicians! Let's go!"

We loaded up. I instructed everyone to pull their vehicles away from the stage and park along the street past the canopy. I told Joni to get behind the wheel of the van and be prepared to haul ass. I had some unfinished business with Pudgy.

All activity underneath the canopy ceased when I interrupted Pudgy's conversation with a real estate agent.

"Hey, motherfucker!"

Pudgy looked startled by my explosive outburst.

"Fuck you and your fuckin' project!" I yelled. "We ain't gonna be treated like a buncha goddamn field hands that can't drink the water or sit in the fuckin' shade with the rich folks. We're leaving!"

I unleashed a verbal barrage of every filthy insult I could think of to provoke Pudgy into taking a swing at me so I could legally knock him on his ass and claim self-defense.

The agent talking with Pudgy turned and ran screaming, "Call security! Call security!"

Pudgy was oblivious to everything except when I said we were leaving.

"You can't leave! We got three hundred people comin'! They're expecting a band!"

"Ya shoulda thought about that before you started runnin' your mouth," I said. I headed for my van, climbed in and told Joni to step on it because they had called security.

By the time we made it to the freeway, the project manager had called. She turned out to be Pudgy's ex-wife and apparently was still his boss. No wonder Pudgy was such an asshole.

Ex-Mrs. Pudgy threatened to sue me if I didn't turn around immediately and come back and play the event.

"Ha! A big company like yours suing a little ol' blues band for refusing to take your shit? *Sue me!* Please sue me! I need the publicity!"

She lowered her voice to a very sensuous, sexy tone. "I'll give you an extra hundred!"

I cracked up laughing. "Lady, do you realize how stupid you sound? You're a multi-million dollar company, building million dollar houses, and you think you're gonna entice me to turn around and put up with your disrespect for a measely hundred bucks? You're crazy as hell! Tell ya what. Take your hundred bucks and shove it up Pudgy's fat ass!"

"If you don't turn around right now," she yelled, "I know a lot of powerful people and I'll see to it that you never work in this town again!"

"I'll take my chances!"

I hung up the phone and turned off the ringer.

## KILL SHORTY

In the spring of 2002 a club owner I had previously worked for in Galveston opened a second location in Baytown and asked my band to perform for the grand opening. The new club was on a peninsula, overlooking the Houston Ship Channel and surrounded on three sides by water.

The owner insisted we promote the event to our biker following. "Be sure and let them know that we are a biker-friendly establishment and have plenty of bike parking," he said.

On the night of the grand opening the owner never bothered to show up at his own event. I was forced to deal with his cocky new manager, "Shorty."

Shorty was a short, fat guy in his mid-thirties, who obviously suffered from a severe case of short-man syndrome. He was another smartass food and beverage guy who obviously hated dealing with musicians. The plan was for the band to perform outside in the courtyard area overlooking the marina, but the early spring weather turned unexpectedly cold with a brisk wind blowing in from the bay. Shorty and I mutually agreed to move the band inside.

Three of the walls were twelve foot tall solid glass with a magnificent view of the giant cargo ships gliding in and out of the Houston Ship Channel. Unfortunately, the glass walls combined with the stone tile floor caused a painful echo that was an acoustical nightmare.

Any professional musician can assess a room's acoustic possibilities automatically. It's second nature. We knew we were going to have a sound problem and tried to adjust accordingly. No matter how quiet we tried to play or how we tried to adjust our system, the music bounced off the glass walls and stone floor. It circulated the interior of the building with no place to go except around and around. We heard our own music ping-ponging back at us from the other end of the room.

The echo of live music, combined with hundreds of voices trying to talk over the music and the rattling of dishes, created a horrible roar. The waitstaff complained they couldn't hear their customers' orders. Shorty insisted we turn down. We turned down as low as we could without turning it *off*. Nothing worked. The only place for the sound to go was through the door behind the bar into the kitchen. Even the cooks complained to Shorty about the band.

Shorty kept running up to me during my show, his face beet red, veins popping out of his neck and screaming, "Turn that shit down! They can hear you in the kitchen!"

The mic picked up his rant and blasted it over the P.A. Every time he screamed "Turn it down!" the bikers in the crowd would yell, "Turn it up! Let 'em hear you in the kitchen!" Shorty was furious.

Even though the weather had turned cold, about two hundred bikers showed up on their bikes dressed in black leather. The house was packed. That's when Shorty really screwed himself and the new restaurant.

In his fit of anger, Shorty refused to seat, or even serve, the bikers. Anyone dressed in black leather was left standing in line at the front door, while people dressed in regular street clothes were pulled out of line from behind the bikers and seated. Many bikers stood in line for an hour and a half or more. Insulted by the undignified treatment, many walked out and vowed never to return to that venue.

Bikers who were fortunate enough to be seated were waited on *one time* and one time *only*. I learned later that after their meal was delivered, not a single waitress was allowed to return to service their table. The bikers had to flag down waitresses and demand service or go the bar and stand in line. The bikers were furious and they let the staff know it. There was obvious discrimination toward the very people whose business the owner was hoping to attract. Though they were disrespected, I am proud the bikers maintained their dignity and didn't tear the place apart. If an ethnic group were treated like that, there would have been a riot.

What Shorty did not take into consideration was alot of today's bikers are professional people by day, lawyers, accountants, CEO's, engineers and ride their bikes mostly on the weekends. He also failed to realize most of them carry platinum and gold credit cards.

Shorty disrespected all the bikers, treating them like stereotypical biker trash out of some old '60s B-movie. Talk about racial profiling. Due to his indignant treatment of those RUBs (Rich Urban Bikers), he pissed off many people who held influential positions in the community who could have helped make the restaurant a great success.

While I was on stage, Joni was sitting alone at a table. She had ordered dinner and was waiting for a few friends to join her. Unbeknownst to me, Shorty disrespectfully ordered my wife out of her seat. "You need to move so *paying* customers can sit down!"

Joni told him she absolutely would *not* move because she too was a *paying* customer. Her friends who would be along in a few minutes were also *paying* customers. When Joni went to the restroom, Shorty moved her personal belongings from the table, including her purse. He put them on the floor in the corner and let another group sit at the table.

I noticed Joni standing at the staircase and thought she'd voluntarily given up her table. Her expression told me otherwise. She was furious. When her friends arrived a few minutes later, they had no place to sit. Joni left pissed off before she herself got into it with Shorty.

At the end of the night, as I was rolling up speaker cords and preparing to load out, Shorty marched to the stage area like a little fat toy soldier on a mission. He shoved a check in my hand. "Pack your fuckin' shit and get the fuck out!"

His comment set me on fire since I was already in the process of doing exactly that. I looked at the check, and told him that my contract with the owner specified cash only.

"I don't give a fuck! Take it or leave it!"

I reluctantly took the check thinking it's better to get it now than fight for it later. Shorty refused to cash the check at the bar like other clubs do so I can pay my band. Even though our business was over, Shorty continued to yell at me in front my biker friends and my band as I prepared to leave.

"Your fuckin' band sucks!" he yelled. "I hate all your stupid fuckin' songs and I hate your kind of music! You're fired! I will see to it you never play here again!"

Shorty continued to yell at me and use profanity. Finally, I took a deep breath, dropped the cords, stepped into his face and gave him a dose of his own shit.

"Back off, motherfucker! You're right, I'll never work here again. My choice, not yours. Our business is finished. Now shut the fuck up or you and me's fixin' to get *real personal*."

Shorty ran and hid behind the bar where he stood yelling obscenities at me.

By the time we got our equipment loaded up, four *real* biker friends of mine had stuck around hoping to see me whip Shorty's ass. I told them there would not be a fight. I was leaving and it was over. From behind the bar, Shorty yelled at the bikers to "get the fuck out."

That was the wrong thing to say to a group of hardcore bikers who had just spent well over three hundred bucks in the place. One of the bikers climbed over the top of the bar to whip Shorty's ass. I was standing close and, without thinking, grabbed his belt and pulled him back. They told me to step aside, it was no longer my business. What that meant was Shorty had insulted them directly. The bikers were going to take care of him *their own way*, and I should stay out of it.

The bikers had every right to kick my ass for intruding on *their* business. They informed me even though I was a friend, I was pushing my limits. I asked them to forget about Shorty. "Hell no!" yelled one of the bikers "That sum-bitch is fixin' to git his ass whupped!"

Shorty yelled from behind the bar, "Come on, mutherfucker, come on! I dare you, mutherfucker!"

If Shorty wasn't afraid of four angry bikers, he probably had a gun. I petitioned the bikers to forget about him. I told them if they whip Shorty's ass, cops would be all over us and we'd all go to jail, and that would only justify public opinion that all bikers are trouble makers. The bikers were pissed and out for blood. They stood their ground.

Without another word, three of the bikers grabbed the one trying to climb over the bar and dragged him out into the cold night air. We all left the building at the same time without incident. Shorty locked the doors as we went out and stood there like a chickenshit shooting us the finger and yapping at us like a small dog.

On Monday morning I called the owner. I expressed my discontent about being paid by a check and the disrespect heaped on my wife, my band, our friends and fellow bikers by that asshole Shorty. The owner was not there. I spoke with his assistant, explaining I would never again work for any establishment owned by their company unless I received a professional apology from the owner.

When word got out about what had happened, bikers and community leaders avoided the place like it had the plague. The venue was out of business in two months.

At the time of this writing, I still have not received a return call from the owner with a professional apology, nor have I ever again performed at any establishment owned by that owner. Too bad.

The club owner lost a damn good band with a great biker following.

## ART CAR BALL

In the spring of 2007 I was honored to be invited to perform at the Official 2007 Art Car Ball at the historic Sons of Herman Hall in the Heights.

Upon arrival we learned that vandals had stolen all the copper tubing out of the central air conditioning system, leaving the old auditorium without air conditioning. It was hotter than hell inside the building so the event promoters asked us to perform outside on a concrete slab underneath a large metal pavilion. There were no side walls on the pavilion, just a metal roof about twenty-five feet overhead supported by steel I-beams. Basically it was a giant carport.

By the time we were ready to kick off the first song, the parking lot was jammed with hundreds of art cars. The area around the pavilion had filled with several hundred people dressed in wild and crazy costumes and they were ready to rock!

As we kicked off the first song, a hundred or more people already primed for the all-night event danced wildly.

Before the first song was over, the wind picked up. An evil-looking black cloud rose up in the west and rolled toward us. It was an awesome sight.

By the third song, the beautiful, sunny afternoon was snuffed out by an angry, churning black cloud that unleashed a barrage of jagged lightning bolts. People were running to the stage with cell phone weather reports telling us the storm was going around.

Someone forgot to tell the storm.

In the middle of the fourth song, gale-force winds slammed into our party bending trees backwards and hurling buckets of water sideways under the pavilion. In an instant, every human and every piece of equipment was soaked by a torrential downpour.

People ran screaming for cover. Everything not tied down blew over – signs, statues, props, our speakers, our light stands and mic stands. The wind and rain hit so hard, so fast, that in the few seconds it took me to rip my guitar from around my neck, everything and everybody was soaked to the bone.

Water was pouring into the top of the PA and the amplifiers. The drums were drenched. Wolff's bass rig, on the opposite side of the pavilion, was getting a direct hit. We might as well have been set up in a drive through car wash.

When everything is drowning at the same moment, what do you protect first? If you can only save one child, which one do you pick? Water and electricity don't mix. I unplugged the electrical cords before we were electrocuted by the power strips on the floor.

I grabbed a large tarp from my van and threw it over the PA and amps which were already soaked. The wind was blowing so hard the tarp was ripped from my hands. I literally climbed on the equipment and laid across the tarp in the driving rain in an attempt to hold it in place.

Several good samaritans, including "The Mayor of The Heights," sacrificed themselves and braved the freezing, blinding rain to help hold the tarp over the gear. I felt like we were in a scene in a shipwreck movie, lashing ourselves to the ship and hanging on for dear life.

In the chaos and confusion, I neglected to pick up $800 worth of guitar effects pedals drowning in the rising water on the concrete slab.

Finally I managed to weigh down the tarp with concrete blocks and set about trying to salvage the rest of the already soaked equipment. Water poured out of the silver can stage lights. Good thing I had yanked the cords.

In the meantime, Wolff had managed to move his amp inside the concession stand and was rolling up cords. Sid's drums still sat unprotected in the blowing rain. Looking around, I saw he had taken refuge in the concession stand, along with a couple of hot chicks.

I yelled for him to come cover his drums with my other tarp. He just grinned, and yelled, "They needed washing anyway!"

By the time the forty-minute torrential downpour subsided, the party was definitely over.

My clothes were soaked and I was freezing. Water poured out of our gear as we loaded up. Over the next few days I took all the electronic equipment apart and dried the circuits with fans and hairdryers. Once everything dried out, it all worked like new. It's hard to kill a Peavey amp with a little water.

The only thing I lost was one Ibanez guitar effects pedal.

## 80 dBs Of Hell

On Friday, March 30, 2007, we performed at the 11th Street Cowboy Bar in Bandera, Texas. We had played there many times with great success for previous owners, but this would be our first performance for the venue's newest owner.

During the same weekend, a motorcycle rally was taking place at the Bandera Fairgrounds. We knew there would be thousands of bikers in town and we knew alot of our friends would be at the show. We were looking forward to a large crowd, as well as performing on the newly-remodeled outdoor concert stage.

The new owner met us in the parking lot. Before we even began to unload, he informed us Bandera had issued a sound ordinance and ordered us to keep the volume down. If we did not abide by the ordinance, we would have to pay a $1000 fine imposed by the city.

The Marshall Tucker Band was scheduled to perform at 11th Street the following night. Having been billed with them on past events, we knew how loud they played so we didn't give the club owner's warning much thought. We'd never had a sound problem at 11th Street before. We blew off his warning as typical club owner paranoia.

We rigged up on the beautiful, new amphitheatre-style stage underneath an overcast sky. We did a brief sound check, then went to our hotel rooms to kick back for a couple of hours.

At show time, we kicked off with our usual trademark, explosive version of "Big Legged Mama." Several hundred bikers had ridden in the pouring rain from all over Texas and a dozen other states to party with us. They began yelling and dancing as light drizzle fell on the concrete dance floor. We were off to a hell raisin' great start, despite the bad weather.

Within seconds of kicking off the first song, our road manager Buddy Love appeared in front of the stage signaling us to turn down. Over the next half hour, Buddy, Joni and the owner would rush the stage at the beginning of every song, telling us to turn down.

Buddy and Joni were catching hell from all sides. The owner kept badgering them at the beginning of each song to turn down. We got mad and frustrated each time they approached the stage. The fans wanted our usual loud and energetic show and complained they couldn't hear us. We kept turning down, down, down. Finally we unplugged our 18-inch sub-woofers and turned off the amp and drum mics. Our stage volume sucked. We could barely hear each other play. "I play louder than this with an acoustic guitar in my living room!" I said.

Many fans came to the stage demanding we turn up the volume. Some ranted, "I didn't ride all the way here to listen to this shit!" Others said we might as well not be playing at all.

Scores of bikers who had ridden hundreds of miles in bad weather were chompin' at the bit to blow off the stress of a hard ride. They wanted to raise some hell, but they couldn't even hear us. Not realizing the restraints forced upon us, they were frustrated by our lackluster performance and yelled, *"Crank it uuuuup! We can't hear youuuu! Rock 'n roll, muthafuckrrr!"*

Instead of our much-anticipated concert of high-energy Southern Rock, we were forced to play at dinner music volume. We struggled through our first set, quietly playing slow blues ballads. For a band like ours to be turned down to nothing, especially at a rowdy, loud bike rally, was miserable. It was *hell*.

As I have said many times, playing at an extremely low volume is like trying to fly a jet plane at 50 mph. It can't be done. Our enthusiasm came sliding to a screeching halt. We were pissed and extremely embarrassed being treated like amateurs in front of a packed house of our biker fans. Buddy and Joni had had enough of being the "messengers" and being "shot at" by the band for delivering the owner's threats.

When we took a break, the club turned the outdoor jukebox speakers up louder than the band had been playing. I made a beeline for the club owner to defend our volume level. I told the owner our fans expected a certain level of performance from us and I knew the following night The Marshall Tucker Band would be playing a hell of a lot louder than us.

So what was the problem?

The owner said the City of Bandera had issued a sound permit for The Marshall Tucker Band for *Saturday night only*! The city refused to issue a permit for our Friday night show. I was also informed that police officers were stationed at the front gate with decibel meters, ready to issue citations for sound ordinance violations if we exceeded 80db (decibels). What is 80db? An alarm clock next to the bed, a vacuum cleaner or a non-amplified acoustic guitar is the volume of 80db.

The club owner said he and I would both be fined a $1000 if we exceeded 80dB. He also gave me the impression that his fines would come out of my pay. That meant it was possible I could leave Bandera $2000 in the hole (his fine plus my fine) and still be responsible for paying my band their salaries and all my expenses.

The rest of the night absolutely *sucked, sucked, sucked!*

Disgruntled bikers, having paid to get in, angrily walked out because they couldn't hear us. They were not having fun. As they left, they revved their bikes in discontent, and were immediately confronted by Bandera police officers, who ordered them to keep their pipes quiet or else suffer the same sound ordinance fines as the band.

Our old friend Outlaw Ray from Sheldon, Texas, had a freight train horn installed in his pickup. When he left, he laid on the horn in protest. It sounded like Union Pacific was plowing through the front gate of 11th Street. Police officers scrambled in his direction, but Outlaw Ray was around the corner and gone like the Lone Ranger. We all knew where the sound came from and cheered his show of rebellion.

We muddled through the rest of the night, professionally embarrassed for getting our nuts cut in front of our fans.

During the show, Joni videotaped our performance from underneath the canopy of a table. Her Harley western hat shielded her face and the camera from the downpour. What she didn't know until we got back to the hotel that night was her hat had funneled rainwater directly into our expensive Sony digital video camera, frying it forever.

Somehow the video survived and now lives on YouTube. Check out the band and the three videos at youtube.com/meangenekelton.

Near the end of our show, a bolt of lightning lit up the night sky and hit a transformer a block away from the club. The explosion rocked the whole city like an atom bomb. I jerked my guitar from around my neck and yelled, "Goodnight!"

We unplugged our gear before something, or someone, got fried as streaks of lightning ripped across the sky. We were loaded and gone in record time and glad our degrading ordeal was over.

I sent out an email to our newsletter subscribers the following week with an apology and a promise.

> *I apologize to all the bikers and all our fans who rode in the rain all the way to Bandera, Texas from different states, and all across Texas, expecting to rock out with Mean Gene Kelton & The Die Hards, only to be disappointed by our lackluster, limp dick performance. We were under strict orders to keep the volume turned down, or pay a $1000 fine if our volume exceeded 80 decibels.*

> *I promise to never again perform at any venue where the integrity of the band is compromised, and where we are forced to submit to performance standards far below what our loyal Die Hard following has come to expect. If we are ever again forced to perform in a manner conflicting with the true Die Hard spirit, we will walk off the stage and take the party with us! Our goal is to give you 100% every time, and we will! Like we used to say back in the sixties, the Establishment can still kiss my ass!*

I was surprised when *Skunk Dots Biker Magazine* thought enough of that email to publish it in its entirety in their May 2007 issue.

To read the email in its entirety, please visit meangenekelton.com.

## KIDNAPPED: "STINKIER THAN HELL" TOUR

On a three-day whirlwind road trip, our road manager Buddy Love was unable to accompany us. At the last minute we recruited our good friend Bucky "Two Notes" Bishop and gave him the title of Assistant Road Manager. We headed off down the Texas Gulf Coast to play a Friday night show at The Last Call For Country in Angleton.

After that gig we headed north for a four-hour drive to Nacogdoches where we were scheduled to play a motorcycle rally at noon on Saturday.

It wasn't until we were north of Houston that Bucky looked out the window and said, "Hey! This ain't the way home!"

In our haste to replace Buddy, we forgot to tell Bucky we would be on the road for *three days*. Thinking we were off to a one-nighter, Bucky didn't have any clean clothes or even a toothbrush. We gave him a band t-shirt and he bought a toothbrush at the next stop. We arrived at our hotel around daylight and got about four hours of sleep.

The next morning on the way to the rally site, Bucky complained about having to brush his teeth with hand soap because he forgot to buy toothpaste. When the laughter subsided we told him we all had toothpaste. All he had to do was ask.

We drove around for an hour looking for the rally site. Even local residents we asked didn't have a clue. We finally found it, well hidden in a wooded area past a very poor section of town.

The promoter's assistant directed us to two forty-foot flatbed trailers parked side by side that would serve as our stage. There was a one-foot gap between the trailers and the wood floors were rotten with gaping, splintered holes every few feet. Any one of us could have fallen through the rotten planks and snapped a leg or ripped off a kneecap.

Our drummer couldn't find a space solid enough or wide enough without holes to set up his drums. I petitioned the promoter to nail down sheets of plywood for our safety. He refused.

The event was poorly located, poorly promoted and poorly attended.

Because of their disorganization, we started late. We played our ninety-minute set to a mere handful of East Texas bikers who also complained about the difficulty in finding the place. After our set, the promoter hid from me for over an hour. When I found him he refused to pay me, citing that we were not a draw. Since he owned a small chain of barbeque restaurants in East Texas, I told him that not honoring his agreement with me might be bad for his business with the biker community. I intended to publicize his dishonest business methods on my website and take our contract to my lawyer.

With cash in hand, we pulled out of Nacogdoches in mid-afternoon for an intense, five-hour drive to west Houston for a Saturday night show. Somehow we managed to start on time at 9pm.

Bucky was delivered back home early Sunday morning in his now well-worn "No Panties" Die Hard t-shirt and everything else he gotten three days' mileage out of. He'd earned his Die Hard Wings, kept his sense of humor throughout the ordeal and now refers to his kidnapping as the "Stinkier Than Hell" tour.

Welcome to the glamorous world of the music biz, Bucky!

## CONTINENTAL AIRLINES BROKE MY GUITAR

In the spring of 2008, Texas Sounds Entertainment, along with 2Getaway Travel in Houston, arranged for Mean Gene Kelton & The Die Hards to perform at the Sandos Caracol Resort in Playa del Carmen, Mexico, in late September of that year.

This would be our first time to play outside the US and we were excited.

The travel agency made a special all-inclusive travel package available to our Die Hard fans to fly to Mexico and party four days and three nights with the band. Our fans were ecstatic, but, for Joni and I, the Mexico trip was plagued with challenges from the git-go.

We had to get passports. That was harder than we thought it would be.

Three months before the trip our drummer quit the band. That meant finding a drummer who already had a passport or who would and could quickly get a passport.

On Friday, September 13, nine days prior to our departure for Mexico, Hurricane Ike devastated the Texas Gulf Coast. Most of Southeast Texas had no power, no internet, no water and no landline phones. Cell towers were knocked out and service was sporadic.

Many of our fans and our band suffered great losses. We had no choice but to postpone the Mexico trip.

Randy Otts, owner of 2Getaway Travel, and I mutually agreed to postpone the Mexico trip until November 2nd. Sandos Caracol Resort was agreeable, but Continental Airlines wanted to charge everyone a rescheduling fee. *The frickin' hurricane wasn't our fault!*

A few of our fans who had signed up to go to Mexico were furious when we postponed the trip. They had already scheduled their vacations and their employers would not let them change dates, not even because of the hurricane. Most of our fans were glad we postponed the event. Some lost everything in the hurricane and were dealing with lost wages, lost jobs, kids out of school, displaced elderly parents, flooded homes, damaged vehicles, insurance adjusters and so on.

We notified people about the rescheduled trip as best we could by cell phone email, since most still didn't have power. Both mine and Joni's phone lines burned up with irate people, ripping us apart when they could not get in touch with Randy at the travel agency. His phone was also out of order and his office was without power.

Tempers flared and ass chewings continued to escalate. People were pissed about the cancellation, postponement and rescheduling fees imposed on us all. The airline would not budge on fees or refunds, even with trip insurance. When Joni and I finally got power, our email was jammed with messages from pissed-off fans.

Then, we had an unexpected family tragedy. On Friday, October 17, in the midst of our hurricane clean-up campaign, Joni and I found my stepdad dead in his home in Liberty.

Though my stepdad and my mom had been divorced for over twenty years, he'd been my stepdad since I was ten years old. My mom took care of funeral arrangements. Until we were able to notify his blood kin, the three of us temporarily moved into his house to protect his property from his vulturous drinking buddies, ex-wives and numerous dysfunctional stepfamilies.

One week before flying out to Mexico, our new drummer took the opportunity to make unreasonable demands that would cost me more money and force the entire band to rearrange its schedule. I fired him on the spot.

Fortunately for us, drummer Jeremy Creed, the son of our Mexico event producer Jerry Creed, already had a passport and was willing to fill in and go to Mexico at the last minute.

Before leaving for Mexico, Joni called 2Getaway Travel several times inquiring about carrying my guitar on the plane and checking it as carry-on luggage. We knew it was done every day, but we didn't want any delays or slipups. She called Continental's Travelers Info Hotline to make sure we could carry the guitar onboard. We thought we were all set.

At the airport, Continental baggage officials rudely demanded I check my guitar as *checked* baggage. We argued we had inquired just the day before, and were told there was no problem carrying the guitar on the plane. They wouldn't hear a word of our argument. I reluctantly checked my guitar. Our bass player, Wolff DeLong, standing at the Continental counter next to us, was told the same thing. He refused to check his bass. A heated argument ensued. Wolff stood his ground. The ticket agent relented and Wolff carried his bass guitar onboard.

By then my guitar was long gone round the bend, and out of sight.

**In Mexico**

On Sunday, November 2, after months of bullshit, a hurricane, losing two drummers, a death in the family, rescheduling and arguing with Continental, we finally arrived in beautiful Cancun, Mexico ready to party and relax.

From Cancun we were shuttled thirty miles to Sandos Caracol Resort by a very happy driver who handed out ice-cold Coronas. We had a late-night show the night before, so the band's flight was a couple hours later than the Die Hard fans making the trip. The band arrived together, three hours later than everyone else. I stepped out of the van with a mucho grande beer buzz.

Our Die Hards fans were there to meet us at the grand hallway and the party was *on*. Free tequila flowed like, well, *free tequila*! We all partied into the night. I drank more in one afternoon than I had in the past five years.

The next afternoon, as we prepared to do a sound check, I opened my guitar case. The headstock was broke off my brand new Gibson Les Paul Studio! It was the only guitar I had brought with me and it was busted.

*Where the hell was I going to find an electric guitar in Mexico?*

Randy Otts worked his magic and found an old Fender Squire Strat that belonged to one of the boys who worked maintenance at the resort. He "loaned" it to us for fifty bucks a night. No argument.

The Strat had rusty strings, corroded inner wiring, and a loose input jack that caused static and buzzing. It plagued us with feedback all night. With its loose heads (tuning keys), it had to be retuned between every song.

Somehow we made it through two nights with a make-do guitar and a last-minute, fill-in drummer who didn't have a clue about our music.

Along with our Die Hard fans and 400 international tourists at the resort, we had a ball.

### Headline Goes Here

Along with our Die Hard fans, we were honored to have Houston blues diva Sandy Hickey, Elvis tribute artist Ray Covey and Texas singer-songwriter Kelley "RoadDawg" Jones make the trip to Mexico with us. Sandy rocked the crowd with "Down Home Blues," Ray kept 'em "All Shook Up," and RoadDawg rocked out with his "Road Dawg Blues".

The resort management forced us to shut the party down, because according to them the success of our party was affecting another event on the other side of the resort.

### Celine

The fun finally came to an end and we packed up for the return to the real world. The first dose of reality hit us when we arrived at the airport in Cancun.

There was some sort of mixup with the tickets. Continental would not allow our friend, Celine Garrett, to board the plane.

The airline said Celine was supposed to be on the early flight the previous Wednesday, while the ticket she held stated she was to depart with us on Friday. Celine would be stranded in Mexico indefinitely until the mixup was straightened out. Celine panicked at the thought of being abandoned in a foreign country. The Mexicans were very lackadaisical about Celine's predicament and offered no solution.

We frantically tried to contact Randy Otts who had left on Wednesday. There was no way to raise him on a cell phone or through any of the Mexican payphones. We were on our own and unable to get any answers. With only ten minutes left to buy the last remaining ticket to Houston, on the last flight out, I bought Celine a one-way ticket to Houston.

Celine got home safe and we sent Randy Otts the bill which, by the way, he paid no questions asked.

Thanks, Randy.

## Returning to Houston

Upon our return to Houston, Joni and I went straight to Continental Baggage Claims to file a claim regarding my broken guitar. We were given a lot of double-talk and a toll-free number to call. After more than a week of calling various numbers, we were instructed to return to Continental Airlines Baggage Claim at Intercontinental Airport at an appointed time, where we would speak to someone in person and our complaint would be investigated further.

## Second Trip To Continental Airlines Baggage Claim

On Tuesday morning, November 18, 2008, Joni and I returned to Intercontinental Airport, guitar in hand. We were instructed by the information desk to knock on the side door to Continental Airlines Baggage Claim office. Entering through the side door would eliminate the need for a security scan.

The lady who worked in Baggage Claims opened the door and led us to the front office to a big, official-looking counter, where she asked us our business. After only ten seconds of listening to my broken guitar story, she threw her hands in the air and yelled, "It's not my job! It's not my job! I have work to do!" With that, she walked out.

Joni yelled, "Lady, this *IS* your work! You *ARE* Baggage Claim and we have *damaged baggage*!" The lady ignored us, leaving Joni and I standing alone in the vacant front office.

Furious at being dismissed and abandoned by the so-called baggage lady, Joni bolted through the front doors of the Baggage Claim office to seek out a supervisor who could help us. About fifty feet away were four Continental Airline employees. She headed straight for them. I could see through the glass windows Joni was having an animated conversation with the employees, pointing back to the Baggage Claim office where she left me standing.

The baggage lady who had abandoned us reappeared at the front desk yelling, "That's a secure area! She's violating National Security! I'm calling security!" She immediately called Security as if Joni was some kind of a terrorist.

Suddenly my brain was flooded with visions of the lady who died in the custody of Phoenix Airport Security back in October 2007. I jerked open the plate-glass door and yelled to Joni to get back in the office immediately because the baggage lady was calling Security.

Joni returned with a supervisor who listened to my story and told us to take a seat while other higher-up supervisors were called. Even she could not get the Baggage Claim lady to calm down and listen. When the Baggage Claim lady started arguing with the supervisor, the supervisor turned around and walked out. We felt like any hope of a resolution walked out with her. Even she couldn't deal with the attitude of the Baggage Claim lady.

Ten minutes later a male supervisor, wearing an official-looking bright red coat, appeared in the waiting room with several other official-looking people. His name tag read "Mike F." Not one of those people had their last names on their name tags. They entered the baggage claim office and asked me what my problem was.

Mike F. and I squared off face-to-face. With my guitar case standing upright between us, I tried to give Mike F. a copy of the fact sheet I had prepared describing my situation. The sheet also included phone calls we made to Continental and the name of the person who told us to be in that office at an appointed time. Mike F. refused to look at it, accept it or touch it.

I started to open the guitar case, but Mike F. ordered me not to. He jumped back like we had a bomb in my guitar case. He and his troop of red-coats went for their walkie-talkies which were hidden under their coats.

After half-listening to my story, Mike F. coldly informed me that, contrary to popular belief, Continental Airlines is only responsible for humans and clothes. That's all. He said people brought other items on board, but Continental was not responsible. He said every time something gets broken they hear about it. Continental would *not* pay for my guitar.

"If you hear all the time your customers have damaged baggage, maybe you'd better look at how your baggage crews handle baggage! The minute Continental demanded my guitar be checked, that's when you became responsible for it. How can you take other people's property in your possession, destroy it, then claim that you're not responsible? *That's crap!*"

Mike F. continued to repeat his canned statement like a pre-recorded tape. He told me to let my homeowners insurance pay for my guitar. He even tried to discredit the value of my loss, saying that I certainly must own more than one guitar.

"My insurance company did not break my guitar," I snapped, *"you did!* And it doesn't matter how many guitars I have, *you* broke *this* one and *you owe me for it!*"

Like a broken record Mike F. defiantly repeated his pre-programmed, brainwashed schpiel. He even had the nerve to imply that I purposely broke my own guitar while en route from the airport in Cancun to Playa del Carmen.

"*Wrong!*" I said. "Why would I break my own guitar? It was the only one I brought to do the show!"

Trying not to be blatantly indignant and use four-letter words on the little wind-up company wimp, I tried to contain my emotions. In my obvious agitated state and intense tone, I lectured Mike F. on the durability of the hard-shell Gibson guitar case. It is designed to survive an impact. However, if it is thrown by a baggage handler, the impact may not affect the case, but the concussion can destroy the fragile guitar inside.

I slapped the guitar case to demonstrate its durability. Evidently my excited tone, aggressive body language and slapping the guitar were construed as an act of aggression. Suddenly three ominous, trigger-happy armed guards, their hands on their guns and tazers, appeared in the doorway ready to charge me at any second. Joni was aware that tazers have been known to kill. She grabbed my arm and pulled me toward the exit in an effort to protect us both from a violent and possible deadly confrontation.

Though I was furious, I took a chance and shoved my hand toward Mike F. to shake hands. He reluctantly reciprocated, and he tried not to flinch as I tried to break his goddamn hand. Now it was an eye-to-eye, man-to-man contest. My firm grip told him in no uncertain terms all he needed to know about my discontent with him and Continental Airlines' disrespect toward its customers.

In my best *Dirty Harry* impersonation, I pulled him face-to-face and told him he had not heard the last of Mean Gene Kelton. Joni pulled me away from the guy.

As Joni and I reached the door, I stopped. "How the hell do you people sleep at night?"

Joni and I found our way outside the terminal. While waiting for the shuttle, we noticed we were under constant surveillance by several armed guards, who circled us like sharks waiting to strike, hands on their guns.

Riding back to Baytown, I was extremely upset and wound up tight. I felt like I had a steel rope wrapped around my body. I'm in excellent health and do not take any medication for *anything*. My blood pressure literally reached the danger level. Two hours after our confrontation with Continental, it was 157/97. Jo Vaughan, a nurse friend of ours, suggested I go to the emergency room immediately.

Instead I did what I knew was best for me.

I went and played a gig at Rooster's Steakhouse in Baytown.

## Continental Airlines Procedures

Continental does not accept responsibility for property destroyed by disrespectful baggage handlers. Its policy gives baggage handlers free reign to abuse customers' baggage any way they want, knowing that regardless of damage, Continental will not have to pay for it.

I do not appreciate Continental Airlines passing the buck and sending us on a wild goose chase. We were trying to file a legitimate complaint. No one was willing to help us or even listen to our grievance. Not a single Continental employee had a clue who the proper contact was, if there even exists such a person or department. All Continental employees seemed scared to death to speak to us and afraid to help us.

I do not appreciate the fact Joni and I were treated like vicious criminals and surrounded by Continental Airlines' Nazi Gestapo ready to draw down on us with their guns and tazers. I do not appreciate the disrespect Continental's personnel show the people who sign their paychecks and keep them in business. *The paying customers.*

## A Die Hard Surprise

On Tuesday, December 16, 2008, one month after the confrontation with Mike F. and the Continental Gestapo, I arrived for my solo acoustic show at Rooster's Steak House in Baytown as usual. The place was packed. As I entered the Derrick Room where I performed every week, the crowd burst into a rousing round of applause like a surprise party.

I was surprised to realized I knew everyone there and almost everyone there had been on the Mexico trip with us. I knew something was up when Randy Otts walked in. I figured the impromptu reunion had something to do with announcing another Mexico trip. I was wrong.

Thirty minutes into my show, Kelley "Road Dawg" Jones borrowed my mic. To my great surprise, Kelley presented me with a brand new Les Paul Studio guitar identical to the one that Continental had destroyed! I could hardly hold back the tears. He announced that everyone who had gone to Mexico with us had pitched in to make it happen.

Turning the guitar over, I saw that everyone who pitched in had signed the guitar, along with the staff at Rooster's. Die Hards are the greatest bunch of people in the world!

Thanks to Kelley and DeLane Jones and all our fans for arranging for the great new guitar.

## Closure and Lettin' It Go

In the summer of 2009, my good friend Rick Rogers, and his lovely wife, Ruth, took my broken guitar story to some of their inside contacts who work for Continental Airlines.

A few days later I got a call from Garry Meckel, manager of Continental Airlines Baggage Resolution Center in Houston. Mr. Meckel was very pleasant and a true professional, unlike those indignant assholes at the airport. I can't believe they all work for the same company.

Mr. Meckel offered me airline vouchers equal to the price of the broken guitar. I hope Continental Airlines is paying Mr. Meckel big bucks because he represents the airline better than it deserves. His job is to iron out alot of wrinkles with pissed off people just like me.

Mr. Meckel's vouchers made it possible for Joni and I to get three round-trip airline tickets to Hawaii. In May of 2010, we took my mom to Hawaii for Mother's Day.

To Rick and Ruth Rogers: *Thanks for picking up the flag and charging into battle.*

To Garry Meckel: *Many thanks. You, sir, deserve to work for a better airline.*

To the SOB's at Continental Airlines Baggage Claim in Houston: *Mr. Meckel's good deeds do not excuse your unprofessional conduct, disrespect and rude, indignant treatment you heaped upon my wife and me. You people at the airport still owe my wife and I a formal apology.*

*Until then, Continental Airlines, I got two words for you...*

Steve Rangel, Joni, Morgan Freeman, me, Curtis Craig and Ground Zero Blues Club owner Bill Luckett, 2002.

A.J. Fee, Curtis Craig and me at Elvis Presley's Memphis Club, 2003

Me and Bucky "Two Notes" Bishop at The Hawg Stop for Tony Lee's Memorial.

A.J. Fee, Mark May, Russell Shelby, Bert Wills (seated) and me at C.J. Garcia's backyard party 1999.

Inside G's Icehouse opening for Johnny Lee. Notice the saddles hanging from the ceiling.

Sherwood Cryer, owner of Gilley's Club and G's Icehouse.

*I-10 Eastbound near downtown Houston*
*Tropical Storm Allison, June 2001*
*Photo by Linda Lawson, Houston Chronicle*

*North of downtown Houston, a few blocks from the*
*Rhythm Room, Tropical Storm Allison, June 2001*
*Photo by Michael Masciopinto, Houston Chronicle*

*Elvis, Johnny and Mean Gene have left the building.*
*The last marquee at Elvis Presley's Memphis Club,*
*Beale Street, Memphis, September 2003*
*Photo Courtesy Frank Jensen and Carolyn Hamilton*

*Mic's eye view of the mayhem at*
*The Bar in Midland, Texas*

*Rick "Biscuit" Maxwell taking a break*
*in front of Ground Zero Blues Club.*

*View from the stage at the Blind Lemon Jefferson*
*Festival, Wortham, Texas 2001. Population: 1713.*
*Festival attendance: Over 5000.*

*The dumbest promo photo I ever did, me*
*on El Toro. I thought I was being cool at*
*the time. G's Icehouse, Deer Park, Texas.*

*The First (and last) Annual "Die Hards Invade Mexico" trip to Sandos Caracol Resort,
Playa del Carmen. Names omitted to protect the guilty and the hungover.
Those not pictured still awaiting rescue from a Mexican jail.*

Pictured top left is the back of the new
Les Paul guitar that the Die Hard fans
signed and presented to me after my
original guitar was destroyed.

Above, me with the new Les Paul,
jamming at Roosters with
Kelley "RoadDawg" Jones after
he presented the guitar to me.

Left, me showing off my new baby.
Thanks, Die Hards!

BOOK EIGHT

# Good Help
# Is
# Hard
# To Find

The old saying "good help is hard to find" holds as true in the music business as any other business. Finding and keeping the right musicians has been an ongoing *Gig From Hell* since the beginning of my music career.

As a teenager I believed the hype in music magazines and on the back of album covers about how members of famous bands met and clicked, how magic happened and they became overnight sensations. In real life it doesn't work that way, at least it hasn't for me.

Since the beginning of my career I've seen bands break up for a million reasons. Personality conflicts, creative differences, emotional undercurrents, style issues, money issues, song preferences, too much work, not enough work, stronger players resenting weaker players, drug and alcohol abuse and many more.

I have seen best friends join the same band and within days try to kill each other over the smallest issue. I have seen musicians forgive sexual indiscretions with another band member's significant other for the sake of keeping a good band together.

Some of the best musicians I've ever performed with were assholes. On the other hand, some of the nicest guys did not meet the needs of my band. The hardest thing about being a band leader is firing a musician I have become good friends with.

In younger days, firings often ruined great friendships and sometimes resulted in a black eye to match the damaged ego. As we have grown older, we've learned not to take it personally. I myself have been fired from many gigs and bands in my life.

During the late 1970s, every band I worked with in Liberty was barred from every honky-tonk in Liberty County just because *I was in the band.* For one, I wouldn't take any crap from club owners who continually tried to screw over the bands. Why is it when a musician stands up for his rights he is considered a troublemaker?

Some club owners said I was too wild and crazy. One club owner said he would "never hire Gene Kelton cause he plays that screamin' shit!" Wow, what an outlaw I was.

In the summer of 1980 I aced an audition as lead guitarist for the very popular Alan Landen Country-Western Band, who worked a house gig at the Carousel Club in Houston. At the audition we jammed on '50s rock 'n roll and classic country. At the gig later that night, they played old, obscure country-western songs I had never heard. I was expected to play them just like the record. I was fired at the end of my first night.

I spent most of the '80s as a single act, only occasionally working with a band on special occasions. After nearly ten years as a one-man band, I was aching to start a blues band.

In 1991, I started seriously looking for musicians for the band that would eventually become The Die Hards. The biggest challenge was finding experienced musicians who could meet my list of requirements.

My requirements include dependable transportation, good equipment, a telephone, professional etiquette, professional attitude and good personal hygiene. Musicians must dress professionally, show respect to our fans and employers and be straight, clean and sober. Band members have to be on time, able to leave personal baggage off the stage and out of the show, be willing to practice and able to sing. I wrote the necessary requirements, rules and expectations in what became *The Die Hard Rule Book*. I present it to all new band members. It began in 1998 as a one-page list. It is now fourteen pages long, and a book in itself.

All those qualities are too much to expect from any one person, much less a whole band. In searching for the right musicians I earned a new respect for women who complain about finding Mr. Right. I almost never find all the right musicians at the same time. I might have a great bass player, but he would be an alcoholic with a bad attitude. At the same time, I might have the nicest guy in the world on drums, who had a messed up clock (timing problem).

## Drugs And Alcohol, Etc.

When it comes to my band, I am totally 100% against drugs and alcohol. I'm no saint. I speak from personal experience and have earned the right to preach.

In the '80s I took a liking to tequila. By the '90s after my second divorce, my drinking got worse. I believed myself to be hot stuff under the influence of a Cuervo tequila buzz as I have documented in other stories.

I gave it up in my late forties after seeing and hearing myself on video. My singing was flat and my playing sucked. It took me a long time to regain the same confidence playing sober that four shots of tequila would give me in fifteen minutes.

My views on drugs, including marijuana and alcohol, caused me to be laughed at and sometimes scorned by musicians who believe it's okay to get drunk, high or stoned before going on stage. I have been called square, old fashioned, redneck and out of touch by my peers.

My stance on substance abuse stems from experience in my early years. I learned I could not perform under the influence of marijuana. I became tone deaf and sluggish. I have learned that pot affects most people about the same way. Even though some musicians claim they play better after smoking pot, I've never yet seen that to be the case. What if a heart surgeon smoked a joint before cutting your chest open or an airline pilot downed four shots of Everclear before starting down the runway in a 747?

I've seen many good friends and great musicians piss their dreams and God-given talent down the toilet and become middle-aged has-beens, diseased invalids and financial burdens on their aging parents because of drugs and alcohol. I've seen them end up living under bridges, go to prison or die young when they could have easily achieved musical greatness by just saying *no*.

I do not purposely or knowingly hire or work with musicians who are drunks, druggies or junkies. There was a time when I believed everything people told me. I was too trusting and too naive (too damn stupid) to recognize the signs of drug abuse. Sometimes a druggie got past me at an audition, but he didn't last long in the band.

I've never understood why any musician would spend years studying their craft, investing thousands of dollars in equipment and thousands of hours away from their families in grueling rehearsals just to get fucked up and make fools of themselves in front of the very audience they aspire to impress. That's like cutting a hole in your parachute just before jumping out of a plane.

There are musicians who have repeatedly asked me for jobs for over twenty years. I never hired them because of their reputation in music circles for drugs, alcohol, marijuana, their bad attitude or their tendency toward to violence.

I tell musicians if they are going to mess with drugs, then do it on their own time. If their habits affect my band and my income, they are fired.

## FIRED!

Other than being drunks, druggies and downright musically incompatible, I have fired musicians for a number of reasons.

I fired a bass player because he never took a bath. He stunk.

I had a drummer who lived with his dog in the back of his pickup in a camper. The only thing holding his old truck together was dried mud and bumper stickers. Wherever we were going to play, he would camp out in that venue's parking lot during the week prior to the gig. He was a nice guy and played well, but he always smelled like a wet dog and looked homeless. I sent him down the road.

I have fired musicians for not learning the songs that make up the core of our shows.

I have fired musicians for stage fright. They might be great in their little neighborhood bar in front of twenty people, but would freeze up in front of TV cameras, on live radio, at recording sessions and at concerts with thousands of people in the audience.

I have fired musicians for refusing to help load in and out. It's not right that one or two guys should do most of the work while the others show up late and leave early and still get the same money. I remedied that situation when I learned to never pay the band before the last piece of gear was loaded.

## FISHNET SURPRISE

In the early nineties, I hired a young drummer about twenty two years old. He said he loved the blues and he sounded great at our blues jam. He showed up to his first gig wearing spandex shorts and fishnet hose. Every song we played sounded like a death metal explosion. I fired him after the last note.

## SPEEDY

A fantastic drummer I had known for over twenty years kept wanting to join the band. I never hired him because of his reputation as a druggie. One year, after his persistent calling and pestering me about a job, "Speedy" and I met at a local restaurant where he assured me since he had reached middle age he had turned over a new leaf.

He told me he wanted to be the best drummer he could, and play with a band that was going somewhere. He told me I'd never have to look for another drummer the rest of my career.

The minute I made the announcement Speedy had joined my band, I received numerous emails and phone calls from his former band mates warning me about his drug abuse. They told me the only gigs he got anymore were when bands called him as a last resort.

In Speedy's defense, I argued, "He said he has turned over a new leaf!" They laughed.

On road trips Speedy refused to ride or roommate with the rest of the band. Regardless of the distance, he always drove his own car and rented his own room, at his own expense. I have no clue how he came home with any money.

Speedy's performances were unpredictable and inconsistent. One night he would be the greatest drummer in the world. The next night he would embarrass us by rushing every song, playing through the breaks and doing inappropriate machine-gun rolls on slow ballads. Sometimes he'd forget the song completely, get up and walk away from the drums in the middle of a song. On bad nights he would be obnoxious and angry and go into a redneck rage, constantly threatening to whip everybody's ass. I reminded him we are a band, not a gang.

After a couple months and several band meetings into his tenure, we refused to take any more of Speedy's crap. I gave him a choice, clean up or clear out.

Without saying a word, Speedy got up from our meeting and walked away. Damn shame.

Speedy could have been one of the greatest drummers in the world, but he allowed drugs to steal his talent and his dream.

## Grits In The Pits

In the early '90s I had a big, fat drummer who insisted on wearing sleeveless tank tops at every show, thinking he was still in the same physical shape he was twenty years before. In the early days it didn't matter much at outdoor gigs, biker events or icehouses. When we graduated to playing nicer clubs, especially where food was served, arguments ensued when I insisted he put on a regular shirt with sleeves.

People in the audience seated on the front row complained about the drummer to the management, who in turn jumped my ass. As the drummer played and began to sweat, his deodorant turned white, balled up and looked like matted grits packed into his armpits.

I had to make a new rule – no tanktops or sleeveless shirts in this band.

## Sneezy

I once had a drummer that convinced me he suffered from allergies. Stupid me. Didn't the fact that he rushed every song at warp speed and left a pile of used tissues on the back of the stage after every gig give me a clue? Like I said, in those days I was naive enough to believe and trust everybody. He eventually landed in the Mean Gene Junkie Pile.

## Homeless

One of the greatest super-drummers I ever worked with ended up homeless, eating out of trash cans, panhandling, stealing and living under a bridge near downtown Houston. All because he preferred to use drugs instead of following his calling to be the greatest damn drummer in the world. Sad.

## Toker

I had a drummer in the band who was psychologically hooked on marijuana and actually believed that he had to smoke dope in order to play. He smoked so much that his teeth and fingers were permanently stained and he constantly reeked of marijuana. He would douse himself with cheap cologne to hide the stench. All the cologne in the world didn't help when we were fired from a gig because the club owner caught him smoking dope on the premises. His habit cost me a steady paying gig.

## Milkshake Nelson

In the fall of 1973, I hired a drummer who was an easy-going "boy next door" type. He was a body builder with perfect "Beach Boy" blond hair and a perfect Donny Osmond toothpaste smile. He never said a bad word, never drank alcohol, never did drugs and never smoked pot.

The band consisted of my brother Ray on bass and Mike Sicola on keyboard. Whenever we were on break and knocking back shots at the bar, our new drummer would be outside on the sidewalk doing sit-ups and push-ups. When we stopped at some greasy spoon after a late-night gig to gorge ourselves on burgers, fries and rot-gut coffee, our drummer would shyly ask for a glass of milk or a milkshake. We named him "Milkshake."

Milkshake Nelson was a well-educated college kid from an upper class, well-to-do family. His well-to-do-ness enabled him to drive a new car and play a fancy set of drums that cost more than the entire band's piece o' shit cars combined. He had an entourage of high-class, hot, rich college girls who followed him everywhere. I have no idea why he wanted to hang out with scrappy riff-raff like us. Maybe he was doing research for a thesis or something.

For a rich kid, Milkshake was a great drummer. Speaking from experience, rich kids can always afford the best gear, but most kids born rich can't play worth a damn.

One night we all went out to scout a possible new gig at the ultra-cool lounge at the Marriott Hotel near downtown Houston. We'd heard it had a great showroom and we felt ready to move up from the skanky little dives we'd been playing.

A ten-piece Las Vegas-style show band was rocking the house as we entered. I felt very out of place in my jeans and denim shirt as we walked into lounge packed with "beautiful people." There were no pool tables, pin-ball machines or neon beer lights, just candlelight and indirect lighting reflected by the floor-to-ceiling mirrors. Cushy leather chairs encircled matching cocktail tables. Giant plants and hanging vines gave the place an exotic look. We waded through the plush, red carpet to an empty table. Waiters and waitresses, in their matching black slacks white shirts and red vests, were ready to take our order the moment we sat down.

Ray, Mike and I opted to split a pitcher of beer. Milkshake ordered a round of hurricanes for himself and his three, hot, centerfold-looking babes who he had brought along.

The moment the waiter delivered the drinks to the table, the girls grabbed them up and quickly sucked them down while Milkshake fumbled with his billfold. The waiter demanded to see the girls' IDs. When none were produced, an argument ensued. The waiter tried to pull the drinks out of the girls' hands. Milkshake grabbed two of the Hurricanes, threw them on the waiter and dropped the glasses on the floor. I was proud of the boy. I didn't know he had that much grit.

The waiter shoved Milkshake in the chest with both hands while yelling, "Security! Security!"

Milkshake responded with a wild swing at the waiter but missed. In the commotion, the girls screamed and jumped from the table, knocking it over in the process. Women at surrounding tables screamed and people jumped up to get out of the way.

All seven of us bolted toward the exit and into the parking lot. We had barely slammed our door and locked them when security guards and bouncers swarmed us, trying to block our getaway as we burned rubber out of the parking lot. Oh, what fun. As with most musicians, we eventually lost contact with Milkshake Nelson shortly after that event.

Three decades later, a heavy-set, bald, fifty-something-year-old businessman in a gray suit approached me at a show at Cosmos Cafe in Houston. He claimed to have once played drums for me. But then again, I hear that from a lot of old guys these days. After a few moments of conversation I realized he was Milkshake. We laughed and reminisced about old times. When I reminded him about how we called him Milkshake he seemed offended and denied any memory of the nickname. He gathered his group of friends and left without saying a word.

Oh well, see ya in another thirty years, Milkshake.

## FISTFIGHT AT THE CACTUS MOON

A bass player "Jimbo" and I were hanging out with a group of musicians at a jam session at the Cactus Moon in Humble. I had been performing there at least once a month for three years. We were drinking tequila and listening to Monica Marie & The Blues Cruizers. Jimbo started playfully punching me and the other guys at the table in the shoulder.

We all told him to stop. He laughed and continued to hit harder with every punch. I told him this was not a schoolyard and we weren't schoolboys trading licks. I also told him he was going to get his ass kicked if he didn't stop. With that, Jimbo drove his fist into my lower right rib cage, cracking one of my ribs and knocking the wind out of me.

I jumped off my bar stool and knocked him on his ass. In an effort to get out of the main part of the club, I dragged him by his long ponytail, kicking and fighting, through the swinging doors that led into the kitchen.

We burst into the kitchen fighting like two enraged bears. We knocked over racks of canned goods, boxes of batter, menus, silverware and dishes. Metal pots and pans clang-banged onto the concrete floor with loud explosions. Kitchen workers ran for cover.

I sat straddle of Jimbo's chest beating the shit out of him. I suddenly felt as if I were being levitated. The club owner, Thomas Gardner, was a big 6' tall, 250-pound guy. He came up behind me, lifted me into the air like a small child and tossed me back through the swinging doors into the club. I hit the floor and rolled.

A split second later, Jimbo came flying through the doors and tumbled beside me. A super-pissed-off Thomas stormed through the swinging doors like King Kong, grabbed each of us by an arm and threw us out the front door into the parking lot. I thought he was going to kick both our asses.

Jimbo's car was parked at Joni's house some twenty-five miles away. I told him he could ride back with me if he would cool off. He was still wound up and screamed and cussed at me all the way back to Houston.

Just before we reached the 610 North Loop, Jimbo sucker-punched me up side my head as hard as he could. I saw stars. I almost lost control of the van. I yelled that if he didn't want us both to end up dead or in Harris County jail, he'd better sit down and shut up.

When we arrived at Joni's house, I had one hand on the steering wheel and one hand trying to keep Jimbo from punching me again. I missed the driveway and skidded into her perfectly manicured front yard. I jumped out and charged around the van.

As I rounded the back of the van, Jimbo met me with a blinding, sledgehammer blow between my eyes. I felt to my knees and fought the urge to pass out. I must have blacked out for a split second because when I came to we were in the next door neighbor's front yard. I was standing over Jimbo pounding his face as hard as I could. With the commotion of us both cussing and yelling at the top of our lungs at 3am, I expected Eyewitness News to show up and film our white-trash Jerry Springer incident for the next day's news.

Expecting the cops to show up at any moment, I let Jimbo up. He ran for his car and took out Joni's cyclone fence backing down her driveway. When it was all said and done, his drinking cost me a bass player and a new fence.

I was barred for the next three years from any performances at the Cactus Moon. This was another perfect example of how someone else's substance abuse caused me the loss of money and employment.

Not to mention the wrath of Joni. She was pissed about us disturbing her beautiful, quiet neighborhood at 3am with our white-trash fistfight, tearing up her manicured yard and destroying her fence.

## THE SMOKIN' TEAM

On many occasions I've hired the best drummer and bass player available, only to find they either hated each other or were not musically compatible. They might be great players, but the band would still suck. Whenever you can get a bass player and drummer who like each other personally and are musically compatible, 90% of your groove problems are over.

I once hired a bass player/drummer team who had played together in a rock band prior to working for me. The groove was tight and we kicked ass. Unfortunately, they teamed up against me when it came to my policy against smoking marijuana at my shows. It was as if they had formed their own two-man labor union.

On every break they and a dozen of their friends would make an obvious mass exodus to the parking lot where a half-dozen joints would be passed around. There would be so much smoke it looked like a barbeque cookoff. Club owners were on my ass, insisting I put a stop to it or lose my gig. I couldn't fire the band until I had replacements.

One night on the way home after a gig, the bass player and drummer were riding with me. The bass player pulled out a joint, lit it up and passed it to the drummer. I told them to throw the joint out the window. I knew if we were pulled over we'd all go to jail and my van and equipment would be impounded. The end result would be a police record and hundreds, if not thousands, of dollars in legal fees. When they refused to throw the joint out, I whipped into the next cheap hotel and forced the two guys out of my van.

I drove off and left them standing in the parking lot, shooting me the finger and cussing me as I drove away.

## BUD WISER KNIFE FIGHT

During my single years I rented a three-bedroom house on Houston's north side that turned into a Grateful Dead-type crash pad where my band, homeless musicians, new-age hippies and hot and cold rotating groupies were in and out of the place around the clock.

The house had a detached garage that had been turned into a game room, complete with air conditioning, wall-to-wall carpet, a fireplace, a pool table, a TV, a stereo system and a wet bar. Impromptu after-gig parties would often carry on until dawn.

Also during this time I was dealing with a bass player who lived at the house. I'll call him Bud Wiser. He was a serious drinker. He would start drinking Budweiser as soon as he woke up in the afternoon and drink until he passed out after 2am. It was hard to keep him sober enough to play a gig.

One night after a gig no one followed us home. Being exhausted I went straight to bed. The drummer, who also lived at the house, disappeared into his bedroom with his girlfriend. I took for granted that Bud would crash as well.

Around 4am I was awakened by the sound of Zydeco music cranked up so loud it nearly blew me out of bed. I thought the cops would soon be knocking on the front door.

I jumped out of bed and went to the game room. The place was empty except for Bud. He was standing in the middle of the room with a beer in one hand, teetering back and forth and staring into space like a zombie. I yelled for him to turn the music down. Though he was looking right at me, he didn't realize I was there. When I hit the off button Bud's glazed-over, solid black eyes burned a hole through me. I noticed a kitchen knife in his other hand. He raised the knife and growled through clenched teeth, "You don't turn my music down!"

I picked up a cue stick from the pool table, drew it back like a baseball bat, and commanded, "Drop the knife!"

We yelled back and forth for a few minutes. He called me every filthy name in the English language. Finally he dropped the knife. I tossed the cue stick aside, then lit into Bud like Mohammed Ali. I needed to get the best of him before he grabbed the knife again.

We fought all over the room. Somehow I managed to pick him up and body slam him down on the pool table, then jumped straddle of him and pinned him down. Through it all he was still holding his beer. I grabbed his beer and poured it on his face and down his throat yelling, "You wanna drink!? You wanna get shitfaced?! Well, here it is!"

Bud was coughing and choking on the beer. Not wanting him to drown, I jumped off him. He jumped to his feet, ready for round two. "You better kill me now, mutherfucker," he screamed, "cause someday I'm gonna kill *you*!"

I grabbed the knife, ran outside and threw it on top of the house.

I told Bud to sleep it off in the game room and I went back in the house. For my own safety and the safety of the drummer and his girlfriend who slept through it all, I locked all the doors and windows in the house. I didn't want him coming in on us as we slept.

Around noon the next day I took coffee and sandwiches to Bud. I tried to talk to him about the situation. I told him if he wanted to stay with the band, he'd have to get sober and stay that way. I also told him for the rest of the week he could only come in the main house to use the bathroom and take a shower and, until he got his drinking under control, he was to sleep in the game room. Bud glared at me. He threw the sandwiches and coffee on the floor and accused me of holding him prisoner and feeding him like a dog in the garage. Garage? It was a game room with every comfort except a bathroom.

Bud walked to the corner store where he apparently made a call from the pay phone. He returned with a twelve-pack of Budweiser. About an hour later someone pulled up in my driveway, picked Bud up and he was gone.

Once again, my band and my career suffered because of someone else's substance abuse.

## TUBBY

In the late '80s and through 2001, I occasionally employed a transient, mercenary bass player who was one of the most unique characters I have ever met.

"Tubby" was a big, fat, slob with serious alcohol and drug problems. He was in and out of the band for about fifteen years. In early years he seldom bathed and would often sleep and play in the same clothes for a week at a time. He always had big, black circles around his eyes. His dirty, shoulder-length curly hair was so thick it looked like a wild, untrimmed shrub mounted on his shoulders.

Back when club owners gave bands free drinks, many told me to never to bring Tubby back in their club because he drank so much. Tubby could drink a whole bottle of Crown by himself and never miss a note. Some made Tubby pay for his drinks, but even that did not slow him down. His bar tab was sometimes more than the salary I paid him for the gig.

Along with his alcohol and drug problems, Tubby was also an obnoxious asshole with a bad attitude and hated every human on the planet. He was always rude, crude and filthy-mouthed when talking to people, especially women. He had no respect for anyone or anything. If he could not eat it, drink it or fuck it, he wasn't interested.

If the guy was such a pain in the ass, why did I keep hiring him back? Because he was, and probably still is, the best damn bass player in the whole frickin' world. I believed in him and hoped someday he would straighten up and we'd have great band.

Other bass players that attended our shows marveled at Tubby's natural abilities. He could slap, pop, funk-out and play any style of music. He could execute intricate jazz and rock solos that blew people away, all the while standing still as a statue without a blink, a smile, a hint of facial expression or bead of sweat.

Tubby was the first bass player I ever worked with who drew his own crowd and had his own fan club because of the way he played. Many people told me they never realized what a bass player actually did until they heard Tubby.

## REDNECK MOTHERS

In the winter of 1988, we had a regular weeknight gig at a little country-western bar in Pasadena called The Diamond Club. It was always a painfully boring gig, what we musicians call a money gig. We wanted to rock out and play the blues, but the situation required us to play old country songs in order to keep a paycheck. Every time we ended a song the room would fall silent. The dozen or so people in the club would sit staring at us like zombies.

One night after we'd ended a song, Tubby grabbed the mic and yelled, "Fuck all you sorry-ass Pasadena redneck motherfuckers that won't clap!"

It was such a surprising outburst the drummer Gerald Handwright and I cracked up laughing. The small, half dead group of zombies didn't even flinch. The owner told me later, "You'd best tell yer boy to keep his mouth shut or he ain't coming back!"

One night we finally got some applause from one guy. Elated we were getting a response, I grabbed the mic and shouted, "Thank you very much!"

When I looked across the room I realized it was just a guy pounding a pack of cigarettes into his hand.

## ENEMAS ANYONE?

At a biker bar in Bacliff, Texas, a girl sat down at the bar between Tubby and me and told us how good we sounded. I said thank you and she and I made small talk. She looked over at Tubby and said, "You're being awfully quiet."

Tubby took a big slug from his beer, blew a big, loud, disgusting belch and replied, "Baby, why don't you and me go somewhere and give each other a Ben-Wah ball enema."

The girl jumped off the bar stool. "You're one sick motherfucker! I was trying to be nice and that's what I get for it."

Tubby calmly replied, "Being nice to me means sucking my dick."

The girl ran out the door screaming.

## MAIL BOX

One night during a break, Tubby, me and the drummer sat at a table talking. As usual, Tubby silently stared off into space, his mind a million miles away. He had been sulking about something for a week. He finally admitted he was pissed off at his girlfriend's boss for firing her. The unemployed girlfriend told Tubby to either get a day job or move out. Tubby hated working day jobs, but he had no other option because he had no place to go.

Out of the clear blue and without any expression, Tubby spoke up. "You know, I think I'm gonna shit in a box for three days and mail it to my girlfriend's boss." I rolled with laughter.

Thinking about it now, he probably did.

## OFFENDED FLAMINGO

In the summer of 1992, we played at The Flamingo Cafe in Clear Lake every Sunday afternoon. While on break, the owner, a big, burly redneck about 6' 4", called me into his office and began yelling at me about the way the band talked to his waitresses. I didn't know what the hell he was talking about. Apparently Tubby had made a rude and disgusting offer to one of the teeny-bopper waitresses. "Hey baby, how'd you like to get licked by a bass player and a sax player at the same time?"

The girl freaked out and reported the incident to her boss who then jumped my ass. I in turn jumped Tubby's ass. Tubby had to apologize to the owner and the waitress or else be fired from the band or we'd all lose our job.

I was told the band could stay, but if Tubby opened his mouth again his ass was history.

On our last night to play at the Flamingo in October of 1992, Tubby stripped off his clothes and ran naked across the parking lot, screaming obscenities at the top of his lungs at the owner. We all jumped in the van and sped away before the cops showed up and before the owner could make his way down from the top deck, across the pier and to the parking lot.

That big dude would have kicked all our asses.

## Locking Horns at The Hop

After leaving the Flamingo on our last night, I went home and went to bed. Tubby and the sax player went to a bar in Clear Lake called The Hop.

Around 1am, the phone rang. It was the sax player. He was drunk and crying like a little girl. He said Tubby had beat him up. He informed me he would never play on the same stage with Tubby again. He insisted I fire Tubby or he would quit.

After the sax player calmed down, I told him we'd talk about it the next day. I laughed when I told my wife what happened and went back to sleep. Ten minutes later the phone rang again. This time it was Tubby with his own drunken version of the fight. Tubby also refused to ever play on the same stage with the sax player and insisted I fire *him*.

What happened? Apparently the pair went to The Hop after our gig and got shitfaced. Drunken horseplay got out of hand and Tubby beat the shit out of the sax player. The club bouncers then beat the shit out of both of them and threw them out.

Tubby and the sax player both agreed to stay in the band for one more major event, the coveted "Party On The Plaza" in downtown Houston, as long as they could be on opposite sides of the stage and did not have to speak to each other. Done.

After the gig at Party On The Plaza, I never saw the sax player again.

## Drummer Takes Tips

Along with Tubby's many faults, he was notoriously lazy. He seldom ever helped move band equipment in or out without me raising hell with him. Even then he moved as slow as molasses and resisted any request to lend a hand.

One night after a gig at the River Queen in Baytown, Tubby sat at the bar drinking while the drummer and I loaded up everything except Tubby's bass rig. Our drummer was a big guy who wouldn't put up with Tubby's crap. He took Tubby's share of the tips and put them in his own pocket. When Tubby came back he asked about the tips.

"They're right here in my fuckin' pocket," the drummer yelled. "I'm doing your part of the work so I'm keeping your part of the tips. If you're man enough to take 'em outta my pocket, you can have 'em. If you ain't man enough, then shut the fuck up cause I'm taking your tips every night that you don't help!"

"Fuck ya'll! I quit!" yelled Tubby. He grabbed his bass gear, shoved it in his car and flipped us the bird as he drove away. I had never seen that fat boy move so fast.

As we stood there laughing, the drummer said, "Man, I'm sorry I made him quit."

"Don't worry. He'll be back tomorrow night." He was.

## Amps For Drugs

When Tubby was near rock bottom, he told me his bass amp had fallen out of his car and busted to pieces. I loaned him a small 4-channel Peavey PA head to play through until he could buy a new amp. Oddly enough, within a week, it was mysteriously stolen from his car at his apartment. I was too trusting and stupid in those days to consider Tubby might have pawned my gear for drug money.

For the next couple of weeks we ran his bass guitar through the PA. We sounded like shit. I started taking ten bucks a night out of Tubby's money to pay for the stolen PA head. With each payroll deduction, Tubby would threaten to whip my ass. He never did.

## Happy New Year

Two days before New Year's Eve of 1992, Tubby called me in a drunken stupor. Referring to the payroll deduction, he accused me of stealing money from him, told me get fucked and hung up. He left me in a bind with only two days to find a bass player for New Year's Eve.

Jerry Carpenter, one of Houston's best bass players, happened to be available and saved our ass.

I did not see Tubby again for eight years.

## The Return Of Tubby

When Tubby showed up on the Houston music scene again around 2000, he had put himself through rehab and was a changed man. He was clean cut and wore clean clothes. He looked me up at a club. He looked me straight in the eye, shook my hand and apologized for the man he used to be. I was impressed.

Two years later I took a chance and rehired him. Though it had been ten years since we'd played together, it only took ten minutes to realize that even though he was no longer a junkie, he was still smoking, drinking and extremely vulgar to our female following. Again he became a thorn in my side and I got a lot of complaints about him.

## Ten Bucks A Smoke

In an effort to try to raise our professional image, I made it law there would be no cigarettes or alcohol on my stage. The only drink allowed on stage was bottled water. Unless you are Keith Richards, smoking on stage lowers the professional image of the band. Beer bottles lined up on top of the amps is worse, even if the show is sponsored by a beer company.

After implementing the "No Booze/No Smoking" rule on the bandstand, a lot of musicians have put me to the test.

After awhile Tubby began to defy my no smoking rule. He took his time between songs to light a cigarette. He'd nonchalantly take a couple of long, arrogantly slow draws, blow clouds of smoke into the air and then meticulously insert the lit cigarette in the headstock of his guitar – all the while giving me a go-to-hell look daring me to do something.

I finally told him, "That cigarette just cost you ten bucks. Every time you light up, it's gonna cost you ten more bucks, so you better enjoy your smoke!"

"You charge me ten bucks a smoke," he retorted, "and I'll whup yer fuckin' ass right here!"

"Maybe you will, maybe you won't. I still get the money before you do and I'm taking ten bucks out every time you bring a beer or fire up on this stage."

He snuffed out the smoke.

## 300 Pound Canary

Tubby hated bikers. He adamantly refused to adhere to our biker band dress code and image. He claimed that he didn't have any black clothes and refused to buy any. In protest he showed up at every biker event wearing pastel-colored barber shirts.

We always give our band members their first band t-shirt for free. It's black. I told him to wear it at every gig. At each event he would conveniently forget the shirt. One night he wore a blinding, bright yellow bowling shirt. He looked like a 300-pound canary. He argued about wearing the second t-shirt I gave him. I reminded him I was the guy signing the checks. That night I deducted the cost of the second shirt out of his pay. He was pissed, but wore the t-shirt at every gig from then on.

Note to musicians: Just like going to work for any established day job, if you join an existing and successful band, you play by their rules. What if you had a chance to work for *KISS*? Do you think you'd be able to perform in a yellow bowling shirt and a pair of flip flops?

## Burn That Bridge

Tubby got his fill of my rules and regulations. One Thursday he called to say his girlfriend had caught him drinking and threatened to throw him out if he didn't quit the band right then.

I had Friday, Saturday and Sunday afternoon booked. I asked Tubby to at least show some professional respect and play through the weekend. He refused. Again he left me in a serious bind. There was no way I could find a bass player in 24 hours that knew my original songs.

Over the next three nights I worked with three different bass players, Brad McCool, J.C. Moore and Larry "Lownote" Johnson. They pulled me out of a bind at the last minute. All three are great bass players and we gave the fans at each show their money's worth.

As for Tubby, I learned he was playing with another band the very next night. That was in 2002. I haven't seen or heard from him since.

I don't care how great a bass player he is or was, Tubby burned his last bridge with Mean Gene Kelton.

## Quickie

In 2002, I hired a drummer in his late thirties nicknamed "Quickie." He earned his nickname because he was a notorious womanizer, always in hot pursuit of the next "quickie" with any female who would give him two minutes. His number one priority was to add another notch to his belt.

Quickie's pickup lines were corny to the point of being ridiculous and down right hilarious. We'd cringe and snicker when he made his adolescent sales pitch to his female prey. More often than not his outdated lines were wasted on women far out of his league and hip to his bullshit. They didn't mince words and busted him like a schoolboy.

One night a young woman came to the bandstand during a break to buy a CD. As I was making the transaction, Quickie said to her, "You have the most beautiful eyes. I could see those beautiful blue eyes all the way across the room – I was so mesmerized I couldn't even keep time on the drums."

The young woman threw him a razor-sharp look and replied, "You must be one really horny mutherfucker, cause my eyes are brown and I haven't heard a stupid line like that since I was in high school! And besides, there's no way you could have seen my eyes cause I was in the back shootin' pool, *asshole!*"

As she walked away, I busted out laughing.

Like a football player with the wind knocked out of him, Quickie recoverd from the serious blow to his ego and within seconds was on to his next victim.

Quickie was always ready with an autographed drumstick, complete with his phone number, for any lady that caught his eye. In his younger days that gesture would have made a teeny-bopper groupie pee her pants. According to Quickie, the drumstick trick always guaranteed a quick roll in the band bus later on. Now at nearly forty, Quickie's antics were obvious and comical to the more mature women who attended our shows.

At one show Quickie threw a drumstick across the large dance floor, expertly planting it under a table of women, striking the women in the legs as it bounced around under their table. On break he made a beeline to the table, inquiring about the drumstick that he "accidentally dropped" (from behind the drums on a stage some fifty feet away).

The band watched in amusement as Quickie made a big show of autographing the drumstick and attempting to give it to the young ladies. They all politely refused to accept it.

With the drumstick in hand, Quickie scurried back to the bandstand with the bewildered expression of a spanked puppy while the ladies snickered at each other.

At a blues festival in Arkansas, Quickie put on his tight, black leather pants and made the rounds to the single women in the audience, presenting them with business cards and throwing down his hook lines. At the end of the night two women came to our booth where we were signing autographs. They publicly chewed Quickie's ass out for being such a transparent whore. We all laughed and kept signing autographs.

Regardless of his turn downs, Quickie had an amazing success rate. "It's just like playing baseball," he said. "If you swing the bat enough times, you'll eventually hit a home run!"

We jokingly told him home runs don't count when it comes to those "skanky double-baggers" he scooped from the bottom of the barrel.

While visiting a music store in Odessa, Texas, Quickie struck up a conversation with three very attractive young women. We could hear him giving them his big star schpiel about the band, who he was and details of our show later that night.

A few minutes later he yelled, "See you guys at the gig!" Quickie took off with the girls.

Later that night the three young ladies showed up at our gig and Quickie introduced them to the rest of us. I inquired about the black "X" marked on the back of each girl's hand.

"That's because we're *minors*," one of them said, rolling her eyes in exasperation.

"Minors!" I blurted. "Just how old are you girls?"

They were fifteen, sixteen and seventeen years old! Quickie had gotten the girls in as guests of the band. I called Quickie outside and read him the riot act. He had ridden around Odessa all day with three underage females. "You dumbass!" I yelled. "You'll get the whole band killed or locked up! Get rid of them, *now!*"

"But all we did was ride around and see the sights!" he argued.

"Don't you know what the word 'statutory' means?" I yelled. "You're forty! They're *kids!*"

I also ordered him not to hounddog any of the West Texas women. I didn't want the whole band buried in a shallow grave in the West Texas desert by some pissed off cowboys because Quickie had a hard-on. He stuck out his bottom lip and pouted like a scolded child.

A few weeks later I had to fire Quickie. He got drunk, passed out and slept for two days, missing a Saturday night show. Thinking it was a Saturday morning, he called to ask directions to that night's gig. Imagine his surprise when I informed him it was already Sunday. We haven't worked together since.

Quickie was an amazingly talented salesman. Many times when we were on the road, he'd jump out of the van at a truck stop. He'd hound the truckers until they bought enough CDs to cover the cost of our gas. He did it for sport and the thrill of the kill. He was amazing to watch when he went into action.

I'm proud to say that Quickie finally cleaned up his act and got married. Today he owns his own successful small business. He's still one the best drummers I've ever worked with and one of the most self-motivated people I've ever known. We are still great friends.

## Doc Bass

In younger days we never thought to ask new band members about their health. After all, we were *young*! As years passed and band members have gotten older, it's become necessary to ask personal health questions and get next of kin and medical info so we'll know what to do in case a band member keels over or we have an accident on the road.

I have worked with alcoholics, epileptics, diabetics, drug addicts (recovering and participating), people who suffer from high blood pressure, obesity, a bad heart, liver problems, loose bowels, heart stents, heart bypasses, bad backs, bi-polar disorders, depression, victim syndrome, Peter Pan syndrome, joint disorders, missing fingers and toes, metal plates, pins, rods, false teeth and hair implants just to name a few.

We started asking about band members' health status after we had an experience on the road with a new bass player. He opened a briefcase lined with dozens of pill bottles, all labeled and neatly organized in little pill bottle holsters like shotgun shells in an ammo case. The briefcase also contained inhalants, sprays, a glucometer and a blood pressure checking apparatus. We began to inquire about his health.

Because of all his pills, we started calling him "Doc Bass." He was obviously a big guy, but when we hired him he conveniently failed to mention he suffered from numerous ailments caused by tobacco, over-eating and sitting on his ass for too many years. And did I mention, he snored like a hacksaw cutting through a tin roof?

Doc Bass weighed about 300 pounds and never exercised. He suffered from smoking-related problems and was always coughing, wheezing, hacking and spitting. He had asthma and was always short of breath. He suffered from low stamina, low energy, insomnia, sleep apnea, diabetes, obesity, hypertension and poor blood circulation.

He also failed to mention he suffered two heart attacks, two bypass surgeries and had a chest full of stents. He was only forty five years old.

I've worked with a lot of people with a lot of problems and most people try to heal their health problems. Not this guy. Depending on where we stopped to eat, we watched him drink beer and eat stacks of hot, buttered pancakes drowning in syrup and chicken fried steaks smothered in gravy.

At Waffle House Restaurants across the nation, Doc would order hashbrowns covered with so much nasty, brown chili, cheese and onions that I told him it looked as though a cow with diarrhea had backed up and shit in his plate. He bellowed a big laugh and ate it anyway.

When his blood sugar shot through the roof, his face turned red and his eyes glazed over. He'd just give a hearty chuckle and tell us not to worry, he had a pill to fix it.

If his blood pressure went through the ceiling, he'd laugh at us and say, "Don't worry, I got a pill for it."

When we were on tour he'd sit up wide awake all night in the passenger seat. When it came his turn to drive, he'd fall asleep behind the wheel within minutes.

On the road we schedule our pit stops to pee and change drivers every two hours. Due to poor blood circulation in his legs, Doc would pull over to stretch his legs and smoke a cigarette every thirty minutes. With him driving, we were going nowhere fast. We had to quit letting him drive.

Not only did his bad health and medications affect his driving, it affected his bass playing. After eight months, Doc still hadn't been able to master all the songs on our CDs and would forget many of the simplest songs we played every night.

After listening to his excuses week after week, I'd finally demanded he learn the songs and pay attention to what he was doing on stage. He finally got tired of my shit and quit the band. We hated to lose him. He was a nice guy.

Too bad Doc didn't have a pill to fix his bass playing.

## MAD SAX

During the mid-nineties I hired a sax player named Al. He was one of the best sax players I'd ever heard and worked with, but he had an explosive temper and a short fuse.

One night on stage he kept complaining about his monitor mix. He grabbed the mic and yelled, "I'm gonna whup somebody's ass for fuckin' up my monitor mix!"

I was embarrassed and infuriated by his outburst. "I own the PA and set the sound. The ass you want to whip is mine, and the season is open year round."

He never said another word about it.

Al loved to walk into the audience with his sax when playing his solos. One night, while standing in the middle of the dance floor, a guy accidentally bumped into him. Al set his sax back on the stage and started after the guy. I had to intervene. The professionalism of the band suffered because of Al's hot temper and nasty mouth.

Al had two equally talented and equally obnoxious brothers. One played slide trombone, the other played the coronet. Though Al was the only one on my payroll, the other two would perform all night long for free for the prestige of saying they were with the band and to get free drinks. The three of them would harass every woman in the place like a pack of dogs.

Even though the three brothers made my band sound fantastic, and two of them played for free, they were more trouble than they were worth. I received complaints from fans because they always started fights, harassed women, and bummed money, cigarettes and drinks.

By himself, Al was never much of a problem. He only showed his ass when his two brothers were there to back him up. I told him he could stay, but his trouble-making brothers had to go. The next day he called to say that he and his two brothers were coming to the gig to whip my ass. I asked him to be there at least ten minutes before show time and would oblige them.

That was in 1996. I haven't seen them yet.

## BEER FOR SAX

In October of 1999 I went in the studio to record my first CD, *Most Requested*. I hired a sax player I'd met at a jam session to play on "Cruisin' Texas Avenue." At the jam sessions he always made the song sound fantastic. His long, wailing notes made it sound great, like the soundtrack from *Eddie and The Cruisers*.

I had told all my players to show up clean and sober for the recording sessions.

The sax player arrived at the studio around noon, already drunk. In one hand was his sax, in the other was a six-pack of beer.

We burnt up an hour of studio time listening to the sax player embarrass himself and make excuses. He never could get it right. He left the studio with tears in his eyes and a beer in his hand. Alcohol took his dream from him.

If you listen to that 1999 recording of "Cruisin' Texas Avenue," you will not hear a saxophone on the song. Too bad. The guy was an excellent player.

Let that be a lesson to all you young musicians. Whatever you do, or *don't* do, in a recording session will last forever.

## WALKING OFF THE STAGE

I had a bass player and drummer who refused to comply with my "No Drinking, No Dope, No Smoking" policies. Finding a loophole in my rules, they would arrive already stoned, claiming they were on their *own* time when they got high. They thought it was funny. Their high time bled over into our playing time and our first sets were horrible.

One night, as usual, our first set *sucked.* Discouraged with their dope-influenced performance I went outside and sat in my van to chill out during the first break.

The drummer, not knowing I was in my van, got into his car which happened to be parked next to my van. He pulled a beer from the floorboard and popped it open, then fired up a joint. I was fuming. I decided to wait until after the gig to confront him.

As we started the second set the bass player walked up on stage with a full beer. I told him to leave it off the stage. He refused, saying he wasn't about to let a full beer go to waste.

I knew it was useless to preach. Without saying a word I took my guitar off, stuck it in the case and proceeded to load up my gear. Both musicians were cussing me, saying I'd better play or else they'd kick my ass because they needed the gig money for gas to get home. I knew they were too fucked up to fight. I just kept loading my gear.

Although I needed the money as bad as they did, there was a principle at stake. I loaded up and drove off. Again, someone else's alcohol and dope problems caused the band to sound like shit, caused me to lose income and cost them their jobs.

## TWO BULLS IN THE SAME STALL

From time to time I've hired musicians who had been leaders of their own bands. They all wanted to get out from under the stress of booking, promoting, hiring and firing and all the other BS that is part of "payin' the cost to be the boss."

Each time I hired a former "leader" I had to listen to them tell me how *they* did it in *their* band, how I was doing it all wrong and how I should run my band and show. In my opinion their way must not have worked, that's why they asked me for a job in the first place. In my band I'm always open to suggestions, but the bottom line, we do things *my* way.

I usually paid them more than they made as bandleaders in their own bands, but all the money in the world does not buy off the bruised ego and the resentment of losing control and being "the Star."

### Bash

One bass player I hired, who had fronted his own band as rhythm guitarist and singer, refused to learn the bass lines to my original songs as they were played on my CDs. Bash insisted he knew a better way. He didn't. He argued about every arrangement and told me my arrangements were all wrong. He was lazy and refused to do his homework.

To top it off, Bash would sit with our fans "bashing" the drummer, the music and me, stabbing me in the back with jealous insults. He'd whine about how I'd robbed him of his creativity. *Creativity?* He was a *copy* musician! He had no creativity of his own. He was a frustrated Neil Young wannabe and constantly complained I never let him play harmonica.

Truth is, Bash's Neil Young impersonations were horrible. Laughable. If he'd stuck to the job he was hired to do things would've been great. I finally got sick and tired of his bashing, back stabbing, cry-baby, lazy, know-it-all ways and fired him.

Years later Bash is still complaining to fans how I mistreated him.

## Bass With A Case

Another bass player and former band leader got pissed off because Joni was going on the road with us for two weeks and his wife was not.

When we discussed the trip on the phone, I reminded him I owned the company and *he* worked for me, his wife didn't. I also reminded him Joni was an integral part of our organization, Vice-President of our record label and in charge of all merchandise sales and management of the shows. Only essential personnel go on the road. No girlfriends, no wives, no good buddies.

He called me a few dirty names, said some very ugly things about Joni and then hung up on me. He made the mistake of calling back and making terroristic threats on my answering machine. I played his threats for the Baytown Police. To this day there is a case number in Baytown with his name on it.

## Lead Bass

After working with me on and off for several years, one bass player felt life was passing him by. His dream was to be a lead guitarist and front his own band. Within a month after quitting my band, he called to tell me how hard it was to find good players, keep them straight and sober and get them to show up on time. *Welcome to my world.*

He offered me $50 a night to front his band while he went back on bass temporarily until he could find permanent players. He is no longer in the music business.

# Dippin' and Chewin'

Early in my career I performed with alot of country-western bands in places where a good ol' boy having a "chaw in the jaw" or a "dip in the lip" was common. I never thought much about it back then.

I even tried dippin' and chewin' myself to see what the fuss was all about. For the first few minutes I enjoyed the wintergreen flavor of the "pinch between the cheek and gum." The high was better than weed. No wonder cowboys always yell "yeeee-haw!" After a few minutes my head started spinning. To the amusement of my friends I spent the next hour heaving my guts up. I swore off dipping and chewing.

To this day, even the smell of Wintergreen Lifesavers automatically makes me want to puke.

I have performed with musicians who kept a spit cup right next to their beer. I've seen experienced spitters drink from one bottle and spit in another, never getting the two mixed up.

In my opinion, dippin', chewin' and spittin' should be kept in barnyards and feedlots and off of professional entertainment stages. Could you imagine going to an Oak Ridge Boys or Kenny Rogers concert in Branson and one of them spitting in a plastic cup on stage?

I had a drummer who chewed tobacco and took my "no dipping, no chewing, no spitting" policy as a personal attack. No matter what I said, he continued to disrespect me, my policy, the band and the fans by chewing tobacco on stage. I got calls from pissed-off club owners because he'd leave spit cups or horse-turd size balls of chewed tobacco on stage after a show.

We played some real nice places and fans were disgusted watching him spit on stage. When we would meet our fans or other music industry professionals, or have photos made, it was embarrassing seeing tobacco on his lips and stains on his clothes. Like the redneck he was, he refused to chew on his own time and "spit responsibly."

We often had to load equipment while walking in his tobacco spit.

## NO STYROFOAM PRODUCTS

We performed a private party at a very ritzy, high-class restaurant where we ate a complimentary meal with the guests before show time. Several waiters with small linen towels draped over their arms attended to our every need, each one serving a different course. Their activities were overseen by the Maître d' who treated us like royalty and spoke with a suave international accent that sounded as cool as Ricardo Montalban.

Our drummer, whose manners may have been acceptable when eating cheeseburgers in a moving semi truck, embarrassed us all by complaining about the fine international cuisine. He refused to eat. When the size of the main dish did not suit him, he commented loud enough for the quiet, candle lit room to hear, "Mah dawg shits more 'n 'at!"

He continued to embarrass us throughout the meal. He topped off his display of barnyard etiquette by pulling a pouch of tobacco from his jacket. To our disbelief, right there in front of everyone, he packed his jaw with what looked like a big brown birdnest. He asked the Maître d' for a Styrofoam cup to spit in. With one eyebrow raised, the Maître d' leaned over and discreetly informed him "the establishment does not carry Styrofoam products."

The drummer went to the van and retrieved a plastic Whataburger cup.

While the rest of us discussed which silver fork to use, our drummer sat at the table making fun of the gourmet food and the waiters and continued spitting in the plastic cup.

Not exactly one of our proudest moments.

## REAL DIE HARDS ONLY

I had a drummer who had a jealous streak a mile wide. He would get furious when we arrived at a gig and the marquee just said "Mean Gene Kelton" and did not include "& The Die Hards."

"What about us?" he complained. "Why duddin' the sign say '& The Die Hards'? You wuddin' be shit without us!"

"I'm not in charge of the advertising," I'd reply.

That drummer was so jealous that without my permission he printed t-shirts at his own expense that said "The Die Hards." My name was not included. "But we're the 'Die Hards,' not you. You're just Gene Kelton." After a heated discussion and some legal mumbo-jumbo about product infringement, he agreed not to print any more t-shirts using my band name.

## MUTINY

Being cursed with a jealous heart and a burning desire to be noticed, the same drummer lusted for fame and glory so much that he began to envision himself as lead singer of his own band. He wanted to put me out of business so bad he contacted my current band members, as well as my own sons, and insisted they all get together, start a band without me and call themselves "The Die Hards."

His plan was to steal my band members, steal my band name and turn my own sons against me. Yet, he had the gall to call himself my friend.

I was proud they all turned him down.

## Stepper's Teeff

Stepper, as we called him, was a damn good drummer. We didn't know he had false teeth. One night in a bar Stepper was singing and his upper teeth fell out, landing on the snare drum. Before he realized it, he brought his stick down striking the side of his teeth. They flipped into the air, across the room and onto the dance floor.

The girls on the dance floor screamed. They kicked Stepper's teeth around the floor like a hockey puck. Stepper jumped off the drums, leaped to the floor and scurried around on his hands and knees, chasing his teeth and yelling, "Mah teeff, mah teeff!"

I know he was embarrassed, but people were rolling with laughter. Stepper snatched up his teeth, doused them with a beer, wiped them on his shirt sleeve and put them back in his mouth. He insisted we start the song over so he could finish it. Now that's the Die Hard spirit.

## Melt Down

There was a big, fat drummer who called me many times through the years wanting to be a Die Hard. He was a nice guy and a good drummer. He was perfect for laid-back blues bands that played small, smokey blues bars, but his style was too tame for us.

Finally I booked him for one gig just to see if he had any hidden talents we didn't know about or any pent-up energy he was dying to unleash on the world. The gig was an outdoor biker event in the summertime and the heat was deadly. From the moment we kicked off he made us sound like a lounge act at a Holiday Inn instead of a blues rock show band. All day we kept yelling, "Hit harder! Hit harder!"

Toward the end of our show, he was gasping for breath and struggling to keep time. I saw his eyes roll back in his head as he looked toward the sky with his mouth wide open. He was not used to playing as hard as we required and he wasn't used to the heat. He was soaked with sweat like a heart attack victim. I bet he melted off twenty pounds that day.

After that gig he never called me again. It ain't easy to be a Die Hard!

## Worst Band

Around 1991, my brother Ray came to play bass play for me in the short lived "Kelton Brothers Band." We hadn't performed together in twelve years. He'd spent several years with a country band in Arkansas and six years with a popular country-western band in Dayton called Southern Breeze. He and I played rock 'n roll back in high school and performed together briefly during the '70s in Firecreek and The Texas Country Bandits. He was a good bass player. I thought with his talent he'd fall back into our former bluesrock groove fairly easy. We hired a drummer from Baytown named Dennis Forbes, whose only musical experience at that time was also with country bands.

So there I was, a blues rocker with a country-western rhythm section. We were a train wreck that happened nightly.

Every blues shuffle sounded like a mutated version of a Merle Haggard country song. I gave the guys blues CDs and cassettes, telling them to listen and learn. It was no use. We still sounded like a country band trying to play the blues. To compensate for their lack of experience, they overplayed to the point that one club owner told us we sounded like a band with a lead guitar, lead bass and lead drums. He said we were the worst band he'd ever heard.

Ray and Dennis were both nice, easy-going guys and good musicians in their own right. I held on to the belief that I could eventually make blues players out of them.

I finally had to face the fact that the club owner was right. *We sucked.*

## WHO DRESSED J.R.?

In the mid-nineties I hired a country-western bass player "J.R." who kept showing up to gigs dressed like a country bumpkin on his way to haul hay. Finally one night I gave him an ultimatum. "Dress accordingly for a blues rock band or you're fired!"

The very next night we had a gig at Lance's Turtle Club in Seabrook, Texas. It was a hot spot that catered to rich, yuppie jetsetters who often drove their cigarette boats and party barges right up to the club's private dock and stepped right into the party. People there wore trendy clothing, fashionable beachwear or bathing suits.

In a spiteful gesture the bass player showed up wearing a turd-brown, three-piece, vintage western-style leisure suit, circa 1975. It came complete with massive bell-bottoms and two-inch cuffs. He wore his "formal" felt cowboy hat with a peacock feather hat band popular during the *Urban Cowboy* days of the early '80s.

The fashion-conscious yuppie clientele of the Turtle Club stared at him all night. I was speechless. I felt like he had worn that suit just to piss me off. After coming from a cowboy band, maybe he didn't realize his suit had been out of style nearly twenty years.

I waited until the night was over before raising hell about his out-of-date outfit. He listened intently to my rant, then calmly replied, "Man, when I wear regular clothes, you bitch at me. When I dress up, you bitch at me. Tell you what. Take this band and stick it up your ass!"

Another paragraph about the "dress code" was added to The *Die Hard Rule Book*.

## ALL DRESSED UP

"Don't dress for where you are, dress for where you want to be." I've heard that saying referred to regarding every kind of business there is, including music.

When breaking into the blues scene in southeast Texas in the early '90s, I noticed how awful the white blues bands dressed and how fantastic the black bands dressed. White bands would perform at the nicest places in sleeveless shirts and raggedy jeans, while the black bands, even at the worst shitholes, were immaculately dressed in three-piece suits, shined shoes and stylish hats turned just right.

Even though an entertainer or band should dress in whatever is appropriate for the occasion and venue, I'm the first to admit to performing in tank tops in my early days in sweltering Texas icehouses.

I soon realized the most successful entertainers dressed for success, no matter the weather or environment. I also believe that no matter what the occasion or venue, an entertainer should always dress so it is obvious they are professional musicians.

Common sense dictates you wouldn't wear a tuxedo to a beach party and neither would you wear a bathing suit to The Ritz. Unfortunately too many musicians don't have a clue what the word "appropriate" means.

When I started insisting that my band dress up and look professional, I was surprised what a *gig from hell* that turned into.

## FLIP-FLOP

At a biker event in Galveston County one Sunday afternoon the bass player, well aware of the Die Hard Dress Code, purposely showed up wearing a sleeveless tank top, cut-off blue jean shorts with tattered threads hanging past his knees and a pair of Dollar Store flip-flops.

When I complained about how he was dressed he replied, "What fuckin' difference does it make? We're just playin' for a buncha stupid fuckin' bikers!"

I was appalled by his answer. Our band was a favorite among bikers. The bass player himself lusted for every bike he saw.

"Man, those guys ride in here on thirty-thousand dollar bikes, wearing a thousand dollars worth of leather!" I argued. "You ain't gonna impress 'em in a pair of shoes that cost less than a beer!"

"They didn't come to look at my shoes," came his disrespectful reply. "They came to hear me play bass!"

He quit the band soon after that performance and got a job driving a delivery truck. I heard they wouldn't let him wear flip-flops at that job either. He's no longer in the music business.

## LESTER THE MO' LESTER

We were befriended by a middle-aged harmonica player, "Lester." He traveled with us occasionally as a non-paid roadie just to get into shows for free and to be seen playing with us. He was a nice guy, a hard worker and a good harmonica player. He used his association with the band as a way to break the ice with single women in the audience.

We began to notice that the females he talked to at the festivals were usually very young, fourteen to sixteen years old. We also began to notice his conversation with us always turned to some disgusting, homosexual, perverted nonsense.

Every time I was distracted, Lester would get next to Joni and lace his conversation with graphic sexual innuendo.

Lester gave Joni the creeps and raised her suspicions. Being an internet sleuth, she did an online investigation on him. He turned out to be a wanted felony child molester in another state. I called some friends in law enforcement. Lester was picked up and put in jail.

## THE REVEREND B

I had a bass player who, in his early forties, looked like Jerry Garcia from the Grateful Dead. He called himself Reverend B. He was every band's answer to the perfect bass player. Nice guy, easy going, always had a big smile. Talented, dependable, experienced, and a good singer. He had good equipment and could play every song in the world.

He was too good to be true, but there was something weird about the wild look in his eyes that concerned me. He had worked in refineries but was on disability so I thought he was always jacked up on medication. Still, I kept telling drummer Dennis Forbes there was something wrong with the guy.

At a gig one night, it finally happened. He snapped. Someone requested "In-A-Gadda Da-Vida." Reverend B glared at me with wild, axe-murderer eyes. He chest began to heave and he trembled all over.

He yelled, "Fuck 'em! Fuck 'em! Fuck 'em all and fuck you! I ain't playing that goddam song! I played it with every piece 'o shit garage band I ever played with, and I ain't playin' it no more!"

Knowing that Reverend B could stomp my ass with his little finger, I still couldn't let him win. He worked for me and this was not a democracy. I yelled back, "Play the goddamn song or I ain't payin' you!"

Reverend B stood motionless like a rhino about to charge. He yelled, "I'll play it tonight but don't ever ask me to play it again!"

He played about a minute of the famous signature bass line, put his guitar down and stormed off stage. When one of the customers tipped him a twenty, I said, "See there, that didn't hurt so bad, did it?" Reverend B was pissed off that I had the upper hand, but he kept the twenty.

A few days later I got a message on my answering machine from the good Reverend B. He spoke in a very low voice as if he was afraid someone on his end might hear him. He whispered, "Hey, Gene. I gotta quit the band, man. My wife is trying to have me committed. I gotta get outta town before she wakes up."

That was in 1993. I haven't seen or heard from him since.

## MID-WIFE

During the early '70s I was asked to play lead guitar for a very successful Hispanic pop-rock band called Magic Sand. The band was made up of two high class, college-educated Spanish guys who played keyboard and rhythm guitar. They both had fantastic voices. Right up front they informed me they were not to be referred to as Mexicans. They were of a pure Spanish bloodline. Okay, whatever.

Since they needed a bass player and drummer, I managed to hook up my brother, Ray, on bass, and our friend, Charlie Taylor, on drums. Practices went well and we were beginning to get gigs in some very nice places.

Both the Spanish guys had exceptionally beautiful and sophisticated wives who hardly acknowledged the three country-ass white boys backing up their husbands. On breaks the Spaniards sat quietly sipping wine with their aloof wives, while we three white-trash boys sat together at another table, drinking beer and telling jokes.

Charlie was a class clown since junior high. He kept everyone rolling with laughter.

One afternoon at a show, the entire band, including the Spaniards' wives, ended up sitting at the same table on a break. Charlie, true to form, was on a roll and had us in stitches.

One of the Spanish girls happened to be pregnant and due any day. In an effort to be funny Charlie announced, "Hey, you know I'm a mid-wife!"

Us gringos laughed, the Spaniards did not. The next day, us gringos was unemployed.

## MIDDLE-AGED CRAZIES

When many men reach their fifties, they go through a mid-life crisis or the Middle-Aged Crazies. Some buy red Corvettes, others leave their wives for younger women. Some buy a Harley and become *Easy Rider* every weekend.

A few years ago I noticed a lot of middle-aged guys buying guitars and trying to break back into the live music scene after not performing since their high school glory days some thirty to forty years prior. In my search for musicians, many Middle-Age Crazies have responded to my ads, showing up with brand new instruments ready for their audition.

I would ask, "How long ya been playin'?"

The usual smoke screen answer was, "I started playin' back in high school."

At first I took that answer to mean they'd been playing music consistently for twenty-five to thirty years. In reality it meant the guy had *not* played *since* high school. Most of those guys were usually good enough to pass an audition playing basic blues songs. When I was in a bind I hired a couple of them by accident.

Middle-Aged Crazies may think they want to re-enter the music business after turning fifty, but when I put them on stage in front of several thousand people they tend to crater. They might have been a CEO with a big company with many employees reporting to them, but when you pick up an instrument you can't delegate. It's all on *you*!

At one show I turned to the band and called the Creedence version of "Suzy Q." The bass player with "thirty years experience" told me he had never played it. *What?!*

At a small concert with about a thousand people, another bass player who often bragged of his lifetime of experience, told me with trembling hands it was the biggest audience *he had ever seen*!

Another bass player who told me he had thirty years experience, would freeze up at every one of our shows. "How many gigs did you play last year?" I finally asked.

"About ten or twelve," he replied, "and they were just jam sessions."

Ten or twelve? I was doing twenty gigs a *month*.

I felt like an idiot for being fooled by the guy and hiring him. He had not been *playing* for thirty years. He had only *owned a bass guitar* for thirty years and lied to me about his experience. I fired him.

I learned the hard way to ask the *right* questions before hiring someone. Today I interrogate the hell out of prospective players. If they don't like my questions, adios. Better to find out up front. If we get past the initial meeting, I give them a CD full of songs to learn, a copy of The *Die Hard Rule Book* and thirty days' probation.

The old saying, "what you don't use, you lose" applies in the music business. Unfortunately, most people think playing an instrument is like riding a bicycle. It's not. The bicycle may still be the same, but your ability to pop wheelies has significantly diminished.

My advice is practice every day. Don't jump back in the music biz too soon. Practice with other players at your level. Hit all the jam sessions and try your luck keeping up with players who stayed with it through the years.

Don't show up with the latest copy of *Guitar Player Magazine* sticking out of your hip pocket. Don't bore people to death with a lot of techno-babble about amps, wattage, tube sizes, who played what gauge guitar strings on so-and-so's album back in *blah, blah, blah*. Knowing all that tech shit does not make you a better player and won't save your ass when some sixteen-year-old Stevie Ray clone cuts your frickin' head off.

Just shut up and *play*!

## DISAPPEARING MUSICIANS

One of the worst things that can happen to a band is for a key member not to show up. In a three-piece band, each member is a key member. Most musicians show some respect when they're going to quit a band and they give some type of notice. With few exceptions I never had much of a problem knowing that a musician was quitting, although it usually happened at their convenience, not mine.

### Ghost

Throughout the '90s I worked with a drummer who would suddenly and unexpectedly disappear into thin air without notice and without a trace, like a ghost. When he'd return to the area, usually after about two years, he'd look me up. He'd give me his sordid schpiel about why he had to leave suddenly, apologizing and promising that if I'd just hire him back he'd be a Die Hard *forever*.

I knew he was full of shit, but I also knew he was one of the best drummers in the business. Like a fool, I always gave the guy another chance.

During the '90s when we were a copy band, Ghost's disappearances were no big deal. Any decent drummer could step in and cover our song list and the public would never know the difference. By 2003 however, after the release of two CDs of original material with harmonies, accents, dynamics and complex musical arrangements, a mercenary drummer could not fake it. Finding a good drummer willing to rehearse proved to be nearly impossible.

At one point we were in the process of preparing to record a live CD and shoot an accompanying music video of the "Panties" song and "The Texas City Dyke." We had a recording crew, camera crew and actors on standby, a script written and dancers ready to choreograph "The Panty Dance." A lot of planning and preparation had been done.

At our next gig Ghost never showed up and never called. He never even called to say he was sorry for committing such a unprofessional, dirty deed to those he called "brother." We were embarrassed in front of our employers and our fans. The band, our fans and *his* fans were hurt that a guy we trusted and treated like family would intentionally and maliciously undermine our plans and leave us hanging.

We've never heard from Ghost since. Good riddance.

All plans for new CDs and videos had to be shelved until we could find another drummer.

Over the next two and a half years, we went through thirteen drummers looking for the right one to add to the Die Hard sound.

## Slippery When Drunk

My never-ending quest for the right drummer turned up a guy who claimed to have played for country music legend Johnny Lee during the *Urban Cowboy* craze. He said he even played on the White House lawn for a president, but couldn't remember for which president.

In our original interview he assured me he did not use drugs and his drinking days were in the past. He was even able to tell me the exact date of his last drink. That should have been my first clue.

At his first gig with us I never saw him take a drink, but he became more shitfaced as the night wore on. His performance was deplorable, sloppy and out of time. He was constantly dragging the beat, blowing through breaks, missing stops and dropping his sticks.

The band and the audience suffered through the gig. During our last break, he disappeared. His truck was gone! The bass player and I waited as long as we could but I finally had to get back on stage and do *something*.

In a desperate effort to compensate for the lack of a drummer, I announced to the audience that, as a songwriter, I wanted to test out some new songs and had instructed the band to sit out the last set. For the next hour I dug out every song and piece of a song I could. I was trying to keep the audience's mind occupied, asking them for their review to help me decide if the new songs were "keepers" or not. It worked. Next thing I knew, it was time to go.

The drummer drove up as we were loading up the last piece of gear. He gave me a long story about how he had given some guy a ride home from the gig and gotten lost on his way back. He opened his truck door and fell out onto the ground. I stuffed half of his money into his shirt pocket and drove off, leaving him passed out in the grass with his feet still in the truck. I never saw him again.

## Shaggy

Another drummer, "Shaggy" was a tall, skinny guy about forty years old. With his thin, scrappy beard, unruly hair and always-shabby clothes, he reminded me of the cartoon character "Shaggy" from *Scooby-Doo*.

Shaggy was an excellent drummer but unfortunately he was a drug addict. Maybe his black front teeth should have given me a clue. He was always rattled and shaky. He always complained of stomach problems.

At every gig he would demand we cut our sets short claiming he had diarrhea and had to run to the restroom and then to his car to take some medicine.

At first I felt sorry for the guy. We soon noticed that he had a never ending case of the shits. After every medicinal treatment, he'd rush every song, sweat profusely and claim that the medicine made him jittery.

Realizing he had a drug problem, I finally told him I didn't care if he shit in his pants we weren't taking a break until I said so.

One night after a gig, Shaggy drove off and we never heard from him again.

## The Mercenary

The unexpected disappearance of Shaggy in mid-June of 2008 left us in a real bind. A four-day stint at the Sandos Caracol Resort in Playa del Carmen, Mexico, in September was only three months away. It meant we had to find a drummer with a passport or able to get one and who was willing to travel out of the country.

Dozens of our Die Hard fans had bought tickets to go to Mexico with us through the travel agency sponsoring the event and we could not cancel just because we didn't have a drummer.

As fate would have it, that same week I was contacted by a drummer, "Boogie." He played for another well-known regional band, but said he was looking for "a real band with balls."

Boogie was a nice guy, about forty years old, who didn't do drugs or alcohol and had a ready-made Die Hard image. He was a good drummer with excellent potential to be a great Die Hard drummer once he learned our music. He already had a passport and was willing to go to Mexico. After doing a couple of fill-in gigs with us, he expressed his desire to be a full time Die Hard.

In mid-July, Boogie told me he had given notice to his other band and would join us full-time in two weeks. Two days later he informed me he was not quitting his other band after all. They had given him a raise. He offered to play for us depending on his availability.

Once again we were in a quandary for a full-time drummer and had to take whoever we could get. Over the next couple of months I divided the shows between various drummers, including Sid and Boogie.

One night in early September I received an emotional voice mail from Boogie. He was screaming into the phone. "I quit that other band! Fuck them! If you guys will still have me, I'm in! I'm ready to be your drummer, *full-time*!"

We welcomed him aboard with open arms. Two days later he quit us, again. He claimed the other band made him a financial offer he couldn't refuse. He said he would work with us as his schedule permitted and still wanted to go to Mexico.

As the Mexico trip drew closer, we scheduled as many shows as possible with Boogie in order to get him in the groove with our music. We wanted to be super-tight in Mexico. Boogie canceled almost every gig with us, all at the last minute, to work with any other band that would pay him a few dollars more.

It became obvious he was what we call a *mercenary*, someone who has no loyalty to anyone and sells their services to the highest bidder. We tolerated his disrespect only because time was too short for us to find another drummer with a passport. And he knew it.

Like a primadonna, Boogie complained about every gig with us from start to finish. The gigs were too far from his house. He burned too much gas. The outdoor gigs were too hot. People were being stuck up. The bass player looked at him funny. He constantly complained at, and about, every gig we played.

On Friday, September 13th, one week before our Mexico trip, Hurricane Ike devastated the Gulf Coast and our trip was postponed until November. New dates and new reservations were set. I emailed the band with the info.

In the middle of all the chaos of hurricane clean up, plus a death in our family, Boogie informed me that since I did not consult with him first about new departure times for Mexico, he would be taking a different flight more convenient to his own personal schedule. He expected me to pay his flight change fees.

I blew up. I was furious. Boogie had crossed the line. He had already lied to us numerous times about joining the band, quit twice, then canceled when he got a better offer. Now he wanted special treatment that was going to cost me more money because I did not *consult with him first*?

I had taken all the crap from him I was going to take. I refused to give in to his demands, waste another dime or another minute or expend another ounce of energy on him. I fired off an email filled with colorful expletives. I stated I did *not* have to consult with him about *anything* and that included departure times. I called him a primadonna, a whiner and an unprofessional mercenary. The final word, "The plane leaves at noon, be on it or don't go!"

Heated emails flew back and forth. Here's one from Boogie you'll get a kick out of:

> *"Gene, Not only are you insecure, you're the most immature 57 year-old I've ever met. It's not my fault that you can't control your temper under fire… spare me all the crap about not being able to handle myself as a professional musician. This is a simple case of old-fashioned band leader vs. progressive sideman… good luck finding another drummer to put up with all the crap. What a shame for me to uncover the real Gene Kelton under these circumstances. After being sworn at, questioned as a musician, I'll never play with you again. I'm not going to Mexico with you because of your unprofessional conduct."*

With regard to him never playing for me again, I wholeheartedly agreed. With regard to my character flaws, I told him, "tell it to *The National Enquirer*!"

With less than a week to find a new drummer, I immediately phoned our Mexico trip producer Jerry Creed. Jerry had produced many shows in Mexico with Houston area bands. Within thirty seconds, I had a new drummer, with a passport. It was Jerry's own son, twenty-four-year-old Jeremy Creed, who served as our drummer for our Mexico shows.

Later that same day I received the another email from the flip-flopping mercenary Boogie:

> *"…if you still want to make this work for Mexico… I'll do everything I can do get to the airport at noon on Sunday… while I concede that I have done my share of flip-flopping, I'm not the type to leave people hanging…"*

I'd heard it all before. He'd already left us hanging too many times.

I replied, "I have another drummer. Have a nice life."

## Pu-King Donuts and The FNG!

At 6' 7" and 265 pounds, thirty-year-old Chris Provost was an intimidating figure as he guarded the door and collected entrance fees at The Howling Coyote in northwest Houston when we started playing there around 2004.

While growing up, Chris had been a roadie for his dad Mike Provost. Mike and his band, The Nighthawks, struggled to support his family on a musician's pay. Having experienced the trials and tribulations of a musician's life first-hand since childhood, Chris always had the bands' best interest at heart. Chris collected door fees for the bands and guarded the entrance with as much attitude and dedication as ancient Roman soldiers in the story of "Horatio At The Bridge." Absolutely no one was going to get past Chris and get in for free, thus robbing the band of income.

At quitting time, Chris could have easily collected his pay and gone home. Instead, he would hang around and help bands load out. Often he would wrap his long arms around the biggest, heaviest piece of gear and effortlessly carry it by himself out the door, down the sidewalk and to the truck. Whenever we offered to assist him, Chris would proudly reply, "Man, this ain't nothin'! I used to do this for my Dad when I was fifteen!"

Over time Chris became a trusted friend and part of our crew. When the Howling Coyote closed in 2008, he began traveling with us and working shows as a door man, roadie and all around hard worker. He became referred to as the FNG (Fuckin' New Guy).

I knew between Chris and our road manager Buddy Love, an equally intimidating figure, I didn't have to worry about anything happening to Joni while I was on stage. Though Chris is proud to claim the title of Joni's bodyguard, he and Buddy both insist it's the general public that they must protect *from* Joni.

On the weekend of September 19th and 20th in 2008, Chris made his first road trip with us to the Live Oak Nudist Resort near Navasota, Texas. Being a natural leader, Chris took over the set up of the gear and the rigging of the sound and lights. The weekend shows at Live Oak are always an adventure and this one was no exception. But, what happens at a nudist resort stays at the nudist resort. It's what happened when we left that was hilarious.

Our Saturday night show ended at midnight. Joni and I retreated to our cabin for a few hours of sleep and told everyone to be prepared to roll at the crack of dawn.

Little did we know, Chris stayed up all night partying with the nudists in the hot tub and had finished off a bottle of Crown Royale mixed with Red Bull. He went back to the room and passed out only an hour before I woke him around 7am.

On the way out that morning Joni rode with Buddy in his truck. Chris rode shotgun with me in the van. Forty minutes after the wake-up call, we pulled into a donut shop in Navasota, operated by an oriental family who waited on us with big smiles. With donuts, coffee and breakfast sandwiches in hand, we climbed back in our vehicles for the two-hour ride home.

Buddy pulled out first and drove toward Main Street. As I made a u-turn in the parking lot of the donut shop to access the side street, Chris yelled, "Stop! Stop!" He jumped out and ran to the rear of the van. I thought he might have left his order on the counter and was headed back into the shop to get it. Due to my u-turn, the rear of the van was positioned just a few feet from the front door of the donut shop.

When I looked in my passenger side rear view mirror, I saw Chris heaving his guts out right there at the front door of the donut shop. The whiskey and Red Bull was taking its revenge.

Suddenly, the vision of a little Chinese man running out the door with a meat cleaver raised high in the air and screaming Chinese obscenities at the six-foot-seven giant puking in his doorway was more than I could handle. I busted out laughing.

In the meantime, Buddy and Joni had pulled over a half-block away to wait for us. My phone rang. It was Joni. From where they were parked they could see Chris at the side of my van and asked me what the hell was going on. I told them Chris was puking in the doorway of the donut shop and the chinese guy was gonna kill him if we didn't get him outta there, right then. Shrieks of laughter blew out of the earpiece.

I hit the horn and started yelling at Chris. "C'mon man, let's get the hell outta here before you get us all killed!"

I knew we had to get away from the donut shop before the cops showed up. I slowly drove toward Buddy's truck which was parked about a hundred yards away. Chris chased after the van, puking as he ran down the street.

Chris caught up with me and climbed in the van. He was sweating profusely and wiping slime from his mouth. I hit the gas. Both vehicles headed for the main highway, hoping to get out of town before the cops caught up with us.

Joni called again. I could hear her and Buddy laughing hysterically. I put them on speaker so Chris could hear. Joni yelled at Chris in a mock Chinese accent, "Ahhh sooo! Yuu no pukeee a my paa-kee lot! Go 'whay! Go 'whay! You run off aww cussomah!"

Chris, sick and hung over, put his hands over his eyes and muttered, "fuck all ya'll!"

The following week we told Chris a surveillance camera had captured his parking lot performance at the donut shop and the Navasota police had issued a warrant for the man who's fuzzy image on the video showed a guy bent over spewing vomit in the doorway of a food establishment. The charges were damaging private property, suspicion of public intoxication, disturbing the peace, loitering, littering, relieving himself in public and violating a sanitation ordinance.

We could barely contain our laughter when we saw the serious, concerned look on his face. Chris knew we were joking and finally started to laugh at himself when I told him, "Oh yeah, there's one more charge, leaving the scene of a "slime!"

## Music Related

Finding and keeping good musicians is not the only hiring dilemma we face in the music business. There is also the challenge of hiring the right recording studio, producer, engineer, soundmen, sound company, roadies, video crew, CD mastering company, video mastering company, graphic designers, web designers and hosts, stage managers, booking agents, publicists, radio promoters, instrument techs, managers, photographers, email services, printers, flyer distributors, assistants, gophers and baby sitters.

Each comes with their own unique flavor of bullshit and potential for a *gig from hell*.

BOOK NINE

# Insignificant Others

As a band leader, not only do I have to deal with personnel problems from band members, I also have to deal with their significant others, wives, girlfriends, husbands, boyfriends, mistresses, groupies, tag-alongs, etc.

How many other jobs or careers are there where wives or girlfriends can go to work with their spouse or partner, sit ten feet from them and ridicule, mock, critique, heckle and become such an embarrassing nuisance they cause that person to be fired?

Imagine if a doctor, lawyer, heavy equipment operator, airline pilot or any skilled professional in any field brought his nagging wife or primadonna girlfriend to work with him. What would happen if she critiqued and heckled his work, bad or good, and then every few minutes yelled out, "Hey baby, you need a drink?"

Or, imagine if every few minutes she invaded the professional's work area, jumped his ass for looking at a female employee, demanded money for a drink in the middle of his work or chewed out his boss on his behalf. It happens with bands all the time.

Why is it because someone sleeps with a band member, they are suddenly an expert on the music business? Why do they think they have any right to represent the band, speak for the band or tell other band members what to do? I don't have a clue, but they *do*.

## Band Wives and Girlfriends

In an all-male band, wives and girlfriends can cause *every* gig to be a *Gig From Hell*. After a while, even women who were initially supportive of their husband/boyfriend's music career feel they are playing second fiddle to his true love, his music.

Next, the women become jealous of the attention to or from fans, other women, other significant others, other band members and groupies and even get jealous of his instrument. In many cases the musician is accused of putting music first and everything else second and made to feel guilty about his dreams, talent and popularity.

Not only does a wife or girlfriend get jealous of her man, but she'll get furious if another band member is getting more glory than her man.

The women usually sit at the same table and gossip *to* each other, *about* each other and each other's man behind each other's backs. If two of them go to the restroom together, you can bet they'll be talking about the other women still sitting at the table and vice versa. Soon, they all hate each other and it's always the guys in the band who suffer and have to listen to a bunch of "he said/she said" bullshit on the way home.

This kind of crap has broken up many a band.

## He Said, She Said

One night on the way home after a gig, my first wife was giving me a long-winded ration of "she-said-he-said-she-said" bullshit that supposedly started with my drummer.

At 2am I dropped my wife off at home. I burned rubber out the driveway and drove twenty-five miles at 90mph to my drummer's house. I drove across his yard, pulled up outside his bedroom window, hit my bright lights and laid on the horn.

He rushed outside where I was waiting. I confronted him about the gossip I'd heard and dared him to kick my ass. He was a big guy and could have stomped me like a bug.

Thankfully he cracked up laughing and said, "Fool! I'm going back to bed! Go home! Call me tomorrow when you sober up!"

We never spoke about the incident again. It was a perfect example of band women running their mouths and starting trouble.

## PUNKIN'

I once had a bass player whose girlfriend called him "Punkin'." He had a limited vocal range so I vetoed most of the songs he wanted to sing. I was only looking out for the band, but Punkin' took it personally and complained to his girlfriend about what an asshole I was.

One night Punkin's girlfriend stood in front of the stage yelling and cussing and publicly accusing me of treating poor Punkin' like a little boy.

In my opinion it was *she* who was treating him like little boy calling him Punkin', fighting his battles for him and acting like his stage mom. The last time I saw her I yelled, "Bitch! Don't let the door hit you in the ass on your way out."

## SHA-MOO

I had a bass player who was married to a 300-pound woman. She would get so drunk at our gigs she would pass out on the table at every show. Club owners adamantly insisted we take her to the car. Since she literally could not walk, and we couldn't get a forklift through the front door, the guys in the band had carry her to the car with her arms over our shoulders and her feet dragging behind her like a wounded soldier.

Once we got her to the car, we had to turn her around with her ass against the back seat and give her a push. Gravity did the rest. Once she flopped down in the back seat, we'd drag her across the seat from the other side. There was absolutely no way to gracefully stuff a 300-pound, unconscious, fat woman in the back seat of a car. It would have been easier to drop her in the trunk. I was glad when that guy quit the band.

## CRACK WIFE

One of my musicians was a real nice, hard-working, well-dressed guy who worked two jobs in order to feed his family. Even with his extra jobs he played in my band to pursue his musical dream. Unfortunately, the poor guy's wife appeared to be a serious drug addict.

She rarely came to gigs with him, but would often show up during our last set, obviously jacked up and looking like a fucked-out alley cat. She was skinny as a rail, had big, black circles around her eyes, and her hair was always a stringy, greasy mess. She looked like a homeless crack ho and was wearing the same filthy clothes every time we saw her.

Crack Wife's arrival to our gigs was always an embarrassment to that musician and to the professional image we were trying to project as a band. None of our crew or other band wives or girlfriends would associate with her for obvious reasons.

Because of her drug abuse, that musician give up his dream of playing music so he could take care of her and his children. I commend him for his dedication to his family. It's just another case of one person's drug problem destroying another person's dreams.

I finally had to lay down the law and add another clause to the *Die Hard Rule Book*. "Any significant other associated with the inner circle of the band, crew, or staff, must adhere to the same rules of conduct, dress and professional etiquette as the band, or else hit the road."

## Cum To Me

During a break at a gig, the band and their wives were sitting together at a table. One of the wives kept staring a hole through me. Finally she blurted out, "I know what you look like when you cum!" Everybody cracked up laughing except me.

I was embarrassed and offended by her remark. "How the hell do you know that?"

"Cause when you play guitar," she said, "you make the same faces my husband makes when he cums!"

I excused myself from the table. For as long as that guy was in the band I never sat at the same table with him and his wife again.

## Swang Yer Partner

Through the years, there have been several musicians in the band who were swingers or wife-swappers. During my single years a musician suggested I bring a girlfriend to his house, watch the girls get it on and then play the wife swapping game. I was repulsed by the thought of having sex with another band member's wife or girlfriend. To me that would be like having sex with a family member or a brother's wife.

I responded, "Man, I can find a dozen willing women who don't mean shit to me, and bring 'em to your little swappin' party. If they're gone tomorrow and I never see them again, big deal, I don't give a damn. But, you still gotta live with your wife and stand next to me on stage every night like nothin' ever happened. Could you live with the thought of us still playin' in the same band after me banging your ol' lady?"

He never mentioned it again.

## Swap Meat

Unbeknownst to me, a drummer who occasionally worked for me was a swinger. He and his wife had their own wife-swapper groupies who followed them to our shows. One day a lady came to me and said, "I love ya'll's music, but I don't want to sleep with any of you."

I didn't know exactly what prompted her comment. I soon found out.

The drummer and his wife were hitting on anyone and anything that breathed, including our fans and my wife. The people who came to our shows on a regular basis had gotten the impression the entire band was nothing but a wife-swapping orgy waiting to happen.

Again I had to put a stop to musicians dragging their extracurricular activities into my business. Thus, another scripture and verse was added to the *Die Hard Rule Book*.

## The Unwritten Rule

It has always been an unwritten rule that band members do not mess with other band members' women or any woman another band member has been with, regardless of their current relationship. That's not saying it didn't happen from time to time. Most of the time it was the women who instigated a sexual liaison with more than one band member.

It's amazing how many women think our "Unwritten Rule" is stupid and how many want to screw the whole band, either for sport or braggin' rights. Morals, self-respect and decency aside, that kind of in-bred mentality stirs up animosity between the band members. The unwritten rule was there to keep from losing good band members over a piece of ass.

During the late '90s, Jamie and Sid often played in my band. They were a couple of handsome young devils in their early twenties and I was in pretty good shape for an old guy in my early forties. I was amazed at how many women, out of purely lustful, demented curiosity, suggested "doing" the father and the sons. To us, it was a disgusting, sickening, disrespectful thought.

One night a little hottie in her early thirties marched to the bandstand and stood in front of us like she was reading the menu at Burger King. Pointing at each one of us, she said, "I don't know if I want the father or the son. Hmmmm?"

Sickened by her comment, I angrily yelled, "Lady, we're a family, not a pack of dogs willing to take turns fuckin' any bitch in heat!"

With a sly grin she turned and pulled down her pants, exposing a perfect, heart-shaped, centerfold-worthy ass and said, "Well, then, that means you don't get none of this!"

Looking at her ass we all busted out laughing. She looked down and saw she had a tampon string hanging between her legs. She ran away screaming with her pants around her knees. The whole crowed roared!

Nobody got any that night.

## THE PIPE

At one show a musician's girlfriend dropped a pipe underneath her chair. I don't know if it was a crack pipe or a pot pipe. The club owner walked by, picked it up and demanded to know who it belonged to. Everyone at the table denied any knowledge.

Right on time the musician walked by and innocently asked his girlfriend, "Hey, why does he have your pipe?"

The band was never asked back because of that musician's insignificant other.

Again, someone else's drug problem cost us money from future gigs lost.

## BAR TAB

During my single years I had a girlfriend who followed me to most of my shows. She loved to drink and enjoyed her status as the band leader's girl by buying rounds for her friends. We, the band, always had plenty of shots of tequila lined up on stage and we enthusiastically imbibed. Unbeknownst to me, all those drinks were being charged to *me*! At the end of the night, my girlfriend would announce she had forgotten her bank card. I would owe nearly half of my personal salary back to the bar. I was going broke, so I got rid of the girlfriend.

To this day I instruct all bar managers that the band does not have a tab. No one is to buy drinks on a band tab and each musician pays for their own drinks.

The *Die Hard Rule Book* states there are *no* band tabs, and if any musician walks their personal tab and if I have to pay it to ensure future bookings I will deduct double the amount of the tab from the next gig's pay.

I'm in the music business, not the booze business.

## SLOTH

I once had a very jealous girlfriend who lied to all the women in the club about me.

Whenever another female showed any extra-special interest in me, my girlfriend would make it a point to tell the interested party what a disgusting sloth I was.

"He lays around the house all day on the couch in his underwear, drinking beer, fartin', scratchin' his ass and watching TV. He won't work and we live off of my day job pay. His band money is just our party money."

When I caught her lying about me, she said she was just protecting her interest.

## PSYCHO SISTERS

At one time we had a road manager with a unique talent for attracting crazy, mixed-up, psychotic, bi-polar, alcoholic, middle-aged divorcees addicted to prescription drugs. If there were a hundred women in a building, he could go in blindfolded and pick the looniest of all.

He once had a lunatic girlfriend who, along with her equally lunatic sister, was hell to all mankind. The sisters would arrive at our gigs an hour before us. By the time we arrived, they were already drunk and had shit stirred up with the owner and clientele. As the night wore on the sisters would argue and fight with each other and start arguments with our fans.

One night the road manager's girlfriend passed out at the front door of the club. We literally had to step over her to load out. We managed to revive her and set her on the curb. She got up and staggered toward the parking lot. Her sister started driving in circles around the parking lot.

The girlfriend then took off all of her clothes and ran naked around the parking lot, chasing the car and screaming obscenities.

We loaded and left before the cops showed up. A few minutes later the Psycho Sisters passed us on I-10 doing about 90mph. I told our road manager to get rid of his girlfriend and her sister or I would. The next day I called the Psycho Sisters and told them to never come back to any of my shows.

Another verse was added to the *Die Hard Rule Book*.

## LET BUSTER SANG!

During the late '80s I occasionally employed a fill-in bass player named "Buster." He was a good bass player, a good singer and a real likeable guy. I liked Buster and we got along well However, I could not tolerate his irritating, loudmouth wife and her equally irritating, loudmouth girlfriends.

Buster was married to a very aggressive, domineering woman none of the band liked. She had a reputation for trying to intimidate musicians and run every band Buster played in. Every time he played for me his wife would tag along and bring a dozen or more of her bitchy girlfriends. They'd push several tables together in front of the band and get shitfaced drunk and obnoxious.

Their attendance and bar tab made me look good to club owners, but I paid the price.

As the women got snot-slinging drunk, Buster's wife would start yelling, "Let Buster sang! Let Buster sang!"

If I didn't let him sing right away she and her herd of heifers would bang ashtrays on the table chanting "We want Buster! We want Buster! We want Buster!"

They would heap this disrespect on us even if I was in the middle of a slow ballad. Their conduct offended other customers and fans and it was embarrassing to Buster. Trouble was Buster was shy as hell. He didn't want to sing and he only knew two songs.

I was not about to let Buster's wife and her drunk girlfriends run my band. Every time they started their crap I cranked up and played loud, fast songs, one right after the other, until the rowdy bitches got tired of yelling.

Then I would let Buster sing his two songs.

I'd asked Buster to talk to his wife about the situation, but he'd just give me that "aw shucks" grin. He never had the balls to stand up to her.

I refused to continue with the embarrassing episodes at my shows. I let Buster go.

## SOCIAL CALENDER

On numerous occasions I have pissed off band wives because I refused to book around *their* personal social calender.

I'm always happy to oblige my musicians and try to book gigs around weddings, family reunions, graduations and things of that nature. But when a musician tells me that his ol' lady wants me and the band to miss a night's work and night's pay because *she* wants him to take her out on the town for a "romantic getaway" – *that ain't gonna happen.*

If a band leader gives in to one band member's wife's demands, then that musician's wife has taken control and the band's ability to work will forever be based on her whims and schedule.

## INSIGNIFICANT OTHERS TODAY

Today we always try to make the friends and family of our staff, crew and band feel like they are part of our Die Hard Family.

We do not encourage nor discourage the band's significant others from sitting together. However, the further apart they are the less bullshit gets stirred up.

BOOK TEN

# Door Deals From Hell

## WHAT IS A DOOR DEAL?

A door deal is when a musician or band is paid either a percentage of the money or the total money taken at the door of a venue.

The three most popular door deals are: bands are paid a small guaranteed salary *plus* a percentage of the door, bands are paid a guaranteed salary *or* a percentage of door, whichever is greater, or bands split the door fees 80/20 with the venue.

Then there is a fourth door deal. *Mine!*

## DIE HARD'S FIRST DOOR DEALS

I produced my first door deal event in the early '70s while I was in high school in Liberty. Our band, The Moven Shadows, could not get a paying gig at that time because we were too young to get into honky-tonks to play for money. We decided to promote our own shows by renting local community center buildings in small towns throughout Liberty County.

We charged one dollar per person at the door and my girlfriend collected the money. Since we didn't sell any concessions we told people to bring their own. We packed those little community centers and had a frickin' blast. With no supervision and no security, which we didn't think about that at that time, situations often got out of hand due to teenage drinking. It was a very educational experience in more ways than one.

At the Hardin Community Center we stacked folded tables on top of each other creating a makeshift stage. We didn't consider that our boot heels and the legs of the drum kit would destroy the table tops.

The lack of supervision and excessive drinking led to several fights. Someone broke the sink completely off the wall in the men's restroom which resulted in the back of the building flooding. Fortunately someone knew how to turn off the water at the wall. Understandably, the folks in charge of the community center kept my $50 deposit and never again rented the building out to anyone who said they were bringing in a band.

## VFW TAKES ALL

I didn't do another door deal until September 1983 when I made a verbal agreement with the officials of the VFW in Baytown. They agreed I could use their building for free to put on my own show. I would work for 100% of the door. At the end of the night they would not owe me anything and I would not owe them anything.

At that time I had been working in advertising and promotions for KBUK radio station in Baytown and had learned alot of promotional tricks. I solicited sponsors to pay for my show in advance. I then published 10,000 copies of a eight-page, tabloid-size magazine, *The Risin' Star,* which included sponsors' ads.

Since the public didn't know who I was in those days, I put my picture holding a guitar on the cover of the magazine. Across the top of the page a bold headline in a big, black letters read, "OLD TIME ROCK 'N ROLL – ALIVE AND WELL!"

If nobody knew who I was at least they'd relate to '50s and '60s rock 'n roll. Hopefully the headline and a photo of a guitar player might spark their curiosity enough that they would pick up a copy and then come to the show. I personally distributed the magazines all over east Harris County as well as parts of Liberty and Chambers counties.

On the night of the show two things happened that turned it into a *Gig From Hell*.

First, in those days, VFW Halls, Elks Lodges and Moose Lodges had a public image of being redneck, country-western establishments. I was trying to put on a '50s rock 'n roll show in that atmosphere. Even though I promoted the hell out of the event there were many tobacco-chewing rednecks who yelled at us all night. "We don't wanna here no rock shit! Play Merle Haggard! Play Willie Nelson!"

Second, the VFW stole our money. My second wife took money at the door. The show was not a sellout, but we pulled in about a hundred people at $5 each. Not a bad paycheck for an unknown band in those days. Since my sponsors had paid all my expenses I had made about $500 profit.

When my wife and I got home and counted the money I was surprised to see there was only a couple hundred dollars. My wife told me that after the show, while I was outside loading up the gear, officials from the VFW surrounded her and demanded she hand over her money box claiming they were in charge of all money made at the VFW. That was not the deal. There was *no* rental fee. We were working for 100% of the door.

I was furious! After all that work, promotion, securing sponsors, typesetting and printing expenses, distributing 10,000 magazines over three counties and playing a four-hour gig, my wife just handed over all the money to the VFW with *no questions asked* without ever asking me. She claimed she didn't understand the details of my deal with the VFW and didn't know she wasn't supposed to give them our money.

I went back to the VFW. I demanded a full refund of my confiscated money. They refused to honor our agreement and refused to pay me the money they stole from my wife. With the exception of performing at a few small benefits, I never again worked with, or for, that VFW.

My wife, traumatized by the experience, said she'd never help me with another door deal.

## WHITES PARK – ANAHUAC, TEXAS

In 1984 I talked my wife into working the door for another door deal event. I rented Whites Park Auditorium in Anahuac, Texas, and put on a big show featuring drummer, Mike Stepp, and lead guitarist turned bass player, C.C. Holt.

I had hired a young soundman, "Spectre." He was twenty-five years old, and had just started up his own concert production company doing sound and lights.

Spectre arrived around noon with a crew of six guys to set up the sound and light show. In no time at all we were ready for a sound check.

At 8pm we kicked off to a few hundred people who showed up more out of curiosity than my ability to draw a crowd on my name alone.

The band was great and we kicked ass all night long. It was a blast! I'll always remember the lights going dark except for one strobe light mounted under Mike's drums when he did an amazing drum solo. The effect was fantastic. Spectre and his crew had done an exceptional job for us.

We didn't get rich that night but didn't go in the hole either. That set the tone for another show and we started building a following for the future. The hardest part about the whole night was having to clean up the building after everyone left or lose my $50 deposit.

I had hired my old friend Terry Rhinehart to handle security. He was a full-time deputy with the Chambers County Sheriff's Department. He grabbed a broom and together we worked til 5am cleaning restrooms, sweeping floors and picking up trash.

Thanks, Terry. RIP, Bro.

## TEXA-VEGAS

In 1985 I took a trip to Las Vegas. I attended numerous shows including Tom Jones, B.B. King, Fabian's Old Time Rock 'n Roll Revue and several others. Inspired but what I'd seen I couldn't wait to get back to Texas and produce my own Las Vegas-style event.

I rented the Baytown Recreation Hall for Friday, September 27, 1985, for *Gene Kelton's Las Vegas Style '50s Rock 'n Roll Show and Rhythm & Blues Revue.*

I secured sponsors to pay for the event. To promote the event I published another magazine I called *Special Edition,* again with my picture on the cover. This time it was twelve pages and I printed 25,000 copies. I presold tickets at $5 each. Several trustworthy friends did a great job of preselling tickets for me.

One so-called friend, "Floor-Man" (he owned a flooring business) insisted he could sell a hundred tickets. I refused to give him that many tickets at one time. Because of his relentless insistence I finally gave him fifty tickets. I told him when he sold those and brought me the money I'd give him some more.

Once again I contacted Spectre for sound and lights. He had done such a great job at our show in Anahuac I wanted to use him again. I knew this show would be bigger and better.

I had two of the hottest musicians in the world playing with me at that time. Chris Bernhard was a red hot, lightning fast, super-drummer fresh from California. Mike Listi, from Highlands, Texas, was a dynamic bass player years ahead of his time in the funky slap/pop style of bass playing. Rodney Wade showed up with Chris and volunteered to play percussion.

In an effort to add a little Elvis to our event I contacted my old friend and part-time Elvis Impersonator, Bert Owen, and asked him to be our special guest.

MTV was new in those days and music videos were a big deal. In an effort create even more excitement and interest in my show I contacted my old friend, Jim Long, a videographer, and asked him to videotape the event. He had videotaped a few weddings but never a full-blown, two-camera music video shoot at a live event.

Spectre had agreed to provide the audio feed from the sound board to Jim's camera so we could capture studio-quality sound for the video. By videotaping the event I was able to create more public interest by promoting that we were going to film an MTV-style music video right here in lil ol' Baytown!

My Las Vegas extravaganza was coming together like clockwork. Until…

The day before the show I called Floor-Man and asked him for the money for the tickets. "Man, I'm sorry," he said, "but I lost all them damn tickets!" He refused to pay me.

The night of the show Spectre arrived at 5:30pm, four hours late with twice as much gear as he had in Anahuac and *no crew.* Even though I was paying him twice as much as the Anahuac show, he said he needed the extra money and decided not to hire a crew.

Spectre had only ninety minutes to set up tons of sound and light gear for a 7pm sound check. The band was forced to serve as his roadies in order to get him set up in time for the 8pm show.

At 7pm we were nowhere near ready for a sound check and people were pouring in.

At 8pm Jim was ready with the video equipment, but Spectre refused to give Jim the audio feed as he had promised. That meant the sound on the videotape would be recorded live using the sound in the room.

By 8:15pm, while Spectre and the band were struggling to get a sound check, I put on my stage clothes. In an effort to stall for time, I made the rounds welcoming everyone to the show and telling them we would be starting in a few minutes.

While making the rounds I spotted Floor-Man sitting with about thirty of his friends at a group of tables. He pretended not to see me. My wife said they all had tickets when they came in. Lesson learned. I never again fronted anyone tickets that weren't paid for in advance.

By 8:45pm, the crowd was getting restless, anxious and mad. So was I.

By 9pm, people were demanding their money back.

Out of desperation at 9:20pm, I insisted we kick off the show *without a sound check*. I told Spectre to mix us on the fly. The mix was horrible. We sucked, sucked, *sucked!*

Feedback ripped through the building like a siren from hell. There was a constant, low-end roar that sounded like a tornado. The stage monitors didn't work. We couldn't hear ourselves sing. We played long solos in an effort to give Spectre a chance set the sound. He never did.

On break Spectre explained he was having trouble because he was experimenting with all new equipment and *did not know how to operate it yet*. In other words, we were his guinea pigs!

Our first set was horrible. *Horrible!* It's a wonder everyone didn't leave.

The second set was just as bad. Chris, Mike and Rodney put on a great show despite the hardships. We were all embarrassed and pissed off. I was so mad that my anger showed through on the video.

At the end of the night Spectre came to me to get paid. I was so pissed off my hands were shaking. I threw half of his money in his face and yelled, "There's half your fuckin' money, you son-of-a-bitch! Let's see you crawl around on your fuckin' hands and knees and see how it feels to be humiliated. You ruined our fuckin' show tonight. You want the other half of your fuckin' money, it's in my back pocket. Whip my ass, and you can have it!"

Spectre started crying like a baby. "Man, I'm sorry!" he sobbed, "I'm sorry!"

I had no mercy as Spectre crawled around on his hands and knees, scooping up his money from the floor. Seeing that I was furious, my band members grabbed my arms and dragged me out the back door. I never saw or heard from Spectre again and I don't know if he stayed in the music business.

I was so embarrassed by that experience I didn't produce another event for ten years.

## COOKIE BITCH

In February of 1995 I once again rented the Baytown Recreation Hall and promoted a very successful show featuring the legendary Louisiana R&B band Cookie & The Cupcakes.

The band, with *all its original members* in their *seventies*, were still kicking ass on their super hits from the '60s like "Matilda," "Got You On My Mind" and others.

The only problem I had with that show was that when I was walking past the VIP section, old Cookie himself yelled at me. "Go get me a beer, bitch!"

I stopped in my tracks. "Do you know who I am?"

"No, muthafucka," he said, "but you kin still gets me a beer!"

"I'm the producer of this event," I said. "I'm the guy that's payin' you and you can go get your own fuckin' beer, *bitch!*"

Cookie started laughing, slapped me on the back and said, "Sho you is! I's jes messin' wit'cha!" He did not call me a bitch again after he realized I was his employer.

The show was a huge success and a great memory. RIP, Cookie.

## Radio Airplay Makes A Band Worth More Money

By the summer of 2000 songs from my first CD *Most Requested* were hitting the #1 Most Played/Most Popular status on over 500 CD jukeboxes across southeast Texas.

*Most Requested* was getting lots of airplay on major-market Texas radio stations as well as hundreds of medium-market and public broadcasting stations nationwide. As a result, attendance at our shows tripled overnight.

I felt the notoriety made my band worth more money. Newer and larger venues started calling, but insisted they should not have to pay any more than the little beer joints paid where we were performing.

I explained to the talent buyers that those little beer joints were booked long before my music gained radio notoriety and I intended to honor all my previous engagements at the price agreed upon prior to my sudden fame. All new bookings would see a rate increase.

Notoriety made our band worth more money, but it also priced us out of many smaller gigs that either could not or would not pay us what we were worth.

Several of my current employers insisted I should continue to work for them for the same measely price they had been paying me for years. One club owner said, "I helped you when you were nobody, you oughtta return the favor."

Club owners *don't do favors*. It doesn't matter how good you are, how good you *think* you are or how much the club owner *likes* you. If your band isn't packin' them in your ass is out the door. That's another subject for another book.

I realized if I wanted to make more money I'd have to start producing my own shows.

## Working Clubs For The Door

Renting a community building or auditorium and producing my own event was one thing, but working nightclubs for the door is a whole 'nuther experience.

Some club owners liked my door deal idea because it relieved them of the responsibility of paying my band, especially if it was a slow night. Other club owners didn't want to do door deals because they'd been making a lot of money at the door and lying to me about it.

### Door Person Stealing Money

During the mid-'nineties we performed regularly at a very nice, full-service bar in southern Harris County with a capacity of about 250 people.

We consistently packed the place long before *Most Requested* was released. After the CD came out and started getting radio airplay, attendance increased to standing-room-only crowds. Many times the place was already packed an hour before show time and still packed when the house lights came on at 2am after we had played an hour overtime *for free*.

The club was charging five bucks a head at the door. Considering the average alcohol sale was about twenty bucks per person, I figured the club was grossing at least $7500 a night every time we played there. We were still being paid the same amount we earned prior to the CD release so I petitioned for a raise.

Like most club owners, this one insisted he was losing money at the door even on packed nights. He explained that because so many people were regulars he was obligated to let them in for free. Anyone with the fire department or law enforcement got in free. According to him, that was the reason he lost money at the door and had to pay us out of his own pocket. He preached about DWI laws robbing him of sales, insisting most people were sipping water. He said this caused him to lose even *more* money which made it impossible for him to give us a raise. Poor bastard. He had a packed house and was *still* losing money?

When I told him to find another band he offered an extra two hundred bucks on our next show *if we packed the house again*. With that statement I was confident I had a raise coming.

At the end of another standing-room-only night the club owner refused to honor his agreement. He claimed he again lost money on us at the door. He even went through the trouble of forging a bogus door receipt showing a loss.

Since I was on salary I told him I didn't give a shit about his door receipts. I reminded him of his promise of a two-hundred-dollar raise if I packed the house. I also told him if he was losing money at the door then his door person was either stealing or letting too many people in free *or both*.

He responded to my accusations with a vaudevillian expression of surprise and sarcastically yelled, "No way!"

A month later he called me to book another date. I refused.

The following year new owners bought the place. They looked over the sales ledger and called me right away. I refused to work for the new owners unless I could work for 100% of the door. I agreed to play only if I furnished my own door person. The new owners agreed.

At the next gig Joni charged *every* person that came in, even off-duty police officers and firemen who were spoiled to the preferential treatment.

"If they're drinking alcohol," Joni said, "they're here to party and they pay!"

That night we made five times our previous salary! That proved I was right about the door person stealing money and letting too many people in for free. It also proved the previous club owner was a liar, a cheat and a thief.

Not exactly a new revelation when it comes to club owners.

## Mustang Sally's

During the '90s there was a very nice nightclub in Baytown called Mustang Sally's.

It was a rockin' club when it was owned and operated by my old friend and fellow musician, Clarence Perry, who played lead guitar in his own house band, The Mercy Blues.

Around 2000 Clarence sold Mustang Sally's to an obnoxious new owner, D.A.

D.A. quickly developed a nasty reputation for firing bands after the first set and refusing to pay them.

Prior to the release of my first CD we had performed at Mustang Sally's a couple of times for a menial salary. As we gained some notoriety I asked for more money. D.A. refused.

He agreed to us working for 100% of the door and I would furnish my own door person.

Three days prior to our performance D.A. called. He insisted we renegotiate our door deal or I would be canceled.

What D.A. didn't know was that his manager had called me letting me know every seat and table had been reserved. The club was even opening the balcony which had never been done before. That meant at least 350 people were expected.

I knew D.A. wanted the door so I quoted him a flat rate four times our previous rate. I insisted on a signed contract with a 50% deposit with the balance payable prior to the first set. I was not going to give him a chance to have a packed house and fire me after the first set without paying me. He refused and hung up on me.

On the night of the show nearly 400 people came and went between 8pm and midnight paying the five dollar cover. D.A. was outraged. He calculated he had "lost" $2000 at the door. He tried to get behind the admission counter to get ahold of Joni's cashbox, saying he needed to count the money.

Joni jumped in his face like a mad cat, cussing him out and never letting him near the money. He retreated behind the bar where he pouted like a scolded child.

While on break D.A. instructed his DJ to play rap and hip-hop. Our bluesrock crowd was infuriated by the ear-splitting noise and many of them demanded their money back. D.A. stood laughing as Joni was forced to refund money to about a dozen people who unjustly yelled at her about the DJ's playlist.

I ran to the DJ booth and told him to play some blues or Southern Rock. He refused saying he worked for D.A., not me.

When I petitioned D.A. to tell the DJ to change his song selection, he yelled over the thundering hip-hop music. "Fuck you, this is *my* club. I play what the fuck I want!"

I yelled back, "You're only fuckin' yourself. You're driving paying customers out the door!"

In an effort to stop refunds the band I bolted back to the stage and played a two-hour set. At midnight Joni went home with the door money and let the remaining customers bitch at D.A. about the hip-hop.

I never went back to Mustang Sally's. The club went out of business soon after and as far as I know D.A. fell off the face of the earth. Good riddance.

**Show Me Your ID!**

Club owners often insist on furnishing their own door person to collect *my* door money using the excuse that they are required to check IDs. They insist on paying a door person and ID checker out of the band's door money. My response to that is *no one* collects my door money except a member of my crew or I don't play. If a club owner is required to check IDs, then the *club owner* must furnish an ID checker. I don't sell alcohol, *club owners* do. Therefore, it is *their* responsibility to check IDs and cover their own ass.

In Texas, TABC (Texas Alcoholic Beverage Commission) requires the person checking IDs must be employed by that venue.

When doing a door deal my band does not work *for* that venue. My band *performs* at that venue and does not receive a paid salary *from* that venue. An ID checker will not be paid by me out of the door money because that person is not a member of the *band* or my *crew*.

One club owner in Tomball, Texas, insisted my road manager Buddy Love check IDs as he collected the door money. I told the club owner that Buddy did not work for him, but if he wanted to hire him for the night to check IDs, I was sure Buddy would appreciate the extra money. I also told the club owner that it wasn't my job to screen his customers. It was my job to get 'em in, his job to weed 'em out.

The owner declined to hire Buddy and sat at the door all night checking IDs himself.

Working the door at various venues, Joni and Buddy have had to deal with every type of asshole and bitch imaginable who tries to get in for free. People use every excuse they can think of. They say they are personal friends of mine, friends of the band, long-lost relatives, friends of the club owner or employees who were called in at the last minute. Two of our favorites are "they just need to come in and use the restroom" or they're looking for somebody for "just a minute but I'll be leaving right away." The girls often flirt with Buddy by batting their eyes and showing their tits trying to get in free.

At one venue a total stranger had the balls to tell Joni he was my best friend and that he ate dinner at my house a couple of times a week. Joni let him ramble on for several minutes. She said over and over, "I don't care, $5 or you don't get in!"

Joni finally extended her hand in a sarcastic gesture and said, "Hi! I'm Joni Kelton, Mean Gene Kelton's wife. I don't know who the fuck you are, so give me the $5 or get the fuck out!" The guy turned and walked back out the door.

All those excuses prompted Buddy and Joni to hang up a sign.

*I don't care who you are or who you are sleeping with*
*I don't care how big your tits are or how cute you think you are*
*I don't care if you work here now, used to work here, or wanna work here –*
*EVERYBODY PAYS TO GET IN!*

## None O' Yer Biz!

A door deal show at a well-known blues joint in Montgomery County, Texas, proved to be an exceptionally rough night at the door for Joni and Buddy.

Drunk rednecks thrown out of other bars in town tried to slip past them with the usual excuses. Realizing they would not be let in for free, the drunks cussed Joni and Buddy out all night in the usual four-letter redneck language and even threatened them with bodily harm.

The general manager harassed Joni all night demanding to know how much money she was collecting at the door. He continually tried to weasel his way behind the counter to get a closer look at the money. By the end of the night both Joni and Buddy had had enough and were ready to get out of there. As we were loading up the gear, the manager sent a young barback to ask Joni how much she made at the door. Joni was in no mood to be interrogated.

Joni got in the kid's face. "None of your fuckin" business!" she yelled at the top of her lungs. "Now get the fuck outta here!"

I thought the kid was going to pee in his pants. He wheeled around and scrambled back across the gravel parking lot and into the club.

Moments later the general manager came storming out the door and across the parking lot. It was an "oh shit" moment. The general manager was a big guy in his mid-forties who could have easily been a professional linebacker. Not knowing what to expect, Buddy and I automatically stepped forward and braced ourselves.

"I need to know how much money ya'll made!" he demanded.

Before Buddy or I could respond, Joni pushed between us and screamed, "It's none of your fuckin' business! We don't ask you how much you made at the bar. We're not coming back to this shit hole, *ever*. Get outta my damn face and leave us alone!"

Even though the guy could have easily stomped all our asses without breaking a sweat, he just shrugged his shoulders and went back inside without another word.

## Where Eagles Dare

In the fall of 2004 I was contacted by the Eagles Lodge in La Porte, Texas, to do a New Year's Eve show. They were used to hiring really cheap bands and protested my price as if I were trying to rob them.

The lodge had a fantastic showroom that would accommodate about a thousand people. It had an equally impressive stage. I could see myself doing a show there. Even though I had learned a hard lesson about dealing with lodges many years before. Against my better judgment I agreed to play, but only if I could do a door deal.

The Eagles Lodge insisted that if I was going to promote my own show and keep 100% of the door, then I should pay them a rental fee for the use of the building. I refused. I told them I would work for 100% of the door and they could keep 100% of their liquor sales. They agreed. New Year's Eve tickets were $20 a person.

One week prior to the show the Lodge manager insisted I give Lodge members a considerable discount because many were senior citizens, veterans and disabled people on fixed incomes. He felt they shouldn't be charged as much as the general public because most of them would leave early anyway. I agreed to sell him 100 tickets at $5 each with the understanding that the previously-mentioned senior citizens would be given complimentary tickets by the Lodge.

The Eagles Lodge managed to put a whole new twist on screwing a band out of money.

On the night of the show Eagles Lodge officials set up a table next to ours at the door selling their 100 discounted tickets for $10 each to anyone willing to pay, while we sold our tickets for $20 each right next to them. Which would you buy?

I had tried to be considerate of their members on fixed incomes when I sold them the 100 tickets for $5 each with the understanding they were to be given for free to those members.

There was mass confusion and heated arguments at the front door. Nobody wanted to pay Joni $20 a ticket when they could buy a ticket from the Lodge for $10. The Eagles Lodge purposely sabotaged our door deal by refusing to cooperate and honor our agreement. They lied about their intentions to give those discounted tickets to their members on fixed incomes.

We lost hundreds of dollars at the door and we were embarrassed in front of our following because of the arrogance and greed of the Eagles Lodge.

Two years later the same Eagles Lodge called and asked us to play another New Year's Eve show for a set salary. I quoted them an outrageous price. They never bothered me again.

### Just For The Record: Regarding Lodges

Throughout my career I've performed at dozens of VFW's, American Legion Halls and Eagles, Moose and Elks Lodges without any problem.

In fact, around 1988 I was drafted by the Moose Lodge in Pasadena. I had a blast playing there as a single act for a lot of crazy people every Wednesday for about two years. They insisted I had to be a member to perform there so they passed the hat to pay my sign up fee.

I went through the initiation process with about a dozen other new members. We marched around in circles carrying the American flag reciting the Pledge of Allegiance and took an oath to adhere to the rules and regulations of the Moose doctrine and to uphold truth, justice and the American Way or something like that. The hundred or so people attending the ceremony then bowed their heads as the ceremony leader mumbled a whiskey-tainted prayer.

Immediately after saying "Amen!" the leader shouted, "Bar's open! Let's drank!" And the party was on.

# The Door Deal Agreement

In the beginning of this book I mentioned there was a fourth door deal option, *mine*.

In a nutshell, I work for 100% of the door. I furnish my own door person. The club will furnish and pay their own ID checker. *Nobody* gets in free. If the DJ plays any music other than our format during our break causing anyone to demand a refund, we will pack up and leave on the spot and direct disgruntled patrons to get their refunds from the manager.

Since drawing up this door deal agreement we haven't had one single misunderstanding with a club owner. When we do a door deal the club owner must agree to and sign our Door Deal Agreement, or we don't play their venue.

GENE KELTON'S

# Old Time Rock & Roll Show

LIVE MUSIC BY "THE ROCKABILLY BLUES BAND"

PLAYING THE HITS OF THE 50's & 60's
BY:

ELVIS - CHUCK BERRY - JERRY LEE LEWIS -
JOHNNY RIVERS - CREEDENCE CLEARWATER -

WHERE: WHITES PARK PAVILION: ANAHUAC, TEX
WHEN: FRI. NITE, JAN. 21, 1983 - 9:PM TO 1:AM
(\$5.00 PER PERSON AT THE DOOR)

SET - UPS AVAILABLE...BYOB
All Concession Proceeds Benefit:
The HANKAMER VOLUNTEER FIRE DEPT.

*Lights & Sound by: Spectra Public Address Co.*
For More Information, Contact:
R&D Management—(713) 427-2225

"LIVE BAND"          "LIVE BAND"

*Above, Road Manager Buddy Love guarding the stage. Below, Buddy Love guarding the public from Even Meaner.*

*Above left, hand-made flyer for Whites Park show, January 1983.*
*Below left, Chris Bernhard and below right, Rodney Wade and Mike Listi.*
*Both pictures were taken at the 50's Rock 'n Roll show in 1985.*

*Tickets and the hand-made poster for the
50's Rock 'n Roll
Rhythm & Blues Revue in 1985.*

Sept. 1983

VOL. I.
FREE

# THE RISIN' STAR

Dedicated to the Preservation and Promotion of Old Time Rock 'N Roll...and the Artist who made it Great.

# "OLD TIME ROCK 'N ROLL ALIVE AND WELL!"

GENE KELTON

Mississippi born Rockabilly, Gene Kelton, brings his Old Time Rock n' Roll Show and Rythym and Blues Revue to Baytown's V.F.W. Post 912, Friday, September 23, 1983 at 8pm. Due to popularity of this peticular style of music, V.F.W. officials are expecting a record attendance.

Thanks to recent hits by such musicians as "Bob Seger", and "Stray Cats", whose music reminds you of the fifties, and also radio stations such as Houston's own KNUZ (12:30 AM) where they "Rock Around The Clock" with 100% Old Time Rock n' Roll, there has been a mass revival in this style of music which has now become the #1 music in Europe and is once again sweeping the U.S.A. just like it did back in the fifties. Many musicians are now jumping on the "bandwagon" and trying to do what Gene Kelton has been doing all of his life: Old Time Rock n' Roll and Rockabilly.

"Rockabilly music is not something I do strictly by choice," explains Gene Kelton, "it's what I am. I tried working with hard rock groups and they all said I was just too country for rock, but yet.... the country bands I worked with said I was too much rock n' roll. I was really gettin' fustrated. I almost gave up on music completely. Finally, I decided to do what felt good to me and to hell with everybody that kept telling me what music I should do, -- and it worked! Now, all of a sudden, everywhere I work, those Rockabilly Blues lovers are coming out of the closets."

Gene Kelton was born in Booneville, Miss. and lived his early years on a cotton plantation where he was exposed to heavy doses

cont'd

*Front page of an eight-page, tabloid magazine published to promote Gene Kelton's Old Time Rock 'n Roll show at the Baytown, Texas VFW, September 1983. It was my first attempt at magazine publishing, typed on a typewriter rented at the library.*

# BOOK ELEVEN

# Sicker 'n Hell

Some of the worst *Gigs from Hell* I ever played weren't because of the gig itself, but rather because I was sick as hell and should have stayed home in bed.

As a professional entertainer, especially the leader of a band, I don't have the luxury of being able to take a single day of sick leave. If I get sick and cannot perform, not only do I lose income but so does every member of my band as well as the venue where we were scheduled to perform.

In earlier years when we were a copy band playing mostly beer joints, canceling a gig due to illness was no big deal. I had a few good friends who fronted their own bands who were always willing to step in to front my band so my musicians would not lose any income.

Michael Stephens who fronted a band called Toonz from Clear Lake and Professor Blues from Baytown were two guys I always called first if I was sick.

If I couldn't find someone to step in for me, there were plenty of other bands who could take a copy band gig at the last minute. It didn't make much difference.

As the years have passed and the notoriety of Mean Gene Kelton & The Die Hards increased and our original songs have become more popular, a lot more people are affected if I miss a show. Promoters, agents, the venue, our fans, my family, and, of course, the band members and their families are all affected.

Even though talent buyers understand unforeseen occurrences befall us all they still get pissed when a band cancels regardless of the reason or seriousness of an emergency. They often hold any cancellation against the band and future bookings may be affected at that venue. Because of that and the fact that I needed the money, I can't count the times I suffered through a show sicker 'n hell with a high fever, a bad cold, the flu, chills, heat stroke, food poisoning or coughing my head off.

My doctor, who happens to be a biker and loves live music, understands my situation. Often I've pushed his professional ethics to the limit demanding to be jacked up with powerful antibiotics and whatever else I can talk him out of so I can get through a weekend.

## THE CREEPIN' CRUD

In November 2004 I came down with the worst case of the Creepin' Crud (flu) I ever had.

With bills to pay and a band that depended on me, I kept getting up and going to work. Just as I would start getting better I'd have to go back to work. I kept relapsing. The Crud hung on four long months. Every gig from November 2004 through February 2005 was a *Gig From Hell.* Being on the road was miserable, being at home not working was miserable. Outdoor shows in the night air were painful and playing in smoky bars was practically suicide.

At the Janis Joplin Birthday Bash in Port Arthur, Texas, in January of 2005 I was so sick I could barely talk, much less squeak out three songs before introducing our featured singer, Monica Marie. Harmony vocals? Forget it!

Two weeks later we performed on an outdoor stage in 40 degree weather at the Galveston Mardi Gras. Every cell of my body ached.

The following weekend we performed in a freezing, wet tent at the World's Championship Barbeque Cookoff at the Houston Livestock Show and Rodeo. I was in mortal pain.

It was a miserable winter. It's a wonder I didn't get pneumonia again.

But the show must go on, *and it did*!

## HEAT STROKE

In July of 2000, while doing an early morning workout underneath my carport, I suffered a severe heat stroke.

When I entered the house Joni took one look at me and freaked out. She put me on the floor and covered me with cool wet towels. I couldn't make it up the stairs to the shower. Against her wishes I refused to go to the ER.

It took four days for my temperature to return to normal. The severe effects of the heat stroke forced me to cancel all outdoor gigs until October that year. The income of the band and the attitude and morale of my players suffered a major blow.

For the next couple of years I'd wake up in the middle of the night sweating like a marathon runner and shaking like a dog shittin' a peach seed. My heart would be pounding like a jackhammer. Some mornings I'd wake up trembling so uncontrollably I'd have to hold on to the wall while taking a leak in fear I was going to fall down or pass out.

Depression was my worst enemy. I thought I was either coming down with some dreaded old man's disease or was on the verge of becoming an invalid. At that time I didn't know what I know now about electrolytes, minerals and your body's reaction when those get out of whack. That's another book.

Over the next several months Joni took me to three different doctors looking for answers. Not one doctor found anything wrong with me.

One doctor said my fears were all in my head and insisted I take Zoloft for stress. After the effects of the first pill wore off I threw the whole damn bottle in the trash. I hate drugs, even prescription drugs. I will never take that crap again.

The second doctor diagnosed me as being hypoglycemic and suggested I eat peanut butter crackers whenever I started trembling. Over the next three years I gained thirty pounds by taking his advice. I have my "fat" pictures to prove it.

My regular doctor explained my condition in musician terms. "You cooked your insides and fried all your wiring," he said.

It took over three years before I started feeling normal again and I was finally able to start working out again.

I lost the extra weight and I feel great.

I still must be very careful about outdoor shows in the summertime in Texas.

## OPERATION BASS PLAYER REMOVAL

After years of hard work honing my craft and building a reputation as a tight, kick-ass band, it's depressing and stressful to do shows with less than average musicians who undermine years of hard work and sacrifice. The old saying "a chain is only as strong as its weakest link" is true in the music biz. A band is only as good as its weakest (worst) member.

One year I hired a bass player who was overcome with stage fright at every show. The more we played the worse he got. Drugs? Alcohol? I don't know. All I know is I was stressed to the max. The quality of the band was shit. The stress took its toll on me in a strange way. I literally lost my vision. It would come and go, one eye at a time.

One night while Joni and I were sitting in a restaurant, suddenly I could only see out of one eye. Afraid I was having a stroke, she hauled my ass straight to the ER.

After a trip to the emergency room, three days in the hospital and $30K worth of tests, so-called medical experts found absolutely nothing wrong with me. Even though my diagnosis was perfect health, the doctors prescribed Plavix, Lipitor and two 81mg aspirins everyday for the rest of my life. "Just to be on the safe side," they said. *Safe side?* Don't they know what the hell they're talking about?

Like I've said, *I hate drugs*! I refused to take any of their prescribed medications, especially since they had said I was in perfect health.

While lying in the hospital bed, I analyzed my situation. I picked up the phone and fired the bass player. My symptoms soon went away and I haven't had any vision problems since.

I should have sent the bass player the bill.

## Food Poisoning

In April 2002 I suffered a horrendous case of food poisoning. On a Thursday afternoon I ate some bad chicken at a barbeque cookoff. Within a couple of hours I was doubled up on the floor puking my guts up. I sincerely thought I was going to die. I spent all night and most of the next day in the bathroom in excruciating pain.

The band was booked for Friday and Saturday night at Westfield's. I called the club owner and tried to cancel my gig. The club owner was furious and insisted I come anyway.

"I'm dying here!" I told him.

The club owner said people already had tables reserved and he couldn't get another band on such short notice. He promised to pay full price if I would just come in and do two sets.

Again Joni came to my rescue. She made an organic blueberry smoothie that temporarily settled my stomach. A couple of aspirins and an ice-cold shower temporarily brought my fever down.

The moment we arrived I shot to the restroom while Joni took charge of the stage setup. We played short sets with a trash can next to me on stage for emergency purposes. Thank God I never had to use it. That would have been a show.

Joni said every time I approached the mic to sing she was sure it was all over. There were many songs where we played a five-minute intro because I wasn't sure what was going to happen when I opened my mouth to sing.

On the second night, still running fever and feeling like crap, I played one set, canceled the rest of the show, took a pay cut and went home.

By our gig Sunday afternoon at another club, I was extremely exhausted from a weekend of puking, sweating, dizzy spells and shittin' like a tied coon. Somehow I made it through.

I was glad when the weekend was finally over. I spent the next few days resting. In photos taken during that weekend I looked like death warmed over.

## Falling Off Stage

We kicked off our Thursday night jam at Marguerite's Club in north Galveston County at 9pm. Customers immediately started sending tequila shots to the bandstand. I did two shots. Within minutes my head was spinning. I was slurring my words and couldn't keep my balance.

Forty minutes into our first set I fell off the stage, staggered across the room and ran into the shuffleboard table. The neck of my guitar got tangled in the chain that supported the dangling neon beer sign hanging over the table.

In my efforts to jerk loose, the light swung back and forth violently with me attached, making quite a show for the amused on-lookers.

A wave of nausea swept through me. I set my guitar down and headed to the parking lot where I heaved my guts up. It was the first and only time in my career I ever got sick from drinking at a show. It was also the first and only time I did not finish a show due to drinking.

It was a full house and the club owner was very pissed off I could not finish the show. She was certainly within her rights not to pay the band. However, she did pay the bass player and drummer half their salary for playing one set.

I woke up the next day on a friend's couch not knowing how I got there and without even the trace of a hangover.

To this day, I still insist that somebody spiked my drink.

## TOXIC FOG

As a non-smoker performing in beer joints and nightclubs for over a half of my life, I have major concerns about the long-term effects of second-hand smoke. Jogging in fresh air seems to help keep my lungs clear and I thank God and Nike I have a clean bill of health.

I have played in nightclubs that were so thick with smoke that the band should have been wearing HazMat suits and oxygen tanks. Many times after coming home from a gig I've undressed outside or in my garage and left my clothes outside the house.

One club was so thick with smoke I told the band we needed fog lights and a police escort just to find our way to the restrooms.

In recent years I'm glad that most of our shows are outdoor events like bike rallies, Blues Festivals and county fairs thus eliminating smoke-filled environments.

On the occasions we end up in a smoky little blues joint I've noticed that I develop a *nicotine hangover*. I'm tired and exhausted for days with dark circles under my eyes like a heroin junkie. As a result I try to follow the advice my sweet mother gave me when I was still a teenager. "Stay outta them places!"

Performing at a barbeque cookoff is a whole different kind of smoke. At least I can partake of the savory results of what the smoke is smokin'. After contact with barbeque smoke the band equipment smells like barbeque for weeks.

Once the band was set up on a flatbed truck next to the exhaust fan of a restaurant kitchen, belching fryer fumes. For days our equipment reeked of fish grease and french fries.

Setting up on an outdoor stage or amphitheater always poses a threat from Mother Nature. Except for the occasional rainout, a fast-moving thunderstorm that passes in twenty minutes is preferable to an all-day dust storm.

We once played a gig in a pasture where tractors had turned the soil in a surrounding field into a fine, sugary powder. Vehicles coming and going sent a constant cloud of dust that covered us like ash from a volcano. After the gig our equipment had to be professionally cleaned. My harmonicas were full of mud. I felt like my lungs were full of mud as well.

Dust, second-hand cigarette smoke and cooking fumes are not the only toxic fog we have to deal with. Clubs are always coming up with something new to put on their dance floor so dancers can slip n' slide. I've seen salt, sawdust, corn meal, corn starch, dry grits, sand, Oil Dry and shuffleboard powder used to make them slick. Those products eventually get ground into a fine powder that floats into the air when stirred up by the dancers. Ever seen lint floating in a sunbeam? Same thing, only worse. Rarely have I ever seen any club use the one product actually *designed* for the job, a product aptly named *Dance Floor Wax*.

Since dance floors are always right in front of the band, the toxic cloud ends up in our nose.

At a party our friend Diane Naski sprinkled granulated sugar on a garage floor that was doing double-duty as a dance floor. *It worked great!* All night long dancers complimented Diane on her ingenuity. Unfortunately, the next morning the garage floor was covered with billions of excited ants who must have thought that manna had fallen from Ant Heaven.

I've played numerous shows where baby powder was sprinkled on the dance floor. It's absolutely the *worst product ever* to put on a dance floor. It creates a fine, lighter-than-air dust that wafts into the air at the slightest disturbance. As people dance and ceiling fans whirl baby powder fills the room like a fog. The room smells like a baby's ass as the dust finds its way into every crack and crevice of our equipment, clothing, eyes, ears and other body parts.

Baby powder cakes when it gets damp. My mouth, nostrils and lungs get filled with it and it turns to mud. My harmonicas have to be washed. Imagine having something in your mouth and nose that moments before was mixed with the dirt on a barroom floor.

For several days after inhaling second-hand baby powder my voice sounds like Marlon Brando in *The Godfather*. And wet baby powder tastes like, well... go do a line of baby powder and let me know what you think.

## BAND MEMBERS SICK

If one of my band members is too sick to play, most of the time I can find another player to get through a couple of shows provided the gig isn't a major event where too many of my original songs are required.

In the spring of 2006 my friend and radio DJ, Mark Moss, invited us to perform live on his radio show on KACC 89.7 FM, "The Gulf Coast Rocker" in Alvin, Texas.

Band performances on Mark's show are heard locally as well as streamed live over the internet. A webcam allows performing bands to be viewed by people all over the world.

Unfortunately, our drummer suffered an injury a week before the show. Since it would have been an all-original show we were not able to use a sub-in drummer who didn't know our material. The show was canceled. Too bad for us. We were going to cut a live CD of that performance.

It never happened.

### Dog Bites Drummer

In February of 2002 I received a frantic call from my drummer, a young guy named Andy Rogers. He couldn't play the gig that week because his hands had been mauled trying to break up a dog fight.

At the last minute I found drummer Curtis Craig. When Curtis played his first gig with us he played as if he'd been with us all his life.

He became our Die Hard drummer for the next three years before he moved to California.

### Always Sick Keyboard Player

During the late '80s I played lead guitar for a very popular, semi-celebrity keyboard player in Houston I'll call "Doc" because he was an expert on prescription medicine. He sincerely believed he had every disease TV commercials suggested you "ask your doctor about."

At every show he would line up at least a dozen prescription bottles on top of his keyboard in plain view of the audience. It was his way of getting sympathy and attention from his fans. The pill bottles made great conversation starters especially when other hypochondriacs in the audience recognized one of the medications as their own.

Doc would waste twenty minutes between songs while he and his kindred spirit indulged a sick-fest. Each would try to out do the other, comparing the number of life threatening diseases they were currently battling and the effects of different drugs.

Along side the impressive display of prescription bottles Doc showcased throat spray, lozenges, mouthwash, aspirin, headache powder, reading glasses, contact solution, eye drops, ear drops and nose drops. He had no qualms about applying any of them in front of the audience. He make a big production out of it, grunting and grimacing as if in dire pain and possibly taking his last breath. Also on display were boxes of tissues from which he would yank handfulls. He'd blow his nose long and loud in full view of the audience.

Doc would hold the tissue open, examining the contents like a goldminer panning for gold. He'd then toss the used tissue in the general direction of the trash can under his piano. Most of the tissues missed the trash can and piled up on the stage, where he stepped on them while patting his feet to the music.

If he wasn't blowing his nose, he would hack and gag until he hawked up a big loogie and then spit in the trash can while I played a lead break. He'd ruin my concentration every time.

Then there was his container of cotton swabs. He regularly stuck the swabs in his ears like he was checking the oil in his car. Just like the tissues, he examined the results of his probing by holding the used swabs up to the stage lights for the whole audience to see.

We learned the hard way to never ask Doc how he was doing. He'd actually *tell* you. You'd spend the next half-hour hoping World War III would start so you'd have an excuse to escape Doc's filibuster about his aches, pains, allergies, ailments, surgeries, medications, blisters, pimples, warts, ulcers, hemorrhoids, hangnails, gas attacks, rashes and the diseases he'd inherited from his ancestors as well as those he just found out he had from a TV commercial he saw the night before.

When I started the *Die Hard Rule Book*, I remembered Doc.

In his honor regarding stage etiquette I wrote:

> *Absolutely no hacking, hawking, spitting, nose blowing, butt scratching, ball scratching, ear fingering or hair combing. There will be no display of personal hygiene items or medical supplies, including tissues, Qtips, fingernail clippers, mouthwash, aspirin, deodorant, cologne, prescriptions, salve, spray, etc. There will be no medical procedures performed on stage; i.e. fingernail biting, fingernail clipping, ear probing, nose picking, butt digging, crotch adjusting, pimple pinching, inserting of contact lenses or taking insulin shots. If any musician has an emergency, request an emergency break but don't disrespect and/or embarrass the audience or band or make and fool of yourself in public.*

I don't know how Doc ever got famous.

## Back Surgery

One morning during the summer of 2010, while on his way to band practice, Die Hard drummer Ted McCumber stopped by his doctor's office for his regular scheduled checkup for his back problems.

Ted had forgotten he was scheduled for more than just a check-up. He was scheduled for outpatient back surgery. Imagine his surprise when he found himself face down on a table, shot full of anesthetic and cut open by a doctor who began whittling away on his discs on his L-4 and L-5 vertebrae. He got a steroid injection, stitches and was sent on his way.

After the procedure Ted drove straight to band practice. He creeped into the practice room bent over and looking pasty white.

With one hand against the wall and the other on his back, Ted grimaced with pain and was barely able to utter his situation to us. Needless to say, we canceled practice and sent him home to recuperate.

When we asked why he didn't just call and tell us what was going on, he replied, "I couldn't let you guys down."

That's what I call the "Die Hard Spirit." Imagine where this country would be if more people in the workforce had that kind of loyalty toward their company and fellow workers.

That day, Ted McCumber earned his Die Hard Wings.

**Crash Test Winner**

On Sunday, October 17, 2010, we were scheduled at the Hawg Stop in Houston starting at 3pm. At 1pm my cell phone rang. It was Die Hard bass player Ed Starkey. He shouted into the phone, "I've been in a major car wreck! I think I'm hurt! I can't make the gig! The ambulance is here. Gotta go!"

The connection went dead. Frantic, I called him back.

Ed repeated, "I've been hit! My van is torn to pieces! The police and ambulance are here. Can't talk!"

Again, the connection went dead.

I didn't know where Ed was or how bad he was hurt. With an obligation to my employer I called several bass players and waited on more news from Ed.

A few minutes later Ed called back. He had been hit from behind by an "unsober, undocumented, unlicensed, uninsured motorist" who left the scene of the accident.

Ed's van was completely destroyed. Miraculously he and his gear were okay and he was on his way to the gig in a rental car. The band started on time.

As the day wore on the reality of the near-death situation began to take its toll on Ed. He said he had sore places where he didn't know he had places. Fortunately, bass players Wolff DeLong and Ray Kelton showed up and stepped in to give Ed a break.

Ed could have chosen to go to the emergency room to be checked out, but instead he crawled out of a wrecked vehicle and made it to the gig on time. What else would you expect from a seasoned road warrior and a Vietnam veteran?

Ed Starkey earned his Die Hard Wings.

## No More Sicker 'N Hell

I use every preventative I can to stay healthy and I'll never suffer through another gig from hell due to sickness.

Today talent buyers can fire me, sue me or blackball me. I don't care.

I refuse to perform sick for any reason. It's just too painful, and can lead to far worse problems. I don't bounce back like I used to. I don't heal like I used to. If I lose money from not playing a gig, so what. The loss of one gig won't make or break me.

Ever since I played my first song in public back in 1971, I have been asked to perform at hundreds of benefits and fundraisers for every conceivable reason and cause. Whenever possible I have gladly done so with no questions asked.

We musicians wholeheartedly believe in donating our time and talents to help a worthy cause. Believe it or not, most of us realize that our musical talents are a gift from God and He probably didn't intended for us to use our talents to sell alcohol in beer joints.

Whenever someone asks me to perform for free for a worthy cause, I feel it's my way of giving something back to the community, helping someone in need and hopefully making a few "God points" at the same time.

However, there are differences between a charity *fundraiser* and a *benefit*.

## FUNDRAISERS

Fundraisers are usually held by organizations to raise money for that particular organization or foundation. They usually have corporate or local sponsors to help pay the expenses incurred. These types of events are usually organized by professional event planners and almost always pay their bands a minimal fee.

We've played for hundreds of corporate-sponsored fundraising events for organizations like The March of Dimes, Muscular Dystrophy, Multiple Sclerosis, B.A.C.A. (Bikers Against Child Abuse), B.A.D. (Bikers Against Diabetes), Bikers Out For Blood (a blood drive organization), Texas Equusearch, Make-A-Wish Foundation and many more.

Even well planned, corporate-sponsored events can result in a *Gig From Hell*.

### Flight Of The Wheelchair King

During most of the '90s, we had a standing gig every March at Kevin Harrington's March of Dimes event held at Walter Hall Park in League City, Texas.

The executive producer of the event was Kevin Harrington, a man of boundless energy who in those days got around in a manually-operated wheelchair propelled by the mere strength of his arms. He was a superb showman whose physical challenges never slowed him down. From his wheelchair Kevin could spin around in dizzying circles, cut donuts, pop wheelies and turn on a dime and give you nine cents change. His showmanship, big smile and contagious enthusiasm kept a long line of women ready to jump in his lap for a spin.

At one event we were performing on an outdoor stage about five feet off the ground. Several hundred people were packed in front of the bandstand listening to us. Kevin was on the front of the stage making announcements.

He wowed the crowd with his amazing wheelchair stunts. He began racing back and forth extremely fast from one end of the stage to the other. The crowd would gasp, then burst into applause as Kevin came to an abrupt halt just inches before flying off the end of the stage.

The more the crowd cheered, the more daring Kevin became. Zooming toward the end of the stage, he missed his braking procedure as he neared the edge. To prevent a bone-crushing crash off the end of the five-foot high stage, Kevin cut a sharp left turn and slammed into the back of our stack of PA concert speakers. He hit a Peavey SP-1 speaker on wheels stacked with a Peavey SP-2 on top. Together they were the size of a stacked, full-size washer and dryer. The stack went tumbling off the front of the stage.

Kevin's wheelchair flipped over backwards. He lay flat on his back in the stage lights with his trademark "Bozo The Clown" shoes sticking straight up in the air. His 20-ounce "Big Gulp" that always sat between his legs poured out over his chest and face.

Kevin's crew ran to pick him up and checked him for damage. Kevin came up coughing, gagging and spewing his drink out of his nose. Laughing harder than the rest of us, he grabbed the mic and announced, "It's okay folks, that's the way we rehearsed it!"

A cheer went up from the crowd.

I jumped off the stage to see if the half-ton load of speakers had fallen on anyone. Thank God they only landed in the dirt. But did they work? Once they were placed back on the stage and plugged back in they worked fine. And why not, they were Peaveys. The jacks were still in the back of the speaker boxes, but the two 50-foot speaker cords had been ripped in half like kite string.

These days Kevin's mascot is a little bulldog dressed in a little biker hat and sunglasses. "Damn Good" (because Kevin says he's a damn good dog) rides calmly in Kevin's lap and doesn't seem to mind the spinning.

Kevin has retired from producing big charity events. He can still be seen frequenting establishments around southeast Texas supporting live music. His new 21st-century wheelchair is a battery-powered, high-tech, space shuttle cockpit on wheels. Kevin operates it like an F-14 Fighter Jet. He still wears his trademark bright red Bozo the Clown shoes, is still a showman and the chicks still line up begging for a ride.

Ask Kevin how he's doing and he'll always enthusiastically reply, "Hat-ta-Chaaaa Cha-cha-cha-chaaaaa! Every day is a good day!"

**Honda Drop**

One of the most interesting charity events I ever played was the "Honda Drop." It was held every year at a little biker bar in La Marque called Murphy's On Main.

Every spring the owner, Wayne, would receive donations of a couple of hundred wrecked Honda motorcycles from various bike shops and salvage yards. The Hondas were piled in the center of the bar's parking lot. The Hondas were then hoisted a hundred feet in the air by a crane. The rowdy crowd of Harley ridin' bikers would count down and the unfortunate rice burners would be released mid-air. The Hondas would slam to the concrete parking lot exploding into a million pieces upon impact. The crowds went wild.

Hundreds of rambunctious bikers with their kids showed up for this highly-anticipated annual event. The bikers enjoyed the camaraderie, the live band playing in the parking lot, the barbeque and the ice-cold beer. It was a hoot. It was the next best thing to going to a Viking beer bust. It's dangerous, violent and fun as hell! What else would you expect a bunch of rambunctious Harley riders to do with a Honda?

One of the most fun parts of the event was when the kids were given sledge hammers and allowed to beat the hell out of the broken Hondas. Some of them swung the sledgehammers until their little arms couldn't move anymore.

Money raised from this event was donated to the Shriner's Burn Center for Children in Galveston, Texas.

You go, Wayne!

### Fire In The Hole!

In the spring of 2006 I accepted an invitation to perform at "Ridin' For The Rose," a fundraiser for a brain cancer research organization.

Arriving on location in rural Brazoria County, I was surprised to see the event was taking place at a little country-western honky-tonk at the crossroads of nowhere, about 100 miles southeast of Houston.

Since the beer joint was very small we were instructed to set up and play on the big ranch-style front porch that encircled the building. The porch made a perfect outdoor stage to play to the hundreds of bikers in the large parking lot.

As we rigged up and prepared for a sound check, Wolff DeLong's bass amp literally burst into flames like a grease fire on a barbeque pit. Wolff yanked the power chord from the wall and tried to slap the flames out with his hands, burning them in the process.

At the other end of the stage the lights on our PA mixer flashed on and off, then went dark *forever*. Blue smoke hung in the air. The entire area smelled like an electrical fire. We all stood with our mouths open.

I immediately sought out the bar owner. He was an old redneck who, in his overalls, looked like a seventy-year-old Walter Brennan just returning from plowing the back forty with a mule.

When I complained about his electrical system being faulty and burning up our equipment, he stuck his thumbs in his overalls, spit off the porch and muttered, "Aint nuttin' wrong w' mah lec-triss-dy, boy. Ya'll just use whut 'cha got and give them thar biker fellers some music. We don't wanna lose this crowd!"

"You don't get it, mister!" I said, "All our gear is burnt to hell. Your electrical system must be screwed up!"

"I done told ya, boy! Ain't a goddamn thang wrong with mah 'lec-triss-dy." he snapped. "Maybe you boys jus' playin' on piss-poor shit. Looks okay to me. Now, you boys go 'head 'n play, ya hear?"

"Goddammit, *we can't play!*" I yelled. "All our shit is burnt up, *destroyed!* We are out of business cause your electricity on this porch is fucked up. You, sir, owe me for three thousand dollars worth of equipment!"

He chuckled, spit off the porch again and moseyed back into the building.

Fortunately Wolff had recently purchased his bass rig from a music store that had a great exchange policy. He got a whole new bass rig with no questions asked.

My PA mixer was a different story. Its guts were melted together. Peavey had quit making that particular unit so I couldn't buy another one just like it. Fortunately, Joni found an identical model on eBay in Canada.

When I asked the bar owner to reimburse me for the cost of the new PA, I got him on tape telling me to stick it up my ass. I contacted two so-called music business lawyers and both of them wanted more money up front than the whole damn thing was worth. I passed the old redneck's sentiments on to them.

I knew it would be hopeless to pursue a small claims case in the county where the incident took place. It's almost impossible for an outsider to sue someone in their own backyard in redneck-land where everybody is in-bred to everybody.

The insurance company reminded me my policy had a $1000 deductible. I was forced to eat the loss.

Our biker friends who witnessed the incident insisted on throwing a benefit to help us raise money to buy new equipment. Though we were honored by their heartfelt intentions we declined their kind offer. I believe benefits should be done for people who are suffering physically or financially due to illness, catastrophe or death. We were perfectly healthy working men capable of overcoming a *Gig From Hell* and pulling ourselves up by our bootstraps.

We choose to save the benefit efforts for those less fortunate who really needed it.

## Hotter'n Hell At The Hawg Stop

Since 2004 my band has performed dozens of Sunday afternoon shows on the small stage inside the main building of one of Houston's most popular biker icehouses, The Hawg Stop.

Each time we perform there, the parking lot fills with bikes and Die Hard fans fill the seats. The beer is the coldest in Texas. When the music starts, biker babes always end up dancing on the stage or on the bar where they show off their best moves and then some. What a party! Our Sunday afternoon shows usually turn into a hell-raisin' one-day music festival.

With the popularity of live music at The Hawg Stop, the owner Delmer Barkley built a giant amphitheater at the rear of the property to bring in bigger shows. We have headlined many bike rallies and blues festivals on that stage and shared the bill with legendary bands like Ten Years After, Canned Heat, Bad Company, Black Oak Arkansas and many more.

In January 2009, Joni and I made a deal with Delmer to produce our own Southern Fried July 4th (SFF) event, benefitting Texas Equusearch, Harley's Angels and Toys for Tots.

Texas Equusearch, founded by our friend Tim Miller, searches for lost and abducted children and adults. Harley's Angels is an all-female motorcycle club that raises money for breast cancer research. Toys For Tots raises money and collects and distributes toys each year as Christmas gifts to needy children in the community.

With seven months to promote the event, we figured we'd have everything ready for a great music event, and be able to support our three favorite charities at the same time.

Over the next few months, every waking moment of our daily lives became a *Gig From Hell*. Joni and I, along with Vickie Music and several other Die Hards, worked fourteen to eighteen-hour days securing sponsorships, booking bands and selling advertising. Volunteers had to be found and organized. Portacans had to be ordered. A million phone calls had to be made, press releases written and thousands of emails sent promoting the event.

Joni designed a website, banners, posters and t-shirts and a twelve-page, tabloid-size magazine. We printed 30,000 copies and distributed them across southeast Texas.

We learned the hard way that even with all the planning, Mother Nature was still the boss. By July, a record-setting and excruciatingly painful heatwave scorched southeast Texas with 100-plus degree temperatures and heat indexes up to 110 degrees.

On July 4th, Joni and I, along with an army of volunteers, arrived at 7am. The heat and humidity were already sweltering. By mid-morning, it was so damn hot you could fry an egg, or a brain, inside a motorcycle helmet.

Based on previous attendance at our shows at the Hawg Stop, we were still optimistic about the event. The gates opened at noon, and we expected a crowd of at least 5000. However, only a few people trickled in.

By 3pm, a small crowd had braved the heat to hear the first band, The 4-Barrel Ramblers. A rockabilly band from the Clear Lake area, the Ramblers did a great job despite the minimal crowd and mid-day heat. The situation wasn't any better for local rock band Clovis that played at 4pm.

At 5pm, Sandy Hickey and Brother 2 Brother took the stage. By then, the heat was claiming victims left and right. Most fans left on their own, but it soon looked as if the local ambulance service was running a shuttle service from the Hawg Stop to the ER. It was so hot that a biker pulled up next to the front entrance, dropped his kickstand, and dropped unconscious to the ground just as he climbed off his bike.

Out of every three people who came through the gate, at least one left complaining about the heat. Even our road manager Buddy Love was overcome by the heat. He was sweating profusely, and his face turned blue. Joni thought he was having a heart attack and a heatstroke. He took refuge in Tim Miller's Texas Equusearch Command Center that they had on display at the SFF. It took Buddy several months to completely get over the heatstroke.

We stretched water hoses to the stage and sprayed the appreciative audience, which had a double benefit from a man's point of view. The girls took off their tops when they got sprayed.

You'd think that several hundred over-heated, hellraisin', beer drinkin' bikers and flashing girls would have balked when Biker Preacher "Uncle Dave" Lancon took the stage at 7pm to bless our event. I felt very proud when the crowd stood up, got quiet, took off their hats and bowed their heads. Uncle Dave reminded us of what the 4th of July was really all about and offered a word of prayer for our fallen soldiers and their families.

The headliners, Larry Grisham and The Beat Daddys put on a great show as the sun went down. Even after dark, the heat continued to smother. Wolff, Ted McCumber and I closed out the night. All the bands were great. The crowd had a great time, despite the heat.

As the months passed and the pain of the miserable heat was forgotten, fans asked if we planned to do another 4th of July extravaganza. That's easy. "Hell no!"

## BENEFITS

While *fundraisers* raise money for organizations or foundations, *benefits* are events put on by friends and family members of an individual who has recently suffered a catastrophic loss due to accident, a fire, a storm or a death in the family. Bands usually play benefits for free.

In order to get us to play a benefit all day for free, musicians are enticed with offers of free food, free beer, and, of course, that magic word, *exposure*. Yes, there were times when we are even offered drugs and sex in exchange for playing a benefit.

For me, just bring on the homemade banana puddin' and I'm there.

Sometimes you just gotta say no to a benefit. Here are a few examples of benefits I have declined to play.

I was once asked to do a benefit for a man whose trailer house had burned down. Turned out he had been cooking dope and his house caught on fire. Among other things he needed money for a lawyer.

My response? *NO.*

I was once called to help a local musician raise money. He claimed his music equipment had been stolen. I was ready to jump in and help until I heard that he had been on a two-week drunken binge, beat up his wife, went to jail, lost his job and pawned all his gear.

My response? *NO.*

A local nightclub owner asked me to perform at a benefit to help his popular, young bartenderess, a single mom trying to support her three-year-old daughter. I was ready to jump onboard. I quickly found out the bartenderess had been locked up for possession and distribution of cocaine. The benefit was to raise funds for her bail.

My response? *NO.*

## Mr. Liver Transplant

I was asked to host a benefit for a man who needed a liver transplant. He was a personal friend of one of our band members so naturally I agreed to play. No questions asked.

I arrived at ritzy, upscale nightclub in north Houston. The parking lot was full of hot new sports cars and SUVs. The club was packed with people in expensive clothes looking like they had just stepped out of a magazine. The DJ music was blaring, the party was rocking and the venue was obviously making a fortune selling overpriced whiskey.

I learned the hard way about not asking more questions about the day's events beforehand. Ron, my band member who booked the event had committed our band for the entire *six hour event*! The rest of the band and I were *not* happy about that.

Food was catered by one of the city's most reputable restaurants for a $20 donation per plate. The band was informed we could eat only after *paying customers* had been served. We were told band members would receive a 50% discount on food and drinks but our crew had to pay full price. We were pissed. That is *not* how things are done for a band donating its time, equipment and talent to a benefit. It is understood that bands and their crew always eat and drink *free* when they donate their time and tons of gear to play *for free*!

All day long Mr. Liver Transplant's co-workers kept interrupting our show to make endless, heartfelt speeches. They professed loyalty and love for their dear, dying co-worker and made desperate pleas for more donations to help save his life. They all seemed to be trying to out do each other. Their comments started to sound like a crock of sugar-coated bullshit just so they could garner a little public attention at the mic for themselves.

As they took turns speaking I couldn't help but notice how well-dressed and articulate everyone was. I asked Ron what company these people worked for. It turned out Mr. Liver Transplant was a senior VP at a major well-known Texas computer company and commanded a salary of a quarter million dollars a year.

"A quarter mill!" I snapped! "XYZ Company! Surely he has medical insurance?"

"Sure he does," came Ron's nonchalant reply. "We're here to help cover his twenty percent deductible."

It was then brought to my attention that Mr. Liver Transplant was sitting at the end of the bar, snot-slinging drunk with a cigarette in one hand and a drink in the other.

When he saw us looking at him he made an effort to raise his glass to us and grinned a glassy-eyed, shitfaced grin.

"Bullshit!" I yelled, "Fuckin' bullshit!"

My blood pressure soared to the boiling point. "We [the band] got no insurance, we got no benefits, we're performing for *free and* getting charged ten bucks a plate to eat. We're supposed to be raisin' money for a *corporate drunk* who makes a quarter-million bucks a year and *has insurance?*! *That's bullshit!* Far as I'm concerned he can pay his own goddamn twenty percent!"

I yelled to the band, "Pack up, we're outta here!"

I thought we'd have to fight our way out the door. It wouldn't be the first time. The yuppie snobs scattered like scared rabbits as we dragged our equipment across the dance floor through the crowd and out the front door.

The club owner was enraged. He knew that with no band, the crowd would soon leave and his much anticipated profits would be zilch! Did he offer to pay us to keep playing and keep putting money in his pocket? Hell no. He played the part of the poor, victimized club owner in front of the crowd cussing us all the way out the door and accusing us of stealing from the poor, sick cancer victim at the end of the bar whose life depended on a blues band.

When that didn't work the club owner made the ultimate and final threat that *all* club owners use that cause us musicians to tremble in fear: *"You'll never work in this town again!"*

We laughed. How original is that?

The club went out of business the following year. I also heard that Mr. Liver Transplant never pursued his surgery and is doing just fine, thank you. What does that tell you?

Mr. Liver Transplant's benefit caused me to rethink my benefit performance policy. Now I insist promoters furnish all equipment and we'll donate one forty-minute set.

We'll help anybody in need provided they have a *need*.

*Top Left:*
*The Wheelchair King*
*Kevin Harrington and his*
*sidekick Damn Good Dog.*

*Top Right:*
*Joni Kelton and*
*Tim Miller, founder of*
*Texas Equusearch*
*texasequusearch.org*

*Bottom:*
*Tim Miller receives a donation*
*for Texas Equusearch*
*from the*
*Southern Fried 4th Poker Run*
*by Poker Run Coordinator*
*Lonny Loehr*

# BOOK THIRTEEN

# Runnin From The Law

It is not uncommon for musicians to have run-ins with the law. The following are situations where I found myself a resident at the Many-Bar Hotel.

## LOCKED UP IN LIBERTY

In late October of 1973 I was twenty years old. My first wife, who had just turned eighteen, and I had been married a couple of weeks.

We were driving through Liberty on the way to play a back porch party at her parents' home. The sudden wail of a siren and the flashing lights in my rear view mirror alerted us we were being pulled over by the law.

Stepping out of the vehicle I immediately recognized the officer as "Sam the Parts Man" from the Liberty John Deere dealership where I had worked part-time in high school. Sam worked full-time for John Deere and on occasional weekends for the Liberty Police Department flagging traffic at funerals and fairs.

Since Sam and I were old friends, I never saw him as a *real* cop. I thought he was joking when he pulled me over. I stepped out of my car. "Hello Sam, how ya… "

In mid-sentence he grabbed me by one arm and by my shoulder length hair slamming my head against the car and knocking the breath out of me. He yelled, "Gene Kelton, we have a warrant for your arrest for blah, blah, blah…"

Sam's partner stood with his hand on his pistol and spouting off various charges against me. Sam read me my rights, cuffed me and shoved me in the back of his police car.

We were only two miles from the jail, but Sam turned on the lights and siren and drove like he'd just captured the world's most wanted criminal. I must have been his first collar.

Sam's sawed-off partner, a cocky, smart-ass little rooster who reminded me of Barney Fife on speed, yelled over the backseat as we flew through town, "We been a-watchin' fer you a long time, boy. We figgered you'd show yer hippie ass 'round here sooner 'r later. We gon hafta teech you-a lesson."

I didn't have a clue why I was being taken to jail. All I knew was I was handcuffed in the back of a police car with two redneck cops who had a problem with my shoulder length hair.

Rooster Cop badgered me all the way to the police station trying to get me to confess to a list of unsolved crimes that he read off from his clipboard. When we arrived at the station I was charged with an outstanding traffic ticket I had completely forgotten about and I was locked up with a couple of elderly town drunks.

In the meantime my wife was left stranded on the side of the road. The officers were so eager to take me to jail and show off their "catch of the day" they were not the least bit concerned with her safety. They didn't even bother to find out if she was capable of driving, handicapped, sick or if she even had a driver's license. At that time, she did not. They left her on the side of the road with no assistance.

When the officers drove away with me, my wife drove our 1968 Chevy Nova to her parents' house twenty miles away. Her dad came to the police station, paid my fine and bailed me out.

On the way home her dad started singing an old country song, "I'm In The Jailhouse Now." We had a good laugh.

I found out later that Sam was still working during the week behind the parts counter at the John Deere dealership and played part-time cop on the weekends. My father-in-law went to the John Deere place the following Monday morning and called him out. He called him out not for locking me up, but for leaving his teenage daughter stranded on the side of the highway with no concern for her life or safety.

Rumor has it that Sam hid in the back of the building until my "John Wayne" father-in-law left the premises.

Knowing my ex-father-in-law, Sam's decision to run and hide was a wise one.

## CHRISTMAS EVE 1985

On Christmas Eve in 1985, I was on my way to play an early evening Christmas party when I was pulled over for speeding in La Porte. Since it was Christmas Eve the officer intended to only give me a warning. But, when he ran my license, the report came back I had an outstanding speeding ticket in La Porte from 1978.

The officer was very apologetic for having to slap handcuffs on me on Christmas Eve. He apologized repeatedly, saying, "Man, I'm sorry, I know it's Christmas Eve. I sure hate to have to do this."

In fact, he was feeling so bad about arresting me on Christmas Eve that *I* actually felt sorry for *him*. I was locked in a cell just as they were serving a Christmas TV dinner of turkey and dressing. I spent a couple of hours in jail until my wife bailed me out.

I made it to my gig and started about an hour later than originally planned. I was surprised at how many people at the party hugged me or shook my hand and told me about when they were in jail. It was as if I had passed some sort of a secret initiation and was now accepted into a very elite society of Jailbirds.

As I got ready to play, my first request was "Jailhouse Rock."

## MAYBERRY – MAYBE NOT

In the summer of 1987 I ran through a four-way stop sign in the small East Texas town of San Augustine.

I was pulled over about a mile south of town by a Texas State Trooper. I handed him my license and gave him the usual answers to the usual questions. He was a nice guy and asked me about the music business after I explained to him I was a musician on my way to a gig.

After running my driver's license, he said, "Man, I don't think you're gonna sing anywhere tonight except our jail."

I had an outstanding warrant for a traffic ticket from somewhere in west Texas and he had to take me in.

I told him my music equipment was in the van and I didn't want to leave it sitting on the side of the road. He wouldn't allow me to drive my van to the jail, but called two other Troopers who were close by. One of them drove my van.

"Don't worry," said the officer, grinning. "We won't charge you a towing fee."

I stood at the side of the Trooper's car ready to assume the position to be searched and cuffed. Instead, the Trooper opened the passenger side front door like a valet and politely motioned me in.

"What? You're letting me ride in the front seat and no handcuffs?"

"Naw, you seem like an okay guy. We're only two minutes from the jail and I don't think you'd do anything I'd have to shoot 'cha for 'tween here and there," he said jokingly.

We both laughed.

I sat in the front seat next to an arsenal of shotguns, billy clubs and other weaponry. In less than two minutes we were at the San Augustine City Jail on the Courthouse Square.

Once inside the lobby looked like a waiting room at a doctor's office from a by-gone era. There were paintings on the walls, magazines on a coffee table, a TV in the corner and several big, comfortable chairs bound in burgundy leather.

Pointing toward the chairs the officer cheerfully said, "Have a seat," as if I were a guest in his home.

"I got paperwork to do in the back. Would you like a cup of coffee?"

"Sure." I replied.

I couldn't believe that my arresting officer actually brought me a cup of coffee.

"There's cream and sugar in there on the counter," he said.

There I was sitting in an antique leather chair, watching TV, drinking coffee and joking around with the officers who heard I was a professional musician. The officers shared their war stories about late night confrontations with drunks at places where I'd performed. I felt like I had gone to jail in Mayberry and wondered if Aunt Bea was going to show up with a big slice of homemade apple pie.

Mayberry? Well, maybe not. While I was being distracted by the hospitality of my new law enforcement friends, my arresting officer was in the parking lot searching my van.

Moments later he came in the front door carrying my pistol that he'd found under the seat. He gave me his obligatory lecture about carrying guns, but since everyone in East Texas carried a gun he simply laid it on the counter and said, "You'll get this back later."

I was detained for about an hour before the fax machine and the teletype completely cleared me of any other criminal acts against humanity.

After paying my fine I was handed a fresh cup of coffee in a Styrofoam cup and allowed to leave. The officers, still laughing and telling war stories, walked me to my van, handed me my keys and my pistol, shook hands and wished me great success in my music career. They all promised to come see me on their next night off.

If I ever go to jail in Texas again, I'm gonna ask to be transferred to San Augustine.

## COP ROCK

In 1988, the band was asked to do an oldie rock 'n roll show in the parking lot at a hamburger joint on Alexander Drive in Baytown for Bayshore Fine Rides Vintage Car Club.

Hundreds of people and hundreds of vintage cars filled the parking lot as we cranked out hits from the '50s and '60s. It must have been a slow night for crime in Baytown because suddenly a dozen cop cars wheeled in and surrounded the band. We thought we were going to jail. We were told to stop playing while the event promoters were questioned. A few minutes later the police superintendent approached me and asked, "Just what kind of music do ya'll play anyway?"

"Old time rock 'n roll," I replied. "Elvis, Chuck Berry, Fats Domino, Jerry Lee Lewis…"

"That's my favorite music!" he yelled. "You boys keep on playing. I'll take care of the complaint."

Once again, rock 'n roll saved the day.

## MOTHER'S DAY 1999

On Mother's Day in 1999, the band was performing an early afternoon show on the patio at Dick Head's Bar (yep, that was the name) on North Shepherd in Houston.

It was a miserably hot day. While setting up my gear I couldn't resist the temptation to chug a couple of ice-cold draft beers in a chilled, frosty mug. They went down too easy. I forced myself to stop after the second mug because draft beer gives me horrible headache. I didn't drink any more beer that day.

By 9pm I headed north on Shepherd Drive to Joni's house in the Heights ten minutes away. Just as I was crossing the I-10 overpass, a fifty-something-year-old lady in a Ford Escort made an illegal left-hand turn from the center lane and plowed into the right side of my van. The impact knocked my van over the curb and into the parking lot of an abandoned gas station where a Houston cop just happened to be sitting. I almost hit his car.

When the officer questioned the lady she said I had crossed into her lane and hit her.

"Bullshit!" I yelled, "I was gonna make a left-hand turn at the next light. Why the hell would I move to the center lane?"

The officer turned to me, pointed his ballpoint pen between my eyes and shouted, "Shut up until I ask you!"

When he did ask the usual questions I confessed I had drank two mugs of draft beer about seven hours earlier. That answer prompted a roadside sobriety test that had me performing like a chicken on a hot plate at a circus sideshow. Next thing I knew I was in the back of his police car and being hauled downtown. I was never arrested or handcuffed.

At the police station I was locked in a small room that was freezing cold. I thought I was going to die of hypothermia. I figured the room was kept ice cold because the officers wear bullet-proof vests under their uniforms. I'm sure it also helps keep down the stench of the reeking human riff-raff they kept dragging in.

After an hour in a holding area with a couple of bloody Mexicans and a young black guy who mysteriously disappeared after getting belligerent with the officers, I was moved to a testing room.

A wall-mounted video camera recorded my every move as I blew into a Breathalyzer and was ordered to recite the alphabet while standing on one foot touching my nose with my right forefinger with my eyes closed. I passed all the tests with no problem.

Around 1am I was ushered to a front room where several officers stood cross-armed and solemn. Thinking I was about to get my ass kicked, a wave of nausea rushed through me. To my surprise, the presiding officer pointed toward the door and said, "You are free to go!"

As I stepped toward the door he told me there was an officer waiting to talk to me on the front steps at the main entrance. "Go see him now!" he ordered.

That sounded fishy to me. Since when do law enforcement procedures require a free man to meet an officer on the front steps of the jail at two o'clock in the morning?

I got suspicious and scared. What the hell were they up to? Maybe a PI charge?

The moment I left the holding area, instead of turning left and going around to the front steps, I turned right and bolted down a dark alley as fast as I could. I felt like a hunted fugitive because I had purposely defied an official order and ran from the cops.

I had never been allowed a phone call all night. I was already five hours late when I found a pay phone and called Joni. She knew my gig was only a mile and a half away. She answered by yelling, "Your ass better be in jail!"

Imagine her surprise.

Joni picked me up and when we got back to her house at 3am the phone rang. It was the officer I was supposed to meet on the front steps of the jail. He was pissed. In a very official tone he ordered me back downtown immediately for what he referred to as official business.

In the safety of Joni's house I felt very brave and said, "Man, meeting you on the front steps at in the middle of the night sounded crazy to me! Ya'll must be looking to pin another charge on me!"

"Mr. Kelton, we have your car keys!" he announced. "And there is some paperwork I need to give you. I highly recommend you get down here, *now*."

I took a shower, changed clothes, grabbed some coffee and back to jail we went.

I was met by two very aggravated officers just inside the front door. One handed me my keys, billfold and personal belongings along with the phone number of the towing company that towed my van. The other officer handed me a ticket for no insurance.

"I have my insurance card right here in my billfold!" I argued.

"Tell it to the judge!" snapped the officer. "Now get outta here!"

A couple of months later I was tried in court by a jury of my "peers."

Since I was never charged with DWI, never arrested, never handcuffed, never fingerprinted and never allowed a phone call I figured I had a very simple, cut and dried winning case. I represented myself.

I drew diagrams of the intersection where the accident occurred. I got statements from the Houston traffic bureau with statistics about the number of accidents just like mine that happened at that same location all the time.

I took photos of the intersection showing that there were no street signs indicating a required "Left Turn Only" from the left lane nor any sign indicating a middle lane left turn option. On the day of the trial the frickin' judge refused to see any of my evidence citing that I did not follow legal protocol for the submission of evidence.

"Next time," he thundered, "hire a lawyer!"

The Assistant District Attorney represented the lady who hit my van. He tried to prove the accident was my fault by arguing that even though I did not register "drunk" when I was tested at the police station, I was "probably" drunk at the time of the accident.

The jury of my so-called peers, a dozen sleepy-eyed old codgers who looked like they had been dragged in from the morgue, bought his story and found me guilty of "possibly being intoxicated at the time of the accident."

I was never convicted of a DWI, but the verdict still cost me $600 and my insurance had to pay for the lady's piece-o-shit car.

That's why today I rarely drink alcohol when I will have to be driving. In the event there is ever a next time, I will definitely hire a lawyer.

## COPS REQUEST STEVIE RAY VAUGHAN

In 2001 Joni and I bought a house in an older section of Baytown. I soundproofed the garage for band practices with Styrofoam panels on the walls and ceiling. Regardless of the soundproofing every time we had band practice the lady next door called the cops.

I have been based in Baytown for over twenty years and performed a lot of shows and benefits so most of the cops knew who I was. They would stop by and make a show of reading me the riot act while the lady next door watched through the wooden fence.

Since we were not breaking any laws and promised to quit by 10pm there was never a problem. Before leaving the cops would almost always ask us to play something by Stevie Ray Vaughan. The lady next door would get furious.

When I wrote the song "Give Blues A Chance" for the *Mean Guitar* CD, I purposely changed the lyrics. *"Somebody called the cops when the band began to play… the cops showed up and requested Stevie Ray."*

From then on every time we had a band practice I would call the cops in advance. I'd tell them my dogs were tied up, the front gate was unlocked and just come on in.

## THE NATCHEZ TRACE

It was a clear, crisp, mid-October afternoon in 2002 as Joni and I drove across Mississippi on our way to an event near Tupelo. Since we were ahead of schedule we decided to take a leisurely drive up the beautiful Natchez Trace Parkway where the speed limit is 50 miles per hour and strictly enforced. Commercial traffic is not allowed on the "Trace" and there are no businesses to mar the natural beauty of the scenic route through the countryside. We rolled down the windows, set the cruise control on 50mph and Joni drove along the winding road while I absorbed the fresh air and viewed passing scenery from the passenger side.

About an hour north of Jackson I was dozing on and off. Suddenly Joni yelled, "I'm being pulled over!"

I raised up and checked the passenger side rearview mirror. I saw the flashing lights of a police car right on our tail and it wasn't trying to pass.

Joni pulled the van off the side of the road. We were approached on each side of the van, an officer at each door. From nowhere a third officer appeared directly in front of the van staring into the windshield with his hand on his gunbelt. The officer on Joni's side said he stopped her for weaving and asked if she had been drinking or was on drugs.

"No!" she responded. "I've got the cruise control on fifty – and I was not weaving either."

The officers opened our doors and told us to get out. Joni was taken to the front of the van while I was escorted to the police car behind the van. We were being interrogated and searched separately when two more police cars arrived with lights flashing.

While Joni was subjected to a humiliating roadside sobriety test I watched as all of our belongings and band equipment was dragged out of the van and onto the ground. The police searched inside every container, speaker box, cord bag, trash bag and ice chest. They went through Joni's purse and even dug through the bag that contained our dirty clothes.

The officers stood with their hands on their guns as they instructed me to open my guitar case – "slowly." They must of thought I had a bomb in my guitar case since they asked me to open it. As instructed I slowly opened the guitar case. I handed one of the officers my guitar and jokingly said, "don't point this at anybody."

The officers solemn expression cued me he was not in the mood for my humor. Another officer made an effort to rip the felt liner out of my guitar case.

After twenty minutes of searching, interrogating and running checks on us, all the officers found were some vitamins, a bottle of bee pollen, dirty clothes and an ice chest containing bottled water, grapes, bananas and carrots.

Once they concluded we weren't drunk or smuggling drugs or Mexicans from Texas, the officers dropped their John Wayne macho act and the tension eased.

Speaker boxes, amps, guitars, and personal items strewn along the side of the roadway. It looked like we had rolled the van. The officers never offered to help reload the van. The officers stood by as we tried to repack our belongings, watching us and asking questions about the music business.

Before we left, I offered the officers one of my CDs. They refused, jokingly saying I could be arrested for trying to bribe a federal officer.

"Then I'll just leave it laying here on the ground, and you guys can pick it up when we leave," I said.

"Then we'll have to charge you with littering Federal property," one of them joked.

I handed them all a business card and we drove away. We got off of The Natchez Trace at the next exit.

The officers suggested there was a possibility we could be stopped again if we stayed on The Natchez Trace. They informed us The Natchez Trace is a national park patrolled by U.S. Federal Marshals which they were.

The Marshalls never would tell us the real reason why we'd been stopped. They eluded to the D.C. sniper who was killing people in Washington D.C. and reported to be driving a white van.

We still love the Natchez Trace. Nowadays, we take the freeway.

*Photo by Joni Kelton*

# BOOK FOURTEEN

Musicians are always playing jokes on each other.

In most cases a practical joke is designed to create an embarrassing moment for a certain member of the band in front of an audience. There is something about being in front of an audience that intensifies even the smallest situation turning it into a hilarious event.

I confess! I'm guilty of playing practical jokes and dirty tricks on my fellow musicians.

## The Joy Of Sax

One night in the summer of 1992, we were playing "My Baby Don't Wear No Panties" at a nightclub in Pasadena when a very large woman took off her panties and threw them at the band. That in and of itself was hilarious. Her panties looked like parachute. I hung them on the headstock of my guitar and waved them back and forth like a Confederate battle flag. The crowd laughed roared with laughter.

At quitting time no one saw me stuff the giant panties deep into the bell of our sax player's horn. We all loaded up and went home.

The next morning I woke up with a case of the summer flu. I called my old friend Professor Blues and asked if he could front my band for our Saturday night and Sunday afternoon shows so my guys would not miss a payday. He heartily agreed.

I thanked him, and took my usual home remedies and slept for two days completely forgetting about the panties in the saxophone.

The following Monday afternoon my drummer Dooley called to check on me and give me an update about the gigs I had missed.

In the course of our conversation, he said, "Oh yeah, something really weird happened Saturday night! All night long, Lips kept messing with his saxophone. He kept twisting all the knobs and going over to the PA board tweaking his settings. He was pissed off all night about his sound. At the end of the night I saw him turn up the sax and look into the bell. Man, he pulled out that same big pair of panties that fat girl threw at us the night before!"

As bad as I felt, and under the influence of medication, I rolled with laughter. The drummer continued.

"Lips was pissed off. He looked right at Tubby and accused him of messin' with his sax. They almost got into a fight right there on stage. The crowd was laughing their asses off. Nobody could figure out how those big-ass panties got in the sax."

Laughing to the brink of uncontrollable urination with tears rolling down my face, I finally confessed that I was the one who put the panties in the sax.

At the show I missed I'd planned to let Lips play three songs and make a big deal out of how bad he sounded. I was going to encourage him to look inside the bell where he would discover the panties. I thought it would be hilarious! Unfortunately, I fell ill and forgot.

It was a couple of years after he quit the band that I confessed the dirty deed to Lips. Up until that time he thought either the fat girl or Tubby did it. He swears someday he will have his revenge. Bring it on Lips! But remember, "You can't out-step a stepper!"

# GUITAR HERO

In the spring of 1986 I lived on the second floor of the Quail Hollow Apartments in Baytown. I was gigging four to five nights a week getting home around 3am.

On the first floor underneath my apartment lived a single mom with her teenage son. He was a tall skinny kid about seventeen. Since I worked nights and the kid's mom worked days I seldom saw her. I'd see the kid sitting in a lawn chair outside their apartment all day while MTV blasted out through the open door. He didn't work. He didn't go to school. He seemed to be a loner and I never saw any other kids his age hanging around. Whenever I spoke to him as I went in or out, he never said a single word in reply. He just glared at me through greasy locks of unkempt, dirty blond hair that hung down over his thick, black-rimmed glasses.

The kid knew I played guitar because he saw me carrying mine up and down the stairs all the time. I was surprised he never said anything about it, because he also played guitar – every frickin' night!

For whatever reason every night when I got home from a gig around 3am the kid would be up and wide awake. Sometimes he'd be sitting outside in his lawn chair smoking a cigarette. Just about the time I laid down to sleep he'd fire up his little amplifier and electric guitar. He was never very loud, but because his bedroom was underneath mine he sounded like he was right under my bed. I don't know if he was trying to impress me, aggravate me or just fill his need for attention. Whatever it was, he was pissing me off every night.

On several occasions I politely asked him not to play late at night because he was keeping me awake. He'd just stare blankly at me, go inside his apartment and shut the door without saying a word.

I told my wife to watch out for that weird kid and not to open the door when I wasn't home. The kid would probably be an axe murderer someday.

One afternoon I had the unique pleasure of meeting the kid's frustrated psychotic mother. I asked her to put a stop to her son's guitar playing at 3am. She exploded into a fury about the hardships of raising a disrespectful teenage delinquent son by herself and how his deadbeat dad wouldn't help her. She blew off my complaint saying she never heard him play even though she slept on the couch in the living room so the kid could have the bedroom in the one bedroom apartment.

It immediately became obvious to me why she never heard him play. She was strung out on pills. Before slamming her door she yelled, "I have my own fuckin' problems! Mind your own goddamn business!"

After that I called security every night about the kid. Security would show up, have a few words with the kid and as soon as the officer drove away the kid went back to playing. Tired of my constant calling they told me there was nothing they could do legally and suggested I move to another apartment.

The daytime manager made the same suggestion. I was furious because I was the one being treated like a trouble maker, not the kid!

Finally one night, I brought in a 50-watt Marshall tube amp. I plugged in my guitar, turned the distortion, treble and volume up to TEN, laid the amp face down in the floor right over the top of the kid's bedroom and waited.

With guitar in hand I crouched beside my bed like a sniper ready to strike. I listened for the kid to make the first move. I sat holding my weapon steady, patiently waiting, waiting, waiting, for the perfect kill shot. I remember thinking I wish I could be a fly on that kid's wall when the shit hit the fan.

Gritting my teeth, I could hear the sound of my own heart beating as the adrenaline pulsed through my veins in anticipation of the deed I was about to commit. My hands were sweating and my guitar playing fingers were itching to rip through the strings and blow the plaster out of the ceiling below. I grinned to myself and I thought about Clint Eastwood's famous line in the movie *Dirty Harry*. I mumbled to myself, "C'mon kid, make my day!"

Finally I heard the kid play through a couple of notes. That was my cue. I unleashed an explosive blast of heavy metal, land-leveling power chords that shook the rafters. I grinned with evil delight as I envisioned the kid shittin' in his pants while plaster blew out of the ceiling and all over his room. I followed with a volley of wall-piercing, razor-sharp machine-gun notes with the intention of sending the kid diving for cover. For good measure I finished off with one long, screaming blast of ear-splitting, blood-curdling feedback that would break the glass on a shower door! My heavy metal ambush lasted about ten seconds. Then I abruptly stopped. I went silent and put my ear to the floor to listen.

Suddenly I heard the shrill screaming of Guitar Hero's mom obviously resurrected against her will from the depths of her nightly near-death, pill-induced coma. My frenzied guitar bomb had blown her ass off the couch. I could here her bare feet stomping across the floor as she apparently charged into sonny boy's room finding him with guitar in hand. I'm sure she jumped to the conclusion that he interrupted her induced slumber. I could hear her voice loud and clear coming through the floor as she tore into the kid with a verbal attack of a vicious she-devil.

"Wha-tha fuck are you doing you little shit?" she screamed. "Don't you know I gotta get up in two hours! Where we gonna live if you get us kicked outta here? Tomorrow you can go live with yer piece 'o shit father!"

Before the kid had a chance to reply I heard his bedroom door slam so hard the concussion rippled through my floor.

After that I never heard another peep out of the kid. Every time I saw him outside he would stop dead in his tracks and glare at me as I passed.

Mission accomplished.

## GETTING THE JUMP ON JOHNNY DEE

Johnny Dee & The Rocket 88's is one of the most famous '50s and '60s rock 'n roll show bands to ever come out of Austin. They are in great demand at major festivals and events all over the south and put on a great, high-energy show. I am proud to say that my distant cousin "T-Bone" Kelton is their bass player and one of the founding members.

In the winter of 1997 or 1998, my band was the opening act for Johnny Dee & The Rocket 88's at a large retro-rock venue, called The Hop on Houston's north side. I was excited to be a part of the show.

Apparently Johnny Dee did not know he had an opening act and was not happy when he found out. Just before show time I introduced myself to him and tried to make small talk, while the sound man was making last minute adjustments. Johnny was aggravated and not interested in having a conversation with some peon opening act. He was down right rude and his demeanor toward me was one of aloof sarcasm.

Cousin "T-Bone" tried to cover for Johnny and told me not to worry about it. Johnny's arrogant attitude toward me and my band had done pissed me off! After all, we were playing for free for "exposure" and he was the big star getting paid. I thought the least he could do was to show us a little respect.

At exactly 9pm we took the stage. As I picked up my guitar, I noticed Johnny Dee's song list for his first set laying on the stage. As luck would have it I knew *every one of his songs!*

"I'll show his ass," I thought.

I turned to the band, Jamie and Sid, and said, "Forget our set list, I'll call the songs!"

The announcer boomed, "Ladies and Gentleman, put your hands together for Gene Kelton & The Die Hards!"

I blazed into the signature intro of Chuck Berry's "Johnny B. Goode."

For the next forty minutes we packed the dance floor playing every song on Johnny Dee's set list. Through the smoky haze I could see Johnny Dee standing off to my right all dressed up in his '50s rock 'n roll costume with an Elvis pompadour hairstyle and Roy Orbison shades. I could tell he was furious.

We finished the set with the crowd yelling "One more, one more!"

I exited the stage feeling very cocky and triumphant. I recalled actor Dennis Quaid's portrayal of Jerry Lee Lewis in *Great Balls Of Fire* in the scene where Jerry Lee Lewis was pissed off for having to be the opening act for Chuck Berry. To upstage Berry, Lewis set his piano on fire. Upon leaving the stage Lewis sarcastically challenges Berry when he says, "Follow that, Killer!"

As I passed Johnny Dee he looked like he was mad enough to knock me on my ass. I said in my very best Dennis Quaid/Jerry Lee Lewis impersonation, "Follow that, Killer!"

Doing Johnny Dee's first set of songs was me being an asshole and taking a personal shot at Johnny Dee. In the end it was Johnny Dee who proved to be the true professional.

His band has an extensive repertoire and me stealing their first set didn't affect their show one bit. They rocked the house. I stayed all night and enjoyed their show. In the years since Johnny Dee and I have become great friends sharing billing on many shows.

Rock on, Johnny.

## VANESSA & THE WILD CACTUS BAND

I met Vanessa around 1987 when I was performing as a single act at the Rambling Bushes Club in Pasadena, Texas.

The club owner David Porter approached me and said, "There's a little girl here who wants to come up and sing."

Knowing that cute little kids have a natural ability to excite an audience I said, "Sure!"

When Vanessa approached the bandstand she was not the little girl the owner's description seemed to imply. Instead, she was hot, sexy young brunette in her early twenties and built like a Playboy centerfold. She had a natural, sultry beauty that movie stars pay thousands of dollars to get.

I looked at the owner, and said, "Your idea of a little girl and my idea of a little girl are two different things."

David shrugged his shoulders, grinned and walked away.

Vanessa and I agreed on a song we both knew and I asked her what key she sang it in.

"What's a key?" she asked.

That one question from an amateur singer is a professional band's worst nightmare.

Vanessa had never heard of a *key*. She had never sang on a mic and had never sang in public. Lucky me.

"I sing it the same as they do on the radio. I sing along with the radio all the time."

People who sing along with their car radios turned up loud are often under the misconception they can actually sing. When it's just your voice alone the singing experience becomes a whole different world. I asked her to sing a little bit of the song just to me so I could find her key.

When we kicked off the song she turned around to see a hundred sets of eyes looking at her for the first time in her life. Her adrenaline kicked in and threw her voice into overdrive. Instead of singing she blurted out the words in a key that did not previously exist in the universe. She knew the words, but her pitch, timing and key were all over the place. She wasn't a bad singer and definitely not shy, just inexperienced.

From a musician's point of view our first effort together was a disaster. Thankfully her good looks made it easier to deal with. The audience was drunk and cheered her on.

When Vanessa left the stage, I figured that was it and she'd never be back. Wrong.

The following week Vanessa was back and insisted on singing again. She was back again the next week, the next week and the next. Each week we struggled to find her key, but it was always the same train wreck.

I could've told her to hit the road, but there was something about her I was attracted to far beyond her cute looks. It was her persistence and burning desire to achieve her dream of being a singer even at the risk of suffering public humiliation. Vanessa's refusal to give up reminded me of myself when I first started out in the music business.

Finally I said, "Look, if you're gonna to be a singer, you need to learn what *keys* are."

After that, each week we would take my guitar out to the picnic tables behind the club and practice her songs in private. I explained to her about keys and so on.

Within a few weeks Vanessa was doing great. We had a good set of about six songs. It was a fantastic experience watching her grow becoming better and more confident as weeks passed.

In the process of working with Vanessa, I got to know her family who always came out to support her. I became good friends with her dad who was the epitome of a true southern gentleman. He was quiet-spoken, well-dressed and charming, most of the time.

When it came to Vanessa, like any protective papa bear, he went into attack mode when forced to discourage overly-interested cowboys who got too close to his little girl. When it came to her singing, Papa Bear was quick to proclaim Vanessa's talent as a singer to everyone within earshot. He never had anything good to say about any other female singer, amateur or professional. Even when superstars like Dolly Parton and Reba McIntire were played on a jukebox they became victims of his ridicule.

"If they ever heard Vanessa sing that song, they'd never open their mouth again," he'd say.

Not even Vanessa was spared Papa Bear's brutal criticisms when he thought she was having an off night. I knew he was only trying to make her stronger, but he was as tough on her as a drill sargeant.

Over the next ten years, Vanessa honed her craft by sitting in with dozens of bands, including mine. Often her dad would accompany her when she sang with my band. Before the night was through he would always offer me his uncensored, razor-sharp commentary. "You outta quit playin' that rock 'n roll hippie shit and play country like Vanessa. You might get somewhere."

By the mid-nineties, Vanessa's career was growing by leaps and bounds and she started her own band, "Vanessa & The Wild Cactus Band." They released several CDs.

Papa Bear automatically assumed the role as manager and actually did an excellent job of promoting Vanessa's struggling music career on a regional level.

# GIGS FROM HELL

In March of 1998, I got a call from concert promoter Kevin Herrington regarding his annual March of Dimes outdoor benefit concert held at Walter Hall Park in League City. He asked if I knew a good country band to headline the event. I recommended Vanessa & The Wild Cactus. It would be her very first show as a concert headliner. She would be performing on the main stage complete with lights, a sound man and stage crew. I was very proud of Vanessa. I felt I had helped her grow from a terrified amateur to concert headliner.

On the same night of Vanessa's debut as a headliner, my band would perform on another stage which sat at the far edge of the concert grounds, up a hill about two hundred yards due west of Vanessa's main stage.

Our band was not provided with anything. No lights, no sound man and no crew. Believing the bands were far enough apart, Kevin scheduled both bands to perform at the very same time. Being in different sections of the park and playing two different styles of music, should not have been a problem for either band. People who like country music could go see Vanessa, while people who liked Southern Rock and blues could see my band.

Just before show time, Papa Bear showed up behind my stage. His expression was that of a stone-faced executioner. His eyes were like cold steel. He showed no emotion as he spoke down at me in a tone that didn't show the slightest hint of our many years of friendship.

"You boys might as well pack up and go home right now. Cause when Vanessa starts singin', that hill over yonder's gonna be packed with people who love her and country music. Her band is the best in Texas. Even better 'n ya'll. When they start playin', ain't nobody gonna come up here and listen to ya'll's rock 'n roll hippie shit."

At first I thought Papa Bear was joking. I quickly realized he was as serious as a mafia hitman on a mission to eliminate the competition. I'd seen him rake other people over the coals when it came to protecting Vanessa, but why me? After all the years I'd worked with her, even back when she didn't even know what a key was. And, not to mention the fact I'd helped her get the very gig where she was now the headliner and I was the side-stage act.

I couldn't understand why he had suddenly turned on me.

I gritted my teeth and kept silent as he walked away. I felt deeply hurt by the comments of someone I saw as a friend. I remember thinking, "if you want a battle of the bands, mister, I'm fixin' to give you one hell of a battle. We'll see who plays to nobody!"

Vanessa's stage was at the bottom of the hill and faced away from us at a ninety degree angle. Unfortunately for her, the stage builders had positioned my stage facing straight down the hill with her stage directly in my line of fire.

Since it was an outdoor gig, I had brought out my biggest concert sound system, two Peavey SP1s and two Peavey SP2s. Like an artillery gunner, I strategically readjusted my speakers and aimed them straight at Vanessa's stage. I placed a mic on every instrument and told the band to turn it up.

We could barely hear Vanessa's band when they kicked off a few minutes ahead of us. About sixty people immediately congregated on the hill in front of her stage.

Before playing our first song, I bowed my head and said to myself, "Vanessa, you know I love ya girl, I'd do anything for you. I hope someday you'll forgive me for what I'm about to do. But you can thank your cantankerous ol' Daddy for what is about to happen."

With that said, we spent the rest of the night unmercifully bombarding Vanessa's stage with wave after wave of high-energy Southern rock 'n roll.

From my stage, I could see the hill that Papa Bear proclaimed was going to be packed with adoring Vanessa fans. Except for him and a couple of the band's wives, the hill was bare.

The area in front of my stage looked like a reenactment of Woodstock. No brag, just fact.

Halfway through our show we took a break and I walked over to the hill where Papa Bear was sitting on the grass. I started sarcastically mocking his words.

"Yeah, man! This hill is gonna be packed with people who l-o-o-ove Vanessa and country music. Best band in Texas. Even better 'n us. I might as well just pack all my shit and go home, cause when Vanessa starts singin' ain't noooobody gonna listen to my rock 'n roll hippie shit!"

If looks could kill, I'd have been shot dead by Papa Bear's deadly glare. I forced a maniacal laugh.

"I gotta go. I have a thousand fans on my hill waitin' to hear more rock 'n roll hippie shit!"

I learned later that every time Vanessa's band stopped playing our sound would wash across their stage like a tidal wave. Her drummer had trouble giving the right count. They had trouble staying on key and their timing was all over the place. Vanessa & The Wild Cactus Band suffered a *gig from hell*, delivered personally by me.

I hated to be that cruel. Vanessa was someone I truly cared about and I sincerely wanted her to be successful. But her dear old daddy needed to be put in his place for insulting me, my music, my band and disregarding everything I felt I'd done to help Vanessa through the years. After all, it was Papa Bear who issued the challenge.

Sometimes you gotta do what you gotta do. He never gave me a problem after that.

Vanessa, if you ever read this, know that I still love ya girl and I sincerely apologize for messing up your show. As I recall, you and your band were great back then and handled yourself like true professionals throughout the ordeal.

One more thing, I still like ol' Papa Bear too. I know he was just lookin' out for you.

## SHIT PILLS

My bass player was riding with me to a gig one afternoon and saw me open a bottle of white pills and pop a couple in my mouth. Without hesitation, he grabbed the bottle and popped a handful.

For a few minutes we rode along in silence.

Finally I asked, "Don't you wanna know what you just swallowed?"

"Naw! If they're good enough for you, they're good enough for me."

"But you should always know what you're taking before you pop something in your mouth, cause you just never know…"

"Ok, ok!" he snapped not wanting to hear my preaching, "What the hell were they?"

"Shit pills!" I snapped back. *"They make your bowels move!"*

"*Shit pills*?" He yelled.

"Yeah!" I laughed, "How many did you take?"

"Four or five, maybe six. Hell, I don't know! A whole damn handful!"

"Man, you're not supposed to take more than one or two of those!" I said. "Two will just loosen you up, four will turn shit into water, but a *whole hand full*? Man, in about an hour you're gonna be blowin' shit outta your ass like a fire hose right there in front of the audience. There won't be a damn thing you can do about it!"

He turned white as a ghost.

"You son of a bitch! You son of a bitch!" he shouted. "You shoulda told me what they were! If I shit on stage I'm gonna whup your ass!"

I was laughing so hard I could hardly see the road. "See why you should always ask before taking somebody else's pills?"

He was freaking out. I was laughing until tears ran down my face.

When I saw he was about to jump out of the van I said, "Hey, dude, I'm just joking! What you took was Chromium Picolinate for energy. They speed up your metabolism. You'll be okay. They won't make you shit."

"You're lyin!" he said. "If I shit in my pants I'm gonna whup your ass!"

I laughed all the way to the gig. He didn't shit on stage and he never took anything else I had in the van.

## Marking Their Territory

During an afternoon show at Michael's Ice House in Texas City, two big bloodhounds came wandering through the big, open doors into the building. They made their rounds among the tables where people tossed them potato chips and beef jerky.

The dogs were stirring people up. People whistled for them as they happily bounced around taking handouts. A few women who were afraid of dogs screamed and climbed on the tables. The happy-go-lucky dogs were having a wonderful time.

While on break Sid went to the bar. I hung out near the stage with several other musicians. I took a bottle of water and sprinkled a few drops on the side of Sid's kick drum.

When he came back I pointed at the water on the drum, and said, "Sid, one of those dogs pissed on your drums."

He looked at the water and started screaming, "I'll kill them sons-a-bitches! I'll kill 'em!"

He turned red as a beet as he dug through his hardware case for something to hit the dogs with. We were all laughing our asses off.

"How come ya'll let them piss on my drums?" he yelled.

We rolled with laughter.

"It ain't funny! Why don't I piss on ya'll's amp? How would you like that?"

"Haa! Haaaaaaaaa!" We could not contain our laughter.

Sid pulled out a piece of chrome drum hardware, stood up and scanned the area for the dogs. Before he could get himself in trouble with the dog lovers in the house, I wiped the water from his drum with my bare hand and held up my bottle of water for him to see.

Furiously, he tossed his weapon back in the case and walked away.

We all busted out laughing!

## Wet Money

I once had a bass player who had no sense of humor. *None.* He never smiled, never laughed and couldn't take a joke. At the end of a gig, I took his money in the restroom and ran it under the water. I told the band to watch as I counted out the wet money to him. As I walked away after I paid him he yelled, "Why's my money wet?"

"Oh, sorry man," I said, "I was taking a piss and dropped your money in the toilet."

He threw all his gig money on the floor and his hands in the air. "You son of a bitch!"

He realized it was a joke when we all cracked up laughing. He still didn't smile.

# BOOK FIFTEEN

Through the years I've been flashed and mooned hundreds of times by hundreds of women of all ages, sizes, shapes and colors. I've been asked to autograph every part of a woman's body. That's right, *every* part. You may wonder how some private parts can be autographed. Well, you just draw a circle around something that doesn't have a smooth surface and initial it on the side. Use your imagination.

I have been very fortunate that no boyfriend or husband has ever confronted me about leaving my "mark" where he has been leaving his. The number of men who approach me insisting I sign their wife's or girlfriend's breasts has been a major surprise to me. Oh well, whatever turns people on.

At one rally a man stood behind his wife, reached around her and held her breasts in his hands so I would have a firmer surface on which to write. He stared at me over her shoulder with a wild, glassy-eyed look while I quickly scribbled my name on her endowments. I think he was getting off watching me touch his wife's breasts. It was too weird.

I couldn't get away fast enough.

## Painted On Smile

One night in the late '90s at the world-famous Lance's Turtle Club in Seabrook, a face painter was painting flowers on all the young ladies. As the night wore on shirts came off and women were walking around topless with their breasts painted with all kinds of designs. The painter was very good and obviously loved his job. It was good for me too!

One young lady pulled her shorts and panties down around her ankles and draped herself over a bar stool to have her ass cheeks painted. The painter was positioned directly behind her. He looked over his shoulder and winked at us when we insisted he move just a little to the left for our benefit, of course.

When he finished painting her butt cheeks, the young lady ran to the front of the stage, turned around, dropped her pants and bent over exposing the beautiful globes of her painted ass. Her left cheek read, GENE KELTON, and her right cheek read, AND THE DIE HARDS. The crowd burst into applause. I was honored. Too bad I didn't have a camera.

## Mama's Boy

At a biker bar in Baytown in 2003, the dance floor was packed. In between songs a young guy about twenty and his somewhat older girlfriend rushed to the stage to request a song.

The young man yelled, "Hey man, play some of them songs that'll make these bitches take their clothes off! I wanna see some titties. Play that song about the girl with no panties. That'll get 'em going!"

"It's a little early for that," I said. "Let's wait awhile and see what happens."

"NO! *Do it right now!*" he insisted.

Then he turned to the woman he was dancing with and shouted, "Show 'em your tits, Mom!" And she did.

## What Big Titties You Have, Grandma!

In 1983 I was working as a single act at the City Club in Baytown when a lady in her late sixties approached me to request a song. While talking to me, one of her rowdy male friends, appeared beside her, put his arm around her shoulder and said, "Show that boy them titties!"

I could not believe what I was hearing. At that time I had never been flashed by anyone in my life, much less someone old enough to be my mother or grandma. The man kept harassing her, pulling at her sweater and shouting, "Skin to the wind, baby!"

Finally she said, "Oh hell, alright!" She pulled her sweater up over two large breasts encased in a bra big enough to cover the front end of a Volkswagen.

"Bullshit! He can see a bra in a Sears Catalog! Show that boy them big titties!"

The woman grabbed her bra and pulled it up. I expected her breasts to plop to her waist, but to my surprise, she exposed two of the most beautiful, perfect, extra-large, all-natural breasts I'd ever seen at that time in my life. She might have been in her sixties, but her breasts didn't look a day over twenty-five.

I grew up believing by the time people reached their sixties they automatically became benevolent grandparent types, old women tended to their flower gardens and old men went fishing. Not so at this place. Somebody must have been spiking the Geritol because all the senior citizens that frequented the place danced, drank whiskey and raised hell like teenagers at a frat party. Good for them. Never again did I believe all that stereotypical crap about how people slow down as they age or that all women lose their figure.

Grandma had it going on.

## Spread 'em, Granny!

Around 2003 we were performing to a packed house at Morgan Freeman's Ground Zero Blues Club in Clarksdale, Mississippi.

During the middle of a set I noticed a skinny, seventy-something-year-old lady caught up in the spirit of the music, dancing uninhibitedly in front of the stage. She was wearing tennis shoes and a peach-colored t-shirt dress.

Over and over she yelled, "Play 'My Baby Don't Wear No Panties'! That's my favorite song! I drove all the way from Arkansas to hear it!"

Finally we played her request. She shrieked and leaped on top of a short rail at the edge of the stage and landed directly in front of our bass player, "Hollywood" Steve Rangel.

Bumping and grinding like a New Orleans stripper, she pulled her dress up to her neck to reveal that she was not wearing *anything* underneath. Standing on the elevated rail, her fuzzy gray crotch was only inches away from Hollywood's face. Hollywood never wore glasses on stage. He should have. Without his prescription glasses all Hollywood saw was a female body dancing on the platform in front of him. He stepped forward to get a closer look and realized he was face to face with a seventy-year-old crotch. He wheeled around in shock, bolted to the rear of the stage and buried his head in his bass amp. The whole place erupted with laughter!

Suddenly a bouncer appeared, grabbed Granny around the waist, threw her across his hip like a small child and headed for the front door pushing people out of the way like he was running for a touchdown.

Caught firmly in the bouncer's grip Granny unleashed a blood-curdling scream. Flailing her arms and legs wildly, she inadvertently spread her legs as wide as she could exposing her gray bird-nest to everyone, in all its antiquated glory.

Women screamed. Everybody laughed hysterically. Over the PA system, I managed to get the bouncer's attention and convince him to let Granny stay if she promised to behave herself. After all she was just having a little harmless fun and she put on a much more memorable show than we ever could.

Granny was allowed to stay if she promised to remain seated in a chair at the side of the stage for the rest of the night. Poor little Granny could hardly contain her enthusiasm when the music played, but she minded her manners and squirmed in her chair until closing time.

## Tangled Tits

In the winter of 2001 we performed at a country-western honky-tonk near Livingston, Texas. At first the good ol' country folks just sat and stared at us as we went through our blues-oriented song list. As the night progressed and the booze hit its mark, they began to yell, "We want sum kuuunt-tree!"

We kept throwing blues and some '50s rock 'n roll at them. Occasionally a couple would get up and two-step to one of our blues shuffles.

There were three women at one table who seemed to really enjoy our music. Two were in their fifties who had obviously been hotties in their younger days. Both sported bleached-blond hair, piled high and feathered back in a style popular in the seventies. Their Rocky Mountain jeans and tank tops were way too tight for the rolls of fat that bulged over their jeans like too much ice cream in a waffle cone. The third woman turned out to be their lil' ol' gray-haired Mama who was probably in her seventies.

None of the men ever asked them to dance so all three women would hit the dance floor and do their own thing. As the whiskey and the excitement of the music took effect, the two daughters made uncoordinated efforts to recreate the moves of their younger days. When they couldn't get the moves right, they unbuttoned their shirts and started flashing their tits.

Mama got upset that her girls were being "sinful." Each time one of them showed her tits, Mama ran out on the dance floor to button her daughter's shirt. Then she'd preach the gospel and shout Bible scripture to force the daughter off the floor. While Mama was busy with one daughter, the other would show her tits. This kept Mama running back and forth between the two girls. From the band's point of view it was hilarious.

The whiskey and frustration was more than Mama could take. Next thing we knew Mama was on the dance floor, mocking her daughter's titty dancer moves and trying to pull her t-shirt off. As she pulled her t-shirt over her head, it got tangled in her bra straps and caught under her chin. With her arms sticking straight up in the air and caught in the twisted clothing, she fought to get loose but couldn't.

The t-shirt was stuck over her head and covered her face completely. Mama's seventy-something-year-old breasts were exposed to the onlookers. She panicked started screaming at the top of her lungs while spinning around in circles and thrashing back and forth like a washing machine agitator. The frantic contortions caused her sagging breasts to flip-flop back and forth against her body like two wet socks. She looked like a cat gone wild with its head stuck in a bag. Her two daughters came running across the dance floor, screaming with hysterical laughter to rescue Mama.

Still hog-tied in her own tangled mess, the daughters dragged Mama off the dance floor and into the restroom. She cussed, screamed and kicked all the way.

We were laughing so hard we couldn't finish the song. In fact, we couldn't finish the set.

## NUDIST RESORTS

Since 2001 the band has performed at numerous nudist resorts across the country.

I know you want to read about wild sexual adventures with hot young vixens. In that case, go read *Penthouse Forum*. The only difference between performing at nudist resorts and any other place is people at nudist resorts are just plain folks who happen to be naked, that's all.

People at nudist resorts have always been extremely polite and professional to us and have always treated us with utmost respect. We've never met anyone who seemed offended, intimidated or embarrassed by the fact we were dressed. In return we show them the same respect. We've never seen any sort of deviant sexual behavior, orgies or any of the other sexual acts that most uninitiated people seem to think goes on. Not saying it doesn't happen in private, but so far we've never seen it in the open. Even if we did see something that might be considered wild and crazy, the unwritten code states, "Whatever happens at a nudist resort, stays there!" Here's one story I *can* tell you about.

### Fire Dancers

During one of our nudist events, a man and woman performed a "Hawaiian Fire Dance." They had flaming torches fastened to both ends of a rope about six feet long. As the music played, they swung the torches around over their heads, around their waist and between their legs making for a really cool light show.

The extremely well-endowed nude woman was covered with a glistening sheen of sweat that reflected the firelight which made her body sparkle like she was covered in a million multi-colored diamonds. She was spectacular. With all the lights out, watching her spin around lighting up the night with her whirling flaming torches was a very impressive, artistic sight. The man, however, was a different story.

Though equally talented, he was obviously impaired by too much alcohol. He should have known that alcohol and fire don't mix. His performance was sluggish compared to the woman's dynamic demonstration. The flaming torch apparently got too close to his pubic region because suddenly the night air filled with the harsh stench of burning human hair.

A collective "oooohhh" and "peee-uuu" came from the audience as they retreated to a safer distance. The men cracked up laughing at the thought of the poor guy roasting his nuts over an open flame.

The next time Jack jumps over the candlestick he'd best take a lesson from the woman, either shave or jump a little higher.

### A Taller Table

Joni always sets up a booth at our shows to sell merchandise and that includes our shows at nudist resorts. Since people are naked, they don't have any pockets to carry money and nowhere to put their merchandise even if they *did* buy something. Sales are usually minimal at a nudist resort.

At the first nudist resort we played, Joni informed me that the next time we would need a taller table. It seems when naked men came to our booth *their* merchandise dangled over the edge of *our* merchandise and appeared to be sniffing the table like curious little "weenie dogs." She moved her CD displays to the back of the table and said next time she'll either bring a taller table or a fly swatter.

### Does The Band Play Naked?

In regards to nudist resorts, we are always asked, "Does the band play naked?"

Can't say! *Won't* say!

Remember what I said about what happens there stays there. The next time we advertise a public invited show at a nudist resort, just show up and see for yourself. We'll play that old country-western song by John Anderson "Just A-Swangin'."

Our motto is *"If you wanna know, you gotta go!"*

# SWINGERS

In 1973, at the tender age of twenty, I had my first encounter with swinger's clubs.

Without going into detail, suffice to say it was an exciting but short-lived experience for a young man at that stage of life.

By 2000 I released *Most Requested* containing many songs with strong sexual innuendos like "My Baby Don't Wear No Panties," "My Blow Up Lover," "The Texas City Dyke," "Let Me Pump Your Gas" and others. As a result of those salacious songs we were asked to perform for various swinger's parties, swinger's clubs and nudist resorts around the country.

## Swang Yer Pardner

Recalling my experiences with ultra cool and very posh swingers clubs from the '70s where everyone looked like centerfolds out of the pages of *Playboy Magazine,* I was excited about the prospect of more of the same when we were offered a gig at a swingers club.

Imagine my disappointment when we arrived. My first swingers club gig in over thirty years was in an old, run-down, deteriorating strip center on Houston's far northwest side. That area was better known for junk yards, used car lots and roadside taco stands.

The gravel driveway was dotted with potholes. The sign over the door was lit by one dim, naked porch light. The club, with its dirty, raggedy red carpet, was a dump that reeked of stale beer, urine and cigarette smoke.

Though the club was empty when we arrived, the DJ insisted on playing the "Panties" song at ear-splitting volume *over* and *over* and *over* as we set up for the gig. He told me their regulars were looking forward to our performance.

As the place started to fill up the first thing I noticed was the absence of any classy, hot vixens like the ones I remembered in the swingers clubs in the '70s. Instead, most of the women looked like they were featured on PeopleOfWalmart.com.

Many of our Die Hards showed up out of curiosity.

After our first set the whiskey and sexual energy in the room took control and people loosened up. Women of all shapes and sizes retreated to a large dressing room in the back of the building and came out wearing all sorts of "sexy" lingerie. It was the first time I'd seen a 350-pound woman in a see-through negligee and thong stuck in the crack of her ass. Every time she took a step it looked as though her butt cheeks were trying to chew the string in two.

By the third set things got really weird. All sorts of debauchery began taking place inside the building. Not like I hadn't seen weirdness before, but *DAAAAMN*!

People were bumping and grinding to the music, humping each other's legs and feeling off whoever was closest. Women bent over exposing their naked asses, while the men (still fully dressed) grabbed the womens' hips and did the booty-bump from behind.

A big guy, about 6' 2" in his mid-forties lifted his petite, topless girlfriend onto his shoulders and positioned her so that her crotch was in his face. He pressed her against the wall and buried his face in her crotchless panties. She arched her back against the wall. With one hand against the ceiling, she held onto the back of his head with her other hand. The music drowned out her obvious moans as she bucked against his face to the beat of the music. She reminded me of Debra Winger riding the mechanical bull in *Urban Cowboy*. The band was mesmerized but we kept playing until she melted and slid off the wall like hot molasses. The big guy then carried her off into the darkness like King Kong carried away Fay Wray.

Meanwhile, back on the dance floor, women were humping each other's thighs. The DJ would shine the spotlight on dancers involved in various sex acts which only encouraged them to be more daring and deviant. Sometimes it became a competition to see who could be the kinkiest while in the spotlight.

At one point two guys grabbed a young, topless girl by the arms and legs, pulled her spread-eagle and swung her back and forth exposing her treasures to the band. She shrieked with delight. I thought they were going to toss her right on top of the drums.

At the bar a lady leaned over and performed oral sex on a guy while he nonchalantly sipped his beer and chatted with the guy sitting on the bar stool next to him. I hope she had been properly introduced.

Other sexual acts were taking place at the tables and in the dark corners of the room. Use your imagination.

## Strap-on Cucumber

During one of our breaks, a straight back chair was placed in the middle of the dance floor. The DJ called a young woman who was celebrating her birthday to the middle of the room. She was in her mid-thirties, but was so anorexic she was no bigger than a twelve-year-old and looked like a walking skeleton. It was obvious she had a severe drug habit.

"Boney Moroney" was so skinny that her breasts, if she ever had any, had withered away to near nothing. In her tiny black leather bikini you could count her ribs. Her hipbones stuck out like handlebars. Her arms and legs looked like toothpicks with lumps for elbows and knees. She had large, dark circles around hollow, black eyes that sunk back in her head. She was a sickly sight and looked like death.

Boney Maroney was commanded to sit in the chair. Her friends had ordered a male stripper to dance for her. The male dancer certainly earned his money that night. Imagine bumping and grinding for a skeletal corpse. She was nearly incoherent as he danced around her wearing only his black satin g-string, cowboy hat and cowboy boots.

Boney would grin a big skeletal grin through a mouth full of rotten teeth and lips coated with thick red lipstick to cover up massive cold sores. It was a sickening sight. The stripper grabbed her by the back of her head and rubbed her face against the obvious bulge in his satin g-string. It was ugly like a bad wreck, but we couldn't tear our eyes away from the horrible scene playing out before us.

For the grand finale the male stripper strapped on a dildo made to look like a Texas-sized cucumber. In the flashing strobe lights and ear-splitting disco music, he danced around, humping like a dog in heat and masturbating the cucumber while the women screamed. He smeared the cucumber with Cool-Whip and stood in front of Boney Moroney. She leaned forward, took the green, frothy monster in her mouth and began to slowly slide up and down on it. All her girlfriends on the sidelines cheered on her performance.

Suddenly the male dancer grabbed Boney Moroney by the back of her head, got a good grip on her greasy, black mane and slammed his green monster down her throat like he was trying to punch a hole through the back of her skull.

Riding her face at full gallop, the male dancer repeatedly slammed against Boney Moroney's face while waving one hand in the air like he was riding a wild bull. Her eyes bulged out of her head as she fought to escape his death grip. The fury of his sudden violent, deep thrusts was choking her to death. Cool-Whip covered her face.

In her frail condition, Boney Maroney's efforts to fight him off were futile. Her drunk screaming friends misinterpreted her struggle as some sort of morbid sexual ecstasy. The cheering crowd failed to realize that what had started out as fun had turned into a violent, public oral rape and she was about to drop dead from the face trauma and suffocation.

The oral attack lasted only a few seconds. The male dancer finished, turned and ran toward the dressing room. He tossed the spit, blood and Cool-Whip smeared strap-on cucumber on the *band table* as he passed. We jumped back as if he tossed a live grenade.

Joni screamed, "You son-of-a-bitch!"

She tipped the table, dumping the cucumber, drink glasses, and bottles onto the floor with a loud crash. We blamed the mess on the male dancer who bolted from the premises as if the place was on fire. He probably headed straight for the free clinic.

We vowed to never to return to that club again.

## Raining Rat Shit

Even though we vowed never to return, it's hard for a full-time musician to turn down a paying gig when someone is throwing good money at you. After a few months we found ourselves back at the same seething little shithole for another exciting adventure.

Upon arrival a light rain had turned the gravel parking into a sloppy, muddy mess. As we were setting up we tracked in mud and gravel and no one seemed to notice or give a damn.

By the time we played our first song at 9pm the house was packed. Outside the light drizzle had turned into a torrential downpour. Inside, the raggedy, old ceiling began dripping rainwater every few inches. The ceiling was missing many acoustic panels, exposing the underside of the metal roof, steel framework and duct work. The exposed wiring was coated with decades of dust, mold and wet cobwebs that hung like Spanish Moss.

Looking up I was disgusted to realize the rainwater dripping on us was being filtered through a maze of filth from decades of rats and roaches living, breeding, birthing, pissing, shitting, dying and decomposing in the ceiling.

Customers seemed to take it all in stride as if it was part of some exotic adventure. They repositioned their chairs and placed empty glasses and ashtrays to catch water that dripped onto their tables. I always wondered if the leaks splattered into their drinks.

Water had to be constantly mopped up from the dance floor. Regardless of the inconvenience nobody wanted to leave because they were afraid they might miss some sexual extravaganza that the place was famous for.

On the bandstand the nasty, brown water dripped all over us and all over our equipment. The bass player and I were able to reposition our amps and mic stands to avoid a direct hit, but unfortunately our drummer Curtis Craig was not so lucky. There was no way he could reposition his entire drum kit to be completely out from under the filthy water dripping on him and his drums. During every song as he struck his cymbals and toms, gross dirty water would splatter all over hiss drums and into his face.

Curtis was an easy going, jovial guy who seldom got mad at anything. At first he made jokes about the rainwater running down the crack of his ass. He played down the situation and laughed it off until I reminded him that the water dripping onto his drums and splattering into his face was *liquified rat shit*.

The change of expression on his face was priceless. He became furious. We all were. The club owner refused to allow us to put a tarp over the band. "It won't look good," he said.

Rain, mud, stench and leaks – but a tarp wouldn't *look good*?

After about an hour, the leaks subsided as the rain let up. We were able to finish our gig to only an occasional drip.

The following week our drummer got a tetanus shot to help fight off any infection he might have picked up from having liquified rat shit splattered in his face, on his lips and in his eyes. We never went back to that club again.

## Swingers House Party

A group we met at the swingers club asked us to play a private swingers party and promised it would be a lot more fun than the club. We accepted the gig.

We arrived at a beautiful home in an upper class neighborhood. I was glad to see our employer had hired an armed security guard for the event. As people arrived he would check IDs and compare them with the printed invitations. We set up in the backyard next to the swimming pool. The band started playing as the sun went down. After about an hour the pool filled with naked people. Another hour passed and things started getting *wild*.

A beautiful young woman in her early thirties danced naked. She stood spread-legged in front of the band having a great time all by herself, if you know what I mean.

People in the pool were experimenting underwater. Two women put on a fantastic show, oblivious to the onlookers. It's a wonder we could remember our lyrics.

The moment I called for a break our drummer "Quickie" ripped off his clothes, streaked past me in a blinding flash and dove into the pool. I choose to keep my clothes on and made my way to the kitchen where there was tons of food at the buffet.

Down the hall I saw two women exit from the bathroom followed by our bass player. He was covered with sweat. He looked surprised and embarrassed when he realized I spotted him. As he walked passed he smiled, winked and said, "Sometimes, ya just gotta go for it."

I shook my head and grinned in disbelief. He was usually such a shy and bashful guy.

I picked up a paper plate and surveyed the usual buffet options, assorted meats, cheeses, fruits, vegetables, chips and dips. I tried to ignore all the naked people standing around carrying on conversations like it was a church social.

A low moan at the other end of the kitchen caught my attention. I turned to see a seventy-something-year-old man backed up against the counter with his pants around his ankles. Two naked women, also in their seventies, were on their knees in front of him. They were dipping his penis in a glass of what appeared to be Bailey's Irish Cream. They'd take turns licking Bailey's off of him, then they'd re-dip and start over. Gripping the counter as if his life depended on it, the old codger's eyes rolled back in his head and his rickety old legs were shaking like a stop sign in a hurricane.

I suddenly lost my appetite. I tossed my plate of food in the trash without even taking a bite and rushed to the bandstand as fast as I could.

At the end of the night I couldn't find our drummer to give him his money. Someone told me he was in the back bedroom and to go on in. I'd always thought I was a pretty wild and opened minded guy until I opened the door to see a pile of seething, naked bodies. I couldn't tell where one body stopped and another started.

I slammed the door and took off down the hall, jumped in my van and hauled ass feeling like a little kid that had seen something I wasn't supposed to see.

I paid the drummer the following week.

## VAMPIRE SWINGERS

During the summer of 2002 a group of swingers began to follow the band all over southeast Texas. We've had our share of followers who adhere to the swinger lifestyle, but most tend to be very discreet. This particular group was an obnoxious, overly-aggressive clan of hell-raisin', lust-filled sexual vampires on a relentless hunt for new victims.

One of the first things we noticed about the group was the contrast between the looks of the guys and the girls. The girls were red-hot vixens in their mid-twenties looking like they stepped out of a *Penthouse* centerfold. The guys looked in their mid-forties dressed like pipefitters and were as homely as hound dogs.

In my humble opinion, there are only two things that would make hot young vixens cavort with a pack of ugly hound dogs – money and drugs.

Every time the "Vampires" showed up to one of our shows, they demanded to hear the "Panties" song, over and over. Each time we played it the girls slithered like snakes in a pit, fondling, bumping, grinding and dry-humping each other on the dance floor. They would rudely impose themselves on other people, grabbing them by the hand and dragging them from their table. On every dance they'd slide up next to someone already dancing, invading the dancers' space. They'd hit on everyone at our shows with promises of wild parties they'd never forget.

### Vampire Swingers Eat At Joe's

When the Vampires first started following the band we mostly performed at nightclubs where their raucous, sexually charged antics were no big deal. But when they showed up at an early afternoon show at Joe's Crab Shack restaurant on I-10 East in Houston, that was a whole different story.

We were playing on the deck and it was packed with families having dinner. Children played in the playground area next to the deck. The Vampires arrived already jacked up and insisted on hearing the "Panties" song, "Texas City Dyke" and other adult songs in our repertoire. We refused to play those songs with children present. When they finally gave up on us playing those songs, the group sat at their table disappointed, sulking and guzzling beer and mixed drinks while the girls flirted with our drummer, Curtis Craig.

Since the beginning of their infatuation with our band, the Vampirettes had been hustling Curtis. He was the only member of the band or crew who would socialize with them. The rest of us kept our distance. Curtis beamed when he told us that the girls invited him to go sailing on Galveston Bay aboard their private party barge. I told Curtis the girls didn't give a shit about him, they were only bait to lure him out on the boat because the guys were a bunch of faggots who were after his ass.

"Does 'squeal like a pig' mean anything to you?" I asked.

Curtis just laughed off my accusation and told me I was wrong. I told him they'd get him five miles out in the bay and give him two choices. I didn't think he could swim five miles. I also reminded him there were sharks in Galveston Bay. Again, Curtis just laughed it off.

The music and the whiskey finally got the best of the Vampires. Right there on Joe's Crab Shack deck in front of the families and children the Vampirettes started bumping and grinding all over each other. One of the guys jumped up on a picnic table and mooned the audience. We were appalled by their disrespect toward families with children. Then the guys started dancing together, humping each other's legs and groping each other's crotches.

We were sickened. I turned to Curtis and yelled, "I told ya they were a buncha faggots! You still going sailing with 'em?"

Curtis wasn't laughing anymore.

Fortunately Joe's Crab Shack employed a very large security guard named Scott Hamilton who was also a Houston Police officer. Scott was obviously a bodybuilder. At around 6' 6" he was an intimidating presence. He was built like a Roman Gladiator with biceps as big as beer kegs and a chest like a Sherman tank.

When Scott rounded the corner in his uniform, the Vampires took flight.

## Vampires Howl At The Cactus Moon

A few weeks later the Vampires showed up at a Saturday night show at the Cactus Moon in Humble. As the music played they fell into their usual routine. To the band their routine had gotten boring and disgusting.

When we played the "Panties" song the Vampirettes tossed their panties on stage. One girl in particular imposed herself upon an older couple sitting at a front table. She sat down at their table, faced the band, spread her legs and began ramming her fingers into herself while her friends cheered her on. The couple was horrified.

The blues-loving crowd was rightfully offended and angered. They were there for a blues music show not a sex show. Thomas Gardner, the owner, threw the entire group out. The audience cheered as he marched the group toward the exit. The girl who had been fingering herself pulled her miniskirt up around her waist and walked out naked from the waist down. Well, not entirely naked. She was wearing stilettos.

I knew I had to put a stop to the Vampires coming and disrupting our shows. Our jobs were threatened and fans told us if the Vampires showed up they would leave and not come back.

Since it's a free country and clubs and restaurants are open to anyone who wants to come in, how could the band bar anyone from a public place? Our job is to get customers in to a place not censor their activities. That's the job of the venue owners.

I took it upon myself to get rid of the Vampire Swingers. The next time they showed up I told them to get lost and to not come back. Thankfully that's all it took.

Haven't seen 'em since.

# BOOK SIXTEEN

# Miscellaneous

## DEVILS ROB ANGELS

It was a dark, rainy evening a few days before Christmas in 1978 when I stopped at Angel's Restaurant in Pasadena. To avoid long distance charges from my home, I wanted to call my keyboard player from a payphone before leaving town. The restaurant was filled with people, mostly families with kids apparently taking a break from their Christmas shopping.

I sat down at the counter, ordered a cup of coffee and asked for change from the sweet, old lady behind the counter. She was probably in her seventies, but projected a vibrant, youthful energy as she spouted orders to the waitresses, busboys and cooks. She seemed to know all her customers personally, calling them by name and exchanging Christmas greetings as people came and went.

I downed a couple sips of coffee, fumbled with my change and stepped over to the payphone on the wall about ten feet from my seat. I called my keyboard player to set up a practice session with our band, Texas Country Bandits.

Leaning against the wall with the phone at my ear, I suddenly heard screaming behind me. I turned to see two masked men with guns drawn rushing through the front door, straight to the counter where I had been sitting.

One masked man tossed a cloth bag at the old lady, stuck a pistol in her face and yelled, "Gimme all yer money, now! *NOW!*"

The old lady stood speechless, staring at the gunman. Everyone started screaming.

The other masked man stood facing the main dining room with a pistol in each hand like Jesse James robbing a train. He yelled, "Everybody shut the fuck up and nobody will get hurt! Put all yer money on the table!"

"This is a joke, right?" the old lady said. Apparently she thought she knew the gunmen and called them by name, believing it was a prank.

"I know who's behind that mask," she said as she grabbed one of the masks and tried to rip it from his face. The gunman slapped the old lady in the face, knocking her backwards against wall. She grabbed her face and screamed in terror.

"This ain't no fuckin' joke, bitch! gimme all yer fuckin' money, now!"

Hypnotized by the unbelievable events playing out before me, I stood at the payphone, mesmerized and still holding the receiver to my ear. My keyboard player was talking away on the other end, but I couldn't focus on what he was saying. Realizing the gunmen might think I was calling the cops, I slowly placed the phone back in the cradle.

The gunman at the counter spotted me just as I placed the receiver in the cradle. He must have thought I was reaching for the phone instead of putting it back. He turned and aimed his pistol directly between my eyes.

In a split second a million thoughts flooded my brain. I guess that's what happens when you're staring down the barrel of a gun and believe death has come calling. I don't remember being afraid. The only emotion I remember was *rage*.

Rage, not fear, flooded my brain. Rage, because I was helpless and at the mercy of a two-bit piece of shit gunman who had the power to take my life and rip me away from my family, sending them into turmoil and causing my two sons to grow up without me. Prior to this experience, I didn't know I could actually want to kill someone with my bare hands. But if I could have reached the gunman, I would have tried.

A vision flashed through my mind. I could see my wife and two little boys sitting on the couch at home, watching TV and waiting for me to come home from work. I could see my little boys' smiling faces as they peered through the window, waving as I drove into the driveway. I could hear their bare little feet stampeding through the house on the old hardwood floors. I could see my wife opening the front door, giving me a hug and a kiss and telling me that supper was on the table. My boys, already in their pajamas, pouncing on me ready to wrestle around in the living room floor before their mom calls "time-out, let's eat."

I was staring into the eyes of the devil himself.

The gunman yelled, "Down on the floor, fella! Down on the floor! Now!"

Terror ripped through me like a lightning bolt. I thought I was about to be executed. With my hands in the air, I slowly dropped down to my knees and got face down on the floor.

A moment later people were screaming, "Call the cops! Call the cops!"

People started running all over the room, jumping over me as I lay on the floor. I looked up. The gunmen had fled.

The reality of my near-death experience set in. My hands trembled and I could hardly breathe. My knees were so weak it was a struggle to get to my feet. Nausea swept through me like a tidal wave. Staggering on my shaky legs like a drunk, I rushed into the men's room and reached a stall just in time to heave my guts out.

When I exited the restroom, the restaurant was full of cops. Everyone was babbling at the same time. I waded through the chaos, went out the front door, found my car and drove away.

I don't remember the hour and fifteen minute drive from Pasadena to my home in Raywood. When I arrived, real life played out exactly as in my earlier vision. After the boys went to bed, my wife, expressing concern, asked me if I had lost my job that day because I was acting so strange. I could no longer hold back the flood of tears. I hugged her as I told her the story. Later that night, just before passing out from exhaustion, I said a silent prayer. I thanked Almighty God in Heaven for sparing my life and allowing me to return home to my family.

As few days later at a band practice when my keyboard player arrived, the first thing he said was, "Hey, man, why the hell did you hang up on me the other night?"

## Purse Snatcher

In the fall of 1979, Firecreek played a little roadside beer joint on Houston's notoriously rough north side called Wall's Icehouse. It was a typical, rough neighborhood bar, complete with a rough neighborhood crowd.

On our first night we watched from the stage as a drunk, male customer in his mid-thirties reached over the bar, snatched the barmaid's purse and bolted out the front door.

"Come back here you son of a bitch!" she yelled. She leaped over the bar and was out the front door in a single bound.

Everybody in the place rushed to the big plate-glass window in the front of the beer joint and watched as the thief tried to escape across the pothole-filled parking lot.

The barmaid closed in on him like a cheetah. She caught him by the hair of his head and brought him to the ground flat on his back. The purse snatcher threw the purse across the parking lot, probably hoping the barmaid would go after it and leave him alone. Instead with one hand, she held the guy's head against the ground and, with her other hand balled into a fist, she pounded the guys face into a bloody pulp.

The barmaid returned to the cheers of the small crowd and yelled, "Now, which wunna you son-of-a-bitches wanna try that?!"

Everybody just laughed. And the band played on.

## Kick Pedal Goes Swimming

At a gig on the top deck of the Flamingo Cafe, our drummer Dennis Forbes dropped his kick pedal into the water. Dennis was frantic.

"That's my best kick pedal! It cost me a hundred dollars!" We fashioned a grappling hook out of a claw hammer, three forks, a length of string and duct tape and managed to fish the damn thing out of the ten-foot-deep muddy water before Dennis had a hissy fit.

## Don't Touch My Wife

While hosting blues jam sessions around Houston in the early '90s, a drummer named Dwayne became a regular jam slut that followed our band to many of our shows. One night in 1992 at Frankie's Club in Baytown, Dwayne was dancing with my wife while I was performing. I never had a problem with my wife dancing, but this time was different.

At the end of the dance, Dwayne threw my wife over his shoulder caveman-style and carried her screaming and kicking off the dance floor. I knew it was all in fun, but it still pissed me off. I could feel the fire exploding inside me as the room fell silent. Every eye was on me, watching for my response.

It took all the willpower I could muster to keep my cool. I turned to the band and called another song. After a few more songs, I thought everyone had forgotten about the incident. I called Dwayne to the bandstand. He scurried to the bandstand like a little puppy thinking I was about to ask him to sit in. When he got close, I stepped away from the mic, motioned him up close and said in my best *Dirty Harry* voice, "If you ever touch my wife again, I will *stomp – your – ass*! Do you understand me?"

Dwayne was a hefty fellow and would've been a formidable opponent, but sometimes it's not about who can whip whose ass. It's about respect and right and wrong. What Dwayne did was wrong and disrespectful to me, my wife and to our friendship, and he knew it.

To make amends, Dwayne did two things that were right. He apologized and he disappeared. I never saw him again.

## Drummer's Truck Stolen

While performing at the Club Rave-On in Baytown, Dennis Forbes received an emergency call around midnight from his wife to tell him the Houston Police Department had just recovered his stolen truck. He insisted his truck was sitting outside in the parking lot and ran to check. Sure enough, the truck was gone.

While he was on stage, thieves had stolen his truck, driven it to the other side of Houston about fifty miles away, stripped it and left it on the side of the road.

## Stranded

Car trouble is a way of life for musicians on the road.

I could go on and on about changing flat tires in the pouring rain and unloading all the band equipment to get to the spare, only to realize that the spare too, is flat.

Once we broke down in the middle of nowhere. Mike Sicola and I walked five miles in the freezing winter rain to get help while Ray and T.J. stayed with vehicle and the equipment.

Another night, while Sid and I were on the way home from a gig, the engine blew up in a U-Haul truck we'd rented. Sid and I were left stranded on top of an overpass in downtown Houston at 3am. There was no way down to the ground (fifty to sixty feet high) for a mile in either direction. Fortunately, a roll-back wrecker came by who loaded us up and took us home. For fifty bucks of course.

## Jumpa Cayba No Reesch

One winter night in 1983, I was on my way to a meeting of the Houston Chapter of the Nashville Songwriters Association International (NSAI).

I pulled into a gas station near the Houston Astrodome. After filling up and paying for the gas, my car wouldn't start. I turned the key again and again. Nothing. I looked under the hood and jiggled the battery cables. Still nothing.

I asked the two oriental station attendants if they would give me a jump. I told them I had my own jumper cables.

"Give one minute," one of them replied.

I went back to my car at the gas pump and waited. I could see both men through the store window. They remained sitting, nonchalantly watching TV and slowly eating something out of a Styrofoam box. After ten minutes, I went back in and again made my request.

The same guy answered me with an aggravated tone, "I say, you give one minute!"

"That's what you said ten minutes ago!" I replied.

I returned to the car and started asking other customers if any could give me a jump. Everyone refused. After another ten minutes, I started whistling as loud as I could and waving my hands at the two attendants who were ignoring me.

Finally one of them came out, jumped in his car and burned rubber around the station. He pulled up twenty feet away from my car. I motioned for to him drive closer, but he refused.

He then jumped out of his car, waving his hands in the air and yelling, "Aaah, no! Jumpa cayba no reesch! No guud! Jumpa cayba no reesch!

I yelled, "Drive closer and they'll reach!"

He yelled back, "Jumpa cayba no reesch!"

He jumped back in his car and peeled back around behind the station.

I was left standing there, holding one end of the jumper cables. The other attendant stood at the door of the station, shrugged his shoulders and said "Jumpa cayba no reeesch! Move caah now! Push 'way pump!"

"I can't move the goddamn car if it won't start!" I yelled.

Several more customers, including a big, obnoxious black wrecker driver, refused to give me a jump. I offered to pay the wrecker driver but he replied, "Muthafuckka, you crazy as hell, you can't pay me 'nuff money to jump yo ass off!"

My mind was now going berserk. My wife was in the car and she had started to panic. We were the only white folks in a low-life ghetto section of town. It was getting dark and we were getting the once-over by a group of gangster-looking black guys who were lurking around the station's restroom doors. It was obvious we were out of place and stranded. I felt like we were in danger of being robbed or worse.

About that time, a young, black kid about seventeen screeched to a halt at the next pump. I offered him five bucks for a jump.

"What if it don't start, I still get da five bucks?" he asked.

"You bet!" I said.

Thankfully the car fired right up. I handed the kid five bucks. As I left the station, I shot the finger at the two guys who stood laughing at us from behind the safety of their plate glass window. Lesson learned, always fill up with gas before leaving your area of town.

Strangely enough, I never had any more trouble out of that battery.

**No Brakes!**

Looking for a place to eat at 2am after a gig in Galveston, I approached a red light on 61st Street. I hit the brakes, but the pedal went all the way to the floor. The van didn't slow down. It was a three-lane street and, fortunately, there was very little traffic. The middle lane was empty so I aimed for it and plowed through the intersection between two cars.

I whipped into a shopping center parking lot and brought the van to a stop by using the emergency brake. Since the raggedy old van was full of equipment and I had to tie the side doors shut with a rope, I slept in the van.

The next morning, I called a tow truck.

## COFFEE IN MY PEAVEY

On New Year's Eve in 1997 we performed at a small club in Houston called The Spot. At midnight we played the usual Auld Lang Syne and took a break while the club served the traditional black-eyed peas, cornbread, cabbage and coffee.

As we started our last set, a lady with a large cup of steaming, hot coffee leaned against the table supporting our 12-channel Peavey 1200-C powered mixer I had purchased new in 1987. The table tipped over. The lady fell backwards, tossing her coffee into the air-intake vents on top of the mixer.

The sound in the speakers went from crystal clear to a muffled, low frequency roar like a tuba with a towel stuffed in it.

I was pissed. The measely salary I was making that night had to go for repairs. We finished out the night playing instrumentals.

The following week I took the mixing board to Armando Garcia, one of Houston's top factory-authorized Peavey equipment repair technicians. His report was if it had only been black coffee, a hair dryer would have fixed the situation in a matter of minutes. Unfortunately, the coffee was loaded with cream and sugar and had covered the circuitry with a gooey coating.

Armando and his crew went through the board with cotton swabs, toothbrushes and alcohol, cleaning every single tiny part. When they plugged it back in, it worked great.

As a testament to the quality and durability of Peavey products, we used that mixer for another ten years.

## ETHNIC SLURS

In the redneck beer joints and biker bars we played in the early '90s, the clientele was mostly middle-aged, Caucasian, blue-collar rednecks. There was no such thing as political correctness. However, in the upscale Clear Lake area nightclubs that catered to multi-ethnic, white-collar professionals mostly associated with NASA Space Center, political correctness was a fact of life.

During our last set at one of those uppity drinking establishments, a large, black man in a white shirt and tie approached the stage and requested "The Thrill Is Gone" by B.B. King.

Before doing the song, I decided to introduce it by telling the small, late-night audience the story of how B.B. King got his stage name.

"His real name is Riley B. King," I said, "but early in his career he played and sang for tips on Beale Street in Memphis. He became known as The Beale Street Blues Boy. He was often referred to as 'Blues Boy' King, which was later shortened to B.B. King."

As I was telling the story, the big, black guy stopped his pool game, walked to the front of the stage and stood there glaring at me with his pool stick in his hand. I had no clue what his problem was and thought I was about to get hit with a cue stick.

As we kicked off the song, he went to the end of the bar where the club owners were. I could tell by his body language he was pissed off and raising hell about something. The second we ended the song, the owner's wife came running to the bandstand. She stood directly in front of me, turned red as a beet, pointed her finger in my face and screamed at me at the top of her lungs, "There will be no ethnic slurs in my club! You do not insult my customers by using ethnic slurs! We will fire any band using ethnic slurs in my club!"

She was obviously putting on a show for the black guy's benefit.

Once she said her peace loud enough to impress anyone who gave a shit, she turned and ran and hid behind her nerd-for-a-husband who was letting his wife do the talking. The nerdy husband gave me the evil eye as long as the big, black guy stood next to him.

I had no clue what their problem was. I could feel the rage racing through my veins as I stood there gritting my teeth. I was humiliated and embarrassed to be a forty-year-old professional musician and scolded like a kid in front of my audience. We still had twenty minutes to go before quitting time. I turned to my band and said, "Pack your shit, boys, nobody talks to me like that!"

I grabbed the mic and yelled, "Lady, I don't know what the hell you're talking about! We quit! Nobody talks to me like that in front of my audience!"

The small audience, amused by the excitement, applauded my unexpected retort to the previous insult.

I put my guitar down and headed to the bar to collect my money. The owners wanted to argue with me and dock my pay because I quit twenty minutes early. The argument became heated. They eventually offered to pay me in full if I would just shut up and leave.

As tempers calmed down, I learned the black guy, in his drunken condition, had misunderstood my use of the word *boy* in the B.B. King story and took offense. Being a regular customer, he threatened to take his business elsewhere and spread the word to "his people" that the club condoned language offensive to blacks.

In an effort to keep the black guy's nice green money from walking out the door, the owner's wife made a fool of herself by running to the stage and making a big show of putting me in my place. They apologized for the misunderstanding, paid me in full and offered me another gig. I declined.

Within a few days, a grossly exaggerated rumor spread throughout the Clear Lake nightclub scene that suggested I got in a barroom fight with a black guy for using an ethnic slur on stage. Because of that misconstrued rumor, I was barred from performing in Clear Lake area nightclubs for over two years.

Lance Stephens, owner of Lance's Turtle Club, broke the curse when he listened to my side of the story and put me back to work.

Thanks, Lance.

## BIKER WANTS TIP MONEY BACK

A dollar in the tip jar is always appreciated by the band. Occasionally, however, a patron will think a dollar in the tip jar gives them ownership of the band and that person will harass a band all night demanding song after song.

Often when we don't know a song, I'll offer a patron their money back. Most people will tell us to just keep it. Whether we know the song or not it has always been my policy when money is placed in the tip jar, it's like putting money in my pocket. It's mine.

Around 2002 at a biker joint in Baytown called Rocky's Pelican Junction, a big biker dropped some money in the tip jar and wanted to hear "Sittin' On The Dock Of The Bay."

I told him thanks for the tip, but we hadn't performed the song in many years, and declined to play it until we had time to brush up on it.

Nothing was said until the end of the night when we were rolling up chords and loading out. The big biker came to the stage and demanded his money back. He claimed he had dropped a hundred dollars in the tip jar. The tip jar did have over a hundred dollars in it, but it had been passed around several times. I had already split the money with the band.

The bikers claim of putting a hundred dollars in the tip jar was just him saying so. There was no proof. I swallowed hard and told him I didn't do refunds once the money was in the jar.

"Gimme back my fuckin' money or I'll stomp yer goddamn ass right here!" he yelled.

"I've already split it with the band," I said. "I can't give it back."

Bass player Terry Dry and drummer Andy Rogers looked like they were about to shit in their pants when the biker shook his fists at them.

"I'll whup the whole goddamn band!"

I knew for a fact the biker could whip us all with one arm while drinking a beer with the other, but I stood my ground.

"Fuck you! I'll see you 'fore you leave, mutherfucker," he warned us.

I turned to Terry and Andy and yelled, "What the fuck ya'll waitin' on? Load up! Let's get the fuck outta here before he comes back!"

The following week we were back at Rocky's and so was that same biker. He sat at the bar glaring at me as we set up. I walked over to him, bought him a beer and said, "Today, you get a hundred dollars worth of "Sittin' On The Dock Of The Bay."

We sang that song once every set and never had another problem with the guy. In fact, I'm proud to say that me and that biker became pretty good friends after that.

## KONK

In April 1993, drummer Russell Shelby, bass player A.J. Fee and I performed at a mexican restaurant in Webster, Texas, called The Jalapeno Tree. The stage was in the corner of the building and not much bigger than a window display at a Five & Dime store.

Even though we were only a three-piece band, the stage was still too tiny for us. Setting up was a logistical nightmare. We kept bumping into each other and arguing about where and how to set up gear. We managed to put up only one light stand to cast a little light in the otherwise dark corner. We were jammed together like the proverbial "three men in a tub," absolutely no room to maneuver. Russell had to climb over my amp in order to squeeze his larger-than-life self behind the drums.

Fortunately, A.J. and I were relatively skinny in those days and were able to stand side-by-side on the front of the stage. However, if A.J. got too excited, I risked getting smacked in the face with the headstock of his guitar. If I got too excited, the headstock of my guitar would bang into the wall on my left. If either one of us took one step back, we'd fall over the drums. There we were, all scrunched up and trying to put on a show. We suffered through the night as best we could and were glad when it was over.

Dismantling the gear in such tight quarters proved to be the same logistical nightmare as setting it up, only in reverse. Again, the three of us were literally tripping over each other.

In the chaos and confusion of tearing down, the light pole was knocked over and the corner of it smashed into the top of Russell's head with a deadening *konk*. The six-foot-something, 250-pound former bouncer dropped to his knees like a rock. Blood poured from the top of his head and ran down the side of his face.

Dazed, Russell came up swinging furiously at anyone who happened to be in his way. Dizziness and nausea sent him staggering toward the restroom. After a few minutes, we went in to check on him. We found him puking his guts up and pouring water over his head in the sink. He finally realized it was just an accident and got over being mad.

Since that night, every time I set up light poles I anchor them with bungee cords and tie them to anything I can find to avoid another accident like that.

## BREEEEATHE, MUTHERFUCKERRRRRRR!

In June of 2003 the Die Hards were invited to perform on *Joe's Roadhouse*, which was broadcast live every Saturday afternoon on Houston's KPFT 90.1 FM. The show was broadcast from the Rhythm Room, a deteriorating old warehouse-turned-nightclub on Washington Avenue. It was one of the best sounding live music rooms I've ever played.

We had spent most of the winter and spring on the road performing in blues clubs and casinos across the mid-south. We utilized those long, boring days in the hotel to practice fifteen new original songs for the CD that became *Mean Guitar*.

Performing seven nights a week all winter made the band as tight as a knat's ass. We were excited to be home and playing new material in front of our Texas fans at the packed-out Rhythm Room, and our fans on the radio and internet.

Unfortunately, the air conditioning system in the Rhythm Room was not working worth a damn. A packed house, combined with its low ceiling made it hotter than a Choctaw sweat lodge. Under tons of flashing lights, the stage was even hotter.

Bass player A.J. Fee and drummer Curtis Craig had arrived two hours before me. They sat drinking at the bar until I arrived. The stifling heat made their ice-cold beer and mixed drinks go down far too easy. I didn't realize until we were about to go on stage, and on the air, that they were both blitzed.

The announcer, Joe Montes, yelled into the mic and over the air, "Ladies and gentlemen, put your hands together for Mean Gene Kelton & The Die Hards!"

The crowd roared and we kicked off hard and fast. With my adrenaline pumping and the air on stage hot and thick, I felt I was trying to breathe through a hot, wet blanket. I was dizzy and gasping for breath. A.J. didn't realize he was standing in front of an open mic when he yelled, "Breeeeathe, muthafuckerrrrr!" His enthusiastic comment was broadcast live across the Texas Gulf Coast and around the world live on the internet. The crowd roared with laughter! Somehow, we were not reprimanded by the FCC or the station.

Every now and then someone will remember that show and yell, "Breeeeeathe Muthafuckerrrrr!"

## I'LL KICK YER ASS

While making last minute preparations to go on stage at a big biker rally near Houston, a giant biker in full road-warrior gear forced his way back stage and roared, "Which one a-you is *Mean Gene*?"

Silence fell over the entire back stage area. Our band, crew and entourage stopped dead in their tracks. I felt like David being called out by Goliath. At least David had a slingshot.

I took a deep breath, reluctantly stepped forward and confessed my identity. In a gruff voice he commanded, *"C'mere!"*

I cautiously walked toward the angry giant, watching him very closely.

When I got within arms length, he extended his hand as if to shake hands. As I responded to his gesture, he grabbed my hand with a vice-like grip, pulled me to him and threw his arms around me. He lifted me off the ground and hugged me like a long, lost child.

When he put me down, the giant biker placed his hands on my shoulders and looked me straight in the eye. In his sandpapered voice he whispered, "I jes wunted to say thank-ya fer writin' that song, 'Tears On My Guitar.' "

His lower lip began to quiver and tears rolled down his cheeks and into his beard. He told me a story about a recent break-up with the love of his life and how the song made him think of her. Placing a sympathetic hand on my shoulder he said, "Man, you shore musta went through the same hell to be able to write a song like that!"

I just nodded. Before he left, he again grabbed my hand and pulled me toward him. He then leaned over and told me something he didn't want my apprehensive crew to hear.

I felt a chill run through my soul as he stared at me with the ice-cold sincerity of a hit man. In a voice as serious as death he whispered, "I love ya man, 'n I love yer song, but if you ever tell anybody I was cryin', *I'll kick yer ass!*"

I could only nod. When I tried to speak, it felt like my nuts were stuck in my throat.

For that very reason, his name and location of that rally will forever remain a mystery.

## BUTCHERIN' THE HAG

During the late '70s I played lead guitar for Firecreek. Since we mixed country music with blues and southern rock, our band was considered social outcasts. We found it difficult to get a gig in the staunch country-western honky-tonks. Imagine our surprise when we were invited to do a show at the very redneck Liberty County Elks Lodge.

From the start it went great. All night long we kept the Kickers two-steppin' round and round in a big circle as we played old country classics and hits of the day. Toward the end of the night, as the alcohol had all the cowboys and cowgirls hoopin' and hollerin', we started adding more rock and blues to our show. Nobody complained and everybody was dancing no matter what the song.

We decided to perform Bobby "Blue" Bland's blues version of Merle Haggard's "Today I Started Loving You Again." We could've played Jimmy Reed songs all night, but the minute we applied Haggard's lyrics to a blues shuffle the country-western crowd took offense. They were ready to "git a rope!"

Liberty County Sheriff Buck Echols moseyed up to the stage and announced, "We throw drunks in jail round here. Ya'll must be drunker 'n hell to butcher up a Merle Haggard song like that. If you boys don't wanna go to jail tonight, ya'll had better play that song again – and this time – git it right!"

We played the song again, Merle Haggard style, but we still narrowly escaped jail and an angry group of young, drunk cowboys a-hankerin' to whup our asses. Sheriff Echols and Elks Lodge officials stood guard as we loaded up our gear.

Various members of the band went on to play with other bands that often played the Elks Lodge, but I was personally not asked back for over twenty years.

I learned the hard way there are two things you don't do in Liberty County. You don't roll a joint using a page from the Bible (even a blank page) and you don't butcher up a Merle Haggard song.

## A Cross Canadian Redneck

In 2008 we did a show at the Sandos Caracol resort in Playa del Carmen, Mexico. There were about 400 tourists at the show from all over the world. The show went great and we were well received. One of the songs we played was our infamous blues version of Merle Haggard's "Today I Started loving You Again."

The next day the band was hanging out at the pool. Numerous people came by to shake hands and compliment us. We all noticed a big, bear of a man in his sixties at the other end of the pool staring at us. Finally he approached us. In a very strong Canadian accent he asked, "You's da boys frum da band lass night, eh?"

Expecting another pat on the back for our musical efforts, we confessed that we were.

The big guy crossed his arms, stood solid as rock, looked me right in the eye and said, "Well, I hafta tell yah, yah fuckin' butchered da shit owdda dat Merle Haggard song lass night! I'm an ole Merle Haggard fan from way back. Ay got all his records don't 'cha know. I know how it s'posed t' sound, and that weren't no Merle Haggard I heard comin' frum yas. I wanted to whip da piss owdda you boys fer da wey yah played dat song. If Merle Haggard was dead, he come back right now as a ghost and kick ya in the fuckin' balls fer butcherin' his song like ya did!"

We roared with laughter. It was 1978 all over again. Some things in this world never change. The seasons, the tides, day and night – and Merle Haggard's international redneck fans. We bought the guy a drink and thanked him for his honest opinion.

See meangenekelton.com for Mean Gene's interview with the Cross Canadian Redneck.

## The "C" Word

I say the word *pussy* in a skit I do with a particular song at my adult-only shows. In the context the word is used it's not vulgar, just funny. It always draws a big laugh from the crowd.

After doing the song at a show at the Cactus Moon in Humble, I was called into the kitchen by the owner, Thomas Gardner, and his wife. I felt like a kid being called to the principal's office. Mrs. Gardner was furious I had said that word, and was raking me over the coals. Thomas stayed out of the way and shrugged his shoulders. He winked as if to say "let her have her say and get it out of her system."

"You offended my female customers using that kind of language!" she yelled.

"It's part of the song," I explained. "Besides, this ain't no damn church. This is a beer joint. Everybody here says a lot worse than *pussy*. And everybody here is drunk, either trying to *get* some pussy or *give some away*!"

Thomas cringed and tried to discreetly motion for me to shut up while his wife continued reprimanding me and threatening me with my job.

Finally I said, "Okay, okay, I'll quit saying *pussy* and go back to using the original word."

"And what word was that?" she demanded.

"*Cunt!*" I shouted with a big grin (of course I was kidding).

Mrs. Gardner ran out the kitchen door screaming. Thomas just shook his head and said, "Man, why the hell did you have to say *that*? Don't you know I have to live with her?"

## BUS TRIPS FROM HELL

### Blind Drunk at Blind Lemon

In September of 2000 we were invited to play at the Blind Lemon Jefferson Blues Festival in Wortham, Texas. We chartered a bus and sold seats to the first fifty people who wanted to go with us. We sold out in a matter of days.

On the day of the event, everyone showed up at the bus terminal with lawn chairs and ice chests filled with beer and whiskey. Excitement was running high. Everybody was laughing, joking and drinking.

We all got loaded in more ways than one. We climbed aboard the bus, ready for our big trip. Before we could get out of the terminal, the bus broke down. For nearly two hours, fifty people sat on the bus drinking and raising hell. By the time we got on the road, most people were shitfaced and some were already running low on booze.

Finally we were on the road to Wortham, four hours north of Houston. Three hours later, people demanded the driver pull over at the first liquor store he saw. When he finally found a liquor store and stopped, fifty people made a mad dash for restrooms, beer coolers, whiskey and ice. The store owner was beaming. He said it was the best sales day he'd ever had.

The festival was in downtown Wortham, a small town with entire population of about 2000. There were already over 5000 people jammed together in the middle of Main Street. All eyes were on our bus as the doors opened. Fifty extremely happy, shitfaced people stumbled – some fell – out the door onto the sidewalk, staggering through the festival gates with their coolers and ice chests in tow.

One lady, who was not used to keeping up with the Die Hard's partying ways, had puked red sloe gin all over her white blouse just before we arrived. You can imagine the looks she got when she teetered off the bus.

Another lady passed out in the aisle of the bus. She had to be revived and practically dragged into the festival before she got her snap back.

Yes, we Die Hards were a sight! I was proud of each and every one for living life the Die Hard way.

### Another Drunk Drives The Bus

On June 23, 2001, one day after Joni and I got married, we were scheduled to play at the Navasota Blues Festival in Navasota, Texas. We had chartered a bus and bragged that we were taking fifty of our closest friends on our honeymoon with us.

Once again the rolling party was on! Only this time, the bus driver decided he wasn't going to be left out of the festivities. Unbeknownst to us, while we were doing our show the bus driver was drinking beer and smoking dope with some Die Hard fans. By the time we were ready to leave the festival, he was drunk. We tried to sober him up with food, coffee and sodas. Thinking the driver had sobered up enough to drive, we loaded the bus and headed out.

Turning out of the festival grounds too fast, the driver cut the bus way too short to the right, missing a culvert and dropping the right front side of the bus down in a ditch. The bus pitched violently. The driver floored the gas pedal, forcing the bus out of the ditch. The right rear tire then went off the culvert and again the bus jerked violently back and forth until it eventually got back on the road.

Snacks and personal belongings flew all over the bus. Peoples heads slammed against the windows. Those people walking in the aisle that weren't in their seats were thrown on top of others. Fortunately, no one was hurt.

All the way home, the driver kept us on the edge of our seats. He drove on the edge of the road, on the shoulder and on top of the "drunk bumps" between the lanes. Someone had to stand next to him all the way to Houston, talking to him to keep him alert.

Some of us even considered a mutiny. There were a couple of professional, CDL-licensed drivers with us that were ready to take the wheel. The bus driver refused to let anyone else drive the bus, saying his insurance wouldn't let us.

We chose not to report the driver because he would surely incriminate some of our Die Hards fans who had obviously carried marijuana on the bus, unbeknownst to me.

We never used that bus company again, and we haven't done another bus trip since.

See meangenekelton.com for video of the Navasota Blues Festival.

*The Rhythm Room in Houston, during the CD release party for Mean Guitar. I'm cutting heads and showing off with Die Hard bass player A.J. Fee.*

*Linda Rose and Forrest showing their Die Hard colors at the Wortham Blues Festival in Wortham, Texas.*

BOOK SEVENTEEN

# Groupies From Hell

## Groupies or Fans: What's The Difference?

A music fan is someone who enjoys and respects the talents and skills of a particular performer enough to buy CDs and attend shows by that artist.

In the music business, the word "groupie" usually brings to mind the stereotypical, adolescent screaming female who follows a male musician or band to every event. In reality, groupies can be either male or female. Groupies can be organizations, clubs or groups from all walks of life who follow a band or artist just because they like the music. Case in point, legions of fans referred to as the "Dead Heads" followed The Grateful Dead for decades.

Since the beginning of time, every charismatic person in every profession, has had groupies. Lots of preachers, politicians and famous athletes have been brought down because of questionable activity with a trusted groupie. Some groupies can't wait to brag about their involvement with someone they view as famous, because they themselves have no life and never will, or they want to blackmail their victim for personal gain. Their only claim to fame is being a destroyer of someone who trusted them, regardless of the consequences.

Some groupies want to get close enough to become a friend and to be able to hang out with or be seen with the band or artist so they can claim braggin' rights. Others may even infiltrate the inner circle and become trusted associates, a member of the crew or street team and, in some cases, even a manager, booking agent or promoter.

Some groupies are just plain freako nutcases – male *or* female – who pretend to be a trusted friend but at the same time will do everything possible to destroy the life of the very person they "worship." Some, jealous of the artist's fame, become dangerous stalkers and have gone so far as to kill the artist they were enamored with. Remember what happened to John Lennon and Selena?

And yes, some groupies, for whatever reason, just want to have sex with a famous person. A couple of these types of groupies have even written books about having sex with their celebrity idols. So far, I've not encountered a groupie that's tried to kill me, but have encountered all the rest, and then some.

I'm often asked if I ever took advantage of the women who threw themselves at the band. Let me put it this way. I'll never be nominated for sainthood.

During the late nineties I was recently divorced from a twelve-year marriage. For months at a time I would go through phases of severe depression when I had absolutely no interest or desire to be involved with anyone. I lived alone, went home alone and preferred to be left alone to lick my wounds and heal my soul.

There were times I didn't see a single human for weeks at a time, except at a gig. For some reason, I still felt married.

One night about two years after my divorce, I watched the front tables fill with available, attractive women who had be vying for my attention. Standing on the stage scanning all that potential, I reminded myself I was divorced, single, and lonely in more ways than one.

It was time to go fishing with dynamite!

For the next couple of years, I fished every pond and didn't throw none of 'em back. I kept no secrets and didn't give a damn who knew what I was doing or who I was doing. I refused to play high school head games with recent divorcees who hadn't had a date since the tenth grade. I was not after true love. My policy was simple. No strings attached and *who's next*?

I was surprised at how many women were willing to openly share, take a number, take turns, get in line, climb in, climb on and pile up. I should be writing stories for Penthouse Forum. They all knew about each other and made a big joke about whose night it was.

Personally, I didn't care. Next...

## JUST DO IT!

I once gave a girl a ride to her apartment. It was late and the complex was dark, so I walked her to her door. As I gave her a little hug and a goodnight peck on the cheek, she grabbed my shirt and pulled me inside the apartment.

The apartment was very small. I could see her kids as they lay sound asleep on pallets on the living room floor in front of the TV that was still on. As I stepped back toward the door, she blocked my way, turned her back to me, bent over, pulled her dress up and insisted I go for it right then and there.

No way! Not with her kids only ten feet away.

"They'll never wake up." she insisted in a demanding whisper, "Just do it!"

I couldn't. I didn't. I left.

## SNEAKIN' OUT

Back in the days before cell phones, I let my drummer drive my van home one night while I stupidly went home with a girl I'd only just met. She made me promises of a wild night I would never forget. She was right.

Once at her apartment, she turned into a raving lunatic. She screamed, "You son of a bitch, you don't care about me. You just wanna fuck me!"

She was right, but I thought that was why we were there.

I suggested we forget the whole thing. I asked her to drive me home or at least let me use her phone to call for a ride.

"Fuck you!" she yelled. "You ain't going nowhere, motherfucker! You make a move and I'll call the cops!"

I got real scared. I prayed she didn't have a gun. She might suddenly get paranoid with a stranger in her house and shoot me.

We spent the rest of the night laying on the carpet in front of her stereo and listening to recordings of her awful singing as she played dozens of stupid songs she wrote. She was horrible, but in an effort to keep her calm I complimented every song. Afraid for my life and a possible Lorena Bobbit incident, I fought to stay awake. Every time I dozed off, she'd straddle my chest, grab my shirt collar and shake me while screaming in my face, "Wake up motherfucker! I'm playing my songs for you! Don't you insult me by falling asleep!"

She finally passed out around the crack of dawn. I slipped out the door putting my boots on at the bottom of the stairs. After having spent a night in fear for my life with the devil's psycho-bitch daughter, I was hungover, exhausted, hungry and thirsty. I had to walk three miles in the sweltering August heat to the nearest payphone.

Lessons learned. Never go home with someone you don't know. Never be without your own transportation. With the invention of cell phones, never leave home without one.

## BONUS PLAN

In the mid-nineties there was a young lady who followed me to many gigs. Her conversations were always laced with flirty, sexual innuendo. Though she was married, she was always putting her hands all over me. I tried to keep her at a distance. I didn't want her husband to get the wrong idea. She asked me to play a backyard party for an upcoming family event. Once she got my number to discuss the details, she started calling me all the time. The phone conversations got crazy.

Finally one day she caught me at the right moment. I told her to meet me at a certain restaurant parking lot. When I got there, I pulled up next to her car and told her to get in my van. She got in, and without a word I drove her straight across the street to a motel, rented a room and twisted her into a pretzel for the rest of the day.

When I dropped her back at her car she commented, "Whew, and I thought all we were gonna do is have lunch."

"Well, baby, " I replied, quoting a line from an Andrew "Dice" Clay comedy routine, "You got the bonus plan!"

## MAGGIE MAY

In the spring of 1973, I was twenty years old. I was performing as a single act every Friday and Saturday night at the Yellow Wagon Cafe, a small truck stop on Almeda Road about twenty miles south of Houston.

One night, a fortyish-year-old brunette came in wearing skin-tight, white jeans, high heels and a shiny, black blouse tied together just under her breasts. She was not what you would call a raving beauty, but she was sexy as hell. I was surprised I was immediately attracted to her because she was my mom's age. But damn, she looked good. I couldn't help but stare at her every time she came in and she came in every weekend.

To the delight of my raging hormones, the attraction was mutual. One thing led to another and soon we became more than casual friends. Being fresh out of high school, my sexual adventures had only been with girls my own age.

This was my first time to be involved with an older woman. I was insanely curious and desperately seeking any wisdom in the area of sensual delights that an older woman might divulge. As it turned out she was just a lonely housewife starved for attention and I was willing to give her all the attention my youthful spirit could muster. Plus I was pretty good at musterin' in those days.

As far as her imparting any sensual secrets, all she wanted to do was go parking near Sims Bayou like a couple of teenagers in heat. Hell, I was already doing that with country girls back home.

The only thing I learned from her was to never allow myself to become an unattentive sloth of a husband like the one she complained about all the time. "He's a fat ass who doesn't like to do anything 'cept watch TV," she'd say.

Our relationship reminded me of Rod Stewart's song, "Maggie May." When "Maggie" told me she intended to leave her husband and wanted us to get an apartment, that was my first clue to run.

One night my Uncle Charlie and a couple of his buddies from his neighborhood were sitting with me at a gig. Maggie's 250-pound truck drivin' husband showed up, grabbed her by the arm and dragged her outside. My second clue to run. Fearing for my life, I opened a buck knife underneath the table. Uncle Charlie promptly took it away from me.

The next day Maggie told me that since I was just a "kid," her husband didn't suspect me. Instead, he accused her of screwing my uncle. I rolled with laughter telling my uncle about the big trucker's suspicions. The expression on his face was priceless.

I immediately broke off my relationship with Maggie before anyone got hurt. She continued to stalk me for a several months. Thankfully, she finally moved on.

## JAILBAIT!!!

In 1985 a voluptuous young strawberry blond watched me perform at a small club in Pasadena. She was always with an older man who was more interested in playing pool than sitting with a young hottie.

One afternoon, while her sugar daddy was shootin' pool, she began to show more than just a passing interest in me. As the alcohol hit her, she stared seductively at me over her glass and laughed at all my silly stage jokes, even when I knew they weren't funny.

On break I walked over just to say thanks for sending drinks and tips to the stage. She exuded a sexiness that reminded me of young Marilyn Monroe. Every time I tried to excuse myself, she would grab me by the arm and ask me another question about nothing.

Finally I said, "Hey, I better go before your boyfriend gets pissed off, and finds out you're buying me drinks with his money."

"He's not my boyfriend!" she exclaimed, "He's my *dad*! People always think he's my boyfriend. He gets so drunk I always have to drive him home."

She leaned over and whispered in a sultry voice, "When he falls asleep, I do what I want!"

"He's your dad?" I asked. "How old are you?"

"Fifteen, going on sixteen," came her matter-of-fact reply.

"Fifteen!" I blurted. I felt faint. I was thirty-two. I thought she was at least twenty-three. I told her not to buy me drinks anymore, and I got away from her as fast as I could.

## SCRAPBOOK

Through the years I've been honored by folks who chose to document my career with their own personal scrapbooks. I knew people did that for their favorite celebrities, but I never saw myself as a celebrity. The first time I ever saw a scrapbook about me created by a total stranger it freaked me out.

I was performing an outdoor festival in Southeast Texas in 1987 when a lady showed up at my booth. I was signing autographs and selling copies of my most recent 45rpm record. The lady looked like a Pentecostal woman with her hair was piled high and wearing a long, homemade-looking dress that almost touched the ground and no makeup.

The lady stared at me with no expression in her eyes as she opened a large book as thick as a family Bible. Inside were dozens of photos of me taken without my knowledge. She shoved it across the table at me and pointed to a space for me to sign. This was early in my career and I was blown away.

There were also newspaper clippings and advertisements mentioning my name that I'd never seen. She never said a word. She just gave me an icy stare. It was creepy.

I felt naked as she seemed to look right through me. I tried to make small talk about the scrapbook, and I thanked her for making it.

The lady never said a word in acknowledgement. She turned and walked away. I never saw her again, at least not that I know of.

## DANITA

Moving to Nashville in 1986 I hit the ground running. I hustled every place I could for a gig as a single act. My style of playing made it possible for me to play a lot of non-tourist venues where the locals would hang out.

At one of the nicer venues, my music caught the attention of a very energetic, attractive young woman named Danita. She was the ringleader of a group of hot, young professional women in their mid-twenties to early-thirties who loved to party together. Danita and several of her girlfriends began following me to venues all around Nashville. They would even show up at places I warned them to stay away from. I was concerned Danita and her classy girlfriends would be so out of place in some of those shitholes that the regular clientele might give them a bad time.

Undaunted, fearless Danita and her entourage charged in and took over every little hole-in-the-wall I played. They were always welcomed with open arms because they were all sexy vixens and always the life of the party.

At a very rough little beer joint called The Madison Grill, Danita laughed until tears rolled down her face when she told me there were footprints on the toilet seat in the ladies restroom. Apparently the rough-cut hillbilly women who frequented the joint preferred squattin' to sittin'.

Danita became a great friend. She had a beaming smile that lit up the room and a contagious trademark laugh that made people beg to know what was so funny. She was very outgoing, never met a stranger and was not afraid of anything.

Because of her enthusiasm for my music, Danita became my unofficial manager, trying her best to advance my career in Nashville. She promoted me as if she were running a political campaign and I was the candidate. She made cold calls to people in high places on my behalf and petitioned all her friends to do the same.

When I told my wife about the dynamic young woman I'd met and how she was trying to help my career, my wife became very jealous and suspicious. But then, my wife was always very jealous and suspicious of *everyone* I met.

If I was five minutes late getting home, I'd be interrogated about every minute of my time, about everyone I saw and forced to account for every cent *not* in my pocket. I'd have to explain the smallest detail over and over to test me to see if I told the same story the same way twice. Nashville was tough on our marriage. I was there to do whatever was necessary to pursue my career 24/7, not just to work gigs like I did back in Texas with a definite start and stop times and hurry home.

I always went straight home to my wife as soon as possible after a gig except one night when I had downed way too much tequila to drive home. Danita was at my show that night. Even though she had to work the next day, she poured coffee down me until I was sober enough to make the twenty-mile drive home. I don't remember if I called home or not, but I arrived there far later than expected and I'm sure I reeked of tequila.

The silent treatment from my wife over the next week was more than I could stand. Shortly after that situation, she insisted we move back to Texas. Because her dad was seriously ill back in Texas and afraid I would lose her if I refused, I packed without argument.

As much as I wanted to contact Danita to tell her I was going back in Texas, I didn't. I was afraid that contacting her would have a negative effect on my marriage. Danita didn't try to contact me, or so I thought.

Several months later I discovered a letter from Danita that had been forwarded from our Nashville address. It had been opened, obviously read, then stashed on the back of a shelf.

In the letter Danita adamantly insisted I return to Nashville because her promotional efforts had paid off with some very positive interest from some high-powered music executives.

When I confronted my wife about intercepting and hiding my mail, I was accused of alot more than friendship with Danita. I was crushed to think my wife may have possibly blown a big break for us because of her jealousy. I don't recall if I ever replied to Danita's letter. The forwarding order finally expired and that was that.

Danita was a great friend and a dynamic promoter who believed in me and went to bat for me. I would like to publicly say thank you to her for her efforts way back then.

Wherever she is and whatever she is doing now, I'm sure she is taking charge, taking names and kicking ass doing it all with her famous sunshine smile and filling the room with her contagious laughter.

## WORKING GROUPIE

Diane Naski grew up fast, fearless and tough on Houston's notorious North side. As a young, single mom she scraped out a living for herself and her son, Shaun, as a waitress for Denny's Restaurants. For over fifteen years she served burgers and coffee to rough-talking truckers and raucous, late-night partiers. The experience taught Diane how to meet people, sell product and hustle tips as a means of survival against some really tough customers.

Diane climbed aboard the Die Hard train in the mid-nineties and followed us to every gig. Everywhere she went she was the life of the party. She danced every dance, even if she had to dance by herself. Often Diane would encourage people to get up from their table and dance until the dance floor was packed. Diane knew how to instigate a party.

Diane jumped in to help sell t-shirts and CDs at our merchandise booth. Her sales skills learned from her many years at Denny's automatically kicked in. Instead of standing behind the merchandise booth waiting for a sale, she'd grab an armload of t-shirts and CDs and wade into the crowds. She'd zero in on an unsuspecting prospect and boldly ask, "What size t-shirt do you wear?" Whatever the reply, Diane would shove a t-shirt in the person's hands and say, "Thanks very much, will that be cash or charge?" She sold the hell out of merchandise.

Diane sang backup on two of our CDs, *Most Requested* and *Mean Guitar*. She is the voice screaming at the very beginning of "Party On The Levee" on *Mean Guitar*. Diane traveled with us on and off for nearly ten years. She was a hell of a lot of fun to have around and tells everyone she is the World's #1 Die Hard Fan.

One day in the spring of 2004, Diane packed an overnight bag, bought a one-way ticket to Hawaii and disappeared into paradise where she is now writing a book about her life.

Aloha, Baby.

## EIGHTY AND CRAZY

After my move from Nashville back to Texas, I searched for gigs at little bars around East Texas. Being fresh from Nashville I enjoyed a short-lived celebrity status as a "Nashville Star" and landed a gig in the very small lounge at The Lake Country Inn in Center.

One night at the Lake Country Inn I heard a woman's voice yell from the back of the darkened lounge. "Damn, boy, you's a purdy thang, if I's forty years younger, I'd chase yer little ass in circles round this room!"

The crowd exploded with laughter. I was thirty-three. The lady yelling at me was eighty years old. She continued to heckle me the rest of the night. The more she drank, the more sexually graphic she became. Her advanced age made the situation funnier than it really was.

The East Texas Bible Belt whiskey drinkers were amused by the lady's straight forwardness and my obvious embarrassment. On my break her daughter, a beautiful former East Texas beauty queen about fifty-five, approached me to apologize for "Mama."

As the weeks passed the mother and daughter were at every show. Mama started bringing me expensive gifts, including a gold chain to wear around my neck, a wallet and cologne.

My jealous wife was furious with me for accepting the gifts. How do you tell an eighty-year-old woman *no* when it made her happy to give me expensive gifts? She insisted I return the gifts, but I refused. From that day on, my wife refused to allow me to wear my favorite cologne, Aramis, only because an eighty-year-old woman had bought me a bottle.

## 70 Year Old Stalker

While performing as a single act at The Lantern Restaurant in Etoile, Texas, a seventy-something-year-old lady sat all alone watching me intently from the rear of the room.

On my break I made it a point to say hello and make her feel welcome. Being cordial turned out to be the wrong thing to do. Though I was less than half her age, she took my kindness the wrong way and began to follow me to all my shows across East Texas. She too began buying me presents.

Since everybody in Shelby County, Texas, seemed to know everyone else, she knew my mother-in-law and soon began showing up unexpectedly at her house where my wife and I were living. She would always say she was "just passing by." I would hide in the rear of the house, but she always demanded to see me before she left. She'd present me with a new gift right there in front of my wife and mother-in-law.

The moment the lady left, my wife and mother-in-law would jump all over me as if I'd invited her over. It was freaky being stalked and wooed by a lonely septuagenarian. I felt sorry for the old gal, but finally had to tell her to stop buying me gifts and following me.

She responded by weeping and wailing as if we were teenagers breaking up. It was weird.

## Kicked Out

It was October 1987 and my second wife and I had been married for almost five years. With letters coming from Danita in Nashville and strange old ladies buying me gifts and stopping by the house, my wife and her mother packed all my belongings. They threw them out in the driveway and told me to leave immediately or they would call the law.

They kicked me out and ran me off like a stray dog.

I was literally a basket case as I drove to my gig at the The Silver Dollar Club in Lufkin that night with everything I owned crammed in my van. I had planned to stay at a local hotel after the gig, but that night fate took a different turn.

### Naked In The Dashboard Lights

A girl who had been following me to many of my East Texas performances showed up that night at the Silver Dollar Club. I told her my situation and that I was looking for a temporary place to stay in East Texas while I finished out a string of local gig commitments. When she realized I was suddenly single, she apparently arranged for her friends to leave and asked me for a ride home.

"Why not?" I thought. After all I'd just been kicked out of my mother-in-laws' house with everything I owned. I had no one to answer to and no other place to stay.

Just past midnight, the girl climbed in my van and told me she had the key to a friend's weekend hunting cabin near San Augustine some twenty miles away. We both had been drinking tequila. I was buzzed, but she was blitzed. As we drove she turned up the radio and began to undress. It was great fun at first, but I freaked out when she threw all her clothes out the window as we crossed the Sam Rayburn Reservoir bridge.

Completely naked, she leaned back in the passenger seat. She stuck her right leg out the window and her left foot on the middle of the dash. Within seconds she was moaning, groaning and putting on a show. I slowed down to about 30mph in an effort to keep the van between the ditches while I enjoyed her performance. She was a glorious sight to behold in the glow of the dashboard lights. I thought about that old song by Meatloaf. My only concern was trying to explain my situation to a police officer if we got pulled over.

The cabin turned out to be one of a group of cabins used by hunters during deer season. I parked the van around back and gave the girl one of my shirts. We staggered in. Being as drunk as we were I didn't expect anything to happen between us. I'll spare you the details, but she was still passed out and reeking of tequila when I snuck out the next morning.

With her clothes scattered somewhere along side of the road, I've often wondered how she got out of there. I never saw her again.

Driving away from the cabin into the gray October dawn, I realized I had no place to go. I thought seriously about going back to Nashville. Returning to Nashville at the beginning of winter would mean working some miserable day job through the winter and not landing a steady paying gig until the following spring.

Instead, I headed for Houston where I knew I could go right to work playing music five nights a week. It proved to be the right choice at the time. My wife and I got back together a few weeks later. She moved to Houston with me. We finally split in the summer of 1994.

## THE SHRINE

In the early nineties, a very sweet young lady named Deborah followed my band all over Texas and took dozens of pictures at every show.

As time passed, rumors of a Gene Kelton Shrine began to surface by other musicians who had seen Deborah's photo gallery. Their stories were like rumors of Bigfoot and UFOs. I had never seen the so-called shrine and questioned the credibility of those who claimed they had.

After hearing about the Shrine for several years, Joni and I finally had the opportunity to visit Deborah's home and see her photo collection. There where hundreds of photos of me as well as other musicians who'd been in my band through the years.

The photos were posted, pasted, pinned, taped and stapled to the walls, doors, mirrors and every nook and cranny. They were every size imaginable. Some were cut-outs, others were life-sized blowups.

Along with the photos, there were show posters, flyers, leaflets, business cards, bumper stickers and articles documenting every facet of my career. There were even broken guitar strings and guitar picks I had used.

I knew people had done that sort of thing with regards to Elvis, the Beatles, KISS and so on, but Gene Kelton? C'mon, who the hell is *he*?

Though honored, I still couldn't believe it.

Some years later I saw Deborah's collection again. By then she'd begun to include memorabilia from other Texas bands. She could have started her own Gulf Coast Music Museum. One very special piece is the very first Gene Kelton t-shirt, designed and owned by Deb. The artwork on the t-shirt is an airbrushed drawing of my Fender Telecaster and says, "If This Guitar Could Talk."

Deborah's love of music certainly qualifies her as our official Die Hard photographer and music historian. Today, whenever I need an old photo of one of my ancient gigs for a story or an article, I call Deborah.

Many of her photos are included in this book.

## DOWN AND DIRTY

If you saw *Porky's* then you will remember a scene where a girl and guy were having sex in a laundry room. The girl was driven into a sexual frenzy by the smell of men's sweaty socks and jockey straps. During my single years I was amazed to learn how many women are really like that and insist on doing the wild thing anywhere, anyplace and anytime, without a bath or shower.

Personally, I don't like to have physical contact, especially after a gig, until I have showered, no matter what the situation. However, I encountered one groupie who refused to let me shower after a gig and insisted we "do it" right then! Right there! Right away!

The worse I stunk, especially after a hot, sweaty gig in the summertime, the better she liked it and the freakier she got. I'd never met anybody like that in my life.

Hope I never do again.

## BACKFIRED BOOTY BLUFF

In the '90s a very homely frail little woman around forty followed our band to every show we played around Galveston County. She wasn't homeless, but she looked that way in her shabby clothes and long, greasy, brown hair.

For some reason I always felt sorry for her. She lived in her own reality and I'm sure that there was a loose wire somewhere or maybe a prescription that needed a refill.

I knew the poor girl was harmless and just wanted some attention, but she was driving me to my limit of trying to be nice. On every break she was either right in my face or running along behind me like a little puppy, constantly yapping with a barrage of questions and comments. She never said anything that made sense to me, just jabber, jabber, jabber about everything. I couldn't have a conversation with anyone without her interrupting.

I learned the only way to get rid of her was to make a sexual suggestion. Then she'd go running for cover and not bother me for a while.

She constantly pestered the whole band, insisting we let her sing. She said it was her dream to sing with a band. At one of our jams we let her sing, hoping she would leave us alone.

She took the mic for the first time in her life and stared blankly at the audience. When the music started, she yelled into the mic, off key and out of time. She was filled with so much stage fright that she peed in her pants right there on stage. The crowd roared with laughter. Oblivious to the crowd and that she had just peed all over the stage, she just kept hollerin'.

We stopped the song, shooed her off the stage and doused the puddle of pee with a pitcher of beer. She didn't seem the least bit embarrassed. Believe it or not, she returned to the stage a few minutes later demanding to finish her song.

A couple of weeks later as I was loading up after a show, she was in my way and running her mouth. "Yakkity-yakkity-yakk!" I was hot, tired and ready to go home. I remembered that a simple sexual suggestion would send her running and thought if I said something very sexually explicit she would go away and leave me alone forever.

As she stood there jacking her jaws at a hundred miles per hour, I blurted, "Hey! Do you have a couch where you live?"

Caught off guard, she stopped talking and stared at me with a puzzled look on her face and replied, "Well, yes…"

Hoping she would be repulsed by my extreme vulgarity and run away, I said, "Then let's go to your apartment. You get on your hands and knees and we'll fuck like dogs in heat!"

Her head jerked back and her eyes flew wide open. Her face turned completely white. Her mouth fell open and her bottom lip began to tremble as she gasped for air. Her sudden silence seemed like an eternity as I waited for her to run away as she had always done. But this time she just stood there staring at me with a look of shock and surprise.

Finally, she took a long, slow, deep breath and wiped the sweaty hair from her brow. Regaining her composure she replied in a soft consenting tone, "Okaaaay."

Words can hardly express my sudden terror. My plan had backfired. With one word she had called my bluff and upped the ante. Everything around me went silent. The only thing I could hear as I contemplated my fate was my own teeth grinding together.

I broke out in a sweat like a man facing the firing squad. I felt my muscles tighten up as my body automatically switched into the "run for your life" survival mode. I tried not to show fear as I suddenly realized what a fly must feel like staring into the eyes of a hungry spider.

"Plan A" didn't work and there was no "Plan B."

"Stay right here," I said, "I'll be right back!"

I snuck out the side door, bolted around the building, jumped in my van and made my escape. The following week she was back. She acted like nothing ever happened.

From that moment, I never called another woman's bluff.

## THANKSGIVING DINNER

In 1996, the band and I were performing every Thursday night at a giant, country-western nightclub in north Galveston County near the Gulf Greyhound Park, called Marguerite's. After two years, we knew most of the regular clientele.

One night in the middle of a show shortly before Thanksgiving, the waitress brought a large, white box to the bandstand with a card that said, *To Gene Kelton.*

The crowd cheered as I opened the box. In it was a dozen long stemmed red roses with a note that read, *"Please come to my house for Thanksgiving dinner. Love, Molly."* A phone number was included for an RSVP. I knew most of the women who frequented Marguerite's, but I didn't recognize the name "Molly."

The audience demanded I read the card out loud. Not knowing the sender, I just smiled as if I had a secret I wasn't telling. The crowd continued to razz me with all sorts of sexual innuendos about the roses. Though I didn't have a clue who sent the roses or why, my reputation and ego were getting a good stroking. After all, it's definitely rare for a man to receive roses, especially in such a public forum. Molly obviously knew I would be on stage in the middle of a show.

Later that night I gave single roses away to ladies who I thought would give them a good home. I threw away the invitation and forgot the whole incident.

The following Thursday night I found a card stuck on my windshield with the same Thanksgiving dinner invitation and phone number. Again, it was signed by the mysterious Molly.

Curiosity got the best of me. A couple of days later I decided to call and find out who Molly was and the reason for such an elaborate effort to invite me to dinner. After several rings, the answering machine picked up the call. I didn't feel comfortable leaving my name and number so I chose my words very carefully.

"Hi, I received your invitation, but I already have Thanksgiving plans. Thanks anyway."

I hung up without leaving my name or number, thinking that'd be the end of it.

In 1996 caller ID was new technology and very few people had it. I didn't give it a second thought when I made the call. Just my luck, Molly had caller ID.

A few days later my home phone rang. A female voice screamed into the phone, "You stupid motherfucker! You been fuckin' that goddamn Molly! Spike is looking for you! He's gonna kill your stupid fuckin' ass!"

"Hey, whoa! Wait a minute!" I yelled. "Who the hell is this?"

It was a waitress from Marguerite's and she was calling to warn me a biker named "Spike" was putting the word out around Galveston County he was going to kill me. He was Molly's boyfriend and he had been at her house when I called. He saw my name and number pop up on the caller ID and naturally concluded that I was bangin' his ol' lady.

After the waitress's description, I remembered Spike. He was a biker who occasionally showed up to our gigs in Galveston County. He and I rarely exchanged more than a nod. He would always sit alone, sipping his beer and watching his girlfriend dance.

I suddenly remembered Spike's girlfriend. She was a wild, crazy girl who'd always dance by herself to every song we played. I remembered being the focus of Spike's brooding stare every time Molly came to the bandstand and requested a song. I always kept my distance from both of them.

"There's no way I'd mess with that girl!" I yelled.

I explained the situation with the roses, the Thanksgiving dinner invitation, the mysterious card on my windshield and the reason for my phone call to Molly.

The waitress insisted I was lying, but gave me Spike's work number. She hung up with a final warning. "You better not ever come back to Galveston County, or you are gonna *die!*"

My hands were shaking as I dialed Spikes' number. What the hell was I going to say? He already had me tried and convicted. When he answered, I mustered up all the courage I could and spoke very firmly.

"Spike, this is Gene Kelton. I hear you're lookin' for me."

"You heard right," came his blunt reply.

"Man, I ain't screwing your old lady."

He was very quiet, like the calm before a storm. As I explained to him about the Thanksgiving dinner invitation and the reason for my original phone call, he did not respond. Finally I thought I'd try to appeal to the logic of the way us men think.

"Look man, I'm single. I live alone on the north side of Houston seventy miles from where you are. I got pussy parked in my driveway every night when I get home from gig. Why the hell would I drive seventy miles to mess with somebody else's old lady when I got bitches knockin' my goddamn door down?"

"You tell me," he replied. "I know you play down here sometimes."

I wasn't getting anywhere with Spike. My hands were sweating. I knew he could make good on his threat or simply make a call to his buddies with the same result. I couldn't afford to cancel my gigs in Galveston County to run and hide over something I hadn't done. I needed another approach.

"Tell ya what, Spike," I said. "You call your ol' lady and tell her to meet us at your shop. I'll drive to Galveston right now, look you straight in the eye man-to-man and we'll get to the bottom of this stupid bullshit!"

Spike got quiet. Finally, he said, "Okay, man, I believe you. If you're willin' to drive all the way down here and come to my shop and talk to me man-to-man knowin' I was after you, you must be tellin' the truth."

When we hung up I thought everything was cool. A couple weeks later my phone rang around midnight. It was my bass player, A.J. Fee. He was calling to warn me Spike was on the warpath again and spreading the word he was going to put me in an early grave.

I don't know what had happened to reignite Spike's anger and suspicions, but the next day, I was on the phone to him. This time he wouldn't listen to reason and threatened to stomp my ass the next time he saw me. Since my first conversation with Spike, I'd seen Molly at one of our shows cavorting with a local radio DJ. Since it ain't cool to rat on someone, even to save your own ass, all I said was, "You need to look a little closer in your own backyard. That's all I'm gonna say."

I hung up and called the DJ I'd seen with Molly. I could hear his wife in the background as he started bragging about his bullshit. I told him to shut up and listen real close and to just answer *yes* or *no*. I told him about my volatile situation with Molly's boyfriend.

I said, "Look, dawg, a lot of people saw you and Molly at Marguerite's. It's just a matter of time before Spike realizes it was you, not me, she was seen with at a Gene Kelton show. I don't know if you're fuckin' her or not and I don't care. But, here's the deal. If I get my ass whupped because of you, I'm passin' the ass whuppin' on to you, *double*. If you don't like the sound of that, you better fix it *now*! You understand?"

"Yeah!" he snarled and slammed down the phone.

A few nights later at my gig at Marguerite's, Spike showed up and said he wanted to talk to me outside. I didn't know what to expect, but I felt my nuts draw up as we headed out the door. A.J. grabbed my arm and asked if I needed backup. Even though my inner voice was silently screaming "*heeeelllppp meeeee!*" like *The Fly* in the old '50s Vincent Price movie, I just shook my head no.

I walked out into the humid night air a few feet behind Spike. Whatever was about to happen, right or wrong, I had to face him with manly dignity and put an end to this shit for good. I felt like I was walking to my death, but it ain't cool to show fear – even though I was about to shit in my pants.

Sweat was rolling down the side of my face as we reached Spike's truck at the far end of the dimly-lit parking lot. My heart was racing and nearly jumped out of my chest when Spike opened his driver's side door and reached under the seat.

A million thoughts flashed through my mind, sending my brain into panic overload. My survival instincts were telling me to *run*! I felt my legs shaking and heard my pulse pounding in my head. What was I going to do if he turned around with a gun or a knife? I knew I'd have only a split second to kick the shit out of him and run like hell. Would he chase me? Would he shoot me in the back as I dodged bullets between parked cars?

When Spike turned around, the look on my face must have been stark terror because he cracked up laughing. In his hand was a brown paper sack.

"Here!" he said, shoving the sack at me. "This is my favorite brand of whiskey and I want you to have it as my way of sayin' I was wrong about you."

My muscles were drawn up so tight I could hardly speak.

"Thanks, man," I said, trying to sound cool and confidant as I pulled the bottle from the paper sack. I glanced at the bottle cap, trying to see if it had been tampered with. Fortunately the cap popped when I twisted it off. I shoved the open bottle toward Spike.

With a big, forced smile, I blurted, "In honor of this event, the first drink is *yours*."

Spike wasn't stupid. He knew exactly why I was giving him the first drink. He looked me straight in the eye and turned up the bottle. Without any expression or reservation, he chugged three huge gulps and shoved the bottle back at me.

Not to be outdone, I returned his icy stare, took three huge gulps, swallowed hard and never blinked as a four-alarm blaze seared down my throat.

After a silent handshake, Spike climbed in his truck and drove away. I never saw him or Molly again.

## THE PIRATE'S DAUGHTER

During the late '90s, we often performed at a small beach bar near Galveston where every show, without fail, an attractive woman in her mid-thirties, "Nita," would show up and attach herself to the band until quitting time.

Nita was always accompanied by her elderly father who she lived with and cared for. "Daddy" was a seventy-something-year old cantankerous, whiskey drinkin', ex-Merchant Marine. His weathered skin, like tanned boot leather, was covered with ancient scars from a lifetime of near-death experiences and faded tattoos that had grown blurry with time. He reminded me of an old pirate with his war stories about life-long adventures on the high seas.

He watched Nita like a hawk. The band joked about the possibility of him pulling out a black powder pistol and killing any land-lubber who got near her. Whenever he got drunk, Nita would take him home, put him to bed, sneak out of the house and come back alone.

Nita would zero in on me with her flirtin' and flauntin' and tell me way too much personal information about musicians she knew from all over Texas. I concluded she was the unofficial one-woman welcoming committee whenever traveling bands passed through.

As a result of her unfiltered disclosures, I always dodged Nita's persistent suggestions to get together after a show. Sex can also be like that proverbial box of chocolates, you never know what you're gonna get, or catch.

One night Nita had been teasing me. I'd drank just enough tequila to not give a shit. She was standing at the bar, flirting with the guys in the band. I walked over, took her by the hand and said, "C'mon babe, let me take you away from these heathens."

Fifteen minutes later I pulled into the driveway of a rickety, three-story beach house that had survived its share of hurricanes. The crooked old steps creaked as I followed Nita to the top deck and through the sliding glass door into her bedroom.

The first thing I noticed as we tip-toed into the house was that it was freezing cold. Looking around, her bedroom was a music museum. The walls were covered with album covers, autographed posters, t-shirts, banners and Mardi Gras beads. After a shower I had to endure an hour of sitting cross-legged in the floor while Nita showed off her collection of music paraphernalia. She pulled old records, CDs, guitar picks, broken strings, bandanas, cigarette lighters, sun glasses, belts, socks, rolling papers, watches, rings, earrings, hair ties, business cards, photos – you name it – from a large, old steamer trunk. Nope, I didn't see any condoms, new or otherwise. Damn wonder.

"All my stuff is from bands that have played here."

I knew many of the musicians personally that Nita named as she showed off her treasures. I figured most of them had once sat in this very spot, but it was too late to turn back.

Nita's bed was a tiny, twin bed. When she saw me looking at it she giggled, shook her head and pointed toward the wall.

She whispered, "Daddy's bed is on the other side of that wall."

She led me downstairs into the equally-freezing living room. In the faint glow of the stove light in the kitchen she opened a fold-out couch.

"I won't be here when you wake up," she said as she slid under the covers. "If Daddy finds me down here he'll be pissed. Just leave as soon as you wake up."

The next morning I was jolted awake by the loud blast of prehistoric squawks. My eyes flew open. It was just past daylight. Too much tequila and only two hours sleep made it difficult to get my bearings. I suddenly realized the grinding, choking sound was coming from the Old Pirate who stood hacking, harking and spitting in the kitchen sink not more than ten feet from me. Apparently he was too sick and hung over to notice the couch had been let out or that a naked man lay shivering underneath the thin sheet. As promised, Nita was gone.

As I peered from beneath the sheet, the first rays of morning sun burst through the window, and reflected off of a collection of knives and swords hanging on the walls. "Damn!" I thought. "The old son of a bitch really is a pirate!"

I envisioned Old Pirate grabbing a sword and chopping me to pieces. A sudden wave of nausea and panic swept through me. Fear for my life and last night's tequila were about to make my presence known. Where the hell were my clothes? My keys?

Barely breathing, I lay motionless with the sheet pulled up to my eyes. I watched the Old Pirate's every move as he balanced himself against the wall with one hand and held his baggy underwear up with the other. It took forever for him to inch his way down the hallway and into the bathroom. The sounds that reverberated through the open door told me he'd be preoccupied long enough for me to escape. I leaped out of bed, jerked on my jeans and bolted shirtless out the door into the blinding sunlight, my boots in one hand and keys in the other.

As I hit the landing at the bottom of the steps, the next door neighbors were having coffee on their deck. They offered up a rousing cheer and round of applause. Obviously, it was not the first time they'd witnessed a terrified musician fleeing from the wrath of Old Pirate's razor-sharp cutlass.

Looking back, I'm sure my t-shirt is now hanging on Nita's wall, and my underwear is safely tucked away forever among the souvenirs in her old steamer trunk.

## NADINE THE WHISKEY QUEEN

In the mid-nineties an unlikely groupie attached herself to our band in the form of a high-class, boisterous forty-something former beauty queen named Nadine. As a very successful entrepreneur, she moved in financial and social circles far above our rough-cut, blue-collar existence.

It's still a mystery to me why she fell in love with our band and religiously followed us.

In her spike heels, movie star smile and her tight-fitting, low-cut dresses exposing glorious mounds of luscious, milk-white cleavage, she reminded me of Delta Burke, the former Miss Florida turned movie star.

When Nadine made a grand entrance into the many sweaty, little juke-joints we played, she looked so out of place that everything came to a screeching halt. People stopped playing pool, stopped talking, stopped mid-drink and beheld her magnificence. She loved the attention, even if it did come from us lowly peasants.

Nadine definitely stood out in the crowd. Her hair and makeup were always perfect. Her perfectly manicured, candy-apple red, razor-sharp claws could puncture a mud-grip tire. She never went anywhere that she wasn't dripping in diamonds. *Real* diamonds and lots of 'em.

With all those diamonds and that big movie-star smile, I once told Nadine that she lit up a room with more sparkle than a Christmas tree in a department store window.

It was a sincere and innocent compliment. But for years afterward, every time she came to a show feeling down and depressed, she would firmly insist – no, she would *demand* – I repeat that very compliment to her. I could have won an Oscar. Once I recited the sugar-coated accolade to her satisfaction, *presto*! That famous smile would instantly appear and she'd traipse back to her table happy for the rest of the night.

I sensed a dark storm brewing somewhere behind those sparkling green contacts. Many times I wished I'd just kept my damn big mouth shut.

Nadine loved whiskey as much as she loved attention. I've never known a woman who could guzzle as much whiskey as she could and still function. If we played a place that didn't serve liquor, she always had a full bottle of "only the very best" in the trunk of her Cadillac.

When she was sober Nadine was a charming, proper professional woman. However, the drunker she got the more her rural upbringing, southern accent and extensive four-letter-word vocabulary would overrule her sophisticated charm-school facade. Over time, a volatile mixture of diet pills and whiskey turned her into a ferocious, domineering demon from hell who demanded the universe bend to her will and kiss her ass.

At every show Nadine sent drinks and money to the bandstand. She demanded we play only the songs *she* wanted to hear, no matter how many times we'd already played them. If I wanted to wait until the next set to re-play a song, she'd yell, "Long as I'm payin' for 'em, you play 'em! I wanna hear *my* songs, *now*. If somebody wants to hear somethin', let *them* sons-a bitches pay you. They'll never give you as much as I do!"

Whenever the band took a break Nadine would get furious if I didn't speak to her first before making my rounds greeting other fans. She told me for the amount of money she put in our tip jar every night, I should show her more appreciation.

Nadine watched me like a hawk, critiquing my every move, my clothes, every song I sang and every word I said on stage or off. It was as if she'd appointed herself my personal manager and image consultant.

As time passed Nadine grew extremely possessive of me and my time and insanely jealous of anyone I talked to. On many occasions she interrupted my conversations with fans. She'd dig her razor-sharp nails into the back of my arm and drag me away like an schoolmarm dragging a child away for punishment. She'd pull me to the bandstand where she'd glare into my eyes and snarl, "Break time is over! I didn't drive way the fuck out here to watch you waste my time talking to a bunch of goddamned white trash or listen to the jukebox. Get your ass back up there on that stage and play, *now*. I wanna hear some Gene Kelton music, *NOW!*"

I was in between marriages at that time and, believe it or not, people actually thought Nadine was my wife. The moment the music started her satanic expression would dissolve into her beautiful movie star smile and all would be wonderful again in Nadine's World.

Nadine was used to getting her way. There were times when the whiskey made her so obnoxious she'd force total strangers to move from any seat she wanted, telling them they were at the band table. We lost a lot of fans because of her.

Being a gorgeous woman Nadine was spoiled. She had her pick of lonely, rich widowers who knocked themselves out trying to be with her. It seemed to be a major blow to her controlling ego that I always turned down her persistent sexual invitations. She never left me alone, even when she showed up with one of her aging sugar daddies. I'd asked her how she could talk to me that way while her date was waiting at their table.

"Oh, hell," she'd laugh, "He falls asleep in his chair every night. He ain't worth a fuck in bed, but he's filthy rich. Me and you could have some good times on his money!"

I was never sexually attracted to Nadine. Maybe I was turned off by her gold-digging ways toward the lonely old guys who'd worked their entire lives to have something and I felt she was taking advantage of them. Maybe I thought she was a psycho-nutcase who carried a ton of negative baggage around in her inebriated brain. Or, maybe because she took every opportunity to belittle me saying, "Gene Kelton, you ain't good for shit 'cept playin' a guitar and fuckin'. I don't wanna be your girlfriend cause you ain't got no goddamn money and you never will. But if you fuck like you play that guitar, someday 'fore we get too old we gonna hav'ta fuck just to see what it's like!"

I wanted no part of her. Not even for a one-night stand. Though she insisted someday I would give in. I was content to keep our relationship strictly on a musician/fan basis.

As time passed Nadine grew more aggressive. She was more determined than ever to snare me at a weak moment.

One night at a show I walked into the middle of the dance floor during my guitar solo. Nadine got behind me, grabbed my hips and started grinding against me. One of her three grown daughters straddled my right leg while another daughter straddled my left. Mother and daughters were humping me like bitches in heat. Nadine's younger sister was in front of me, bumping and grinding like a titty dancer. It must've been a hell of a sight to see four horny hotties humpin' on me from every direction. The audience was going wild and I was having a blast. They made me look like King Stud.

When the song was over Nadine pulled my head back by my hair. Her talons dug into my scalp as she growled in my ear, "Goddamn you, Gene Kelton! One of these days you gonna have to break down and fuck *one* of us. We can't take this shit no more!"

I was blown away by her bold statement. She had just given me permission to screw any female in her family, including her barely-legal-age daughters. I just laughed it off and pretended she was joking.

I hastily retreated to the safety of the stage.

### Who The Fuck Are Ya'll?

In May of 2002, we were booked as the opening act for legendary country-music outlaw David Allan Coe at the Garden In The Heights outdoor concert arena in Houston. That show was a *Gig From Hell* from the very start.

While unloading our band equipment, the band came under attack by a swarm of bees from a hive next to the unloading zone. Several members of our entourage were stung. Our bass player "Hollywood" Steve Rangel was highly allergic to bee stings. He received so many stings he began to sweat profusely and his eyes began to swell shut. Like a true Die Hard, Steve fought back the nausea and soldiered on.

After setting up and doing a sound check, we got off the stage.

Nadine arrived just as Coe's band took the stage to do their sound check. She was already hammered by her usual combination of pills and whiskey. She hastily made her way to the stage looking for me. Not recognizing any of Coe's musicians, she charged on stage like Joan of Arc and yelled, "Who the fuck are ya'll? Get the fuck off this stage! Ya'll ain't Mean Gene Kelton & The Die Hards. Get the fuck outta here. I'm with Mean Gene Kelton and I'm telling ya'll to *get the fuck off this stage, now!*"

Surprised by a hysterical woman's screaming tirade, Coe's band stood motionless. They stared back her in disbelief. Over 2000 people in the open-air amphitheater roared with laughter as Nadine's voice was picked up by the live mics and broadcast over the outdoor concert PA system.

I bolted onto the stage and took Nadine's arm before one of Coe's musicians bitch slapped her. The moment she realized I was standing next to her, she became as calm and gentle as a little lamb. With a broad smile she gently took my hand and softly cooed, "Oh, there you are!" Her bottom lip began to quiver, and like a lost child she meekly whispered, "I was looking for you and I couldn't find you anywhere!"

I patted her hand, smiled and softly said, "It's okay, baby, I'm here now. Let's go."

The glazed look in her eyes told me that even though the lights were on, there was nobody home. Pills and whiskey had claimed another victim.

I winked and nodded at Coe's band members who responded with nothing more than a solemn stare. Arm-in-arm, I slowly led Nadine from the stage like walking a bride down the aisle. I handed Nadine over to her daughter who drove her home.

We finished our opening set just as a blinding rainstorm blew sideways across the stage, shutting down the event for about an hour. We and our gear were drenched. When the rain passed, we stood soaking wet in the mud to watch David Allan Coe.

I gave Nadine a couple days to sober up.

I called her to tell her how embarrassed I was by her actions toward Coe's band. She denied any knowledge of having ever been to the David Allan Coe show. I went on to express my disdain with her conduct at our shows over the previous couple of years. I told her that every time she got blitzed, she became a hateful, vicious bitch to me, to my new wife and to all our fans. I reprimanded her for intruding into my conversations with fans, for stalking me, for insulting my financial status and sexually harassing me while pretending to be my wife's friend. I suggested she take six months off from coming to our shows and seek professional help to get off the pills and whiskey before they killed her. I told her I didn't want to see her at any more shows until she cleaned up.

Without argument she politely apologized for her actions and hung up. She probably never had a man talk to her like that before.

In the months that followed rumors surfaced that Nadine had started a "Mean Gene Kelton Hate Campaign," complete with a website where she blamed me for her addictions. Did I care? Hell no. Where ever she is today, I wish her good health and happiness in all aspects of her life.

I never saw Nadine The Whiskey Queen again.

# ZENA

In the '90s "Zena" started following the band to every gig. She was tall, tanned, big-boned and well endowed with long black hair who reminded me of *Xena, Warrior Princess.* She loved to get shitfaced drunk and dance uninhibited all night, all by herself, to every song we played. She would sweat profusely. When she'd swing her head from side to side to the music, her long black hair would sling sweat like a lawn sprinkler.

Sometimes Zena would place her forehead against one of the main speakers, grab ahold of the sides and bump and grind like a stripper doing a pole dance. I don't know what kept her eardrums from bursting. Sometimes when she was lost in the music and oblivious to the rest of the world, she'd let out a blood-curdling scream, louder than the band.

From a musician's perspective, Zena was a beautiful site. We wished for a million more fans following us around just like her.

Over time Zena and I became good friends. When she was sober she was an intelligent and caring person. Our growing friendship caused me to be concerned for her safety when she was under the influence of alcohol.

One night during a rainstorm, she had been sweating from constant dancing and had gone outside to cool off. She was so drunk she laid down in a rain-filled ditch. She screamed with delight and splashed the ditch water like a baby in a kitchen sink. She leaned her head back and drank the rain as it fell. Needless to say, I felt obligated to see she get home safe that night.

On another night while driving home north on I-45 toward Houston from a gig in Texas City, Zena was following me. Suddenly, her headlights flashed in my rear-view mirror and her car zig-zagged from lane to lane. I pulled over on the shoulder and Zena pulled up behind me. I ran back to see what was wrong.

At that same time an off-duty Texas State Trooper, in his personal vehicle, pulled in behind her. He and I both reached her at the same moment. The Trooper made Zena get out of her car and questioned us both about why she was all over the road. She said she had the radio cranked up loud and was turning the steering wheel back and forth to the beat of the music.

"You could kill somebody!" he yelled. "I'm calling a unit to pick you up."

I could see the lighted sign of a Kettle Restaurant about a mile ahead at the Dickinson exit. I told the Trooper I'd just got off work and was going to the Kettle for a hamburger and coffee. I offered to take Zena.

The Trooper obviously knew Zena had been drinking. He ordered her to leave her car parked on the side of the road and go with me to the restaurant. He told us if Zena's car was moved in less than an hour, he would hunt us both down and lock us up.

We were obliged to follow his instructions to the "T."

After another gig in Texas City, I had plans to go to my girlfriend's apartment in Houston. Zena was drunk and wanted to hang out and talk. I snuck out of the club, jumped in my van and drove away. Zena caught up with me a few miles north of Texas City on Highway 146. There was no way my raggedy-ass old 1983 Chevy van could out-run her new car.

Zena pulled up next to me, rolled down her window and yelled, "Pull over! Pull over!"

I refused. Zena was all over the highway and all around me like a Kamikaze. She even drove 70mph through ditches on both sides of the road trying to make me stop. I was afraid she was going to hit a culvert and flip over. Trying to lose her I drove twenty miles past my intended turn. I didn't want Zena to know where my girlfriend lived.

I finally had to pull over for gas. Zena pulled in behind me and asked me to wait for her while she went inside to pee. I seized the opportunity and drove off. I couldn't out run her, but I lost her in the abandoned neighborhoods of Mount Belvieu, Texas. I finally made it to my girlfriend's apartment about 5am.

After a couple of years of Zena's antics, I became less and less sympathetic when she got drunk. One night she was tired and went to take a nap in her car. She asked me to wake her up when it was time to go, and she would follow me home.

At the end of the night I drove off, leaving her passed out in the front seat with her feet hanging out the window.

### A Naked Zena Donut

One miserably hot night at Del's Lookout, a beach front bar in Surfside, we were the opening act for Dallas bluesrocker Bugs Henderson. Anxious to see Bugs for the first time, we quickly moved our gear off the stage the moment we finished our set.

While Bugs and his band were setting up, Zena asked me to walk with her to the beach to wade in the water and cool off.

It was a pitch-black, moonless night. The gulf breezes were blowing as hot as a hair dryer. As we walked down the beach the only light was the distant glow of neon at Del's. Shining in the darkness the lights from the club made the place look like a multi-colored flying saucer that landed on the beach.

About 150 yards from Del's, Zena and I waded ankle-deep into the water with waves splashing up around our knees. I could faintly hear the band doing a sound check and wanted to hurry back, but Zena wanted to keep walking a few more minutes. She was drunk and I didn't want to leave her on the beach alone. Suddenly Zena stripped off her clothes. She then ran naked and squealing into the white-capping waves.

"Oh, shit!" I thought. I had a vision of the beginning of *Jaws*. I yelled at her to come back, but she swam out farther and farther. I could hear her squealing with delight, "It's wonderful, it's wonderful!"

All I could think about was *sharks*. Fearing she'd drown, I fought against my own survival instincts and my fear of sharks, stinging jelly fish and rip currents. I charged in after her.

I swam toward the sound of her hysterical laughter. Once I found her, I grabbed her by the arm and yelled, "Let's go! Let's go!"

She pulled away from me yelling, "No, I wanna stay! It's so spiritual!"

I dug my toes into the sandy bottom. With the help of the waves, I managed to drag her to the beach. Zena fought me all the way. We were both exhausted as we fell on the beach. She began to roll around in the sand laughing and yelling, "That was fun! Let's do it again!"

Zena's wet, naked body was coated with sand. In the dim glow of the even more distant flashing neon lights, she looked like a giant sugar-coated donut.

We came out of the water a hundred yards further down the beach than where we went in. We could not find her clothes anywhere on the dark beach. She giggled about being naked and how free she felt. I was aggravated I was missing Bugs Henderson.

The booze and the exhausting swim took its toll on Zena. She was on the verge of passing out when we finally found her clothes. She outweighed me by at least fifty pounds. With both of us under the influence of alcohol, getting her dressed was a chore. I managed to get her back to the band house behind the club. I put her in the shower to wash off the remaining sand where it clogged the drain. Zena demanded to go back in the club, but only made it as far as the bed where she dropped like a rock.

I made in back into the club just in time to catch Bugs Henderson's last song.

## LOLLIPOP

Around 1985, a tall, stocky, corn-fed gal from Iowa showed up to a gig in Pasadena. Her name was Lollie, but everyone called her Lollipop. Legend has it that a guy grabbed her ass one night and she popped him in the eye, thus the name Lollipop.

Lollipop was probably around thirty years old when I met her. She epitomized the spunk and spirit of the true mid-western American pioneer woman. She was a tough, fearless, fist-fightin' biker chick who rode her own. That might not sound like a big deal in today's biker culture, but in the '80s it was very rare to see a woman on a motorcycle unless she was ridin' bitch. For you non-bikers, "ridin' bitch" simply means riding on the back. There weren't no 'lectric starters in dem days. Kick startin' a Harley was no easy task for alot of men, much less a woman.

Lollipop always insisted that women who love to ride should take charge of their own life and ride their own bike. In those days, women riders often fell victim to the razzing from macho guys who felt challenged by gals who rode their own. On many occasions, after making some derogatory comment to her about her riding her own bike, I saw Lollipop send smart-mouth cowboys retreating with their egos drawn up between their legs.

Lollipop rode an old Harley that backfired every time she kicked it. Her ability to be or not be thrown off depended on how drunk she was. Many nights, after I loaded my van at 2am, we took turns trying to kick start her bike until we were both worn out. Once the bike fired up, I watched with great admiration as she burned out of the parking lot and disappeared into the night with her long, blond hair flying in the wind.

How Lollipop was able to keep her high spirits and zest for life in those days is a mystery to me.

When I first met Lollipop she was homeless. She had two things, her bike and a rusty old car. Her bike was her first love and her only transportation. The old car was her *home*. She often told me about having to continually move her car around Pasadena to keep it from getting towed and keep herself from being locked up. I felt bad because there was nothing I could do for her. She wouldn't allow me feel sorry for her.

She'd say, "Aw hell, things can't do nuttin' but get better from here."

Like I said, true pioneer spirit. We could all take a lesson from her positive outlook on life.

In those days, I was just starting out as a one-man band and had not yet built a following. There were many nights when Lollipop was the only person in the audience at the little beer joints along Pasadena's Spencer Highway where I played. Even though she was homeless, broke and unemployed, she was always in great spirits and cheered every song in an effort to make me feel better in spite of the lack of attendance. It was always a pleasure to see her. Our relationship was one of mutual admiration and never more than just great friends.

Being a big girl, Lollipop became my unofficial bodyguard. Whenever a woman in the audience got too friendly, Lollipop would firmly let the interested female know I was happily married and that she was a friend to my wife. The interested party would leave me alone.

If some redneck male was hassling me, fearless Lollipop would be in his face like a wildcat, threatening to whip his ass if he didn't shut up. Once a redneck sarcastically asked me, "You gonna let a woman do yer fightin' fer ya?"

"He fights his own fuckin' fights!" she interjected. "But I'll whip your ass just cause I want to, motherfucker!"

Not another word was said.

One night a drunk cowboy was popping off about his dislike for me and my songs. Lollipop stepped in front of him like a gunfighter and yelled, "Hey, motherfucker! If you don't shut the fuck up, this is what I'm gonna do to your head!" In a flash, she ripped a beer can in half and handed the guy the two halves.

The drunk cowboy never said another word.

In a dark little club in Webster, I heard Lollipop let out a shriek. Looking into the audience, I saw she had one hand around the throat of a guy in a wheelchair and her other hand drawn back in a fist. The whole room heard her yell, "Motherfucker! You don't grab my goddamn tits! I don't care if you *are* in wheelchair, I'll knock you on your fuckin' back!"

You could've heard a pin drop just before everybody busted out laughing.

By 1988 I had known Lollipop about three years. I was in the process of writing the first version of "The Texas City Dyke" and stupidly thought a funny line in the fourth verse of the song should be, "She got herself a cute little girlfriend, sweetest thing you ever saw, takes her ridin' on her Harley, cause she likes to show her off."

Unfortunately, everybody in that area, including Lollipop, thought I had written that line – and the song about *her* because she rode a motorcycle. Truth is, *I did not*.

I remember her coming to me as I was on stage, angrily stabbing her finger in my chest and plainly stating for all to hear. "I ain't no goddamn *dyke*!"

Everybody knew she was not a dyke and I was surprised when people jumped to the conclusion the song was about her. I was only trying to write something funny, but I had unintentionally hurt Lollipop's feelings.

I embarrassed Lollipop publicly and screwed up our great friendship. I felt horrible and learned the power of the pen, *the hard way*. I also learned a misguided effort to be funny can wield a lot of pain when consequences are not considered well in advance.

As more and more women started riding their own bikes, I felt it wise to rewrite the verse as it is today. "*She got herself a cute little girlfriend, sweetest thing you ever saw. She brings her down to our old hangout, cause she likes to show her off.*" Unfortunately, by the time I rewrote the verse I had already permanently damaged my friendship with Lollipop. She never came to any more of my shows.

As the years passed, Lollipop landed a great job with a petrochemical refinery. She became financially successful, bought herself a new home, a new car and a new bike that she didn't have to kickstart. In the few times she accidentally showed up to where I was playing, her response was very cool and polite and not like two old friends who used to watch each other's back in the old days.

So Lollipop, if you ever read this, let me say for the millionth time. *The Texas City Dyke was not about you*. I truly miss our friendship and I publicly apologize for any pain and embarrassment I may have unintentionally caused you.

## THE SORCERESS

There was a young woman who followed the band to every gig for about three years. In her long black robes, scarfs and capes and black eye shadow and black fingernail polish, she always looked like she was going to a Halloween party. She claimed to be a Sorceress.

Often we'd find her in the parking lot after a gig, waving her arms in the air, chanting and spinning around in circles. She'd stand in front of our van making hand gestures with beads and flowers and speaking in tongues. Using her fingers, she'd draw astrological symbols in the dust on the hood and windows of the van. She claimed to be blessing our van so it would keep us safe on our travels. No harm done.

I guess it worked. So far, so good.

## WANDA THE WITCH

I was fifteen years old in 1968 when I encountered my first groupie. She was a very attractive, well-endowed seventeen-year-old named Wanda. I'd seen her walk past my house many times. Her long, dark hair blew in the breeze while her breasts led the way.

Wanda saw me playing my guitar outside on my lawn one afternoon. She stopped and introduced herself. Later she showed up with her own guitar. We became good friends and played music together almost every day.

As time passed and we became more comfortable with each other, she confessed to me that she was a witch. Not an evil, broom ridin' Halloween witch, but a *good* witch.

Occasionally Wanda took strands of my hair, fingernail clippings, threads from my clothes, broken guitar strings and guitar picks home with her. I never gave it much thought. I figured she was making a voodoo doll with my name on it with all that stuff and was trying to put a spell on me. Sometimes she'd call me a dozen times a day to tell me she was having a vision or reading my mind at that moment.

Sometimes I wondered.

The sixties were a wild, weird experience for all of us who were teenagers during that time. A freaky girl who claimed to be a child of the universe and a mind-reading witch was no big deal. I was always amused by Wanda's eccentric philosophies. I tolerated her hippie folk songs and flower-child, psycho-witch babble merely for a chance to get her naked.

If she could really read my mind, then she should have known that.

When she announced to me that she and I were meant to be together forever, I began to dodge her. I hoped she would get tired of chasing me and move on. Wanda refused to give up and showed up at my house every day. If she wasn't knocking on my door, she'd be driving by in her dad's car blowing the horn or calling me on the phone. I refused to answer the door or her calls.

In the summer of 1969 my family moved from Houston to Liberty. I figured my relationship with Wanda was finally over. I was wrong. She stole her daddy's car, ran away from home and showed up on my family's doorstep with a suitcase. She reminded me again we were meant to be together, *forever*.

My folks should have sent her packing. Instead, they felt sorry for her. After insisting she call her parents, they let her spend the night in our guest room.

For the next year, Wanda and I went back and forth between Houston and Liberty. I enjoyed her company and her weirdness. We had some good times and reveled in our youth, but I was never *in love* with her. Wanda, on the other hand, became obsessive to the point of being psychotic and scary. I finally ended our relationship cold turkey.

For the next two years, Wanda continued to show up unexpectedly at some of my band gigs, bringing some of her weird, freaky friends with her.

Wanda continued calling me every year on my birthday even after I married my first wife. When my first son was born, she sent gifts. Concerned that Wanda had put a spell on the gifts, my wife and I threw the gifts away.

That was the end of Wanda, or so I thought until thirty years and three wives later. An anonymous email popped up on my computer screen. I immediately recognized the weird, cryptic message. *Wanda The Witch was back*!

Within a couple of months, Wanda began showing up at my shows again, telling our fans she was my former high school girlfriend. On band breaks she tried to monopolize all my time. It was as if Wanda had come back from the dead to reclaim her long lost property, *me*!

Then she said, "There are matters of great importance we need to discuss."

Echos of the past rang loud in my head when she restated "We were meant to be together, *forever*!"

She was freaking me out.

I tried to be nice to an old friend from my past, but it was obvious being nice was misinterpreted by Wanda as a desire to rekindle an old flame that existed only in her mind.

Wanda seemed so sad and so lonely. I felt sorry for her. I explained to her I was happily married and planned to stay that way. We were *not* supposed to be together forever. I firmly encouraged her to go back to her own life. I told her any "matters of great importance" would have to stay buried in the past.

Wherever she is now, I'm sure Wanda's "witch senses" have alerted her I wrote this story. Right now she's probably stabbing a voodoo doll that looks like me.

If she can still read my mind, she knows I wish her good health, peace and happiness.

## Swingin' From The Rafters

In the '90s, Blondie's Club in La Porte had a very low ceiling with exposed steel I-beams. Musicians had to be careful removing guitars over their heads, because if they weren't paying attention, they'd bump the ceiling or ceiling fans and damage their instruments.

One hot night as I stood at the front of the band, a very large, drunk, sweaty, thirty-something-year-old woman, wearing a dress too short for her big ass, approached the bandstand to make a request. On impulse, she reached up and grabbed both sides of the I-beam. She lifted her feet into the air, threw both her big legs around my neck and locked her thighs around my head.

She wasn't wearing any panties and I was suddenly looking straight into her crotch. Even though her thighs covered my ears, I could still hear the sound of muffled shrieks of laughter from the audience.

One of my musicians came around behind me. He grabbed the lady's ankles and gave them a yank, slamming her sweaty crotch into my face. I was holding my breath and struggling to get loose, but her thighs had me a headlock. Along with the muffled laughter, I could hear her laughing and hollering with the excitement of the moment.

Suddenly she started screaming that she was losing her grip and about to fall. Fortunately, the musician behind me finally let go of her ankles and she put her feet back on the floor. If she had lost her grip on the I-beam with her legs wrapped around my head, she would've fallen, taking us both down, probably breaking her back and snapping my neck like a twig.

I was glad to finally be free and breathing *only* secondhand smoke.

## Curb Service

Late one night after a gig before going home, I pulled around behind the club where we'd just played to use the water hose to put water in my radiator. I had a full view of the club's parking lot.

I noticed one of my musicians standing next to the driver's side of a parked car. After filling the radiator, I slammed my hood of my van. The musician looked in my direction. I waved. He waved back, and I drove off.

When I got home an hour later, my phone rang. It was the musician from the parking lot. "What the fuck you doin' spyin' on me from behind the club?"

When I convinced him I wasn't spying on him and was just putting water in my radiator, he fessed up.

According to him, a very persistent groupie had been chasing him for a week and waited in the parking lot that night until he came out of the club. As he headed across the parking lot, she pulled up between him and his car and made him an offer for sex. When he declined her invitation, she offered curb service if he'd just "stick it through the window" while she serviced herself.

'Nuff said.

## That's Him! That's Him!

It was December 1999. I had *zero* celebrity status as an entertainer.

Except for a few close friends and a small, dedicated group of loyal fans, nobody knew who I was. I hadn't recorded anything for commercial release in nearly twelve years. I was not pursuing a songwriting or recording career. I had accepted my fate to be nothing more than a beer joint guitar player who scratched out a living playing copy songs to people in bars who didn't give a crap about the band.

My lack of notoriety was about to come to a screeching halt.

Joni and I were Christmas shopping in the perfume section of a large department store in Houston's Northwest Mall. Suddenly a young woman about fifteen feet away let out a blood curdling scream that scared the shit out of everybody within earshot, including me. People ducked behind racks and counters, probably thinking a robbery was in progress.

The young woman was screaming at the top of her lungs, *"It's him! It's him!"*

Customers were looking all around to see who *him* was. It was definitely an *oh shit* moment when I realized she was pointing at *me*!

"She must think I'm somebody else! Maybe she thinks I robbed the place!"

The woman continued screaming. "He's that singer! He's that singer that sings *that song*!"

Obviously the woman had seen me perform somewhere and was uncontrollably star struck. Why, I don't know. I was nobody, remember?

With one finger pressed over my lips, I attempted to shush the woman, while motioning with my other hand for her to lower her voice. She kept screaming, "He's that singer! *He's that singer!*"

Joni peered from behind a clothes rack to watch the scene play out. I was on my own.

Finally, the woman calmed down. Never in my life have I seen anything like that. She was trembling, whimpering and gasping for air in short, quick breaths.

As she calmed down, people began to flock around me. A mob mentality ensued as I was besieged for autographs by people who didn't have a clue who I was but apparently thought I must be *somebody* famous since I had caused a woman in a shopping mall to go into a screaming fit.

It was a weird experience. After signing a few shopping bags and Christmas lists, Joni and I were able to escape before the mall cops arrived to see what all the ruckus was about.

## Cow Tang Sisters

Around 2002 the band and I were introduced to Head Nurse Nancy. She was an extremely large woman in her early forties who claimed to be head nurse at one of the local hospitals. She had extremely large breasts, which she flaunted in front of the band at all times by wearing very low-cut and tight v-neck shirts. She had so much cleavage it looked like she had a fat man's naked ass sticking out of her chest.

After a while, Nurse Nancy began to show another side. She would call my cell phone and ask me to meet her at my driveway, because she had something *special* for *me*. She started stopping by the house unexpectedly. She'd bring cakes, pies and homemade cookies. Harmless enough, I thought at first. Soon it became an annoying routine.

When Joni was busy selling merchandise or working the door at a show, the good Nurse Nancy would seize the opportunity to disrespect my new bride by whispering extremely vulgar, sexual suggestions in my ear.

I was repulsed by Nurse Nancy's total disrespect for my marriage and grossed out by her filthy mouth that went far beyond kinky. She was a sicko. She claimed her experience in the medical field gave her special intimate knowledge of the human body. She assured me she could make my toes curl and my eyes roll back in my head. I tried to laugh it off and pretend she was joking, but Nurse Nancy was relentless in her pursuit of a liaison. I tried to avoid being alone with her in any situation.

Though I never said anything to Joni, her radar was telling her to watch out for Nurse Nancy. When Joni voiced her suspicions to me about Nurse Nancy, I just laughed it off. I pretended I hadn't noticed Nurse Nancy's interest in me. Joni got pissed that I wasn't taking her suspicions seriously. Women have a sixth sense about these kind of things, right?

I was always polite to Nurse Nancy. I looked past her bullshit for a long time for the sake of putting more money in the cash register at places we played. She and her "plus-size" girlfriends could put away enough booze to cover the band's entire salary.

Some of her bullshit I didn't know about was that Nurse Nancy would barge into a club like a bulldozer, announcing to the management that she was with the band. She'd demand a better table, free drinks, free cover at the door and anything else she could get away with.

Nurse Nancy also developed a notorious reputation for being extremely rude and verbally abusive to club waitstaff. She would constantly send half-empty drinks back to the bartender, demanding more booze be added because it was "weak" and a "ripoff." Once she forced a whole table of fans at their reserved table to get up and move, telling them they were at a table reserved *exclusively* for the band. As a rule, we never have a reserved "band" table.

The band and crew were too busy setting up gear, merchandise and selling CDs to notice Nurse Nancy's antics – until one night. At The Howling Coyote, owners Mit and Laura Truax came up to Joni, profusely apologizing for not having our band table ready. Mit and Laura offered to comp the band's tab, especially since a "member of our entourage" was upset and had just walked out without paying the band bar tab.

"What band table?" Joni asked. "What band tab? The band is on stage, and our crew is either working the door or selling merchandise. We don't do band tabs!"

Joni asked Mit and Laura to describe this woman. It was none other than Head Nurse Nancy.

Joni told Mit and Laura in no uncertain terms, "That woman is *not* with the band. She just shows up. She pays a cover charge and pays her tab just like everybody else."

Mit and Laura then told Joni about Nurse Nancy's disrespectful conduct toward them and their staff every time she came in. Joni apologized to them for the trouble and the misunderstandings Nurse Nancy caused. She paid Nurse Nancy's bar tab.

When Nurse Nancy showed up at our gig the next afternoon, I demanded repayment for her bar tab. I also told her Mit and Laura had enlightened us to her treatment of them, their staff and our fans. She cussed and yelled, and magically started putting "the cry game" on us. We didn't buy into all the drama.

To add insult to injury, the next week I got a call at home from a prominent City Council member, giving his deepest apologies and sincere concern for my separation and impending divorce from Joni. *What?*

Nurse Nancy had been overheard at a local restaurant saying that she and I were secret lovers and I visited her at all hours, before and after *all* my shows. According to her, I hated to go home to my wife. She told everyone I was in the process of a divorce and would soon be moving in with her.

I was not amused.

I had to put a stop to Nurse Nancy's twisted, psycho crap before we found a dead rabbit boiling in a pot on her stove or, worse, before we found *Joni* boiling in a pot on her stove, ala *Fatal Attraction.*

I called Nurse Nancy and unleashed my wrath. In told her in no uncertain terms that I was happily married and planned to stay that way. I told her that I had not, never had been, nor *ever* would be sexually interested in her. I told her she never *was*, or ever would be, *with the band*. I told her to *get* lost, *stay* lost and to never come back.

I don't like being mean to people, but Nurse Nancy forced me to put her in her place for the protection of my wife, my marriage and my band's reputation.

I didn't see her again until two years later.

## FREIDA FREAKENSTEIN

By the summer of 2004, we hadn't seen Nurse Nancy for two years. She unexpectedly showed up at one of my gigs with her freaky, equally fat, equally big-tittied, equally warped-minded twisted sister, Freida Freakenstein.

We had previously met Nurse Nancy's forty-something-year-old sister Freida when she came in town to visit Nurse Nancy. We called her Freida Freakenstein because when describing her to people, we jokingly referred to her as Tammy Faye meets The Bride of Frankenstein on steroids. We weren't trying to be cruel, but it was an accurate description.

Freida's jet black hair was always teased high and fanned out like a spray of peacock feathers. She wore massive amounts of tacky, sparkly blue eyeshadow and thick, black eyeliner that looked like it was applied with a four-inch wide paint brush. Combined with blood-red lipstick on a face caked with an inch of white baking powder, Freida looked like a bad Halloween hangover.

Freida was a gen-u-wine backwoods hillbilly from somewhere in the deep south which was evident by her hick-billy drawl and lack of common courtesy or good manners in the presence of civilized city-dwellers. She always had a bad attitude and cussed like a sailor. She had a deep, manly voice like a pro wrestler. She proudly displayed the same humongous tits and Grand Canyon cleavage as her baby sister, Nurse Nancy.

After two years with no Nurse Nancy or Freida Freakenstein sightings, here they were at our show. When they arrived, they sat at a table in the back and started sending drinks to the stage. The waitress brought a note to our drummer.

My plan was to ignore them.

During a band break, Freida ambushed me when I came out of the restroom. I tried to ignore her, but she had been waiting for me. She stepped directly in front of me like a giant troll and growled, "Hey! Yew still mayreed?"

"Yep," I said, as I tried to squeeze past her.

"Well, tha's jus too gawddamn bad!"

"Why's that?" I asked. Looking back, that was a stupid thing to say.

"I'm happily married to a sweet little woman who treats me like a king. I don't see that as a bad thing."

With a defiant sneer, she glared at me through big, black-ringed, angry eyes. Already blocking my path, she stepped forward, pressed her giant tits against my chest and expelled her whiskey-tainted, cigarette-smelling hog breath in my face.

Freida gritted her teeth and in a low, guttural, hick-billy growl, she snarled, "Cause I wuz gonna take yew home with me t'night and fuck yer brains out!"

"No thanks!" I replied. I bolted back to the bandstand.

I remember thinking, "How the hell could that fat, nasty bitch possibly think I'd be interested in her big, sweaty, ugly, stinkin', cow-tang ass?"

I called the band to the stage. I was grossed out when I told them what had just happened with Freida. The drummer then handed me the note the waitress had brought him earlier. It was an invitation from Nurse Nancy to meet her and Freida after the show for an orgy.

The drummer told me while Freida had me cornered at the men's room, Nurse Nancy had the gall to proposition him, right after he'd introduced her to his new girlfriend sitting in the audience. It pissed me off to think those two cows were on a mission to conquer the Die Hard Band that night. The bitches actually believed we'd be *interested*.

Nurse Nancy was up to her old tricks again. I was disgusted with the whole sorry mess. I posed a hypothetical question to the band just before we kicked off our last set, "How could these nasty bitches possibly think we'd wanna jump off in their nasty cow-tang?"

The guys roared with laughter at the word "cow-tang." I told the band to stay close because after the last song, I was going to confront Nurse Nancy and Freida Freakenstein and put an end to their bullshit *forever*, and I needed witnesses.

When we played our last song, Nurse Nancy and Freida were sitting at their table, watching us like a couple of giant lusting heifers. While the band and a few close friends stood by, I called the "Cow-Tang Sisters" to the stage. They jumped up and excitedly came to the front of the stage.

When they reached our group, I pointed my finger at Nurse Nancy. I yelled, "I don't wanna fuck *you*…" and I turned and pointed at Freida, "…and I don't wanna fuck *you*! In fact, nobody here wants to fuck either one of you fat nasty bitches! *So, get the fuck outta here!*"

Taken by surprise, the Cow-Tang Sisters both turned and headed for the exit. Nurse Nancy ran out the door and disappeared.

Freida took ten steps, stopped and then turned around facing me. She looked like a mad bull ready to charge. She stormed back across the dance floor and stopped just inches from my face.

"Yew maaht scare mah stupid sister with that kinda tawk yew stupid asshole, but yew don't scare me, yew little piece 'a shit! Yew sorry little short dick mutherfucker! I'll whup yer got-damn ass jus like I whupped my got-damn ex-husband, yew no good piece 'a dried-up fuckin' dawgshit!

The band and our entourage listened to her rant until she ran out of wind and headed for the exit. No one said a word until the door closed behind her.

"Well, I guess that's that! Let's go home!" I said.

Everybody busted out laughing and began repeating Freida's enraged oratory, trying to copy her hillbilly accent. It was hilarious.

By the time I got home, Freida had already called my voicemail. She left a couple of ranting terroristic threats, repeating her backwoods rant. It was funny until her threats said she knew where I lived and that she would do harm to me and to Joni.

I took a copy of the voicemail message to the Baytown police department. The police woman called Freida and threw the fear of God into her, telling her the police had a copy of her threats on file and a case number on her.

Freida was informed if she and her sister ever showed their faces around me, my wife or my band again, they would suffer the consequences. They've never been back.

**Outlaw Dave Plays The Backwoods Rant**

A few weeks after my confrontation with Head Nurse Nancy and Freida Freakenstein, I was a special guest on Outlaw Dave's afternoon drive-time radio show on Houston's KIOL Rock 103.7FM. Outlaw Dave played Freida's threatening voicemail message in its entirety, beeping out the "seven dirty words" that can't be said on commercial radio.

Even with all the bleeps, it was still hilarious. Houston went crazy over it.

If you'd like to hear and download a copy of Freida Freakenstein's uncensored, vulgar, verbal attack on me, go to meangenekelton.com. Adults only, please.

It's the nastiest use of the English language you'll ever hear from the mouth of a female.

## Psycho Sybil

"Sybil," like the schizophrenic psycho in the movie, had been around Michael's Ice House in Texas City since we had started playing there every Sunday beginning in 1994.

Sybil was an attractive woman in her late thirties and always friendly. We never had much to say to each other except a passing hello. I found it strange that the mild-mannered girl with such a pretty smile had a notorious reputation for getting drunk and turning into a hell-raisin', fist-fightin' psycho. I never saw anything weird about her until one night when I hung around to talk business with Mr. Michael after a gig.

The place was nearly empty except for a few stragglers sitting at the bar including Sybil. As I exited the office and walked past her, she said, "Hey, c'mere."

I walked over to her. She put her arms around my neck, pulled me close and softly whispered, "I wanna fuck you right now."

Startled by Sybil's unexpected bluntness, I jerked loose from her embrace. I backed up and looked at her with a surprised expression.

"Whatsa matter?" she asked sarcastically. "Don't 'cha like-ta fuck?"

Before I could respond, she leaned forward and looked me dead in the eyes. In a voice loud enough for the other customers to hear she firmly stated, "I been watchin' you for a long time! I wanna fuck you right now!"

I was speechless. At first, I thought Sybil was joking and just trying to get a reaction out of me in front of the people at the bar. Then I saw that her eyes were glazed over like two solid black marbles. I felt like I was staring into the eyes of a demon. Her voice changed to a demonic growl, as if an entity had taken over her body.

Sybil began to scream at the top of her lungs. "I wanna fuck you right now, you muthafucker! Goddamn you, don't walk away from me, muthafucker! I wanna fuck you right now you son of a bitch. I'll fuck your goddamn brains out!"

Expecting to see her head spin around three times and spew out green vomit, I yelled, "I gotta go!"

I turned and ran out the door to the sound of people laughing behind me. As I drove away I could still hear her screaming as if she was burning at the stake.

"Come fuck me, you chickenshit motherfucker!"

When I saw Sybil at our gig the following week, she smiled, said hello and acted as if nothing had ever happened.

**Escape From Sybil**

A few weeks later, four women stayed after the gig. They were waiting for me to load up. Each one had promised me a good time.

Two girls sat together at the bar and promised me a three-way I'd never forget. Another girl was a titty dancer, who rubbed her crotch and deep throated her fingers while she danced in front of me. The fourth one was that crazy Sybil.

Not to be outdone, Sybil climbed into my van as I loaded up and refused to get out.

I was in a serious dilemma. Regardless of what I did, there'd be hell to pay. My bass player sat at the bar, sipping his beer and laughing at me.

"Man, I can't wait to see how you're gonna handle this one," he said.

He and I both knew if I dragged that crazy Sybil out of my van, she'd probably go berserk, start fighting and probably beat the hell out of the other girls and me too. As luck would have it, she eventually climbed out of my van to go to the restroom.

I took the opportunity to jump behind the wheel and escape. Alone.

## Sybil Calling

Sybil managed to get my home phone number from a waitress who worked at Michael's Ice House. She would get drunk and call me all hours day and night. She's leave highly-charged, detailed messages regarding her sexual demands. I wish I'd saved those tapes. I could've made a mint selling them as downloads.

One cold, rainy morning around 7am, the phone next to my bed jolted me awake. I barely whispered hello when a female voice screamed in my ear, "Come fuck meeeeeee! Come fuck me right now, motherfucker!"

I cringed at the sound of Sybil's voice. "It's 7am! Don't call me!"

"Hey, wait a minute," she yelled. "My girlfriend is here and her car won't start. If you bring some jumper cables, we'll both fuck your brains out!"

It's amazing how fast the mind of a healthy heterosexual male works. Even in my exhausted and confused state, my eyes flew wide open at the possibility of being intertwined with two uninhibited, sex-crazed nymphos.

However, in that same split second, my Guardian Angel kicked me in the gut. Simple logic suggested since Sybil was a certified psycho nutcase, her girlfriend probably was too. At 7am they had both probably been up all night doing God knows what and some pissed-off man was probably looking for the girlfriend. Suddenly the thought of being with those two freakos made me sick.

I jerked the phone cord out of the wall, turned over and went back to sleep.

## I Quit

When I woke up later that morning after hanging up on Sybil, I raised up in bed and looked around. I felt amazing and more alive than I'd felt in years. I felt renewed. Refreshed. I didn't know why. It was as if a fever had broke and I could see clearly for the first time in years. I thought about Sybil's phone call.

Suddenly the mere thought of touching another coke snortin', dope smokin', beer guzzlin', whiskey drinkin', fist fightin', shit talkin', pill poppin' schitzo-nympho freako nut case, kinky, bi-polar, bisexual, psycho-demon possessed monster-bitch from hell made me sick.

Following my Guardian Angels, my gut feeling and hanging up the phone signaled to the universe and my soul that I was tired of being a whore and I wanted to be a better man. I truly felt if I answered another booty call, I would surely die. I knew my Guardian Angels were tired of protecting my sorry ass from my self-inflicted misadventures.

I walked away from my wild, crazy lifestyle cold turkey and I've never looked back.

## CAN MEN BE GROUPIES?

Yes, men can be groupies. Though we men are less obvious than stereotypical female groupies (we don't throw our Fruit-Of-The-Looms on stage at rock concerts) we fellas still have our favorite bands, musicians, movie stars, actors, athletes, comedians, NASCAR drivers and other notables whose achievements and careers we follow.

It doesn't matter if the object of groupie fascination is male or female, human or animal. It might be a fast car or motorcycle whose logo we tattoo on our biceps. If we like and respect a person, place or thing we make an effort to see that person, place or thing whenever possible.

When female groupies go crazy, they can usually be dealt with easily and sent on their way. However, when a psycho biker or a bipolar, six-foot-four Vietnam veteran with alcohol and anger management issues follows you to every gig, screams in your face, threatens your life and tells you what a fuck-up you are, then you have a serious male groupie problem.

### Mad Max

In 1983, I performed as a single act every Tuesday night at a small club in Baytown called The Showcase. One night, Max introduced himself. He was a husky, stout-looking guy in his early forties who reminded me of Jack Nicholson. He wanted to talk music. He said he played a few chords on the guitar, but wasn't very good. He expressed a great interest in my music, especially the blues.

From that moment we met, Max followed me to every gig in the Houston area. He would always sit alone at the bar, chugging beer and staring a hole through me with his beady snake eyes. He'd grind his teeth and talk to himself all night. Though he seemed like a nice guy, he always looked pissed off. He was scary.

Every night Max and I talked about the Blues. He didn't know the names of any blues artists except B.B. King. He told me whenever I played blues, especially when I played the harmonica, it affected him deep down in a way he could not describe.

"You're a great blues player," he'd say. "Why do you wanna waste your time playing that cowboy shit when you can play the blues like you do? Play your harmonica and take us across the tracks tonight!"

I'd try to explain to him that, in 1983, a white boy couldn't make a living playing a full diet of blues. I had to play that "cowboy shit" in order to make a living. I'd sprinkle in a little blues whenever I could get away with it.

Max soon began to monopolize all my break time with lengthy, emotional lectures about why I should play nothing but the blues. He would get drunk and rant and rave until he had talked himself into a raging tirade. He'd pound his fist on the bar and yell, "Fuck them goddamn cowboy goat ropin' motherfuckers that don't like the blues. Play that harmonica. Take us down across the tracks. Play the *blues!*"

Sometimes I'd leave Max sitting there yelling and hustle back to the stage before he got both our asses whipped. Max was not the least bit concerned with making a scene. When he mixed pills and whiskey with inner rage, he'd stand flat-footed and fight the devil himself.

One numerous occasions Max showed up to my gigs bruised and beat all to hell. He'd laugh and say, "You oughta see the other guy!"

One night Max got into a fight over a pool game. He grabbed his opponent in a headlock and tried to shove a cue ball in the guy's mouth. It took a half-dozen people to pull "Mad Max" off the guy. That fight cost the loser several thousand dollars in dental bills.

Over the next few years, many of my breaks at my gigs were consumed by Mad Max as he interrogated me with millions of questions about the music business. He meant well with his suggestions about my career, but until a person has to derive evey cent they earn from a musical instrument, they don't have a clue about the business of music and aren't qualified to give advice. My breaks would always end with him ranting about why I should play the blues all night, just because he *wanted* me to.

The VA put Mad Max on several medications to keep his blood pressure and heart rate under control. He took other meds to control his unpredictable mood swings and uncontrollable rage. Mad Max was a ticking time bomb, and that time bomb had attached himself to *me*.

One night he showed up and announced, "Your worries are over, now you can play nothing but the blues! *I just bought you a nightclub!*"

Mad Max had bought the Remember When, an ailing nightclub on Market Street in Old Baytown. He insisted I put together a new band and play nothing but blues, for nobody but him, five nights a week, *forever.*

A musician will never turn down a steady gig and I was aching to stop being a one-man band and have my own full band, so I took the bait.

I got a bass player and a drummer and we started rehearsals. Mad Max insisted I quit playing anywhere as a one-man band until his grand opening so we could bust out with the all-new Gene Kelton Band. I told him unless he wanted to pay me *not* to play, I still had to make a living until the grand opening. Against his will, I kept playing wherever I could right up to opening night at Remember When.

Over the next couple of months, as Mad Max renovated his new club, he called my house a dozen times a day. He would demand I drop whatever I was doing and rush out to the club to discuss new renovation ideas.

Mad Max had theories about new carpet, artificial plants, decorations and wall paper. What type of cosmetic lighting in the women's restroom made a woman look younger? What color paint makes a person spend more money and buy more drinks? Which snacks would make people drink more? Would new faucets to add a touch of class to the restrooms? Would mirrors make the club look bigger?

I realized Mad Max was a control freak who wanted to monopolize my life. Because of the incessant phone calls and so-called emergency meetings with Mad Max, I could not get any rest, do any rehearsals or spend time with my family. I started taking my phone off the hook. The calls and meetings had nothing to do with my specialty, playing music.

I put together a band featuring Jivin' Gene Ganus on piano, Chris Bernhard on drums and Mike Listi on bass.

Opening night, the Remember When was packed with a standing-room-only crowd. Every song packed the dance floor and we rocked the place with nothin' but houserockin', butt-bumpin' blues until the house lights came on at 2am.

All night, as we rocked the packed house, Mad Max stood in the back of the room, silent and still as a statue. He was sweating profusely and staring angrily at the band through his evil, Jack Nicholson snake eyes. On every break he'd motion me into his office where he'd scream at me about our performance.

When the last customer left the building, Mad Max tore into us like a tornado, screaming about everything he'd found wrong with our performance. Truth was, there was *nothing* wrong with our performance.

Mad Max was just a control freak who knew nothing about music or how to entertain an audience. He was trying to intimidate us. His meds must have worn off because he stayed pissed off for the sake of being pissed off.

As weeks passed, we tolerated Mad Max's dictatorship and constant temper tantrums for the sake of a steady paying gig to get us through the winter. We ignored him as much as possible. From the bandstand, we watched numerous waitresses run out the door crying when Mad Max would "go mad" and scare the shit out of them.

Mad Max was a scrapper. We saw him break beer bottles over the heads of many customers and beat the hell out of them for whatever reason he saw fit on any particular night. He lost a lot of good paying drunks doing that.

After every show Mad Max insisted on taking the band to breakfast. We dreaded going to breakfast with him. He would always go off into his rant, pounding his fist on the table and splattering coffee while telling us what sorry pieces of shit we were. Mad Max's fit would cease only after the restaurant manager would threaten to call the cops.

Mad Max would remind us again and again that his life savings was invested in the club. He'd threaten to fire us if we "kept fuckin' up." We weren't fuckin' up. We were a damn good band and packed the house every night. We didn't have a clue about what Mad Max was talking about.

Every day Mad Max would call me to talk about the show the night before, telling me to come in early so we could have a private meeting to discuss band problems. *He* was the only frickin' band problem. Again, I started leaving my phone off the hook.

Two months into the new club, Mad Max had a mild heart attack. I went to see him in the hospital. He was in good spirits, laughing, joking and strapped down to a bed with a catheter and an IV. I chose that time to tell him I was tired of his temper fits, bad treatment and disrespect.

I also told Mad Max I was tired of his numerous phone calls demanding I drop everything to be at his beck and call to discuss stupid shit like cosmetic lighting, wallpaper and things that didn't have anything to do with the band.

I told Max, "I quit!"

"You wait 'til I'm flat on my back to tell me that shit?"

"Well, I was gonna have to tell you some time, but this works for me."

I drove straight to the club and loaded up all my gear. A few months later the club folded. By the following summer Mad Max was back to working construction. I moved to Nashville.

When my travels led me back to Baytown twenty years later, I bumped into Mad Max at a gas station. I barely recognized him.

The years of booze, meds, health problems and inner boiling rage had eaten Mad Max alive from the inside out. He had lost most of his teeth. The once-mighty street fighter was hardly more than a sickly, dilapidated, slumped-over old skeleton, hobbling along on shaky legs. I could hardly believe that rickety old codger was once the same intimidating control freak who scared the hell out of us.

Standing in the parking lot exchanging news of the past two decades, Mad Max told me he was retired and just "piddled around" these days. He asked what I was doing.

I replied, "I play the blues for a living."

Max grinned a big snaggle-tooth grin, nodded approvingly and mumbled as he slowly shuffled away, "I always knew you would."

## TOR-LET PAPER

One afternoon in 2002, Joni and I were shopping at Wal-Mart in Baytown. Since I don't wear my show clothes when we are out and about, if you didn't know me, you'd think I was just another Bubba redneck in my denim cap and faded jeans.

We were nonchalantly pushing our buggy through the aisles when suddenly a big, burly fifty-something-year-old man dressed in camouflage hunting clothes stepped in front of me. He snarled, "Hey! Ain't 'chu Mean Gene?"

After admitting my identity, we properly introduced ourselves and made small talk. He kept commenting about how he couldn't believe he'd run into a famous person at Wal-Mart. Joni stood close by and pretended not to know me as she snickered under her breath.

The man yelled to his wife shopping at the end of the aisle, "Hey, hon, lookie here, it's Mean Gene Kelton!"

She came running down the aisle pushing her buggy with a big smile on her face. The guy noticed the huge 24-roll pack of off-brand toilet paper prominently sticking out of our buggy like the Empire State Building. He put his hand on the package and exclaimed, "Lookie here, hon! Mean Gene uses same kinda tor-let paper we do!"

With a big grin, he then said to his wife, "Take a picher o' me 'n ol' Mean Gene stannin' here by this here tor-let paper!"

From deep in the caverns of her large purse, the wife retrieved a camera and snapped a couple shots of us with our hands on the "tor-let" paper. After shaking hands, the couple went their merry way, content we had a special bond because we used the same brand of ass-wipe.

Somewhere deep in the heart of East Texas, I just bet there's a framed picture hanging on the wall of a double-wide trailer showing two rednecks proudly standing on each side of a huge, 24-pack of off-brand toilet paper, looking as if they were two mighty hunters who had just bagged the biggest deer of the century.

## STARMAN RIDES AGAIN

I first met fifty-something-year-old biker Lonny "Starman" Loehr around 2005. He approached me about performing at a benefit he was producing for his chosen charity The United States Marine Corps Toys For Tots.

Lonny, an avid live music lover, began showing up at many of our shows across Southeast Texas and beyond. So much so that he joked about becoming a male groupie. We became great friends.

Lonny had been riding motorcycles since he was a kid and proudly wears the scars earned from years of professional competition. I also learned Lonny was a two-time U.S. Army vet.

Lonny always showed up to our shows with a big smile. He'd buy the band rounds and pass out cigars as if he was celebrating something. Everyday was a celebration for Lonny, He was a guy always surrounded by friends and who never met a stranger.

Along with our friend Bucky "Two Notes" Bishop, Lonny went with me the day I bought my first Harley at Stubbs Cycles in Houston. Since then, Lonny has been to my house numerous times to help me customize my bike. When he saw the tools I was using were rusty pieces of crap, he gave me a brand new set. That's just the kind of guy he is.

Lonny is a fantastic chef and loves to cook. He has often invited the band and Die Hard friends to come eat, just cause he felt like cooking up a mess o' ribs, steaks or shish-ke-bobs. Yep, life is always a party with Lonny around.

In November 2007 the good times caught up with Lonny. He was diagnosed with heart problems, and had his first heart stent operation. Three months later, another stent was put in.

Within a few months, we noticed a change in Lonny for the worse. He was no longer the happy-go-lucky, good-timing, free-wheeling guy we knew and loved. He had developed a short fuse, a hair trigger and an explosive temper. The smallest comment would send him into a rage.

As months passed, Lonny's personality changes caused even lifelong friends to fear him and keep their distance. Increasingly, Lonny showed up to my gigs beat to hell from fights, some with his best friends. Often the fights were caused when concerned friends would try to take his keys to keep him from driving after drinking. We all feared we'd get *that* dreaded phone call in the middle of the night. Once, he dropped his bike even before he got it started.

Other times, Lonny would make obscene insults or threaten people until somebody finally popped him. It wasn't long before he found himself barred from most of his favorite neighborhood waterin' holes where he'd been a welcome customer for years.

At our shows, Lonny would become obnoxious and insist on singing. He is *not* a singer. He'd get irate when we would't let him have his moment on stage. During this dark period, Lonny scribbled out a song he wanted me to decipher and sing. It was written single-spaced on legal-size paper and was thirteen pages long.

Like alot of our friends, I tried not to get involved with Lonny's personal life. I kept my distance – until it got personal.

On the way home from a gig, Joni was madder than hell. She told me how Lonny sat next to her at the bar and scared the hell out of her. She said one minute he was fine and the next minute he flew into a maniacal rage. He raised his fists like he was about to hit her and then pounded them on the bar. He screamed in her face and made threats of violence against her and our friends. At one point, yelling in Joni's face, Lonny picked up a bartender's tip jar on the bar and violently threw it against the wall across the room.

Joni thought Lonny was going to hit her. She said she knew he wasn't drunk, *he wasn't even in there,* as she put it. In other words, Lonny didn't seem to know what he was doing.

The next day I called Lonny around lunchtime. I knew that time of day he would be the most rational. I asked him if he remembered his conversation with Joni.

"No," he calmly replied.

Lonny didn't even remember seeing Joni. I asked him if he knew why he was getting kicked out of his favorite bars.

"I don't know," came his puzzled reply.

I asked him if he knew why his best friends were kicking his ass.

"I've wondered the same thing," he said. "All I know is I wake up with bumps and bruises all over me."

Lonny said that since his first heart stent, details of his life were fuzzy and his brain had been lost in a fog. His life seemed surreal. He said he felt confused, detached and couldn't focus. He suffered blackouts and was unable to remember where he'd been and what had happened.

I could hear Lonny's disbelief when I described his violent tirade toward Joni. He poured out an emotional apology and told me that he never meant to scare Joni or anyone else.

Concerned about my friend and knowing about his recent medical issues, I asked him how many doctors he was seeing and how many prescriptions he was on. His answer was startling. Three separate doctors with three separate sets of prescriptions.

"Does each doctor know about the other two?" I asked. "Does each doctor know what the others are prescribing?"

Lonny got real quiet, as if a light had come on.

"I don't know!" he muttered. "All my doctors in the same office, they have to know. No, come to think of it, I don't think so!"

Over the next few days, Lonny arranged a face-to-face meeting with all three doctors at one time in the same room. Not aware Lonny was being seen by the others, the three doctors came to the conclusion they'd nearly killed Lonny by overdosing him on anti-rejection drugs, anti-depressants and blood thinners. When mixed with Lonny's daily after-work ritual of a couple of friendly beers, the lethal mixture of prescription drugs and alcohol turned him into a raving maniac.

Once the doctors compared notes and got him on the correct medications, Lonny's problems quickly disappeared. Soon he was back to being his old happy-go-lucky self. He was passing out cigars, cooking out on the grill, promoting charity bike runs for Toys for Tots and enjoying friends, family and life to the fullest. Great to have ya back, Starman.

I interviewed Lonny before writing this story. We mutually agreed I should publish it in hopes his experience may help prevent someone from suffering a similar situation with a possible worse outcome.

Lonny's message – make sure all your doctors know about any other doctors you may be seeing, for what reason, and all other prescriptions you may be taking. Ask a million questions. Do not be intimidated by doctors and always get a second opinion. You are hiring them, not the other way around. Remember doctors are people too and make mistakes.

Confidentiality is one thing, but lack of shared information can kill you.

## My Wives: Groupies?

Just for the record, none of my three wives were ever groupies. I did not meet any of them at a gig or at a bar and none of them chased me down an alley with their panties in hand.

My first wife was my high school sweetheart. The moment we were married, she expected me to give up my life-long dreams of playing music.

Didn't happen.

My second wife was a secretary for a small, independent recording studio. I was stupid enough to think she worked there because she loved the music business. Wrong. It was just another day at the office for her. When she got fired, she was through with the music business and expected me to quit as well.

Didn't happen.

I met my third wife at a computer seminar I attended in an effort to become computer literate. She was giving a lecture on publishing and graphic design. I was the publisher of *Texas Blues Magazine*. I thought she was a cute little computer nerd and she thought I was a Neanderthal. We were both right, and I hired her to design *Texas Blues Magazine*.

Rumor has it I married her so I wouldn't have to pay her.

*"Even Meaner" Joni and Mean Gene*
*Photo by Jim Shortt, RIP*

*Me with a couple of willing groupies.*

*Ass me how I know!*

*One of our fans, Jeff Vandall, bought "Panties" t-shirts for the guys at his family reunion. The guys put the shirts on and surprised Jeff's parents with their rendition of the "Panties" song!*

*Halloween with the Die Hards, Debbie Maxey and Diane Naski, 1996.*

*Me and Celine Garrett with a mess o' frog legs in Charleston, Mississippi.*

*Die Hards Deb and Susan show their Die Hard colors at Southern Fried 4th, 2009. Photo courtesy Ken Fontenot*

*Both Pictures, New Years Eve, LaPorte, Texas 2003*
*On left, Kerry and Terri Laramore; Far back, Carolyn Hamilton and Frank Jenson. Front, left,*
*Charlotte Emigh, Lynn Garcia, Jeaneanne Ray, Bucky "Two Notes" Bishop (with panties on his head)*
*and Missy Bishop. Notice the donations of panties on the guitar...*

*Front, left to right: Lynn Garcia, Jeaneanne Ray,*
*Bucky "Two Notes" Bishop (panties still on his head) and Missy Bishop, Donna Tremont.*

Pictured above, me with Deborah McAllister, the Die Hard "photo historian." The other two photos are of her custom-made airbrushed t-shirt. This was the first official "Die Hard Band Shirt."

Handcuffed to a kinky groupie
at the Turtle Club, 1996.

Getting the royal Die Hard treatment at the
South Mississippi Bike Rally

*Right, top: Die Hards CJ and Lynn Garcia at The Balinese Room. CJ is the video historian, with hundreds of tapes of Die Hard shows that he's taken since 1999.*

*That's Lynn below, doing the Die Hard shuffle with me at a club in Clear Lake, Texas in about 1999.*

*A picture is worth....*
*Frankie's Club, Baytown 1993*

*Former Elvis Presley's Memphis General Manager*
*Judith Parra, at the CD release party at*
*Coyote Ugly, Memphis, August 2007.*

*Denise Chatham and Joni dancin' on the*
*bar at Coyote Ugly, Memphis, 2007.*

*Kathy Adams and Vickie Music running the show*
*at Southern Fried 4th, 2009.*

# BOOK EIGHTEEN

# Musicians Commandeer Funeral

R.I.P.
Tony
Lee

*Musicians are disrespected enough while they are living. The following story isn't a Gig From Hell from a band or show standpoint. However when our friend and fellow Texas Blues musician Tony Lee passed away, what happened at his "final appearance" would turn into just that, a gig from hell.*

*The story was published on the "Unkommentary" section of my website and relieved overwhelming response and an outpouring of support for Tony, Monica, me and the guys at the funeral.*

*Since I started writing this book, many people have requested that I include this story.*

## MUSICIANS COMMANDEER FUNERAL AND SEND PREACHER PACKING

After losing a long battle with colon cancer, on Monday, March 12, 2007, we laid to rest our very dear friend and fellow Texas Blues musician, Tony Lee, 55, of Houston.

Tony Lee and his wife Monica Marie with their band, Monica Marie & The Blues Cruizers, were a driving force in the Houston music scene for over twenty years. During that time, they performed over 200 shows a year and traveled around the world many times entertaining troops at USO shows. They were always first to volunteer for benefits.

In 2002 Monica Marie & The Blues Cruizers won the Houston competition of the Blues Foundation's International Blues Talent Competition put on by the Houston Blues Society. The band earned the title "#1 Blues Band" in Houston. The Houston Blues Society sent the band to Memphis, Tennessee, to represent Houston and to compete against blues bands from all over the world. Although they did not win in Memphis, Monica Marie & The Blues Cruizers made us all very proud here at home.

I had personally known Tony and Monica since our days jamming together at Billy Blues in Houston since 1993. Through the years our bands shared many stages, not to mention the countless bottles of tequila and millions of laughs. We lost a great friend and a journeyman blues warrior when Tony passed.

The Chapel of Angels at Forest Park Funeral Home on Lawndale in Houston was filled to capacity with Tony and Monica's families, life-long friends, musicians and people from all walks of life who'd been touched in one way or another by Tony's music, charm and his contagious sense of humor. I was honored to be one of seven close friends who served as Pallbearers.

At 2:30pm, the Pallbearers were led to our seats at the front of the chapel as "Simple Man" by Lynyrd Skynyrd played through the sound system.

For the next few minutes the audience suffered through what I consider the worst eulogy and worst funeral sermon by the worst preacher I've ever heard in my life.

In my opinion, the Reverend Paul G. Whitlatch of Epworth Parker United Methodist Church performed the "one-size-fits-all" generic eulogy where all he had to do was fill in the blanks with the name of the current deceased and pick up his check as he left.

The sermon lacked conviction, lacked passion, and lacked respect. It lacked anything about *Tony*. The Reverend was preoccupied, uninterested, unprepared and completely *unqualified* to speak about our dear friend, Tony Lee Zeisemer. The Reverend rambled, stammered, lost his place and lost whatever point he was trying to make more than once.

Instead of talking about Tony, the Reverend babbled on about his own life, his wife, his kids, his travels and various other subjects that had nothing to do with Tony. When he realized he had lost his train of thought, he would quickly quote a scripture like a gambler pulls an

Ace from his sleeve, tossing it into the crowd that ached for comforting praises of Tony. Praises never came. Only hot air and bullshit.

The only thing worse than listening to the Reverend's lackluster drivel was the sound of hammers banging on the walls from the other room. The music to be played during the service by Bread, Elvis and others, specially chosen and planned by Monica and Tony himself, was drowned out by the sound of power saws and construction renovations in the next room.

Without warning the service came to an abrupt halt. The Reverend announced, "Thank you all for coming. For those of you going to the gravesite, please return to your cars and get in line."

There was no invitation for anyone to step forward to share any memories about Tony. The service was finished. "Voodoo Chile" by Jimi Hendrix played through the intercom, as mourners were signaled to get up and leave.

The crowd filed out the front door, looking as surprised as the Pallbearers by the sudden end to the service. Carrying Tony's casket, the Pallbearers were led out the back door where we silently loaded the casket into the hearse under the whispered instructions of the funeral directors.

I felt empty inside. Unfulfilled by the Reverend's empty words, I felt robbed of the opportunity to stand up and say a few words about my friend Tony. I felt guilty and angry at myself for not having taken the initiative and forcing my way to the podium. Now that Tony was in the hearse, my chance to speak about him was lost forever. I was pissed!

I turned to the Pallbearers standing closest to me. "I think that preacher is full of shit!"

Galen Medlenka, a life-long friend of Tony's and former bass player for the Blues Cruizers spoke up. "Yeah, man, you're right! He didn't say nothing about Tony! I wanted to get up and say something about Tony. Nobody gave us the chance."

Bucky "Two Notes" Bishop, who had been studying guitar under Tony, agreed with us. "Man, that just ain't right. He never said nothing 'bout Tony. He shoulda let other people get up and talk."

No longer able to contain my anger I announced, "Boys, when we get to the gravesite, we're taking over. We're sending that preacher's ass packin'. We're gonna say our piece about Tony and nobody's gonna stop us."

Both guys heartily agreed. "Just give us a signal," they said. "We're with you all the way."

## At The Gravesite

Arriving at the gravesite, Galen suggested we get Monica's blessing before turning Tony's funeral into a rumble. Monica seemed very agitated, but we figured it was all part of the stress she was going through losing Tony and dealing with funeral arrangements. She agreed to let us talk about Tony, but had no idea we were going to run that preacher's ass off.

As the family was seated under the tent and the crowd gathered around, Galen and Bucky waited for my signal. I suddenly felt like we were three courageous swashbucklers about to draw our swords to save the day and defend the honor of our friend, Tony Lee.

As the Reverend opened his Bible, I walked up to him face to face. I placed a firm grip on his shoulder, pulled him up close enough that he could smell my breakfast in his face and in my very best Godfather/Biker voice, growled, "Hey, buddy. Me and the boys here are taking over. We gotta few things we gonna say 'bout Tony. Step aside, we'll take it from here."

I'm sure the good Reverend was not used to being told what to do by an angry biker-looking dude wearing black leather at a funeral and who was obviously not impressed or intimidated by his title, his double-talk or his bullshit. With me in his face, Galen on one side and Bucky on the other, the Reverend stared back at me like a deer in the headlights.

He meekly replied, "Oh, okay, yeah, sure, sure, I have to be somewhere anyway… I really have to go… I… I… I… I can't stay… I really have to…"

"Get outta the way, Preacher," I growled.

In an effort to earn his thirty pieces of silver, the Reverend made the fastest obligatory graveside prayer I'd ever heard, rushed through his artificial condolences and hauled ass.

I stepped forward and gave my humble speech about what Tony's friendship had meant to me. Following me, Galen, Bucky, Dennis Ray and Monica's mom Mary Eddins all took their turn speaking. Overall, a dozen people came forward and spoke great things about Tony.

Monica was last to speak. Her words were beautiful as she tearfully quoted lines from a song, talked about her and Tony's life together and thanked everyone for coming.

We finished the service by honoring Tony the way every musician should be honored, with a standing ovation.

As we left the gravesite, Bucky, Galen and I were proud of our little coup d'etat. However small it may have seemed to the universe, it was a big deal to *us*. We felt like conquering heroes. It was fulfilling, cleansing to the soul and we all hoped somehow Tony could feel the love in the words that were spoken by everyone that day.

## Monica Goes Head-To-Head With The Reverend

After the graveside service, Monica told us how proud she was we had taken the initiative to stand up and speak. What we didn't know before our little takeover was that Monica had already suffered a verbal confrontation with the Reverend prior to the service.

Monica told us she had asked the Reverend about letting some of Tony's friends get up and say a few words about Tony. Her request was rudely denied. *Denied!*

The Reverend stated it makes for a long, drawn-out service and that he had to leave in twenty minutes to be somewhere else.

Monica was hurt and infuriated. "You mean to tell me that my husband was on this earth for fifty-five years and you're gonna sum his life up in twenty minutes? And not even let his friends to get up and speak?"

According to Monica, the Reverend told her, "That's the way things are done. Get a grip on reality and live in the real world."

Instead of being a compassionate man of God and trying to honor the requests of a grieving widow, the Reverend dismissed Monica like a she was an annoying schoolgirl. He actually told her, "Now go sit down, relax and enjoy the funeral that we've prepared for you. It's in our hands now." In other words, Monica was told her musician friends would not be allowed to speak and to sit down, shut up and mind her own business so he could finish and leave.

To top it all off, according to Monica, the Reverend had gone behind her back and changed the music to suit himself. Before the hearse left for the gravesite, Monica asked the funeral director why the songs had been changed. The funeral director told Monica that Reverend Whitlatch said that he was the only one who approved *all* music.

Not only was Monica suffering the great loss of her husband, but now she was pissed off, offended and disrespected by the Reverend who was supposed to lead all by his example of exemplary Christian conduct. Yeah, right.

When we decided to take the services away from the Reverend, we had no idea all this had happened prior to the funeral.

## Monica Marie Owed A Public Apology

It is a shared opinion that Forest Park Funeral Home and the Reverend Paul G. Whitlatch both owe Monica Marie Ziesemer a public apology and compensation for added stress, public embarrassment, indignity, disrespect, arrogance and indifference and for allowing a construction crew to destroy Tony's service with the sound of hammering that echoed through the walls of the Chapel during the entire service.

*Above: Tony Lee and me cutting heads at Outlaw Dave's Birthday Bash, Baytown, Texas.*
*Below: Tony's benefit at Fenders, l to r: Thurman "P-Funk" Robinson, bass; Norm Uhl, keys;*
*in back, Dave Nevling, harp. Front, Rick Lee, guitar; Tony Lee, guitar.*

## In Closing

For the record, for every *Gig From Hell* there have been a hundred great gigs and hundreds of great people who have helped me along the way. I hope you have enjoyed the adventures in *Gigs From Hell*.

The end of this book does not mean the end of my story. Life goes on and I'm sure there'll be other gigs from hell and more stories that will keep us all glued to the edge of our seats.

Thank you all for your friendship, support and for being Die Hards.

As for me, I've had a blast and wouldn't change anything. I plan to keep on rockin', cause "I Love My Job!"

*Stay tuned for the further adventures and the never ending saga of
Mean Gene Kelton & The Die Hards.*

*Southern Fried 4th, 2009  Photo by Ken Fontenot*

*Thanks
Mean Gene Kelton*

# For More Photos, Stories, and Gigs From Hell Merchandise, go to meangenekelton.com

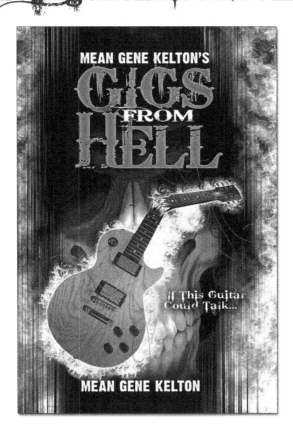

## FOLLOW US:

### TWITTER: MEANGENEROCKS

### FACEBOOK FAN PAGE: MEAN GENE KELTON & THE DIE HARDS

### WEB: MEANGENEKELTON.COM